*Cottages and Common Fields*
*of Richmond and Kew*

# Cottages and Common Fields of Richmond and Kew

Studies in the Economic and Social History
of the Manor of Richmond up to the mid-Nineteenth Century

## JOHN CLOAKE

with very best wishes

John Cloake

PHILLIMORE

*For John and Mary*

2001

Published by
PHILLIMORE & CO. LTD.
Shopwyke Manor Barn, Chichester, West Sussex

ISBN 1 86077 195 5

Printed and bound in Great Britain by
THE CROMWELL PRESS
Trowbridge, Wiltshire

Colour printed by
ST RICHARD'S PRESS
Chichester, West Sussex

# Contents

*Appendices*

# List of Plates

# List of Illustrations in the Text

# Acknowledgements

The sources of illustrations and acknowledgements for their use are shown in the captions. Where no source is indicated, the item is from the author's own collection.

The maps specially drawn for this book were all conceived and originally drafted by the author, and are in his copyright. But, except for those at plates 5 and 9-12, they have been redrawn far more artistically by the cartographer Geoff Gwatkin.

The coloured version of 'The Prospect of Richmond' used on the book jacket was kindly supplied by Peter Bland of Lavender Picture Framers, Wandsworth Common.

# List of Subscribers

Ian Day Adams
Clive Adamson
Asgill House Trust
David Attenborough
Janet Backhouse
D.S. Baird-Murray
Hilary and David Barnfather
Alyson Barr
Mr. and Mrs. Ron Berryman
David Blomfield
Iris Bolton
Grahame and Valerie Boyes
R.C.H. Briggs
Gary B. Bullard
Dr. and Mrs. J.D.K. Burton
Helena Caletta
Dr. T.H.R. Cashmore
Edward Casaubon
Mr. and Mrs. Patrick Clackson
Jennifer Cloke
Andrew Constantine
Cllr. and Mrs. David Cornwell
Robert Cowie
Tom Craig
William Dacombe
Hilary Denness
Mr. Henry G. East
Peter Edmonds
Graham and Susanna Edwards
Henry F.A. Engleheart
Margaret Evans
Edward C. Flann
Peter Foote
John Fothergill
Richard E. Fothergill
Patrick Frazer
Colin Ganderton

Christina and Bamber Gascoigne
Jane Gibson
Dr. Tom Greeves
Ernst J. Grube and Eleanor Sims
Johnny van Haeften
David M. Harper
Jean and Michael Harris
John L. and Katharine C. Hart
Daniel Hearsum
Richard Maria and Grace
    Hebblethwaite
F. Nigel Hepper
Peter and Sunny Hills
Historic Royal Palaces
A.T. Hoolahan, QC
Ken and Teresa Howe
Patton Howell
Noel Hughes
Keith Hutton
Derek Jones
Paul J. Kershaw
Angela Kidner
Ronald S. Knight
Simon and Sally Lale
J.M. Lee
Janet Locke
Prince and Princess Rupert zu
    Loewenstein
Cllr. Serge Lourie
Mark Loveland
Walter McCann
Robert and Donna McDonald
David F. McDonough, OBE
David and Elizabeth McDowall
Tony McSweeney
Richard Meacock
Richard Milward

Museum of Richmond
C.F. Pagnamenta, OBE
Christopher Palmer
Adrian and Hilary Parsons
Ann Pearson
John and Rosalind Pickston
B.J. Pincott
Laura Ponsonby
Christopher and Jenny Powell-Smith
Roy and Martha Price
Norman Radley
Emma and Mike Reeve
Mr. and Mrs. William Reid
Anthony and Marjorie de Reuck
John Richardson
The Royal Parks Agency
John Safford
Judge and Mrs. John Samuels
Esther and Richard Savinson
A. and L. Simcock
Barney Sloane
Ronald Smedley
Eleanor Stanier
Ian and Deborah Taylor
Dr. Jenny Tonge, MP
Valerie Treasure
Eileen and Rodney Turner
David and Patricia Urch
Paul and Elizabeth Velluet
Ian F. Watts
Michael J.C. Watts
Ian D. White
Bernard Wigginton
Kim Wilkie
Sir David Williams
Iain Winning
Zoë Woolrych York

# Introduction

STANDING ON THE northern, Surrey, bank of the River Thames and looking across the river to its southern, Middlesex, bank one sees the river flowing almost due west on its way down to the sea! This complete inversion occurs by the site of the former Richmond Palace, for the river – winding its way around and through the modern London Borough of Richmond upon Thames – does indeed follow a most devious course. The new Borough adopted as its logo a capital letter R depicted as a winding river, and if this slightly exaggerates the topography it does indeed symbolise both the geographical reality and the vital part which the river has played in the development of the communities on its banks formerly in Middlesex and in Surrey, now joined in the London Borough.

This book deals with just one of those communities: the Manor of Shene (or, from 1501, Richmond) in the County of Surrey. Because it was, from the early 14th century, a royal manor it has been fortunate in the preservation of its records, mostly now in the Public Record Office. In *Palaces and Parks of Richmond and Kew* I dealt with the history of the royal estates in the area. In *Cottages and Common Fields* I shall record and attempt to analyse some of the wealth of information that can be derived, mainly from these manorial records, about the properties and lives of the inhabitants of the village called Shene (or Richmond) which grew up round the royal palaces and of its little isolated hamlet at Kew.

As with *Palaces and Parks* my main aim has been to set down, so that it may be shared with others, some of the product of my researches over the years since my wife and I bought our first home in Richmond in 1963.

There has been very little published about patterns of land-holding in Surrey. For Richmond and Kew there is information available which enables one to follow some of the holdings in a continuous sequence from the 15th century. Unfortunately, there are gaps in the records which make it impossible to trace all the manorial 'tenements' so far back, let alone to link them with the very full picture of the Manor in the early 14th century which is captured for us in the first surviving manorial document. But one can present a detailed study of the development of the village into the town; and of what happened to its fields up to the moment when they disappeared under rows of new suburban villas.

This book has a ragged ending. To complete the story of the economic and social life of the town in the 19th and 20th centuries requires another volume and perhaps another author (for here we would be on ground that I have no particular claim on; my research has tended to concentrate on the period before 1800). Yet I needed at least to follow the fate of the fields, and that required mention of the coming of the railway and a glance at the activities supporting the enlarged communities. But I have abandoned the story of the schools in 1825, of the pubs in 1830, of local government about 1850. I have hardly touched on the shops or all the new churches, let alone developments of the 20th century.

I have said much about the early history of houses in the town – but little about their architecture. It is still my hope and intention to turn next to that aspect of the town's history.

A note on spelling. In the first appendix I have listed the many variations which I have found in the early documents of the names of Shene and Kew. In this book I have used original spellings in direct quotations or where there is a clear documentary context. Otherwise I have standardised on 'Shene' and 'Kew' – both relatively late forms, but easily readable. When on Henry VII's direction Shene adopted the name of his Richmond earldom, there is again a wide variety of different spellings to be found. Almost any permutation of the following can be found somewhere: i or y in Rich; o, u or ou in mond: d or t as the final consonant; an additional e at the end of either syllable (or both). Again, there are wide inconsistencies in the spelling of personal surnames – manorial records have a different spelling from parish registers; one year's entry even in the same records differs from that of the year before. I have tried to introduce some consistency even at the cost of slight inaccuracy of transcription. In particular I should note that I decided always to spell Capell with two ls; as also Michell (although the charitable trust these days uses only one).

As always I owe a great debt of gratitude to Jane Baxter, the librarian in charge of local studies, for her willing and effective help. And to the staff of the Public Record Office (especially those in Chancery Lane in the 'good old days' before computers). I am also indebted to Anne Pearson for some last-minute help with research when I was unwell. My wife has been a tower of strength throughout – and has typed, retyped, criticised (a little) and encouraged (enormously).

# I

# *Shene: Setting the Scene*

THE RECORDED HISTORY of Richmond, anciently called Shene, begins with the will of Theodred, Bishop of London, made about the year 950. It is but a brief mention, in a section dealing with the disposal of the estates which he held as bishop rather than those which were his personal property. He had apparently been a successful trustee:

> And it is my wish that at London there be left as much as I found in the estate, and that what I have added to it be taken and divided into two, half for the minster and half for my soul, and all the men are to be freed. And the same is to be done at Wunemanedune [Wimbledon] and at Sceon [Shene]. And at Fulham everything is to be left as it now stands, unless one wishes to free any of my men.[1]

We have no inkling of the size of the Bishop's holding at Shene, nor of its history in the next century. By the time of the Domesday Survey Shene was a part of the royal manor of Kingston (and had presumably been so in the time of Edward the Confessor). It is not mentioned by name in Domesday Book, but it is possible, as I have suggested in my book *Palaces and Parks of Richmond and Kew*, both that Shene was the site of the manor house of Kingston, and that the two hides and a fishery held, under Walter FitzOther, by a man of the jurisdiction of Kingston who had charge of the King's forest mares, were in the Shene area.[2] Shene and Kew were, however, cut off from the main part of Kingston manor by the small manor of Petersham which had belonged from the early eighth century to Chertsey Abbey.

In *Palaces and Parks* I attempted to trace the ownership of the manor of Shene from the time when it was legally separated from Kingston by King Henry I and granted to John Belet. It remains to record what little else is known about the manor and its inhabitants during the two centuries before it returned to royal ownership. First, however, let us consider what we know or can deduce of the physical characteristics of Shene in Norman times.

The ancient boundary of the manor of Shene survived until quite recent times as parish and borough boundaries, but it may be useful to trace it out in modern terms. Starting from the south, it left the river bank at a point just inside the riverside Buccleuch Gardens, ran north-east for some 200 feet, then turned back to the south-east to reach Petersham Road just south of the *Rose of York* public house. It then turned north-east again, running up the slope of the hill including most of the building of the *Petersham Hotel* and the whole of The Wick and its grounds, but excluding Wick House. On reaching the pavement of Richmond Hill it turned back to the south-east, passing through Richmond Gate close by the lodge and on into Richmond Park for nearly 600 yards to a point just outside Sidmouth Wood. From there it ran a little east of north to the spring on the southern edge of Conduit Wood. It then followed the course of the stream running north from that spring (Black Ditch), which flows today on the surface only as far as the park wall against Richmond cemetery. Thereafter the stream now runs underground, but its course (and the boundary) can be followed from the cemetery gates, along Grove Road and the eastern edge of Pesthouse Common and then, cutting through the grounds of Courtlands, to a point just east of the traffic lights at the junction of Queen's Road and the Sheen Road. Thence the boundary ran northwards along the eastern side of Manor Road and Sandycombe Road to the crossroads with Broomfield Road and Kew Gardens Station Approach. It then continued up the eastern side of Atwood's Alley and the first part of Forest Road, up to the bend; then along the foot of the railway embankment to a point some 90 yards from the riverbank. From there it turned south-easterly to follow a line roughly parallel with the river for 600 yards or so, passing to the north of the Public Record Office building, and finally turning back 120 yards to the river.

To the south lay the small manor of Petersham, which remained in the hands of Chertsey Abbey until the reign of Henry V, and to the east was the Archbishop of Canterbury's large manor of Mortlake (or Wimbledon, as it was later called), which included Mortlake, Roehampton, Putney and Wimbledon. A bank of earth, called in later times 'Mortlake Bank' or 'Bailey's Bank', stood along most of the boundary with Mortlake, and was within that manor.

✠

*Plate 5*     If one looks at a relief map of the area of Richmond and the land to its east and south one sees the River Thames winding in a flat plain to the west and north of two blocks of hills, separated by the valley of Beverley Brook. The westerly block, of Richmond Hill, Coombe Hill and Kingston Hill, is now largely within Richmond Park. It has a steep escarpment on its western side, but falls away more gently to the north and east. Its highest point, 56 metres above sea level, is between Pembroke Lodge and the Sidmouth Plantation in Richmond Park, and is separated by a dip (at Ham Cross) from the Coombe and Kingston hills. The easterly block, between the valleys of Beverley Brook and the River Wandle, is the area of Putney Heath and Wimbledon Common, with a more extensive flat plateau.

In the river plain to the north of these hills large areas in Barnes and Chiswick, along the river by the borders of Kew and Mortlake, around Brentford Docks and in the grounds of Syon House and along the Surrey bank from the Isleworth Gate of Kew Gardens up to Richmond Bridge – lie below the 5-metre contour line. There are relatively narrow belts of low-lying land along the river's edge in Twickenham and from Petersham Meadows around the river bend that encircles the western side of Ham. It is possible that in ancient times this low land was either within the bed of a river wider then than it is today or was marshland. Another extensive marshy area lay further inland at the foot of the northern slopes of Richmond Hill, around the border between Shene and Mortlake and extending from what is now the Lower Mortlake Road southwards as far as the lower part of Queen's Road, Richmond, and Pesthouse Common.

Beverley Brook was the only important Surrey tributary of the Thames that was near to the manor of Shene, though wholly outside its boundaries. There were, however, a number of streams which had their origins in springs in the hilly ground in the area. The Sudbrook (or South Brook) rose in the northern slopes of Coombe Hill and flowed down through Hatch (the area around Ham Common) and Petersham to join the Thames near the end of River Lane. A small brook, from a spring near Richmond Church, followed the line of Red Lion Street and Water Lane, and was named (in manor roll entries of 1496 and 1535) as 'Mochebroke'[3] and later as 'Midbroke'. A stream which ran down Richmond Hill probably gave its name to the Moorbrook estate on the slope between Richmond Hill and the Petersham Road.

From the area near the 'White Conduit' in Conduit Wood in Richmond Park the Black Ditch stream which formed for much of its length the boundary between Shene (or Richmond) and Mortlake ran northwards to discharge into the marsh. Another 'Black Ditch' ran from the village pond (on the site of Dome Building) along the Kew and Mortlake Roads and also discharged into the marsh. From the eastern slopes of the Richmond Hill uplands some small streams ran down to join Beverley Brook.

There were also of course other ditches which drained the cultivated fields and the meadows, but whether any of them had a regular flow of water cannot now be determined.

The islands in the River Thames were once more numerous than they are today. Some have been joined together, some taken in to the river bank. Many of these 'islands' or aits (or eyots) were in fact mere bullrush or osier beds, the ownership of which was however important when bullrushes and osiers were a commodity in demand for basket-weaving. Others served as the bases for fishing weirs.

Along the river bank were water meadows – stretching in a thin ribbon around the riverbend to the north-east of the hamlet of Kew, and possibly in another ribbon round the bend by what is now Isleworth Ait, but was then a cluster of smaller aits. The hamlet of Kew grew up at the Surrey end of a major ford across the River Thames from Brentford where there was some solid ground on both sides of the river – the lowest point at which an army could ford the Thames at low tide.

The area around Kew was probably mostly woodland and heath, though a small field reserved exclusively for the Kew inhabitants was evidently reclaimed from the waste at quite an early date. The two main cultivated fields of the manor stretched downwards on the northern slopes of what today is Richmond Hill and across the flat land west of the marsh about half the way up to Kew. The village of Shene developed close to the manor house, on the western side of these fields. To the north and north-west of the manor house lay the demesne lands and the Lord's hunting grounds – an unenclosed warren of rough heathland. To the south-east of the fields the Great Common of Shene stretched into what is now Richmond Park, and a smaller common lay on the western slope of the hill between the fields and the river.

✠

Before considering the holdings of land in the manor of Shene we should look briefly at the system itself under which this land was held. The manor was the basic unit of local administration throughout the country; the word, of Norman origin, had been easily applied to the broadly similar existing English system of vills and villages. What the Normans had done was to impose over this system a more rigid feudal structure. Under the king, who was the ultimate landowner and landlord, were the great earls (the old Saxon word was used here instead of the Norman 'count') whose holdings were 'counties' (replacing the English 'shires'). In each county a vice-count or shire-reeve (sheriff) acted as tax collector and government accountant.*

The earls and the other great barons held their lands directly from the king and in return owed him the service of the armies which they could raise. In their turn they granted land to lesser magnates who were responsible for providing the men, arms and horses to constitute those armies. And so the system proceeded downwards to the lord of the manor, who was himself the vassal of a greater lord, but the lord of his own tenants. The average manor was rated for 'one Knight's service', so that in time of military necessity the lord of the manor himself – or a substitute provided by him – would have to muster a fully-armed knight in the service of his lord, and ultimately of the king.

That was the basic theory, but there were many variations from it. Many manors were still controlled by the king himself, and their lords held 'from the King', usually by knight's service but sometimes by serjeanty.

Serjeanty was the provision of a civil, rather than a military, service; and was of two kinds. Grand serjeanty required the provision of a given specific service, such as that of acting as the king's cupbearer at his coronation (Shene was held from the king by this serjeanty). Petty serjeanty required only the provision of some specified object at a specified time. In practice, when money taxes were being levied, serjeanties were equated with knights' service, so that the holder of Shene and the holder of Coombe (by one knight's service) would each be assessed for the same amount. Some of the

---

* Although the Latin records continued to refer to this post as 'vice-comes', the English term sheriff won general acceptance as the title, leaving the word viscount to be revived much later as a rank of nobility between baron and earl.

free tenants of the manor were assessed for tiny fractions of a knight's service – and it was quite common for smaller sub-manors to be rated at, say, one-quarter or one-fifth of a knight's service.

The lord of the manor was, under his own lord or the king, in theory the owner of all the land within his manor. Some of this land would be reserved for his own direct use as 'demesne' land. Some would be laid out in open common fields, usually in strips, for cultivation by the manorial tenants. This land was granted to them and they enjoyed (in theory at least) the protection of their lord – in return for labour services to help the lord cultivate his demesne land. In some manors the labour obligation was ill-defined and almost open-ended; in Shene it was, at least by 1314, fairly clearly defined and not unduly onerous. Other land in the manor would be stipulated as 'common land' on which the manorial tenants had recognised rights such as the pasturage of animals and the collection of firewood, although such commons were in the lord's direct ownership. Whatever was left over was the manorial waste, again in the ownership of the lord – and over large tracts of which he might be granted the right of warren (or hunting on unenclosed land – it was later that 'warren' developed the narrower sense of a breeding ground for game, especially rabbits, and then of a complex of rabbits' burrows).

The normal grant of land to a manorial tenant was a 'whole tenement' consisting of a messuage (house) with a small amount of ground (the curtilage) around it*, a virgate of land (being approximately the amount that one tenant and his family could be expected to cultivate with their own resources) and an allocation of meadow. Some tenants had only a half-tenement. In the typical English open-field system the virgate of land would be a collection of separate strips, each of an acre or half-acre in extent, scattered throughout the fields. The two or three main fields would be subdivided into smaller units, the names of which varied from region to region, but which in Shene were either 'shotts' (presumably the length of a bowshot) or 'furlongs' (the length of a plough furrow).

The 'ideal' acre strip in such a shott would be a furlong (220 yards) in length by a chain in width (the chain of 22 yards being four rods, poles or perches and the rod, etc, being the length of a yoke of a team of oxen). In practice the dimensions of the shotts and the strips might vary considerably and a 'one-acre' strip might be anything between a half and one and a half times the statute acre. Such fluctuations were sometimes the result of geographical features such as roads or streams which formed convenient boundaries; it may also be that they resulted from a rough and ready attempt to make allowances for the quality of the land. The dispersion of the strips meant both that all tenants might have a reasonable share of good and poor land and that their overall holdings were probably much the same in total area despite the variation in size of particular notional 'acres' or 'half acres'.

* The term 'capital messuage' was in origin simply the 'head house' of such a whole tenement.

# 2

## *Shene in the Thirteenth Century*

THE FIRST LANDOWNERS in Shene, other than the Belet family, whose names are recorded, were Hubert de Burgh, the king's chamberlain, and John de Valtort in the year 1200.[1] Of their holdings, or what was the nature of the case in the King's Bench in which they were involved, other than that it concerned land at Shene, we know nothing. In 1204 we have the name of another inhabitant, who was presumably a man of some importance, Richard Palmer. He had excused himself from attendance at another legal suit on grounds of illness – a matter which required the despatch of four knights to 'Sienes' to check the story. They reported that he was indeed unwell, and that they had set a new date for him to appear at the Tower of London.[2]

Then at an unspecified date during his lordship (*c*.1207-1214) Michael Belet gave a charter to Walkeline de Caneton granting the latter a virgate of (free) land in the manor of 'Scenes' held by widow Wolinns and half a virgate formerly held by Geoffrey Dipere. The document, very clearly written in a minuscule script, bears the name of many witnesses, but they do not seem likely to have been Shene tenants.[3] In 1214 occurred the case in which Michael Belet was found to have illegally disseised (dispossessed) Roger de Burun and his wife Matilda of common pasture in 'Scien' which belonged to their free tenement in that village.[4] Henry Cocus and Geoffrey de Ware were guarantors for the fine imposed on Belet; de Ware and At Ware are ancient Kew family names – 'Ware' being almost certainly a corruption of 'weir'.

The list of serjeanties compiled in 1244, from information which, in Surrey at least, dated back to the time of Michael Belet, recorded that the Templars held one virgate in 'Shenes', and Robert de Bello Campo (Beauchamp) another.[5] Dugdale's *Monasticon* cites a gift to the Templars by 'John Vautort (Valletort) and his forebears' of ten shillings of annual rents and seven acres of arable land in Shene.[6] (The ten shillings' rents might well be the yield on the remaining part of one virgate.) It seems likely that the Templars had disposed of this holding by 1250, as there is no mention of them in the document of that year discussed below. In any case, whatever land was still held by the Templars was seized by Edward II when he suppressed the order in England in 1308.

6

The efforts of Alice, widow of Michael Belet, to pursue her dowry claims yield some further information on land holdings. On 17 February 1218/9 she reached agreement with the Prior of Merton to grant to him and his successors six acres of (arable) land and three acres of meadow in 'Scenes', part of her dowry, in return for an annuity.[7] In 1220 she claimed from William de Colevill and his wife Matilda as her dowry a one-third share of one carucate and one virgate of land in 'Shenys'.[8] Ten years later, she and her new husband Roger de la Dune were claiming as her dowry 8½ virgates and 12 acres of land and two shillings of rents in Shene.[9]

It is not until 1250 that a detailed return of serjeanties (which were to be commuted into money rents) first gives us a significant list of main landowners and some sub-tenants in Shene, after the division of the manor between Emma Oliver and Alice de Valletort, the daughters of John Belet.[10] The return notes that their serjeanty 'is in part alienated' and goes on to detail the assignees, who fall into a number of groups.

1.  Ralph Postel and his undertenants. Ralph Postel of Kingston was the descendant of a long line of Ralph Postels who had, since the time of Henry I, held a hide of land at Coombe by the serjeanty of being 'collector of the Queen's wool' – a service that is recorded in Domesday Book as then held by one of the villeins of Kingston under the charge of Humphrey the Chamberlain. By 1250 this holding, which was always separate from the former Belet holding at Coombe, had passed into the hands of one Peter Baldwin, but Ralph Postel had invested in some land in Shene. He owed for this land service of 1/20 of a knight's fee; and in addition he paid, on his own behalf and by their agreement that of the sub-tenants, an annual fine of 7s. 8d., being a third part of the annual value of the property. The landowners listed in this group were:

| | | |
|---|---|---|
| Ralph Postel | 8ac | worth 4s p.a. |
| John Syser | 1ac | 8d |
| Robert Merchant | 1ac | 8d |
| Gilbert le Kersere | 4ac | 4s |
| Simon den de Amur | 5ac (& 1 perch) | 5s |
| Ralph Wakelein | 1ac (& 12d rents) | 2s |
| William Marshall (of Kingston) | 1ac | 12d |
| Simon Yve | 1½ac | 9d |
| Robert Merchant (again) | 1ac | 12d |
| William (son of Edwy) | 1 messuage | 2s |

A total of 23½ acres, one house and 12d. rents worth £1 1s. 1d. per annum.

2.  Nicholas Premerole held 14 acres worth 9s. p.a., and paid a fine of 3s. p.a. and owed service for 1/70 of a knight's fee.

3.  William de la Strode (a former bailiff of Kingston) held half a virgate worth 5s. p.a. and paid a fine of 20d. p.a. and owed service for 1/60 of a knight's fee.

4.    Ralph Wlvrich (*sic*) held 4½ acres worth 2s. 6d. and paid a fine of 10d. p.a.

5.    John de Valletort and sub-tenants. John de Valletort, husband of Alice Belet, owed service of half a knight's fee for their manorial land which was not alienated. On his own behalf and those of the sub-tenants he paid an annual fine of 4s. – one-third of the 11s. 10d. value of the alienated land – all in Alice's part of the manor. The holdings were:

| | | |
|---|---|---|
| John de Valletort | ½ virgate & 7ac | worth 8s p.a. |
| Edith, daughter of Adam | | |
| de Taurente | 5½ ac | 20d |
| John Lambard | 1½ ac | 6d |
| Adam de Tarante | 5½ ac | 20d |

6.    Sub-tenants of Emma Oliver, who herself owed service for half a knight's fee, and who paid on behalf of these tenants of her part of the manor a fine of 8s. p.a. The holdings, with a total value of two marks p.a., were:

| | | |
|---|---|---|
| Roger de Senes | 4½ ac | worth 20d p.a. |
| Walter Cissor | 1 virgate | 5s |
| Geoffrey de Wherry | 4 virgates | 20s |

7.    The Prior of Merton held 41 shillings worth of rents and 8½ acres of pasture and one acre of mead, worth 10 shillings, and paid a fine of 15 shillings per annum. (The land was probably that granted by Alice Belet, though the description is not quite identical.)

The total property listed as alienated amounted to six virgates and a further 75½ acres of land, one messuage and 42 shillings' worth of rents. All this must be assumed to be freehold property – and, in origin, demesne land of the manor, much of which had probably been originally split off as dowries and subsequently sold to realise its value. The values given for the different parcels of land measured in acres vary considerably, from under 4d. an acre to as much as 12d. an acre. (We will leave aside for the moment the question of how many acres constituted a virgate at this time, but the land in the holdings of Walter Cissor and Geoffrey de Wherry was almost certainly at a valuation of only 3d. (or a little over) per acre.) This variation makes it virtually impossible to attempt to translate the Merton rents into terms of land; however, there was evidently a significant acreage owned by the Priory but let to sub-tenants.

It is interesting that, in this final commutation of the serjeanty service for Shene into money rents (or knight's service fees), no reduction was made in the knight's service due from Emma and Alice, or their husbands, on account of the alienated land. Not only was an extra 2/25 of a knight's service due from three of the assignees, but money rents totalling 40s. 2d. a year were levied in addition. The serjeanty was commuted to an annual rent of 4s. levied on each half of the manor, or 8s. in all.

It is not clear from which part of the manor the holdings of Postel, Premerole, de la Strode and Wlvrich arose; but in 1253 the suit brought by Emma against Alice and her husband resulted in the recognition by Emma of one carucate of land in 'Westshenes' as being a part of Alice's dowry.[11] This would be about equivalent to the total of the land listed in groups 1-5 above. Emma's remaining land, after she had surrendered the manorial rights to Gilbert de Clare in 1264, was also one carucate (and a messuage), which she and her last husband William de Wylburham sold in 1270 to William le Zuche, brother of Adam, first Lord Zouche, and a former Sheriff of Surrey (1261-66).[12]

The lordship of the manor was, as related in *Palaces and Parks*, sold by Hugh de Windsor in 1271/2 to Robert Burnell, the Chancellor, and by him in 1275 to Sir Otto de Grandison with the provision that it should revert to the Burnell family if Grandison died without heirs.[13] In 1279 Grandison was given a grant of free warren in his demesne lands of Shene.[14] When he set off to the Crusade in 1290 he reinvested Burnell conditionally with the manors of Shene and Ham (also purchased by him from Burnell with a similar condition). The *post mortem* enquiry into lands held after Burnell's death at Berwick on 25 October 1292 while Grandison was still away therefore showed Burnell as holding Shene (among a total of 82 manors). The description of his share of the manor and its annual income was as follows:[15]

|  | worth p.a. |  |
|---|---|---|
| Capital messuage, garden, dovecote and park | 0 | (because of resumption)* |
| 200 acres of arable land at 4d an acre [demesne] | 3.6.8 | |
| 16 acres of meadow at 1s 6d an acre [demesne] | 1.4.0 | |
| a several pasture [demesne] | 3.0 | |
| a rabbit warren | 13.4 | |
| assised rents of free tenants | 16.11 | |
| assised rents of customary tenants | 1.16.10 | |
| the works of customary tenants | 10.6 | |
| pleas and perquisites of the Lord's Courts | 4.0 | |
| a free fishery | 1.0 | |
|  | 8.16.3 | |

Grandison had returned and reclaimed his land by 1295 and in the following year was granted permission to lease out the manor of Shene; which it appears that he did to Edward, Prince of Wales.[16] The other portion of the manor (without the rights of lordship) had meanwhile remained in the hands of John de Valletort, husband of Alice Belet, who died towards the end of 1300. The inquest on his property, held on 22 April 1301,[17] listed:

---

* Both here and at Ham certain items were said to have a nil value 'because of resumption'. This presumably meant that no rent would accrue to Burnell or his heirs as Grandison was about to reclaim his estate.

|  | worth p.a. |
|---|---|
| 200 acres of arable land at 2d an acre (*sic*) | 16.8 |
| 12 acres of meadow at 1s an acre | 12.0 |
| pasture in a little island of the Thames called la Wynyard | 1.0 |
| assised rents of 6 free tenants | 2.12.2 |
| assised rents of 13 customary tenants | 1.10.1 |
| the works of the customary tenants at harvest | 1.3.3½ |
| and – held of Otto de Grandison at a rent of 6d p.a.: | |
| a messuage with a garden worth p.a. 1s | |
| 20 acres of arable worth p.a. 3s 4d | } 5.4 |
| 1 acre of meadow worth p.a. 1s | |
| | 7.0.6½ |

As Edward I's confirmation of Burnell's sale to Grandison (dated 6 January 1279/80) mentioned that he had purchased 15 acres of meadow from Robert (*sic*) de Valle Torte,[18] it would seem likely that Alice's share of the manor contained almost all of the original meadowland. It is also noteworthy that the rents of free tenants in this part of the manor amounted to over three times that in Burnell's part. While no exact calculation can be made equating these rents with those mentioned in 1250, it is perhaps worth noting that the sum of the annual values of the lands held in 1250 by Postel, Premerole, de la Strode, Wlvrich, the Prior of Merton and the three direct sub-tenants of de Valletort amounted to £2 13s. 5d. This is quite close to the £2 12s.2d. listed in the de Valletort inquest – the difference could be explained by a small part of the Merton lands being in the other half of the manor. There is, however, no easy way to reconcile Burnell's rents from free tenants of only 16s. 11d. with the annual value of £1 6s. 8d. given for the alienated lands in Emma's part in 1250.

As for the customary tenants, it is interesting that, while the money rents owed by them are higher (by 6s. 9d.) in the Burnell part of the manor, the value of harvest works is far higher (by 12s. 9½d.) in Valletort's portion. Presumably the process of commution of labour services to money rents had proceeded more rapidly under absentee landlords, for John and Alice de Valletort seem to have lived at Shene while Emma Belet and her five husbands had regularly leased out their property.

A problem which cannot be resolved is the actual amount of demesne arable land in the Valletort portion. The original inquest document reads quite clearly: 200 acres at 2d an acre – 16s. 8d. There may have been an arithmetical slip and the value should have been given as 33s. 4d.; or the holding may have been only 100 acres; it is most unlikely that the land was worth only 1d. an acre. Although one might expect that the land would have been equally shared between the two sisters, the apparent preponderance of meadow in the original Valletort portion suggests that this was not the case. As meadow would have had a far higher value than arable land, there may have been a balancing discrepancy in the arable – so perhaps the '100 acres' hypothesis is the most likely.

The picture of the manor of Shene that emerges in the second half of the 13th century is sketchy, but has some clear features. The manor house has a garden and an enclosed park (probably quite small). There is a stretch of land devoted to a hunting and rabbit warren. There are either 300 or 400 acres of arable demesne land, plus some extra but quite small pieces of pasture and a total of 28 acres of demesne meadows. There is a fishery (probably the one granted by Henry II to Robert Belet in 1164-65).

There are a number of free tenants – perhaps nine or ten – who between them hold some 5½ virgates and 60 acres (excluding John de Valletort's own holding), and perhaps some 25 to 30 customary tenants who pay rents totalling £3 6s. 11d. and also owe harvest labour worth a total of £1 13s. 9½d. Of the land farmed by these customary tenants, however, we as yet know nothing. Merton Priory has a significant stake in the manor, with 9½ acres of land in its own hands and rents from other properties amounting to no less than 41 shillings a year. The total value of the manor is about £16, not counting the manor house and its park.

✠

In the first years of the 14th century three incidents ruffled the rural calm of Shene. The first was the execution by hanging of John de Pynkeney. We do not know who he was or what crime he had committed; only that the value of his forfeited goods was the large figure of £24 10s. 0½d., and that sum was required to be paid by the township of Shene; until in April 1302 a pardon was granted to the inhabitants and they were let off the payment.[19] Three years later John, son of Walter Paroles of Shene, was killed (by accident or design?) by Simon, son of Maurice of Petersham, who was held in the Marshalsea Prison,[20] but who was subsequently pardoned.[21]

The third incident was a juicy bit of gossip, recorded in the registers of Bishop Woodlock of Winchester. In November 1310 Elianore, wife of John Vautort of Schene, laid a complaint that her husband had committed adultery with Dionysia (Denise) Le Ladde, daughter of the constable of Shene. In February Dionysia was publicly excluded from church on account, not of her guilt in this matter, but of her 'insolence displayed before the commissioners of our court'. The probable cause of Dionysia's attitude emerged three weeks later when Elianore, the complainant, was excommunicated for slander.[22]

This incident occurred just a year after John de Vautort (or Valletort) had been pressured into selling for 100 marks to Hugh le Despenser his entire estate, described as 'one messuage and one carucate of land and twenty acres of meadow and 7 marks of rents in West Shene, Cumbe and Baggashete'.[23] (As the Coombe and Bagshot holdings of the Belet family had long since passed out of their hands, the property listed can be read as relating solely to the Valletort holding at Shene.) The 7 marks of rents (£4 13s. 4d.) compares with £4 2s. 3d. from free and customary tenants given in the 1301 inquest, but perhaps there had been some further commutation of labour services in the intervening ten years.

# 3

# *Shene in 1314*

BY 1313 THE WHOLE MANOR of Shene was reunited in the hands of King Edward II. Sir Otto de Grandison had retired to his original home by Lake Geneva, obtaining licence to quit England for good – and probably surrendering his rights to Shene when he did so. Hugh le Despenser had handed over to the king the other half of the manor which he had acquired from John de Vautort, and also the reversionary rights of the Burnell heirs to Grandison's portion. These he had obtained in 1312 after marrying his daughter to Bishop Burnell's grandson Edward.* On 7 October 1313 the king granted the custody of his manor of Shene, during pleasure, to John de Boseham.[1]

A recent development in manorial practice at that time was the recording in writing of the labour services due ('custumals') and the compilation of manorial surveys ('extents'). It is very probable that the return to the Crown and the granting to John de Boseham of the manor of Shene was the occasion for such an exercise, so that Boseham should know exactly what the revenues should be, what services should be performed, and what outgoings in wages and food allowances would be incurred.

The document, preserved in the Public Record Office[2] which records an 'extent' of the manor of Shene at this period is written on both sides of a single large membrane in a clear but small script, in Latin with many abbreviations. It has no heading or date, but appears to be a part of a manorial court roll – no doubt preserved when the rest was destroyed because of its intrinsic importance. It notes which of the free tenants were present at the court, and concludes with a record of four transactions 'at the court'.

The 'extent' had probably been prepared to be checked and attested at the court. This part of the document contains several deletions, marginal additions and interlineations which may well be last-minute corrections made after consultation with the jurors. It concludes with a marginal notation of the names of three villein tenants who had perhaps vouched for its accuracy.

The document not only lists all the tenants, free and villein, by name, their holdings, the money rents paid and the labour services due (in full detail), but it also illuminates in various ways the life in the village at that time. It also provides us with the first hard

---

* See *Palaces and Parks*, ch.1.

evidence of the existence of a small hamlet at Kew, for five of the tenants are named 'de Cayho' or variants thereof.*

Apart from the intrinsic likelihood that such an extent and custumal would have been drawn up by, or for the benefit of, John de Boseham as the newly appointed keeper of the manor, the very first entry helps to confirm the dating. It refers to the fact that Walter Waldeschaft held two carucates of land in Turbeville 'as of the manor of Shene'. Turbeville was not in the manor, but was a small separate estate or sub-manor in the vicinity of Tolworth. It had been acquired, as had Shene, by the Burnell family in the late 13th century and in 1313 John de Berewyck had died seised of the manor of Turbeville which he held 'from the heirs of Philip Burnel, as of the manor of Shene'[3] (which meant that, for administrative convenience, its accounts etc. were included with those of Shene).

Berewyck's heir in 1313 was a young cousin Roger Huse, who being a minor was placed in wardship. A Hubert de Swynesford took over the manor, but his title was contested and alleged fraudulent. He, however, granted Turbeville to Walter Waldeschaft. Then the younger Hugh le Despenser (who already owned Tolworth and had his eye on Turbeville) stepped in. According to a petition presented by Roger Huse in 1331, Despenser put pressure on Waldeschaft, saying that he held Turbeville without the king's licence and was depriving the king of his rights and income from the wardship. Waldeschaft promptly gave way and surrendered the manor to Despenser who held it until his execution in 1326. It was then seized by the Crown and regranted to the Earl of Kent, so Roger Huse never regained it.

Although the precise dates of Waldeschaft's tenure are not established, it was clearly brief and likely to have been soon after 1313. We can therefore with some confidence assign *circa* 1314 as a date for our extent of the manor of Shene.

A full translation is given in Appendix 2, but the main details can be summarised here.

The freehold tenants (those present at the Court are marked +) were:

|  | Annual Rent |
|---|---|
| Walter Waldeschaft – the sub-manor of Turbeville (2 carucates of land) | 18s |
| +Ralph Postel – one messuage and 3 acres | 0 |
| William atte Church – one messuage and a curtilage (also liable for some labour at harvest and haymaking) | 2s |
| John le Clerke – one messuage and half a curtilage (also liable for some labour at harvest and haymaking) | 13d |
| +Mary widow Parole – one messuage and half a curtilage | 6d |

---

* What appear to be the earliest references to the place name occur in the Pipe Rolls for 1201 and 1202. They are, however, in the form of personal surnames and their relevance to Kew in Surrey is uncertain. William de Cahiho owed money for land at Aylesford in Kent in 1201. John de Caiho, a citizen of London, was joint sheriff of London and Middlesex in 1202.

+Isabell de Bingates – one messuage and 10 acres, and 1 acre meadow          6s 8d*

John le Walsche – one messuage and 9 acres, and 1 acre meadow          12d

John le Schephurde – one messuage and 4½ acres and a rood          15½d

+Henry le Meleward – one messuage and 1½ acres and a rood          3d

John Valentyn – one messuage and 10 acres (also liable for some labour at harvest)          2s

+Stephen Lombard – one messuage and 8½ acres and a rood, and 1 acre meadow          2d

Denis le Lad – one messuage and 5 acres, and 1½ acres meadow (and holds pasture land)          2d

Richard de Valtort – one acre and one rood          1d

Thomas atte Bosco [Wood] – 36 acres, and 4 acres meadow          14d

+Alice widow of Henry Warre – 4 virgates          8s

The villein tenants (all of whom owed labour services in addition to money rents) were:

|  | *Annual Rent* |
|---|---|
| Richard de Cayho [Kew] – one messuage and 20½ acres, and 2 acres meadow | 3s 10d |
| Alice de Cayesho [Kew] – one messuage and 18 acres, and 2 acres meadow | 2s 10d |
| John Ho – one messuage and 14½ acres, and 2 acres meadow | 3s |
| John le Clerke de Cayesho [Kew] – one messuage and 18 acres, and 2 acres meadow | 3s 5d |
| Richard Love – one messuage and 9 acres, and 1 acre meadow | 2s |
| John Cayhow [Kew] – one messuage and 9 acres, and 1 acre meadow | 18d |
| Alice widow Carpenter – one messuage and 9 acres, and 1 acre meadow | 18d |
| Isabell Binnegates – one messuage and 9 acres, and 1 acre meadow | o |
| William le Drivere – 9 acres, and 1 acre meadow | 2s |
| Christen widow Simon – one messuage and 9 acres, and 1 acre meadow | 18d |
| John Goionn – one messuage and 9 acres, and 1 acre meadow | 18d |
| Gilbert Binnegate – one messuage and 9 acres, and 1 acre meadow | 18d |
| Thomas le Thrishere – one messuage and 9 acres, and 1 acre meadow | 18d |
| John Ermite – one messuage and 9 acres, and 1 acre meadow | 18d |
| Gilbert Ho – one messuage and 13½ acres, and 1½ acres meadow | 2s 8d |
| Adam Ladde – one messuage and 13½ acres, and 1½ acres meadow | 2s 3d |
| Anne widow Wary – one messuage and 18 acres, and 2 acres meadow | 3s |
| Gilbert Vagge – one messuage and 18 acres, and 2 acres meadow | 4s |
| Maud le Palmer – one messuage_and 18 acres 'as above' [?2 acres meadow] | 3s |
| Maud de Binnegates – 'as above' [?1 messuage and 18 acres and 2 acres meadow] | 3s |
| Adam Bigge – 'as above' [?1 messuage and 18 acres and 2 acres meadow] | 3s 6d |
| Gilbert de Cyho [Kew] – 'as above' [?1 messuage and 18 acres and 2 acres meadows] | 3s |
| William Thomas – 'as above' [?1 messuage and 18 acres and 2 acres meadow] | 4s |
| John Pargent – 'as above' [?1 messuage and 18 acres and 2 acres meadow] | 3s |

* After the name of Isabell de Bingates is a deleted entry for Christen de (?Nautarum Sinus). Nautarum Sinus was Rotherhithe — but the reading is dubious.

Maud Balis – 'as above' [?1 messuage and 18 acres and 2 acres meadow]        3s

Gilbert Bonde – 'as above' [?1 messuage and 18 acres and 2 acres meadow]        4s

John Randulph – 'as above' [?1 messuage and 18 acres and 2 acres meadow]        3s

## Additional – from the Court transactions:

John le Walsch – a virgate of land        3s

Robert Ladde – one messuage and 18 acres, and 2 acres meadow        3s

The total number of free tenants was 14, and of villeins twenty-nine. It is interesting to note how many of them were women (not all named as widows) – three out of the 14 free tenants and eight of the villeins – just over a quarter of the total. Only four of the names can be linked to those in the 1250 list: Valletort, Postel, Lombard and de Wherry (now Warre). But, as will be seen later, many more names recur in a tax list of 1332, and some of the names which appear here for the first time are those of families which continued in Shene for hundreds of years (e.g. Byngate, Walshe and Ho – later Hoo, Hough or Howe).

The document shows that this was a transitional time in Shene. Some of the freehold tenants are still liable to perform labour services (though they may have received some pay). There is a very wide diversity in the freehold quit rents, which seem to bear little relation to the size of the holdings. Perhaps this was because some were old-established freeholds while others were only recently enfranchised. For instance Thomas atte Bosco (Wood) paid only 14 pence for his 36 acres while Isabell de Binnegates paid 6s. 8d. for 10 acres plus one acre of meadow (plus perhaps the further nine acres and one acre of meadow which she held in villeinage, for which no separate rent is recorded but which was liable for the full range of services). It is clearly a period of transition when the same tenant has both free and villein holdings.

Two of the court transactions illustrate this point further. Both relate to the Ladde family. Robert Ladde's lands had been seized by the lord because he had falsely claimed to be a freeman. Having admitted, after interrogation, to being a *nativus* (a born bondsman) he was allowed to have his lands back on payment of a fine of 20 shillings – a large sum when a day's labour could be worth only one penny. Another member of the family, Denis Ladde, was however permitted, on payment of a 40-shilling fine, to convert his smaller holding into a freehold on the grounds that his occupation of carter prevented him on occasion from performing the customary services. The treatment of both cases suggests, in the context of the time, a relatively enlightened and liberal manorial administration.

There is much more consistency in the money rents paid by the tenants in villeinage. The norm, from which there are a few but not very large deviations, seems to have been a rent of three shillings a year for a 'whole tenement' consisting of a messuage, 18 acres of arable land and two acres of meadow. A few tenants paid at a rate of four shillings, or a figure between three and four shillings. Those holding three-quarters, or half, of a whole tenement paid *pro rata*. It is possible that those paying at a higher rate had commuted some of the services due – and some cases seem to bear out this theory, but there is no very clear pattern.

There was an additional charge for pannage (the pasturage of pigs) and for the hire of meadows. The normal rate was 1d. a year for pannage and ½d. a year for a lot of meadow, but these charges were levied only if the facility was used. Richard of Kew, who must have been the principal pig breeder, paid a special annual fee of 6d. for pannage.

The labour services due from the villein tenants cover the whole gamut of the manor's farm life, but they were mostly clearly defined and not arbitrary. Moreover they took some account of the individual's need to harvest his own crops while helping the lord to get his harvest in. The services to be rendered were as follows:

**Cultivation**

| | | |
|---|---|---|
| Ploughing | All but three of the villein tenants owed seven days' service. | *Plate 1* |
| Harrowing | In general the holders of whole tenements were liable for half | |
| Hoeing | a day's hoeing; holders of half-tenements had to harrow for half | |
| Digging (ditches presumably) | a day and dig for half a day. | |

**Haymaking**

| | | |
|---|---|---|
| Mowing | Most of the holders of whole tenements had to mow 'daily when needed', but some had a clear obligation to work for one or two days, and the holders of half-tenements were limited to one day's work. | *Plate 6* |
| Lifting | For almost all, this service was 'for as long as needed'. | |
| Carting | For 'as long as needed' in most cases of whole tenements, but not required for half-tenements. | |

**Harvest**

| | | |
|---|---|---|
| Reaping | 'Every other day' in all cases, but the holders of whole tenements had to produce two men rather than one. (One tenant, Adam Bigge, had for some reason to produce five men.) | *Plate 6* |
| Threshing and winnowing | Four bushels for a whole tenement, two for a half-tenement. | |
| Carting | Two days' work for a whole tenement, one day for a half-tenement. | |

**Carting dung to the lord's fields**

This service seems to have been calculated by virgates (of the lord's fields). It is clear that each holder of a half-tenement had to cart dung for a half virgate; whether, as would seem likely, the obligation for a whole tenement was for a whole virgate is not quite clear (as is explained below).

**Carting fuel for the lord**

This obligation applied to only three tenants, all living at Kew (where most of the woodland must have been). Richard of Kew and Alice of Kew 'jointly provide cartage for one cartload of fuel before Christmas, and they may return home on the same day'. John le Clerke of Kew 'carts fuel as the aforesaid Richard of Kew' (though presumably he must have carried a full cartload). What visions that little note about 'returning home the same day' conjures up: the long muddy track from the Shene manor house to Kew – perhaps almost impassable in wintry conditions, certainly dangerous in the early dark of a December afternoon – perhaps there were wolves in the woods. So the Steward reminds himself that 'I must remember to let them go early enough to get home before nightfall'!

**Sheep shearing**

Here the various tasks are distributed among most, but not all, of the tenants, whether they held whole or half-tenements. One prepared the sheepfold, one fetched the sheep, three guarded them, and one 'carried a rod'. Ten put in half a day's work washing and shearing the sheep, and four folded the fleeces.

*Plate 1*

**The provision of hurdles**

Some two-thirds of the tenants had an obligation to provide hurdles – 12 new ones had to be made each year. (Two tenants of half-tenements purchased, rather than made, a new hurdle each.) Most of the whole tenement holders also had a duty to repair existing hurdles.

**Other provisions**

Malt

About two-thirds of the holders of whole tenements had to produce two quarters of malt apiece, and all the holders of half-tenements had to produce one quarter. Adam Ladde, who was perhaps the village maltster or brewer, exceptionally had to produce 5½ quarters (but then he was exempted from any work at sheep shearing).

Eggs

Here there was no variation. Whole tenements provided 10 eggs at Easter, half-tenements five. What the lord did with these 230 eggs is not clear; perhaps they were all or mostly for hatching.

All the free tenants, except John le Clerke and Richard de Valtort, were liable to heriot – an inheritance tax which was normally levied in terms of 'the best beast' or a money equivalent. All villein tenants were liable to pay merchet – a payment made to the lord for the right to marry off a daughter. Though the principle differed little from the king's right to control the marriage of heiresses, the payment of merchet was always regarded as one of the clearest marks of servile status. All tenants, both free and villein, were obliged to make suit of court (i.e. to appear at the manor court) normally every three weeks, but there were some – perhaps the elderly and infirm – who were required to appear only once a year.

One of the four court transactions which follow the extent reads simply: 'All tenants, both freemen and villeins, recognized the lord and gave 20s.' This sum was a communal recognizance, as is made clear by a marginal note, not a charge on each individual. This act of allegiance further strengthens the case for the date of the extent being that of the first court after John de Boseham's grant of the manor. Whether the 20-shilling 'gift' was at that time an established custom it is difficult to say; there is no later reference to any such recognizance in the manor rolls.

So far we have looked only at the tenants' obligations, but the extent also spells out some obligations on the lord's part – the payment of money wages to two of the free tenants who gave service at harvest time (2d. a day for reaping and 1d. a day for lifting hay) and the provision both to them and to other tenants of free meals while working for the lord. John Valentyn's food allowance is spelled out in detail: 'for two days he receives for each day one loaf priced at a halfpenny and fish priced at a farthing; and on a third day for dinner sufficient bread and cheese and two hot dishes of meat or fish and two cakes priced at a farthing.' Richard de Cayho's entry gives the general pattern for remuneration for villeins: '... he hoes for a half day without food, but if he works for a whole day he receives food, viz: one loaf priced at a halfpenny and fish priced at a farthing, and the half day's work is worth 1d. And he mows for two days and receives nothing except a gift of as much grass as he can lift with his scythe,* and the day's work is worth 4d. And he lifts hay for two days without food, and the day's work is worth 1d. If he does not mow or lift the hay he is to receive nothing. And at harvest time he reaps with two men every other day, with food provided by the lord, and for any third day he receives allowances as John Valentyn.' In the entry for John Ho we are given two extra details: '... and for the lifting of the hay the lord provides food which will be carried to the fields – and by custom they have a sheep worth two shillings at the time of the haymaking.' Adam Bigge's entry makes it clear that the dinner worth three farthings is to be provided for all the extra men that he brings at harvest time; and both the entries for John Cayhow and for Isabell Binnegates mention the option of a money payment of three farthings in lieu of food.

It is interesting to compare the manorial revenues from rent with those given a few years before in the post mortem inquisitions of Bishop Burnell and John de Valletort in 1292 and 1301 respectively. Those showed Burnell with an income from free tenants

---

* A not uncommon form of payment – quite a lot of hay could be balanced and lifted on the handle of a scythe.

of 16s. 11d. and Valletort with £2 12s. 2d. – a total of £3 9s. 1d. By 1314 the rent from free tenants (excluding Turbeville) was only 24s. 4½d. A likely explanation is that a lot of demesne land which had been rented out, particularly Valletort's, had now been brought back into the direct control of the lord. The rents from customary (or villein) tenants which had amounted to £3 6s. 11d. (£1 16s. 10d. for Burnell and £1 10s. 1d. for Valletort) had now increased to £3 16s. (including the extra 6s. for the two holdings whose tenure was settled at the court) or possibly £3 19s. (if one transfers 3s. for Isabell Binnegates' villenage holding from the freehold to the customary list). This might indicate either an increase in rents charged or an increase in the cultivated area.

✣

It is evident from the 1314 extent that the 'whole tenement' in Shene was at that date a messuage, 18 acres of arable land and two acres of meadow. The 'virgate'* in Shene in 1314 was therefore 18 acres. Confirmation of this can be seen in the two consecutive entries relating to Gilbert Ho and Adam Ladde. Each held 13½ acres, or three-quarters of the normal eighteen acres, and one and a half acres of meadow. For some unexplained reason Gilbert Ho performed no labour services, but these were done for him by Adam Ladde who 'does service in all respects as above for one virgate and a half of land'. Again, the holding of John le Walshe, which is described as 'a virgate of land' in the court transactions, entails services 'in all respects as the aforesaid Anne' [widow Wary], who was the holder of 18 acres, etc.

Having established the area of the virgate, we can now calculate exactly the amount of cultivated land in Shene held by manorial tenants in 1314. The freeholdings (again omitting Turbeville) amounted to four virgates (72 acres) plus 90 acres – 162 in all. The holdings in villeinage were one virgate (18 acres) plus 404 acres – 422 in all, making a grand total of 584 acres. Assuming that the holdings described in virgate terms also had the usual allocation of meadowland, the notional extent of the meadows was 63½ acres.

The extent appears to provide us with a formula also for calculating the cultivated area in demesne – for the service of carting dung is described in terms of the area of the lord's land to which it is to be applied. However there is a snag. While it is explicit that all the holders of half-tenements (except Richard Love) are to 'cart animal dung in the fields for the lord as above to half a virgate of land', it is not so clear what the obligation is for holders of whole tenements and for Adam Ladde doing service for one and a half-tenements. At least thirteen whole-tenement holders (and Ladde) had an obligation to carry dung. The problem is that 'as above' in the formula just quoted (from the entry for John Cayhow) does not refer back to any previous entry. Dung is mentioned for the first time in John Cayhow's entry. Adam Ladde and Anne widow

---

* The size of the virgate, and the composition of the 'whole tenement' in Shene was to change later in the 14th century, as will be shown in chapter 9.

*Plate 1*

*Ploughing, from the Luttrell Psalter, c.1340 (British Library Add MS 42130 f.170).*

*Sheep in a fold – one being shorn, one being milked – and two women carrying food and drink to the fields, from the Luttrell Psalter (British Library Add MS 42130 f.163 verso).*

*Plate 2*

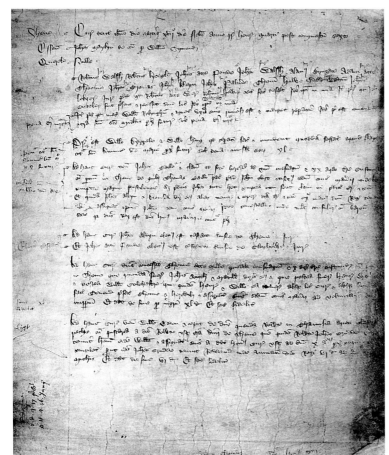

*Page of the roll recording the proceedings of the Manor Court held at Shene on 17 February 2 Henry IV (1404/5). (PRO: LR3/101/1, m.1)*

*Fishing from a boat, from Queen Mary's Psalter (British Library MS Royal 2Bvii, f.73).*

*Plate 3*

*This watercolour by Augustin Heckel shows two lines of stakes in the river to the right of the island. One is almost opposite the town wharf (note the squared-off masonry corner jutting into the river); the other about opposite the point where Friars' Lane now reaches the riverside. They were probably both parts of the same weir. (Private collection)*

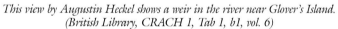

*This view by Augustin Heckel shows a weir in the river near Glover's Island.
(British Library, CRACH 1, Tab 1, b1, vol. 6)*

*Plate 4*

*Anne of Bohemia on her deathbed at Shene Palace. From a copy of Froissart's* Chronicles
*(British Library, Harleian MS 4380, f.22).*

Wary (the first named of the whole tenement holders who are expected to perform this service) 'cart dung as above'. It therefore seems likely that the carting of dung was omitted by accident from the list of duties of the first of the earlier named full tenement holders – in which case perhaps four other such tenants also carted dung. But was the obligation on the holder of a full tenement, as one would expect, twice that for a half-tenement – or is the 'as above' literally correct? If we take the least case, that only those tenants for whom the obligation is clear should be counted, and that every such tenant was liable for half a virgate only, we have 23 tenants delivering dung to 11½ virgates – i.e. 207 acres. If we assume that the obligation varied pro rata with the holding, the 23 tenants delivered their load to 19 virgates or 342 acres. If we bring in the other four tenants the total would be 23 virgates or 414 acres. The lowest figure seems, in the light of the 1292 and 1301 inquisitions, much too small. The largest figure seems too large to leave any room for warren land. So perhaps the middle one is the most likely to be correct.

The demesne land of Shene was to the north and north-west of the manor house, in the bend of the river opposite Isleworth. Judging from a later reference, a part of it may have been within the lower common field. The two open common fields of Shene circled the village on the north and east sides – the Lower Field beginning to the north of the Green (a common waste) and stretching up towards Kew and Mortlake, and the Upper Field on the slopes of the hill. Whether their boundaries were at that time identical with the subsequent ones will be considered later. To the north was the small Kew Field, divided between the inhabitants of that hamlet. To the north of Kew Field was another patch of common waste, triangular in shape – the future Kew Green – and to its east was the waste land of Kew Heath. Between Kew Field and the river on the west side was probably some of the freehold land. Around the bend of the river, opposite what is now called Brentford Ayt and the hamlet of Strand on the Green, lay the thin strip of manorial meadowland overlapping the western end of the manor of Mortlake. There may at this time have been some more manorial meadows opposite Isleworth.

On the eastern side of the Shene fields lay the Mortlake marsh, a part of which spread across the manor boundary into Shene, both north and south of the 'Marsh Gate' on the road leading to Putney. Then, further south again, and stretching up the hillside to the east of the Upper Field, was the Great Common, separated only by notional boundaries from the commons of Mortlake and Petersham, and connected by a quite narrow neck outside the southern corner of the Upper Field with the other stretch of common which ran down the steep western side of the hill to the river on the north-west side of Petersham Common. It is possible that some of the land between the south-west side of the Upper Field and the river was the original park of Shene manor house.*

* See *Palaces and Parks* I, p.49.

The village of Shene at this time would have consisted of little more than two score of cottages, mostly grouped along the south-east side of the Green, but a few others along the road (now George Street) south of the parish church. The church itself was still a chapel of ease to Kingston, served by priests nominated by the Vicar of Kingston (and probably visiting from Kingston), but the existence of Shene as a separate parish seems to be established in a deed of 1220.[4] The church belonged to Merton Priory, but was not yet endowed with the means to support a resident priest. Still, one wonders whether John le Clerke, with his house and half an acre of free land in 1314 (who was not liable for a heriot), might have been a priest and whether William atte Churche was his sexton – but this can be only speculation, and there was certainly no church at Kew to account for John le Clerke de Cayho!

Both John le Clerke and William atte Churche were freemen (though providing some paid labour at haymaking and harvest) and had two of the very small freeholdings listed. It can only be a guess, but perhaps their houses and that of widow Mary Parole occupied the ancient freehold site at the corner of what are now George Street and Church Court.

Some of these small holdings, such as those of Ralph Postel and Richard de Vautort, were evidently relics of earlier, larger, holdings that had been broken up. But some of the larger freeholdings seem to fit the pattern of whole or half tenements. Alice Warre with her four virgates was clearly the successor in title to Geoffrey de Wherry of 1250, whose holding was possibly the carucate claimed as far back as 1220 by Alice Belet as part of her dowry. The 36 acres held by Thomas at Bosco was probably two whole tenements in origin, and the 10-acre holdings of Isabell de Bingates and John Valentyn, the nine acres of John le Walshe and the 8¾ of Stephen Lombard may well have had their origins in half tenements.

# 4

## *The Manorial Courts and Customs*

EVEN IF ALL the manorial court records had survived it is unlikely that they would have shed much light on the history of the freeholdings, unless (as in the case of Denis Ladde) they were new enfranchisements. But the manorial court rolls recorded all the transactions dealing with villein or 'customary' land. As the 'nativus' or born bondsman was, unless specifically freed, tied to his native village and as his land was held by the lord's grant and not by free charter, any disposal of it, whether by sale or inheritance, had to pass through the lord's hands. This transaction was normally conducted in the manor court, which was presided over by the lord's steward and had a body of jurors from the tenants. The court's origin was of course the requirement for a visible and frequent confirmation of the allegiance of the tenants – as was shown by the word used to describe the jury – the 'homage'. But as the lord was the protector and arbiter of village affairs it also became the place where complaints were raised against those who broke the rules – the customs of the manor – in such ways as overgrazing the common pastures, turning out their animals in the meadows before the hay was gathered, obstructing the highways by buildings or dungheaps, failing to keep up hedges or ditches and so on. Any financial penalties levied on the wrongdoers went into the lord's coffers. So did the 'fines' levied on a transaction affecting land. ('Fine' did not originally have the sense of a financial penalty, for which the word was 'amercement'. It was a sum paid on the conclusion – finish – of a transaction.)

When a customary or villein tenant wished to dispose of land by sale or gift he had to surrender the land to the lord 'to the use of' the intended purchaser or recipient, who would then be 'admitted' by the lord to the land and would have to pay a fine on admission. When a tenant died, the custom in Shene, as in many other manors, was that the heir should be the youngest son (or failing a son, the youngest daughter or youngest brother, etc.). This custom was called 'Borough English'. The death of a customary tenant would be 'presented' at the next court, and the identity of the heir established. The heir would then have to appear at the court to be admitted by the lord, paying a fine as above or (originally only for free tenants but later extending also to customary tenants) a 'heriot' of his best beast or the notional value thereof. If an heir was not identified, or failed to appear, the court would issue a proclamation bidding him to make his claim.

The only title deed to such property was a copy of the relevant entry in the manor rolls recording the tenant's admission, so such land gradually became known as 'copyhold' – a term which took the place of 'tenure in villeinage' as labour services were progressively commuted to money rents (although the alternative term of 'customary land' also continued in use). Once a tenant paid only a money rent for his land instead of manual labour, any social stigma involved in holding land on this basis disappeared; and by the time of the Tudors even great nobles were holding property in the manor by copyhold tenure.

Every manor had its own 'Court Baron' as the local manorial court was called. This was the lord's own court and a private jurisdiction. The jurors of the court – the 'homage' – were originally only the free tenants, but in Shene the customary tenants were also jurors by the mid-14th century.

Another court was the View of Frank Pledge, which had its origin in the 'tithings' of Anglo-Saxon times – groupings of a number of households who were communally responsible for the behaviour and presence of each member, and for the payment of taxes. The 'View' ensured that all tenants of full age were enrolled and had pledged their allegiance. The early Courts Baron of Shene were also Views of Frank Pledge, but then this latter function was taken over, from early Tudor times at least, by the Court Leet at Kingston.

The Court Leet was a court of public jurisdiction, but was normally also a manorial court, presided over by the lord or his representative. The right to hold such a court was, however, a privilege granted only to certain manors. It could deal with minor offences such as squabbles between neighbours, nuisances and affrays, the sale of underweight bread or sub-standard ale, etc. And it was at the Court Leet that the manorial officials were elected from among the tenants to serve (unpaid) for a year at a time: the constable who had the job of keeping the peace, the tithingman or headborough who was the tax collector, and the aleconner who tested the quality of ale. Shene had no Court Leet of its own until the 17th century. Until then it was subject to the Court Leet of Kingston – a reminder of Shene's origins as part of that royal manor.

✠

As the manor of Shene – later Richmond – was in royal hands, the records of its manorial courts have been preserved with the national archives, now in the Public Record Office. Even so, up to the late fifteenth century only some sporadic records have survived. Apart from the 1314 document, there are just three years' worth of court records from the fourteenth century, for the years 1348 to 1350 – the time of the Black *Plate 2* Death.[1] Then, made up long ago into a single roll,[2] are what survives from the reigns of Henry IV, Henry V and Henry VI: records for 1404-05, 1413-22, 1445-46 and 1449-52.

From the accession of Henry VII onwards the series is much more complete. There are two main gaps in the reign of Henry VIII, from 1520 to 1527 and from 1545 to 1547; the whole series for the reigns of Philip and Mary (1553-58) is missing, as also are the last 12 years of Queen Elizabeth I (1589-1602). From 1603 onwards every record is preserved.[3] Sometimes information from the missing rolls is quoted, or implied, in a later entry. It is thus possible to trace the history of virtually every property in Richmond back to 1603, of many back to 1485 (with a bit of luck), and of a few back to the early 15th century (making some assumptions such as continuity of ownership in the same family if a property was held by persons of the same surname at different periods).

Apart from their value as records of the transfer of property, the court rolls and books provide invaluable records of the names of tenants, for the jurors are always listed, and occasionally there is a full list of the absent tenants (who were fined for non-appearance). The 'presentments' in the court, often recording offences against the manorial customs, frequently mentioning individual properties or the names of fields, lanes and ditches, sometimes setting out new rules, often recording deaths and identifying heirs, sometimes citing wills or explaining family relationships, sometimes even complaining about oppressions by the lord of the manor, or by a temporary lord who held the manor in lease, shed much light both on family histories and on some of the conditions and problems of daily life in the manor.

What happened to the missing rolls? The early ones presumably just succumbed to the passing of time and were lost or destroyed in the distant past. Some may indeed have been lost in the palace fire of 1497. The later ones may possibly have been required as evidence in some legal case and have been mislaid in consequence. Perhaps some will one day be rediscovered. It appears that the rolls for Queen Mary's reign were still around in 1640, for in that year the deputy steward certified a copy of an entry from the court of 17 October 1554 as having been 'verified with the original'.[4]

Those responsible for mislaying the rolls have much to answer for, but with one exception remain anonymous. There is, however, one named culprit. In October 1621 the homage presented in the manor court 'that divers writings belonging to this Manor remain in the hands of Sir Richard Grobham, Knt, formerly Steward of the Manor'.[5] Grobham was the personal steward of Sir Thomas Gorges who held the lease of the manor from 1596, so it is probable that he was made steward of the manor at about that time. There is no other reference to him in the surviving rolls; he had been replaced by 1604. It is thus very likely that the documents which he had retained were the rolls current at the time of his stewardship, the missing ones for the period 1589 to 1602. It is true that entries in these rolls were being quoted in later entries up to the year 1618, but such references could have been derived from the copies in the hands of tenants rather than from the original rolls. Grobham remains a prime suspect; but he himself was childless and the Grobham-Howe family descended from his sister died out in 1804, so there seems little hope now of tracing any papers he may once have held.

✟

The manorial customs of Shene, Petersham and Ham were codified in 1464.[6] All three manors were then in the hands of the king and were administered (and leased out) together. All followed the same customs, except in respect of quit rents and fines. (By that time all labour services had long since been commuted to money quit rents.) There were 12 heads, which may be summarised as follows:

(1) The court would be held yearly, with two weeks' notice; those not attending to be fined.

(2) The court to enquire whether any tenants have died holding land, and to present the heir.

(3) The heir to be the youngest son, and if no son the youngest daughter, with remainder to next of kin; if no traceable heirs, the property to escheat to the lord who may grant it out afresh, for a new fine.

(4) The widow of a tenant without issue may claim one-third part of the rent during her life.

(5) If a tenant wishes to surrender property during his lifetime he must deliver it into the hands of two fellow tenants who must present the surrender at the next court.

(6) Lands are held by copy of a court roll at the will of the lord, and tenants may lop or fell timber provided they keep their houses in good repair; if houses are not kept in good repair the lord shall take the lands and profits until the repairs are carried out, when the tenant must pay a fine to have them back.

(7) Any tenant suing (or renting) his lands to one outside the manor without the lord's licence shall forfeit all his copyholdings; and no transaction made by an heir shall have any effect until he has been properly admitted by the lord.

(8) The lord may grant any waste or empty ground in copyhold in return for a fine and a yearly quit rent.

(9) All land in the common fields (except certain closes) is considered as common from Michaelmas to Lady Day; the holders of tenements may common three sheep for every acre (or 60 for a whole tenement) and four oxen, three kine, two horses and one mare or gelding; those with a house only with no land may common three kine and one horse or mare.

(10) A tenant mixing freehold and copyhold land with the intent to make the copyhold freehold shall forfeit all his copyholdings.

(11) Any tenant may top wood or fell furze and thorns (portion and portion alike) and carry them home for his own use; no brewer or baker shall be entitled to more wood, furze and thorns than his due portion.

(12) Quit rents and fines:
In West Sheen: quit rent 2d. an acre, 6d. a house; fine – two years' quit rent.
In Petersham and Ham: quit rent 4d. an acre, 6d. a house; fine – one year's quit rent.
In all: fine for a whole tenement 7s. 6d.

A matter on which the customs were silent, but which seems to have been very scrupulously observed by the manor court, was the status of a woman's property. While this, by the law of the land, immediately became her husband's property on marriage, the manor court always considered husband and wife as joint owners, and any surrender of such property had to be in their joint names, the wife having been first examined by the court as to her agreement. It was also common for a man to surrender a property to himself and his wife jointly for their lives, with reversion to their heirs, so that the wife might continue as owner of it if he predeceased her. A problem in tracing property sometimes arises when this happened – if the woman married again and the property thus came into the ownership of a new name without any further transaction being recorded in the manor court rolls.

On occasion the manor court might supplement the customs by making further detailed regulations concerning, say, the pasturing of animals or the gathering of firewood and furze or the digging of gravel. And, if it was necessary, a basic change might be agreed between the lord and his tenants in the court. For instance, the enclosure of much of the commons of the surrounding villages into Richmond Park in the 1630s necessitated new rules on the commoning of animals. There is no Richmond example, but the new rules for Ham were laid down at the manor court held there on 25 April 1637.[7]

Indeed, when the Customs of the Manor of Richmond were recited by the Parliamentary Commissioners in their survey of Richmond Palace in 1649[8] they quoted a document of 1481 which already showed a number of changes from the customs of 1464 set out above. These changes included: the obligation on all copyholders to pay a heriot of their best beast or 6s. 8d.; a limit of three years within which a tenant was allowed to let his property without licence; and the levy of an arbitrary fine at the will of the lord on the first admission of a 'stranger' who had not held land in the manor before. The fact that such fines were usually much larger than those for existing tenants led to a practice, which became very common in the 18th and 19th centuries, whereby a new tenant would first seek admission to a very small piece of property – say ¼ acre or a part share of a cottage – paying a relatively small fine therefor, following this at the next court by his full purchase (for which he would then only be liable to pay the regular fine as an existing tenant of the manor).

There were various schemes which the lawyers evolved in order to get round the customs and the legal conventions of the period. For instance, the 'Borough English' custom of the youngest inheriting could be avoided if a tenant surrendered his property, during his lifetime, 'to the use of his will'. Then the dispositions of the will would in due course take precedence over the manorial custom. To break an entail, or to secure a clear title to a property which had changed beyond recognition since it was last described, an involved process called a 'recovery' was used, in which the property was surrendered in turn to a bewildering number of people (including all those whose rights might be affected) until it was finally 'recovered' with an absolute title (and a new description if necessary) to the original tenant, or occasionally, as a final step, to a new tenant.

Two other procedures should also be mentioned. Mortgages of copyhold land took the form of a 'conditional surrender' and were enrolled as such. If the stipulated condition of repayment was met, the rolls were supposed to be annotated to this effect (but frequently were not); if it were not met, the mortgagee could apply to be admitted to the property which had been conditionally surrendered to him. The same form was sometimes used by elderly parents who would conditionally surrender their property to a son in return for an annuity; if the annuity were not paid the conditional surrender would be voided. When a mortgagee had in this way acquired title to a property and the mortgagor (who might still be living there) died, it was not uncommon for the heir to make a 'release', or a second surrender of the property, to confirm the new owner's title.

The transfer of any freehold land within the manor was not normally recorded by the manor court. Such a transaction would take the regular form of conveyancing practised at the time – a fine enrolled in chancery or the exchequer, or later deeds of 'lease and release', and so on. Unless one can find these deeds, the histories of freehold properties are much harder to elucidate. But there were some occasions when freehold property was noted by the manor court: one such was the simultaneous transfer of two properties, one freehold and one copyhold, but otherwise of similar description. It was evidently felt appropriate to note the fact to avoid future confusion. There were some instances when the status of a property was called in question – was it freehold or copyhold? The ownership of freehold property might be mentioned in the description of an adjacent copyhold. And one can sometimes infer the transfer of a freehold property from a change of name in the lists of the homage.

# 5

## *The Medieval Fisheries*

A FEATURE OF the 1314 'extent of the manor' was the detail which it gave of the meals served to the men working in the lord's fields – and figuring prominently in those menus was fish. The riverside population must have caught and eaten fish from the earliest times. Some fishing was no doubt done from boats with nets, but the way to catch fish in large numbers was by the erection of a static fence in the water.

Already in Anglo-Saxon times the development of fisheries of this kind was causing problems. They could be a great obstacle to navigation. Further upstream an additional hazard was the construction of weirs to divert water into millstreams to work water mills. In the wider tidal waters of the Thames with which we are here concerned mill weirs were not a problem, but fishing weirs were. King Edward the Confessor has been credited with the first piece of river conservancy legislation: 'If mills, fisheries or any other works are constructed [on the four royal rivers of Thames, Severn, Ouse and Trent] to their hindrance, let these works be destroyed and the waters repaired, and the forfeit to the King not forgotten.'[1]

In the Domesday Survey the important fisheries are noted. In this area there was one shared between the manors of Fulham (which then included both Chiswick and Brentford) and Isleworth, so probably sited near the border between those manors; one in Mortlake; one more in Isleworth (which included Twickenham); one at Petersham; four altogether in the royal manor of Kingston (which may have included one at Shene). The Mortlake one, we are informed, had been established by Earl Harold 'by force' in the time of King Edward on Kingston land (Kew meadows) and St Paul's land (probably at 'the Strand' i.e. Strand-on-the-Green).[2]

In these fisheries weirs would be built with stakes driven into the river bed and closely woven hurdles jammed down between them, often in a zig-zag pattern, to block and entrap the fish. Although a passage was always supposed to be left for boats, this might be screened by nets, sometimes suspended from cables, so that a boat's passage could indeed be hazardous.

The one body that could – and did – stand forcefully and effectively for freedom of river navigation was the City of London, whose mainspring was trade – trade which was heavily reliant on river traffic. At the end of the 12th century King Richard

I, in return for 1,500 marks (£1,000) paid by the City, decreed the removal of all weirs in the Thames 'for it is manifest to us that great detriment and inconvenience hath grown to our said City of London, and also to the whole realm, by occasion of the said weirs'.[3]

Eighteen years later Magna Carta confirmed that all fishing weirs should be destroyed in the Thames and Medway. But despite these injunctions the owners of the ancient fisheries, often granted by royal charter, continued to maintain their rights to fish and to have weirs; and in the 13th and early 14th centuries there were constant disputes between the City of London and the fishery owners. In 1327 Edward III granted the City authority to remove all weirs in the Thames and Medway.[4] In 1344 the City appointed a Commission 'to remove piles, hurdles and other engines from the Thames, to afford a free passage between Westminster and Staines'.[5] Staines became in practice the point up to which the City claimed conservancy rights.

One of the problems was that many of the fishery owners were princes of the church or the great monasteries. The Fulham share of the fishery by Brentford belonged to the Bishop of London. The fishery at the western end of Mortlake (confusingly also known as the 'Brentford' fishery) was granted in 1173 by King Henry II to Merton Priory.[6] A few years before, in 1164, a fishery had been granted to one of the Belet family – its location is not recorded, but it was probably the Shene manor fishery, and just upstream of the Merton one.[7] The base for the Merton fishery was almost certainly the Ware Ground (?Weir Ground) on the eastern side of Kew Green; just to its west was the meadow a part of which still bears the name of 'Westerly Ware', which was presumably the western weir, belonging to Shene manor.

The grant to Merton also conflicted with an ancient right claimed by St Paul's to a tithe of every fish caught in their sub-manor of Sutton in Chiswick. In 1223, following a law suit, an accommodation was reached between Merton and St Paul's under which the Prior of Merton granted limited rights to the Canons of St Paul's and their tenants of Sutton manor to set up fisheries at a distance from their own weirs at Mortlake and Brentford.[8]

Monasteries as powerful as Merton had influence at court and, as long as some passage was left for boats, they were allowed to maintain and enforce their fishery rights. In 1241 there was a dispute between Merton and Robert de Beauchamp, guardian of the Belet heiress and acting lord of the manor of Shene. The king was persuaded by the Prior to issue an order to the sheriffs of Surrey and Middlesex to impound all fishing tackle upstream of the Prior's weir. Boats and nets belonging to Beauchamp were duly seized. But Beauchamp also had influence and evidently he reckoned his case, no doubt deriving from the 1164 Belet grant, was a just one. So a new order was issued to the sheriffs to restore to Robert de Beauchamp his boats and nets used for fishing above the Prior's weir. 'And,' added the king, 'if the Prior should object thereto, the matter should be carried to the King's Justices.'[9]

There were other causes of dispute. Overfishing was a frequent one. In 1330 a petition was sent to the king by a number of inhabitants of Barnes, Kew, Isleworth and Shene complaining of the Prior's fishery. They objected that the weir was left in place long outside the proper season (from the feast of the Exaltation of the Cross on 14 September to the feast of St Martin, bishop and martyr, on 11 November) and that it was so closely meshed that it caught all the fish, large or small. The whole stock was being destroyed.[10] (Although not in this particular context, there were frequent complaints at that period of weirs that were catching fish fry which were then fed to pigs.) However, in 1340 the grant to Merton of the 'Brentford' fishery was confirmed.[11]

It was not only the static fishery owners against whom complaints of overfishing were levelled. Some of the local fishermen were themselves equally at fault. In the 1380s the City of London took action against John Maykyn of Shene and two other fishermen of Kingston and Walton for the use of unlawful nets 'to the destruction of small fish called fry'.[12]

*Plate 2*

In the 1390s a renewed dispute over freedom of navigation arose between the City of London and Merton. The Lord Mayor wrote to the Prior that he was informed that 'the course of the water of Thames is so stopped by the Prior's weir at Brentford that boats, skouts (?scows) and other vessels coming with wood and other provisions to the City of London could not have passage, to the great delay of the provisions, injury of the City and in contravention of the franchise thereof'.[13] The Prior's reaction was simply to appeal to the king to uphold his rights to the fishery.[14]

Ten years later the City took stronger action. They charged the Prior with placing branches of trees in the Thames between his weir and the Surrey bank, to the obstruction of the passage of vessels, and ordered their officer who was 'Supervisor of the Water of Thames' to retaliate by seizing and holding a skout, a long boat and a wherry belonging to the Priory. Three persons stood surety for the Prior in the amount of £40 to get the boats released, but two years later they forfeited their recognizance as they 'failed to give sufficient answer for the Priory'.[15]

Merton was not the only influential fishery owner in the vicinity. The Bishop of London, as has been noted, had a fishery in Brentford. The Priory of St Swithin's at Winchester had a fishery at Kew – but this, I believe, may have been not in the river itself but may rather be the origin of the pond in the corner of Kew Green. The difficulty in sorting out these fisheries is compounded by the fact that Kew was called in the Priory's accounts 'Kayho-juxta-Braynford' and sometimes just Braynford for short. The first mention in the accounts occurs in 1327,[16] but the fishery was mentioned in charters of 1205 and 1243,[17] and may date from a grant allegedly made by King Ethelred in 996 to the Church of Saints Peter and Paul in Winchester of 'half a fishery in the Thames at Brentford'.[18] From the 1350s onwards the Winchester fishery was leased to Merton[19] – but it was unlet in 1533 which is the last time it figures in the accounts – shortly before the Dissolution.[20] It seems to have been overlooked in the post-Dissolution survey of the Priory's possessions – and the small piece of land which went with it seems to have been subsumed in the larger adjacent Merton holding.

Within the five years from 1410 to 1415 three new fishery grants were made, two of them in connection with Henry V's foundation of new monasteries in the area. Both the Shene Charterhouse and the Briggitine House of Syon were given initial foundation charters in 1414 and revised charters a year later. The revised charters include the fisheries. To Shene went the weir at Petersham with half an acre of land attached, and 'all our fishery of Shene'.[21] This must have been the manor fishery: in the accounts drawn up after the Dissolution it is described as 'Croft Mead* in Kewe with the fishery in the Thames and adjoining the said croft and fishery to the water of Thames from the lane called Paternoster Lane on the west to the land called Hokehawe on the east'.[22] To Syon were granted Ham weir with some adjacent meadow, and 'all fisheries within the water opposite the aforesaid parcel of land [the old site of Syon, later Twickenham Park] viz between the two banks of the said water; also a certain rout situated opposite the same parcel for taking the fishes in the same water'.[23]

The Priors of Shene seem to have successfully avoided serious disputes over their fisheries, but the Shene manor court complained twice in the 1440s that the 'Abbess' of Syon had 'not repaired her fishpond' (and fined her 40 shillings) and in 1452 that she had 'obstructed the passage of the Thames ... at Cayo'.[24]

Far more serious, however, was the dispute that erupted about 1412 or 1413 between the inhabitants of Shene and Kew and their temporary lord, Thomas Holgill. Holgill, a member of King Henry IV's household, had obtained a grant from the king on 3 December 1411, to himself and his intended wife Elizabeth Lasyngby, to permit them to 'make a weir on the King's soil across the river Thames where they please between the town of Stronde [Strand-on-the-Green] and the town of Mortlake, saving a reasonable passage for all vessels, and to fix piles and sluices and all other necessaries ...'.[25] In May 1412 Holgill bought the estate called the Grove 'in Sutton and Stronde in Chiswick',[26] and also acquired a ten-year lease of the manor of Shene.[27] With a secure footing on both banks of the river, Holgill proceeded to construct his weir. He seems to have disregarded the precise terms of the grant, for he built it from Strand to the Kew meadows and he apparently left no passage for vessels. Not content with blocking the river, he evidently then went a step further by constructing channels, for the easier taking of the fish, in the Kew meadows. These meadows were not of course the sole property of the lord of the manor, let alone a temporary 'farmer' of the lordship, for the manorial tenants had property and rights in them. There was an outcry from the inhabitants – especially those of the tiny hamlet of Kew. What followed

* Later called 'Stony Close'.

is best told in the words of the inhabitants themselves, in a petition which they addressed to their real lord, the king.[28]

> Your unfortunate tenants and loyal liegemen Adam Simonds, William Simonds the Elder, William Simonds the Younger, Richard Walton, Alayn Byngate, Thomas Mille, John Lockyer and other of your tenants of Shene, Robert Lydgold, Robert atte Were, John Ponde and Clement Makyn* beseech most humbly and by these presents show as follows.
>
> Your petitioners declare that they are grievously oppressed by Thomas Holgill Esquire both in pocket and in chattels and that their meadows are quite destroyed by the said Thomas Holgill by means of ditches made by the men of the said Thomas and his weirs set in the Thames to the very great injury of your unfortunate tenants and to the utter destruction of your stream of Thames, so that no vessels, for some time, will pass towards Shene and Kingston unless some strong remedy is applied. And that the said Thomas has set his weirs in such manner that no other things whatever can pass the weirs of the said Thomas Holgill, to the utter destruction of your stream. And moreover the said Thomas has maliciously made a way into your tenants' meadows so that his animals may destroy their meadows.
>
> And because they complained the said Thomas resorted to force of arms and came to meet your tenants at Cayu and there fought with the said Robert Lydgold and would have killed the said Clement Makyn, save that he was not to be found. And so he went to Shene to raid your honourable Manor and by force of arms arrested eight people who remained in the hands of his men, and made known that he intended to kill the said Robert Lydgold and Clement Makyn wherever he could find them. Therefore, most noble and redoubted Lord, your said tenants do not dare to go out to seek their living for fear of the said Thomas and his men.
>
> May it please your Honourable Majesty to command that the said Thomas should come before your just presence so that your said tenants may enjoy the grace of peace and so that retribution may be exacted for the extortions he has made and is unhappily still making, against the rights of your said tenants and against God's law and against all charity.

The king does not appear to have been swayed by this impassioned appeal for Holgill remained as 'farmer' of the manor of Shene until 1425, and the manor court continued to arraign him each year until 1418 for misdeeds concerning his fishery. It is at least comforting to note that Robert Lydgold and Clement Makyn continued to figure in the lists of tenants. However, the fishery was eventually demolished – perhaps with the intervention of the City authorities.

For half a century later the City secured a notable triumph in 1468-69 when King Edward IV licensed his kinsman the Earl of Pembroke to make a weir across the Thames 'called Overithwart Were in the place where Holgyllys Were used to be'. The

---

* Lydgold, atte Ware, Ponde and Makyn were all inhabitants of Kew.

City protested and the king cancelled the grant. He apologetically explained that he had been informed 'that he was entitled to a weir called Holgilles Were, now broken and utterly destroyed; but William Taillour, the Mayor, and the aldermen have shown that they have the conservance of several statutes within the said river from the bridge of Staines to the said city; and the rebuilding of the weir would be contrary to the same and to the liberty of the City.'[29]

However, the other fisheries remained, and those in monastic hands were leased to laymen after the Dissolution of the Monasteries. If the City could impose its will on Edward IV it had a harder nut to crack in Queen Elizabeth I, but it tried and not without success. One must admire the courage of the Lord Mayor who was summoned before the Queen's Council in 1580 to account for the number of weirs between London and Staines, and how many were new; the Queen had been annoyed by some 'stop' on the river opposite Richmond Palace. The Lord Mayor retorted that 15 hatches and six stops had been erected on the orders of Mr Comptroller to supply lampreys and roaches for the Queen's household; and that the four great weirs, at Isleworth, Twickenham, Kingston and Hampton, were all the Queen's, from which she derived rents – and were all harmful because they caught fry and because of the 'driving each year of new great piles or posts with great hurdles into the ground within the said weirs'.[30]

Four years later new orders were issued for the conservation of the river: no new wharves, banks or walls were to be built obstructing passage; no dung, rubbish or other filth was to be thrown into the river; no posts or stakes were to be driven in; and the 'fairway was to be kept as deep and wide as heretofore'.[31]

Despite the weirs, the Thames remained abundantly stocked with fish. The chronicler Holinshed wrote:

> This noble river, the Thames, yieldeth not clots of gold as the Tagus doth, but an infinite plentie of excellent, sweet and pleasante fish, wherewith such as inhabit neere unto her banks are fed and fullie nourished ... Salmon in such plentie after the time of the smelt be passed and no river in Europe able to exceed it ... Barbels, Trouts, Pearches, Smelts, Breames, Roches, Daces, Gudgings, Flounders, Shrimps, etc, are commonlie to be had therein ... It seemeth from time to time to be as it were defrauded ... by the insatiable avarice of the fisherman ... but the more it looseth at one time the more it yieldeth at another ... Oh! that this river might be spared but even one yeare from nets, etc; but, alas! then should manie a poor man be undone.[32]

We hear of no more serious disputes involving the fisheries, but several weirs in the Thames in this area survived well into the 18th century. One near Glover's Island and one between Cholmondeley Walk and the island facing it were both clearly *Plate 3* shown in drawings by Augustin Heckel in 1754.[33]

# 6

# *The Black Death*

AT ABOUT THE TIME when John de Boseham took over the management of Shene manor the English weather was misbehaving badly. Rainfall was heavier than usual and the summers were cold and stormy. The price of wheat rose sharply in 1313 and 1314 and in 1315 the harvest was a total disaster. There was a great famine throughout the land which continued throughout the following year and was only partially relieved in 1317. The livestock was also affected and, despite an attempt at price fixing by the Parliament in 1315 the murrain that killed off much of the stock drove up the cost of meat. Holinshed wrote of the year 1317:

> Victuals were so scant and dear, and wheat and other grain brought to so high a price, that the poor people were constrained to eat the flesh of horses, dogs and other vile beasts; and yet for default there died a multitude of people in divers places of the land. Fourpence in bread of the coarser sort would not suffice one man a day. Wheat was sold at London for four marks the quarter and above. Then after this dearth ensued a great death and mortality of people.[1]

Though the harvests in 1317-19 were better, the cattle sickness continued and there was renewed famine in 1321 and 1322, though not quite as severe as that of six years earlier.

For this period there are very full accounts for the manor of Shene, which are analysed in Appendix 3.[2] The prices for grain and livestock demonstrate clearly the fluctuations due to the dearth in 1315-17 and 1321-22. Wheat rose from 6s. a quarter in 1313-14 to 20s. in 1315-16, had dropped back to 6s. 8d. by 1320-21, but rose again to 17s. in 1321-22. Cows costing 10s. in 1314 were fetching 22s. by 1317. There are, as it happens, no accounts extant for the year 1318-19 when a different kind of disaster appears to have struck the local farmers. When John de Boseham was making up his final accounts in the year 1326-27, consequent on the handing over of the manor to Queen Isabella, he included an item for the sale of rye in 12 Edward II (1318-19) to 'the Prior of Merton and the poor men in his district because the rye growing on the land turned into darnel' (i.e. ryegrass).[3] It is good to know that the King's granaries held reserve stocks and that the king's agent (he is described at this time as 'late bailiff of Shene') was prepared to release them to remedy a local need.

35

For the rest, it is interesting to note some of the prices mentioned, and to compare them with labour costs. The comment by Holinshed that four pennyworth of bread would not suffice a man for a day can be more clearly appreciated in the light of the knowledge that a skilled craftsman such as a carpenter, thatcher or tiler would be fortunate to earn more than fourpence for a day's work, and that mowing an acre of hay would earn the mower just threepence. One could wish there had been more information about the price of fish; but it appears that a farthing would about purchase two herrings, even if a salmon would have cost a skilled workman at least a week's pay – and double that during the famine. But only the richest inhabitants would have been able to afford salmon. One wonders whether the nine-gallon brass pot for which the manor house paid 12 shillings was for cooking the salmon! The solitary sturgeon was caught at Mortlake, and promptly sent to the king in Nottingham.

A point that emerges from study of the prices is the comparative cheapness of livestock in relation to grain or other food staples. Of course the cows, pigs and sheep of that time were small and scrawny creatures in comparison with their counterparts today. However, in good times one could buy a cow (even it seems a horse) for ten shillings – less than two quarters of wheat at six shillings a quarter. Two sheep cost less than a quarter of peas or beans, a pig could be had for less than a quarter of barley, and a lamb for the price of five or six pounds of apples. Small wonder that most of the tenants kept at least as much livestock as they were allowed to pasture, or that their cottage gardens would have been full of vegetables and fruit trees rather than flowers.

A tax assessment made in 1332 provides us with a rather different list of the principal inhabitants of Shene, for it was for a lay subsidy of 'fifteenths and tenths' and shows the relative wealth of the villagers in terms other than land holdings. Townspeople were generally assessed for one tenth of their assessed value in movable goods; country people for one fifteenth. It is of interest therefore that the inhabitants of Shene, described as a 'villata' or town, were originally assessed twice – on both bases. The first entry was among the towns; the second, which was subsequently erased, was among the villages of Kingston Hundred. The names in both lists are the same (though there are some minor spelling variations). Unfortunately for the people of Shene it was the one tenth rather than the one fifteenth rate which was ruled to apply to them. Those whose goods were valued at less than ten shillings were exempted.

In order of wealth, the list – and the one tenth assessments – are as follows:

| | |
|---|---|
| Gilbert de Bynegate | 6s |
| William Thomas | 6s |
| Adam Goion | 4s 6d |

*Plate 5*

*Relief Map of the area from Isleworth and Twickenham to Putney and Wimbledon*

*Note: a few roads are shown, which existed in ancient times, to help with identification of localities.*

Richmond Park

Boundaries of the Manor of Richmond

Scale

Heights in metres

55-60
50-55
45-50
40-45
35-40
30-35
25-30
20-25
15-20
10-15
5-10
0-5

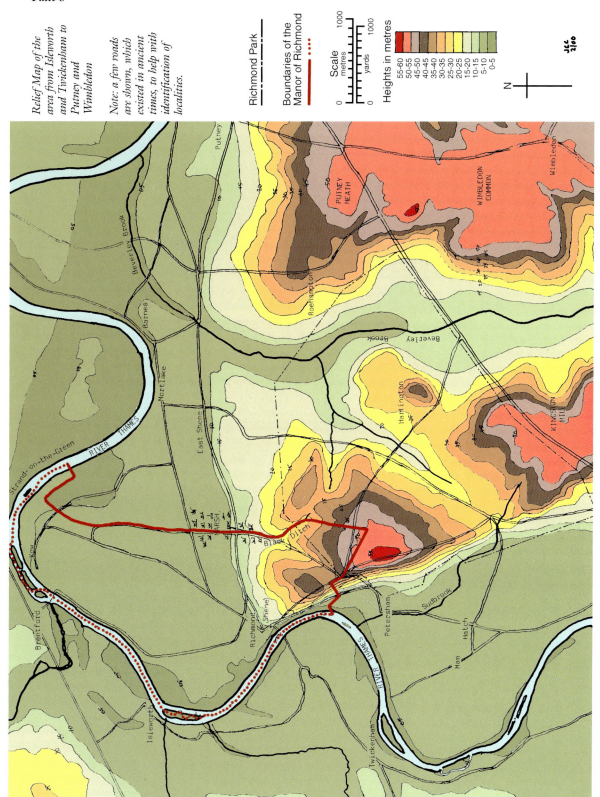

*Plate 6*

*Haymaking – mowing, from Queen Mary's Psalter, early 14th century. (British Library, MS Roy 2 B vii, f. 76)*

*Harvest – reaping the corn, under the bailiff's supervision, from Queen Mary's Psalter. (British Library, MS Roy 2 B vii, f. 78 )*

Plate 7

*Richmond Palace and houses below and above Ferry Hill. Detail from a painting by an unknown Flemish artist, c.1630. (Fitzwilliam Museum, Cambridge)*

*Plate 8*

*View by Joseph Farington, published by Brydell, 1793.*

*View by William Westall, published by Rodwell and Martin, 1823.*

*View by William Westall, published by Ackermann, 1828.*

| | |
|---|---|
| William Hankyn | 4s 6d |
| Richard Vautort | 4s 2d |
| Amice Ireland | 3s 9d |
| Alice atte Wodehall | 3s |
| Adam le Kesere | 3s |
| Gilbert le Vag | 3s |
| Christine le Drivere | 3s |
| Adam Richard | 2s 7½d |
| Thomas Chaplain | 2s 3d |
| John le Clerk | 2s |
| Gilbert Johan | 1s 6d |
| Thomas le Taylour | 1s 6d |
| Richard Stormy | 1s |
| Joan Stormy | 1s |
| Agnes le Drivere | 1s |
| Adam le Lad | 1s |
| Adam Bigg | 1s |
| Cecilia Heghes | 1s |
| Adam Plonte | 1s |
| Henry Parmyd | 1s |
| William le Shepherde | 1s |

The total to be collected from Shene was £2 19s. 9½d.[4]

Two years later Shene's total was increased by one shilling to £3 os. 9½d. An idea of the prosperity of Shene relative to some of its neighbours can be gathered by comparing this total with those for: Kingston town (£21 2s. 1d.); 'Ham and Petersham' – but excluding those under the next heading, so mainly Ham – (£1 18s. 2d.); Villeins of Chertsey Abbey in Petersham village (£1 1s. 6¼d.); Mortlake (£4 15s. 0d.). The total for the entire county of Surrey was £587 18s. 8d.

Of the 22 surnames in this list, half figure in the 'extent' of 1314 as manorial tenants, and one other (le Kesere) appeared (as le Kersere) in the 1250 list. But it is quite clear that by no means all of the manorial tenants were rich enough to have to pay the tax, so there may well have been a good many other families among the 1314 tenantry who were still holding land at this time. As this subsidy was only paid by lay people we can be reasonably sure that this John le Clerk was not a serving priest (though he might possibly be the son of John le Clerke of 1314 rather than the same man), nor was Thomas Chaplain (whose name is given in the Latin form Capellanus) the chaplain of the parish church.

After the revised assessment the rate for this tax remained fixed, by totals for localities, for over 200 years and there are no further assessments giving individual names. It was presumably the task of the local authorities to work out how the burden should be shared. The concept that only the laity should contribute appears to have been abandoned. In Shene, after the foundation of the Charterhouse, the 1422 tax returns note that 6s. 8d. of the £3 0s. 9½d. total was 'for the goods of the prior and convent of Shene'. After the Dissolution of the Monasteries, Richmond, as Shene had then become, was allowed a deduction of 11 shillings, and had to pay only £2 9s. 9½d. in 1540.[5]

✛

The earliest surviving court rolls for Shene (except for the extent of *c.*1314) are for eight or nine courts held in the years 1348 to 1350 – the time of the Black Death.[6] That first and most devastating nation-wide visitation of the plague appears to have struck Shene early in 1349 and to have continued for about a year. The rolls are in poor condition and are very difficult to read in some places – indeed there are whole passages where the ink has been so rubbed away as to become totally illegible. Even some of the headings and dates are indecipherable. But enough remains to enable many of the tenants' names at that time to be recorded, and to establish a broad picture of the deaths and the regrants of manorial lands.

The first court in this period (held on the Friday after the feast of St Michael the Archangel in 22 Edward III, i.e. 3 October 1348) appears to reflect a normal situation. There are quite a number of regular 'presentments' for various minor offences. Some eight totally illegible lines are followed by a partly legible entry and then by a surrender (from Gilbert Byngate to the use of William Walsh) of what appear to be two half-tenements (10 acres of land and one acre of meadow; and a messuage, 10 acres of land and a half-acre of meadow). The second court (date illegible) follows a similar pattern: presentments, a fine of 8d. for four acres of land, a grant of land to John son of John Hoge (Howe) of Kayhoe.

Then the pattern begins to change. At the court held on 13 February 1348/9 four deaths of tenants appear to be recorded. On 13 October 1349 there are nine entries of which sufficient is legible to establish them as recording deaths and there are what may well have been three other similar entries in this list. The next court (date illegible) records at least two more deaths. There thus appear to have been some 18 manorial tenants (and possibly a few more) whose deaths were recorded in the space of a year.

No attempt seems to have been made to admit the heirs during this year (though these were often identified), but on 20 July and 25 November 1350 there are lists of new grants and of one or two claims for admission. The total number of such entries (allowing six for a totally illegible passage in the November roll which is about one and a half times the length of a passage recording four grants) equals at least approximately that of the recorded deaths. The records of the two courts whose proceedings are on the last membrane of this roll are not sufficiently legible to allow more than the picking out of a few names.

It appears probable that about half the customary tenements of the manor changed hands during these two years – and from that it may be argued that at least half the population of Shene died from the pestilence.

In those cases where it is possible to read the full entry, whether a record of a death or of a new grant, the holdings are all (with one exception which refers only to a single cottage) in terms of a messuage and one virgate or a messuage and half a virgate. There is no single entry which enables us to determine for certain the size of a virgate at this period – but the surrender (plus meadow), of two units of *ten acres* (plus meadow) by Gilbert Byngate in 1348, mentioned above, causes one to wonder whether a change had in fact taken place since 1314 when there were two half-tenements held by villenage in the Byngate family (Gilbert and Isabel), both explicitly of nine acres of arable land and one acre of mead. There is also a reference back to this period in the roll for the court held on 17 February 1404/5, when a John Taille claimed successfully a messuage and *20 acres* 'of which his father Thomas Taille died seized at the time of the great pestilence'.[7] (Thomas Taille's death may have been one of the now illegible entries.)

☩

All over the country the Black Death was followed by a period of social unrest. There is some evidence of this in Shene. On 10 October 1353 a commission of oyer and terminer was issued when certain disturbers of the peace had broken into the manor of Shene.[8] On 18 June in the following year a similar commission gives full details of the incident. Twelve inhabitants of Twickenham, East and West Brentford, Acton and other places had 'entered the manor of Shene which the King's mother Queen Isabella holds for life, of his grant, broke her close and houses and hunted in her free warren there, carried away her goods as well as hares, conies, partridges and pheasants from the warren, assaulted her men and servants there and at Kyngeston, followed them to the dwelling place of the manor and besieged them, so that they dared not go forth to serve her, whereby her land remained untilled and other business was left undone for a long time, and hindered other of her ministers so that they could not do their office and make her profit.'[9]

Queen Isabella repaired the Shene manor house in 1356,[10] but died in 1358. Within a couple of years after her death Edward III began the process of turning the manor house into the royal palace of Shene.[11] This new turn of fortune probably saved the village of Shene from suffering the economic depression that hit most of the country. Although we have no surviving manor rolls to document it, there was likely to have been an influx of craftsmen some of whom may have taken up residence in the village, buying out tenements from the widows and daughters who were in several cases the heirs of the plague victims. There is no evidence in Shene of any reduction in the cultivated area, and the presence of the royal court cannot but have contributed to the prosperity of the village. Edward III himself made much use of his new palace, in which he died in 1377; and for his successor, the young Richard II, and his wife Anne of Bohemia, Shene became a favourite home.

A most curious incident occurred at Shene in the year 1388-89. Stow noted it in his *Annales*:

> A fighting of gnats at the King's manor of Shene where they were so thick gathered that the air was darkened with them. They fought and made a great battle – two thirds of them being slain fell down to the ground. The third part having got the victory flew away, no man knew whither. The number of the dead was such that they might be swept up with brooms, and buckets filled with them.[12]

The plague seems to have become virtually endemic in England after the Black Death. There were renewed outbreaks in 1360, 1366, 1380, 1390 and 1393. But the shock to the inhabitants of Shene when Richard II's beloved wife Anne died of the plague on Whit Sunday 1394 in the palace there was not limited to the loss of a royal patron. On Richard's instructions the palace itself was demolished – although the agricultural buildings in its outer court were apparently spared and the life of the manor continued under temporary lords who held it 'in farm' (by lease).

As Henry IV confirmed in office for life the gardener of Shene Palace appointed by Richard II, it is likely that the gardens also continued to be maintained. But it is a possible hypothesis that the original park of the manor house was carved up at this time. If, as suggested in *Palaces and Parks*, the area called in 1499 'South Park' on the hillside between the upper and lower roads to Petersham was a remnant of this park, it must originally have extended up as far as that from the manor house along the river.

The land by the river called Windeyarde (Vineyard) Close first appears by name in the manor rolls in 1445 when it was stated to have been 'formerly in the occupation of John Coteler'. John Coteler, who presumably gave his name to Cutler's Hill (as the road up Richmond Hill was called in the late 15th century) appears as a member of the homage in 2-10 Henry V (1414-22) and might even have been the first grantee of this land. It may also be that the two long freehold closes lying between the edge of the Upper Field and the road up the hill were also remnants of this first park; it is the most plausible explanation for this rather odd feature of the local topography.

Another logical inference from this hypothesis would be that the first grants of land on the south-west side of what is now Hill Street might also date from this time. All this is, of course, pure conjecture, as there are surviving records for only two manor courts (in 1404–05) during Henry IV's reign, and they give no clue on this point.

*Plate 4*

Shene remained neglected by the court until the accession of Henry V. Then came a great new burst of activity, for Henry not only determined to rebuild the palace (and meanwhile remove to the Shene riverside his timber manor house from Byfleet to serve as temporary accommodation), but also proposed to found three monasteries in the area – two on the Middlesex bank of the river and one at Shene itself.

King Henry's foundation grants (the original one in 1414 was revised in 1415) for the Charterhouse of Jesus of Bethlehem of Shene resulted in a major alteration to the local map. A large area in the bend of the river opposite the Isleworth aits was taken out of the royal demesne land and transferred to the ownership of the Carthusian order. This was later enlarged by grants from Henry VI of 64 acres in 1442 and from Edward IV's queen, Elizabeth, of 48 acres in 1479. On the north-west side of the Green Henry VI enclosed the 'New Park of Shene' by 1437. This new park, triangular in shape, was bounded by the river on the south-west and by the road which led from the Green to the Charterhouse on the north, and may have contained about forty-five acres. It was at once stocked with deer.

The works of building the new palace and the Charterhouse introduced a new industry in the area, for some of the buildings of the palace were of brick, and the cost of importing bricks from the brickworks just outside Calais was almost double the cost of the bricks themselves. Accordingly a brick kiln was established at Petersham, to make use of the local clay.[13] Some twenty years later another kiln was established, under the control of William Vesey, brick master, in the royal demesne land to the north-east of the Charterhouse site.[14] There is one indication that a tile kiln, rather than a brick kiln, may already have existed in Shene, for the accounts for the building of the lodge in Isleworth Park in 1375-7 include a payment of six shillings to 'John Brounyng of Shene for 150 tiles called 'holltyll' bought from the same, price the hundred 4s'.[15] But we have no other knowledge of John Brouning – or indeed of locally made tiles until two hundred years later – so whether he actually made his tiles at Shene remains unconfirmed.

It was King Henry V who brought Petersham and Ham into a closer relationship with Shene, for he acquired both manors to extend his estate in the area. The deal with Chertsey Abbey was a complicated and circular affair. Chertsey was prepared to give up Petersham to the king, but wanted in exchange the appropriation of the church of Stanwell in Middlesex (the lands of which belonged to the Priory of Newark (near Woking in Surrey) and the advowson to Sir Richard Windsor). Windsor wanted the manor of West Bedfont in Middlesex, which belonged to Newark. And Newark wanted to be compensated by the appropriation of the church at Ewell in Surrey, which belonged to Chertsey. All this was duly sorted out in a series of deals which took from 1415 to 1421 before everyone was finally satisfied. But the first steps, not surprisingly, involved the grant to the king by the Abbot and convent of Chertsey on 23 May 1415 of the manor of Petersham (and the advowson of Ewell church).[16]

The acquisition of Ham was much more straightforward. The king purchased the manor of 'Hemme Upkyngeston' on 14 June 1415 from the then lord of the manor, Sir Hugh Burnell. The price was £200, or 300 marks. As the king had already borrowed 200 marks from Sir Hugh, the collectors of the wool subsidy at the port of St Botolphstown (Boston, Lincs.) were instructed to pay Burnell out of the proceeds of the subsidy the total sum of 500 marks.[17]

Thereafter both Ham and Petersham became, for the next two hundred and fifty years or so, 'members of the manor of Shene' (i.e. sub-manors, administered with Shene).

# 7

## The Village in the Fifteenth and Sixteenth Centuries

WE KNOW RELATIVELY LITTLE about the history of Shene, other than the Palace and the Shene Charterhouse, in the 15th century before the reign of Henry VII. There are the sparse surviving manor rolls for 1404-5, 1413-22 and 1445-52, and a few references in patent and close rolls – mostly to the appointments and remuneration of palace officials and craftsmen.

It is, however, clear that both Palace and Charterhouse were the cause of some significant alterations to the local geography. Apart from the new buildings themselves, initiated by Henry V – and described in *Palaces and Parks, volume 1* – there were two major encroachments on the Green. In 1444-5 the royal clerk of works made a 'new great quadrangle' with a gatehouse for the Palace and a new brick wall round the King's garden – bringing the front of the Palace forward by some 270 feet.[1] In 1466 the Charterhouse was granted, for a conduit head for a new water supply, all the plot of land which is now occupied by Old Palace Terrace and the shops on both sides of Paved Court.[2]

On the north-western side of the Green, Henry VI established his New Park of Shene and the land to the north of it was granted from the royal demesne to the Charterhouse in 1414-15 and in 1442.[3] Whether the inhabitants of Shene would have had any access to these royal lands before the grants is uncertain – they were probably a mixture of arable, pasture and meadows – and perhaps the meadows at least had had some manorial tenants, accounting for that generous 14th-century allocation of two acres per tenement. The manorial warren lay to the north of these demesne lands (see the plan at Chapter 9, page 89) – but another 48 acres of this was granted to the monks in 1479.[4] The warren was open heath land – even if the game in it was reserved to the Lord of the Manor.

To the east of the Palace, part of what had probably been the old park of the manor house and the Plantagenet palace was now occupied by the Byfleet buildings and, as suggested in Chapter 6, part may have been granted out for new houses and as the 'windeyarde' close by the riverside.

The building works would have brought craftsmen and labourers to Shene; the rebuilt Palace would have attracted some courtiers to find dwellings there. The village

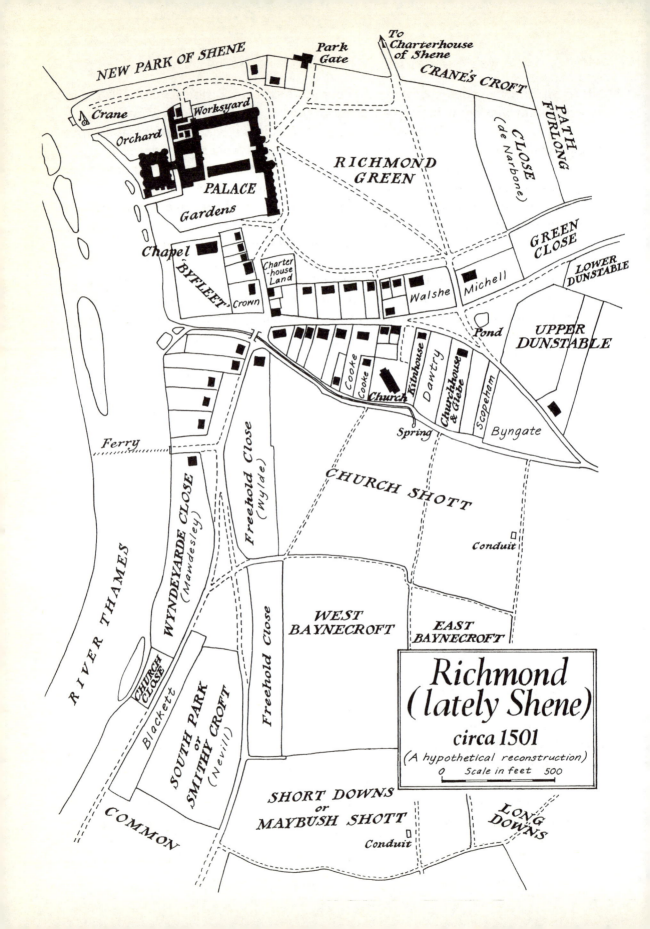

NEW PARK OF SHENE

Park Gate

To Charterhouse of Shene

CRANE'S CROFT

PATH FURLONG

Crane

Worksyard

Orchard

CLOSE (de Narbone)

RICHMOND GREEN

PALACE

Gardens

Chapel

*'BYFLEET'*

GREEN CLOSE

Charter-house Land

LOWER DUNSTABLE

Crown

Walshe

Michell

UPPER DUNSTABLE

Pond

Cooke

Cooke

Kirkhouse

Dawtry

Churchhouse & Glebe

Scopeham

Byngate

Church

Spring

Ferry

WYNDEYARDE CLOSE *(Mawdesley)*

Freehold Close *(Wylde)*

CHURCH SHOTT

Conduit

RIVER THAMES

CHURCH CLOSE

Blackett

SOUTH PARK or SMITHY CROFT *(Nevill)*

Freehold Close

WEST BAYNECROFT

EAST BAYNECROFT

Richmond (lately Shene)

circa 1501

(A hypothetical reconstruction)

0    Scale in feet    500

COMMON

SHORT DOWNS or MAYBUSH SHOTT

Conduit

LONG DOWNS

inevitably expanded – though its population was still probably under 250 at the end of the century. Some new houses were built in the curtilages of the ancient 'capital messuages', others on new ground. In the early part of Henry VII's reign the lands of the manor grange, mainly to the east of the parish church but a small part on the west side of the churchyard, were granted out for development.[5]

The parish church itself was rebuilt. In 1487 'Sir' William Hyne, the parish priest, left a bequest of 20 shillings towards building the tower,[6] and in the following year John Prein left 3s. 4d. for the 'steeple'.[7] In 1504 King Henry VII gave £10 to the parish priest towards the building of his new church and in the following year another £10 for 'the beleding of their church' (the laying of lead on the roofs suggests that the work was nearing completion).[8]

The actual date of the foundation of St Mary Magdalene's church is unknown. The deed granting Kingston vicarage to Merton Priory in the early 12th century was lost: in a deed dated during the priorate of Henry de Basinges (1231-38) it could only be described as 'long ago' (*a longis retro temporibus*).[9] Whether or not Kingston's four dependent chapelries of Petersham, Shene, East Moulsey and Ditton existed at the time of that original grant is therefore uncertain. (Petersham church, but none of the others, is mentioned in Domesday Book.) The earliest indication of a church at Shene is a reference to 'the parish of Senes' in a lawsuit in 1220.[10] A list of the lands of Merton Priory dated about 1242 includes an entry for 'church and land of Schenes' (yielding a revenue of 20 shillings a year).[11] A lease granted in 1258 of two virgates of land and an acre of meadow provides that the annual rent of 15 pence should be paid 'at the church of Shene'.[12]

Of this first church nothing remains. There is no reason to think that it was not on the same site as the Tudor building, but it was no doubt smaller and lost within the rebuilding. This process seems, from the references quoted above, to have started with the building of a tower ('steeple' in the usage of the time does not necessarily imply a spire). The tower, now refaced with flint over the original stone, survives; but the rest of the Tudor church has all been replaced. Its chancel at least survived until 1903-4 and engravings of it give a clue as to the style of the rest of the building. Moses Glover portrayed the church in his map of Isleworth Hundred in 1635, but his detail cannot really be relied upon.

The churchyard had elements of the manorial grange lands on both sides of it – which suggests that a part of these lands may have been allocated for the original building of the church and for its churchyard (which was smaller than now until extended on the south side in 1746).

The church at Shene, even if it had its own parish, was still only a chapelry of the vicarage of Kingston, served by priests appointed by the vicar of Kingston. Indeed it was not until 1375 that any proper arrangements were made for a resident chaplain. A dispute had arisen between the Prior of Merton and the Vicar of Kingston over

*Richmond parish church in 1635.*
*Detail from Moses Glover's map of*
*Isleworth Hundred at Syon House.*
*(By kind permission of His Grace*
*the Duke of Northumberland)*

responsibility for repair of Kingston church and the chapels (all but Petersham were said to be in a very bad state). This led the Bishop of Winchester to intervene. Agreement was reached on a new basis for sharing the tithes and other church revenues between the Priory and the vicar, and on their mutual responsibilities for the chapelries. The Priory gave land for a manse and a glebe for each chapelry and agreed to build the manses (which the vicar was then to maintain). The Priory also agreed to repair, or rebuild if necessary, the chancels of the chapels, while the vicar was to provide suitable chaplains and meet all the other ordinary expenses.[13]

The land provided for the manse at Shene was about an acre and a quarter on the north-east side of the grange land. (In modern terms its frontage to the highway was the whole of Lower George Street, and it stretched back to Paradise Road between St James's Cottages and Eton Street – including the whole site of Eton Street.) It was probably at this time also that provision was made for the future maintenance of the church by the grant from Merton Priory of the lands that became known as the 'church estate' (which were actually misappropriated, through a misunderstanding, in the 19th century to become a charity for relief of the poor).[14]

During the 16th century it is probable that the population of the village more than doubled, rising but slowly in the first half of the century but then expanding more rapidly in the second half until it was about 600 by 1603 (see Appendix 5 for the calculations by which these very approximate figures have been arrived at). This growth was in part due to the frequent presence of the court at the Palace which Henry VII had rebuilt and which he had renamed Richmond in 1501. The manor being also renamed, the village inevitably followed.

A feature of the new growth was the emergence of Kew from the obscurity of a tiny hamlet to become the site of the homes of many of the court grandees. They included at various times: the Courtenay Earls of Devon and Edward IV's daughter

Princess Katherine; Henry VII's daughter Mary (both as a child and when, as widow of the King of France, she married the Duke of Suffolk); the Earl of Worcester, Chamberlain of the Household to Henry VII and Henry VIII; Sir Edward Seymour, Viscount Beauchamp, brother of Queen Jane Seymour and later to become Duke of Somerset; Henry VIII's daughter Mary, the future Queen; Sir John Dudley, Viscount Lisle and future Duke of Northumberland; Sir Robert Dudley, favourite of Queen Elizabeth who was to create him Earl of Leicester; and, after the arrival in England of James I of England and VI of Scotland, his daughter Princess Elizabeth, from whose marriage to the Elector Palatine derived the Hanoverian claim to the English throne.

There were, however, for most of the century, only a handful of large mansions and little more than half a dozen riverside cottages at Kew. It was not until the last decade of Queen Elizabeth's reign that the hamlet began to spread along the north and south sides of Kew Green, by the grant of lands from the edges of the Green itself.

Such grants of waste land began to become more frequent in Richmond also. They are considered in Chapter 12.

The presence of the court and the expanding population called for the setting up of new hostelries. There are references to a *Star and Garter* and a *George* in the early 16th century, but their sites are unknown. The *Bell* in what is now George Street and the *Red Lion* (at the corner of George Street and Red Lion Street) were the principal inns in Queen Elizabeth's time and were requisitioned to house the suite of the Duke of Anjou when he visited her at Richmond in 1581. Other inns or taverns known to have existed before the end of the century were the *Lily Pot* (at the corner of Brewer's Lane and George Street), the *Cross Keys* on Richmond Green and the *Goat* (at what are now 1-5 Sheen Road). The *Queen's Arms* (later *Queen's Head*) at the corner of King Street, and the *Golden Hind* opposite it, were also probably in business before Elizabeth I died although their names are not found until 1603 and 1607 respectively.

While the Palace itself would have provided accommodation for many of the court officials – and with primitive sanitary arrangements could not be used for more than a few weeks at a time – other courtiers and suitors would stay in the inns or rent rooms from the inhabitants of the village. A new service industry was born – catering to visitors. And it was undoubtedly highly profitable. In 1555 the Venetian ambassador complained to the Doge and Senate of Venice in an official report of 'the exorbitant cost of everything and the very narrow lodgings' and 'the expense of two houses [one in London and the other in Richmond] which exceeds his means'.[15] But Queen Mary had on this occasion stayed at Richmond Palace for a record period of no less than two and a half months on end.

The normal way of reaching Richmond from London at this time was by the river. Many Richmond men earned their living as watermen, and the London watermen would bring visitors down, probably as a rule travelling according to the tides – up river with the flood tide, down with the ebb – for the tides, which at this time probably reached about as far as Hampton Court, were quite strong. In 1530 a crew of 16 watermen were paid a total of 10s. 8d. (or 8d. each) for the passage from York House in London to Kew.[16]

The river was crossed, at Kew and at Richmond, by ferry. The ferry between Kew and Brentford, which had replaced the great ford over the Thames, was an informal affair operated by Brentford watermen until December 1536 when King Henry VIII granted a monopoly to John Hale – causing an outcry from the Brentford men. In a petition to the Duke of Norfolk they complained that they had enjoyed free passage over the river to Kew with their boats until this grant was made. But now John Hale 'will suffer no man to pass with a boote but only in his boots exactyng a certain some for every passage for every horse and man an halfpenny and for every man woman and child a farthing'. Hale, it was alleged, had imprisoned Richard Cokyng for using a ferryboat.[17] The petition was unavailing. Hale kept the ferry and after him it was held in succession by Morgan Lewes and Dr William Awbery. Hale's charges were actually quite moderate, for the Earl of Devon had paid 6d. for the ferrying of six horses across the water to Kew in March 1518/9 'when my Lord dined at Mr Belknap's place with the ambassadors of Burgogne'.[18]

The crossing could be hazardous. John Dee recorded in his diary in 1579: 'October 9th, 10th, 11th, 13th, great rayne for three or four dayes and nights. October 13th, this day it broke up; the fote bote for the ferry at Kew was drowned and six persons, by negligens of the ferryman overwhelming the bote uppon the roap set there to help, by reason of the vehement and high waters.'[19]

A ferry was also set up just to the north of Isleworth Ait – perhaps originally in order to carry bricks across from the Shene brick kiln for the building of Syon. In 1443 the Convent of Syon was granted permission 'to carry materials by all the highways commonly used in the King's Warren called le Conyngyerd within the manor of Shene and to and from the wharf of the bricke ooste unto and upon the water of Thames'.[20] In 1539 the Isleworth ferry was listed among the possessions of the dissolved Charterhouse of Shene.[21] Thereafter ownership of the ferry was tied to the leases of the former monastic site.

The origins of Shene (or Richmond) ferry are unknown. The first documentary reference that has been traced is the appointment of John Yong in January 1442/3 as 'Keeper of the boat and ferry over the Thames at Shene Manor' in succession to Thomas Tyler, 'he nowise bound to find a boat'.[22] This sounds rather as though the ferry at the time was a service dependent on the Palace – with a keeper rather than a lessee. The next reference was differently worded: the ferry and the toll were granted to Richard Scopeham in February 1479/80 'with all profits, rewards, eatables and drinkables, provided that nothing be taken for conveyance of the King's household'.[23]

In 1520 the ferry with all profits was granted to John Pate[24] and in 1536 to David Vincent.[25] A grant in 1566 to Thomas Burgess for 21 years specifies a revised annual rent of 13s. 4d. (with a fine for the grant equal to four years' rent) and lays down that Burgess should be responsible for repairs to the boat.[26] Similar terms were included in the grants to William Hatfield in 1579[27] and to John Williams in 1594.[28]

*Plate 13*

Although the river was the first choice, there were of course roads both for local traffic and for the cartage of goods. When Queen Elizabeth moved to and from Richmond Palace many of the heavy goods were carried by cart. Sometimes road had to be used instead of river. In January 1578/9 when the Earl of Leicester's company were putting on a play at Richmond Palace a horse had to be hired for two days, 'the frost being so grate no bote could goe'.[29] Richmond was not on any main route, but was the hub of a local network. There was a lane to Kew meadows, a footpath from Richmond Green to the Kew ferry and a lane to Mortlake, a rather more important road through East Sheen to Putney, Clapham and London and another through Petersham and Ham to Kingston. The route to Kingston had been the subject of improvement, as the old road to Petersham at the foot of the hillside was liable to flooding. Exactly when 'the upper causeway', leading up the hill to the common and thence down into Petersham village, was built we do not know. The first reference to it as 'the causey' in the manor rolls appears to be in 1566[30] – and the first mention of Petersham Road as 'the lower highway' in 1569.[31] These entries suggest that the construction of the causeway (which is now of course Richmond Hill) may have taken place about the middle of the 16th century; but it should be noted that it was only about then that grants of waste land in this area were being made which necessitated some description. All these roads were unpaved, and such drains as existed were just open ditches.

In the village itself there was the lane on the south-east side of the Green; a track which probably ran straight across the Green from the Palace gate to the end of what is now Duke Street; a lane from there to the Charterhouse site (Shene Lane); the lanes between the Green and what is now George Street, now represented by King Street, Brewer's Lane and Duke Street; the lane from the corner of George Street and King Street down to the river, which continued a path from the churchyard beside the stream (on the line of Red Lion Street); the bottom of the Hill (now Hill Street); and the steep lane down to the ferry (Ferry Hill).

There were also of course some field paths or worples between some of the shotts in the fields. Though none can be actually identified as existing in the 16th century, it is likely that the Vineyard, Friar's Stile Road, Mount Ararat Road, Albany Passage, Paradise Road and Church Terrace-Patten Alley, as well as Worple Way, are all on the lines of such ancient field paths.

Up to the middle of the 16th century there are few mentions of the names of the shott or furlong divisions of the common fields. But the terrier of Sir John Raynford's holdings drawn up on his death in 1559[32] (though the last page which should have included Kew is missing) gives us a fairly complete list of the Richmond fields as they were known at that time.

The Upper Field included:

Church Furlong

East Furlong (which began at the old Shene Charterhouse conduit head – approximately on the site of the present Mount Ararat Road – and continued up to the marsh)

Shorte Downe Furlong (later called Red Conduit Shott or Maybush Shott)

Longe Downe

Easte Downe  
South Downe  } (which together became Heath Shott)

West Baynecrofte

Easte Baynecrofte

Upper Downstede  
Nether Downstede  } (later Upper and Lower Dunstables)

The Lower Field included:

Pathe Furlong – divided into three sections: north side of path; south side of path; against the King's Lease hedge (toward the northern end)

P..don Way by Shepperd's Crosse (later the shott by Baylie's Bank)

This listing omits two of the divisions in the Lower Field: the shott on the east side of the 'horse lane' to Kew (now Kew Road) which was later called Middle Shott, and the shott between the lanes to Kew and to Mortlake, later called Lower Shott. Of the divisions of the Kew Field at this time we have only the indications of West Deane in 1504, East Deane in 1517, Deanhead in 1578, Foxholes in 1553, and Tinderland in 1577 (these are the earliest dates at which these names are found in the manor rolls).[33]

What is known of the history of the houses in the village up to 1603 and of the holdings of land in the fields before 1620 are the subjects of the next two chapters.

# 8

# *Richmond and Kew in 1603*

As THE MANOR ROLLS all survive intact from 1603 onwards, it is possible with a fair degree of accuracy to establish what houses were standing in Richmond and Kew at that date. In many cases there is sufficient evidence in the earlier rolls to trace their histories back to the 15th or 16th centuries. In doing so there is inevitably some element of speculation because of the gaps in the rolls in some years of Henry VIII, the whole reign of Mary I and the last 14 years of Elizabeth I. (This gap is particularly irksome in respect of properties in Kew, where many of the initial grants of waste for building around Kew Green probably date from the period 1589-1602.)

In the 'directory' of Richmond and Kew in 1603, which follows below, an attempt has been made to summarise what is known or can be deduced about the history of the houses before 1603 and their ownership in that year. In many cases the next disposal of the properties after 1603 has been mentioned as it is relevant to establishing the ownership in 1603. Some of the houses listed were the 'capital messuages' of tenements or half-tenements of land in the fields – and references to 'tenement No. x' apply to the numbering adopted in Chapter 9 and Appendix 7. Other houses were built on land granted from the manorial waste.

Richmond Palace was of course still standing and occupied in 1603. The directory *Plate 7* starts by its north-west corner and follows roughly the geographical order of listing later adopted by Richmond rate-collectors. There is however one important difference: the north-west side of George Street is here considered together with the houses on the south-east side of Richmond Green. Many of the original capital messuages of tenements were in this area, with their grounds stretching through from the Green to George Street. The main houses faced the Green; the few cottages that had yet been built along George Street were in their grounds, sometimes on parts of the land which had been sold off.

References to George Street and other modern street names are of course anachronistic in 1603, but it seemed easier for the modern reader to use such names in the sub-section headings and in describing the location of the sites.

To cite all the references to the manor rolls would involve footnotes almost as lengthy as the text, so these have been omitted. A key (by dates) to the Public Record

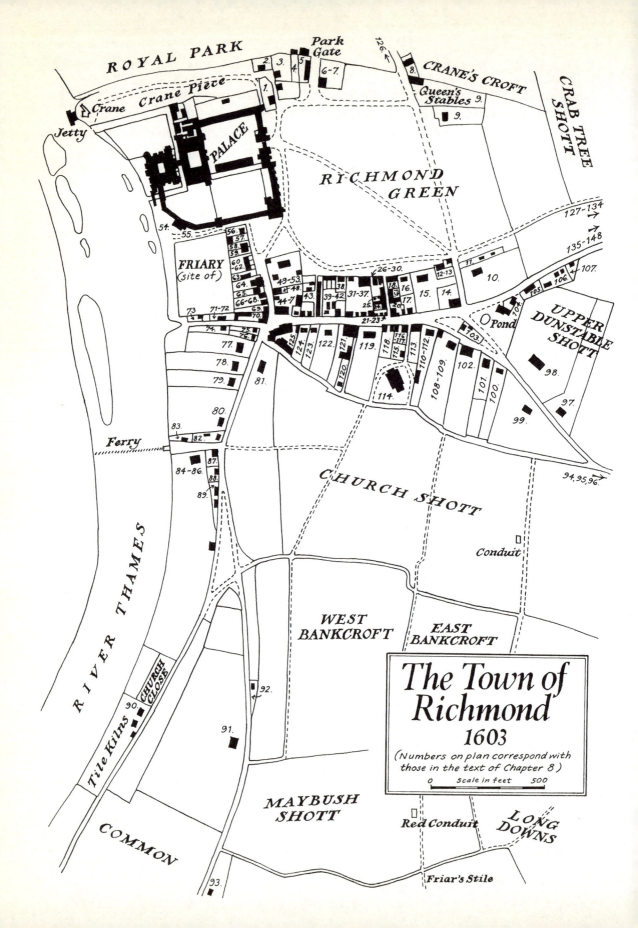

ROYAL PARK

Park Gate

CRANE'S CROFT

CRAB TREE SHOTT

Crane Piece

Crane

Jetty

PALACE

Queen's Stables 9.

9.

RICHMOND GREEN

127-134

135-148

FRIARY (site of)

54.

55.

56.
57.
58.
59.
60-62.
63.
64.
65.
66-68.
69.
70.

73

71-72

49-53.
44-48.

38

26-30.

11.

12-13

10.

107.

106.

105.

104.

UPPER DUNSTABLE SHOTT

43

39-42.

31-37.

25.

18.
19.

16.

17.

17.

20.

15.

14.

103.

O Pond

98.

21-23.

74.

75.
76.

77.

78.

79.

81.

125.

124.

123.

122.

121.

119.

118.

116.
117.

115.

113.

110-112.

108-109.

102.

101.

100.

97.

120.

114.

99.

80.

83.

82.

Ferry

84-86.

87.

88.

89.

94, 95, 96.

CHURCH SHOTT

Conduit

RIVER THAMES

92.

WEST BANKCROFT

EAST BANKCROFT

Tile Kilns

90.

CHURCH CLOSE

91.

**The Town of Richmond 1603**

*(Numbers on plan correspond with those in the text of Chapter 8)*

0    scale in feet    500

MAYBUSH SHOTT

Red Conduit

LONG DOWNS

COMMON

93.

Friar's Stile

Office references for the manor rolls and books will be found at Appendix 6. References to documents other than the manor rolls (dealing with Crown or other freehold properties) are included.

✠

## A. Richmond

### The north-west side of Richmond Green

**1** (Site of the old Theatre Royal, by the corner of Old Palace Lane)
The original grant of this piece of land, outside the wall of the Clerk of Works' yard at Richmond Palace, has not been traced; it may have been in the reign of Mary I. By the beginning of Queen Elizabeth's reign Thomas Denys had a substantial house on it (as can be seen in Wyngaerde's drawing of the Palace from the Green in 1561-2). *Plate 13b* Denys's widow Joan was given a life interest in the house (with remainder to her son Benjamin and ultimate reversion to the parish of Richmond for the benefit of the poor), but in 1569 she and her new husband Nicholas Beneson sold the house to Henry Harvey. William Thomas and his son Robert were admitted to the property in 1601. In 1604 they secured their title by a recovery process involving the heirs of Robert Welsh (see at 2 below), when the property had been recently rebuilt and was described as 'a mansion house newly erected'.

**2** (Site of 1-7 Old Palace Lane)
There were three known grants of land here: the first (44 by 26 feet) to Thomas Fysshe in 1493; the second (57 by 30 feet) to George Hallywell in 1529; and a third to Henry Harvey in 1566. Fysshe's land was acquired in 1528 by Henry Parkyns who built a cottage on it; it was then regranted to Hallywell along with the extra land. After the death of Hallywell's widow Alice in 1538, the cottage was inherited by her brother Robert Welsh. The latter's widow left it in 1563 to Richard Bradshaw who sold it three years later to Henry Harvey. Harvey's grant of land to extend the property included both land on the side facing the lane, leaving 'a sufficient way to the Queen's timberyard' and land on the north-east side between his house and and No. 3 (below). William Thomas and his son Robert were admitted to this property, as also to No. 1, in February 1601.

**3** (Site of Cedar Grove)
The original grant here has not been traced, but in October 1510 a cottage on the site was inherited by Joan Burton from her father Thomas. Joan married Thomas Marre, and in 1535 mortgaged the property to Elizabeth wife of Harmon Goldstone, who was admitted to it in 1538. (Elizabeth Goldstone may have been Joan's daughter.) The Goldstones sold the property to Henry Harvey in 1569. Meanwhile, to its north-east

King Edward VI had leased to Henry Todde in 1552 'a cottage and two gardens' between Richmond Green and the wall of the park. In 1581 Henry Harvey was presented in the manor court for many misdeeds including occupying these gardens 'which belonged to the Keeper of the Park' – but they appear to have become a part of this property from then on. What happened between 1589 and 1602 is lost with the manor rolls, but on 9 June 1603 Sir John Stanhope, Vice-Chamberlain to James I, sold the cottage 'lately in his tenure and formerly in that of William Ballott' to Stephen Peirce. (Stanhope, a nephew of the Protector Somerset, was created Lord Stanhope of Harrington in 1605; his daughter Elizabeth married Sir Lionel Tollemache and was an ancestor of the Earls of Dysart. Stephen Peirce was Keeper of the Wardrobe at Richmond Palace.)

**4-5** (Approximate site of 1 and rear of 2 Pembroke Villas)
There were two houses on the south-west and north-west sides of the gate into the park, occupied originally (see the grant to John Bury in 1437)[1] by the Keeper of the 'New Park of Shene' and by the Clerk of the King's Works. They were still in use as such when the Palace and James I's park were sold in 1649-50. There was also a bakehouse belonging to the Palace on this site.[2]

**6-7** (Approximate site of 2-10 Pembroke Villas and Park Gate)
On the north-east of the park gate two grants of land outside the park pale were made to Bartholomew Neall in 1583 and 1585. The first, of a square plot measuring 54 feet each way, was specifically 'for building a new house 12 feet by 12 feet'. The second was of land 63 feet by 12 feet on the west side of the former. In 1586 Neall surrendered these to William Park. Thomas Keyes purchased these plots of land at the end of Queen Elizabeth's reign and built on them 'a capital messuage and a cottage'. Then in 1604 he obtained a new grant of some half an acre of land outside the park wall stretching all the way up to Sheen Lane, the road which led from the Green to West Sheen.

**North-east side of Richmond Green**

**8** In the latter part of the 16th century (date unknown but before 1585) Richard Eustede had a grant of land at the corner of the Green, on the north-east side of Sheen Lane (which led to the Charterhouse site), on which he built a barn. Immediately to the south-east of this another grant was made in 1585 to Gilbert Polleston, of the 17 feet of land remaining between Eustede's barn and the Queen's Stable (see 9). Polleston probably built a cottage on it, but the subsequent history is unclear.

**9** The Queen's Stable (site of 5-17 Portland Terrace)
A grant of land at this corner of the Green was made to Massie Villyard (joint lessee

of the Manor of Richmond and joint Keeper of the Palace, the Wardrobe, the Garden and the New Park of Shene from 1522) and on it two houses were built.[3] After his death one of the houses was demolished, but its site with a one-acre close and the other 'fine house with a fine garden' were leased to Elizabeth Philpot. In 1546 Anne of Cleves, as Lady of the Manor, leased this property to David Vincent,[4] who also had a lease of the manor and a grant of the several keeperships. In 1550 new stables were built for the Palace on the site of the demolished house.[5] Vincent exchanged his lease in 1552 for a grant of lands elsewhere,[6] but he appears to have retained the house as a sub-tenant until his death in 1565. The house itself was by then known as 'The Queen's Stable'; it was re-leased in turn to various court officials, including eventually Edmund Beck, Yeoman of the Spicery, who had a lease, which also included some adjacent royal land, in 1597.[7] When James I wanted this adjacent land to add to his new park Beck was paid £80 in compensation and was given a new lease in 1607 of the Queen's Stable only.[8] (By that time the royal stable complex had been moved to Sheen Place, the mansion developed from the old Charterhouse of Shene, but the name still attached to the house on the Green.)

## South-east side of Little Green

**10** The main property on the south-east side of the Green north of Duke's Lane was a freehold, containing some 1½ acres, and extending through to the Kew Road and to the open space where the village pond and the cattle pound (or pinfold) were situated. It is therefore probably the freehold 'cottage and garden adjoining the pinfold' which was made over in 1497 by Johanna, widow of William Hunt, to her daughter Elizabeth and son-in-law John Michell.

Nothing more is known of its ownership until 1581 when it belonged to 'Mr Duke' (Thomas Duke, heir to the Wylde-Raynford estate, who died in 1608). It was one of the capital messuages of this estate (tenement 11). Whether it was Thomas Duke or his son William who built the large mansion seen in the 'Prospect of Richmond' engraving (1726) is uncertain – but it appears to be of late 16th- to early 17th-century date. The Michell connection of 1497 is interesting in view of the later 17th-century ownership of this house by the Michell family, but this may be pure coincidence.

**11** On the outside of the Duke property several grants of waste from the edge of the Green were made in the reign of Elizabeth I. An initial grant on which William Parker built 'a mansion house' has not been traced, but in 1581 he received two further grants to extend his property, and Richard Eustede received a small adjacent grant. Then in 1583 Alexander White was given some land to the north-east of Parker's, part of which he sold in 1586 and the other part of which was regranted in the same year to Paul Rising (who promptly sold it to George Bosley). By 1628 all this land belonged to

Nathaniel Giles and had a cottage on it – but Giles had probably acquired it, and built the cottage, before 1603. What happened to Parker's house is uncertain; it appears to have been abandoned – the land was regranted in 1672.

**South-east side of the Green and north-west side of London (now George) Street**

**12-13** (Sites of 1-3 The Green and 5-6 Duke Street)

A plot of land 30 by 16 feet was granted from the Green, by the corner of Duke's Lane, in 1579 to Richard Sewell, who built a cottage, with a shop. Next to it was a smaller grant (20 by 14 feet) to John Goodgrome, who made it over to Sewell in 1580. In 1585 a grant (20 by 16 feet), adjoining Sewell's land, was made to Gilbert Polleston 'to build a house', and Sewell sold him a piece of his land. Then in 1586 Polleston was granted more land, which brought his holding to a total frontage on the Green of 58 feet by 23 feet deep. He purchased (probably between 1589 and 1602 from John Hynde or Sir Hugh Portman, see 15) a tract of land behind these grants, stretching through to Duke's Lane; and then built a large house on the site of Nos. 2-3 The Green. This had come into the ownership of Jacob Irish by 1603, and was inherited by his grandson William Irish in 1604. Sewell's shop (with a plot of land just 20 by 10 feet) was inherited by Augustine Sewell on his father's death in 1598-9 and he sold it to Joan widow of Jonas Harrold. Joan Harrold sold this in 1609 to Thomas Snow, who was Richard Sewell's nephew. Sewell's cottage appears to have been on part of the land sold to Polleston, and was probably sold to Snow by the latter before 1603. By 1612 Thomas Snow had both cottage and shop on the site of No. 1 The Green.

**14** (Sites of 41-45 George Street and 1 Duke Street)

This site may have been that of the capital messuage of a half-tenement or may have been associated with 15 below; its history is unknown until 1585 when Edward Charlton forfeited his house and garden there to the lord of the manor for the misdeed of having let it out without a licence. He was readmitted in the following year and his son Walter Charlton inherited the property in 1595. It was later to become the *Rose and Crown* inn.

**15** (Site of 4-7 The Green, 46-50 George Street and 2-4 Duke Street)

This property, which almost certainly included originally most of 12-13 (above) and possibly 14 also, is so large in comparison with most of its neighbours as to suggest that it was the accretion of several capital messuages of tenements – perhaps as many as three. The south-western end of it, at least, seems to have belonged to John Walshe or Welsh in 1505 – and his house may have been the messuage of tenement No. 16. By the second half of the 16th century the whole property was in the hands of Augustine Hynde and then his son John Hynde. It may be that in expanding his estate Augustine

Hynde deliberately acquired some tenements whose houses adjoined his. As the first tenement he acquired was No. 4, the houses of tenements Nos. 6 and 8 may have added to the site. He may have then rebuilt a single mansion on the enlarged site. Together with the rest of the Hynde estate this property was acquired by Sir Hugh Portman, who was on 9 June 1603 granted a licence to let 'his messuage abutting the Green on the north, Jacob Irish on the east and Edward Miles on the west'. (When Hynde or Portman sold to Gilbert Polleston the land behind Nos. 1-3 The Green, the section abutting the central part of Duke's Lane was retained. If 14 was indeed originally a part of this property, it had presumably been sold off earlier.)

**16** (Site of 8-9 The Green)
This, together with 17, was probably the garden of John Walshe's capital messuage belonging to tenement No. 16. In 1505 the section facing the Green was surrendered by William Tyler to William Brice and his wife Joan as 'a parcel of land behind the tenement of John Walshe containing 116 feet north to south and 56 feet east to west, abutting Thomas Fysshe west, the Green north and John Walshe east'. A house was 'new built' when William Brice's daughter Alice inherited it on his death in 1515. From the Brices it passed to George Burton, then to Peter May (1561) and his son Thomas (1565) and then to Ralph Burstoe (1580) and his daughter Mary. By 1603 it belonged to Edward Miles who surrendered it to John Baker on 28 May 1606.

**17** (Two houses on site of 51 and part of 52 George Street)
Though probably in origin a part of the same property as 16, nothing is known of the history of this holding until four members of the Mann family (as joint heirs – possibly of Robert Mann buried 8 November 1603) surrendered it to Thomas Larkyn alias Flint on 2 May 1604. The houses had presumably been built by 1603.

**18** (Site of 10-12 The Green and 11-13 Brewer's Lane)
This was owned by Thomas Fysshe in 1505 (see 16) and was, together with 19, the capital messuage of his tenement (No. 21). The house had become separated from the tenement by 1559 when it was left by Thomas Denys to his wife Joan for her lifetime with remainder to his son John (and with an ultimate reversion to the parish if John had no heirs). On 11 April 1572 Joan and her new husband Nicholas Beneson sold the house, by then a tavern under the sign of the *Cross Keys*, to Henry Naylor, from whom it was inherited by Mary Crome who was the owner in 1603. This was one of the properties in dispute between Mary Crome and the Richmond Vestry in the 1620s.

**19** (Site of 5-9 Brewer's Lane and a rear part of 10 The Green)
This part of the capital messuage appears to have been passed on with 18, but from 1561 to 1576 there was a series of suits in the manor court over its ownership, the

Benesons' rights being challenged by John Parkyns and then his son Henry Parkyns, the successors in title to Thomas Fysshe's tenement No. 21. Henry Parkyns emerged victorious in 1576, by which time the cottage on the site was occupied by William Meryall. A William Brewer had acquired the title to the cottage by 1603 – probably in the period 1589-1602 – and in October 1611 the manor court recorded the death of William Brewer and the succession to the property of 'William Brewer alias Merriall, his reputed son'. The William Brewer who died in 1611 was undoubtedly the one who gave his name to Brewer's Lane, but his heir's name presents us with a small problem. William Brewer was perhaps the second husband of William Meryall's widow, whose son William was born posthumously and later took the name of his stepfather.

### 20 (Site of 52-54 George Street and 1-3 Brewer's Lane)

This site at the corner of George Street and Brewer's Lane was that of the *Lilypot* inn and later of the parochial school (established in 1713). It had been the capital messuage of South's half-tenement (No. 5) in the mid-14th century and appears to have been separated from the land during the reign of Henry VII. In 1502 Thomas Knolles surrendered the tenement and garden 'called South's' to John Smith and his wife Alice; and it remained in the Smith family until 1547 when sold to William Glasborough who sold it on to Robert Stockden two years later. The first mention of the '*Lilly Pott*' came when Stockden and his wife made it over to their daughter and her husband Robert Storer in 1567. By 1603 the property belonged to Robert King (who in 1614 failed to redeem a mortgage to George Charley who then took title).

A number of small cottages had been built in the back yard of the inn, some facing Brewer's Lane, by the 1620s. Some of them may have been in existence by 1603, but there is no clear evidence of this. The house on the southern part of the site of 52 George Street was described as 'new' when sold off from the rest of the property in 1614.

### 21-23 (Site of 55-58 George Street)

This property, together with 24 and 25, was probably the site of a half-tenement capital messuage, but had been separated from its land before the end of Queen Elizabeth's reign when most of it belonged to Seth Goldstone. In 1604 he sold '3 little cottages' – the George Street frontage – to John Cogdell and his wife Jane.

### 24 (Site of 4-6 Brewer's Lane)

The single small cottage here was already separated from the rest of the Goldstone property by 1603 when it belonged to Robert Dye. Dye left it ('the messuage wherein he dwelled') in trust for his four daughters when he died in September 1612.

### 25 (Site of 8-10 Brewer's Lane)

In 1607 Seth Goldstone, who had previously mortgaged the single cottage on this site for £8 2s. 6d. to Ralph Fletcher, sold 'the messuage in which James Wicherly [the parish clerk] lived' to Henry Cookney.

**26-30** (Site of 13-15 The Green and 12-18 Brewer's Lane)
This had probably been the capital messuage of a half-tenement. In 1596 it was surrendered by John Feare alias Deere and Thomas Smyther to Alice the wife of Ralph Tye. No details are available as this surrender, which would have been recorded in the missing manor rolls, is only known by being referred to when John Tye inherited the property from his mother Alice in 1617. By 1617 – and probably in 1596 – the property consisted of 'one messuage divided into two' (facing the Green) and 'four shops' (facing Brewer's Lane). It seems likely that this was Richmond's main shopping area at the end of Queen Elizabeth's reign.

**31-37** (Site of 16-20 The Green and 59-65 George Street)
This large property was the capital messuage of one of the whole tenements (No. 25) held by William Cooke about 1500. By the time that his son Thomas Cooke died in 1539 there were eight cottages on the property in addition to the main house. Thomas Cooke's daughter Katharine, wife of John Hall, surrendered it to Henry Naylor on 4 May 1551. Naylor's heir was Mary Crome who was owner in 1603. In 1614 it was recorded that she held 'the messuage called the *Crown* abutting Richmond Green [16-17 The Green] and six cottages: one on Richmond Green [18-20 The Green] and five on London Street – the six cottages were formerly eight'. The three cottages knocked together into one house were probably at 18-20 The Green.

**38** (Site of 21 The Green)
This property was probably in origin a part of the next (39), but by the reign of Queen Elizabeth it was owned by Edward Lovell (who may have been a brother of John Lovell, the Palace gardener). Lovell died in April 1584 and all his property was inherited by his son Ralph. On Ralph's death in 1604/5 his younger son Thomas Lovell Junior inherited 'one messuage'.

**39-42** (Sites of 22-25 The Green and 66-73 George Street)
This (with 38 probably) was the capital messuage of one of the tenements (Nos. 35 and 36) surrendered by William Blackett to Richard Brampton in 1491. Three generations later Thomas Brampton surrendered them to Thomas Gisby in 1581.

Gisby divided the holding, selling the main house facing the Green to Bartholomew Knaresborough in 1582. Knaresborough developed and further subdivided this property, selling it in three separate parts in 1584-87. The main house at the northern end [site of 22 The Green] went to Reginald Edwards and from him to Lord Cobham in 1587. By 1603 it was owned by John Symonds, whose brother Robert Symonds inherited it in 1604.

The central portion of Knaresborough's land, with a cottage on it (site of the *Cricketers*) was sold in 1584 to Richard Reading who passed it on in the following year to Isabel Spurling. She was still in occupation in 1603.

The southern section with a cottage and shop (site of 25 The Green) was sold to Alexander Whyte, who lived there until his death about 1606.

The George Street frontage Gisby mostly kept for himself, but he sold off a cottage at the northern end (site of 66 George Street) to Isabel Spurling in 1586. All the rest passed on his death in March 1607/8 to his son Thomas. It is not clear whether there were by then any buildings on it.

**43** ('Pensioners' Alley' – sites of 26 The Green and the *Prince's Head*, Golden Court, and part of Dickins and Jones store including the former 74-77 George Street)

On 18 April 1621 the Richmond manor court, having been 'charged to inquire whether certain tenements in Richmond called Chanon Row alias Pensioners' Alley be concealed fully from the Prince or enjoyed by any lawful title', reported that, 'They have inquired thereof, but do not find how it was passed away, altho of late times it hath been held by Coppy.'

The implication that this had been royal property seems to be controverted by what is known of its earlier history, which suggests that it was the capital messuage of a tenement (No. 30) which had belonged to the Constable family and was regranted to John Pyke in 1485. In 1517 Matthew Clyderowe's house (see at 44-46 below) abutted to the east 'the messuage and garden of John Pyke, formerly of Robert Constable'.) In 1571 John Davies and Nicholas Snow had gardens on the site, but they were probably under-tenants, as this whole tenement descended into the ownership of Henry Harvey, who is noted as owner of this property in 1582. Sir Robert Wright was admitted to ownership in 1596 and on his death in 1610 the property was described as 'divers cottages, erections, stables and garden plots called Pensioners' Row or Channon Row'. There is no clear evidence as to how many cottages were on the site at this time or how they were disposed on the site. Nor is it known who built them or who were the pensioners for whom they were intended. The later supposition that this might have been royal property suggests a tradition that they were built for pensioners of the Palace.

**44-46** (Site of former 78-81 George Street, now part of Dickins and Jones store)
This property, together with 47 and 48, was the capital messuage of tenement No. 13, and belonged to John Gryffyn in the late 15th century. No. 48 was sold off in 1494 (see below) but the remainder was purchased by Sir William Tyler and surrendered by him as 'a cottage and garden' to Thomas Wastell in January 1500/1. From Wastell it passed to Matthew Clyderowe (or Clitheroe).

Clyderowe sold off two parts of the property in 1502. One was 47 (below). The other, sold to William Cope, was a 'new built' house standing in the large yard (the entrance to which was between 78 and 79 George Street). Clyderowe himself retained a house on the rest of the property until 1532. Its history for the rest of the 16th century is obscure.

The little cottage at 78 George Street belonged in 1633 to Anne Wilks who had inherited the property of Isabel Spurling, who was therefore probably the owner of this cottage in 1603. The rest of the George Street frontage (with its side on King Street) became the inn which was first called the *Queen's Arms*. This was surrendered by Robert Wright to William Haynes and his wife Alice in 1603. The yard and the house and other buildings in it had by then been reunited with the main property.

**47** (Site of 25-26 King Street)
This was sold as undeveloped land by Clyderowe to Thomas Herford in 1502. A cottage had been built on it by 1509. It appears to have descended in the Herford family (whose name became changed to Harvey) and was owned in 1603 by the tilemaker Henry Harvey.

**48** (Site of 22-24 King Street)
The land was sold by John Gryffyn to Thomas Burton in 1494. There was a cottage on it by 1514, and Burton's heirs, the Marres, passed it on to Harmon Goldstone in 1536. By 1583 it was in the hands of the Slaney family and passed from Alexander Slaney to his brother Jasper in 1607.

**49-53** (Site of Old Palace Terrace and Paved Court and 18-21 King Street)
This parcel of land contained the conduit head granted to Shene Charterhouse in 1466.[9] It had until then been part of the Green. The Charterhouse developed five cottages on it before the Dissolution in 1538. These cottages were then leased out by the Crown to various tenants until George Kirkham obtained a 60-year lease of all five in 1596.[10] In 1605 George Kirkham was described as holding 'a mansion house and three other houses in his own possession and one other mansion house in the occupation of Anthony Lynton, all formerly belonging to the late Monastery of Shene'.[11] It is not certain at what date Kirkham replaced the five houses by the single mansion which can be seen in Moses Glover's map of Isleworth Hundred drawn in 1635. The documents continue to refer back to the lease of the five houses until 1650, but in his will made in February 1610/1 George Kirkham left to Robert, son of his cousin Edward Kirkham, 'the house in Richmond'[12] – so the rebuilding was almost certainly completed by then.

*Plate 13a*

*Plate 14b*

## Friars' Lane

**54** (Part of the site of the Queensberry House flats)
Land outside the garden galleries of the Palace (and also outside the wall of the

Friary) was granted to Henry Harvey on 14 April 1569. His 'mansion by the King's wall' was mentioned in 1581. This house which was – confusingly – known as 'the Friars' existed until the 1730s, but in 1649 it was being used as a chandlery for the Palace.[13] Whether or not it was in private ownership in 1603 is not known. It can be clearly seen, with its double gables, in Hollar's engraving of the Palace in 1638.

*Plate 14*

**55** (Part of the site of the Queensberry House flats)
Hollar's engraving also shows another two-gabled house next to 54. Nothing is known of it in 1603, but it may originally have been a part of Harvey's house. It is almost certainly the 'little very old tenement' which was occupied by Mrs Anne Darley a century later, in 1703.

## The southern corner of the Green

**56** (At the present entrance to Friars' Lane and the site of 'Friars' Way')
Only a narrow path separated the Palace from the first of the houses facing the little corner of the Green at the west end of King Street. The house belonged to John Lovell, the Palace gardener, and his wife Katherine in 1529. It seems likely that this land was a grant, either to Lovell or one of his predecessors as gardener. The house was inherited by the Lovells' son John on Katherine's death in 1571 and by the latter's son, a third John Lovell, in 1590. John III's brother Thomas Lovell succeeded to the ownership in 1603.

*Plate 13*

**57** (Site of 'Beaver Lodge')
The cottage 'in which remains the former wall of the Priory of Observant Friars' was separated from 56 in 1529 when John and Katherine Lovell surrendered it to James Manning. James's son John Manning sold it to Nicholas Bird in 1579. It was inherited by John Bird who sold it to Thomas Huishe in 1607.

**58-59** (Site of 'Old Friars')
This property and Nos. 60-63 were the site of the capital messuage of tenement No. 19 – formerly of Robert Hoo, then of John Maykyn and surrendered by the latter's widow Isabella to Richard Scopeham in 1489. Richard's son Edmund Scopeham, having inherited the property in 1501, sold the three houses which by then stood at its western end to John Wray, Sergeant of the King's Ewery, in 1502-3. John Wray's heir Richard Wray with his son Philip sold them in 1532-33 to Thomas Lord Darcy. One of these houses appears to have been treated at that time as a freehold, but its origin as such is unknown.

There is some uncertainty about the ownership of the houses after the death of Lord Darcy (who was beheaded for treason in June 1537). The copyhold houses seem to have reverted to another John Wray, while the freehold one came into the ownership of Thomas Denys. Denys left it to John Burton and in 1561 Joan, widow of Thomas Denys, and her new husband Nicholas Beneson 'released' to John Burton this 'tenement which he had by gift after the death of Thomas Denys'.

The copyholds meanwhile had been claimed by Robert Humphrey who obtained title after John Wray's death in 1538 – and who promptly sold them to Thomas Dover. From him they passed to Geoffrey French in 1571, then to Thomas French, who sold them to Robert Dover in 1579. In 1580 Dover sold them to John Burton, who had thus reunited the former Wray and Darcy property. In the process the fact that one part of the property had been freehold appears to have been forgotten by the manor court who insisted in 1617 that Burton had never been properly admitted to two of his houses – they were now regarding them all as copyhold. (Presumably Burton had built a second house on the freehold property.) There were now four houses and a stable yard in total. The two former freeholds were on this site (58-59).

Thereafter, the fate of these two houses is clear. Burton's daughter Grace, wife of John Wayland, was retrospectively admitted to the two properties in 1617. She then surrendered the more westerly one to Humphrey Child who had been living in it ever since Burton had sold it to him in 1590. The other passed through several hands before coming into those of Thomas Mercer in 1607. (The owners in 1603 were Richard Turner and his wife Margery.) The Waylands surrendered their rights to the house to Thomas Mercer in 1620.

## 60 (Part of 'Old Palace Place')

For the early history, see 58-59. This was an empty plot of land which John Burton had surrendered to Simon Purdew before 1603. In May 1604 when Purdew sold it to George Kirkham it was 'a parcel of land on which a new house is to be built'. By October 1606 it was 'land on which a house is begun'. It was finally acquired by Thomas Mercer in 1607 and his rights in the house were confirmed in the surrender by the Waylands in 1620 (so possibly the land had been a part of the original freehold). It was part of the decorated outer plaster wall of this house that was discovered when a door was opened between 'Old Friars' and 'Old Palace Place' in World War I – the panel, painted with flowers, is now in the Museum of Richmond.

## 61-62 (Part of 'Old Palace Place')

For the early history, see 58. The other two Burton houses were clearly copyholds. They were surrendered by Burton and his wife to John Atkinson and his wife in 1586. Between 1589 and 1595 they changed hands twice, first to Robert Moulsworth, then to Henry Goodgrome, from whom they were acquired by Sir Robert Wright and his wife Dorothy in January 1595/6. On his death in 1610 Sir Robert left them to Dorothy for her lifetime, with reversion to his brother Richard Wright. When he made his will in 1608 they had been occupied by John Note, a plumber, and one Bourne, a barber.

## King Street (south-west side)

### 63 (Site of Oak House and 15-17 King Street)

For the early history, see 58. This stable yard was surrendered, about 1589-90, by Burton to Edward Spencer, Yeoman of the Royal Scullery. Spencer died in February 1591/2 and his son, another Edward Spencer, sold it with 'the divers buildings' in it to William Haynes, landlord of the *Queen's Arms*, in 1604. It is uncertain whether the 'divers buildings' included any residential accommodation; there was no house as such, but there might have been rooms for stable hands or grooms over the stables.

### 64 (Site of 11-14 King Street)

The remaining properties along King Street as far as No. 3 (64-69) were all part of the Scopeham estate, but appear to have been the site of a separate capital messuage called the *Crown*, which may derive from another unidentified tenement. At the time of Edmund Scopeham's sale to John Wray in 1502-03 (see 58-59 above) the adjacent property on the east was 'a barn of Edmund Scopeham called the *Crown*'. Its history for the next 60 years is untraced, but in 1565 the property was granted to Alexander Slaney as 'a cottage called the *Crown* in the tenure of Thomas Tye and a garden called the *Crown* garden in the tenure of Cornelius de Vase'. (The *Crown* may have been, at least by this time, a tavern.) Slaney divided up the property, selling the first 60 feet of frontage to Seth Goldstone in 1579. (Goldstone must have mortgaged this to John Cogdell; in 1604 Cogdell surrendered the same property back to Seth Goldstone.) By 1604 it had 'buildings' (unspecified) on the land. By 1618 these are identified as 'a messuage of 11 rooms called the *Angel*'.

### 65 (Site of 9-10 King Street)

The *Crown* garden – save for a cottage at its eastern end (69) – was sold by Alexander Slaney to Seth Goldstone in 1580, but was sold back to Slaney two years later. In 1584 John Slaney, Alexander's brother, inherited. In 1585 he sold a small cottage with a 26-foot frontage to the road (a width diminishing to only 11 feet at the rear by the Friary wall) to John Bond. By 1603 the property was in the hands of Thomas Biggs, who died in 1612 – by which time the single cottage had been divided into two dwellings.

### 66-68 (Sites of 4-8 King Street)

The rest of the *Crown* garden remained in the ownership of John Slaney until his death in 1607. By then (and probably by 1603) he had built three houses on it: a larger one on the site of 8 King Street and small cottages on the sites of 4 and 5. (The sites of 6 and 7 King Street were first built on between 1610 and 1620.)

### 69 (Site of 3 King Street)

The cottage at the eastern end of his land – possibly the original *Crown* – was made over by Alexander Slaney to his son John in 1583. John sold it a year later to John Feare alias Deere, who died in 1596. By 1603 the cottage was in the ownership of John Matthew and his wife Grace, who sold it in 1610 to Thomas and Thomasine Blemell.

**70** (Site of 1-2 King Street)
A grant of waste land on the south-east side of the Friary wall and of the Scopeham property was probably made to Thomas Denys (Senior) in the early years of the 16th century, but has not been traced. In 1520 Thomas Denys (Junior), his son and heir, surrendered this land to Henry Parkyns, who then in 1528 surrendered it as 'a cottage and garden' to John Aman. In 1536 the property was described as 'a cottage, barn, garden and half an acre of land at Temes [Thames] Croft in Richmond'. In 1544/5 John Aman mortgaged the property to Augustine Hynde, and must have failed to redeem the mortgage, for John Hynde, Augustine's son, is recorded as owning the property in 1572 and in 1586. John Hynde must have sold it between 1589 and 1602 to Edward Standen, who in 1607 left to his son Lawrence 'the messuage called the *Golden Hind* in which Thomas Tye, butcher, dwelled'. The *Golden Hind* was an inn (which was renamed the *Feathers* in the early 17th century). The name evidently celebrated the ship in which Drake circumnavigated the world in 1577-80, but one wonders if there was not also an element of punning on the name of the owner of the property.

## Water Lane, north-west side

**71-72** (Site of part of 1 King Street and 2-14 Water Lane)
This had been a part of 70, but had two extra cottages built on it by 1603. In 1607 Edward Standen bequeathed to his son John a cottage at the corner of the lane from the highway to the Thames, with a garden, occupied by Edward Standen, and a cottage and backside adjacent in the said lane, formerly occupied by Robert Standen deceased, son of Edward. (Robert Standen had died in August 1602.)

**73** (Site below 14 Water Lane)
John Sexton died in 1608 seized of one small cottage erected on a parcel of waste 'lately granted to him'. His widow claimed a life interest by virtue of an entry in the manor court roll of 31 March 1600 (now missing), so it is probable that the cottage was built by 1603.

## Water Lane, south-east side

**74** (Site above Riverside House)
The land on the south-east side of Water Lane (including 75 and 76) was former wasteland granted in 1514 to Nicholas Gray, the Clerk of Works at Richmond Palace,

and his wife Mary as 'a tenement near the King's Manor, called Timber Hawe on which a messuage was built by the said Nicholas'. 'The house in which Nicholas Gray lately dwelt' was granted to John Pate in 1520 and to David Vincent in 1536. After Vincent it seems to have returned to Pate ownership. In 1560 'the messuage of William Pate' (John's son) was granted to Massie Stanton, and nine years later the house of Massie Stanton was said to be to the south of the land between the Friars and the river granted to Henry Harvey (see 54). The house again reverted to Pate after Stanton's death; the land at the end of Water Lane granted for the construction of a town wharf in 1586 lay 'between the land of Henry Harvey on the north and the land of William Pate on the south'. William Pate died about 1590 and his widow Alice in 1602. Their heir was their son John Pate, who was admitted retrospectively in 1606. He had already surrendered all his father's property, without being admitted himself; so now new surrenders had to be made to the current owners to set the record straight.

One of these was to Robert Bayley of 'the land formerly called an eight on which Robert Bayley waterman lately built a house and converted the residue into a wharf ... parcel of the hereditaments of William Pate and descended to John Pate, and came to Joan Deere alias Fryer widow and since to Robert Bayley'. No separate grant of this ait has been traced; it was probably a 'bullrush bed' at the river end of the property granted to Nicholas Gray.

**75** (All the rest of the south-east side of Water Lane and sites of 1-3 Hill Street)
Another surrender made by John Pate in 1606 was to Richard and Katherine Sherratt. They at once passed it on to Thomas and Jane Fuddes. The property (which included 76 below) was 'the messuage, garden, orchard and piece of land adjoining the messuage on which divers buildings are erected, now in the possession of Richard Sherratt and his wife Katherine in her right, and formerly of widow Deere alias Fryer'. The exact site of the messuage and the nature and extent of the 'divers buildings' are not known.

## Hill Street, south-west side

**76** (Site of 5 Hill Street)
By 1617 there was an extra house at the north-east end of the Fuddes property (see 75) 'in which George Charley lately dwelt'. It was probably one of the 'divers buildings' in 1606 and was very likely already there by 1603, but one cannot be certain.

**77** (Site of 7-11 Hill Street and of Whittaker House, Whittaker Avenue)
This had been the capital messuage of the tenement (No. 33) belonging to the Osey family and later to Sir Richard Guilford and his son Henry, which came into the ownership of John Pate in 1530. It was inherited in turn by William Pate and the latter's son John. In 1606 'the great capital messuage with garden, barn, orchard and stable

yard' was surrendered by the second John Pate (see 74) to Ralph Fletcher who was already in occupation.

## 78 (Site of Old Town Hall and down to river)

This had probably been the capital messuage of the half-tenement No. 34. In 1487 it was left by William Hunt to his wife Joan (who later married a Hosey – or Osey – from next door) with remainder to their son Edmund. It had previously belonged to a John Yonge (probably keeper of the ferry – see page 48).

Edmund Hunt sold it to Hugh a Deane and his wife Agnes in 1502, and Agnes sold to John Sharpe in 1509. Between 1521 and 1527 it came into the hands of John Crewe who in 1531 made over a life interest to his wife Elizabeth with reversion to John Pate. In 1536, John Pate having died, William Pate was admitted, but surrendered to Elizabeth Stede (ex Crewe) for her lifetime – and she leased the house to Pate. By 1575 when William Pate surrendered the site to Nicholas Bird and his wife Bridget the cottage had gone and the description was 'land called a Shepehawe* near Ferry Hill between Pate's own tenement and that of Nicholas Byrd'. The Birds built a new mansion which their son and heir, another Nicholas, sold to Dr Henry Atkins, Physician-in-Ordinary to King James I, in 1607.

## 79 (Sites of 13-15 Hill Street and Hotham House)

The next house to the south was in 1489 in the possession of John Drewe. On 16 July of that year the manor court demanded that he repair the hedge between his croft and the tenement of Johanna Hosey *alias* Hunt; and another reference at the same court was to 'the watercourse in high level of Thames against his [Drewe's] tenement'. Drewe was noted as a manorial tenant from 1485 and this would appear to have been the capital messuage of his half-tenement (No. 23). After his death in 1494 the house and tenement went to his nearest heir Elizabeth, daughter of John de Bury, wife of Robert Cornwalys. The tenement then passed through several hands into the ownership of Hugh Denys, an 'esquire of the King's body' in 1501. Thereafter the history of the house is obscure. It was probably sold after Denys's death in 1511, as instructed in his will. For reasons explained below it may then, or a bit later, have been acquired by Henry Parkyns and merged into the next property.

This was the capital messuage of tenement No. 20. (It may have been the 'messuage with a virgate of land' inherited by William Hoo from Constance Hoo in 1449.) By 1487 it was in the ownership of John Hough (his land was stated in 1499 to lie on the north side of Pykwell's – see below at No. 80). Though Hough, who died in 1501, partly split up his lands, the house and 16 acres appear to have been in the hands of his son Humphrey Hough by 1512. In 1513/4 Humphrey Hough sold all his property

---

* Hawe is used here in the sense of a close of land

to Henry Parkyns (in 1518 the former Pykwell house (now Pyke's) had Parkyns as its northern neighbour). In 1544 Henry Parkyns received a grant of waste land 'on Ferry Hill containing 3 perches from the highway on the east to his croft against the Thames on the west and 6 perches from the house called Shypcott on the north to the Lord's common on the south'. This grant suggests there was originally some 50 feet (three perches) of waste land between the eastern boundaries of the holdings south of No. 78 and the roadway. But 100 feet (six perches) is surely too wide a frontage for a single holding – hence my suggestion that by 1544 the Parkyns holding included the site of Drewe's house as well as Hough's. Henry's son John Parkyns sold this house to John Gwyldmyn, probably in the reign of Mary I. In 1570 John's son Henry Gwyldmyn sold it to Anthony Pope as a 'messuage formerly of John Gwyldmyn and before of John Parkyns' and in 1573 John Brockhouse inherited it from Pope as 'a messuage formerly of Henry Gwyldmyn and once of Humphrey Hough' – so its antecedents are well corroborated. Brockhouse sold the house in 1575 to Henry Mewes, who sold it on to Nicholas Bird two years later. The Bird family sold the house to Sir Robert Wright between 1589 and 1602.

**80** (Sites of 17-19 Hill Street and Heron House and most of Heron Square)

This land had also been the sites of two capital messuages of tenements (Nos. 7 and 29). John Pyke acquired tenement No. 29 with its messuage from John Vernon in 1492; then he purchased from John Pykwell in 1499 the cottage adjacent on the north side which had belonged to half-tenement No. 7. In 1518 both were sold to Owen Holland. It was probably a son of the same name who sold them to Henry Harvey in 1576. The Birds acquired ownership between 1589 and 1602. When John Bird sold the site to Sir Robert Wright in 1604 the original houses had long since gone, but so had the mansion which had replaced them. The description read 'a close of two acres with a great barn – at the time of Nicholas and Bridget Bird was one new great messuage and before that was flat'.

## Hill Street, north-east side

**81** (The entire north-east side of Hill Street and of Hill Rise up to the Vineyard)
A large freehold close of some five acres lay between the edge of Church Shott of the Upper Field and the road leading up the hill. It stretched from Red Lion Street to the Vineyard and was about 100 yards wide at its central point (where Ormond Road is today). Within it, probably at or near the corner of Hill Street and Red Lion Street, stood one large mansion. This was the principal house of the freehold estate in Richmond and Kew (tenement No. 11) which had belonged to the Wylde family of Camberwell and then, in right of his wife, to Sir John Raynford. In the terrier of Raynford's lands drawn up in 1559 the close is listed under the heading of 'Church Furlong' (of which it was not in fact part, but which clearly indicates the location) as

'a close of Sir John Raynford's late Wyld's joining on the backside of the house, containing five acres'. Lady Raynford's heir was Thomas Duke, who in 1576 divided the estate with one Wyatt Wilde (an uncle or cousin – see pages 95-97) .

It is probable, though not certain, that this house and close together with the lands in the Richmond fields were Wyatt Wilde's share. By 1603 the Richmond lands had been acquired by Duncan Jones; and in 1604 the close was in the occupation of Jones's tenant William Dawborne. The Jones family held the former Raynford lands in Richmond throughout the 18th century.

### Ferry Hill (now Bridge Street), north-west side

**82** (Corner of Hill Street and Bridge Street)
At the top of Ferry Hill on its north-west side was a piece of land with a barn. The land was probably part of tenement No. 17, but it never appears to have had a house on it until the mid-17th century. The land was a 'hempstall ground'.* The then owner Robert Sanders died in 1564 leaving the barn and land to his widow Anne for life, with remainder to Roger Richbell. In 1577 Richbell, by then in occupation, acquired a little more land by grant; and in 1599 he sold this property to Edward Spencer. (The rest of the tenement seems to have gone to his daughter Katherine Gisby.) In 1604 Spencer's son, also Edward, sold the barn and land to William Haynes.

**83** (Approximate site of Tower House)
Lower down Ferry Hill a grant of land was made in October 1553 to Seth Goldstone. He built a cottage on it which he still owned in 1603.

### Ferry Hill (Bridge Street), south-east side – and Petersham Road

**84-86** (Site of Northumberland Place and 15-49 Petersham Road, and the garden by the bridge)
A large stretch of land on the south of Ferry Hill, between the river and the lower road to Petersham, was probably first granted to John Coteler (or Cutler) in the reign of Henry IV. (It may have been part of the original park of the manor house.) In 1445 the manor rolls describe it as 'a cottage and garden called Wyndeyarde formerly of John Coteler now in the occupation of Richard Chester'. In 1500 William York inherited 'a cottage and two crofts called the Windeyarde' from his father and sold them to Gilbert Mawdesley. Mawdesley's son John sold the property to Thomas Warde in 1532 and Warde's son Richard sold it to Edward Hatfield in the early 1540s. A surviving 'copy'[14] of a court roll entry of 17 October 1554 (a date for which the original roll is lost) records the death of Edward Hatfield and that his heir was his 12-year-old son William. When William died in 1588 he again left a minor son William as heir. In all

---

*   The word 'hempstall' is not given in the *Oxford English Dictionary*. Possibly the hempstall ground was a place where hemp was gathered, stored and/or sold.

these entries the land is referred to as 'the Windeyarde'. In 1608 the latest William Hatfield sold the property to William Pitts and three years later Pitts surrendered it to himself and his wife Susanna as 'a messuage and closes of land adjacent and two cottages on part of the said land, formerly called the Vineyard and lately in the occupation of William Hatfield'. This land probably was a vineyard (Windeyarde being a corruption of the name). Its location on a south-west facing slope by the river would have been very suitable. It is not quite clear where all three houses mentioned in 1611 were located or when they were built; but the main house (in existence by 1603) was almost certainly on or near the site of the later Northumberland House, by the Petersham Road, and it is most probable that one of the cottages was at the foot of Ferry Hill.

**87** (Site of *Joe's Tavern* and 1-9 Hill Rise)
In 1572 Thomas Burgess was granted a long triangle of waste land between the road to Petersham and William Hatfield's land. It had a 32-foot frontage to Ferry Hill at the top end, tapering to a point along a 300-foot frontage to the Petersham Road. This grant covered Nos. 87-89. Burgess built a barn and stable in the middle part of the land and then in 1574 sold the northern end to Nicholas Bird. In 1607 John Bird, son of Nicholas, sold the house which had by then been built at the top of Ferry Hill to Henry and Dorothy Holloway, and in 1609 he sold them some more land with a stable and two sheds.

## Hill Rise (west side) and Petersham Road

**88** (Site of 11-13 Hill Rise)
See early history at No. 87. The remainder of John Bird's land, with the barn and stable, was sold to William Holmer in 1610.

**89** (Site of 1-13 Petersham Road)
The southern end of Thomas Burgess's land was sold to William Hatfield in 1577. On the site of 1-13 Petersham Road Sir George Wright built his almshouses (known as Queen Elizabeth's) in 1600. His purchase of the land and vesting of it in trustees must have been recorded in the missing court rolls. The earliest mention in the existing rolls is in 1621 when Stephen Peirce as surviving trustee made over the land to new trustees. (The southern tip of the Burgess triangle was absorbed by Hatfield into the Windeyarde land.)

**90** (Site of former *Three Pigeons*, boathouse and adjacent car park)
There was just one other development along the riverside by 1603. South of the Windeyard land was the close belonging to the parish church. Then to the south of

this a grant of one acre of waste land was made to Henry Harvey in 1569. On this land a tile kiln and a cottage had been built by 1597 when John Feare alias Deere left the property to his widow Joan, who held it until her death in 1623. This was the beginning of the tile-making industry along the Petersham Road which flourished until the 1760s.

## Richmond Hill

**91** (West side from No. 19 to Hewson Terrace)
The land called originally 'South Park' and then 'Smithy Croft' was granted to Robert Nevill, a bricklayer and brickmaker, in 1499. It may have once been part of the original park of the Shene manor house. It was regranted in 1552 to Harmon Goldstone. By 1573, when Goldstone died, a mansion had been built and the estate had been renamed 'Moorebrook'. Harmon's son Seth Goldstone sold it in 1574 to Nicholas Snow, from whom it was inherited by Lawrence Snow in 1583. When Lawrence Snow was executed at Kingston in 1596 for horse-stealing, his lands would have forfeited to the lord of the manor, and it seems probable that Moorebrook was then granted to Nicholas Bird. Bird sold the property to Seth Goldstone in 1602, although the sale was not fully completed until 1604. (This land was later the site of Richmond Wells.)

**92** (East side – site of Nos. 50-58 Richmond Hill and of the front part of Richmond Hill Court)
There was probably a cottage almost opposite the Moorebrook house in 1603. On the south-west of West Bancroft Shott of the Upper Field there was a long freehold close, as yet undeveloped, and between this and the 'upper causeway' (i.e. Richmond Hill) another narrow tapering close, formerly waste, stretched from the Vineyard (the lane of that name), where it was 32 feet in breadth, some 750 feet up the hill, where it finally came to a point. It had probably been granted in the reign of Queen Mary to Edward Lovell, from whom it was inherited in 1584 by his son Ralph Lovell. Some 300 feet at the southern end of this close was sold by Ralph Lovell to William Arnold in 1586. Arnold died in 1596 but it was not until 1617 that his son Robert claimed his admittance to the land which by then had a cottage on it. It is most likely that this cottage had been built by William Arnold.

**93** (East side – Nos. 114-142 Richmond Hill)
In 1603 the narrow strip of former wasteland between the 'upper causeway' and Heath Shott of the Upper Field, to the south of the fieldpath which is today Friar's Stile Road, belonged to Seth Goldstone. (The original grant has not been traced, but what seems to be the same property was sold by Thomas Gisby to John Feare alias Deere in 1587 – and was presumably sold by him to Goldstone. It may have been granted

to Gisby in the reign of Queen Mary.) In 1613-17 Goldstone disposed of it in several separate parcels. There was a single house on the northern part of the land by 1617, but whether it already existed by 1603 is unknown. There were no other buildings on the hill in 1603. The Great Common lay on the south-east of Heath Shott; the Hill Common on the south-west of Goldstone's strip.

## Marshgate (eastern end of Sheen Road)

### 94 (Site of Courtlands)
A grant of land (200 feet in length by 44 feet in breadth at one end and 32 feet in breadth at the other) was made here to Clement Maunder between 1589 and 1602. It is probable that he had built a cottage on it by 1603, but the existence of the cottage is not proven until his widow Emm Maunder surrendered the reversion of it to her son Rowland and his wife in 1638.

### 95 (Site of 178-186 Sheen Road)
The first house on the south side of the Marshgate (now Sheen) Road, on the west side of what is now Queen's Road, was only built between 1603 and 1615; but there were already in 1603 two buildings on the north side of the road near the gate (95 and 96). An acre of waste land, between the end of Upper Dunstable Shott and the green lane leading up to the Kew meadows (now Manor Road) had been first granted out in 1563. It remained undeveloped until sold to Henry Pencost in 1580. He then built a house on it which he sold in 1581 to Roger Richbell. By 1603 it was in the ownership of William Deacon who died in 1605, leaving the house to his son Thomas.

### 96 (Site of Black Horse Garage)
The easternmost half-acre strip of Upper Dunstable was acquired by Roger Walter between 1589 and 1602. In 1604 when Walter sold it to John Preston it had on it a small cottage 'lately built'.

## Marshgate (now Sheen) Road

### 97 (Site of Lichfield Court – eastern part)
Coming into Richmond from Marshgate, the next building encountered in 1603 would have been a barn on the north side. Next to this was a freehold property within Upper Dunstable Shott, part of a half-tenement of 10 acres (No. 26). It had belonged to Robert Walshe in 1481 and was sold in the following year by his son John to Thomas Denys. It appears to have already had a house on it at that time. This house and half-tenement was owned in 1603 by Mary Crome and was one of the properties unsuccessfully claimed from her by the Vestry in the 1620s. The continued existence of this house in the fields is attested by the manor terrier of *circa* 1620.

**98** (Site of Lichfield Court – western part)

The next house on the north side stood in a close of 2½ acres at the west end of Upper Dunstable Shott. It was part of the large estate of 80 acres or so which belonged in the first part of the 16th century to the Parkyns family and which had been known as 'Scopeham's lands' but then became 'Parkyns's Farm'. The house, built in the fields (at an unknown date but almost certainly later than 97) was probably not an original 'capital messuage'. The whole estate was acquired in 1563 by Thomas Lovell, whose brother Henry became owner in 1577. In 1606 Henry Lovell sold the house and estate to James Fitch, the vicar of Kingston.

**99** (Site between Sheen Road and Paradise Road, from the Christian Science church to the footpath beside Spencer House)

There is no actual evidence of any house built in the large freehold close on the south side of the Marshgate Road before the late 17th century, but it seems likely that there would have been one (possibly as the capital messuage of tenement No. 12 which had 30 acres of free land). The close was part of the freehold estate that had belonged to David Vincent and that was purchased by Richard Wright in 1608 from Ezekiel Culverwell.

**100** (Site of 11-21 Sheen Road and through to Paradise Road)

A house on this site was mortgaged by Edmund Bird to Edward Miles in 1606, Miles taking full title in 1608. It may have been the capital messuage of tenement No. 32. The only known fact is that the land belonged to John Byngate in 1503, as did that tenement.

**101** (Site of 1-9 Sheen Road and Eton Street (east side) to Paradise Road)

This was a close of land, part of Lockyer's tenement, in the reign of Henry VII. (Lockyer's tenement was possibly No. 24.) A cottage and stable had been built on it by 1533. In 1579 it was acquired by Thomas Gisby and when he sold it four years later to William Boone it had become a tavern under the sign of the *Goat*. It remained in the ownership of William Boone and his widow Cicely until 1633.

**102** (Site of Eton Street (west side), 1-5 Lower George Street and Eton House, Paradise Road)

This was the original glebe of the house allotted for the priest of Richmond's parish church, granted for the purpose by Merton Priory in 1375. As far as is known, the 'parish house' was still occupied by the parish priest in 1603, and until 1647.

## Middle Row

**103** It was Henry Harvey who first built on this little island of land between the roads to Kew and Marshgate, but the first formal grant was made to Nicholas Beneson and his wife Joan in 1569 of 'a cottage newly built by Henry Harvey on waste by the street leading to London and a garden newly enclosed adjoining the cottage'. In 1605 William White, blacksmith, enlarged and then divided the cottage, selling off 'four newly erected rooms and a shop and shed' to pay his debts. The original cottage remained a smithy, the rest became an alehouse.

## The 'horse road' to Kew (now Kew Road)

### 104 (Site of 44-50 The Quadrant)
This site and 105-107 appear to be grants from the waste between the Upper Field and the lane to Kew (then known as Fagge Lane), probably all made in the period 1589-1602.

On the east side of the village pond (which was where Dome Building now stands) there was a large barn belonging to Richard Eusted, and then, by its north end, a stable which belonged in 1604 to William Snow.

### 105 (Site of 38-42 The Quadrant)
There were stables here, inherited in 1604 by William Irish from his brother Jacob, whose house was on the Green (see 12-13).

### 106 (Site of 30-37 The Quadrant)
The history of this site has not been traced before 1628 when Thomas Bun was admitted to all the property of his late father Thomas Bun, who had died in February 1612/3. That property included three houses and two stables, but was not all on this site. However it seems probable that Thomas Bun Senior was the original grantee and was occupying the site in 1603. By 1647 it is clear that Thomas Bun Junior had two cottages and a stable here, but what existed in 1603 is unknown.

### 107 (Site of 29 The Quadrant)
This, the last site yet developed along the lane to Kew, was granted to William Tye in 1599. When he died in 1603 his son William inherited 'a little cottage near Fagge Lane gate, lately erected on part of the waste'.

## George Street (south-east side)

### 108-109 (Site of 35-38 George Street, St James's Cottages and 4-16 Paradise Road)
The land between the parish glebe and the churchyard (which also included 110-113) belonged until the reign of Henry VII to the manor grange. In 1496 two acres were granted to William Dawtry 'to build on the north part' (the south part being part of Church Shott on the other side of Paradise Road). However, there is no evidence of

any building by 1521 when the land was owned by Dawtry's daughter Elizabeth and her husband Robert Dawker. The Dawkers' daughter Elizabeth married Thomas Edlet (or Edlen) and by the time of her death in 1575 the property included a house with a quarter-acre garden and a one-acre close. By 1603 Elizabeth's grandson Richard Edlet or Edlen owned two houses on the site. One he sold to Thomas Smythe in 1603, the other, with the close, to the same buyer in 1606.

**110-112** (Site of 32-34 George Street and Church Walk)
This part of the former grange was granted in 1496 to William Turns. In 1502 it was described as the 'Cylnhouse', so it is likely that a brick kiln or lime kiln was established here – perhaps to supply material for the rebuilding of the church. By 1528 the property consisted of a house called the Cylnhouse and two cottages. (The latter were two halves of a single house built on the southern part of the land facing the churchyard.) By the end of the 16th century the property was owned by Humphrey Stafferton. In 1604, following his death, his widow inherited a life interest, but the property was thereafter to be divided between his son Charles (the house on George Street) and his two daughters (who each got one of the cottages by the churchyard).

**113** (Site of 29-31 George Street and Church Court – north side)
This land, presumably also part of the grange, with a stable on it, was first granted out in 1505. It was regranted (the stable having meanwhile been demolished) in 1529, and by 1536 a cottage had been built. This was acquired in 1570 by Nicholas Snow. In 1614, when William Snow (probably Nicholas' son) failed to redeem a mortgage to Thomas Larkyn, the house contained 'alerooms', but there is no other evidence of its use as a tavern.

**114** (The parish church and churchyard)
The church in 1603 was still as it had been rebuilt at the end of the 15th century. The first enlargement (the original south aisle – later rebuilt) was not added until 1614. The churchyard was narrower on the south-west side than it is today.

**115** (Site of 1-6 Church Court – south side)
In 1496 this was sold as 'part of a garden belonging to John Walshe'. By 1543 a cottage had been built on it. This was acquired by Henry Deacon, Sergeant-Plumber to the Queen, in 1577. It passed to William Deacon, who died in 1605, when his son Thomas Deacon inherited.

**116-117** (Site of 25-28 George Street)
This was an ancient freehold property. It may well have been in 1314 the site of the messuage and curtilage of William atte Church, the messuage and half-curtilage of

John le Clerke and the messuage and half-curtilage of widow Parole. The whole property appears to have belonged to Miles Acracker about 1510-20, subsequently to John Stoughton and then (in 1548-50) to Henry Aleyn. From him it passed through the ownerships of George Annesley and Nicholas Beneson to that of Walter Hickman, whose name appears as owner from 1612 to 1643. There were two cottages on the property in 1548-50, and probably also in 1603.

**118** (Site of 24 George Street)
This appears to have been a garden belonging to John Walshe in 1496 when a part of it was sold off (see 115 above). Its subsequent history is not very clear. Thomas Herford owned a cottage on the front part of the site in 1567, which was sold to Edward Lovell in 1571 and by Lovell to Henry Deacon in 1574. The ground between the cottage and the churchyard was acquired by Deacon (with 115) five years later.

Deacon built up a large estate on the south-east side of George Street between the path to the church and the *Bell Inn* (see below). Although there is evidence of the early history of some of the component parts it is not very clear to which tenements they may have belonged. Nor is it clear which houses were retained, rebuilt or demolished by Deacon or his successor. On his death in 1592 Deacon's heir was his only daughter Joan, wife of Robert Clarke, an attorney of the Inner Temple (who had become Steward of the manor of Richmond by 1603). Clarke added to the estate, but on his death in 1606 the property left to his brother Richard was simply described as 'a great capital messuage and two cottages' (and land in the fields). The exact location of these is uncertain. Thereafter, the descent of the various elements in the estate can, however, be clearly identified. Noted below at 119-122 is what can be determined of the previous history, but the locations given are necessarily somewhat tentative.

**119** (Site of 18-23 George Street and Red Lion Street from Churchyard to north-east side of Victoria Place)
In 1413 John Waler surrendered to John Frawnceys a messuage and orchard 'near the close formerly of Robert Howe and the Church hawe' together with a virgate of land (probably tenement No. 22). By the 1490s these had come into the hands of William Cooke, to whom was also granted in 1496 a contiguous parcel of the manor grange land on the south-west side of the churchyard, measuring 13 perches 4 feet north to south and 31 perches plus 3 feet east to west.* These passed through the ownership of Cooke's widow (1505) and then his son Thomas (1532) to Ralph Annesley (1535). The latter's grandson in 1571 surrendered the reversion of two whole tenements and three cottages to Henry Deacon.

---

* 218ft. 6ins. by 60ft. 9ins., assuming a 16½ foot perch.

**120** (Site of entrance to Victoria Place from Red Lion Street)
A cottage about here 'adjoining the Bell Inn on the west' was owned by the Herford family from 1509 to 1571 and then by the Stockden family. It was acquired, at an unknown date, by Henry Deacon.

**121** (Site of 15-17 George Street and south-west side of Victoria Place)
This was the site of the 16th-century *Bell Inn*, first recorded in 1535 when it was inherited by Anthony Cope from his father Stephen. It had probably been the capital messuage of a tenement, but there is no clue as to which. In 1569 the *Bell* was regranted to John Burton who sold it in 1572 to Peter May. The latter's successor Thomas May (a London goldsmith) sold it in 1580 to Henry Harvey who disposed of it immediately to John White, a London grocer. White sold it in 1586 to Lawrence Snow. After the execution of Snow for horse-stealing in 1596 (see at 91 above) the premises must have been regranted to Robert Clarke. They ceased to be a tavern, but may have provided the nucleus of Clarke's 'great capital messuage'.

**122** (Site of 11-14 George Street, through to Red Lion Street)
A cottage in this area was sold by Lyonell Redman to Sir Thomas Nevill in 1562 and by him to Henry Harvey in 1573. It had belonged at some previous time to John Parkyns, and may therefore have been the capital messuage of one of his tenements (possibly No. 19). Its history after 1573 has not been traced, but it had become part of Robert Clarke's estate by 1606.

**123-4** (Site of 7-10 George Street and Lion House, Red Lion Street)
This was probably the 'messuage, cottage and garden' inherited by William Hoo on the death of Constance Hoo in 1449 (which was additional to another 'messuage and virgate' (tenement No. 20 – see at 79 above). If it had once been, as seems likely, the capital messuage of a tenement or half-tenement, it had become detached from its land before 1449. At the end of the 15th century it belonged to William Hough (a son of William Hoo of 1449?). In 1497 he divided it into two parts. The more southerly, which was still a garden, with frontage of 39½ feet to the main street and 41 feet 4 inches to the 'way called Midbroke' (now Red Lion Street), he sold to John Heron, subsequently knighted. In 1536 Sir John Heron's younger son John inherited the land, now with a house on it; and in 1547 he sold house, garden and stable to John Gwyldmyn. The northerly section contained William Hough's own house. In March 1511/2 the manor court recorded that he had died 'long since' leaving the property to his wife Joan, and that the latter's heir was Milicent, wife of James Dale. The Dales were admitted to the cottage in 1516. The next 30 years of the site's history has not been traced; but in 1547 one Henry Rydon surrendered to John Gwyldmyn 'two cottages

with a garden and orchard and two pieces of land called a garden platte at the back of the houses of the said Henry Rydon, between Mydbrook Lane on the south and the land of the said Henry Rydon next the highway on the north'.

John Gwyldmyn now held both the two contiguous pieces of land which had belonged to William Hough, with one house and two cottages. They were inherited in due course by his son Henry Gwyldmyn (after a lawsuit between him and his mother and her second husband). In 1568 Henry sold the combined property to John Sturtivant who sold it on at once to Michael Blaye. Blaye sold in 1583 to Thomas Keyes, who then owned what was by now described as 'one messuage and one cottage' until his death in 1611.

**125** (Site of 1-6 George Street and through to Red Lion Street)
This whole area was occupied by the *Red Lyon Inn*. Its precise origin is uncertain. The site was apparently in the ownership of John Pyke in 1497, but the first identifiable record of a house on it dates from 1510 when Joan Burton inherited it from her father Thomas. It was probably in origin the capital messuage of a tenement or half-tenement, but no obvious link has been found. Joan Burton, who married Thomas Marre, made over the house in 1535, after his death, to Elizabeth wife of Harmon Goldstone (possibly Joan's daughter). In 1563, when Harmon and Elizabeth Goldstone sold the house to Alexander Slaney, it was for the first time described as 'called the *Lyon*'. It is probable that Alexander Slaney sold or mortgaged the premises at some date between 1589 and 1602 (when he died) to Elizabeth, wife of William Boone. After her death the inn, by now called the *Red Lyon*, was inherited in 1605 by her son by a previous marriage, Michael Merriall. In 1615 a great-nephew of Alexander Slaney laid claim to the premises 'lately divided into one messuage now called the *Red Lyon* and divers barns or haylofts, stables and yards adjoining, and two cottages to the said premises next adjoining'. However Merriall remained in possession.

**126** Sheen Place
The mansion formed from the remains of Shene Charterhouse was still in 1603 in the occupation, by royal grant, of Sir Thomas Gorges and his wife the Marchioness of Northampton. Its previous and subsequent history has been related in detail in *Palaces and Parks of Richmond and Kew*. Part of the buildings had been adapted for use as stables and coachhouses for Richmond Palace, and the terms of the royal grant enabled the sovereign to take over all but Gorges' own house, if required, when the court was at Richmond. A few years later it was rented from the Marchioness by Henry Prince of Wales, perhaps with the intention of using it as a base while alterations were made to the palace.

## B. Kew

### Riverside and north side of Kew Green

**127** (South of Brentford Ferry Gate of Kew Gardens)
By 1603 the mansion of the Earls of Devonshire and Suffolk Place had both been demolished and their grounds had by then all been absorbed into the estate of Sir Hugh Portman. Remaining, however, by the river, just south of the ferry, was a freehold capital messuage belonging to Thomas Duke. This had been part of the former Wylde/ Raynford estate and remained in Duke's hands when he split the estate in 1576 (see at 81 above), though leased for 43 years to William Wright. That lease, by a series of assignments, was held in 1603 by William Hickman (who was probably occupying the house himself). In 1609 Thomas Duke's son William sold the freehold to William Hickman's son Walter – who sold it on to Sir John Portman three months later.

**128** (Site of part of car park just north of Brentford Ferry Gate)
The next house was one in which John Hales, proprietor of the Kew-Brentford ferry from 1534 to c.1566, had lived and was immediately north of the ferry place. By 1603 this had come into the hands of Sir Hugh Portman along with the Dudley estate (see 129-131).

**129-131** (Site of car park by riverside)
The story of Kew Farm (or Kew House), by 1603 the largest house by the riverside, has been told in detail in *Palaces and Parks of Richmond and Kew** and need only be summarised here. It was also a freehold. It had been the mansion of Thomas Byrkes (for whom a private chapel was licensed in 1522). His son Anthony sold it to Henry Norris, executed in 1536. Regranted to Edward Seymour, Viscount Beauchamp (the future Duke of Somerset), it was sold by him in 1538 to Thomas Cromwell, by him to William Byrche and by Byrche in 1542 to John Dudley, Viscount Lisle. It then passed through several hands before being granted in 1558 to Sir Robert Dudley (the future Earl of Leicester). Dudley sold the house in 1562. The estate was purchased by Lord Buckhurst 15 years later, sold by him to Anthony Mason in 1591 and by Mason to Sir Hugh Portman in 1592. Hugh Portman's father-in-law, Sir John Puckering, Speaker of the House of Commons, was already leasing the house by 1591 when he entertained Queen Elizabeth there, as he did again in 1594 and 1595. In addition to the main house and the ferry house, the estate also included a stable (the former chapel), a brewhouse, the 'dairy house' and two extra cottages – all freehold. It is possible that these cottages were two of the three freehold cottages that had stood to the south of the ferry at the beginning of the 16th century, all of which belonged to Thomas Byrkes, but there is no way to pinpoint the precise location of these long-vanished freehold properties.

* See Vol 1, Chapter XI, and Vol 2, Chapter XIX and pp.225-6.

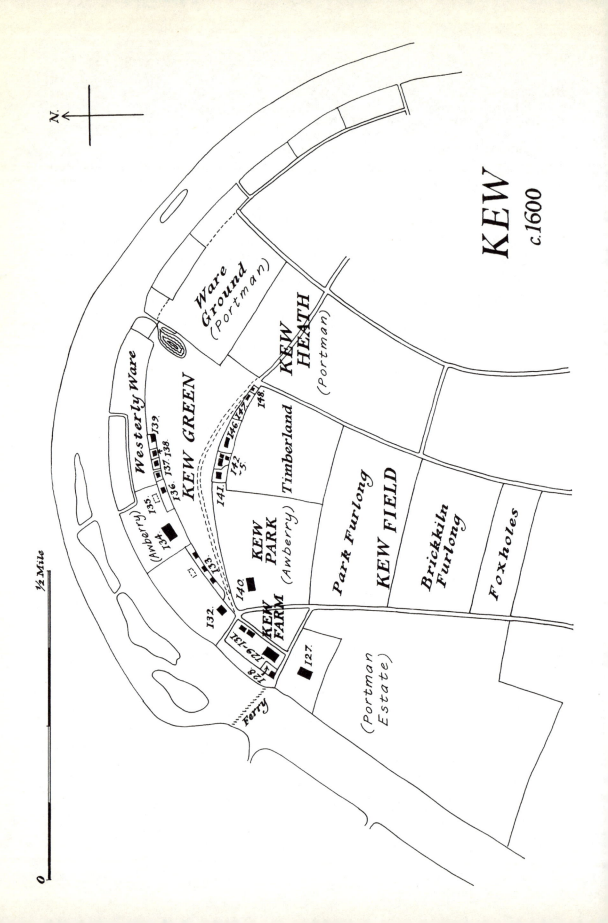

KEW
c.1600

Ware Ground
(Portman)

KEW HEATH
(Portman)

Westerly Ware

KEW GREEN

Timberland
(Awberry)

(Awberry)

139

137.138

136.

135

134

133

141

142
5

146 147

148

Park Furlong

KEW FIELD

Brickkiln Furlong

Foxholes

KEW PARK

KEW FARM

140

132

129·131

128

127

(Portman Estate)

Ferry

N.

½ Mile

0

**132** (Site of Kew Palace)
To the north of Kew Farm Sir Hugh Portman also owned two of the copyhold
cottages (or their sites) which had been capital messuages of tenements (Nos. 9 and
10) in Kew Field and which had belonged about 1500 to Robert Markyn and Robert
Lydgold. It is probable that by 1603 one of these houses had been demolished and
the other rebuilt as a forerunner of the 'Dutch House' which was to replace it in 1631.

**133** (On north-west side of walk from Kew Gardens main gate)
A long 'panhandle' of Kew Green stretched south-westwards right past the front of
the Portman copyhold property at 132. Some grants of land from the edge of the
Green had, however, been made in Queen Elizabeth's reign: one at an unknown date
to William Awberry, renewed to William Merriall *als* Brewer in 1599; one to Thomas
Adams in 1582, another to William Awberry in 1579. On the last of these a cottage had
already been built in which Thomas Adams was then living. By 1603 the cottage and
its land, and the central portion, had come into the hands of Nicholas Saunders. He
was buried in May 1603 and William, his son and heir, died in the December following,
leaving the property to his sister Elizabeth, wife of John Lane.

**134** (Approximate site of Sir Joseph Banks building and Nash Conservatory)
The next house, proceeding eastwards along the north side of the Green, was another
of the ancient capital messuages of a Kew tenement (No. 27). It was sold by Thomas
Byrkes to Sir Charles Somerset (later Earl of Worcester) in 1505 and was inherited by
the latter's son Sir George in 1526. Sir George Somerset appears to have sold the house
(but no record has been traced – perhaps the sale was in the reign of Queen Mary).
It next appears in the records when sold by Thomas Barnes to Hugh Pope in 1562 as
a 'capital mansion house ... formerly of Sir George Somerset'. A year later Hugh Pope
died and the house was inherited by his son Hugh, who sold it to William Awberry
in 1574. William Awberry (a Doctor of Laws and father of the antiquarian John Aubrey)
and his wife presented it to another son Morgan Awberry in 1588, probably on the
latter's marriage to his wife Joan. They were still in occupation in 1603, but sold the
property to Sir Arthur Gorges in 1605.

**135** (Rear part of site of Herbarium)
Beyond this was the former capital messuage of a half-tenement (No. 28) owned,
perhaps since the 14th century, by the 'At Ware' (or At Weir) family. William at Ware
inherited it from his father Stephen in 1501, and made it over to himself and his wife
Joan for their lives in 1531. A Ralph at Ware was the likely owner from 1532 to about
1552. It seems probable from an only partially legible entry that his widow Joan had
remarried Thomas Adams and, having been again widowed, made over the house to
her son James at Ware in 1577. Ten years later James Ware (he had dropped the 'at') sold
it to Morgan Awberry. There is no further record of this house, whose land became

part of the ground (later all called Somer's Close) attached to No. 134 but whether or not it was still standing in 1603 is unknown.

### 136 (Front part of site of Herbarium)

There had also been a number of grants from the Green in front of Nos. 134 and 135: a fairly small one to William Awberry at an unknown date, and in 1582 a large one to Edward Somner (the original Somer's Close). This was held after his death by his widow Elizabeth (who had a son James Netherwood by a second marriage). By February 1605/6 when Elizabeth Summer (*sic*) and James Netherwood mortgaged the property to Alexander Prescott, there was a messuage and a barn on it. It was mainly on this front land that two large houses were later built (after the demolition of Nos. 134 and 135), one of which housed Peter Lely and the other of which was replaced by the mansion that is now the Kew Herbarium.

### 137 (Site of 57 Kew Green)

An untraced grant (between 1589 and 1602) was presumably the origin of the parcel of land with tenements, buildings and outhouses sold by Nicholas Smith to Stephen Smith in 1615. There is no earlier record, but there was probably at least one cottage on the site (now that of 'Hanover House') in 1603.

### 138 (Site of 59 and 61 Kew Green)

The earliest record of a house on this site is in 1635 when Beatrice wife of Thomas Higgs inherited it (and a parcel of land formerly waste) from her father Nicholas Maynard. The untraced grant of waste was probably made in 1589-1602, so it is likely that the house was built by 1603.

### 139 (Site of 63-67 Kew Green)

Again the earliest record here is of the inheritance by Oswald Franklin, a minor, from his father Thomas Franklin in 1617 of 'a cottage, formerly waste'. By the same reasoning as at No. 137, the cottage probably existed in 1603, and would have been the last house on the north side of the Green in that year. Although the present houses on the site have gardens stretching back to the riverside, in 1603 these houses stood on the narrow strip of land granted from the Green and behind them were the Kew Meadows.

## South of Kew Green

### 140 (Site of house marked by sundial in lawn opposite Kew Palace)

The 19-acre Kew Park appears to have been enclosed out of the western end of Tenderland Furlong of Kew Field by Sir George Somerset in the 1520s. In it he built a hunting lodge. After his death and that of his widow Thomasine, his youngest son William Somerset inherited the park and lodge in 1560, and sold them to Dr William Awberry in 1566. Like the mansion at No. 134, the park and lodge were given to Morgan and Joan Awberry in 1587 and sold by them to Sir Arthur Gorges in 1605. The lodge would eventually become the 18th-century royal residence known as 'The White House'.

**141** (Part of site of 49 Kew Green)
While nearly all of the copyhold lands in Kew formerly owned by Charles Brandon Duke of Suffolk reverted after his death to the merchant Augustine Hynde, who perhaps held a mortgage on them, some 7½ acres appear to have descended through Suffolk's daughter Eleanor, Countess of Cumberland, to her daughter Margaret, Countess of Derby, and from her to the Earls of Derby. This land comprised two parcels of the Tenderland Furlong. On a grant of land between the western parcel and the Green a cottage had been built by 1603, in which year it and the 7½ acres were sold by William, the 6th Earl, to Alexander Prescott.

**142-145** (Site of 47 and part of 49 Kew Green)
A grant of land on the south side of Kew Green, 'between the highway and the Kew Field hedge' was made in 1578 to William Ware. He had built a cottage on it before his brother James inherited it a year later. In 1580 James sold the undeveloped western half of the land to John Burden. Burden had built three cottages by the time he sold this property to Dr William Awberry in 1583, and these were passed on to Morgan Awberry in 1587. James Ware in 1583 sold the cottage in which his widowed sister-in-law was living to Stephen Mudgett, and Mudgett sold it to Morgan Awberry in 1593. All four cottages were sold by Awberry to Sir Arthur Gorges in 1605.

**146** (Site of 33-45 Kew Green)
A grant of land from the Green 22 rods (363 feet) in length was made to James Ware in 1586, but does not appear to have been developed until 1604-06 when a number of cottages were built on it by Robert Dye.

**147** (Site of 23-31 Kew Green)
This land is recorded as belonging in 1609 to Henry Peake, who surrendered it, with a cottage built on it, to Johanna Atkins in 1626. As the original grant of land cannot be traced, it was probably made in 1589-1602; and it is therefore likely that the cottage had been built by 1603.

**148** (Site of 17-21 Kew Green)
The story here is similar to that at No. 147. The land belonged in 1609 to John Langley; he surrendered it with a cottage to Richard Jordan in 1628. If the cottage had indeed been built by 1603 it would have been the last one on the south side of Kew Green in that year. (The land on which 1-15 Kew Green were developed was not granted out until 1609.)

**Kew Green – east side**

No land on the east side of Kew Green had yet been granted for building by 1603, and there is no trace of any buildings in the meadows or closes there at that period.

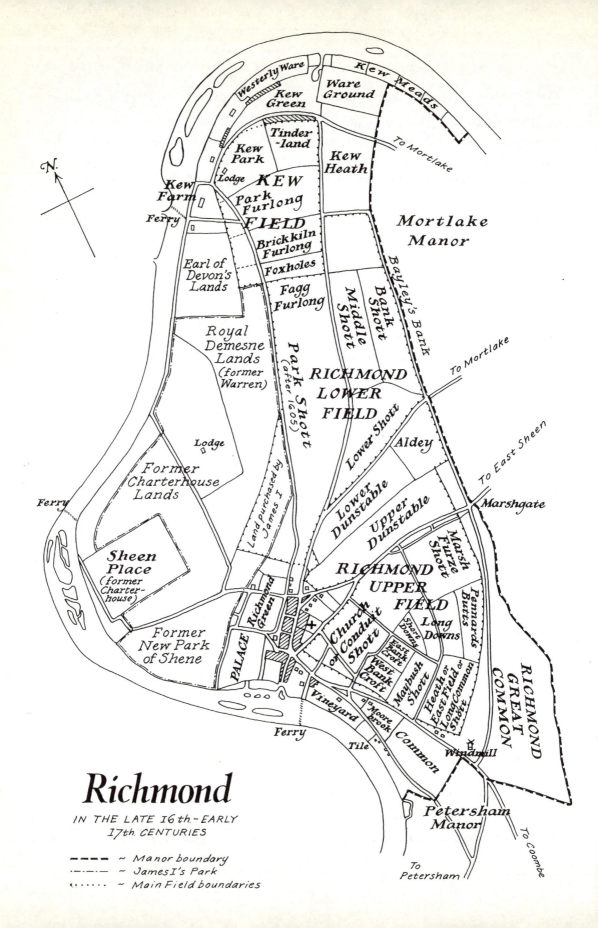

# Richmond

IN THE LATE 16th.–EARLY
17th. CENTURIES

- - - - ~ Manor boundary
- · - · - ~ James I's Park
· · · · · · ~ Main Field boundaries

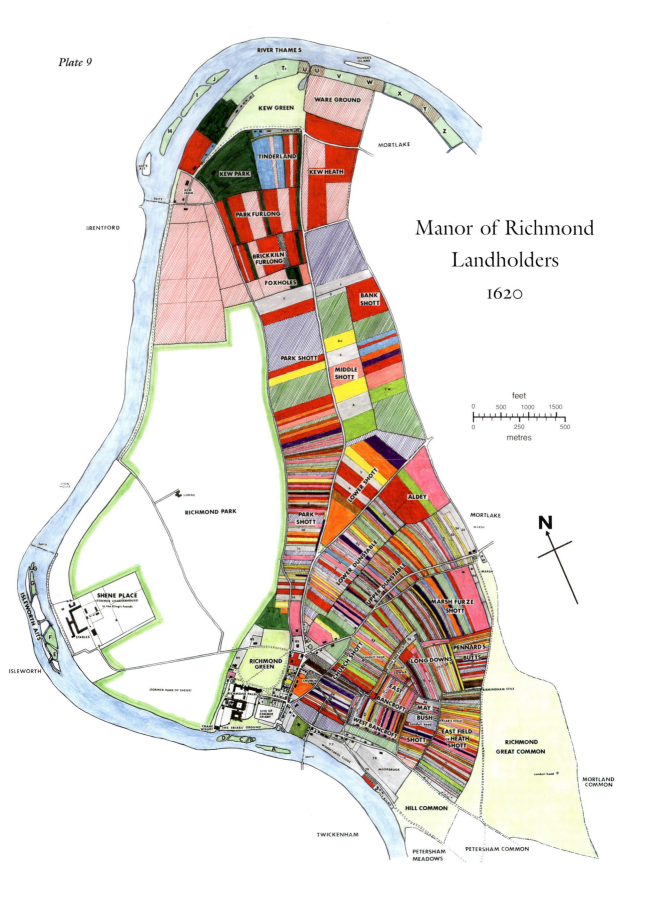

*Plate 9*

RIVER THAMES

OLIVER'S ISLAND

J

I

H

T₁   T₂   U   U   V   W   X   Y   Z

WARE GROUND

KEW GREEN

MORTLAKE

LOT'S AIT

TINDERLAND

KEW PARK

KEW HEATH

BRENTFORD

KEW FARM   ferry

PARK FURLONG

BRICKKILN FURLONG

FOXHOLES

BANK SHOTT

PARK SHOTT

MIDDLE SHOTT

AC

## Manor of Richmond
## Landholders
## 1620

feet

0   500   1000   1500

0   250   500

metres

ISON HOUSE

LODGE

RICHMOND PARK

ferry

LOWER SHOTT

PARK SHOTT

ALDEY

MORTLAKE

MARSH

N

ISLEWORTH AITS

G

F

E

SHENE PLACE
(FORMER CHARTERHOUSE)
In the King's hands

STABLES

LOWER DUNSTABLE

UPPER DUNSTABLE

MARSH FURZE SHOTT

MARSH

ISLEWORTH

RICHMOND GREEN

(FORMER PARK OF SHENE)

CHURCH SHOTT

CHURCH

SHORT DOWN

PENNARD'S BUTTS

LONG DOWNS

BIRMINGHAM STILE

RICHMOND PALACE

SITE OF FORMER FRIARY

'THE FRIARS' GROUND'

CRANE WHARF

D   C

A

B

VINEYARDS CLOSE

MOORBROOK

EAST BANCROFT

WEST BANCROFT

MAY BUSH

FRIAR'S STILE

EAST FIELD or HEATH SHOTT

RICHMOND GREAT COMMON

MORTLAND COMMON

conduit head

HILL COMMON

ferry

TWICKENHAM

PETERSHAM MEADOWS

PETERSHAM COMMON

*Plate 10*

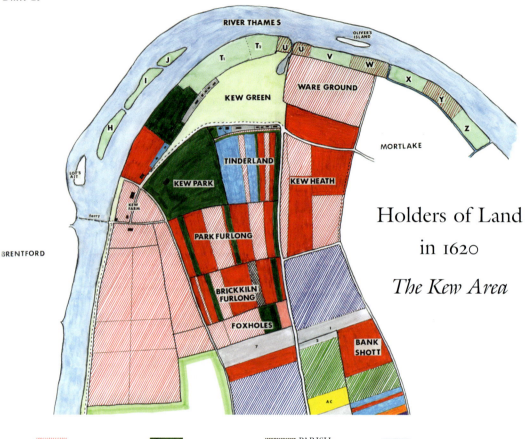

Holders of Land
in 1620

*The Kew Area*

| | | | |
|---|---|---|---|
| PORTMAN free | GORGES copy | PARISH CHURCH free | OTHERS (numbered) |
| PORTMAN copy | CLARKE copy | CHARLEY copy | river |
| JONES free | PAYNE free | THOS SMYTHE copy | meadows & islands |
| CROME free | PAYNE copy | BART SMYTHE copy | commons & wastes |
| CROME copy (including 4ac of Arthur Crome – AC) | WRIGHT copy (including 4ac of Thomas Wright – TW) | PEIRCE copy | King James's Park (borders) |
| | | BURD copy | –·–·– field boundaries |

**OWNERS OF ISLANDS**
A  Bullrush Bed – James Standen
B  Ait opposite Palace – William Bayley
C  Ait opposite Palace – James Standen
D  Ait opposite Palace – Augustine Reading
E  Ait by Shene Wall (south) – James Standen
F  Walnut Tree Ait – William Bayley
G  2 aits 'by Shene Wall' (north – Thomas Redriffe
H  'The Hill' at Kew – John Hudson
I  Brentford Ayte – Ezekiel Prymer
J  Mattingshaw Ayte – in hands of Lord of Manor

*For key to other owners see page 85.*

**OWNERS OF MEADOWS**
**Freehold meadows**
Sir Henry Portman
U  *Twiggetts*
W  *Two Hayes*
Υ  *Five Pits*

**Standing Lots in**
*Westerly Ware (T1)*
Duncan Jones (free)          8
Sir H. Portman (free)         4
Rebecca Payne (free)          7
Mary Crome (free)             1
Parish Church (free)          1
William Portman (copy)        4
John Lambe (copy)            ½

**Running lots: 18 each in**
T2  *Westerly Ware*
V  *Short lots*
X  *Hachetts*
Z  *Red Ledes*
Sir H. Portman (free)         12
Duncan Jones (free)           8
Rebecca Payne (free)          7
William Portman (copy)        13
Stephen Peirce (copy)         8
Sir Arthur Gorges (copy)      8
John Burd (copy)              6
Henry Clarke (copy)           4
Dorothy Lady Wright (copy)    3
Mary Crome (copy)             2
Henry Cudeney (copy)          1

*Plate 11*

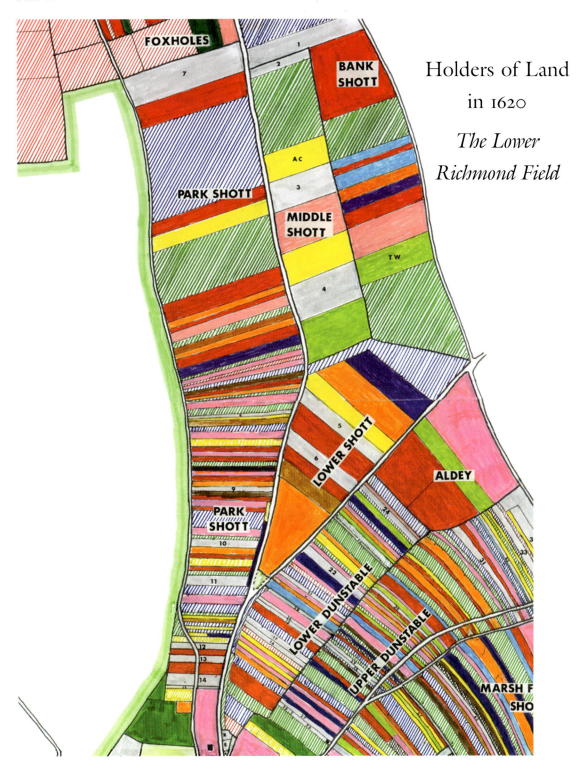

FOXHOLES

BANK SHOTT

PARK SHOTT

MIDDLE SHOTT

AC

TW

LOWER SHOTT

ALDEY

PARK SHOTT

LOWER DUNSTABLE

UPPER DUNSTABLE

MARSH F SHO

Holders of Land
in 1620
*The Lower
Richmond Field*

Plate 12

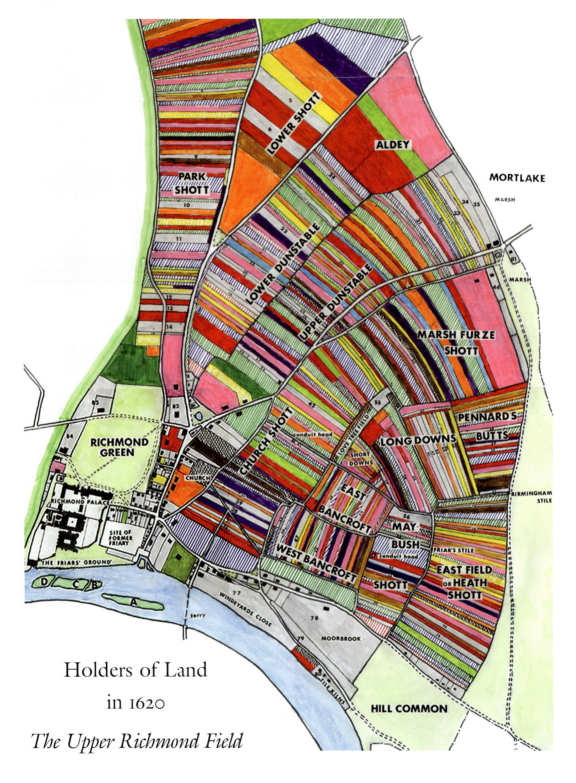

Holders of Land

in 1620

*The Upper Richmond Field*

# *OTHER LANDOWNERS,* whose lands are numbered on the map

**Bankshott**

| | | |
|---|---|---|
| 1 | Walter Hickman | 5 ac |

**Middle Shott (N-S)**

| | | |
|---|---|---|
| 2 | William Bonner | 1 ac |
| 3 | Ann Wilkes | 3½ ac |
| 4 | Lott Peere | 5 ac |

**Lower Shott**

| | | |
|---|---|---|
| 5 | John Keele | 2 ac |
| 6 | Henry Collins | 2 ac |

**Park Shott (N-S)**

| | | |
|---|---|---|
| 7 | Henry Cuckney | 5½ ac |
| 8 | Richard Lovell | 1 rood |
| 9 | William Boone | ½ ac |
| 10 | Dorothy Holloway | 1 ac |
| 11 | Judith Baylie | 1 ac |
| 12 | Thomas Booker Jr | 3 roods |
| 13 | John Keene | 3 roods |
| 14 | Thomas Booker Sr | 1 ac |
| 15 | Thomas Booker Jr | 1 rood |

**Lower Dunstable (W-E)**

| | | |
|---|---|---|
| 16 | George Hudson | ½ ac |
| 17 | John Smythe | ½ ac |
| 18 | Judith Baylie | ½ ac |
| 19 | George Langley | ½ ac |
| 20 | George Langley | ½ ac |
| 21 | widow Hill | ½ ac |
| 22 | George Marshal | 1 ac |
| 23 | Richard Lovell | 1 rood |
| 24 | Lott Peere | 1 ac |

**Upper Dunstable (W-E)**

| | | |
|---|---|---|
| 25 | Thomas Booker Sr | ½ rood |
| 26 | Henry Mann | 1½ roods |
| 27 | John Keele | ½ ac |
| 28 | John Smythe | ½ ac |
| 29 | Judith Baylie | ½ ac |
| 30 | Henry Collins | ½ ac |
| 31 | Dorothy Holloway | 1 ac |
| 32 | Henry Collins | ½ ac |
| 33 | Lott Peere | 1 ac |
| 34 | John Preston | 1 ac |
| 35 | William Jeffrey | 1 ac |

**Church Shott (W-E)**

| | | |
|---|---|---|
| 36 | Charles Sedwell | ½ ac |
| 37 | Charles Sedwell | ½ ac |
| 38 | Charles Sedwell | 1 ac |
| 39 | Charles Stafferton | 1 ac |
| 40 | Charles Sedwell | ½ ac |
| 41 | Anthony Lynton (crown lease) | ½ ac |
| 42 | John Smythe | 1 ac |
| 43 | Richard Lovell | ½ ac |
| 44 | Lott Peere | 1 ac |

**West Bancroft (N-S)**

| | | |
|---|---|---|
| 45 | John Keele | 1 rood |
| 46 | John Smythe | 1 ac |
| 47 | Thomas Downing | 1 ac |
| 48 | Charles Sedwell | ½ ac |

**East Bancroft (N-S)**

| | | |
|---|---|---|
| 49 | Giles Hill | ½ ac |
| 50 | Robert Trotter | 3 roods |

**Maybush Shott (W-E)**

| | | |
|---|---|---|
| 51 | Lawrence Goldstone | ½ ac |
| 52 | Lawrence Goldstone | ½ ac |
| 53 | Thomas Booker Sr | 1 rood |
| 54 | Charles Sedwell | ½ ac |
| 55 | Giles Hill | ½ ac |
| 56 | Ann Wilkes | 1 ac |

**Short Downs (W-E)**

| | | |
|---|---|---|
| 57 | Robert Trotter | 1 rood |
| 58 | Giles Hill (at end of Love Tree Field) | ½ ac |

**Long Downs (W-E)**

| | | |
|---|---|---|
| 59 | John Keele | ½ ac |
| 60 | Thomas Redford | 1 rood |
| 61 | William Duke (free) | 1 ac |
| 62 | William Boone | 1 ac |
| 63 | Henry Collins | ½ ac |
| 64 | Henry Collins | ½ ac |
| 65 | George Rutter | ½ ac |
| 66 | John Keele | ½ ac |
| 67 | Thomas Redford (headland at north) | 1 rood |

**East Field – 1**

**Pennard's Butts (N-S)**

| | | |
|---|---|---|
| 68 | George Rutter | ½ ac |
| 69 | Robert Trotter | ½ ac |
| 70 | Robert Trotter | ½ ac |
| 71 | Thomas Bigge | 1 rood |

**East Field – 2**

**Heath Shott (N-S)**

| | | |
|---|---|---|
| 72 | William Snow (with footpath) | 1 rood |
| 73 | Thomas Redford | 1 rood |
| 74 | Charles Sedwell | 1 rood |
| 75 | William Duke (free) | 1 ac |
| 76 | John Leaver | 1 ac |

**Closes between the Upper Field and the river**

| | | |
|---|---|---|
| 77 | 'Windeyarde Close' | William James |
| 78 | 'Moorbrook' | Lawrence Goldstone |
| 79 | William Snow | |
| 80 | The tilekilns | Joanna Fyre *als* Deere |

**Grant of land at Marshgate**

| | | |
|---|---|---|
| 81 | | Clement Maunder |

**Closes by the Green**

| | | |
|---|---|---|
| 82 | | William Duke (free) |
| 83 | 'Queen's Stables' | George Allington (crown lease) |
| 84 | Alexander Wilson | |

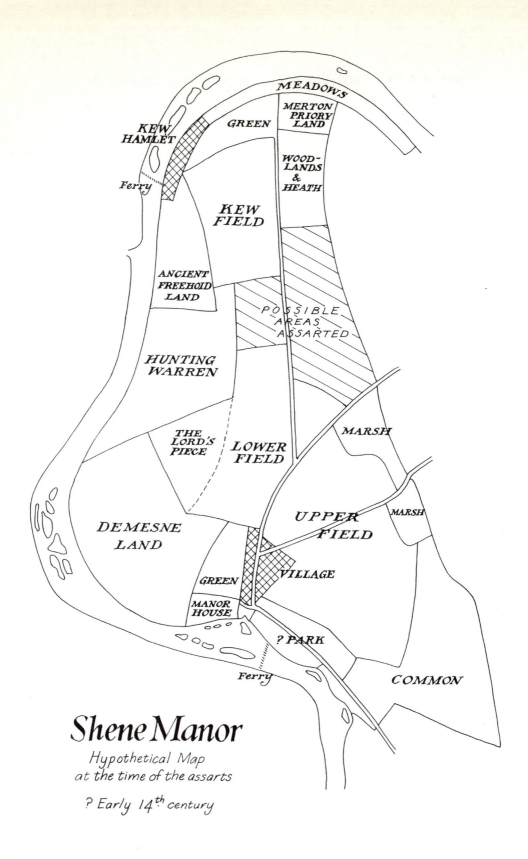

MEADOWS

MERTON
PRIORY
LAND

KEW
HAMLET

GREEN

WOOD-
LANDS
&
HEATH

Ferry

KEW
FIELD

ANCIENT
FREEHOLD
LAND

POSSIBLE
AREAS
ASSARTED

HUNTING
WARREN

THE
LORD'S
PIECE

LOWER
FIELD

MARSH

UPPER
FIELD

MARSH

DEMESNE
LAND

GREEN

VILLAGE

MANOR
HOUSE

? PARK

COMMON

Ferry

# Shene Manor

*Hypothetical Map
at the time of the assarts*

*? Early 14th century*

# 9

## *The Fields in 1620*

IN OR ABOUT the year 1620 a terrier was drawn up listing all the lands in the fields of the manor of Richmond.[1] This gives some new field names. The full list as given in the terrier is as follows:

| | |
|---|---|
| Kew Field: | Tenderland Furlong |
| | Park Furlong |
| | Brickhill Furlong (*sic* ?Brickkiln) |
| | Foxholes |
| Kew Heath | |
| Lower Field: | Shott butting on the Baylie's Bank |
| | Shott butting the highway to Kyo |
| | Shott butting the highway to Mortlake |
| | Shott butting on the Parke west |
| Upper Field: | Church Furlong |
| | Upper Dunstable |
| | Lower Dunstable |
| | East Field Shott |
| | Long Down |
| | Short Downes |
| | East Bancroft |
| | West Bancroft |
| | May Bush Shott *alias* South Down |
| Meadows: | Westerly Ware |
| | Twigghayes |
| | Short Lotts |
| | Two Hayes |
| | Hachett's |
| | Five Pits |
| | Redlades |
| The Ware Ground at Kew. | |

Looking back to the names used in the mid-16th century (p.50), there are quite a number of changes. East Furlong has disappeared into an expanded Church Furlong, which will soon be divided again into Church (or sometimes Conduit) Shott and Marsh Furze Shott, the division coming a lot further to the east than the old one. Short Downe Furlong has been renamed Maybush Shott or South Down (or sometimes Red Conduit Shott) and the name of Short Downs has been given to a small triangle of land at the west end of Long Downs. The former South Down and East Down have been merged into East Field Shott, more commonly called Heath Shott or sometimes Long Common Shott. The former East Down was sometimes regarded as a separate shott and called 'Pennard's Butts' – which suggests that it may have been where the manor's archery butts were located. The Baynecrofts have become Bancrofts and the Downstedes (Upper and Nether) have transmuted into Dunstables (Upper and Lower).

In the Lower Field definitive names for the shotts have yet to be found, but the former Path Furlong is now reidentified by its proximity to King James's new Park. (The part of Path Furlong on the north-west side of the 'path' – the Kew foot lane – has all but disappeared completely into the Park.) In the manor rolls there are indications of two other names used before the formation of the Park: Crabtree Shott for its southern end and Fagge Furlong for its northern. Crabtree Shott only occurs once (in 1621,[2] but that was probably a reference back to an earlier entry). Fagg occurs as a placename in the manor court roll of 1404/5, when two tenants are instructed to repair ditches there.[3] Fagge Furlong occurs in 1550[4] – and Fagge Lane as a name for the horse lane to Kew is found several times in the second half of the 16th century.[5] As 'fag' in this sense means a left-over piece, like the fag-end of a cigarette or of a bolt of cloth, the name suggests that the northern end of Park Shott was the last piece of the fields to be recovered from the waste. That may have remained true until 1569 when Henry Naylor was granted 4½ acres from the marsh (at the end of East, Church or Marsh Furze Shott).[6]

The other area whose name suggests it had been part of the marsh was Aldey at the eastern end of Lower Dunstable Shott. Aldey means 'island of alders'. When this area was reclaimed is not known – by 1620 its 20 acres were held in just three closes, two of nine acres each and one of two acres. The name is first found in the manor rolls in 1491 when William Hough was presented at the manor court for felling whitethorns there,[7] but the first definite indication of a tenant's ownership (of one of the nine-acre closes) comes in 1562/3.[8]

In Kew the old divisions of East Deane and West Deane seem to have vanished altogether. West Deane may have been the part of the field that lay to the west of the foot path from Richmond and which was perhaps incorporated into the freehold closes that lay between it and the river. Kew Park since its formation, probably in the 1520s, was also taken out of the fields, but gave its name to Park Furlong which lay to the south of the Park and of what was left of Tinderland (or Tenderland) Furlong. Brickkiln Furlong evidently owed its name to a brickkiln there – the parish of Richmond owned 1½ acres in this shott 'near ye brickhouse', but a rueful note in 1621 records that 'making bricks for the parish has made the three half acres in Brickkiln Shot of less value than heretofore'.[9] Foxholes, a curious little shott only half the normal width, is a name that was already in use by the mid-16th century.

✠

From the terrier, with some cross-checking against the entries in the manor rolls and books, it is possible to draw up an accurate map of all the holdings in the fields in 1620, showing the ownership of every parcel.

Plates 9-12

It is at once apparent that an intricate pattern of one-acre and half-acre strips (and a few of just a quarter-acre) still survived in the whole of the Upper Richmond Field (except Aldey and the recently developed area at the end of Marsh Furze Shott) and in the southern part of Park Shott in the Lower Field. This is evidently a true picture of the early medieval division of the land. However the pattern at the northern end of Parkshot and in the other three shotts of the Lower Field (especially Middle Shott and Bank Shott) is very different. Here the parcels of land are considerably larger, some being as large as 20, 18 or 13 acres.

Though some consolidation of holdings may have taken place, the difference is so striking that it suggests that these larger parcels must derive mainly from a process of assarting (reclaiming arable land from the waste) after the original allocation of strips. This may have taken place in the 14th century – perhaps at about the time when the normal tenement holding was changed from 18 acres of arable and two acres of meadow to 20 acres of arable and one acre of meadow. The total of arable holdings, free and villein, recorded in the 1314 survey was 584 acres. The total area for Kew Field and the two Richmond Fields recorded in the 1620 terrier was 603¼ acres; but to make a fair comparison one should add to this figure 19 acres for Kew Park, some 60 acres for the block of freehold land at Kew and some 35 acres for land purchased from the fields for James I's park – and subtract five acres for the grants in the marsh. This gives a figure of some 712 acres in 1620 to compare with 584 in 1314 – a difference of 128 acres, to be accounted for by new cultivation.

The area at the north end of Parkshot held in large parcels is about 43 acres, the areas of Middle Shot and Bank Shot add up to 120 acres. (Lower Shott would add another 38 acres, but the difference in pattern there is not quite so marked.) This total is evidently larger than the difference of 128 acres mentioned above; but some of the assartings may have already taken place by 1314.

If these speculations are correct, it may be noted that they appear to leave Richmond with one large field (the Upper one) and one very small one (the Lower, if reduced only to the southern end of Parkshott, plus possibly a bit of the Lower

Shott). But to this must be added the 35 acres or so purchased by James I for his park and also, most probably, the 36 (or 46) acres of the 'Lord's Piece' (or Pieces) which references in 1538 and 1555 place as within 'the common fields'.[10] This goes a long way to redress the balance (see map at p.86). It is also possible (though there is no evidence of any kind) that Lower Dunstable Shott was originally considered as part of the Lower Field – which would make Upper and Lower Fields almost identical in area – and was reallocated after the assarts had added to the Lower Field.

In Kew Field, it is probable that the larger than normal holdings were simply the result of early consolidation; they are still intermingled with one-acre and half-acre strips.

✠

The other notable feature emerging from the terrier is that some 90 per cent of the land in the fields in 1620 was in the hands of just ten families. Of the remaining 10 per cent of 'small holdings', though some can be traced back to grants of land, most derive from the break-up of three estates in the late 16th-early 17th centuries. Until the late 16th century the pattern of 'whole tenements' and 'half-tenements' that characterised the villein land in the 14th century had been preserved virtually intact in the later copyholdings. Indeed in the surviving manor rolls up to the time of Elizabeth I nearly all the transfers of land (as distinct from houses) are in terms of 20-acre tenements or 10-acre half-tenements. (This, incidentally, is very different from Petersham where many of the original tenements appear to have been fragmented at a much earlier date.)[11]

Ownership of the houses in the village of Richmond does, however, show a rather different pattern. As noted in the previous chapter the ownership of only a few of the 'capital messuages' of tenements remained linked with their lands in the early 17th century. Often the divorce of the land from its capital messuage appears to have taken place in the 15th or early 16th centuries.

✠

Described below are the main estates in 1620 with brief notes of their histories up to that point and on some of the families concerned. A more detailed history of the separate tenements will be found at Appendix 7.

As even the fragmented estates came partly into the hands of significant landowners this review covers all the known tenements in the manor. (The numbers allotted to them are arbitrary, in order as they occur here, to facilitate cross-referencing to the appendix and to the houses listed in the previous chapter.) The fact that many of the tenements continued for years to be known by the names of previous owners has made it possible to connect up, at least tentatively, some of the later recorded history with names – and even in some cases properties – mentioned in the early surviving manor rolls.

⊹

## 1. The Portman estates

In 1620 the freehold Portman lands were held by Sir Henry Portman, second baronet of Orchard Portman in Somerset, and the copyhold lands by his youngest brother William (who was to succeed also to the freeholdings when he became the fifth baronet in 1630). They were nephews of the Hugh Portman who acquired the estate in Richmond in the early 1590s. Hugh's grandfather (died 1555) had been Lord Chief Justice of England. His father-in-law Sir John Puckering, Speaker of the House of Commons, had probably already been leasing the house 'Kew Farm' when he entertained Queen Elizabeth there in 1591 (being knighted a few months later). By the time he entertained the Queen again in 1594 and 1595 the house had been purchased by Hugh, who was himself knighted in 1595. After Sir Hugh's death (his will was proved in March 1603/4), the property passed to his brother John. John Portman was knighted in 1605 and made a baronet in November 1611. He had four sons, Henry, John, Hugh and William, who each in turn inherited the baronetcy, and the freehold lands. By the 'borough English' custom of the manor of Richmond, the copyhold lands went straight to the youngest son William.

**A.** *The freehold lands* appear to derive from three main sources:

i. The former Suffolk and Devonshire estates at Kew (see tenements 1 and 2 at Appendix 7). Most of the land in these was consolidated in the large block of freehold land between the west side of the Kew Field and the river. This was by 1620 attached to the house known as Kew Farm (see page 79). It was not counted as part of the manorial fields in the 1620 terrier. Some of the freehold land in the Kew Field may, however, have derived from the former copyhold tenement (No. 1) granted in freehold to the Earl of Worcester in 1517. These freehold lands were all purchased by Hugh Portman from Anthony Mason in 1592.

ii. Those parts of the former Wylde-Raynford-Duke estate (see tenement 11) which remained attached to the Duke house at Kew until sold by William Duke to Walter Hickman in November 1609 and by Hickman to Sir John Portman three months later. (It is possible that these included some free land in Kew Field as well as land immediately adjacent to the house.)

iii. The former holdings of Merton Priory (tenement No. 3). These included the 'Ware Ground' on the east side of Kew Green and the three freehold meadows at Kew. There was also land in the Richmond fields, known at the time of the Priory's dissolution as 'Prystes' lands' [i.e. Priests']. The 1620 terrier shows Sir Henry Portman as holding 9½ acres in the two Richmond fields, but several of these holdings were later disposed of as copyhold, so may have been incorrectly identified in the terrier. (Alternatively the distinction may have been blurred in the Earl of Ancram's rush to sell off the estate in the late 1650s and early 1660s.) The Merton holdings had been granted out almost immediately after the Dissolution of the Priory. They were acquired in 1546 by Augustine Hynde whose son Rowland Hynde sold them to Hugh Portman in 1594.

**B.** *Kew Heath* is listed separately here as there is some doubt as to its status. It stretched from the Ware Ground southwards to the northern end of the Lower Richmond field, and had been demesne land until granted out in the 1580s. According to the 1620 terrier 15 acres of it were held by Sir Henry Portman as freehold, and 25 acres by William as copyhold, but the designation of 15 acres as freehold may have been an error. Grants (not stated to be freehold) had been made in 1583 of 22 acres to John Hynde and in 1585 of 13-3/8 acres to John Bond. These excluded a further 5 acres immediately adjacent to Kew Green, which must be assumed to have been granted out in 1589-1602. Hugh Portman presumably acquired the whole from John Hynde along with the copyhold property. Later in the 17th century Kew Heath was considered to consist of two parcels, both copyhold: 10 acres between the Ware Ground and the lane from Kew Green to Mortlake (now the Mortlake Road), and 35 acres to the south of this lane.

**C.** *The copyhold estates.* These were purchased at some time between 1589 and 1602 (most probably in 1594) by Hugh Portman from John Hynde, the youngest son of Augustine Hynde. Apart from Kew Heath, this large estate, assembled by Augustine Hynde (a London alderman, Master of the Clothmakers' Company in 1545, and Sheriff in 1550-1), was essentially the accumulation of three whole tenements, some two-thirds of two others, and two half-tenements, as listed below.

i. *Walton's tenement* – 20 acres and 1 acre of mead (tenement No. 4). Several Waltons are mentioned in the manor rolls of 1413-18 and 1445-52, including Alice, widow of John, who held a messuage and 20 acres in 1418. This later passed through the ownership of John Makyn, Thomas Aleyn and Adam Halydaye. Adam's heir, William Halydaye, sold it to Augustine Hynde in 1539.

ii. *South's half-tenement* – 10 acres and ½ acre of mead (tenement No. 5). John South was a manor tenant in 1348-50. In the 15th century 'South's tenement, passed through the hands of the At Mill (or Mille) family to the Harts, and then in 1506 to John Oxenbrigge, a chaplain (and later a Canon of Windsor). Oxenbrigge's heir, a relative named William Horethorne, sold the half-tenement to Augustine Hynde in 1542.

iii. *A (nameless) tenement* of 20 acres and 1 acre of mead (tenement No. 6). In 1485

Thomas Hart acquired a half-tenement (different from ii above) from Robert Mille and another half-tenement from William Hunt. He seems to have amalgamated these as a 'whole tenement' which, like (ii) passed to Oxenbrigge and was bought by Hynde in 1542.

iv. *Pykwell's half-tenement* of 10 acres and ½ acre of mead (tenement No. 7). John Pykwell was named as a manor tenant in 1414-22 and 1445-52 (in which year he died). His grandson John Pykwell sold the cottage separately in 1499 and then sold the land in 1500 to Robert Fawkon, who sold it to Hynde in 1542.

v. *Thorne's tenement* of 20 acres and 1 acre of mead (tenement No. 8). Five members of the 'At Thorne' family are mentioned in 1413-19, including Roger Thorne who in 1419 inherited a messuage and 20 acres from Richard at Thorne. This is probably the tenement that became the property of William Lawles in 1486 and was then granted to Alice wife of John Man (late wife of Thomas Denys) in 1504. Thomas Denys Junior, her son, mortgaged to Augustine Hynde the reversion to 13½ acres of land and the acre of mead, and sold off the rest. Hynde gained full possession of his 13½ acres in 1550.

vi. *Maykyn's tenement* of 20 acres and an island (tenement No. 9). The Maykyns were early inhabitants of Kew, John Maykyn being mentioned in 1385. This tenement at Kew belonged in the 15th century in turn to Clement, Stephen and Robert Maykyn. In 1491 it was split between Robert's two daughters as co-heirs, but was reunited by 1535 in the ownership of John Becke. In 1539 Becke surrendered it to Augustine Hynde, who sold it on immediately to Charles, Duke of Suffolk. However Hynde probably retained a mortgage, for on Suffolk's death in 1545 the land reverted to Hynde's ownership.

vii. *Lydgold's tenement* of 20 acres and an island (tenement No. 10). Robert Lydgold was a manor tenant in 1404-22 and John Lydgold in 1413-19 and 1449-52. In the early 16th century the tenement (entirely at Kew) passed by inheritance to the Staynford family. Thomas Staynford appears to have sold it to Sir George Somerset (probably in 1521-27 for which years the manor rolls are missing). In 1538 Sir George sold it to John Becke who promptly mortgaged it to Augustine Hynde. A year later Becke and Hynde sold it to the Duke of Suffolk. In this instance it appears that the Duke only mortgaged 12½ acres and the island back to Hynde, to whom they reverted in 1545. The other 7½ acres became eventually part of the John Burd estate (see 8 below). They had been inherited by Suffolk's daughter Eleanor, Countess of Cumberland, and then by her daughter Margaret, Countess of Derby. They were sold by William, 6th Earl of Derby, in 1603 to Alexander Prescott whose widow married John Burd.

✠

## 2. *The Jones freehold estate ('the George Farm')*

The terrier shows Duncan Jones as holding 85½ acres of freehold lands in the Richmond fields (none in Kew). This estate was in scattered holdings – some large, but many in original strips of one acre or half an acre. All of these, except for 11 acres at the northern end of Parkshot and 8 acres in the Lower Shott, are identifiable with holdings in the Raynford terrier of 1559, which also included a further 6½ acres in Path Furlong (which can be equated with the 5½ acres and 27 perches, when accurately measured, sold by Jones to King James I for his park). The 8 acres in Lower Shott may well have been listed on the missing last page of the Raynford terrier which would also have included holdings at Kew.

The estate may have had its origins in a 12th-century dowry. A carucate or four virgates of free land is mentioned several times in the 13th and early 14th centuries. To this 80 acres another 20 were probably added by 1478 when the documented history begins (in the Hildyard papers deposited in the Nottingham University Library). In April 1478 there was a recovery by William Gray to John de Orkan of 'one messuage, 100 acres of land, 8 acres of meadow and 3 acres of wood in Kayo'. This is followed rapidly by another document in which the property is described as exactly double: a sale by Sir Thomas Urswick, chief justice of the King's Bench, in March 1478/9 to John Aleyn, citizen and goldsmith of London of '2 messuages, 200 acres of land, 16 acres of meadow and 6 acres of wood in Shene and Kayo, formerly of John Goyeon'. It was not unusual for a sale of freehold land to be deliberately overstated in this way and it seems likely that the property had passed from John de Orkan to Sir Thomas Urswick without any actual change in its composition. Were John de Orkan and John Goyeon the same person?

Aleyn sold the property in 1489 and shortly thereafter it came into the hands of the Wylde family of Camberwell. The name of Wylde occurs at various times in the Richmond manor rolls from 1498 onwards. A foot of fine dated 18 November 1522 records the sale by Henry Wylde, son of John Wylde, of 3 acres of freehold meadow in Kew. (The names of Sir Henry Wyatt and his wife Ann are linked with that of Henry Wylde in this document. Wyatt had been a tenant of the manor since 1500. His name was also linked with those of Thomas Wylde and John and Roger Wylde in the purchase of an estate at Godstone in 1527. A family link seems probable – especially as a Wyatt Wylde appears in 1555.)

At some date before 1535 Thomas Wylde, who had held the whole estate at Kew and Richmond formerly belonging to Sir Thomas Urswyck and John Aleyn, died – and his widow Winifred married John Raynford (knighted by 1539). Raynford's name appears in the manor court rolls as a tenant at various dates from 1535 to 1554 – usually as a defaulter for not attending the court. On 11 December 1539, however, is recorded a 'conditional surrender' (i.e. mortgage) by John Raynford, Knight, and Lady Winefrede of all their lands to John Hale of Cayo, and on 25 April 1552 Sir John was presented at the court as 'tenant in right of his wife Winifred, formerly wife of Thomas Wylde' because they had demised their lands to John Hale for a term of 40 years without the Lord's licence. Raynford died in September 1559, which was the occasion for the drawing-up of the terrier of his lands at Richmond. On 14 July 1561 Sir George Howard was granted 'custody of Winifred, late wife of Sir John Raynford deceased and daughter of John Pimpe late of Nettlested, Kent, a lunatic enjoying lucid intervals ... with custody of her lands in Kent, Suffolk and Surrey from Michaelmas last'.

Exactly who held the lands for the next 15 years is uncertain – Sir George Howard's name does not appear as a manorial tenant in the rolls, but that does not necessarily mean that he was not one. The lands at about this time appear to have acquired – perhaps from him – the name of 'the George Farm'. On 4 April 1567 the manor court recorded that 'the homage finds that the George lands are customary, as are the lands called lots or meads belonging to them'. This was of course quite unfounded, but it was not until 1576 after the death of Lady Winifred that the error was challenged and corrected. The court roll for 13 April 1576 records:

> Lady Winifred Wylde widow, late wife of John Raynford Kt and formerly wife of Thomas Wylde, held for her life by free charter 2 messuages, 200 acres of land, 16 acres of meadow and 6 acres of woodland in Richmond, Shene and Keyo at a rent of 22s 2d a year; and on her death Thomas Duke paid a relief of 22s 2d. And Thomas Duke came to the court because someone had said that the tenements were customary and not free, and he showed the charter and proved his title and that they were free property.

Unfortunately the Hildyard documents do not contain a copy of the Wylde charter, but they include the record of a recovery process dated 8 February 1575/6 by which Thomas Duke 'recovered' the estate (thereby breaking an entail) and then surrendered a moiety (half) of it to Wyatt Wylde. The estate was described in this document as '5 messuages and 5 gardens, 200 acres of land, 30 acres of meadow, 10 acres of pasture and 12 acres of wood in Shene *als* Richmount, Kayo and Kingston on Thames'. The extra houses and land may have been in Kingston (mentioned here for the first time), but have not been traced.

Thomas Duke, of Cossington in Kent, was the son of George Duke of Cossington and of Camberwell and his wife Ann, daughter of William Wylde of Camberwell. Ann Wylde had a sister Winifred who married a Matthew Poyntz. William Wylde's wife was named Dorothy: their names are linked in a series of feet of fines dealing with property in Croydon and Godstone between 1543 and 1552, then in 1555 comes the combination of 'Dorothy Wylde widow and Wiatt Wylde gent' in a Croydon sale.

Attempting to link these clues, my guess is that a William Wylde of Camberwell (who is noted as a servant to the Archbishop of Canterbury)* had at least two sons:

---

* According to a paper in the collection of the Society of Genealogists (but which Archbishop and when is not stated).

Thomas, who married Winifred Pimpe of Nettlested, but died without living issue; and William who married Dorothy (perhaps a daughter of Sir Henry Wyatt) and had a son Wyatt. William also had daughters Anne, who married George Duke, and Winifred (Poyntz). Thomas Wylde had acquired or inherited the property at Richmond and Kew and left it to his wife Winifred for her life, with reversion to their niece Ann Duke and their nephew Wyatt Wylde. Ann died before Winifred Raynford (formerly Wylde) and Ann's son Thomas Duke then became the heir to her share – but gave up half the estate to his uncle Wyatt Wylde. (See the family tree.)

## Wylde, Duke and Michell families
### (probable relationships)

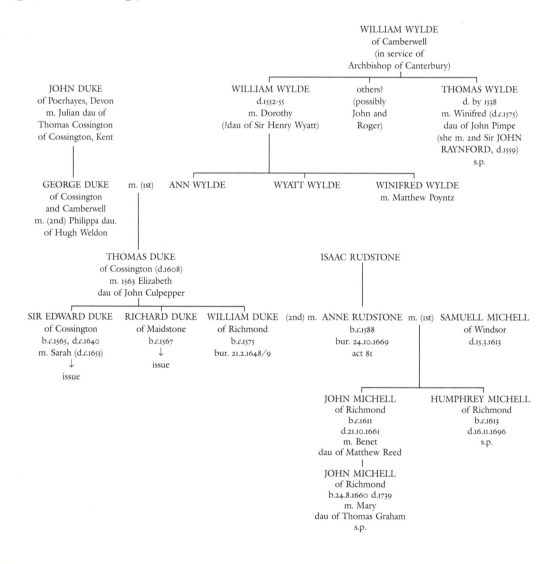

The half of the estate surrendered to Wyatt Wylde may have been the 'George Farm' lands in the Richmond fields, together with the house (No. 81 in the 1603 list) which stood in a five-acre close at the bottom of the east side of the hill. This land was probably purchased by Duncan Jones towards the end of Queen Elizabeth's reign, but when it first figures in the 17th-century manor rolls it (or much of it) was in the occupation (by lease?) of William Dawborne. There are several references between 1604 and 1617 to land in Dawborne's tenure – all identifiable with Raynford holdings in 1559 and Jones holdings in 1620 – but it was Jones who sold the land to the King for his park in February 1606/7, so it is probable that Dawborne was only a tenant of Jones.

The George Farm estate descended through several generations of Jones heirs (paying a quit rent of 11s. 1d., which was exactly one half of that recorded as paid by Winifred Raynford) to a John Jones who split up the estate in 1705. (By then it had temporarily acquired the name of 'Wayland's Farm' under which it is listed in the tenure by lease of Edward Allen in the manor survey of 1703; but all the documents which have been traced dealing with the sale of parts of the estate refer to them as 'formerly part of the George Farm'.)

Thomas Duke evidently kept the house and lands at Kew, together with just two acres in the Richmond fields and the freehold house by Richmond Green (No. 10 in the 1603 list). His son William Duke sold the Kew estate in 1609 to Walter Hickman, who sold it on to Sir John Portman three months later. The house by Richmond Green was, however, inherited by William Duke's step-sons John and Humphrey Michell.

✠

## 3. The Wright and Payne estates

The Wright family of Richmond at the end of the 16th and the beginning of the 17th centuries had some rather complicated inter-relationships (see table).

Sir Robert Wright, who owned property in Richmond from the 1590s, is said by Sir James Whitelocke, a contemporary judge and journal keeper,[12] to have been 'meanly born' in Shrewsbury. However, he got an education, and apparently became a tutor to the young Robert Devereux, who became Earl of Essex in 1576. Wright remained in the Earl's household until Essex was appointed by Queen Elizabeth to be her Master of the Horse in 1587. Essex had Wright appointed as 'Clerk of the Stable'. Their friendship persisted until Essex's execution in 1601. In his will,[13] dated 21 November 1608, Robert Wright (who had been knighted on 17 May 1605) left to 'my Earl of Essex [Robert Devereux's son] in token of my unspotted love to the most worthy Earl his father, the basin and ewer of silver and gilt, which his lordship gave me at my marriage'.

Robert Wright married in 1588 Dorothy (née Walwyn), the widow of John Farnham of Nether Hall, Quorndon in Leicestershire. Sir Robert died in 1610, but she long outlived him, dying at a ripe old age in 1638. They had no children of their own, but Dorothy had had children by her previous marriage to John Farnham, including a son Humphrey who inherited at Quorndon, and a daughter Dorothy. This younger Dorothy Farnham married (at Richmond) on 10 August 1597 one George Wright, whose relationship (if any) to Sir Robert – other than by this marriage – is unknown. Dorothy brought with her a dowry of lands in, surprisingly, Kent.[14] George Wright (who was probably born about 1572, was knighted on 4 July 1604, and died in 1623) was said by Whitelocke[15] to have been the son of Thomas Wright, vintner, of the famous *Boar's Head Tavern* in Eastcheap. He was a fellow student of Whitelocke at Merchant Taylors' School and at St John's College, Oxford.

George and Dorothy Wright had children and George was in some respects Sir Robert's successor. He took over the appointment as Clerk of the Stable; in right of his wife, he took over Sir Robert's mansion by the river in Richmond. But Sir Robert's legal heir (after a life interest to widow Dorothy senior) was his brother Richard who lived in Walthamstow and died in 1617, leaving sons Robert and Lionel. This younger

## The Wright Family of Richmond

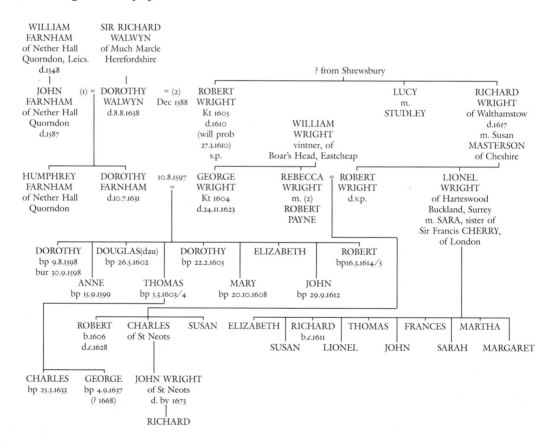

Robert had married a Rebecca (said in the Surrey visitations of 1623 to be the sister of Sir George Wright), but died before his father – whereupon Rebecca took another husband, Robert Payne.

Both Robert Wright the younger and his brother Lionel had children, but by his will Richard Wright left a life interest in his property at Richmond (partly inherited from Sir Robert, partly purchased by himself) to his widowed daughter-in-law Rebecca. Thus it was that in 1620 much of the Wright estate was in the hands of Robert and Rebecca Payne, though entailed to revert later to Lionel Wright and then to Robert the younger's son Charles Wright.

In 1620 the Paynes were shown in the terrier as holding 90½ acres of free land and 1½ acres of copyhold land. However, in addition, Dame Dorothy Wright (senior – the widow of Sir Robert) held 15¼ acres of copyhold land in her own name and another four acres jointly with Thomas Wright her grandson (son of Sir George).

## A. The freehold land

In fact the terrier was in error for 10½ of the 90½ acres of allegedly free land held by the Paynes were actually copyhold. The origin of the 80 acres of freehold land lay in a grant made to David Vincent, Keeper of the Wardrobe and of Richmond Palace, in 1549 of the lands which had previously been held by Peter de Narbone and his son John (John having died without heirs). The Narbone holding had been 30 acres freehold and 50 acres copyhold, but the whole 80 acres was granted to Vincent in freehold.

*The freehold 30 acres* (tenement No. 12) is first identifiable in a sale by William Skerne to Richard Marshall in 1451. It appears to have been sold to Peter de Narbone about 1490. Narbone's *copyhold land* consisted of:

(i)     *a whole tenement* (No. 13) of 20 acres formerly belonging to John Gryffyn and then to Sir William Tyler, who sold it to Narbone in 1500;

(ii)    *another whole tenement (No. 14) called Heron's*, sold by William Blackett to Narbone in 1490;

(iii)   *a half-tenement* (No. 15) which was perhaps the one sold by Blackett to William Gardner in 1487 (and then by Gardner to Narbone?).

Vincent sold the estate in 1556 to Nicholas Culverwell, a merchant and haberdasher of London, said in the *DNB* to have been Queen Elizabeth's wine merchant. In 1569 Nicholas bequeathed the property to his second son Ezekiel, who became a well-known Puritan divine. In 1608 Ezekiel Culverwell sold it to Richard Wright, with reversion to the latter's son Robert and his wife Rebecca. In addition to land in the fields the Vincent estate acquired by the Wrights had included two important freehold closes outside the fields, each of about three acres. One was at the east end of the village between what are now Sheen Road and Paradise Road and was probably the site of the capital messuage of the 30-acre tenement; the other lay between West Bancroft Shott and the causeway leading up Richmond Hill.

## B. Copyhold land

i. 11½ acres of copyhold land and an acre of meadow were sold by Ezekiel Culverwell to Richard Wright, with the same reversion as the freehold mentioned above, in 1609. Ten acres of this was the *half-tenement (No. 16)* held by Gilbert Binnegate in 1314, surrendered by him to William Walsh in 1348 and sold by John Walshe to Thomas Denys in 1492. The latter's son Thomas sold it to Nicholas Culverwell in the reign of Queen Mary I and in 1559 also sold to Culverwell an adjacent barn and 1½ acres in Upper Dunstable.

ii. In 1609 Richard Wright was granted a piece of land at the southern end of Parkshott which had been acquired by the King for his park but had in the end been left outside the new park pales. This was a little over one acre, abutting a 4-acre close (now also sold by Ezekiel Culverwell to Wright) on the north side of the Green.

iii. On the death of Sir Robert Wright in 1610 his brother Richard was proclaimed his heir, but Sir Robert's widow Dorothy had a life interest in nearly all his property, including his mansion standing in a two-acre close on the north side of Ferry Hill (Nos. 79-80 in the 1603 list) and two houses on the site of old Palace Place (Nos. 61-62 in the 1603 list). The only exception, which went straight to Richard Wright, was the collection of cottages and stables called Pensioner's Alley (No. 43 in the 1603 list) which Sir Robert had acquired in 1596.

iv. The copyhold lands in the fields that belonged to Sir Robert and then to Dorothy Wright were 5 acres purchased from Humphrey Stafferton in 1602 (which were a part of the ancient *half-tenement (No. 17)* – identifiable with the half-tenement held in villenage by Isabell Bynnegates in 1314), and 10¼ acres purchased from John Bird in 1606 (see at 8 below). The purchase had been 11½ acres but Wright sold 1¼ acres to the King in February 1606/7, at which time he also sold 1½ acres of meadow on the banks of the Thames outside the pale of the old park.

v. By 1620 Dame Dorothy had purchased two other pieces of land, but in both instances she joined her grandson Thomas (son of Sir George Wright and her daughter Dorothy) in the title. One, purchased in 1614 from Seth Goldstone, was a long triangle of waste land between Ferry Hill and the grounds of the Wright mansion house. The other was a 4-acre holding in the Lower Field, purchased from Thomas Tye in 1615. In 1619 Dame Dorothy made over the mansion house itself to her daughter Dorothy, Sir George's wife, for her lifetime, with reversion to Thomas.

☩

## 4. Stephen Peirce's estate

The terrier shows Stephen Peirce, Keeper of the Wardrobe at Richmond Palace, as holding a total of 72 acres. This includes a close (or two closes) of 9 acres at Aldey at the eastern end of Lower Dunstable Shott and a close of 3 acres at the western end of Upper Dunstable. It does not however include 'Green Close' of some 2½ acres which lay between the horse lane and the foot lane to Kew by the southern end of Parkshot (and on the north side of the Duke mansion). This was possibly the site of Peirce's house.

The larger part of this holding was called 'Scopeham's lands' or 'Parkyns' Farm'. When sold to Peirce in 1612 by the Rev James Fitche, Vicar of Kingston, it was said to consist of 'a messuage, two barns, three stables, one garden and one orchard, four closes whereof one lies between one of the said barns [?the one in Upper Dunstable], two lie in a field called Aldey and the other lies near the pinfold and against the said messuage, and 4 acres of meadow called 8 lots in Kew, and 46 acres of arable land lying dispersed in the common fields of Richmond'. Fitche bought this estate in 1606 from Henry Lovell, at which time the four closes were said to contain altogether 12 acres and one rood.

Lovell had sold quite a lot of land to King James I for the latter's new park. There were two tranches, of which the accurately surveyed areas were '4½ acres and 20 perches' and '4 acres and 21 perches' respectively. The nominal acreage was probably quite a lot more – 10 acres at least.

There is however some difficulty in reconciling Peirce's holdings exactly with what we know of the previous ownership. Peirce already owned some land before the purchase of 'Scopeham's'. In the period 1589-1602 he had acquired 10 acres from Anthony Mason – originally part of William Pate's estate (see 9 below) – and 3 acres from Henry Naylor (see 6 below). He later acquired the other 1½ acres of Naylor's 4½ acre grant 'in the Marsh' by exchange with Richard Clarke for 2 acres elsewhere. He seems to have had at least another 1¾ acres from other sources, and to have sold before 1620 another 1¾ acres. So at least 13 of his 72 acres had not been part of the land he bought from Fitche. The remaining 59 acres ties in fairly closely with the 46 acres in the fields and 12¼ in separate closes.

Add to this some 10 acres for the sales to the King, and we should have about 70 acres all told (including the closes) for the property of Henry Lovell before 1605. Its descent from John Parkyns seems clear. In 1562/3 he sold to John Hopkins and Bowes Thelwell (who sold on in April 1563 to Thomas, son of Gregory, Lovell) the 'messuage and tenement called Scopeham's lands and a close and barn and 60 acres of arable land and 7 acres of mead or pasture (3 in a former close before the doors of the house and 4 in the Lott meadow at Kew) and a piece of land in the common field called Aldey containing 9 acres'. Thomas Lovell's sister Francesca inherited the land from him in 1565 and their brother Henry inherited from her in 1577. This gives a total (apart from the Kew meadows) of 72 acres plus whatever is included with the house – which was presumably the 2½-acre Green Close. It must be assumed that Henry Lovell had got rid of some 5 acres or so before 1603.

When Henry Parkyns died in 1533 he left 'three tenements and cottages' to his widow Elizabeth for her life (she died in 1547) with remainder to their son John. It may be, however, that there was more land inherited by John as there appear to have been four (or possibly five) tenements all or part of which were in the ownership of Henry Parkyns. John Parkyns may have sold some land during the reign of Mary I. The four acres of mead associated with this property suggest that there were at least four tenements involved in its make-up.

i. *Gylle's tenement* – 20 acres and an island (tenement No. 18) Robert Gylle was a manor tenant in 1445-52 and his wife Mary was mentioned in 1445. They were probably the parents of the Robert Gille who left a tenement of 20 acres and an island to his wife Margery in 1491. Margery sold this to Henry Parkyns in 1494. Parkyns sold off the island in 1502 to John Foxe.

ii. *Scopeham's lands* including a tenement of 20 acres and 1 acre of mead (tenement No. 19). The family of Hoo, Hough or Howe were landowners in Shene throughout the 14th and 15th centuries. John Ho and Gilbert Ho were manor tenants in 1314. Thomas, Robert and John Howe figure in 1404-22, Constance Hoo and her heir William Hoo or Hough in 1449-52; John Hoo or Hough from 1487 to 1499. In 1485 John Makyn left to his wife Isabella a whole tenement of a messuage and a virgate of land 'formerly of Robert Hoo'. Isabella sold this to Richard Scopeham in 1489. Richard Scopeham's will in 1501 left all his lands in Richmond to his son Edmund, and Edmund two years later left them to his wife Elizabeth. Unfortunately no detail is given of the lands thus inherited in 1501 and 1503; but it seems likely that the Scopehams had also acquired the former Lockyer tenement (or half-tenement) as Edmund sold off its cottage and curtilage in 1503. (This may be tenement No. 24 – see at 5iii below.) But if so either the Scopehams or the Parkyns must have sold off the lands and not retained them.

There is no record of any transfer of the Scopeham lands from Elizabeth Scopeham to Henry Parkyns – and it is indeed probable that Elizabeth, widow of Edmund Scopeham, became Elizabeth, wife of Henry Parkyns. In any case it is clear the Scopeham lands came into the hands of Henry and John Parkyns. The Raynford terrier of 1559 lists no less than nine separate pieces of land abutting his as owned by 'Parkyns late Scopeham'.

iii. *John Hough's tenement* – 20 acres and 1 acre of mead (tenement No. 20). John Hough died in 1501, having just sold 4 acres of land to Sir William Tyler (who sold them on to Peter Narbone). He left to his wife Isabella, with remainder to his son Humphrey a cottage and 5 acres – to which Humphrey gained full title in 1511. In the meantime he had been engaged in 1509 in a suit against Henry Prym over a house and 11 acres (presumably the rest of the original tenement). In February 1513/4 he sold to Henry Parkyns 'all his lands'. Whether that was 5 or 16 acres is uncertain – but there is no other trace of what might have happened to the 11 acres if Prym had retained them.

iv. *The Fysshe tenement* (20 acres or 10 acres?) – tenement No. 21. In September 1487, John Turner and his wife Joan having both died, their son William Turner was admitted to 20 acres, with reversion to Thomas Fysshe. It is not absolutely clear whether Fysshe ultimately inherited the full 20 acres or only half of it. (The house and curtilage associated with this tenement appear to have been of 'half-tenement' size.) On his death in 1505 his half-brother John Kyte was proclaimed his heir, but it was found that Fysshe had surrendered the property to his daughter Elizabeth and her husband John Cave. The Caves sold it to John Knolles, who sold it to William Hartopp who sold it to Henry Parkyns in 1528.

✠

## 5. *The Clarke estate*

The terrier shows Richard Clarke as holding 37 acres and one rood, but it also shows a ¾-acre holding as 'George Charley/Robert Clarke', and this can be counted as Clarke's making a total of 38 acres. Richard Clarke had inherited 40 acres of land and 2 acres (4 lotts) in Kew meads from his father Robert in 1606. He sold some 2½ acres to the King for his park, but gained an extra half-acre in his exchange of land with Stephen Peirce in 1614.

Robert Clarke of the Inner Temple, steward of Richmond manor, acquired his estate and interest in Richmond by his marriage with Joan, the only daughter and heir of Henry Deacon, Sergeant Plumber to Queen Elizabeth. (Deacon died in 1592.) Deacon had purchased two whole tenements, each of 20 acres and 1 acre of mead (one called 'the Catherine Wheel') from George Annesley in 1571. At least one of the capital messuages of these tenements was located in the area between what are now George Street and Red Lion Street, to the south-west of the church. Deacon and Clarke also acquired a lot of neighbouring town property in this area, but without further land in the fields. On this land Robert Clarke built a large mansion (possibly based on the *Bell Inn*, which may have been granted to him after the execution of Lawrence Snow in 1596).

The Annesley holding derived from Thomas Cooke who surrendered 'a cottage and garden and 2 virgates of land' to Ralph Annesley in 1535. Annesley's widow, who was left a life interest in this estate, apparently then married Jeffrey Perryns (whose name appears as a manor tenant in 1550 and 1554 and in the Raynford terrier) and then, shortly before her death in 1559, a Mr Cartelage. Her heir was proclaimed at the manor court in July 1559 as George Annesley, the son of Robert deceased, who was the son of Ralph Annesley.

The origins of the two virgates of land lie in one whole tenement and two half-tenements as follows.

i. *Waler/Frauncys tenement* of 20 acres and 1 acre of mead – (tenement No. 22). This was surrendered by John Waler to John Frauncys in 1413, it being noted that the messuage and orchard was 'near the enclosure formerly of Robert Hoo and the Church hawe'. A Hugh Frauncys was noted as a manorial tenant in 1445-52. By the 1480s this holding had come into the hands of Henry Stokes, who disposed of it in two halves, in June 1490 and October 1491, both to Richard Goodyere (and both noted as having once belonged to John Frauncys). Goodyere sold one of the halves to a John Blythe and the other half in 1494 to William Cooke. In 1496 William Cooke reunited the property by buying out John Blythe.

Cooke died in 1504, leaving his lands for life to his widow Katherine. She married twice more, first to Edward Skerne and then to Sir William Tyle (*sic* – ?Tyler). When she died in 1532 her son Thomas Cooke was acknowledged as her heir to the 20-acre tenement, but with one Clement Twyford as his guardian. (As Thomas must have been at least 27 years old by this date, the need for a guardian suggests that he was of unsound mind.)

ii. *Drewe/Denys half-tenement* of 10 acres and ½ acre of mead (tenement No. 23). John Drewe was noted as a manorial tenant from 1485 to 1492. In 1489 there was a reference to a hedge between John Drewe's croft and the tenement of Joanna Hosey and another reference to a 'watercourse in the high level of Thames against John Drewe's tenement' (page 67). Drewe died in 1494 and in 1496 his 'half-tenement of a cottage and 10 acres in West Shene and ½ acre of mead in Kayho' was granted to Elizabeth, wife of Robert Cornwalys, daughter and heir of John de Bury, as the nearest heir to John Drewe. (This John de Bury was probably a son of the man by that name who was Keeper of the New Park of Shene from 1440 to 1452.)

Robert and Elizabeth Cornwalys sold the half-tenement in 1497 to John Kempe, who passed it on a year later to Thomas Thorpe. It then appears to have been sold by Thorpe to Edward Jones in 1499 or 1500 and by Jones to Hugh Denys in May 1501. Hugh Denys, an 'esquire of the King's body', died in 1511. Although in his will he instructed that his house in Richmond was to be sold, it appears that the half-tenement remained in the ownership of his widow Mary and her new husband Sir Giles Capell.

iii. *Half-tenement* of 10 acres and ½ acre of mead (?Lockyer's): (tenement No. 24). Sir Giles and Mary Capell must have acquired another half-tenement, but its history prior to 1533 cannot be identified. For no better reason than that, I suggest that it may have been Lockyer's tenement (the history of which I have been unable to trace, except that its cottage with curtilage was sold by Edmund Scopeham in 1503 – see 4ii above). Perhaps Scopeham or Henry Parkyns sold the land to the Capells. In June 1533 Sir Giles and Mary Capell summoned the Steward of Richmond manor to their house at Rayne in Essex to receive their surrender of 'a half-tenement in the possession of ... Cooke and of a tenement consisting of a cottage and 10 acres of land and ½ acre of mead' to the use of Clement Twyford. 'Master Twyford' was listed as a manor tenant in 1535-36 and, as noted above, was guardian to Thomas Cooke. There can therefore be little doubt that these two half-tenements (ii) and (iii) went to form one of the whole tenements surrendered by Thomas Cooke (or by Twyford on his behalf) in 1535.

✝

## 6. Mary Crome's estate

Mary Crome, widow, is shown in the terrier as holding 28¾ acres. This was mostly derived from two tenements, a copyhold whole tenement of 20 acres and a freehold half-tenement of 10 acres, which she owned as heir to Henry Naylor.

i. *Whole tenement* (No. 25). 20 acres and 1 acre of mead. John Prein (or Prym) who died in October 1488 left his house and lands to his wife for life with reversion to John Walshe (who was probably his son-in-law and was an executor of his will). This whole tenement had perhaps belonged to a former John Prynne who was a member of the homage in 1422. In January 1501/2 John Walshe surrendered the property to Robert Elyott, an official of Henry VII's court and his wife Joan. After Elyott's death (about 1510) it seems probable that Joan married John Mellyneck (bailiff of the manor court in 1520-33) and that they sold the property to Owen Holland. Holland may then have sold it to Thomas Cooke. Cooke died in 1538 leaving as heir a daughter Katherine who was still a minor. In 1550 Katherine, now the wife of John Hall, was admitted to the tenement (which now included eight cottages). Four months later they sold a half-acre to John Gyldmyn and the remainder to Henry Naylor.

ii. *Half-tenement of free land* (No. 26). 10 acres and ½ acre of mead. This was the free half-tenement that had belonged to Isabel de Binnegates in 1314. It was surrendered to William Walshe by Gilbert Byngate in 1348. It descended in the Walshe family and was inherited from Robert Walshe by John Walshe in 1491. John Walshe promptly sold it to Thomas Denys who was the owner in September 1492. The latter's son Thomas Denys deeded this property in August 1558 to trustees for the parish church – and had the deed noted in the manor rolls. Despite this, Denys's widow and her new husband Nicholas Beneson appear to have sold the property to Henry Naylor – and it was not until the 1620s that Mary Crome's claim to it was challenged by the Vestry. They won their case, but somehow Mary Crome managed to retain the land.*

Naylor had other lands than these two tenements: some from William Pate (see 9 below), some by grant (including 4½ acres of the marsh) and some which is not

---

* For the details of this case see John Cloake, 'The Curious Story of the Church Estate' in *Richmond History* No. 13 (1992), pp.2-16.

identifiable. The difficulty is compounded by the fact that he evidently disposed of some of it (including the marsh) in the years 1589-1602. Of her inheritance from Naylor, Mary Crome sold 3¾ acres to James I for his park, but otherwise she seems to have kept it all until her death in 1636.

✠

## 7. Sir Arthur Gorge's estate

In 1620 Sir Arthur Gorges held Kew Park of 19 acres (not included in the terrier) and a further 8¾ acres in Kew Field. These lands were derived mainly from two tenements:

i. *A tenement of 19 acres* with an acre of mead (No. 27) sold by Thomas Byrkes to Sir Charles Somerset in 1505. When Sir Charles, ennobled as the Earl of Worcester, died in 1526 he left his lands to the widowed Countess for her life with remainder to his son Sir George Somerset. George also inherited the tenement granted to his father in freehold in 1517, together with a 3 acre close, ½ acre in the East Dene and ¼ acre in the West Dene. This enabled him to effect some juggling and consolidation of his lands, concentrating all the freehold into closes on the western side of Kew Field and all the copyhold into a small park at the western end of the Tinderland furlong. Both of these thereafter ceased to be considered as parts of Kew Field. The freehold land was sold, with Worcester's mansion, to the Duke of Suffolk in 1538. The park was inherited by Sir George's son William in 1560 and sold by him to Dr William Awberry in 1566.

ii. *The 'At Ware' half-tenement* of 9 acres in the fields, an extra 1 acre close and ½ acre of mead (tenement No. 28). A member of the 'At Ware' family of Kew is mentioned as early as 1234, and there are many further mentions of the name (which is surely 'at the weir') throughout the 14th and 15th centuries. William at Were inherited the half-tenement from his father Stephen in January 1501/2. His successor in title was Ralph at Ware who seems to have left the land to Joan Adams (probably his daughter) and her husband Thomas. On Joan Adams's death James at Weere became the owner. Between 1578 and 1583 James Were (or Ware – his is the first usage of the name without 'at') disposed of the holding: half an acre went to John Hynde; all the rest save the cottage was sold, in five separate transactions, to Dr William Awberry. In 1587 the cottage was sold to William's son Morgan Awberry.

In that year Dr William Awberry and his wife made over both the park and the lands acquired from Ware to Morgan Awberry and his wife Joan. (It was probably a wedding present.) The park and all but one acre of the Ware lands were sold by the Awberrys to Sir Arthur Gorges in 1605.

William Awberry had also acquired a further acre in Tinderland and another 3 roods in the fields from other sources. These too passed to Gorges, who did, however, give up one half-acre by the edge of the park in 1606.

✠

## 8. *The Smythe and Burd estates (formerly John Bird's)*

The terrier shows Thomas Smythe as holding 10¼ acres, his son Bartholomew Smythe as holding jointly with his wife 12¼ acres, and John Burd and his wife as holding 15 acres. Apart from John Burd's 7½ acres in the Kew Fields which derived from Lydgold's tenement (see at 1, vii above) this property had been part of the estate held by John Bird at the end of Queen Elizabeth's reign.

This estate comprised elements of six former tenements, but these were already becoming fragmented.

In 1587 Nicholas Bird acquired from William Pate 8 acres which had come from Pate's tenements (33 and 34) discussed at 9 below. These were inherited by John Bird. Between 1589 and 1602 Nicholas or John Bird acquired 41 acres and 2½ acres of mead from Henry Harvey and 20 acres and 1 acre of mead from Ezekiel Culverwell. The sources of these were:

i. *A whole tenement* of 20 acres and an acre of mead (No. 29) which was sold by Thomas Vernon to John Pyke, goldsmith in 1492. (Its earlier history has not been traced.)

ii. *A half-tenement* of 10 acres and ½ acre of mead (No. 30) which had belonged in the 1420s to William Constable, then to his son Robert and descended to a John Constable. The latter's heir, William Osburne, died without heirs before his admission to the property, which was then re-granted in 1485 to John Pyke. These two holdings (i) and (ii) were sold by Pyke in 1518 to Owen Holland and his wife Elizabeth. It was probably not this Owen Holland, but a son of the same name, who sold both tenements to Henry Harvey in 1576.

iii. In the meantime Harvey had acquired just over half of another *whole tenement* (No. 31). This had belonged to Elys (or Elias) Hawes, who died about 1501 leaving it to his wife Margaret and then his daughter Margaret. In 1534 the daughter Margaret and her husband Robert Moger sold it to Henry Herford. The latter's son Thomas Herford inherited in 1563 and sold off seven acres two years later. In 1567 William Herford inherited the cottage (next to the *Bell Inn*) and 13 acres, and an acre of mead and at once sold two more acres to William Smythe. In the following year Henry Herford was admitted to 11 acres and one acre of mead. By the 1570s he was spelling his name Harvey rather than Herford. This holding, which, together with i and ii above, amounted to 41 acres and 21 acres of mead, Henry Harvey appears to have sold to one of the Birds between 1589 and 1602.

iv. The *whole tenement* (No. 32) owned by Maud de Binnegates in 1314 probably descended in the family until Thomas Byngate was admitted to it on the death of his mother Joan (widow of John Byngate) in 1529. Thomas passed it on at once to his daughter Sibyl, but on her death in 1539 it was inherited by Thomas's sister Alice and her husband Thomas Lawrence. From them it passed to Robert Lawrence and in 1564 to the latter's brother William. It was probably leased at this time to George Vernon. In December 1565 the tenement was sold by Thomas Foster, a Groom of the Chamber (who was probably acting as an attorney for William Lawrence) to Nicholas Culverwell. That this was the Lawrence tenement becomes clear when on Nicholas's death in 1570 his younger son Nicholas inherited 'a messuage and 20 acres formerly of William Lawrence', and when in 1584 Ezekiel Culverwell was admitted as heir to his brother Nicholas to 'a messuage and 20 acres of land which their father Nicholas Culverwell held from the surrender of William Lawrence'. Between 1589 and 1602 Ezekiel Culverwell sold this tenement to Nicholas or John Bird.

By 1603 the Birds had disposed of 9¾ acres (probably 8 acres to Richard Wright, 1½ to Thomas Smythe and ¼ to Henry Naylor). In 1605-06 John Bird sold off a third of the remainder: 2 acres to Henry Holloway, 8 acres to Thomas Smythe and 11½ acres plus 1½ acres of mead to Sir Robert Wright and his wife Dorothy (see at 3 above). He then in May 1606 surrendered to William Haynes and Thomas Smythe as trustees the remaining 38 acres and 2 acres of mead) 'formerly of William Harvey [*sic* – should probably read 'William Pate and Henry Harvey'] and afterwards [*sic* – 'previously'?] of Owen Holland'.

Haynes and Smythe promptly sold off 8 acres to Alexander Prescott (which were held in 1620 by John Burd (or Bird) and his wife – who was Prescott's widow). In the next six months another 8 acres were sold to Henry Cuckney, half an acre to John Preston and 3 acres and 34½ perches to King James I (for his park). In 1612 Haynes and Smith sold one more acre to John Leaver and the 2 acres of meadow to Sir Arthur Gorges. This left 17 acres which they divided between themselves in April 1613, each getting 8½ acres.

Thomas Smythe had inherited 3 acres from his father William in 1582. He obtained 1¼ acres in 1606 from Robert Edlet (?his father-in-law). In all he received 18 acres from the estates of Nicholas and John Bird. By 1620 he had sold off 10½ acres and had given 2 acres to his daughter-in-law, for his son Bartholomew had married Winifred the daughter of William Haynes. Haynes died before he could be admitted to his share of the residue of the Bird estate and Winifred was his heir. With the addition of another 1¾ acres that Haynes had previously acquired, Bartholomew and Winifred Smythe held 12¼ acres in 1620 while Thomas Smythe held 10¼ acres.

## 9. George Charley's estate – (a) the former Pate estate

William Pate had held one whole tenement and one half-tenement.

i. *A whole tenement* of 20 acres and an acre of mead (No. 33). This had belonged to the Osey family, established in Shene by the first years of the 15th century. Philip Osey (*floruit* 1445-52) and after him John Osey held this tenement, but it then went to John Leghton and his wife Elizabeth and then to Thomas Hart. In 1486, after the surrender of Thomas Hart, William Bracebrigge, a London draper, became owner. He sold it in March 1497/8 to Sir Richard Guilford, Controller of Henry VI's household. Sir Richard died at Jerusalem, on pilgrimage, in 1506, and his son Henry (later one of Henry VIII's closest courtiers) sold the property in 1509 to Matthew Clyderowe (or Clithero). From Clyderowe the tenement passed to Richard Broke and then in 1530 to John Pate. William Pate was pronounced heir to his father in 1536, but John Pate's widow Anne held the property for a while with her second husband (?Thomas) Aleyn.

ii. *A half-tenement (No. 34).* A John Yong (probably the ferry keeper – see page 48) held this tenement in the mid-15th century, followed by William Hunt. Hunt died in 1486. His widow Joan, who then married a Hosey (?or Osey), left the property in 1497 to her son Edmund Hunt, who sold it to Hugh a Deane in 1502: It then went to John Sharpe, then John Crewe who in 1531 surrendered the tenement to his wife Elizabeth for her life, with reversion to John Pate. William Pate became owner in February 1544/5 on the death of Elizabeth Stede (formerly Crewe).

From these properties William Pate sold 3 acres to Henry Naylor in 1557/8 (see 6), 10 acres to Thomas Lord Buckhurst in 1578 (see 4), and 8 acres to Nicholas Bird in 1587 (see 8). When his son John had to be admitted retrospectively in 1606 he surrendered to Ralph Fletcher 9¾ acres of land and 1 acre of meadow. (An additional ¾ acre had been acquired from an unknown source.) All but the meadow and ¼ acre of land were sold by Ralph's son William Fletcher to George Charley in 1615 and 1616.

## 10. George Charley's estate – (b) the former Gisby estate

Of George Charley's total holding in 1620 of 24 acres, as recorded in the terrier, nearly two-thirds came from two tenements which had been Thomas Gisby's. These were:

i. *Thomas's tenement* of 20 acres and an acre of mead (tenement No. 35). A William Thomas held a whole tenement in 1314. There are various mentions of members of the Thomas family in the manor rolls of the 14th and early 15th centuries.

ii. *Freeman's tenement* of 20 acres and an acre of mead (tenement No. 36). A William Freeman was mentioned in the manor rolls in 1415-22.

It is possible that these two tenements, always in one ownership from 1491 to 1581 (see below) came together shortly after 1422 in the hands of Robert Kentford. In 1445 John Kentford, holding the lands formerly of Robert Kentford, died and his sister Cecily was pronounced as his heir. In the following year she was admitted as heir to Robert and John to 'two messuages and two virgates'. However no link can be positively established between the Kentford holding and the next entries.

William Blackett, a member of the homage in 1485, surrendered to Richard Brampton and his wife Elizabeth in 1491 a tenement and 20 acres of land and an acre of mead 'formerly of Richard Thomas', together with another 20 acres of land 'parcel of Freeman's tenement'. (The cottage and garden 'called Freeman's' was by then in separate ownership.) For the next 90 years (despite a lawsuit over the ownership of the lands called Freeman's brought by William's grandson John Blackett in 1542) the property descended in the Brampton family: from Richard to Thomas in 1520-22, to Thomas's son John in 1528, to the next generation John in 1532, to another Thomas in 1572. In 1581 this last Thomas Brampton surrendered 40 acres of arable and 2 acres of mead to Thomas Gisby.

By the time of Gisby's death in March 1607/8 he had disposed of 21¾ acres – mostly in small parcels (which were the source of many of the small holdings in the fields listed in the terrier). I believe these disposals (several of them between 1589 and 1602) to have been as follows:

– 2 acres went to William Boone in 1590. By 1620, having sold ½ acre to the King for the park, Boone held 1½ acres.
– 4¾ acres went to Ralph Tye between 1589 and 1602. In 1620 John Keene held 4 acres and Thomas Wright ¾ acres.
– 6 acres went to Nicholas Saunders between 1589 and 1602. In 1620 Walter Hickman held 5 acres and George Marshall 1 acre.
– ½ acre went to John Jewett. It was held by Giles Hill in 1620.
– 1½ acres went to Thomas Bun – also held by Giles Hill in 1620.
– 2 acres were sold to Thomas Tye in 1605. Of these, two separate half-acres were held by Henry Collins in 1620 and two other half-acres by George Rutter.
– ½ acre was sold to Seth Goldstone in 1605 – still held by him in 1620.
– two sales were made to the King for his new park: ½ acre and 20 perches in February 1605/6, and ½ acre and 31 perches a year later.
– ½ acre was sold to George Hudson in 1606 – held by him in 1620.
– 2 acres were sold to Joan Harrold in 1607 – held by Judith Bayley in 1620.

The remaining estate was inherited by Thomas's son, another Thomas Gisby in 1608. Apart from 1 acre and 3 roods sold by him to Richard Lovell (of which Lovell still held one acre in 1620, while Thomas Radford held 3 roods) all the rest was sold to the Fletcher family: 8½ acres to Ralph Fletcher in 1608 and 8 acres plus 2 acres of meadow to Ralph's son William in 1611. These were all surrendered by William Fletcher to George Charley in 1615-16.

From these known transactions George Charley should have held 9½ acres of former Pate land and 16½ acres of former Gisby land in 1620. In fact he only held 24 acres. I have not resolved this discrepancy.

# 10

# *Inns and Taverns in Richmond in the Sixteenth and Seventeenth Centuries*

RICHMOND WAS ALWAYS well supplied with inns, taverns and alehouses. Strictly speaking, these were three different types of establishment. Inns provided overnight accommodation for visitors as well as food and drink. Taverns were in origin houses where wine and spirits were sold and which in most cases also provided meals. Alehouses were the poor relations – supplying only ales and beers. But even by the 16th century the distinctions were becoming blurred. Larger alehouses were serving food and using the name of tavern, some taverns with a room or two to let were calling themselves 'inns'. It is often uncertain to which category a licensed house in Richmond should belong – frequently we only know its name and location and perhaps some of its proprietors. The latter may be described as 'innkeeper' or 'innholder', which is clear enough – as is the description 'alehouse keeper'. A 'common tippler of beer' is clearly at best an alehouse keeper. But in most cases they are 'victuallers' or 'licensed victuallers' and their establishments might have been either taverns or alehouses – or even inns. So in this account of these early 'public houses' (a term which did not come into general use until the 19th century) the terms are used quite loosely.

✛

On 12 May 1634 the Justices of the Peace for Surrey addressed a letter to the Privy Council. At their last session, they recalled, they had had letters from the Lords of the Council 'for suppressing the multitude of alehouses in that county'. However they had already issued licences for Kingston and Elmbridge hundreds – for 25 alehouses in 15 parishes. They went on to note that 'within Richmond, by reason of the Prince's Court often residing there and being a place of much resort and recreation for divers gentlemen and citizens, of the 25 they have licensed ten there'.[1]

It is possible to identify with reasonable accuracy these ten inns, taverns or alehouses. The first three such establishments of which there is any trace in the records had already vanished: the *Star and Garter* at which some court officials dined together at Christmas 1509[2] makes no other appearance in the records; nor does the *George* at which Sir Edward Guildford obtained hay and oats on a visit to Richmond in 1519.[3] Their locations are unidentified. The *Bell*, however, which stood on the site of Nos. 15-17 George Street, is first mentioned in the Richmond manor rolls in 1535 and last mentioned in 1596.[4] Its last owner, Lawrence Snow, was executed at Kingston in 1592 for horse-stealing. His property was forfeited. The *Bell* appears to have been regranted to Robert Clarke, but there is no further indication of its use as an inn.* Its proudest hour was in October 1581 when it was one of the two Richmond inns taken over for the accommodation of the suite accompanying the Duke of Anjou on his visit to Richmond to seek the Queen's hand in marriage.[5]

Thirteen more inns and taverns are identifiable in Richmond before 1634 and ten of these were still in business in that year. They are probably the ten then licensed (although it is possible that this number included one or two which do not appear in the manor rolls until a later date).†

Plate 15

The *Red Lyon*, at the corner of what are now George Street and Red Lion Street, was Richmond's main inn in the 16th century. It was also taken over for the Duke of Anjou's suite in 1581. Although it is first mentioned by name (as the *Lyon*) in the records in 1563 when its ownership was transferred from Harmon Goldstone to Alexander Slany,[6] its origin as an inn was probably shortly after the admission of Harmon Goldstone and his wife to the property (then simply described as 'a cottage and garden' in 1538).[7] By 1581 its name had become the *Red Lyon*.

The inn had bad times as well as good. In 1630 it was confiscated by the lord because its owner had 'allowed it to go to ruin', but 18 months later it was regranted to the late owner's son.[8] It had evidently recovered by 1638 when William Crowne and William Dugdale were created respectively Rouge Dragon Pursuivant and Blanch Lyon Pursuivant Extraordinary at the inn.[9] In 1664, it was rated for 12 hearths.[10] It was empty again in 1734 and '35, but in 1736 a lease was taken by Henry Fudge.[11] The *Evening Post* for 28 February 1736/7 contained a notice that 'the old *Red Lion Inn* ... kept by Henry Fudge, peruke-maker, is now opened where Gentlemen, Ladies and others will be entertained in the best manner'. However, its days were numbered. It closed for good in 1739-40, though a part of it became briefly the *Plough* tavern which continued until 1748.[12]

The *Lily Pot* was probably established about 1560. In 1553 Robert Stockden was admitted to the property, at the northern corner of Brewer's Lane and what is now George Street, as 'a cottage and garden'.[13] In 1567 he surrendered 'the messuage called the *Lily Pott* and garden adjoining'.[14] By 1624 it had become 'the *Three Pigeons* and *Lillypott*, occupied by widow Tucker and containing 11 spaces, viz: hall, parlour, kitchen,

---

* The manor rolls from 1589 to 1602 are lost. By 1606 the property was in the hands of Robert Clarke, a lawyer and steward of the manor.
† It should be noted that the dates given below for 'the first mention' of various inns may be many years after their actual establishment.

buttery, shop, cellar and five chambers, with three stables and a courtyard'.[15] It was rated for 11 hearths in 1664. The name, sometimes just as the *Three Pigeons*, remained unchanged until the end of the century, when it was changed to the *Castle*.[16] In 1710 it was sold as 'the messuage in Brewer's Lane, occupied by James Seymour, formerly called the *Three Pigeons and Lilly Pot* and lately called the *Castle and Trumpet*'.[17] Three years later it was purchased by Lady Vanderputt as a site for the new charity school.[18]

The *Cross Keys* on Richmond Green (site of Nos. 10-12) belonged to Thomas Denys who died *circa* 1558. Whether it was then an inn or not is uncertain, but by 1572 his son John Denys sold the reversion to it as 'the messuage called the *Cross Keys* now occupied by Nicholas Beneson' (who was his mother's second husband).[19] By 1626 it was described as the house 'which was the *Cross Keys* now occupied by William Smith, parish clerk',[20] so presumably it had ceased to be a tavern by then. The business, however, had been transferred to another house on the Green (site of Nos. 18-20) in the same ownership, which is mentioned under this name in the manor rolls for 1644 and 1650,[21] so the latter could have been one of the 1634 alehouses.

The *Goat*, on the site where Nos. 1-5 Sheen Road now stand, was first mentioned in the manor rolls in 1583.[22] It appears to have closed just before the 1634 licensing as it was still 'the messuage called the sign of the *Goat* with barns, stables, outbuildings and an orchard' in May 1633,[23] but was 'heretofore known by the name or sign of the *Goat*' on 30 April 1634.[24]

The *Queen's Arms* at the corner of what are now George Street and King Street (No. 81 George Street, now part of Dickins and Jones) is first mentioned in June 1603.[25] At the end of the 1650s it seems to have been split into a number of small separate residential units, but they all remained in the same ownership and had been reunited as an inn, under the new name of the *Waterman's Arms*, by 1671.[26] By 1703 the name had changed again to the *Queen's Head* and under this name it survived (with a complete rebuilding in 1854) until 1960 when it was purchased by Gosling's department store.

Opposite the *Queen's Head* at Nos. 1-2 King Street stood the *Feathers*, which began its existence as the *Golden Hind*. The reference to the ship in which Sir Francis Drake circumnavigated the world in 1577-80 suggests that it may have dated from the 1580s, but there may also be a punning reference to the owners of the property at that time: Augustine Hynde and then his son John Hynde. The first mention of the *Golden Hind* in the manor rolls is not, however, until 1607.[27] At an unknown date between 1611 and 1633 the name was changed to the *Feathers*, presumably an allusion to the crest of the Prince of Wales.[28] (Richmond Palace was the seat first of Henry, Prince of Wales until 1612 and then from 1617 until he ascended the throne in 1625 of Charles, Prince of Wales.) The *Feathers* was assessed for seven hearths in 1664. In the 18th century a large assembly room was built at the rear of the inn. It went out of business in 1778 and the premises were divided up as shops and offices in the 1780s. The building was demolished for road widening in 1907.

*Head of a Tudor door from the* Feathers Inn *(Museum of Richmond).*

The first reference to an alehouse in Middle Row, the little island of property between Sheen Road and Lower George Street, occurs in 1610 when Ralph White was granted 'part of a mansion house containing four rooms and a shop ... now occupied by John Keele, blacksmith, and Richard Coles, alehouse keeper'.[29] White promptly sold the property to John Keele. In 1647 Keele was granted a licence to let it for 21 years to Thomas Lucas, under the name of the '*Flour de Louis*' (?*Fleur de Lys*).[30] The licence to let was extended to 31 years in 1656.[31] There is no real evidence of its continued use as an alehouse, but John Tinsley, a 'tapster', was one of the residents of Middle Row in 1664. However, it is a probable candidate for the 1634 list.

There is a single reference in the manor rolls in 1614 to a 'messuage with alerooms' on the site of 29 George Street.[32]

The *Crown*, at 16-17 the Green, is first mentioned in 1614.[33] It was still described as such in 1636,[34] but in 1639 it was 'anciently called the *Crown*'.[35] It may, however, have had a new lease of life as it appears in 1653 as 'anciently called the *Crown* and now the *George*'.[36] There is no further reference to this house by either of these names.

The *Angel*, at 12-14 King Street, belonged to Seth Goldstone in 1618 and then had II rooms.[37] In 1664 it was assessed for 12 hearths. By the end of the century it had changed its name to the *Half Moon* and was being redeveloped as three separate houses,[38] which were sold in 1707 to Nathaniel Rawlins.[39] It is not clear whether there was a hiatus (other than that caused by the rebuilding) in the use as an alehouse at this time, but by 1724 the centre one of the three new houses (13 King Street) was a tavern called the *Thistle and Crown* (or *Crown and Thistle*).[40] It was damaged by fire in 1753, but continued under this sign until 1786 when it changed its name to the *New Ship*.[41] The *New Ship* was finally closed in 1893.

The *King's Arms* at 4-6 Brewer's Lane was first mentioned in 1619 when it was bought by Reed Corderey, a brewer of Kingston.[42] Its last appearance in the rolls as the '*King's Arms*' was in 1650.[43] On the next transfer of ownership (in 1665) it was simply described as 'a cottage'.

There are four references in the period 1624-1633 to 'a messuage called the *Flying Horse*' on the north side of a plot of empty ground which lay to the north of the *Angel*.[44] This had been in the ownership of members of the Wright family since 1595, but in 1632 it was sold to Sir William Parkhurst[45] who incorporated it with its two northerly neighbours to form the original mansion that later became 'Old Palace Place'.

The *Black Bull* on the site of 22-24 King Street was first named in the manor rolls in 1626 when Reginald Hadwell (who had inherited the house from his father in 1615) died and his brother Nicholas Hadwell became owner.[46] When Hadwell sold it to John Gregory in 1633, the *Black Bull* was in the occupation of Robert Arnold, who was fined at the Court Leet in 1637 for selling musty beer.[47] Arnold died in 1642.[48] In 1656 John Gregory sold the *Black Bull* to Thomas Eling, a butcher.[49] It seems that Eling converted the premises into a butcher's shop, building a slaughterhouse in the yard; there is no further mention of the *Black Bull* after 1656 (but the house was assessed for nine hearths in 1664).

It would appear, therefore, that the ten taverns licensed in 1634 may have been: *Red Lyon*, *Three Pigeons and Lilypot*, *Cross Keys*, *Queen's Arms*, *Feathers*, *Fleur de Lys*, *Crown*, *Angel*, *King's Arms* and *Black Bull*.

The next tavern to make a (fleeting) appearance in the 1630s was the *White Lion* (up an alley behind 51 George Street), which is mentioned once in 1638.[50] There are no other references to this name in any of the records of changes of ownership in the 17th or 18th centuries, but in 1721 and 1741 known victuallers were named as its occupants and comparison of the licensing records from 1724 and the rate books from 1726 onwards establishes that it was still called the *White Lion* in 1734, though changing its name to the *Swan* in 1735.[51] It and the adjacent buildings were rebuilt in 1751-53 when it ceased to be a tavern.

There may have been an alehouse at 5 King Street in the 1630s and '40s. William Gray, 'a common tippler of beer' (the word 'tippler' is here used in the sense of beerseller, not that of imbiber) was fined in 1642 for selling beer below strength.[52] His home (inherited from his father of the same name in 1634) until 1647 was a cottage at 5 King Street,[53] but this is never described as an alehouse in the manor records. (In 1658 Gray was licensee of the *Queen's Arms*.)

The *Swan*, at 25 King Street, was a more substantial tavern. It makes its first appearance, between the *Queen's Arms* and the *Black Bull*, in 1644 when John King (listed as an alehouse-keeper in 1646) mortgaged the property.[54] It was assessed for seven hearths in 1664. It continued in business until 1700 when it was inherited by the six-year-old Francis Russell[55] (grandson of the victualler who had held the licence – but was not the owner – in the 1650s). Francis Russell's mother and guardian rented it to a poulterer (in occupation by 1703) and by 1708 it was described as 'formerly the *Swan*'.[56]

The *Rose and Crown*, which stood at the corner of George Street and Duke Street (41-43 George Street and 1 Duke Street) is first mentioned in the manor rolls in 1653.[57] It is one of the few taverns in Richmond for which the names of many of the publicans before 1724 can be positively identified: George Wilde 1653, his widow Margaret Wilde 1654, Ralph Ditchfield 1663-4, John Darley 1677-84, Moses Campion for some years up to 1720. It had eight hearths in 1664. It continued until 1787, having by then quite extensive stabling at the rear, but by 1790 it had become 'the late *Rose and Crown*'.[58] Its name was transferred to the *Angel* in Middle Row about 1805.

The *White Horse* at 22 The Green first appears in 1658,[59] but was probably opened a few years earlier. It had ten hearths in 1664. It is uncertain when the name and licence was transferred to the premises in George Street which later became the *Greyhound*. The house on the Green was still listed as the *White Horse* in the manor survey of 1703; but the old house was pulled down in 1725 to be replaced by the pair of houses which still stand on the site.[60]

The *Glass Bottle* at 4 King Street was probably opened in the early 1650s though it is not mentioned by name in the manor rolls until 1680. Christopher Towne, who was described as an 'alehouse keeper' in 1646 and as a 'victualler' in 1658,[61] acquired the premises in 1650[62] and was in occupation of them himself in 1656.[63] There were six hearths in 1664. Between 1683 and 1691 the name was changed to the *Ship*.[64] This first *Ship* closed about 1720, when the name was taken over by the former *Six Bells* next door (see below).

With the *Plough*, first mentioned in 1659, we come to the earliest Richmond tavern which has a continuous history as licensed premises up to the present day. Standing at the corner of Ferry Hill and the Petersham road, the *Plough* was purchased by George Layton, victualler, in April 1659[65] – but he was already in occupation, so may have started the business some years earlier. It was quite a small alehouse with only four hearths in 1664. The name was still the *Plough* in 1702,[66] but by 1733 it had become the *King's Head*.[67] It was rebuilt as a much larger house about 1750 and was again enlarged in the 1770s and the 1830s;[68] and it continued to flourish as the *King's Head* until 1967 when the name was changed to *Christie's Tavern*. It became '*Joe Beaulais*' in 1988 and just '*Joe's*' in 1991.

A former *King's Head*, just below the *Plough* on Ferry Hill, appears on the evidence of trade tokens issued in 1666-67 to have had a brief existence as an alehouse.

Thomas Cogdell, who in 1654 acquired the property on the south side of the top of what was later called Compass Hill[69] was given in 1664 a grant of extra waste there 'at the north end of his tenement called the *Spread Eagle*'.[70] By the 1730s, when the house was owned by one of Cogdell's grandsons, it had changed its name to the *Three Compasses*.[71] The name was transferred in 1782-83 to the former *Rising Sun* tavern at the bottom of Compass Hill. There is no evidence that the old *Three Compasses* ever reopened as an alehouse, although it had continued associations with the liquor

*Plate 13*

*The only known contemporary depiction of houses in Richmond in the mid-16th century is in these details from Wyngaerde's drawing of Richmond Palace in 1561-2. The left-hand one shows the houses on the sites of Old Palace Terrace, and from Old Friars to Friars' Lane, then comes the banqueting house and corner tower of the Palace. On the right are houses on the sites of Garrick Close, the end of Old Palace Lane and Cedar Grove. (Ashmolean Museum, Oxford)*

*The Richmond ferry – a drawing by James Marris, c.1770. Although this is a late 18th-century drawing, the technology would have been much the same in the 15th or 16th centuries. (Private collection)*

Plate 14

*Houses beside Richmond Palace – looking towards the parish church (on the right). Detail from an engraving by Wenceslaus Hollar, 1638.*

*Some parts of Richmond in 1635 can be seen in this detail from Moses Glover's map of Isleworth Hundred at Syon House. On the left, between the tree and the armorial obelisk, is the parish church and what are probably houses facing the Green and George Street. To the right is the Green with the Palace, and houses along its north-west side where they back onto James I's Park. The remains of the Shene Charterhouse, still vaguely monastic in layout, are farther right. In the south corner of the Green Mr. Kirkham's mansion stands on the site of Old Palace Terrace; and George Street, King Street, the scaffold sign of the Red Lyon Inn, Water Lane and Ferry Hill are readily identifiable. The 'lower almshouses' are just above Ferry Hill, then the road continues up 'Richmond Banke' to the windmill. By the riverside is the tile kiln. (By kind permission of His Grace the Duke of Northumberland)*

*Plate 15*

*The* Red Lyon *as shown in 'The Prospect of Richmond' (1726).*

*Courtyard of the* Greyhound Inn, *c.1800, watercolour by Jean Claude Nattes. (LBRUT Orleans House – Ionides Collection)*

*Plate 16*

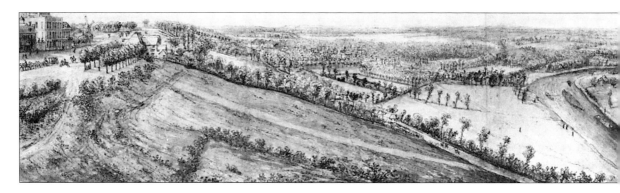

*Leonard Knyff,* View from Richmond Hill, *pen and brown ink, with grey wash. (Private collection)*

*Detail of a view from Richmond Hill by J.H. Muntz, c.1760, showing a game of cricket being played on the waste ground between Doughty House and the top end of the lane across Pesthouse Common. That waste ground is now the forecourts of the* Richmond Hill *and* Richmond Gate *hotels. (Present ownership untraced)*

business. It was owned very briefly in 1805-06 by the brewers W. and E. J. Collins[72] and its owner from 1806, Thomas Taylor, was licensee of the *White Cross* in 1817 and 1818.

The *Six Bells* at 3 King Street was the forerunner of today's *Old Ship*. It was first mentioned in the manor rolls in 1682.[73] It changed its name to the *Ship* by 1720,[74] and became the *Old Ship* after the *New Ship* adopted that name in 1786. It was at about this time that the *Ship* took over a part of the former *Feathers* and expanded to occupy both 2 and 3 King Street. It has flourished as the 'Old Ship' to the present day.

The *Magpye* in Brewer's Lane (now the *Britannia*) is another tavern which has a continuous history back to the 17th century. It first appeared in the manorial records in 1690.[75] The change of name occurred about 1869[76] – perhaps when a new lease was taken by the brewers Phillips and Wigan. Owned by the Crutchley family since 1773 it was sold to Watneys in 1907.[77]

A small alehouse on the top of the hill (on the site of No. 1 The Terrace) had almost as many names as years of existence. It is first mentioned as the *Adam and Eve* in 1693, and again in October 1696.[78] But by January 1696/7, when Nos. 2 and 3 The Terrace were already in course of construction, there are two references to it by different names. Michael Pew, the builder of Nos. 2 and 3, bought it under the name of the '*Half Moon and Key*' – but at the same manor court it is also called the '*Cross Keys*'.[79] There was no time or need to resolve the problem; it was promptly demolished to be replaced by 1 The Terrace.

That completes the tally of taverns and alehouses in Richmond which can be proved to have existed before 1700, but there are a few others, the first mention of which is found in the first years of the 18th century and which seem likely to have been established shortly before the end of the 17th century.

The first of these is the *Two Brewers* at 17 George Street (now W.H. Smith). This appears as 'a messuage occupied by Robert Biggs' on 1 January 1700/1.[80] Biggs, who died in 1715,[81] is known from his will to have been a victualler. By 1724-33, when the occupant was Richard Bonsey,[82] the house can be positively identified as the *Two Brewers*. It appears to have been rebuilt in 1735-36.[83] By 1757 it had changed its name to the *Artichoke*.[84] (It gave this name to Artichoke Alley, the narrow passage between Red Lion Street and George Street that was swept away to be merged with Victoria Place in 1909.) In the rate book for 1860 it is still named as the *Artichoke* but in a directory issued in that year and in the 1861 census it had become the *Forester's Arms*. It continued under the latter name until 1913 and was then taken over by Henekey's (wine and spirit merchants) as a shop.

The *Dog Inn* at 28 Hill Street was flourishing by 1702 when the depositions in a case concerning allegations of a plot against Queen Anne contain references to an 'accidental meeting' there.[85] This was a freehold property and it is uncertain who owned the property in 1702, let alone when it was developed as an inn. It was already quite a large establishment when portrayed in the 'Prospect of Richmond' engraving in 1726. By 1746 it had changed its name to the *Talbot*.[86] By the late 19th century the *Talbot* was one of the town's principal hotels, but it closed in 1908-09. Part of its site was occupied by the Talbot Cinema, built in 1911, and then by the new super-cinema (now the Odeon) built in 1930.

The *White Horse* at 22-24 George Street was listed in the manor survey of 1703 as a house belonging to William Moody (who inherited the premises from his father Matthew in that year).[87] By 1726 it had been renamed the *Greyhound* – probably after

*Plate 15b*

rebuilding. (An early 20th-century advertisement for the *Greyhound Hotel* claims that it was established in 1685, but there is no evidence that it was a tavern in Matthew Moody's time.) It is, however, interesting that the first known licensees of the *White Horse* in George Street were Edward Trippett and then his widow Mary (whose last year as licensee was 1724), while recent licensees of the *White Horse* on the Green were Thomas Trippett (died *circa* 1688) and then his widow Elizabeth – possibly Edward's parents. The *Greyhound* had developed by 1825 to become 'the principal inn in the town'.[88] It was further enlarged in the 1830s and '40s.[89] A Masonic Hall or Assembly Room was already a feature by 1863[90] and in 1869 this hall was rebuilt on a grander scale at the rear of the premises. The *Greyhound* closed as a hotel in 1923 when it was purchased by Messrs Short, wine and spirit merchants. The building was restored as offices in 1982-3.

The *White Lyon* on Richmond Hill (on the site of The Wick) was presumably one of the three cottages sold by Ann Eling to William Hickey in 1700.[91] A manor roll entry of March 1703 states that widow Eling (mother of William Eling) had held 'the messuage called the *White Lyon* on Richmond Hill, sold to William Hickey',[92] although the manor survey made in that year has two separate entries for 'Widow Eling (mother of William) – *White Lyon* on Richmond Hill' and for 'William Hickey – 3 little cottages bought of widow Eling'.[93] By the mid-1720s this had become the *Bull's Head* alehouse.[94] Hickey leased it to the brewer Edward Collins, and it was one of the properties left in his will (dated 1727) to his trustees. The *Bull's Head* can be seen in an engraving by Augustin Heckel to be a ramshackle wooden building. In 1775 it was demolished by the trustees who leased out its site, on which The Wick was then built.

The *Bear*, at 50 The Quadrant, was listed in the 1703 survey in the name of Mary Lever as 'the house with the sign of the *Bear* against the Pond in Richmond'.[95] The house, however, belonged (from 1680 to 1722) to John Gardiner, a baker,[96] so Mary was presumably the lessee and licensee; but there is no indication as to the date when the premises first became a tavern. The name was changed to the *Brown Bear* in 1804.[97] About 1966 its status changed from a public house to a licensed restaurant, renamed *The Garden* in 1982. In 1985 it ceased to be licensed premises and became the Next store.

# II

## *Where did all the Islands Go?*

THE RICHMOND MANOR ROLLS contain references to several islands which no longer exist as such. Six of them can be accounted for as having been incorporated into the river bank. Others have joined up with adjacent islands to become parts of larger units (particularly in the case of Isleworth Ait). Ait, also spelled eyot – and anciently eight, eite or ayte (or even nayte) – is a word particularly used on the River Thames for a small island. The manor records appear to call them aits or islands or 'pieces of land in the River Thames' according to the whim of the clerk at the time. Some of them were in truth no more than bullrush or osier beds.

Only a few ever had buildings on them; for the most part they served two economic purposes. Some were used as a base for fishing; others as a source of supply for the rushes and osiers which were the staple of the basket-makers' trade (an important one in the days before paper bags or plastic wrappings!).

There are a few early references to islands which cannot be positively identified. In 1405 William Osey, who lived probably in a cottage in Hill Street on what is today the northern side of Whittaker Avenue, was granted 'a parcel of land in the Thames formerly of John Aleyn'.[1] There is no evidence as to the location of this – but it is not impossible that it was the nearby ait at the bottom end of what is now Water Lane, where the little Mochebrook stream ran into the Thames. Another unidentified island was the 'parcel of land in the Thames called Nayte' which was owned in 1550 by Christopher Hamond of Isleworth and his wife Elizabeth, who were in that year granted a licence to let the island for 20 years to John Arnold.[2] As the owner was an Isleworth man this may have been one of the several Richmond islands now incorporated into Isleworth Ait.

Some other early entries concern islands at Kew, where the island appears to have replaced the normal 'meadow' element of a whole tenement. These can, at least tentatively, be linked to the later history of the Kew islands and are therefore considered below.

It would be interesting to try to trace all the vanished islands between, say, Kingston and Kew, such as the Crow Ait (Crowett or Crowell) which was part of the manor of Ham and was incorporated into Teddington Lock, or the small sliver of land alongside

Glover's Island which existed until well into the 19th century. Several islands were absorbed by the Twickenham river bank. However, only those islands which belonged to the manor of Richmond really come within the scope of this work. They are considered below in geographical sequence, starting upstream. Fuller details of their ownership can be found in Appendix 8.

We should begin, however, with a Petersham island for it was right by the manor boundary and became part of a Richmond property. In 1636 its owner, William Perkins of Petersham, was 'presented' in the Richmond manor court for encroaching on land which was part of Richmond Common 'lying next Petersham' in order to 'augment his eight at Petersham'.[3]

Perkins was noted as paying 4d. quit rent for an 'eight' in the survey of Petersham made in January 1649/50.[4] This island had been taken into the river bank by the time that it was acquired, on behalf of the Duke of Montagu, by the Rev. Cutts Barton: 'land abutting north and north-west on the Thames, east on the common sewer and land of John Perkins, south on land of John Perkins and on a part of Petersham meadows now enclosed, containing on the north side 280 feet, at the east end 45 feet and on the south side 270 feet, which was formerly an island or parcel of willow ground occupied by Ralph Platt fisherman, but is now together with the said part of Petersham meadows enclosed in the garden of the Duke of Montagu'.[5] This is now part of Buccleuch Gardens.

A similar fate befell the next island northwards, which also lay close inshore, just off the ancient Church Close (now the site of the Bingham Hall Hotel and Nos. 1-4 The Paragon in Petersham Road). This was granted in 1506 to one Richard Richardson as 'a small island, formerly Thorne's, in the Thames near the highway to Kingston'.[6] (Members of the Thorne family appear as manorial tenants from 1413 to 1452 but there is no specific mention of their island in the few surviving rolls.) Of Richardson's disposal of the island there is no existing record; but in 1542 it was surrendered by Robert Fawkon to Augustine Hynde as 'an ayte in the south part of Richmond near the highway to Petersham'.[7] Like most of Hynde's lands it passed through the ownership of the Portman family into that of the Earls of Ancram. In 1659 the second Earl presented it to trustees for the poor of Richmond as 'half an acre of ground' between 'the Thames on the west and the parish land adjoining the highway to Petersham on the east'.[8] Evidently it had by then been reclaimed within the river bank. It was added to Church Close and lost all separate identity. The Earl's gift to the poor was equally lost sight of, for the 'Church lands' (of which the Church Close was a part) were an endowment for maintenance of the Church, not for the benefit of the poor.

What is today called 'Corporation Island', just downstream of Richmond Bridge, has a continuous history traceable back to a grant to John Standen in 1602.[9] It was then called 'the Bullrush Bed near the Ferry Place' and later 'the Bullrush Bed opposite

Water Lane'. It was five perches in width (about 80 feet) and its area in 1771 was given as 1 acre and 20 perches. It was acquired by the Duke of Queensberry in 1802.[10]

Just beyond this, but very close to the Surrey bank, was another ait at the foot of Water Lane itself, probably lying within the mouth of the former 'Mochebrooke' stream. Already by 1606 it was described as 'land formerly called an eight on which Robert Bayley waterman built a house and converted the residue into a wharf'.[11] It seems likely that a further grant in this area of '30 rods of waste on the Thames at the end of Town Lane [another name for Water Lane]', made in 1638 to Samuel Chambers,[12] was also a former ait or bullrush bed, and that the Mochebrooke entered the Thames through a marshy patch with two small islands in it.

Bayley's wharf and house – and the grant to Chambers – must have been on the east side of Water Lane, and the house, if not the wharf, appears to have stood where Riverside House is today – a little above Richmond's 'harbour', the launching ramp for boats and (in the days before the building of Richmond lock and weir) the way up for carts when barges had to be unloaded in the mud at low tide. The western side of this little inlet was the 'town wharf'. A parcel of land by the Thames on the western side of the end of the way from the Quaterelmes to the Thames' (i.e. Water Lane) was granted by Queen Elizabeth in 1586 to William Awberry and others 'to build a wharf for the inhabitants'.[13] A grant of adjacent waste land by the river in 1610 to Thomas Redriffe leads one to wonder whether Awberry and his colleagues carried out their charge or whether the job was left to Robert Bayley, for the land granted is said to abut south on 'the town wharf, now called Bayley's wharf'.[14] It is, however, clear from its subsequent history that Bayley's own property was not where the town wharf was built.

Just a little further north, lying close to the river bank, by the Palace grounds, were three small aits. They were first mentioned in the grant of the Shene manor house to the Carmelite Friars in 1315;[15] they then vanish from historical notice until they were granted in 1542 to John Lovell, the keeper of the Palace gardens.[16] In 1604 they were claimed by the heirs of Sir Hugh Portman who were, however, unable to produce sufficient evidence to uphold their claim in the manor court.[17] They never reappear in the manor records and were almost certainly absorbed in the reclamation of land from the river supervised by Inigo Jones in 1610-11.*

The two very small aits which today lie in midstream opposite the site of the Palace are the remains of one larger ait – which was itself the accretion of three smaller ancient ones. The most southerly of the three was granted in 1560 to Massie Standen;[18] the central one, which was the largest – 30 perches in length by 6 perches in width – and probably the one on which a pavilion had been built for Richard II, was granted to Edward Standen in 1580.[19] These two had become joined into one, in the ownership of Elias Standen, by 1669.[20] This was sold to a trustee for the Earl of

* See *Palaces and Parks* Vol 1, pp.184-187.

Cholmondeley in 1740,[21] and passed from him to Francis Earl Brooke, together with Cholmondeley House, in 1756.[22]

The northernmost ait of the three, 16 by 10 perches, was granted to Augustine Redding in March 1618/9.[23] By 1760, when this ait was sold by the heir of Thomas Perkins, waterman and fisherman, to Earl Brooke it had become 'part of an ayte, abutting south on the other part of the ayte ... now belonging to Earl Brooke'.[24] So the merger into one island seems to have occurred between 1740 and 1760. The channels between these three aits must have been very narrow. Moses Glover in his map of Isleworth Hundred made in 1635 shows only one island with an area of two acres. John Rocque's map of 1745 again shows one island – but by then this was probably correct – stretching from opposite Cholmondeley House to opposite the site of Asgill House.

It is said that it was the Duke of Queensberry (owner from 1804) who then cut the island in two, after which the tide rapidly diminished the size of the two parts.[25] Perhaps the Duke was seeking some relief from the monotony of his view – he is credited (by Wilberforce) with the grumbling comment: 'What is there to make so much of in the Thames? I am quite weary of it; there it goes, flow, flow, flow, always the same.' But the island had already been much reduced in size (from more than seven roods to just over two roods) by 1771; it was still described as one ayte of 2 roods 9 perches in area when surrendered to the King, together with the Bullrush Bed, by Queensberry's heirs in 1831.[26]

Plate 8

The reuse of a previous description is not, however, proof that the property had not changed; and, although it is not always very reliable, artistic evidence may be of some help in identifying when the division took place. A painting by Joseph Farington, engraved in 1793 as an illustration for Boydell's *History of the River Thames*, shows one quite small island with a clump of large trees at each end – and the Bullrush Bed with only scrub vegetation. In William Westall's views published by Rodwell and Martin in 1823, this island appears to be accompanied by an even smaller, treeless, one between it and the Bullrush Bed; and the same feature can be seen in a lithograph by T.N. Baynes published in the same year. But by 1828, when some new Westall views were used to illustrate Ackermann's *A Picturesque Tour of the River Thames*, three islands are clearly depicted (including the Bullrush Bed), all with trees, and the north-westerly one has only one clump of trees left on it. So the attribution to Queensberry of the division may well be correct.

The Ordnance Survey map of the 1860s shows the two tiny aits of today, but also marks shoals, which would have been exposed at low tide, covering most of the area of the former island. The two small aits, together with Bullrush Bed soon to be renamed Corporation Island, were sold to the Richmond Vestry for £200 by the Commissioners of Woods in 1873.[27] The change of name to Corporation Island commemorated Richmond's becoming a borough in 1890.

✠

The story of Isleworth Ait is still more complicated. Today there is one large ait, of which a small piece near the south-east end is considered as belonging to Richmond. The 1960 Ordnance Survey map gives an area of 8.05 acres for the Isleworth part and 0.77 acres for the Richmond part. There is also a very small thin ait by the Middlesex bank at its northern end. Earlier maps show different configurations: the 1860s Ordnance map shows a similar general outline, with the same portion allotted to Richmond, but the main ait is divided into two by a channel about half-way along its length. The 1771 Richmond Manor map shows four elements: the main island divided into two by this same cross-channel, the thin ait at the north-west (much longer than in the later maps), and also a small ait at the western side of the southern section. But the Richmond holding is here shown in a different place – a triangle of land in the northern part of the southern section with its apex stretching right across to the western bank of the island. Moses Glover's map of Isleworth Hundred, made in 1635, shows four islands: one, which equates roughly with the southern section of the main ait, is marked as containing 7½ acres; the other three which, taken together, equate with the northern section, are of three, two and 1½ acres respectively – making a total of 14 acres for the entire complex. There is no sign in Glover's map of the two very small aits mentioned above.

There must, however, have been many more component islands than are shown in any of these maps, for no less than four were part of the manor of Richmond, and there were certainly several others belonging to Isleworth. All four of the Richmond aits were granted out to manorial tenants in 1617. The most southerly (which we will call A) was approximately in the location that is allotted to Richmond today. It was granted at the Richmond manor court to John Standen as 'an ayte near Railshead to the west, and Isleworth to the north, adjoining the ait granted to William Bayley on the north'.[28] It is not necessary to follow all the changes of ownership, but in later 17th- and 18th-century descriptions it is simply called 'an ayte near Sheen Wall' and has another ait belonging to Isleworth on its south side.[29]

The 1617 grant to William Bayley was of 'an ayte on which a walnut tree grows'[30] – later known as Walnut Tree Ayte and was the area, of 3 roods 18 perches, shown as belonging to Richmond in the 1771 manor map. Seventeenth- and 18th-century descriptions mention an ait belonging to Isleworth on its west side.[31]

The other two Richmond islands, at the north-east end of the complex, were granted in 1617 to Thomas Redriffe: one granted in March was 'an eite containing 16 perches by 4½ perches at one end and 3½ perches at the other end, lying near another ancient eite in the same river and adjoining the wear light on the south end of the same'[32] the second, granted in October of the same year, was 'a little eite on the west part of Whitebie's Eite in the same river, abutting Sheene Meadow on the south'.[33]

Though Thomas Redriffe Junior was declared as heir to 'two eights' when his father died in 1654,[34] he was admitted to only one;[35] and the two islands seem to have been merged into one at this time. We shall call this one B. The Redriffe heirs eventually split this holding into two shares (one described as 'an undivided moiety of an ayte near Sheen Wall'[36] and the other described as 'part of an ayte near Sheen Wall adjoining part of another ayte belonging to Isleworth').[37]

By 1765 both parts of ait B had come into the same ownership as that of ait A,[38] and in 1818 both A and B were sold to the Duke of Northumberland for £130.[39] Although they were not listed in the manor survey of 1771, nor shown as Richmond property in the survey map, they were clearly still part of Richmond manor and the Richmond manor court books record this sale and then their inheritance by Algernon Duke of Northumberland in 1851[40] and their enfranchisement to him in 1855.[41] The latter entry has an accompanying plan which shows clearly that A was the small portion near the south-east of the southern main ait, while B was at the north-east corner of the northern main ait. They contained together 1¾ acres, so B was probably just over an acre in extent.

Walnut Tree Ait had become consolidated as part of the southern main ait by 1771 and is described in the 1774 manor rental as 'adjoining north-west and south-west on other parts of the said ayt holden of the manor of Syon'.[42]

The status of the component parts of Isleworth Ait was, however, beginning to confuse the Deputy Stewards or their clerks who were keeping the manor records. When Walnut Tree Ait changed hands in 1804, the description as above was written in the court book, then 'the manor of Syon' was amended to read 'this manor'.[43] That was equally an error. The truth was that Walnut Tree Ait adjoined on the north-west and west on holdings of the manor of Syon, but on the south-west it directly adjoined Ait A, a Richmond holding.

Walnut Tree Ait was never in the same ownership as the other Richmond portions of Isleworth Ait and was still a privately-owned copyhold of the manor of Richmond when copyhold tenure was finally abolished in 1922. It had been in the same family for a century and a half: Henry Bell who acquired it in 1774 left it to his daughter Elizabeth Collett and she to her son James Collett. James's successor in title Elizabeth Eleanor Toby (ex Collett) bequeathed it to her son William James Toby in 1829. On the latter's death in 1892 it went to his nephew Henry George Octavius Collett, whose son Henry Archibald Arthur Collett sold it for £10 to Norton Courlander in 1922.[44]

Within a few years Norton Courlander sold out to the Duke of Northumberland who then at last owned the entire island. It seems that he entrusted its maintenance to the local authority, for a survey report presented to the County Councils of Middlesex and Surrey in 1930 states that 'Isleworth Ait is preserved by the Heston-Isleworth Urban District Council as a public open space'.[45]

In 1933 the Duke sold the island to the Middlesex County Council. Two years later, as part of the Mogden sewage works project, the level of the island was raised about a metre and a stone embankment wall was constructed along its east side. This resulted in the final closure of the narrow channel separating the north and south parts of the island and in a slight narrowing of the southern part. Four penstocks were constructed for the discharge of treated sewage into the river. In 1965 the Greater London Council succeeded Middlesex as owners and in 1986, following the abolition of the GLC, ownership was vested in the Thames Water Authority, who currently lease it to the London Wildlife Trust.[46]

In the meantime strange things had been happening to the notional boundaries on the ait – as appears from a study of the relevant maps. The manor survey of Richmond compiled in 1771 listed only Walnut Tree Ait as being part of Richmond, and showed it as containing 3 roods, 18 perches (0.8615 acres) in the ownership of David Russell. The manor title book,[47] in use about 1771 to 1815, however, lists also the title to aits A and B. When the enclosure map of Isleworth was drawn up in 1818[48] the three parcels of Richmond land were all included as if they belonged to Isleworth. A and B (with areas of 1 rood, 11 perches and 1 acre, 1 perch respectively) were shown as owned by Thomas Forrow, and Walnut Tree Ait (area 1 acre, 23 perches) as in the occupation of James Adams, who was probably a tenant of Elizabeth Collett. Apart from two very small areas on the south-west side, the whole of the rest of the island was by now in the hands of the Duke of Northumberland, who later that year acquired also Forrow's pieces. Thomas Warren's map of Isleworth parish drawn in 1848[49] shows the entire island as belonging to the Duke except for Walnut Tree Ait (now said to contain 1 acre, 1 rood and 6 perches) which is, however, listed as an Isleworth property in the occupation of the Dowager Lady Cowper (presumably as a tenant of W.J. Toby). In all these plans, despite the variations in acreage, the land shown as Walnut Tree Ait in the 1771 map reappears with the same triangular shape in the same place.

The plan in the Richmond manor court book recording the enfranchisement in 1855 of the Duke's portion of Richmond land (A and B, totalling some 1¾ acres)[50] follows almost exactly the same lines as shown for these holdings in the 1818 enclosure map.

Then came the Ordnance Survey 25 inch map of the 1860s. Not only did this again ignore the fact that a piece of land (B) at the north-east end of the island belonged to Richmond, but it produced an entirely new shape and location for the Richmond land in the south. The northernmost four-fifths of Walnut Tree Ait was shown as Isleworth land, while the rest of Walnut Tree Ait plus the former ait (A) were enlarged by the addition of significant pieces of the Duke of Northumberland's land, stretching right down to the southern point of the island – and this new parcel was allotted to Richmond. (Its area was given in 1894-6 as 0.871 acres; in 1960, following the building of the embankment wall, as 0.77 acres.) The same shape and location has persisted in

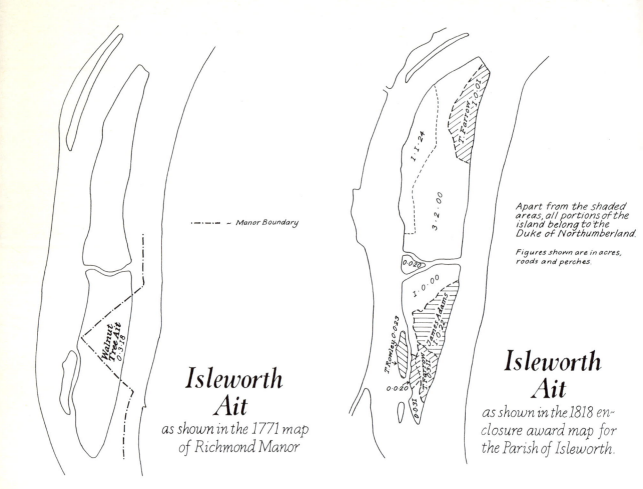

·—·—·— ~ Manor Boundary

*Isleworth
Ait*
*as shown in the 1771 map
of Richmond Manor*

Walnut
Tree Ait
0·3·18

1·1·24

3·2·00

0·0·20

1·0·00

T.Farrow 1·0·01

T.Romley 0·0·23

0·0·20

T.Foss 1·1·11

James Adams 1·0·22

1·0·31

0·0·31

Apart from the shaded
areas, all portions of the
island belong to the
Duke of Northumberland.

Figures shown are in acres,
roods and perches.

*Isleworth
Ait*
*as shown in the 1818 en-
closure award map for
the Parish of Isleworth.*

all later editions of the Ordnance Survey maps. The boundary thus delineated is not just a manorial and parish one, but was until 1965 a county one, and today persists, at least in theory, as a boundary between Richmond upon Thames and Hounslow. But what is the basis for it?

Unless this was a pure aberration on the part of the surveyors in 1863, two questions present themselves, though today they are only of academic interest. Did Richmond lose some two acres of its historic land simply by default? Was there some deal between the Duke of Northumberland and the owner of Walnut Tree Ait in the years between 1855 and 1863 to adjust their boundaries? And if so, was this acquiesced in by the manorial, parochial and county authorities concerned? – it was certainly not taken

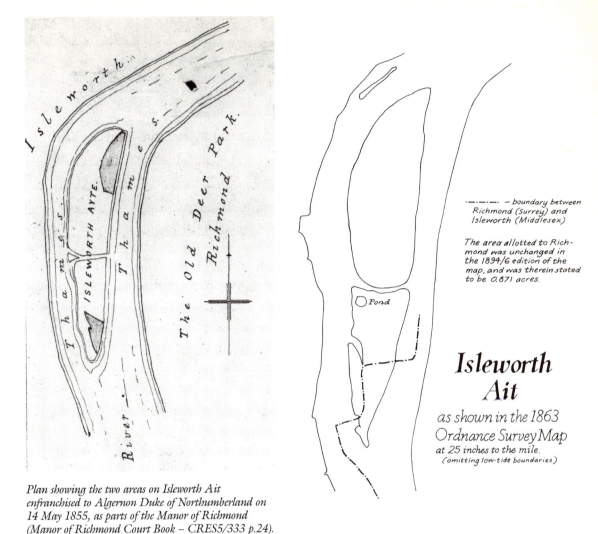

Plan showing the two areas on Isleworth Ait
enfranchised to Algernon Duke of Northumberland on
14 May 1855, as parts of the Manor of Richmond
(Manor of Richmond Court Book – CRES5/333 p.24).

—·—·— – boundary between
Richmond (Surrey) and
Isleworth (Middlesex)

The area allotted to Richmond was unchanged in
the 1894/6 edition of the
map, and was therein stated
to be 0.871 acres.

Pond

## Isleworth Ait

*as shown in the 1863
Ordnance Survey Map
at 25 inches to the mile.
(omitting low-tide boundaries)*

note of by the stewards of the Richmond manor court who continued to describe Walnut Tree Ait by the same time-honoured formula up to 1922.

✠

Lot's Ait was always in Brentford, but Brentford Ait had three component parts, all in the manor of Richmond. It is possible to give them, though only tentatively, a somewhat longer history, dating back to the 15th century.

In 1449 John Litgold leased to William Bower 'an island called Litgold's'.[51] In 1538 John Becke mortgaged to Augustine Hynde the 'whole tenement formerly Robert Lydgold's', together with an ayte (instead of the usual share of meadow), which he acquired from Sir George Somerset.[52] This was made over to the Duke of Suffolk in 1539,[53] but in 1544/5 it was 'released' by Sir George Somerset to Augustine Hynde[54] (who as mortgage holder seems to have recovered all the property sold to Suffolk). This may have been the island called 'the Hill', of which more below.

The second island in the Brentford Ait chain appears also to have been the 'meadow' element of a whole tenement which was inherited in 1491 by Margery Gille on the death of her husband Robert.[55] Margery sold the whole tenement and the island in 1494 to Henry Parkyns,[56] who sold the island alone to John Foxe in 1502.[57] In 1533, on John Foxe's death, it was inherited by his widow Rose, as 'an eyte in the Thames by the Stronde'.[58]

To its east was the third island, called in 1637 'Mattingshawe or Maken Shawe' – a name which may perhaps be a corruption of Makyn's Hawe.* For there was another whole tenement at Kew which had an island instead of meadow, and it belonged in 1445 to Clement Makyn,[59] who invested his son Stephen with the rights in remainder in 1446.[60] As this island was later a freehold, it may subsequently have become attached to the former copyhold tenement which was granted in freehold to the Earl of Worcester in 1517.

Whether or not these tentative identifications are correct, the continuous history of the three aits can be picked up a little later. The westernmost island called 'The Hill' was granted in 1569 to Thomas Burgess,[61] and from that date onwards every change of ownership is documented. It was described as an 'oziery' in the 1630s,[62] and the last occurrence of the name 'The Hill' in the manor records was in 1641.[63] Thereafter it was generally described by reference to the mansion which (from 1631) stood opposite it on the Surrey bank – the Dutch House at Kew. From 1715 its extent was given as three acres,[64] until the survey of 1771 replaced this with the exact measurement of 1 acre, 1 rood and 23 perches.[65] (Perhaps there had been some erosion in the previous sixty years.) Its owner at that time was Walwyn Strudwick, son of William Strudwick, surgeon. It was then known as Walwyn Strudwick's Ait – but never could it have been 'Walwyn's Strudwick', a curious corruption which has been seized upon as a picturesque name by several writers! In 1825 it was given to King George IV by John Ward, the then owner, in exchange for land on the north side of Richmond Little Green.[66]

The central portion of Brentford Ait belonged in 1603 to John Barber,[67] whose acquisition of it must have occurred in the period 1589-1602 for which the rolls are missing. It passed through many hands until it came in 1737 into the possession of Stephen West as 'half an acre of osier ground'.[68] By then it was already joined up to the third island at its eastern end, but it remained separated from 'The Hill' by the channel called 'Hog Hole'.

The third element, Mattingshawe or Makenshawe, also later called Twigg Ayte, containing 1¼ acres of land, was the subject of a case in the manor court in the early

---

* 'haw' was anciently a hedge or an enclosure.

17th century. In 1613 it was recorded as having been held by Sir William Reade, who had alienated it without consent as a freehold, to another manor – and it was therefore declared forfeited to the lord.[69] That the manor court confused its history with that of the island called 'The Hill', and therefore considered it copyhold, was not a deciding factor as even freeholds needed the lord's consent for any sale or gift to another manor. In 1637 a long entry in the manor rolls gives the full (and corrected) story. The island 'planted with willows' had been held, indeed as a freehold, not by William Reade but by William Payne, who had inherited it from John Payne his father. William Payne had granted it by a deed of 22 October 1612 to trustees for the poor of the parish of Fulham and Hammersmith, to fund, after his death, cash distributions to lame or blind persons and apprenticeships for poor men's children. A worthy cause indeed, but this had been done without the consent of the lord of the manor and the property had therefore been forfeit. After Payne's death, the trustees in 1637 appealed to the Richmond manor court; and Queen Henrietta Maria as lady of the manor agreed to grant the property to them to enable them to fulfil their trust.[70]

At that time it had been leased to basket-makers, and this continued throughout the 17th century, but by 1724 it was leased to Stephen West who had built on it a tavern, licensed under the name of 'The *Swan*'.[71] The licence and the lease (and the copyhold tenure of the adjoining part of the island) were held after Stephen West's death in 1746 by his brother Henry West until 1784,[72] then by Henry's widow and his son Henry and the latter's wife until 1793, and then by Thomas Samuel Maycock until his death in 1801.[73]

The *Swan*, or the *Three Swans* as it was later called, was a well-known house and a rendezvous for river outings. But Robert Hunter of Kew, living in the house on Kew Green which was later to become the Herbarium, regarded the island and the *Three Swans* tavern as 'a great nuisance' (see Chapter 16 page 253)). In 1811-12 he purchased both the copyhold part of the island and an assignment of the lease from the trustees.[74] He also obtained a new lease in his own name,[75] then closed down the *Three Swans* altogether, even filling up the old fishpond. When his son, another Robert, sold their freehold house on Kew Green to General Sir Samuel Hulse (as agent for King George IV) on 6 June 1820, 'Twigg Ayte called Mattingshaw or Makenshaw' formed part of the deal.[76] And evidently this included the lease from the Payne Trustees as well as the copyhold land, for on the appointment of new trustees in 1829 their tenant on the island was named as 'His Majesty'.[77] When the next set of trustees took over in 1870 the occupants were 'Her Majesty's Commissioners of Woods, Forests and Land Revenues'.[78]

In 1874, with the consent of the Charity Commissioners, the Payne Trustees sold their 1 acre, 2 roods, 24 perches of freehold land on Twigg Ayte to H M Commissioner of Woods for £650,[79] thus finally uniting the whole of Brentford Ait in crown ownership.

☩

Oliver's Island, though lying in midstream between the Kew meadows and Strand-on-the-Green, was always in Chiswick. In 1777 the height of the island was raised by three feet and a toll house was built on it by the City of London Corporation, who purchased the island for 60 guineas in the following year.

# 12

# *Nibbling Away at the Common Wastes*

THE MANORIAL TENANTS had rights in the commons: the pasturing of animals, the cutting of timber for repair of houses, the cutting and gathering of firewood. However, the waste land, whether recognised common or not, was the lord's and the customs of the manor specifically spelled out his right to 'grant any waste or empty ground in copyhold in return for a fine and a yearly quit rent'.

These wastes were any land that was not in the lord's demesne, in the common fields, in freehold closes or in the curtilages of the tenants' houses. In Shene manor in the 15th century there were the Greens in Shene and Kew, Kew Heath, parts of the marsh, the Great Common and the Hill Common and a few smaller patches around the village pond and up the edge of the lane to Kew, by the stream that led down to the Thames south of the palace, on the hill (Cutler's Hill it was called) and by the riverside.

Although the granting out of waste was an obvious source of potential revenue for the lord of the manor, there are not very many instances recorded before the middle of the 16th century. The principal encroachments on common land were the extension of the palace into the Green in 1444-45 and the grant from the Green of the land around the Charterhouse's new conduit head in 1466.[1] Not quite in the same category, but noteworthy as producing new land for building, was the splitting up and granting out of the manor grange land in 1496 and the grant of South Park to Robert Nevill in 1499. Also in 1499 some land was granted out in the west corner of the Green on the outside of the 'New Park of Shene' and at the north corner (Crane's Croft). In the reign of Henry VIII the land on both sides of the little stream (today represented by Water Lane) was granted out and what had been quite a broad access to the river was reduced to a narrow lane.

From the middle of the 16th century, however, the granting of land became a much more usual practice, and it will be more convenient to analyse it by area rather than chronology, noting that the periods of greatest activity seem to have been the 1580s and '90s, the 1630s, and the 1660s and '70s. (Small grants of a few feet from roadways in front of houses were fairly numerous, but are hardly significant, so have been ignored here.)

# Grants of waste in the Richmond area

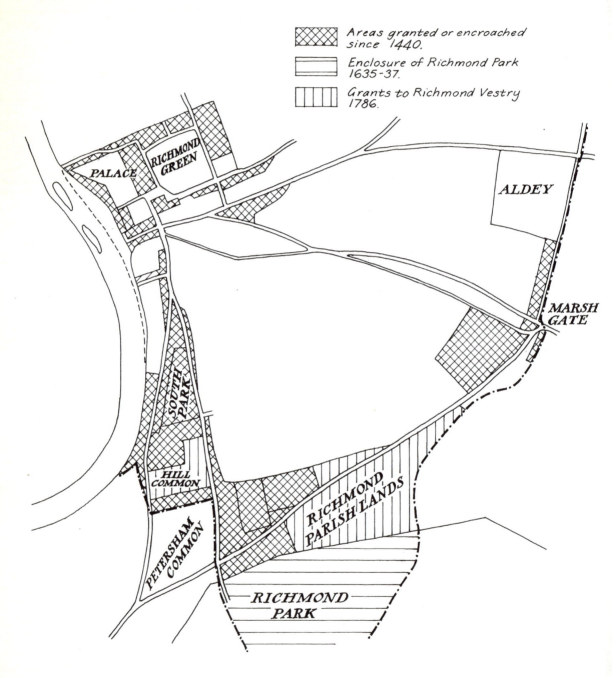

**Legend:**

- Areas granted or encroached since 1440.
- Enclosure of Richmond Park 1635-37.
- Grants to Richmond Vestry 1786.

PALACE

RICHMOND GREEN

ALDEY

MARSH GATE

SOUTH PARK

HILL COMMON

PETERSHAM COMMON

RICHMOND PARISH LANDS

RICHMOND PARK

## Kew Green and Kew Heath

The Green at Kew was originally much larger than it is today. Not only are all the houses around the present Green built on grants of land taken out of it, but it also had until the 1820s a long 'panhandle' stretching down to a point just beyond the front of the present Kew Palace. The grants on both south and north sides of the Green began in the late 1570s. On the south side the first was to William Ware in 1578, followed by one to James Ware in 1586. These covered most of the ground from the corner of Kew Park up to Cambridge Cottage. Behind them lay the headlands of Tinderland Furlong. Further grants in 1606 brought the frontages further out into the Green; then by 1609 three more grants extended the row right up to the end of the lane to Richmond.

On the north side, development was slower. The first grant, at the west end, in 1579 was followed by two more in 1582, and a further four in the period 1589-1602. Between them these produced a row of cottages extending up to the site of 67 Kew Green. A grant made between 1611 and 1619 extended this up to No. 73. Then there was a pause. The sites of 75 and 77 were first granted in 1641 and that of 79 (the *Rose and Crown*) in 1648. Nos. 81 and 83 were built on a grant of 1671 and the *King's Arms* pub was built on a site first granted in 1701. As for the land that now lies below and to the east of the bridge, the first 120 feet was granted in 1702, the remainder not until 1741. On the north side of all these grants lay the Kew meadows.

The land on the east side of Kew Green, on the outside of Kew Heath and the Ware Ground, was developed from the south to north only in the 17th century. The first grant (on the site of Richmond House) was in 1635. The next, originally consisting mostly of a large and dangerous gravel pit, extended as far as the site of No. 18. Two grants in 1669 and 1670 covered the rest of the east side up to the southern edge of the pond, and a last one in the 1670s was of land on the north side of the pond (including the sites of Nos. 52-66).

Kew Heath had been granted out in 1583 and 1585. Though it is clear from the entries in the manor rolls that it was already the practice to lease out the land there and that John Hynde was already tenant of some 22 acres (in three separate blocks) it was only in 1583 that these 22 acres were formally granted to him. Two years later another three pieces, totalling 13 acres and 1½ roods, were granted to John Bond. This patchwork must have been united in the ownership of the Hyndes or Portmans at some date between 1589 and 1602, from which period must also date a grant to them of the remaining five acres of the Heath, abutting the Green, on the north side of the Mortlake lane. The northern boundary of the Heath (where it met the 'Ware Ground') was on the line now marked by the back garden walls of the houses on the north side of Gloucester Road; its southern boundary was at Broomfield Road.

## *The southern end of the Kew Road*

There had originally been a triangular open space – a small green – at the north-east end of what is now George Street. This began where the lanes to Kew and to East Sheen forked and extended up as far as the line of Prince's Street – Waterloo Place. From its northern corner by the Kew lane a narrow strip of waste land stretched up some 300 feet on the eastern side of the lane to the end of Lower Dunstable Shott. The road coming from Richmond Green (now Duke Street) cut across the triangular space to join up with the lane to Marshgate and East Sheen. On the north side of this road was the village pond.

The small island of waste on the south side of the road cutting this green was first built on, apparently without formal permission, by Henry Harvey in the middle of the 16th century. In 1569 the 'cottage newly built by Henry Harvey on waste by the street leading to London and a garden newly enclosed adjoining the cottage containing 60 feet at the west end and 38 feet at the east end and 126 feet in length from west to east' was granted to Nicholas Beneson and his wife Joan.

In 1582 Richard Eusted was granted an empty piece of waste 80 feet by 30 feet 'between the water called Richmond Pond on the south and the way from Richmond to the fields on the north and bounded by ditches on east and west', with licence to build a barn thereon. (This was on the site of the later *Brown Bear* pub – now Next's store.) A series of four grants followed after 1589 along the edge of the lane to Kew until, with the fourth in January 1598/9 to William Tye of land 'by the Fagg Lane gate', the whole strip of waste there was in private hands.

To the south-east of Eusted's barn, there was another series of grants over a much longer period. Grants in 1617, 1638, 1645, 1646 and finally in 1770 left a narrow alley between these properties and the large close at the western end of Upper Dunstable Shott. Another grant by the south-west corner of this close an 1640 provided a site for what was to be for over two hundred years a blacksmith's forge.

In 1744 the jurors of the manor court examined the town pond and found it 'a very dangerous place unless railed at the head, otherwise it will be dangerous to both man and horse'. The 1770 grant mentioned above was of 'waste formerly part of the town pond but some years past filled up by various kinds of rubbage'. Then in 1843 the property 'lately the town pond' was granted to trustees for the building of the proposed Mechanics' Institute. This building, semi-circular and of one storey only, was the base on which 'Dome Buildings' grew – and part of its straight back completed the enclosure of a square piece of ground, on which were just the watch hut and lock-up and the fire-engine shed, and which became known as The Square.

## The Marsh

Another area that was developed in the second half of the 16th century was that of the marsh. Although this was nearly all in Mortlake manor (chiefly between the lanes from Richmond to East Sheen and to Mortlake) its edges spilled over the border into Richmond. In 1656 the jury of the manor court found the bottom end of the common near Marshgate 'to be very full of bogs and founderous places whereby the cattle feeding and depasturing upon the Common are thereon much indangered and sometimes destroyed by sinking into these spungy places out of which they cannot at some times be gotten forth but are thereby destroyed'. They proposed as a remedy that the area be enclosed and granted out.

This was what had already happened to an acre of waste ground on the north side of the lane to Marshgate, between the eastern end of Upper Dunstable Shott and the green lane along the manor boundary, which was granted out in 1564, and to 4½ acres on the south side of the lane, granted to Henry Naylor in 1569. The lane to Marshgate at this time followed the line of Worple Way and continued on this line until it came out onto the Common where it curved a bit to the north round another small pond before crossing the manor boundary (the curve that is today at the bottom of Queen's Road). The eastern edge of the land granted to Naylor was later extended by some 30 feet by three grants in 1646, 1680 and 1692.

On the eastern side of this northern arm of the Common, right by the border of Mortlake, a whole series of grants, large and small, were made, beginning with one between 1589 and 1602, but steadily increasing the size of the property in 1646, 1649, 1666, 1691, 1692 and 1698. With this last grant, the build-up of the land which was to form the Richmond portion of the grounds of the mansion – mainly in Mortlake – which was later known as Kenyon House, then Stawell House and which is now the site of the Courtlands blocks of flats was finally completed.

## Richmond Green

As mentioned above, the first recorded encroachments on the Green were the extension of the Palace in 1445-55 and the grant to the Charterhouse in 1466. The first grants of land to individuals were on the north-west side of the Green and date back to the 1490s. These were in the corner by the lane leading down to the Crane Wharf (now Old Palace Lane). In the 16th century there were some further grants here, stretching up to the gate into the 'New Park of Sheen'. One of these, just outside the northern corner of the Palace, was to become the site of a mansion that was pulled down in the 1750s to build the Theatre Royal. A further grant on the south-west in 1633 completed, for the next century and a half, the development of houses down the lane to the wharf.

Then in 1583 and 1585 came the first grants of land outside the park pale on the north-east side of the park gate. These were relatively small, but in 1604 a whole half-acre was granted, stretching all the way from the gate up to Shene Lane, the road leading from the north corner of the Green out to the site of the former Charterhouse. Some quite small additions were made to this land in 1663, 1671 and 1691 by which time it had become the site of the mansion of Sir Charles Hedges – the future Fitzwilliam (and later Pembroke) House. Most of Pembroke Villas stand on the site of this grant.

In the corner north of Shene Lane there were two grants of waste in the 1580s – to John Eusted who built a barn there (he seems to have had them all over Richmond!) and an adjacent plot to Gilbert Polleston in 1586.

The south-eastern side of the Green was also eroded by grants. At the end nearer to King Street the original line was probably that of the rear walls of the shops on the south-east side of Paved Court. The first identified grant, after that of the land of the conduit head to the Carthusians, came in January 1571/2 when Thomas Audeley, then occupying three cottages on the northern part of the former Carthusian land, was granted a plot 80 feet by 40 feet between his garden and the gardens of John Davies and Nicholas Snow. (This grant is now the site of the *Prince's Head* and Nos. 25 and 26 The Green.)

The existence of these gardens on the north-east side of the grant to Audeley suggests that the next property came forward about as far as the present building line; and indeed there is no evidence that any other properties between this point and Brewer's Lane were significantly extended at the expense of the Green. Nos. 10-12 The Green, however, stand well forward of these and here there are records of two grants to John Turnbull in 1641 and 1650 when he was 'improving' the three decayed cottages that had been the former *Cross Keys* tavern, which together added 18 feet to the property at the Brewer's Lane end and 15 feet at the other end. Again there is no evidence of grants adding to the land of Nos. 4-9 The Green, but it is highly probable that such grants were made (perhaps in 1589-1602) as there is clear evidence again of grants on the sites of Nos. 1-3, in 1579 (two), 1585 and 1586, which were up to 23 feet in depth.

The grounds on the north side of Duke's Lane (Duke Street) of the mansion that belonged to the Duke family, then the Michells, and which later became Richmond Academy, were not themselves directly augmented in the 16th century, but grants of waste from the Green, all 21 feet deep, outside the walls of the mansion were made in 1581 (three), 1583 and 1586 (though the one of 1583 was a regrant of land originally granted in 1581 to John Eusted, who had built a barn on it without the lord's prior consent). In the 1670s and 1690s four more grants were made to John Michell who had by then acquired ownership of the strip of former grants, which in total increased the depth of the property by a further 34 feet.

On the south-western side of the Green the frontages from Friars' Lane to Old Palace Place were brought forward 12 to 15 feet by two grants in 1655 and one in 1663.

## Water Lane and Riverside

In February 1513/4 Nicholas Gray, the palace Clerk of Works, was granted the 'Timber Hawe, a close and two gardens'. This was the land on the south-east side of the brook which ran into the Thames on the course of what is now Water Lane. From a later entry it appears that part of this grant was in origin an ait which had become attached to the mainland and on it a wharf was built.

On the other side of Water Lane the original grant has not been traced, but it appears to have been made to Thomas Denys at a date before 1519. This land was called Thames Croft in 1536. In February 1544/5 it came into the possession of Augustine Hynde, and it was owned by John Hynde his son when the Friary grounds were granted to Percival Gunston in 1572.

After these grants, there were no more in Water Lane itself until 1600. However, in 1569 Henry Harvey was granted the land between the Thames and the Friary grounds, up to the gallery round the palace gardens on one side and to the house of Massie Stanton (on the south-east of Water Lane) on the other. He built his house on the outside of the gallery but then proceeded to perpetrate a series of misdeeds which eventually led the manor court to bring a 14-count indictment against him in 1581. Three of the counts were in respect of encroachment on the Crown property of the Friars and another was that he had made a gate and fence to obstruct the lane from the Four Elms to the Thames (i.e. Water Lane). The outcome is not clear, but the gate and fence were evidently removed and Harvey appears to have abandoned any claim to the end of Water Lane itself. In 1586 a piece of land 245 feet by 45 feet was granted to trustees 'to build a wharf for the inhabitants'. It was bounded by the lane and the property of John Hynde (the former grant to Thomas Denys) at one end and the Thames on the other, by the land of Henry Harvey on the north-west and by the land of William Pate (the former grant to Nicholas Gray) on the south-east.

In 1610 Thomas Redriffe was granted a parcel of waste between the Friary and the river abutting on the town wharf, which suggests that Harvey's land had been taken back. However, the plans of Prince Henry for new gardens for the Palace and the work done in consequence by Inigo Jones in 1611-12, which resulted in a substantial reclamation of land from the river, altered the whole map in this area. By the end of the 17th century all the ground between the river and the sites of the Palace and the Friary was included in leases of those sites.

Some additional grants were made on the north-west side of Water Lane, below the Hynde property, in 1600 and 1611. This land must have been part of that originally earmarked for the town wharf. In 1638 an area of 30 rods by the water on the south-east side of the lane was granted to Samuel Chambers. This, like the lower part of the grant to Gray, had probably been an ait – or a bullrush bed – at the mouth of the stream here.

## Ferry Hill

Development of the waste land on the north side of the road leading down to Richmond Ferry begun in 1544 with a grant to Henry Parkyns of land which brought the eastern boundary of his smaller holding up to the line of those to the north of him (i.e. up to the line of Hill Street). This was followed by grants in 1553 to Seth Goldstone, in 1577 to Roger Richbell and in 1618 to Baldwin Packer of spare land which lay between the road down the hill to the ferry and the established holdings there.

On the south side of Ferry Hill the large riverside close called the Windeyarde is first noted in the manor rolls in 1445 as having previously belonged to John Coteler (whose name recurs in the rolls for Henry V's reign and after whom 'Cutler's Hill' probably took its name). Its origins are lost – whether it had been part of the original park or part of the manorial waste is unknown. It did not, however, stretch all the way up from the river to the road to Petersham. There was quite a wide, but gradually narrowing, expanse of waste between the Windeyarde and the road. This was the subject of two grants in 1550: of a plot 80 feet by 50 feet at the corner of Ferry Hill and the Petersham road and of land of unspecified dimensions to the south of that first grant. This second grant was made to Edward Hatfield who was the then owner of the Windeyarde, and probably absorbed into the latter. It still left an area of 300 feet by 32 feet (at the north end) by the road, which was granted out in 1572.

## The Riverside to the west of the Petersham Road

The Windeyarde close stretched southwards until it met the riverside close which belonged to the parish church (on which 1-4 The Paragon and the *Bingham House Hotel* now stand). Beyond the 'Church Close' was an acre of waste and then another area down to the Petersham border which had possibly once been demesne land as it had the name of 'Northcroft', but which was, by the 17th century at least, also regarded as manorial waste. In 1569 (with a regrant in 1573) the one acre was granted to Henry Harvey. On it Harvey set up a tile kiln – the first of a Richmond industry in this area which was to flourish for two hundred years. In 1638 Richard Pennard, then proprietor of the kiln, obtained a further grant to the south (just two rods or 33 feet wide) to extend the property.

In the same year, 1638, two further grants were made of riverside land, but for some reason leaving a gap of about 150 feet between Pennard's grant and the northernmost of these, which was 143 feet north to south, and which was eventually to become the site of the *Three Pigeons* pub. The gap was filled in 1668 when it was granted to Samuel Rundall, a proprietor of the tile kilns, to build a wharf.

The second 1638 grant, of 110 feet north to south, again left a gap of about 160 feet. It was the first element of what was destined to become the riverside grounds of

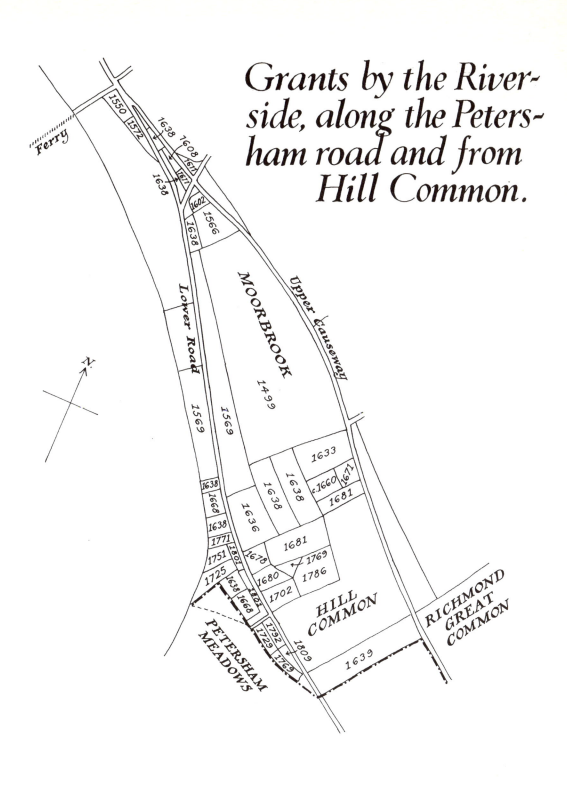

Grants by the River-
side, along the Peters-
ham road and from
Hill Common.

Buccleuch House. These were built up gradually by a whole series of further grants: one to the south in 1668, then extension to the north, progressively filling up the gap, in 1725 (regrant in 1731), 1751 (regrant in 1765) and 1771. Finally more land was granted from the roadside, varying from five feet in the north to 15 feet 6 inches in the south, and round the southern end, in 1801. The first house had been built on this land in the second half of the 17th century. It was rebuilt in 1761 as a mansion by the Earl of Cardigan (later Duke of Montagu), who also obtained a small grant of land from the manor of Petersham to make a straighter boundary to his grounds at the southern end. These grounds and the mansion were inherited by Montagu's daughter and her husband, the Duke of Buccleuch.

This was not, however, the last house in Richmond, along the Petersham road, even if it was the last by the river. The manor boundary sloped back at an acute angle to the Petersham road, creating a long narrow triangle some 46 feet wide at the northern end and nearly 450 feet long. This was progressively granted out in 1729, 1769, 1792, 1809 and 1810. A house was built on it by the fisherman Ralph Platt, the original grantee in 1729. From the 1770s it had a series of noble owners and occupants – the Duchess of Buccleuch (daughter of the Duke of Montagu), Lady Bridget Tollemache, Lady Diana Beauclerk, Sir William Wolseley Bart. and in 1820 the Duchess of Devonshire. Devonshire Lodge, as it became, was eventually purchased and demolished by the Richmond Council in 1968 and its grounds were added to the meadows.

## Richmond Hill and the Hill Common

After the grant of South Park to Robert Nevill in 1499 and its regrant as Smythe Croft or Moorbrook to Harmon Goldstone in 1553 there remained a strip of land some 60 feet wide between it and the Petersham road. This was granted out, as 1½ acres in all, in 1569. (There had been an earlier grant of a 'roddehawe' or 'hoope' of land below Cutler's Hill in 1498, but there is no record of what subsequently became of this and it was probably resumed by the manor.) On the south side of Moorbrook the Hill Common stretched to the Petersham boundary. There was also a large triangle of empty land between the upper causeway and the lower Petersham road to the north of Moorbrook.

The first grant in this triangle was of land on the south side of Compass Hill in 1566 (with a regrant of the same in 1573). This was followed by another in 1602 and a third in 1638, while a little more land was added in 1664. The area of the triangle north of Compass Hill was, except for its very tip, disposed of by grants in 1608, 1611 and two in 1638.

On the eastern side of the upper causeway there were two long thin stretches of waste land: the first lay outside the freehold closes on the west of the upper field, the second was between the road and the hedge of Heath (or East Field) Shott. The exact dates of the grants allocating these are not certain. By 1584 the waste land from the 'lane leading to the Vineyard' up to what is now the corner of Cardigan Road was in the hands of Edward Lovell; by 1587 the land from 'the lane to the Friar's Stile' almost as far as the corner of Doughty House belonged to Thomas Gisby. (A little extra land was added to this from the roadside in 1663.) In 1611 the rounded corner of the close on the northern side of the lane to the Vineyard was squared off with a grant of land which was large enough eventually to provide a site for no less than six cottages.

It was, however, the Hill Common where the greatest disposal of waste land took place. It was eroded from north, west and south. At the north end there were large grants in 1633, about 1660, and in 1671 and 1681, which together reduced the edge of the Common from its original position opposite the lane to the Friar's Stile to where it is now, opposite the middle of Stuart Court. These grants stretched about halfway down the hillside. They were met by grants of land spreading up from the lower road to Petersham in 1636 and 1638. The grants here were mainly to tilemakers who dug their clay out of the slopes of the hill – and set up new kilns on the east side of the Petersham road. Four more grants in 1678, 1680, 1681 and 1702 extended the development along the Petersham road to the point which is now the bottom corner of Terrace Gardens, and took another slice out of the lower part of the Common.

*Plate 16*

The tilemakers, especially Samuel Rundall, Isaac Pigg his son-in-law and Rundall Pigg his grandson, were constantly being accused – and fined – in the manor court for over-enthusiastic extraction of clay from the hillside, not only from the land which had been granted to them but also from adjacent areas which were still part of the Common. One problem was identified in 1651 when the jurors of the court, while protesting that the grants which had been made were a 'manifest encroachment upon the common', complained that Samuel Rundall had not even enclosed the land which he claimed by grant and insisted that he should do so forthwith 'to the end that there may be a just distinction made between that and the remaining common which this Homage finds to be continually decayed and damnified by the digging of clay and thereby made very dangerous to cattle feeding the same'. In 1680 Isaac Pigg was similarly fined for he had 'carried away great quantity of the earth from our said common and converted it to his own use contrary to the custom of our manor'.

The complaints continued – and so did the abuses – until 1766 when the newly established Parish Trustees (see Chapter 20) complained to the King. George III replied through the Deputy Steward of the Manor, Mr James Sayer:

Mr Sayer hath also received His Majesty's further Commands to inform the Earl of Cholmondeley [steward of the manor], that it is his Majesty's Pleasure, His Lordship send proper Notice to the Proprietors of the Tilekilns that they do not for the future presume to dig any more Earth for making of Tiles, and prevent the Common from falling in further by what they have already done, and that if after such Notice given they presume still to continue carrying on their Works, his Majesty's Attorney General will receive orders to put a finall Stop to it, the Consequence of which is, they must Account for every Tile they have sold the Freehold of the land being in his Majesty.

That was enough. In the following year the proprietors of the kilns sold out to the Duke of Montagu, who converted their land into a part of his pleasure gardens. Another small corner of the Common adjacent to the tilekiln land was granted to the Duke in 1769 because 'there is a dangerous precipice to the great danger of cattle feeding on the common', which was the remains of a clay pit and which the Duke had undertaken to fence in securely. The process was completed by the grant of another acre to the Duke in 1786, which produced the boundary between his grounds (now Terrace Gardens) and the Common (now Terrace Field) which exists today.

At the southern end of Hill Common, where it adjoined Petersham Common, a strip some 80 feet wide at the top end by the upper causeway, increasing to about 130 feet wide by the lower road to Petersham, was granted in 1639 to Francis Barnard 'provided he shall make and keep a sufficient fence between Petersham Common and Richmond Common with a gate and stile for passengers'. The purpose of the fence and gate was to prevent cattle straying from one manor into the other. This grant was divided eventually into three parts, represented today by The Wick and its grounds, the *Petersham Hotel*, and the *Rose of York* inn. A path ran straight down the hillside at the edge of what was left of the Common. The Common itself was granted by George III and Queen Charlotte to the Richmond Vestry in 1786. They leased out a small field at the bottom. Then in 1809 Mr Timothy Brent, who had purchased in 1806 the house called Nightingale Cottage or Lodge (where the *Petersham Hotel* stands today) proposed to take over the lease of the small field and, if permitted, at his own expense to divert the roadway around it (and take in a bit more land). This was agreed, and in 1810 Nightingale Lane assumed its present alignment. A smaller portion next to the Petersham road was leased to the Duke of Buccleuch for access to his stables (now the *Rose of York*). Though not technically 'grants' of land, these leases have continued, to the owners of the same properties, for nearly 200 years. The rest of the Hill Common, now called Terrace Field, was rented out for pasture from 1809 until the opening of Terrace Gardens to the public in 1887.

Although they are in Petersham, not Richmond, Wick House and the *Star and Garter* are so closely associated with this area that they may also be considered. The first grant from Petersham Common on the site of Wick House was a mere 4 rods by 2 rods (66 feet by 33 feet) for the building of a cottage in 1750, and this was the full size of the site on which Sir Joshua Reynolds' house was built in 1772. It was enlarged down the hillside by another 90 feet in 1805, and again to its present extent in 1861.

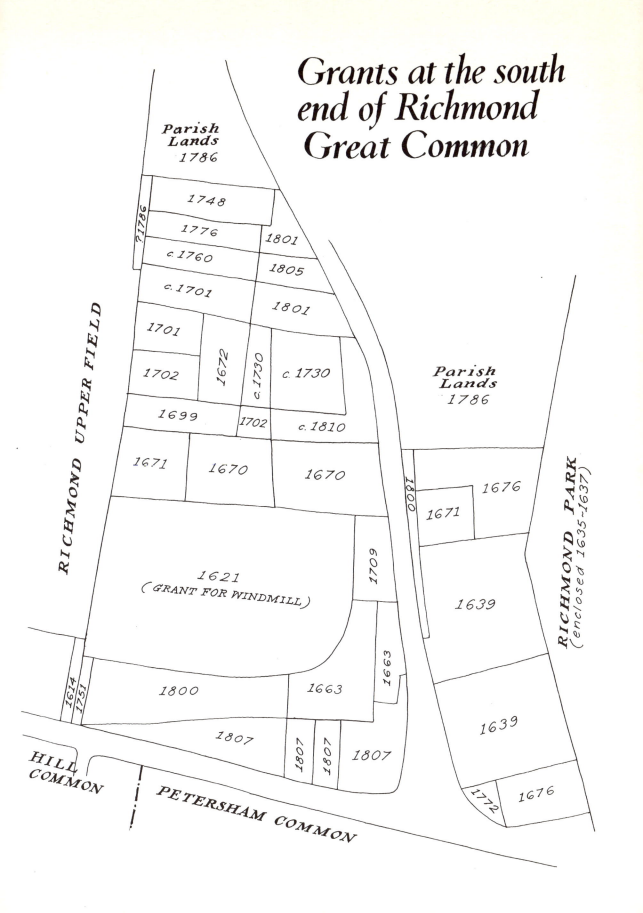

Grants at the south end of Richmond Great Common

Parish Lands 1786

1748

1776

?1786

1801

c.1760

1805

c.1701

1801

1701

1672

c.1730

c.1730

1702

1699

1702

c.1810

1671

1670

1670

RICHMOND UPPER FIELD

Parish Lands 1786

1800

1671

1676

1621
(GRANT FOR WINDMILL)

1709

1639

RICHMOND PARK
(enclosed 1635~1637)

1663

1800

1663

1807

1807

1807

1807

1807

1614

1751

HILL COMMON

PETERSHAM COMMON

1639

1772

1676

John Christopher obtained his grant of land on which to build the *Star and Garter Tavern* in 1738. Its ground was also twice enlarged by new grants; in 1803 to James Brewer and in 1865 to the company that had just taken over the management of the hotel.

## Richmond Great Common

It is not really historically accurate to separate the two Richmond Commons in the context of the early 17th century. Although they were linked by a neck only some one hundred feet in breadth, they were both part of 'the Great Common' in the minds of Richmond inhabitants until after the middle of that century. But it is convenient to consider everything on the south-west of the upper causeway (Richmond Hill) as Hill Common and everything on its north-east side as the Great Common (or Pesthouse Common as it became known towards the end of the 17th century after a pesthouse – or isolation hospital – had been built on it).

The very first grant out of this part of the Common was an extension in 1615 of 15 feet or so in width of the strip of land beside the causeway already mentioned above. But the most important early grant was that made in 1621 to Thomas Mercer of an acre of land 'upon condition that the said Thomas build one Grist Wind Mill upon the same land'. Mercer's acre (in fact he took rather more) is now the site of the buildings – excluding the forecourts – of the *Richmond Hill* and *Richmond Gate Hotels*. This area was enlarged a little on the south-east side by two grants in 1663 and another in 1709. Cottages were built in front of the mill (which stood a little behind the tall house now part of the *Richmond Gate Hotel* and which was demolished in 1725) and substantial houses in the portion of the 'mill close' nearer to the edge of the Upper Field. The land in front of these remained common until 1800 and 1807 when it was granted to the owners of the properties facing onto it.

Plate 16

Richmond Windmill. Detail from Moses Glover's map of Isleworth Hundred, 1635. (By kind permission of His Grace the Duke of Northumberland)

In 1637 Charles I enclosed his new Richmond Park, taking in some 73 acres of the Great Common. The wall of the park was only some 200 feet away from the end of the Mill Close, and almost immediately two grants were made of land outside the park wall near the gate, which reduced to a tight bottleneck the space through which a muddy track passed leading down to Marshgate. To these two original grants of land another was added in 1671 and two more (including a smaller one right by the gate) in 1676. The eastern side of the track (now Queen's Road) was thus developed from the gate as far as the site of the later *Lass of Richmond Hill* pub. When the Duke of Ancaster built his mansion on the site of the two buildings nearest to the gate in 1772 he was given a further grant of a roughly triangular piece of land to round off the corner; and in 1800 Sir Lionel Darrell, then occupying Ancaster House, was granted a strip of extra land from 15 to 18 feet wide along the frontage of the grounds of the house (where the original grants had been a bit shorter than that on which the house itself now stood).

Behind Windmill Close there was a triangle of land between the lane and the hedge of the Upper Field which was about 1,000 feet in length. Its width immediately behind the close was 380 feet. In the top, wider, end of this triangle an estate was built out of a series of grants. The story is a complicated one involving no fewer than 17 separate grants over the period 1670 to 1805. These began right behind the close, then spread gradually northwards for some 400 feet in all, but leaving out bits which served as access lanes to cottages sited away from the road, and which were finally mopped up only after the whole area had come into a single ownership. This estate is now the grounds of Richmond International University.

In 1786 George III and Queen Charlotte granted most of what remained of Pesthouse Common to the Richmond Vestry as a site for a workhouse and a new burial ground and 'for the employment and support' of the poor of Richmond parish. This included the lower and narrower part of the triangle of land on the west side of the lane and all the undeveloped land on the east side down to what is now the northern end of Grove Road. All that was left of the Great Common was the small area of less than four acres which is still known as Pesthouse Common at the northern end of Queen's Road.

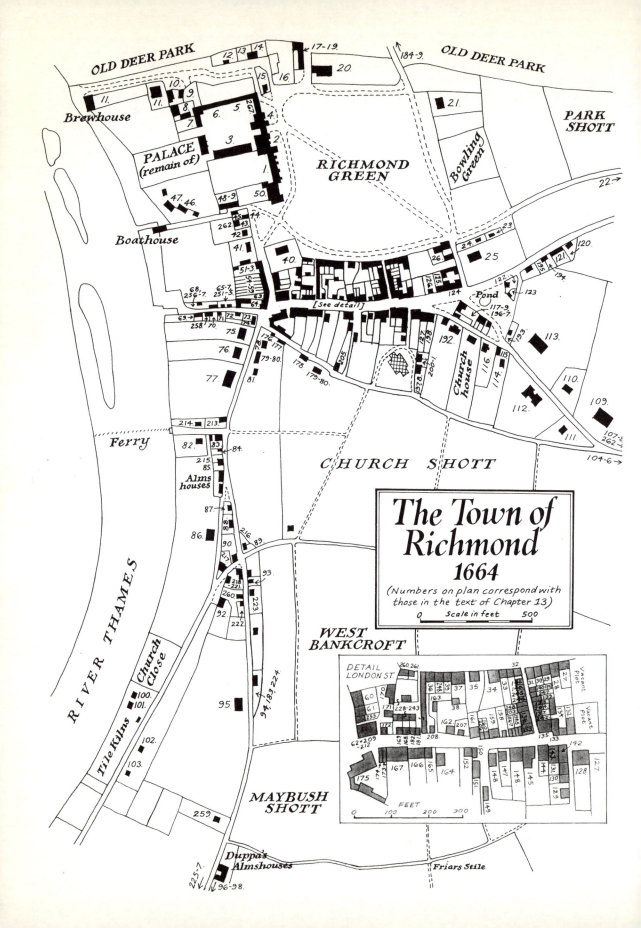

OLD DEER PARK

12 13 14

17-19

20

184-9

OLD DEER PARK

PARK SHOTT

11

10

9

8

7

15

16

21

Brewhouse

11

267

6

5

4

Bowling Green

PALACE
(remain of)

3

2

1

RICHMOND GREEN

22

47. 46.

48-9

50

Boathouse

262

45.
43.
42

44

23

41

40

26

25

24

68.
256-7

65-7
251-3

55.
54-53

24

25

120

121

255

19

51-3

64

122

123

[see detail]

117-9
196-7

69

71-71

72

73
74

258

70

75

127
198

192

193

113

176.
82.

177

205

200-1

200-1

91

115

110

76

79-80

178

179-80.

Church house

112

109

77

81

107-3
262

214.

213

111

104-6

Ferry

82

83

84

CHURCH SHOTT

215
85

Alms
houses

87

88

216

89

86

90

217

93

The Town of
Richmond
1664

(Numbers on plan correspond with
those in the text of Chapter 13)

0    Scale in feet    500

RIVER THAMES

218-
221.

260.

223

92

222

WEST
BANKCROFT

94, 183, 224

95

Church Close

Tile Kilns

100.

101.

102.

103.

MAYBUSH
SHOTT

259.

225-7

Duppa's
Almshouses

96-98.

DETAIL
LONDON ST.

260, 261

32

Vacant Plot

60

70

36

39

37

35

34

33

31, 30 29
246
245

27

28

Vacant Plot

61

255

171

228-243

163

38

162

207

158

159

245
247

135

131

133

142

62+209
-212

172

182

167

166

165

164

152

150

151

148.

147

1+8.

145

144

130

129

153.
131.

127

128

175

173.

FEET

0    100    200    300

Friars Stile

# 13

# *Richmond in 1664:*
# *The Hearth Tax Returns as a Street Directory*

THE 1664 HEARTH TAX returns for Surrey were published (as an alphabetical list of taxpayers covering the entire county) in 1940 as Volume 17 of the Surrey Record Society publications.

They provide an invaluable population list and a clear indication of the size of houses – and therefore of the relative prosperity of their occupants. However the original returns (in the Public Record Office[1]) have an extra interest which was entirely lost in the 1940 publication. For they were drawn up village by village and followed on the whole a logical geographical sequence in many cases, including Richmond – though not Kew. Unfortunately, the many houses and cottages in each locality that were exempted from payment were all grouped together and although a geographical sequence for Richmond can be identified in this group it is different from the main sequence, and somewhat less clear-cut.

The tax was levied on occupants, not landlords, so the names given are either tenants or owner-occupiers. A careful study of the manorial court records of the period, however, enables a significant number of the names to be placed with fair certainty in particular properties, either as tenant or owner. There are some problems: many people owned several houses and it is not always clear which one they were actually living in; some house-owners actually lived in a house which they rented, perhaps next door or close to the one they owned; a few of the entries in the list appear to be for several properties assessed together, perhaps because they were charged to the owner, being untenanted at the time (or perhaps because the owner had agreed with the tenants that he would pay their tax). Nevertheless a clear pattern emerges and it is far too regular and logical to be coincidental. The pattern, once discerned, enables many of the unfamiliar names to be placed simply from their order of listing. So the tax list can serve as a street directory in the same way as the later poor rate lists.

This is, after all, to be expected. A tax assessor in a place as large as Richmond, anxious to ensure that every property was included, would be likely to set them down in a determined geographical pattern. In Kew, on the other hand, there were still so few houses that the assessor just listed them in rough order of the importance of their owners.

The path followed by the Richmond tax assessor in 1664 was much the same as that used by the 18th-century rate collectors. He starts at the remains of Richmond Palace, still the most important building in the little town despite the demolitions and neglect of the past 15 years. He proceeds clockwise round the Green (including a brief detour up the Kew Foot Lane) until he gets back to Friars' Lane. He goes down the lane to include a cottage or two built beside the palace wall, then notes the house on the corner (on palace ground, but not yet listed), then turns back along King Street (to give it its modern name) taking in houses on both sides. He detours down Water Lane and back up, then goes on up Hill Street, past Ferry Hill (Bridge Street) and along the Petersham Road. Turning up Compass Hill, the few cottages on Richmond Hill and the Terrace are noted, then he comes back down to take in the group around the tile kilns by the riverside. Back up to the gates of Charles I's new park, the collector cuts down the track across the Common (now Queen's Road) to the small group of houses at the Marsh Gate at the manor boundary on the road to East Sheen. Then he turns back towards the town, noting the few houses and cottages along the Marshgate (Sheen) Road. From the junction by the village pond, he makes a quick detour up the lane towards Kew to take in the group of cottages at 'World's End'; then he works methodically along the main street (now George Street, but then known as either London Street or Richmond Street), taking small groups of houses on each side alternately. Finally our assessor arrives at the *Red Lion Inn* and notes one or two cottages in the lane behind it (Red Lion Street). Refreshed perhaps by a drink and a bite to eat at the inn, he sets off to West Sheen, the hamlet on the site of the former Carthusian monastery, and records the mansions and cottages there. And so to Kew.

At two points in the list – before and after the visit to West Sheen – there are a few entries which may have been added as 'postscripts', as they seem almost certainly to relate to houses already passed rather than to ones at the point reached. They had perhaps been empty or otherwise considered non-chargeable when the original list was compiled, then later found to be liable. In total, 192 chargeable houses are listed for Richmond.

With somewhat less certainty, a similar but different sequence can be discerned for the exempted, non-chargeable, houses (Nos. 193–258): Marshgate Road, World's End, Middle Row, George Street, the George Street end of Brewer's Lane, George Street, King Street, Ferry Hill, the Petersham Road, Hill Rise, the Hill, the Green end of Brewer's Lane, the Green and Water Lane. But these are nearly all small houses occupied by tenants rather than owners and are therefore less frequently identifiable with any certainty from the manor rolls. They have been intermixed with the others in the listing below at the points where they seem to fit. Uncertain identifications are noted with a query.

At the end comes a list of five empty properties (259–263), all of them positively locatable, and so also inserted in their proper places in the listing below. Houses known from the manorial records to have existed by 1664, but for which no occupant taxpayer can be identified in the tax list, are also noted below. Only one property in the Richmond list has proved totally unlocatable; unless it is an unrecorded house at West Sheen it is probably a 'postscript' entry and may belong to one of the houses whose occupants are unidentified.

At Kew, the list was so small that a methodical geographical approach was unnecessary. The houses are listed (with one or two exceptions) in order of size – 21 chargeable, six non-chargeable, two empty. Of the 29 houses all but five can be positively located, and for those five a reasonably convincing guess can be made.

A point that emerges clearly is that Richmond was a prosperous community. As the table below shows, out of 263 houses only 10 had but a single hearth – the norm for a peasant in the country. More than a quarter of the population had substantial houses of seven or more hearths – and close on a tenth were in mansions of 12 hearths or more. At Kew there are higher proportions of the very poor and the very rich: out of 29 houses there, five had a single hearth but four had 16 or more.

SUMMARY BY NUMBER OF HEARTHS

| No. of hearths | Richmond | Kew | | No. of hearths | Richmond | Kew |
|---|---|---|---|---|---|---|
| 1 | 10 | 5 | | 14 | 2 | |
| 2 | 79 | 8 | | 15 | 1 | |
| 3 | 26 | 2 | | 16 | 2 | 1 |
| 4 | 34 | 6 | | 17 | 1 | |
| 5 | 23 | 1 | | 18 | 1 | |
| 6 | 16 | | | 21 | 1 | |
| 7 | 16 | 2 | | 22 | 2 | |
| 8 | 14 | | | 23 | 1 | |
| 9 | 7 | 1 | | 24 | 1 | |
| 10 | 8 | | | 25 | | 1 |
| 11 | 7 | | | 26 | | 1 |
| 12 | 8 | | | 34 | 1 | |
| 13 | 2 | | | 35 | | 1 |
| | | | | TOTAL | 263 | 29 |

Each property may be shown in the listing below with three numbers: first, its serial number as listed in 1664; second a reference, where appropriate, to the number in the 1603 list in Chapter 8; and third (to enable the link with 18th-century properties to be more easily traced) the number given to it in the manor survey of 1771 and the manor rental of 1774.

I have given a brief history of the properties from the point reached in Chapter 8, showing also the ownership immediately after 1664, and have added a few notes on the occupants where these names occur in the parish registers, quarter sessions records, etc. Many of the names given in the Surrey Record Society publication need a little correction to bring them into line with the manorial and parish records, but they are listed as there printed, with my corrections in brackets.

✠

## The Palace

1.   Villarse, Cr ( = Colonel Villiers)                tenant             17 hearths
(No. 8 in 1771 survey)
Colonel Edward Villiers (knighted in 1680), nephew of George Villiers, Duke of Buckingham, was granted in July 1660 after the restoration of King Charles II, the offices of 'Keeper of West Sheen House *als* Richmond, Co. Surrey, with the wardrobe, gardens and green thereto belonging, Keeper of the Park, lodges and game, also Steward of the Court Leet there, Keeper of the late Monastery of Shene, Steward of the said Manor and Keeper of the Court Baron there'. The manor, formally restored to Queen Henrietta Maria in 1660, had been leased to Villiers for 31 years on 6 April 1663. He thus became 'Lord of the Manor *pro tempore*' (as he is described in the manor court rolls). He seems to have surrendered his lease in 1679 to James Duke of York (who succeeded Henrietta Maria as grantee of the manor).

Villiers lived in that part of the palace facing the Green on the eastern side of the gateway, which had been retained after 1660 in royal hands (the site now of Maids of Honour Row).

2.   Stanlocke, Mr John (also Stanlake)                tenant             13 hearths
(No. 7 in 1771 survey)
In the account of his rents which Villiers drew up *circa* 1677, 'Mr Stanlake's house' is included within a subtotal for 'great house and garden, coachhouses and stables, ye honble house and Mr Stanlake's house', but there is no individual entry under his name. It seems likely, therefore, that Villiers had by then taken over this property also, and that it was another part of the buildings remaining in direct royal control (probably the present Gate House and Old Palace).

John Stanlack, gent, was fined at the Quarter Sessions in July 1665 for allowing his ditches to overflow. (A Richard Stanlake had been fined for a series of similar offences in the previous year. Richard Stanlake and his wife Sarah had several children baptised in Richmond between 1663 and 1669 but there is no mention of John in the registers.)

3.   Rogers, James                                      tenant             10 hearths
(No. 7a in 1771 survey)
This entry probably refers to the Wardrobe. There is no mention of Rogers in Villiers'

list of 1677, and James Rogers has not been noted in any other document. Robert Roane (see below) was occupying the Wardrobe in 1660, but was not granted a new lease.

4.   Washington, Cr ( = Colonel Washington)        tenant        16 hearths
(No. 6 in 1771 survey)
Colonel Henry Washington was a first cousin both of Edward Villiers and of the John Washington who settled in Virginia in 1656 (and was the direct ancestor of the first President of the United States). Henry was the son of Sir William Washington who settled in this area when he bought Wicks Hall in Isleworth. Colonel Henry distinguished himself as a royalist officer in the civil war. He died at Richmond and was buried in Richmond Church on 9 March 1663/4, but the tax assessment is still in his name. His widow soon moved back, with their four daughters, to her native Worcester.

   This substantial portion of the old palace must have been the greater part of the range on the west side of the gateway, called later in the 17th century 'the Gallery' and taken over by Sir James Butler. It is now the site of Old Court House and Wentworth House.

261. Roome, Mr ( = Robert Roane)        tenant        5 hearths
(No. 5 in 1771 survey)                                    (empty)
At the time of the parliamentary survey of the palace in 1649 Robert Roane, the under-keeper, claimed as belonging to his office, 'one ground room without the gate ... and five ground rooms in the gallery... adjoining to the gate ... westwards'. In 1660 he was still in occupation of a house in this area, which must have been in the corner of the ranges on the north-east and north-west sides of Wardrobe Court. The house was empty in 1664 – and probably formed part of the premises leased to John Ayres in 1669 (see next entry).

5.   Steward, Mr        tenant        8 hearths
(No. 5 in 1771 survey)
It is unclear whether this entry refers to a man by the name of Steward or to the new steward of the manor, John Coell, appointed by Villiers when he took over the lordship. The latter seems more likely as there is no trace of any Steward family in other Richmond documents of the period.

   The entry probably relates to the remainder of the buildings at the corner of Wardrobe Court (see last entry) leased to John Ayres in 1669.

6.   Hopper, Mr Simon        tenant        9 hearths
(No. 5 in 1771 survey)
Simon Hopper was one of the first people to move into the palace after its sale in 1650. In April 1653 he was in trouble with the manor court for 'stopping up an ancient

watercourse in the Great Court Yard of Richmond'. When Simon's daughter, Ann Hopper, applied for a new lease in 1696, the Surveyor-General reported that Edward Villiers had granted several leases of the property to Simon Hopper since 1660, the last being for 21 years from 1675. Simon Hopper was buried in Richmond on 25 September 1694.

This property was part of the range of buildings on the north-west side of Wardrobe Court, immediately adjacent to the 'kitchen gate' of the palace. (Now the site of 1–4 Stable Cottages, Old Palace Yard.)

7. Hall, Mrs, Junior             tenant       8 hearths
(No. 7 in 1771 survey)

This property and the four following apparently represent those parts of the former kitchen quarters and domestic offices of the palace which had escaped demolition and were readily convertible into dwellings.

Mrs Hall's property was listed by Villiers in 1677 and was probably the 'little old tenement late Lloyd's' mentioned in documents of 1701 and 1702. The latter adjoined Mrs Hopper's (last) and Mr Godscall's (next) and included the 'kitchen gate' building. The main part of the property had probably been the Clerk of Works' office (by the gate) and the old 'flesh larder'.

Mistress Alice Hall was buried in Richmond on 25 April 1665. As Alice Mander she had married Henry Hall in July 1663. This listing may be for her, though Henry Hall appears elsewhere (see in George Street).

8. Goscall, Mr John ( = John Godscall)       tenant       9 hearths
(No. 7 in 1771 survey)

John Godscall had two houses which formed part of the old kitchen premises (possibly the pantry and the poultry house and some other offices). He also held the lease of a large part of the former Great Orchard on the south-west side of the kitchen premises – which made this the most highly rented property in Villiers' list of 1677. John Godscall's name does not appear in the parish registers but a Mr William Godschall was buried in 1667 and a Mrs Jane Godschall (child) in 1669. Probably both were his children – the 'Mr' and 'Mrs' denoted gentry status rather than age.

9. Spilar, Mr John ( = John Spiller)       tenant       5 hearths
(No. 3 in 1771 survey)

This was probably the old 'Woodyard Lodging' by the side entrance into Crane Piece (now Old Palace Lane). It and the following property had been in the hands of Robert Cross in 1660. Mr Spiller appeared in Villiers' list of 1677, but he died in September of that year. There may have been no tenant thereafter, for the house was 'long uninhabited and in great decay' in 1701.

10.  Peece, Mrs (? = Mrs Peirce)                    tenant              3 hearths
(No. 3 in 1771 survey)
This property, also belonging to Robert Cross in 1660, was the former office of the
Clerk of the Woodyard, standing to the south-west of the Woodyard Lodging.

Mrs Peece is not identified; possibly the name should be Peirce or Pearse, an
important Richmond family in the first half of the 17th century. A Mary Peirce died
in 1679.

11.  Measect, Mr Eriginall ( = Reginald Marriott)    tenant              6 hearths
(No. 3 in 1771 survey)
'Reynol' Marriott was one of the tenants already in occupation of the former palace
buildings by 1660. His house was probably the one-time cistern-house, later converted
to an armoury, which stood just outside the wall of the Great Orchard, in Crane
Piece. He may also have had use of this land and of the old 'rock house' by the river,
later converted into a brewhouse. By 1660 Crane Piece appears to have been enclosed,
save for the lane to the river and a wider patch by the river's edge and wharf. Marriott
also owned (from 1657 to April 1664) a small cottage of three rooms, separated off
from the main house at No. 16 below. It was occupied in April 1664 by Henry Warren
(see below at Brewer's Lane, No. 204). It was reunited with the main Bentley holding
(No. 16) in 1667.

Reginald Marriott was buried in Richmond on 8 October 1677. In Villiers' list of
1677 these properties – house and brewhouse – were occupied by a Mr Kemble. Asgill
House now stands on the approximate site of the brewhouse.

## Old Palace Lane

12.  Chabner, Mr John ( = John Chabnor)              owner               7 hearths
(No. 22 in 1771 survey)
In October 1663 John Chabnor and his wife Elizabeth acquired from Elizabeth, widow
of Robert Rogers, the house on the west side of the lane running down Crane Piece,
more or less facing Mr Marriott's. The land on which it was built was a new grant
from waste in 1633 to Samuel Chambers, resident Clerk of Works at the palace. He at
once built a cottage on it (mentioned in 1634) and sold it to the Rogers family in 1638.
Chabnor sold the house to Sir Richard Chaworth in 1670. It adjoined a stable belonging
to Mr Fifield (see No. 15).

13.  Drake, Deor ( = Dorothy Drake)                  tenant              7 hearths
14.  Short, Mr William                               tenant              8 hearths
(No. 2 in 1603 list; No. 22 in 1771 survey)
Neither Dorothy Drake nor William Short appears in the manor court records, and
Dorothy Drake does not figure in the parish registers. William Short was the father of

children baptised in 1648 and 1649/50; his first wife Mary died in November 1653 and on 16 June 1655 he married Anne widow of George Mawhood. She died in July 1659.

Robert Thomas died in 1645, leaving an only son who was legally declared to be an idiot. In 1652 his property, by then described as 'two messuages and two cottages' (which included No. 15 below), was awarded to the boy's three sisters jointly. When Robert, the idiot, died in 1658, the property had become 'a mansion house' [No. 15] and 'two dwelling houses [each?] containing 6 rooms', with a garden and stable. These are the two dwelling houses, standing just to the south-west of the corner of Old Palace Lane, behind the mansion.

### Richmond Green (north-west side)

15.  Fifield, Mr John                                         tenant                 11 hearths
(No. 1 in 1603 list, No. 24 in 1771 survey)          later owner
In 1665 John Fifield acquired ownership of one-third of the former Thomas properties from one of the three sisters; in 1670 he obtained the other two-thirds. It is evident that he was already occupying the 'mansion house' by 1664.

The baptisms of John Fifield's children appear in the parish register from 1658 to 1668. In 1676 he mortgaged all his property to Anthony Horsmanden who acquired full ownership in 1680. (Horsmanden was the great-uncle of William Byrd, the founder of Richmond, Virginia.) The site of the house was later occupied by the Georgian theatre built in 1765. It is now open space.

16.  Mrs Bentley ( = Mrs Jane Bentley)              owner                 18 hearths
(No. 3 in 1603 list, No. 22 in 1771 survey)
By 1630 when Stephen Peirce (or Pearse) died, the 'cottage' he had acquired in 1603 had become a 'mansion house' – so had presumably been rebuilt by him. It was bought by John Bentley in 1641. As former woodmonger to Charles I, he was alleged to have made £20,000 during the civil wars and the Commonwealth period by selling off wood from the royal parks for his own account. He got away with it – and with having appropriated to his own use 20 acres of the old park which lay to the south of the lane from the Green to West Sheen. He also acquired extra land, extending his frontage to the Green right up to the entrance to the park. (Though the 20 acres were still known as 'Bentley Park' as late as 1696, they were soon detached from this property after the restoration and were separately rented to John Godscall (see No. 8) and then to Sir Charles Hedges (see No. 20) in 1695.

John Bentley, whose sadly damaged memorial is in the parish church, died on 26 February 1660/1. His second wife Jane, who survived him and married *circa* 1668 Edward Bertie, youngest son of the Earl of Lindsey, left the property on her death to Thomas Ewer (possibly her son by an earlier marriage). The site is now that of Cedar Grove.

| 17. | Stanse, Mr | tenant | 3 hearths |
|---|---|---|---|
| 18. | Kindall, Richard ( = Richard Kendall) | tenant | 3 hearths |
| 19. | Jannings, Gilbert (? = Gilbert Grimes) | tenant | 3 hearths |

(Nos. 4–5 in 1603 list; No. 1 in 1771 survey)

These three names as printed are untraceable in the manor records or the parish registers, but Gilbert Grimes appears in Villiers' list and in the Quarter Sessions records, and Richard Kendall also appears in the latter. Gilbert Grymes (*sic*) was bound over in 1662 to keep the peace 'especially towards Ann Grymes, his wife'. Richard Kendall was one of a number of Richmond watermen fined in 1663/4 for failure to repair highways.

In 1660 the three houses were described simply as 'three small tenements in the possession of John Bentley or his under-tenants'. Villiers' list of 1677 shows them as in the tenure of Rowland Corbet, the widow of Gilbert Grimes, and William Beamond. Eventually they were included in the lease to Sir Charles Hedges (see next) and were demolished soon after.

| 20. | Finch, Mr ( = William Finch) | owner | 24 hearths |
|---|---|---|---|

(Nos. 6-7 in 1603 list; No. 21 in 1771 survey)

The land purchased by and granted to Thomas Keyes had three houses on it by 1635. Two belonged to John Fletcher, who died in that year, leaving his infant daughter Hester as heir. Hester later married William Finch. By 1662, when Finch purchased the third property from John Dickins, all three houses had been demolished and a new mansion had been built in their place.

William Finch was a London merchant, perhaps connected with the Finch family who were Earls of Nottingham and of Winchelsea. He died in 1674, when the house was inherited by his son Samuel – and in 1701 by Samuel's brother George. It was rented (from 1694 at latest) by Sir Charles Hedges, Secretary of State to Queen Anne. He bought it from the Finches in 1706.

*Richmond Green (north-east side)*

| 21. | Nott, Sir Thomas | crown leaseholder | 16 hearths |
|---|---|---|---|

(No. 9 in 1603 list; N and (a) in 1771 survey)

All the land on the north-east side of the Green, and extending some way up Parkshot, was acquired by Roger Nott, a rich Londoner, and his son Thomas Nott from Sir Robert Pye in 1639. At the same time they took over from Pye the crown lease of the house known as 'The Queen's Stable'.

Sir Thomas, who was knighted in 1639, was given full title to the lands by his father in 1640, in which year he also acquired the lease of Twickenham Park. He probably lived mainly in Twickenham until 1659 when he sold the lease of the Park and moved to Richmond. He and his father, and his wife Ann (daughter of Sir Thomas Thynne – see No. 76) were all strong supporters of the King. Ann was alleged to have inspired a royalist demonstration in Twickenham in 1648. On the restoration Sir Thomas Nott was made a Gentleman of the Privy Chamber. He was an original member of the Royal Society.

Roger Nott was buried in Richmond on 20 January 1670/1; Sir Thomas on 22 December 1681, and his widow Ann on 17 November 1694. The leasehold property was inherited by their son Thomas and the copyhold by their youngest son Edward and then by the latter's sister Susan Layton. In 1705 and 1709 respectively Thomas Nott and Susan Layton sold the land to the architect and developer John Price, who built the rows of mansions on the north-east of the Green that can be seen in 'The Prospect of Richmond' engraving.

## Parkshot

[Occupant unidentified]
(No. 414 in 1771 survey)
The first cottage to be built in the fields in Parkshot, by the 'foot lane' to Kew, stood on the first strip of land north of the Pye-Nott estate. It was described as 'lately erected' when Thomas Bowker sold it to Thomas Gould and his wife Prudence in 1641. (It does not seem to have existed when Bowker bought the land in 1636.) Prudence died later in 1641 but Thomas remarried and had several more children before his death in 1648. His second wife was possibly Joan (buried 5 August 1679) and there is a widow Gould among the occupants of exempt properties, but she appears to have lived in Pensioners' Alley. The youngest son Richard Gould became owner of this property in 1663 at the age of fifteen.

22. Stredwick, Oliver ( = Oliver Stridwick)      owner      2 hearths
(Nos. 415–7 in 1771 survey)
The next strip of land was freehold. From entries in the manor records concerning the adjacent properties it is evident that it belonged to Arthur Crome in 1641, to John Antill in 1657 and to Oliver Stridwick by 1670. Stridwick died in 1680. Both this cottage and the previous one were on the west side of the 'foot lane' against the park pale. They stood approximately where the A316 passes the end of the road now called Parkshot.

## Little Green

23. Susan Moulam ( = Susan Molam)      tenant      3 hearths
(No. 11 in 1603 list; No. 428a in 1771 survey)
In 1662 William Poynter surrendered to John Michell a cottage occupied by widow

Susan Molam on the edge of Little Green outside Michell's garden wall (see No. 25). Two cottages here had been sold in 1628–29 by Nathaniel Giles to John Young, who had sold this one to William Poynter in 1659.

| | | |
|---|---|---|
| 24. Asgood, William | owner | 2 hearths |

(No. 11 in 1603 list; No. 428a in 1771 survey)
John Young sold this cottage to William Kelly and his wife Judith in 1641. After William Kelly's death, Judith married William Asgood.

By 1672 the cottage had been demolished and the Asgoods and Judith's son William Kelly sold the vacant plot to John Michell. He then obtained a grant of the remaining land along the outside of his house's Little Green frontage and brought his garden wall 22 feet forward to the new alignment.

These two cottages (Nos. 23 and 24) stood approximately where the theatre is today.

| | | |
|---|---|---|
| 25. Duke, Mrs (Anne Duke, widow) | owner | 12 hearths |

(No. 10 in 1603 list; Nos. 423–7 in 1771 survey)
Thomas Duke's house passed to his youngest son William, who married Anne, daughter of Isaac Radstone. William Duke died leaving no surviving children, and was buried in Richmond on 21 February 1648/9. He left the house and his lands at Richmond to his wife Anne who had two sons John and Humphrey by her earlier marriage to Samuel Michell. Mrs Duke lived on at the house until her death on 24 October 1669 when her grandson John Michell (son of John who died in 1661) inherited the property.

The old house was rebuilt in the mid-18th century and became 'Richmond Academy', a school run by three generations of the Delafosse family.

### The Green, south side (actually south-east side)

| | | |
|---|---|---|
| 244. Miller, Richard | tenant | 2 hearths |
| 26. Paniter, Mrs ( = Mrs Dorothy Paynter) | owner | 2 hearths |

(Nos. 12–13 in 1603 list; Nos. 139–141 in 1771 survey)
William Irish sold his house (site of 2-3 The Green) in 1628 to Thomas Withers and his wife Dorothy. After Thomas Withers' death (circa 1631) Dorothy married a Mr Paynter (probably Alexander who died in 1643). The cottage and shop at the corner of Duke's Lane (1 The Green) was acquired in 1661 by Dorothy's son James Withers, a surgeon. She gave up to her son's house part of her garden (which had stretched behind it right up to Duke's Lane). Here a schoolhouse was built before the 'cottage, garden and schoolhouse' were sold by her and James to John Williams and his wife Unica in 1665. At that date, the cottage was occupied by Richard Miller. No more is

heard of the schoolhouse, and it is probable that the property at 1 The Green was rebuilt at this time. When the Williamses sold the property to John Michell in 1690, it had moved up the social scale, being then occupied by Lady Ormsby. (The story that this house had a connection with Shakespeare, having been owned 'by his friend Simon Bardolph', is pure invention.)

Dorothy Paynter was assessed for a fine of £100 in 1644 as a royalist supporter, and her plate was distrained, but she was let off the fine 'as she is not worth £100' and the plate was returned 'because she has helped maimed soldiers'. She died between 1665 and 1675 and her son James Withers inherited the house, which had by then been divided into two. He sold it in 1675 to Elizabeth Stobart, whose family then owned it for nearly ninety years.

[Site of 4–7 The Green, 46–50 George Street]
(No. 15 in 1603 list; Nos. 135-8, 157-60 in 1771 survey)
What happened to the mansion that had belonged to Sir Hugh Portman in 1603 is not known. The site, which had passed in turn to Sir John Portman, Sir William Portman, and the Earl of Ancram, was empty when the Earl sold it to Humphrey Heycocke in 1658. Heycocke had built a new house on it by 1670, but had not apparently done so by 1664.

| | | | |
|---|---|---|---|
| 27. Mr Radford ( = Rev William Radford) | owner | 10 hearths |
| 28. Elliott, Mr James | tenant | 12 hearths |

(No. 16 in 1603 list; Nos. 133-134 in 1771 survey)
The large house on this site (8–9 The Green) was purchased from Richard Baker in 1633 by James Elliott, a Groom of the Privy Chamber, and his wife Juliana. Elliott was buried in Richmond on 21 October 1634, when ownership of the house passed to his widow, with reversion to his son Thomas. Thomas sold the right of reversion in 1650 to Humphrey Michell. In 1663 Juliana Elliott died (buried 8 July) and Michell became owner. He sold the property in the following year to William Radford who obtained a release of claim from the Elliott's son James. Although there is no indication in the manor records that the house had been divided (or another built beside it) it appears from the tax returns that both Radford and Elliott were resident in 1664.

The Rev William Radford had officiated at some marriages at Richmond parish church in 1658 and 1659. In 1662 he obtained a licence to set up a school for boys and founded the Richmond Grammar School, which he ran until his death in 1678. His son, Vertue Radford, an attorney, inherited the property.

| | | | |
|---|---|---|---|
| 29. Caempe, Mrs (? = Mrs Kemp) | tenant | 7 hearths |
| 30. Trumball, Mr John ( = John Turnbull) | owner | 4 hearths |
| 31. Summarse, Mrs (? = Mrs Summers) | tenant | 7 hearths |

(No. 18 in 1603 list; Nos. 130–132 in 1771 survey)

This group is the 'three cottages on Richmond Green anciently known as the *Cross Keys*', which John Turnbull and his wife Rebecca acquired from Mary Crome's son Daniel in 1640. The *Cross Keys* was one of the properties which the Vestry had claimed from Mary Crome in the 1620s and, although their claim was endorsed by the findings of a Royal Commission, Mary somehow contrived to retain the property. She was buried at Richmond on 18 July 1635, and her son Daniel who then inherited it – apparently without any dispute – transferred the name and licence to another house on the Green (see No. 35 below) and had divided the old inn into three separate dwellings by the time he sold it to the Turnbulls.

In 1641 John Turnbull obtained a grant of extra land in front of the cottages 'for their improvement' and he got a further grant in 1651, taking in altogether a strip of land from the Green varying from 15 to 18 feet in depth. John Turnbull died in 1673 (buried 29 March) when the three houses were inherited by his daughter Elizabeth and her husband Robert Brown. They were rebuilt between 1705 and 1715 as Nos. 10–12 The Green.

| | | | |
|---|---|---|---|
| 32. | Dasley, John (? = John Darley) | tenant | 6 hearths |
| [140. | Bower, Alexander] | owner | ? |
| 33. | Mainse, Mr (? = George Mayne) | tenant | 6 hearths |

(Nos. 26–30 in 1603 list; Nos. 93–95 in 1771 survey)

The names Dasley and Mainse are unknown in any other document, but a John Darley, 'of Kew' in 1662 but 'of Richmond' in 1667, buried 30 March 1679, and a George Mayne, buried 1 November 1678, figure in the parish registers.

The 'one messuage divided into two, and four shops' belonging to John Tye in 1617 was developed by him. In 1618 he sold off a new cottage on the corner of Brewer's Lane to John Cole, who passed it on immediately to Robert Deane. This left the 'messuage divided into two cottages' and the four shops to be inherited by his brother Thomas Tye in 1619. Thomas sold the south-westerly cottage to Robert Trotter in 1621 and the central cottage and the four shops to Thomas Lovell in 1623. The corner cottage (site of 13 The Green) was sold by Robert Deane's son Thomas in April 1664 to Reginald Marriott. The cottage on the site of 14 The Green and the shops in Brewer's Lane passed through various hands before all coming together again in the ownership of Alexander Bower by 1662. That at 15 The Green was by 1664 owned by Margaret wife of Richard Allen. All three houses then remained in the ownership of the same three families until the 1690s.

Both Thomas Deane and Reginald Marriott figure elsewhere in this list, as does Richard Allen. All the property of Alexander Bower is assessed together in Brewer's Lane (see No. 140). It seems likely that John Darley and George Mayne were tenants of the Marriott and Allen houses respectively.

34.  Vickes, John ( = John Wickes or Weekes)          owner          7 hearths
(Nos. 31–37 in 1603 list; Nos. 91–92 in 1771 survey)
Mary Crome's son Daniel sold the tavern previously called the *Crown* (but which had
then changed its name to the *George*) in 1653 to John Weekes, a baker. When John
Wickes (as he then spelled his name) died, about 1674, he left the property in equal
shares to his son Charles and his daughter Susan, who married Robert Sherlock – but
it was no longer given a name and had presumably ceased to be a tavern. The property
was physically divided in 1704, when half was sold to John Price who built a new
house on it (No. 17 The Green) which subsequently became Richmond's principal
coffee house.

35.  Gray, widow Alice          owner          7 hearths
(Nos. 31–37 in 1603 list; Nos. 88–90 in 1771 survey)
By 1640 Daniel Crome had transferred the name of *Cross Keys* from its former location
(see Nos. 29–31 above) to this house on the site of 18-20 The Green. In 1650 he sold
it to Thomas Weld, who in turn sold to James and Alice Gray in 1656. James Gray died
in 1662 (buried 25 July) and Alice in 1673 (buried 22 December). The house was then
sold to pay her debts and legacies, and was bought by Alexander Bower.
     James Gray, in the week before his death, stood surety at the Quarter Sessions for
Gilbert Grymes (see No. 19 above).

[36. Owen, Mr Philip – apparently out of order – see below]
37.  Lovell, Mrs Anne          owner          10 hearths
(No. 38 in 1603 list; Nos. 86–87 in 1771 survey)
William Lovell, son of Richard, on his death in 1657/8 (buried 10 February) left the
house, 'called the *White Horse*', to his widow Anne for her life, with reversion to their
daughter Bridget wife of John Child. Bridget died in 1674 before her mother (who
was buried 22 June 1675), and in 1679 the *White Horse* was sold by trustees to William
Cross. His son, another William, rebuilt the property as two houses about 1725.

38.  Powdall, John          tenant          3 hearths
(?No. 38 in 1603 list; Nos. 86–87 in 1771 survey)
The name of John Powdall has not been found in any other document. His relatively
humble dwelling was perhaps a cottage formed out of part of the White Horse
premises.

39.  Wickes, William          tenant          5 hearths
(Nos. 39–42 in 1603 list; No. 85 in 1771 survey)
After the death of Robert Symonds in 1610, his sister and heir sold the house to
Samuel Mercer, who in 1620 put it into the joint names of himself and his wife Ann.

He died in April 1630 and it seems probable that his widow Ann then married a Mr Strickson, as the next identified owner is widow Ann Strickson in 1649 (Ann Strickson was already a widow by 1639 as can be seen in records of other property). She died in 1663 and her heir was Samuel, son of Nicholas and Frances Lidgould – the latter being perhaps Ann's sister. The house was at that time occupied by William Wickes. Lidgould sold it to James Spicer in 1669. It was rebuilt in the early 18th century by Matthew Drew.

| 248. Carter, George | tenant | ?11 hearths |
|---|---|---|

(Nos. 39–42 in 1603 list; No. 84 in 1771 survey)

After many changes of ownership in the first half of the 17th century, this house was purchased from John Osbaldston by William Best in 1656. Three years later, it was inherited by the latter's son, another William Best, and was then stated to be in the occupation of George Carter. The name of George Carter, assessed for 11 hearths, appears in the exempt list (but without explanation as to why). The house on this site was certainly not large enough to account for 11 hearths, so this figure is probably a total including other property chargeable to him – he had at least another house in Brewer's Lane. William Best died in 1679 (buried 26 May) and his widow Katherine then owned the house for another twenty years.

| 36. Owen, Mr Philip | owner | 5 hearths |
|---|---|---|

(Nos. 39–42 in 1603 list; No. 83 in 1771 survey)

The tax assessor seems to have got into a muddle by listing this house before Mrs Lovell's for it was definitely the one next to the house on the corner of Pensioners' Alley (now Golden Court). It had remained in the ownership of the Whyte or White family until 1644 when Alexander's granddaughter Rebecca White sold it to widow Juliana Ireland, who had been occupying it as a tenant and had 'lately' rebuilt it. She sold it in 1653 to Philip Owen (with reversion to the latter's daughter, Joan wife of Daniel Brent). Joan became owner on Philip Owen's death in 1667 and the house then remained in the ownership of herself and her heirs of the Brent and Cotton families for over a hundred years.

## Pensioners' Alley (now Golden Court)

(No. 43 in 1603 list; Nos. 80–82 and 104–111 in 1771 survey)

| 228. Swath, Roger ( = Roger Swarth) | tenant | 2 hearths |
|---|---|---|
| 229. Buddar, widow ( = Anne Rudder) | tenant | 2 hearths |
| 230. Stredwick, Henry ( = Henry Stridwick) | tenant | 2 hearths |
| 231. Wilson, John | tenant | 2 hearths |
| 232. Ball, Richard | tenant | 3 hearths |
| 233. Kindall, Thomas ( = Thomas Kindar) | tenant | 2 hearths |

| | | |
|---|---|---|
| 234. Price, Evan | tenant | 2 hearths |
| 235. Nellamse, Evan ( = Evan Nelhams) | tenant | 2 hearths |
| 236. Morgan, widow | tenant | 2 hearths |
| 237. Halse, Anthony | tenant | 2 hearths |
| 238. Scalse, John ( = John Scales) | tenant | 2 hearths |
| 239. Greenbrow, Edward ( = Edward Greenborough) | tenant | 2 hearths |
| 240. Baylies, Andrew ( = Andrew Bailey), | tenant | 2 hearths |
| 241. Gravener, John | tenant | 2 hearths |
| 242. Boone, Thomas | tenant | 2 hearths |
| 243. Guld, widow ( = widow Joan Gould) | tenant | 2 hearths |

This list of tenants, many of whom can be positively identified as occupants of Pensioners' Alley, occurs in a straight consecutive sequence in the 'non-chargeable' section of the tax list. It is evident that by 1664 the development had almost reached the pattern that is shown on the 1771 manor plan. On the north-eastern side a row of small cottages stretched from the Green to London (George) Street. On the south-western side there were two cottages facing the Green (Nos. 249 and 250) and three slightly larger houses and a tiny cottage (Nos. 118–119 and 181–182) facing London Street. Between and backing onto these some more small cottages faced onto an open yard (Golden Court).

From the Wright family, ownership of the entire development passed to Richard Burnham, a London goldsmith, in 1634–35. After Richard's death in 1666 it was held by his widow Elizabeth. It was not until she split up the property between her heirs in 1680–81 and they subsequently re-divided it in 1683 that the manor records give detailed information as to the occupants of each dwelling.

However, there are other indications. The cottage by the Green next to No. 36 above can be identified from an entry for that property as occupied by Mr Swathe in 1653. (Roger Swarfe [sic] was shown in the parish registers as married in 1633 and Roger Swarth as buried in February 1667/8.) A couple of lists of occupants of Pensioners' Alley fined by the manor court in 1658 and 1659 for throwing sewage into the Alley produce the names of John Edwards and Walter Gordon (see next entry), Roger Swarth, Henry Stridwick, Thomas Kinder, Evan Nelhams, widow Goude, John Morgan and Richard Ball. The 1683 records enable one to compile a complete list of all the then occupants of the line of 11 cottages, several of which coincide with the names above: viz, from north to south – 2 Anne Rudder, 4 John Wilson, 6 Evan Price, 7 Elizabeth Nelham, 8 Andrew Bailey, 9 Sarah Gravener. And on the south side of the yard there were four cottages in 1681, two of the inhabitants being John Scales and Edward Greenborough. From these indications, it can be calculated that in 1664 the cottages in the north-eastern row were Nos. 228–231, 233–235 and 240–243, one was on the north-west side of the yard (232) and four on its south-east side (236–239).

*The Green, south-east side*

| | | | |
|---|---|---|---|
| 249. Goodin, Jane ( = Jane Jordan) | | tenant (non-chargeable) | 1 hearth |
| 250. Mudey, Thomas ( = Thomas Moody) | | tenant (non-chargeable) | 2 hearths |

(No. 43 in 1603 list; No. 80 in 1771 survey)

In 1680 the occupants of the two houses facing the Green at the north-west side of Pensioners' Alley were Jane Jordan and Deborah Edwards. They were probably the widows of Walter Jordan (or Gordon) who died in 1662 and John Edwards (died 1673) who appear in the lists of 1658–59. The name of Edwards does not appear at all in the 1664 tax list, so his cottage may have been sub-let at that time. These two entries, following that for George Carter in the non-chargeable list, evidently refer to the cottages on what is now the site of the *Prince's Head*.

| | | | |
|---|---|---|---|
| 40. Carlisle, the Earl of | | tenant | 15 hearths |

(Nos. 49–53 in 1603 list; Nos. 54–66 and 73–79 in 1771 survey)

Occurring at this point in the list this large mansion must have been the one built early in the 17th century by George Kirkham, occupying what is now the sites of Old Palace Terrace and Paved Court. The house remained in the ownership of various members of the Kirkham family until 1646 when Roger Kirkham left it to his 'servant' John Stokes in trust, to be sold to pay his debts. The house was purchased by John Thorpe in 1650. Thorpe sold it in 1669 to Humphrey Michell, who sold it to his nephew John Michell in 1689. The latter sold it on at once to Vertue Radford who then redeveloped it with the row of houses facing the Green and a row of cottages at the back (Paved Alley or Court). Charles Howard, Earl of Carlisle was presumably John Thorpe's tenant in 1664. A descendant of the Howard Dukes of Norfolk, he had negotiated his way through the last twenty years with some skill. Heavily fined in 1646 for having borne arms for the King, he then changed sides, became High Sheriff of Cumberland (where he purchased Carlisle Castle as his residence) and Captain of the Lord Protector's Life Guards. A member of Barebones' Parliament and of the Council of State, he was enobled by Cromwell as Viscount Morpeth. He opposed the army's move against Richard Cromwell and was imprisoned for treason, but released. On the Restoration he was made a Privy Councillor and Lord Lieutenant of Cumberland and Westmorland and was created Earl of Carlisle in 1661. At the time of the 1664 tax assessment he was serving as Ambassador to Russia, Sweden and Denmark, but his house at Richmond was obviously not empty, and was perhaps occupied by his wife. Later Lieutenant-General of the Forces and Deputy Earl Marshal, he died in 1685.

*The Green, south-west side*

41.  Ray, Sir John (or Rae)                              owner        21 hearths
(Nos. 60 and 61–63 in 1603 list; No. 29 in 1771 survey)
In 1633 Sir William Parkhurst bought the new house built in 1604–06 (which had
passed through seven different owners since 1604), the two houses formerly owned
by Sir Robert Wright (which were still in the hands of one of the latter's nephews) and
the stableyard adjacent to them. By 1641 he had joined the three houses into one,
which he leased to the Earl of Newcastle, Governor of the Prince of Wales. Three
more changes of ownership took place in the 1640s and '50s until Sir John Rae
purchased the mansion from William Bolton in 1663. Rae's daughter Ursula and her
husband William Church sold the house in 1688 to Vertue Radford, who built a
completely new front part, one room deep, but kept the back parts of the original
three houses. Their separate identities can still be distinguished in the interior of 'Old
Palace Place'.

42.  Wood, Mrs ( = Martha Wood)                          owner        14 hearths
(Nos. 58–59 in 1603 list; No. 28 in 1771 survey)
As with No. 41 above, the two houses on the site of 'Old Friars' passed through many
hands before being purchased in 1653 and 1654 by Hugh Wood and his wife Martha.
In 1658 Hugh Wood left to his son John 'two messuages lately made into one dwelling
house'. However, the widow Martha remarried Sir Edward Wingfield, and they
continued to live in the house until their deaths. In 1681 John Wood finally took over
the property which he rebuilt as the house now called 'Old Friars' (the back part dates
from 1687, the front from *circa* 1700).

43.  Wildin, Mr John ( = John Weldon)                    tenant       8 hearths
(No. 57 in 1603 list; part of No. 28 in 1771 survey)
The house (on the site of Beaver Lodge), sold by John Bird to Thomas Huishe in
1607, had been bought in 1642 by Henry Medlicott. He died in 1664 but the house
remained in the ownership of his heirs until 1669 when they sold it to William Radford.
In 1744 it was purchased by William Gardiner, then owner of 'Old Friars', and was
added to that property – being rebuilt by Gardiner as an assembly room with stables
below.
        John Weldon's occupation of the house in 1664 is confirmed by a manor court roll
entry relating to the adjacent property (No. 44). Mr John Weldon was buried in
Richmond on 22 March 1664/5.

44.  Rowles, Dr (or Rolls)                               tenant       8 hearths
No. 56 in 1603 list; No. 27 in 1771 survey)
This entry and the two following refer to the rest of the Lovell property. Shortly

before 1664 John Lovell and his mother Penelope, the then owners, appear to have built a second new house on the east side of the one 'with nine rooms' built in 1622 (see next entry). In 1664 title to all the property was transferred to Gregory Lovell, probably John's brother. The new house was at that time occupied by Dr Rolls. In 1670 Gregory Lovell sold out to William Radford.

45.  Knowldin, Edward                              tenant           11 hearths

(No. 56 in 1603 list; No. 27 in 1771 survey)
In 1622 Thomas Lovell built 'a new brick house of nine rooms' adjacent to the original Lovell house. In 1664 it had been 'lately occupied by Juliana Elliott', but the new tenant – presumably Edward Knowldin – is not named. Knowldin's name does not appear in the manor or parish records. By 1670 he had been replaced as tenant by a Mr Craycroft.

262.  Lovell, John                                 owner            5 hearths
                                                                   (empty)

(No. 56 in 1603 list; Nos. 26–27 in 1771 survey)
The original Lovell house was divided into two cottages after 1622. It is last mentioned in the manor records in 1658 when John Lovell was (belatedly) admitted to it as heir to his father. It was probably demolished shortly after 1664.

*Friars' Lane*

46.  Booke, John ( = John Bauke)              tenant)          1 hearth
47.  Heath, Mrs (? = Mary Heath, widow)       tenant           6 hearths
48.  Cross, John                              tenant           2 hearths
49.  Pew, Michael                             tenant           2 hearths

(Nos. 54 and 55 in 1603 list; Nos. 11–12 in 1771 survey)
It is impossible to identify these four entries with complete accuracy, but it is almost certain that the large one was the house, misleadingly called 'The Friars', built by Henry Harvey on the outside of the Palace garden galleries.

In 1660, when the Surveyor-General reported on the state of Richmond Palace, there were 'four small tenements claimed by Mr Carter' and 'one other tenement claimed by him', which appear to be cottages built onto, or adapted out of, the garden galleries, in addition to the 'one old ruinous building called the Fryers'. Sir Edward Villiers leased the Friars to his steward Edward Holmwood in 1677 and in his rental of that year there are five other entries relating to cottages in this area (two of them rented by John Bauke). It is, therefore, quite possible that two of the entries in the 'non-chargeable' list should figure here.

Bauke was a family name in Richmond for several generations. One John Bauke had children baptised in the 1630s, another from 1660 to 1680, and a third from 1690 to 1702. Mrs Heath is probably Mary (née Edmonds) who married Henry Heath in 1642 and was left a widow in 1661. John Cross (born 1626, died December 1664) was a member of the large Cross family of watermen and fishermen. He was the son of Richard Cross and had brothers Richard and William. Michael Pew (died 1686) was a brewer who later lived in Kew. His residence here in 1664 was probably connected with the brewhouse established by Edward Villiers in the south-east corner of the palace grounds.

## The Green, south-west side

50. Armitage, Mrs (? = Sarah Armitage, widow)       leaseholder       10 hearths
(No. 10 in 1771 survey)

In the 1650s, after the sale of Richmond Palace, Henry Carter built a new house on the site of the former open tennis court and converted the former banqueting house next to it into another dwelling. By 1660 one was in the possession of John Fox and one in that of widow Armitage. (Robert Armitage died in June 1660; a Sarah Armitage, probably his widow, was buried on 6 October 1692.) Mrs Armitage appears to have been granted a lease of both these houses, and she appears in Villiers' rental of 1677. Her daughter Jane Armitage sought a new lease in 1701. These houses faced the Green by the corner of Friars' Lane: now Tudor Lodge, Tudor Place and Tudor House.

## King Street, south-west side

51. Bradley, Mr                                    tenant       5 hearths
52. Trippett, Henry                                tenant       3 hearths
53. Mersham, William ( = William Marsham)          tenant       12 hearths
                                                   Innkeeper

(No. 64 in 1603 list; Nos. 30–32 in 1771 survey)

Turning back into King Street, the next large building past Sir John Ray's house was the *Angel Inn*. By 1620, when Seth Goulstone's daughter, Ann wife of John Murray, sold the *Angel* to John Cogdell, another cottage with five rooms had been built at the back in the north-west corner – and this was excluded from the sale. The *Angel* passed from the ownership of John Cogdell to that of his son Thomas in 1629. The innkeeper of the *Angel* in 1647 was Richard Milton and by 1663 William Marsham (who issued a trade token in that year). It is possible that Marsham took over in 1654, for in that year Ann Murray, by then a widow, sold the five--room cottage to William Marsham and his wife Charlotte, whose son Benjamin inherited it in 1692. Another three-room cottage had been built by John Cogdell on the south-east side of the *Angel*, which was sold off by Thomas Cogdell in 1659 and which was also acquired by the Marshams in 1664, passing to their son James in 1686. Thomas Cogdell remained as owner of the inn until his death in 1697, but by then it had changed its name to the *Half Moon*. The property was then taken over by Henry Trippett, husband of Cogdell's granddaughter, who was a builder and 'architect', and who rebuilt it as three new cottages in 1699 (now Nos. 12–14 King Street).

William Marsham died in September 1691. He had seven children baptised in Richmond between 1649 and 1664.

The Henry Trippett living in the cottage in 1664 was probably the father of Henry Trippett the 'architect', who died in March 1713/4 and had children baptised between 1692 and 1708. Of Mr Bradley nothing is known – he was presumably a tenant of William Marsham.

54.  Burkett, Robert                                    tenant              2 hearths
(No. 64 in 1603 list; No. 33 in 1771 survey)
This cottage belonged to Seth Goulstone's son Lawrence, who made it over to his sister Anne Murray in 1620. It had probably been built by Seth since 1603 on part of the *Angel Inn* site. It was also in William Marsham's occupation in 1654 but was bought in the following year by Thomas Dean, a joiner. Dean sold it in 1663 to Sir John Ray, at which time it was occupied by Robert Burkett, a blacksmith. Burkett was presented at the Quarter Sessions in 1662 as 'a disturber of the King's peace, an oppressor of his neighbours, a common evil-speaker and slanderer and a sower of discord among his neighbours'. Though his neighbours would clearly have been delighted to be rid of him, Sir John Ray was refused admission to the property in May 1663 'because the Court hath been informed by the Homage that this surrender was made merely to defraud the Lord of the Manor'. Ray was presumably already negotiating the purchase of the much larger property which later became Old Palace Place (No. 41 above) and had hoped that paying a much lower fine for admission to this cottage would enable him to be assessed as already a manor tenant when the question of his admission fine for the mansion was considered. He was admitted to both properties at the next court in October and made over this cottage to himself and his daughter Ursula (who owned it until 1688). It was on the site of 11 King Street.

55.  Eling, Henry                                       tenant              7 hearths
(No. 65 in 1603 list; Nos. 34–35 in 1771 survey)
The two cottages on the sites of 9–10 King Street were sold by Thomas Biggs's son Thomas in April 1659 to the waterman Thomas Redriffe. The first was an old one which had been occupied on lease by Redriffe's parents for well over thirty years. The second, built of brick – perhaps by Thomas Biggs Senior, was leased in 1659 to Henry Eling. Eling seems to have taken over the other cottage also after the death in 1659 of Elizabeth, Thomas Redriffe's mother, who had been living in it. The seven hearths is probably the total for the two cottages. Henry Eling died in 1667/8 and his widow

Mary either in 1686 or '89. In 1691 a widow Sarah Eling was living in the first cottage. Thomas Redriffe died in January 1689/90, leaving the brick cottage to William Butcher and his wife Mary (probably Thomas's daughter). Thomas's widow, Avis, who died in September 1691, left the other cottage to her brother John Vernon.

56.  Redriffe, Thomas                                    tenant            7 hearths
(Nos. 66–68 in 1603 list; No. 36 in 1771 survey)
The house built here by John Slaney (site of 8 King Street) passed through six ownerships before coming into the hands of Ann, widow of Henry Brown, in 1638. She subsequently married Joseph Longe. Thomas Redriffe was already occupying the house as tenant in 1671 when Joseph Longe was granted a licence to let it to him on a 21-year lease, but in 1672 Ann Longe died and her heir Frances, wife of John Price, sold the house to Thomas and Avis Redriffe in 1675. On his death in 1690 Thomas left the reversion, after the death of Avis, to his sister Martha Lewis.

57.  Patrick, Robert                                     tenant            9 hearths
(Nos. 66–68 in 1603 list; Nos. 37–38 in 1771 survey)
John Jewett, who bought an open plot of land here from Jasper, son of John Slaney, in 1610, had by 1620 built a house on it (site of 6 and 7 King Street), which he sold to Thomas Redford. Thomas's son William sold it to widow Elizabeth Charley and she left it in 1646 to her sister Ann Strickson. In 1663 and again in 1670 Robert Patrick, a tailor, is noted as the tenant. In the latter year the property was acquired by the butcher Thomas Eling. The house became the *Crown* alehouse in the early 18th century and was split into two separate houses about 1747.

58.  Batmond, John ( = John Bateman)                     owner             6 hearths
(Nos. 66–68 in 1603 list; No. 39 in 1771 survey)
John Slaney's second cottage was sold by Jasper Slaney to William Gray in 1611. The latter's son, also William, was 'a common tippler of beer' found by the manor court in 1642 to have been serving 'false measures'. He sold this house (5 King Street) to John Bateman in 1647. Bateman lived there until his death in 1683 when his daughter Sarah and her husband John Rundell inherited the property. John Bateman, waterman, was one of a group of local inhabitants fined in 1664 for failure to repair the highways.

59.  Towne, Christopher                                  tenant            6 hearths
                                                         former owner
(Nos. 66–68 in 1603 list; No. 40 in 1771 survey)
John Slaney's third cottage (on the site of 4 King Street) was sold in 1610 to Thomas Cooms alias Blower and his wife Elizabeth. Elizabeth's grandson and heir John Linton sold it to Thomas Tooker, haberdasher, in 1643 and the latter's widow sold it to

Christopher Towne in 1650. Towne, a butcher and victualler, sold the house to John Gregory in 1656 but was still living in it when Gregory in turn sold it to Henry Carter in 1658. By the time Henry Carter died in 1680 it had become the *Glass Bottle* alehouse, occupied by Joseph Simons, but we can assume from this hearth tax listing that Christopher Towne was still in residence in 1664. (He died in 1666.) As Towne was a victualler the premises may have been an alehouse since 1650, but when the *Glass Bottle* sign was put up is not known.

## King Street (north-east side)

**60. Eling, Thomas (Senior)**  owner  9 hearths
(No. 48 in 1603 list; Nos. 67–69 in 1771 survey)
Before reaching the end of King Street the tax assessor crossed the road to take in some properties on the other side. Thomas Eling, butcher, purchased the property next to John Thorp's mansion (No. 40) from John Gregory in 1656. It was an inn (traceable from 1626) called the *Black Bull*. In 1663 Eling enlarged his property by buying two stables and a yard behind the inn from Robert King (see Nos. 170–171 below). When the property next appears in the manor records there is no mention of the name *Black Bull* but the outhouses by then included a slaughterhouse, so Eling had probably converted it into his butcher's shop. Eling, serving as a churchwarden, was accused in 1665 along with Matthew Moody (No. 144) of misappropriating parish funds for the relief of the poor. He died in 1696 leaving his son Thomas (Junior) as heir.

**61. Parrat, Thomas**  tenant-innkeeper  7 hearths
(No. 47 in 1603 list; No. 70 in 1771 survey)
Next to the *Black Bull* stood the *Swan*. It had passed through the hands of eight owners since Henry Harvey before being sold by Matthew Moody to Thomas Brooker in 1657. It was first described as the *Swan* in 1644. The tenant in 1657 was Francis Russell, and the next recorded tenant was Richard Freeman in 1666 (whose name does not appear anywhere in this 1664 list). Thomas Parrat was presumably the keeper of the *Swan* between these two. His name is not found in the parish registers or manor records (but a John Parrat, waterman, was one of those fined in 1664 for failure to repair the highways).

**255. Barkes, Matthew ( = Matthew Berkes)**  owner  2 hearths
(non-chargeable)
(No. 47 in 1603 list; No. 71 in 1771 survey)
A small cottage, consisting of 'two lower rooms, one chamber and a closet', was attached to the *Swan*. In 1657 John King, who had sold the inn in the previous year, sold this cottage to Matthew Berkes who was then living in it. After Matthew's death

in February 1665/6 his widow Alice sold the cottage back to John King's son Robert.

| 62. Barnse, Thomas ( = Thomas Barnes) | tenant | 2 hearths |
| 209.Tillman, widow (Susan) | tenant | 2 hearths |
| ?210. Brightridge, John | tenant | 3 hearths |
| ?211. Aman, Thomas (? = Thomas Almond) | tenant | 3 hearths |
| ?212. Milton, Robert | tenant | 2 hearths |

(Nos. 44–46 in 1603 list; Nos. 72 and 99 in 1771 survey)

The next inn in the row, on the corner of King Street and George Street, had been the *Queen's Arms*, which had an extensive yard and stabling, with the main entrance thereto from George Street. John King had acquired this in 1640. On his death in 1657 the property was divided. His youngest son John got the stabling and outhouses and three cottages in the yard (see at Nos. 170–171 below, listed in George Street). His daughter Margaret and her husband William Silver had been given a reversionary interest in part of the main building (7 rooms: 2 lower rooms, 2 shops, 2 chambers and a buttery), but they made this over to Margaret's brother Robert. Robert inherited directly four rooms and a buttery, occupied by William Gray and facing onto George Street. There should, therefore, have been something like a dozen hearths in the *Queen's Arms*. The five entries in the 1664 list, taken together, produce a total of 11, and two (Barnes and Tillman) can be shown as relevant. It would seem that Robert King and his wife decided to close the inn and subdivide the property. In April 1664 they sold to Thomas Eling Junior a cottage occupied by Susan Tillman, with use of the yard held in common, which adjoined the gateway into the yard on the east and the tenement occupied by Thomas Barnes on the west. There is no other obvious location for the other three non-chargeable entries, which probably represent the seven-room portion of the inn.

Robert King died in October 1668 and his widow Mary married John Harris. The property (except for the cottage by the gateway) appears to have been reunited by them under the new name of the *Waterman's Arms*, which they sold to Thomas Eling in 1671. (It later became the *Queen's Head*.) A halfpenny trade token was issued by a John Randell (presumably the new innkeeper) at the *Waterman's Arms* in 1668.

*King Street (south-west side, continued)*

| 63. Antill, John | owner | 7 hearths |

(No. 69 in 1603 list; No. 41 in 1771 survey)

The cottage on this site (3 King Street – now part of the *Old Ship* inn) changed hands four times between 1603 and its purchase by John Antill, a draper, in 1651. He then held it for thirty years. It was probably the next owner (from 1680), Simon Hopper, who turned it into a tavern, called originally the *Six Bells* and later the *Ship*.

64. Street, Philip                                        tenant-innkeeper 7 hearths
(No. 70 in 1603 list; No. 42 in 1771 survey)
By the corner of King Street and Water Lane stood one of Richmond's best known inns – formerly the *Golden Hind*, but renamed the *Feathers* at some time in the early 17th century. Philip Street became its owner in 1672, but he was already in occupation as innkeeper by 1664. Mary Batt let the house to Henry Carter for 21 years in 1647. She married, and was left a widow by Wicks Fitchett, and as Mary Fitchett widow she was licensed in 1669 to let the Feathers for another 21 years, this time to Philip Street who was already in occupation. She sold the property to Street in 1672.

*Water Lane (north-west side)*

65. Gay, Mrs                                      tenant          2 hearths
A small cottage was part of the *Feathers* complex in 1664 (it became a separate property in 1679). It seems probable that Mrs Gay, listed next, was its tenant.

?251. Greene, William                        tenant          2 hearths
                                              (Non-chargeable)
(Part of 71–72 in 1603 list; No. 43 in 1771 survey)
When Edward Standen died in 1607 he left the *Golden Hind* to his son Lawrence but a strip of land along Water Lane outside the wall of the Friary to his son John. This remained in the Standen family until about 1670. In 1663 the reversion after the death of Gilbert Standen's widow Elizabeth (who had remarried Thomas Cogdell) was granted to Gilbert's son Ellis, who subsequently sold to John Antill this cottage at the corner of the *Feathers* property. It was reunited with the inn in 1692. There is no indication of the tenant in 1664. There are seven small properties in the 'non-chargeable' list which seem likely to have been situated in Water Lane. (Of Nos. 251–254 and 256–258 two can definitely be placed there, and most of the others fill what would otherwise be gaps in the list. No. 255 has already been placed in King Street.) William Greene is the first of these owners listed – but he and Mrs Gay could quite possibly change places.

66. Cogdell, Thomas                           owner          5 hearths
(Part of Nos. 71–72 in 1603 list; Nos. 44–45 in 1771 survey)
67. Prise, Richard ( = Richard Price)        tenant          4 hearths
?252. Stoakes, Philemon                    tenant          2 hearths
                                              (Non-chargeable)
(Part of Nos. 71–72 in 1603 list; Nos. 46–51 in 1771 survey)
Two cottages here were owned by Elizabeth Cogdell, Gilbert Standen's widow. She and her husband Thomas Cogdell lived in one until her death in 1666. It was sold by Ellis Standen to John Antill about 1670. The other cottage was sold in 1670 to Richard

Price. Both Richard Price and Walter Mitchell are recorded as occupying this cottage at that time (and by 1676 the property was definitely two cottages). It seems possible that Philemon Stokes, the next listed non-chargeable tenant, fits in here.

| | | |
|---|---|---|
| 253. Martin, John | tenant | 2 hearths* |
| ?254. Booth, Edward | tenant | 2 hearths* |
| (No. 73 in 1603 list; No. 52 in 1771 survey) | *(both non-chargeable) | |

The next two small cottages down Water Lane, one on the Sexton land, and one on land probably granted to Edward Standen, but not yet developed in 1603, had come together into the ownership of Thomas Bun in 1611. In 1654 his son, another Thomas, failed to redeem a mortgage on them to Robert Cross. They were then occupied by one Thomas Hastings. In 1663 Robert Cross died and his heir was his son Cornelius Cross, a merchant tailor of London. When in 1668 Cornelius Cross sold the two cottages to the haberdasher Nathaniel Gardiner, the occupants were John Martin and widow Hastings.

| | | |
|---|---|---|
| 68. Parkins, William | tenant | 4 hearths |
| ?256. Miller, Katren | tenant | 2 hearths* |
| ?257. Warner, Bartholomew | tenant | 2 hearths* |
| (No. 53 in 1771 survey) | *(both non-chargeable) | |

These two cottages on part of the land granted to Edward Standen, built between 1607 and 1614, had both belonged to Robert Bayley, who had left them to different daughters. They were reunited in the ownership of Thomas Darling in 1635. Both had a hall, kitchen and two chambers. One had also a single garret, the other had two garrets and a cellar. In 1661 Edward Darling inherited the properties and granted 21-year leases to their respective occupants, Thomas Drew and William Parkins. (Parkins renewed the lease in 1682 and finally purchased his house from Darling heirs in 1700, but by 1664 Thomas Drew had moved elsewhere; see No. 178). As his house should have had four hearths, it seems possible that it may have been divided when sublet. William Parkins was a fisherman, Bartholomew Warner a waterman.

## Water Lane (south-east side)

| | | |
|---|---|---|
| 69. Brignall, Mrs ( = Elizabeth Bricknall) | owner | 8 hearths |
| (No. 74 in 1603 list; No. 227 in 1771 survey) | | |

Returning up the other side of Water Lane, the strip of land immediately above Bayley's wharf had been sold by Robert Bayley to Thomas Fuddes, a merchant tailor, in 1608. Fuddes built several houses on it (69–74), and when his widow Jane died in 1640 the holding was divided between their daughters.

The first house above the wharf went to the Toldervey family. On the death of Timothy Toldervey in January 1662/3 it was inherited by his aunt Elizabeth, wife of

Henry Bricknall. Between 1680 and 1703 her son John Bricknall developed the holding with four houses.

| | | | |
|---|---|---|---|
| 258. Langley, Mrs | | tenant (non-chargeable) | 3 hearths |
| 70. Dennise, George ( = George Dennis) | | tenant | 4 hearths |
| 71. Martin, Robert | | tenant | 4 hearths |
| 72. Fletcher, Thomas | | tenant | 3 hearths |
| 73. Drake, Mr John | | tenant | 6 hearths |

(No. 75 in 1603 list; Nos. 228–235 in 1771 survey)
The next holding, which ran right up Water Lane to Hill Street, was left by Jane Fuddes to Sarah, wife of Robert Cross. It was still a single house, with orchard and garden, in 1641; but between then and Robert's death in July 1657 it had been developed into a holding of three cottages and gardens, occupied by William Drew, widow Langley and – Dennis. By 1659 Robert's son James Cross had added two more cottages. In 1659 James Cross surrendered the property to himself and his intended wife Mary Gordon, with reversion to his brother Cornelius Cross. There is no further listing of tenants until 1682 when Jane daughter of James Cross died and left her reversionary right to her mother Mary (now married to a second husband William Beauchamp). Of the five tenants then listed only the name of George Dennis survived from the 1664 list. In 1688 the Beauchamps divided and sold the property in four lots. Of the five houses listed in 1664 the largest, occupied by John Drake, would have been the one standing at the corner of Water Lane and Hill Street. Both George Dennis, waterman, and Robert Martin, fisherman, figure in the Quarter Sessions records for 1664.

## Hill Street (south-west side)

| | | | |
|---|---|---|---|
| 74. Bugnise, Mr (? = Buggins) | | tenant | 8 hearths |

(No. 76 in 1603 list; No. 236 in 1771 survey)
This was the last bit of the Fuddes property, inherited in 1641 by the youngest daughter Jane Seaman. When her son Dutton Seaman inherited the house in 1657 it was occupied by Mrs Marsh and Mr Wallis. Dutton Seaman sold it in 1665 to Sir Richard Chaworth who was by then already in occupation. Mr Bugnise (or Buggins?) is untraceable.

| | | | |
|---|---|---|---|
| 75. Duppa, the Lady ( = Jane Duppa) | | tenant | 11 hearths |
| 76. Thinn, Sir Thomas ( = Sir Thomas Thynne) | | tenant | 12 hearths |

(Nos. 77 and 78 in 1603 list; No. 237 in 1771 survey)
These two houses were purchased by Sir William Herrick, jeweller to James I, in 1607 *Plate 17a* and 1608 respectively. In 1626 he sold them to Sir Anthony Mayney; and John Mayney, Sir Anthony's son, mortgaged them to Peter Richaut (Junior) in 1637. Richaut obtained

full title in 1646 at which time they were occupied by James Rosse and Dr James Chambers. Peter Richaut (or Rycaut) was the son of the financier Sir Peter who came to England from Brabant during the reign of James I. Sir Peter devoted his fortune to the royalist cause, and was ruined by the civil war. He died in 1657 – his daughter Mary married John Mayney (created a baronet in 1641) who also ruined himself in the royal cause.

In 1650 Peter Richaut sold the more northerly house to Justinian Isham of Lamport Hall (who succeeded to a baronetcy in the following year). In fact the purchaser was Bishop Brian Duppa, formerly tutor to the Prince of Wales, who had just been deprived of the see of Salisbury on account of his royalist connections. He and Isham were close friends; their correspondence, published in 1955,* reveals that Duppa was already renting the house, but was alarmed when his landlord put it up for sale as he could not afford to buy it himself. Isham offered financial assistance, but in the end Duppa himself came up with the £250 required – explaining, however, that he had caused the title to be put in Isham's name. After the restoration of the monarchy, Duppa was made Bishop of Winchester but retained the house in Richmond where he died on 26 March 1662. On the day before his death King Charles II came to kneel at his bedside to ask a final blessing from his friend and tutor. Duppa had founded Richmond's second group of almshouses in 1661 as a thank-offering for Charles's restoration. By his will he left the house to his widow Jane for her lifetime, with reversion to Doctor (later Sir Richard) Chaworth, to whom Isham surrendered it in 1666.

The more southerly house was sold by Richaut in February 1650/1 to Eleanor, wife of John Bentley. Mrs Bentley left the house to her son-in-law Richard Graves, who sold it in March 1657 to Sir Thomas Thynne. This Sir Thomas was the younger son of another Sir Thomas who was the grandson of the builder of Longleat. When his elder brother James died in 1670 Sir Thomas's son Thomas succeeded to Longleat. He was the ancestor of the Marquesses of Bath. Sir Thomas left the house in Richmond to his daughter Elizabeth, wife of John Hall.

Sir Thomas was also a strong royalist supporter and this 'nest' of royalists was a cause of suspicion to the Commonwealth authorities. In 1659 Parliament authorised the interrogation of Bishop Duppa and a search of his house, and the arrest of Sir Thomas Thynne's butler; but nothing could be proved against them.

Both houses came in 1720 into the possession of Dr Caleb Cotesworth who built in their place the mansion that later became the *Castle Hotel* and on whose site the Richmond Town Hall was built.

77.  Wyld, Mr Thomas ( = Thomas Weld)             owner             14 hearths
(Nos. 79 and 80 in 1603 list; Nos. 238–245 in 1771 survey)
Some of the rest of the area up to Ferry Hill (now Bridge Street) had been acquired

---

* *The Correspondence of Bishop Brian Duppa and Sir Justinian Isham 1650–1660*, edited by Sir Gyles Isham, Bart., Northamptonshire Record Society, 1955.

by Sir Robert Wright and his wife Dorothy from either Nicholas or John Bird before 1603 and a further two acres was purchased from John Bird in 1604. The mansion which Wright had built was sold by Thomas Wright, Dorothy's grandson, to Sir William Acton in 1638. He was a merchant tailor of London and a former City Sheriff, and was another of the royalist group: his East India Company stock was distrained and his house in Richmond seized in 1643–44, but he compounded for a fine of £1,000. His daughter Elizabeth, wife of Sir Thomas Whitmore, Bart, inherited the house in 1651 and sold it six years later to Thomas Weld, a citizen of London. The Welds and the Whitmores were closely linked by at least four marriages, but I have not been able to establish where Thomas fitted into the pattern. The house remained in the Weld family until 1693.

## Hill Street (north-east side)

| | | |
|---|---|---|
| ?78. Crewse, Mr (? = Cruys) | tenant | 8 hearths |
| ?79. Cenner, Nicholas | tenant | 4 hearths |
| ?80. Lambe, Robert | tenant | 4 hearths |
| 81. Burram, Richard ( = Richard Burnham) | owner or tenant? | 6 hearths |

(No. 81 in 1603 list; Nos. 247–257 in 1771 survey)

These four entries cannot be traced in the manor rolls, which suggests the possibility that they were freehold properties. If so, they were probably built on the close of freehold land on the north-east side of Hill Street. This had been the grounds of the former Raynford mansion and was probably in the ownership of Duncan Jones in 1603. A part of this appears to have belonged to Richard Burnham in 1655 (according to a record relating to the adjacent property to the east), but whether as freeholder or tenant is not clear. Apart from Burnham (who died in December 1666) the only name clearly identifiable in the parish registers is that of Robert Lambe, whose daughter was baptised in 1658 and who was himself buried in May 1665; a child named Mary Cruys (parentage not stated) was buried in 1662.

## Ferry Hill (now Bridge Street) (north-west side)

| | | |
|---|---|---|
| ?213. Willis, John ( = John Willetts) | tenant | 6 hearths |

(No. 82 in 1603 list; Nos. 240–241 in 1771 survey)    (non-chargeable)

At the corner of Hill Street and Ferry Hill, south of the Weld property, stood a house which had been built by Edward Farley, on land which had previously been occupied only by a barn, between 1637 and 1647. In 1647 he made it over to Nicholas Scutt and his wife Edith with reversion to their daughter. (Edith was perhaps Farley's daughter.) Nicholas Scutt died in 1655 and Edith remarried John Antill, who then retained ownership of the house until his death in 1695. However, he was obviously not residing in it in 1664 as he was assessed at his house in Water Lane (No. 63). It seems likely, in view of the following entry, to have been rented by John Willetts (or Willis). He was married in Richmond in 1641 and had children baptised from 1642 to 1662. He died in 1665 and his widow in 1679.

214. Peecker, widow ( = Prudence Packer)                          tenant             4 hearths
(No. 83 in 1603 list; Nos. 245-246 in 1771 survey)        (non-chargeable)
The other house on the north-west side of Ferry Hill, near its foot, had been bought by Baldwin Packer, the ferryman, and his wife Prudence in 1621. Baldwin Packer died in February 1624/5 but Prudence retained ownership of the cottage until 1648 when she and her daughter sold it and it was acquired, through an intermediary, by Thomas Weld. It seems probable, however, that she continued to live in the cottage until her death in June 1666. By 1674 it was occupied by Jervis Foster, but in 1664 he was living in George Street (No. 148).

## Ferry Hill (south-east side)

82. King, Robert                                        tenant-innkeeper  8 hearths
(Part of Nos. 84–86 in 1603 list; No. 275 in 1771 survey)

*Plate 17*  Robert King, having carved up the *Queen's Arms* (No. 62 etc) had by 1666–67 apparently opened a new alehouse called the *King's Head* (from which he issued in those years trade tokens with King Charles II's head on them). This appears to have been lower down the hill than the *Plough* (see next). The house was owned from 1663 by William Foxcroft who sold it in 1666 to Edmund Brawne. By 1680 it had been divided into two and was occupied by Brawne and John King (Robert's son). It was sold in 1683 to Abiel Borfett, the minister of Richmond church, and he rebuilt it as the house later known as Bridge House.

83. Laiton, George ( = George Layton)              owner-innkeeper 4 hearths
(No. 87 in 1603 list; No. 276 in 1771 survey)
On the corner of Ferry Hill and the road to Petersham stood a house which John Bird had sold to Henry Halloway (or Hallowell) in 1607. By 1659 when Thomas Hallowell sold it to George Layton it had become a tavern called the *Plough*, of which Layton was already the tenant. Layton remained there until his death in 1690. About 1730 it took the name of the *King's Head*, its original neighbour of that name having long since been replaced by a private house.

## Petersham Road (Hill Rise)

84. Halloway, Thomas ( = Thomas Hallowell) owner                          4 hearths
(Part of No. 87 in 1603 list; No. 277 in 1771 survey)
Past the *Plough* was another cottage, originally part of the same holding. Thomas Hallowell kept this for himself when he sold the *Plough*, and continued to live there until his death in April 1683.

215. Sall, William, Senior (or Sawley)        tenant        2 hearths
                                                 (non-chargeable)

85. Burgis, John ( = John Burgess)        tenant        2 hearths
(No. 88 in 1603 list; No. 278 in 1771 survey)

Two cottages were built about 1640 between Thomas Hallowell's and the Queen Elizabeth's almshouses. In 1662 they came into the ownership of Christopher Yates. From him they passed to Garrett White who sold them in 1673 jointly to Lever Millward and John Child. At that time they were occupied by John Burgess and a Mr Rycroft. The latter does not appear in the 1664 list, but the next name in the list of non-chargeable houses is that of William Sall or Sawley, who died in March 1670/1. Sawley (or possibly his son William – see at 90) was awarded in 1663 a pension of £2 a year as a 'maimed soldier'.

    Queen Elizabeth's almshouses were not assessed for hearth tax.

86. Bradshaw, Mr Robert                tenant        11 hearths
(Nos. 84–86 in 1603 list; Nos. 281–287 in 1771 survey)

Apart from the small holdings listed above the land between the 'lower road to Petersham' and the river, from Ferry Hill right down to Church Close (now The Paragon), belonged from 1633 to John and Elizabeth Child. This was the old 'Windeyarde' (or Vineyard) Close. When Elizabeth Child surrendered the reversion in 1661/2 to Mary wife of Thomas Prestwick, the property was described as 'a messuage in the tenure of Robert Bradshaw and a close of 6 acres'. In 1666 Prestwick sold it to George Carew from whom it passed to Sir James Butler in 1681. The house probably stood on the same site as the later Northumberland House.

## Hill Rise

87. Clarke, Thomas                       owner        3 hearths
(Not in 1603 list; Nos. 297–299 in 1771 survey)

The northernmost portion of the triangle of land bounded by the Petersham Road, Richmond Hill and Compass Hill was granted from the manorial waste to Thomas Redriffe, waterman, in 1633. He sold it, still undeveloped, to Thomas Clarke and his wife Elizabeth in 1651. An objection was raised to their building on the land, but the dimensions of the grant were then altered to ensure that a house should not cause obstruction to the highways. The house had evidently been built by 1664. In 1680 it was inherited by the Clarkes' daughter, Mary Butcher.

88. Best, Henry                           owner        6 hearths
(Not in 1603 list; Nos. 300–303 in 1771 survey)

The central portion of the triangle of land was granted in 1608 to Henry Best who at once built a cottage on it. On his death in 1625 his son, another Henry, inherited the cottage where he lived until he died aged 83 in 1690/1.

| | | |
|---|---|---|
| 89. Pointer, Simon | owner | 3 hearths |
| ?216. Bishey, William (? = William Bishop) | tenant | 2 hearths |
| (Not in 1603 list; Nos. 319–322 in 1771 survey) | (non-chargeable) | |

The tax assessor has crossed to the east side of Hill Rise. Simon Pointer bought his cottage here, just below the Vineyard, from George Rutter in 1638. The land on which it was built was a small triangular piece of waste outside the rounded corner of the freehold close which stretched up from Red Lion Street to the Vineyard. This parcel of waste had been granted to Thomas Nicholas, then tenant of the close, in 1611 on condition that he maintain the field gate and stile which were located there. Simon Pointer died in 1646 but the property remained in his family until the mid-18th century, so references to it in the manor records are relatively few. It next appears in 1687 when Simon's son and heir William has remarried, and by then it had been divided into two. There is no hard evidence that this had been done by 1664 but it is the likeliest explanation for the William Bishey (or Bishop?) entry if the locations given to entries 215 and 217 are correct. The name Bishey is found nowhere else, but a William Bishop had children baptised at Richmond between 1661 and 1668.

| | | |
|---|---|---|
| 90. Sall, William, Junior (or Sawley) | tenant | 4 hearths |
| 217. Excill, Thomas ( = Thomas Exall) | tenant | 2 hearths |
| (Not in 1603 list; Nos. 304–308 in 1771 survey) | (non-chargeable) | |

These holdings are back on the west side of Hill Rise. The southern part of the triangle of land north of Compass Hill was granted in 1611 to Richard Bradley, who had built a house on it by the time he sold it to George Rutter in 1614. In 1660, when George's son William Rutter sold the property to Henry Best, it had been divided and was occupied by William Sawley Junior and Parnell Rutter. Henry Best sold it to Dr John Thompson in 1669. Sawley was still resident, but Parnell Rutter had been succeeded by Cornelia, widow of Thomas Exall (who died in 1669).

| | | |
|---|---|---|
| 91. Carter, Henry | tenant | 5 hearths |
| (Not in 1603 list; No. 331 in 1771) | | |

This cottage stood in the common field at the western end of Church Shott, behind Pointer's house. It first appears in the records in 1654 when John Bayley and his wife sold it and the one-acre strip on which it stood. In 1655 it was purchased by Edward Poulton. From him it passed in turn to two of his brothers. When Henry Poulton sold it to John Spiller in 1670 it was 'in the occupation of Henry Carter'. Henry Carter, described sometimes as yeoman and sometimes as gentleman, was brought before the assizes in 1662 and 1663 for failing to attend church. In 1660 he had been denounced as having been 'the first puller-down of the King's House'; it was alleged that he had sold stone and other materials to the value of over £2,000. It is rather surprising to find him just four years later in such a modest house.

## Richmond Hill

| | | | |
|---|---|---|---|
| 218. Snow, widow ( = Frances Snow) | tenant | 2 hearths* |
| 219. Goddard, William | tenant | 2 hearths* |
| 220. Copshall, John | tenant | 3 hearths* |
| ?221. Right, William ( = William Wright) | tenant | 2 hearths* |

(*all non-chargeable)

(Not in 1603 list; Nos. 361–362 in 1771 survey)

The first plot of land above Compass Hill had been granted out in 1602. It had only one cottage on it by 1631, but this had increased to four by the time that Thomas Cogdell acquired the land, in two separate transactions in 1654 and 1657. Two of these cottages faced the Petersham Road; the largest one was on the corner of the Hill and Compass Hill; the fourth adjoined the third but faced onto the Hill. By 1664 when Cogdell obtained a grant of a small extra piece of land the largest of the cottages was an alehouse called the *Spread Eagle*. Although three hearths seems small for an alehouse, this is likely to be No. 220. It is tempting to suggest that the name Copshall (which is not found in manor, parish or court records) is a misreading for 'Cogdall', but Thomas's son John died as a child, so such a reading would require an amendment to both names. Thomas Cogdell died in 1697 – his heir was James, the only son to survive infancy. In 1670 Thomas Cogdell made over the reversion of one of the cottages to Margaret Ellico. It was occupied by Widow Snow and was on the south side of a cottage occupied by William Goddard. Widow Snow was probably Frances (died 1674), widow of William (died 1660/1). William Goddard, a waterman, was the father of eight children baptised in Richmond between 1662 and 1679. He died in 1708. William Wright had a daughter in 1655 and died in 1672.

| | | | |
|---|---|---|---|
| 260. Abshaw, Mrs ( = Elizabeth Abshaw) | owner | 7 hearths – empty |

(Not in 1603 list; No. 363 in 1771 survey)

South of the Cogdell property was a house built between 1616 and 1626 by William Green. Elizabeth and her husband Thomas Abshaw (died 1642/3) bought it from Richard and Ann Pennard in 1642. In 1660 Elizabeth Abshaw was granted a licence for a long lease to George Carew (see at 92 below), but he must have moved out by 1664. Mrs Abshaw died in 1672, when the house was inherited by her daughter Elizabeth, wife of John Bull.

| | | | |
|---|---|---|---|
| 222. Excall, John (=John Exall) | tenant | 2 hearths |

(Not in 1603 list; Nos. 364 and part of 365 in 1771 survey)      (non-chargeable)

In 1650 Thomas Cogdell purchased from Richard and Ann Pennard a house to the south of Mrs Abshaw's, facing the Hill. He also bought from Richard Hussey some extra land adjoining it. By 1669 when Cogdell sold this property to George Carew it was described as 'late in the occupation of Thomas Exall and Susan Paykins'. Thomas

Exall (who died in 1669) was living elsewhere in 1664 (see 90 and 217 above). John Exall (died 1681/82) was probably his brother. John had children baptised at Richmond from 1662 to 1682.

92.  Carew, Mr George                                     owner          7 hearths
(Not in 1603 list; part of No. 365 in 1771 survey)
George Carew, gentleman, built up a large estate on the lower part of the Hill. One of his first purchases, from Thomas Cogdell in 1660, was a cottage and land next to Mrs Abshaw's. Carew replaced this, and others which he bought from Cogdell, with a new mansion (described as 'newly built' in 1675). This was on the site of the later Harbord House and was purchased by Sir James Butler in 1681.

[Unidentified]
(Not in 1603 list; Nos. 372–374 in 1771 survey)
On the north-east side of the Hill, the first house above the Vineyard was a cottage built between 1614 and 1625. It was inherited by James Cross from his mother in 1657. In 1659 it was described as occupied by one Symons (a name which does not occur in the 1664 list). There is no further note of its occupants until 1688 when Cross's widow (by then Mary Beauchamp) sold it to Sir James Butler. It was then occupied by John Langley and Elizabeth Singleton. (This was later the site of the playhouse built in 1730.)

93.  Mearrick, Margaret ( = Margaret Merrick)     tenant          2 hearths
223.  Gaines, Philip                                   tenant          2 hearths
(Not in 1603 list; Nos. 337 and 378–381 in 1771 survey)          (non-chargeable)
Next to James Cross's house, going up the Hill, a cottage had been built between 1614 and 1617, which had become two cottages by 1640. They then belonged to Robert Arnold who died in 1642. His widow Elizabeth became the wife of Thomas Cogdell and in the 1650s they granted the reversions to two of Elizabeth's children by her first marriage. The reversion of the first cottage was sold by Elizabeth's daughter Sarah Husband to Simon Pointer in 1663, when the occupant was Margaret Merrick, widow. The reversion of the second cottage was sold by Edward Arnold to the Husbands and by them in 1662 to Thomas Cogdell, when the occupant was George Answorth (not in the 1664 list). When Cogdell, after Elizabeth's death in 1666, made over the cottage in 1668 into the joint names of himself and his third wife Isabella the occupant was Philip Gaines. The cottages remained in the Pointer and Cogdell families until well into the 18th century.

[Unidentified]
(Not in 1603 list; Nos. 382a&b in 1771 survey)
This cottage was built in 1615–16 by Thomas Lovell. It was purchased by George

Rutter and his wife Parnel in 1651 and in April 1664 Parnel sold it to James Spicer, who sold it on to George Carew three months later. It was rebuilt by Carew and formed the original nucleus of the mansion that is now the Old Vicarage School. The manor rolls give no clue as to its occupancy; the name Rutter is not in the 1664 list and James Spicer was living elsewhere (No. 163). The next numbers both in the main series and the non-chargeable series are attributable to the houses next following. A possibility is that it was Mr Doutey's house (see page 205 below).

| | | | |
|---|---|---|---|
| 94. | Laiton, Roger ( = Roger Layton) | tenant | 4 hearths |
| 183. | Dalley, John | tenant | 2 hearths |
| 224. | Smith, Ambrose | tenant | 2 hearths |

(Part of No. 92 in 1603 list; Nos. 382c&d in 1771 survey) (non-chargeable)

Robert Arnold inherited a cottage here from his father in 1617. It was bought by Richard Pierce in 1634. Between 1648 and 1654 (when his son John inherited) Richard Pierce had developed the property into three cottages. In 1658 John Pierce sold them to John Michell, 'occupied by Roger Layton, John Dalley and Ambrose Smith'. The same three occupants were listed in 1662 when John Michell died and his son John inherited. (He sold out to Sir James Butler in 1684.) John Dalley's listing towards the end of the list of chargeable entries is probably a late addition; perhaps he was transferred from the non-chargeable list at the last minute.

| | | | |
|---|---|---|---|
| 95. | Warner, Thomas | tenant | 11 hearths |

(No. 91 in 1603 list; Nos. 369–71 in 1771 survey)

Back on the western side of the road, this is the big estate of Moorbrook, on the slope between Richmond Hill and the Petersham Road. Nicholas Bird sold it to Seth Goldstone in 1604 and the latter's son Lawrence sold it to James Martin in 1622 (when it was rented to Sir William Herrick). In 1648 it was inherited by James Martin's daughter Rebecca and her husband John Turnbull. The Turnbulls were granted in 1656 a licence to let the property for 31 years to Mr Thomas Warner, an apothecary. It is probable that it was Warner who first identified the medicinal qualities of the spring water on the estate, which led to the original development of Richmond Wells in the 1670s and their further development as a place of entertainment in the 1690s. Turnbull died in 1673 and left the estate to trustees who made it over in 1680 to Turnbull's daughter Eleanor and her husband Robert Brown. (Warner was still listed as the occupant.)

| | | | |
|---|---|---|---|
| 259. | Goulston, Lawrence (or Goldstone) Junior | owner | 4 hearths |

(Not in 1603 list; No. 580 in 1771 survey) (empty)

Laurence Goulstone (or Goldstone) Senior received a grant of ¾ acre from the Hill Common, adjacent to Moorbrook and the 'upper highway to Petersham' in 1633. By

1659 when he made it over to his son Lawrence (Junior) it had a cottage on it. When young Lawrence died, about 1666, his son John inherited the property – it was the site of the later Lansdowne House, opposite the end of Friar's Stile Road.

[96 Goulston, Henry – this entry should follow 98 – see below]

Duppa's Almshouses, at the corner of Friar's Stile Road, had been built in 1661. They were not assessed for hearth tax.

97.  Allin, Richard ( = Richard Allen)                    owner              4 hearths
(Part of No. 93 in 1603 list; Nos. 602–604 in 1771 survey)
The site on the east side of the road, south of the almshouses, had already a house on it when it was acquired by William Kendall in 1628. He died in 1632/3 leaving the house to his widow Margaret for her lifetime. Her third husband, whom she married in February 1655/6, was Richard Allen. When Margaret Allen died in 1677 her daughter (by her second husband) Ann Wilde was the heir – and she also outlived three husbands. Richard Allen was appointed a collector of the hearth tax in 1665; in April 1667 he was charged at the assizes for illegally exacting tenpence from Thomas Allen of Merstham for issuing the latter with an exemption certificate.

98.  Muggett, Thomas                                        tenant             4 hearths
(Part of No. 93; Nso. 603–606 in 1771 survey)
There was a second cottage – on the site of the *Roebuck* – on the property inherited by Ann Wilde from her mother. Though the name of Thomas Muggett does not appear in the manor records, he was presumably the tenant in 1664.

*Plate 17*  96.  Goulstone, Henry (or Goldstone)                owner              1 hearth
(Part of No. 93 in 1603 list; No. 607 in 1771 survey)
A cottage had been built on the site of No. 1 The Terrace by John Leaver between 1613 and 1615. This was acquired by Henry Goulstone, another son of Lawrence (Senior) in 1643. In 1655 he built another small cottage on the site and was prosecuted by the manor court for encroaching over the ditch onto the highway. It seems possible that there should be an extra entry here, but only one cottage was mentioned in the manor records when the property passed to John Goldstone in 1677.

99.  Best, Arthur                                           owner              2 hearths
(Part of No. 93 in 1603 list, plus newly granted land; Nos. 608–613 in 1771 survey)
Arthur Best in 1664 held all the land between Henry Goulstone's cottage and the windmill (which stood just behind the present *Richmond Gate Hotel*). In 1621 Thomas Mercer had been granted an acre of land from the common by the southern corner of the upper Richmond field on condition that he build a windmill there. In 1629 he

acquired also the southern end of the strip of land between the field and the 'upper highway' (i.e. the sites of 2–4 The Terrace and Doughty House). The next owner William Bayley separated the mill from the rest of holding. The latter came into the hands of Arthur Best by marriage in 1653. The Bests' house, later sold to Henry Goldstone, was probably on the site of No. 3 The Terrace.

[Unidentified]
The next property which should figure in the list is the windmill itself, which was owned at this time by Henry and Richard Crane. In 1665 when John Williams became owner as the result of an unredeemed mortgage, there was a cottage in the mill yard as well as the mill, of which Richard Crane was said to be in occupation. Neither Crane nor Williams appears in the 1664 tax list.

## Hill Common (southern end)

| | | |
|---|---|---|
| 225. Goulstone, Lawrence (Senior) | owner | 1 hearth* |
| 226. Blanckes, John | tenant | 2 hearths* |
| ?227. Kersey, widow | tenant | 4 hearths* |
| (Not in 1603 list; Nos. 587–589 in 1771 survey) | (*non-chargeable) | |

An acre of land in a narrow strip along the southern edge of the Hill Common, where it bordered Petersham Common, was granted in 1639 to Francis Barnard on condition that he should maintain the fence between the two commons and a gate and stile therein. After Barnard's death his widow Ellen married Lawrence Goulstone (Senior). They divided the property, selling off in June 1664 the cottage at the top end (on the site of the Wick) which was then occupied by John Blanckes and Thomas Matthews. Matthews' name does not appear in the tax list.

There were two other cottages further down the hillside. One (on the site of the *Petersham Hotel*) had been purchased in 1656-57 by Samuel Rundall; in 1659 it was said to be in his own occupation; in 1672 it was occupied by Thomas Man. The other, by the lower road to Petersham (site of the *Rose of York*) had been bought in 1649 by Richard Haines. Haines still owned it at his death in 1667 when his son Edward was his heir. There is no mention of an occupant's name between 1649 and 1689. It seems likely that Goulstone and Blanckes were both in the top cottage in 1664 and that widow Kersey was in one of the others. But the next entry after hers in the non-chargeable list is clearly in Pensioners' Alley. It may be that the Rundall cottage was counted in with his other holdings (see 101 below).

## Petersham Road

| | | |
|---|---|---|
| 100. Perkins, James | owner | 5 hearths |
| (Not in 1603 list; No. 574 in 1771 survey) | | |

Land between the Petersham Road and the river, south of the Church Close, was granted in 1638 to Samuel Chambers and Augustine Reading. Chambers sold his land to Samuel Rundall in 1648, but it does not appear to have been built on until the 1680s. James Perkins acquired Reading's plot in 1644 and built a cottage on it. It remained in the ownership of the Perkins family until 1765 when it was sold to become part of the grounds of Montagu (later Buccleuch) House.

101. Randall, Samuel ( = Samuel Rundall) owner        6 hearths
(No. 90 in 1603 list; No. 296 in 1771 survey)
In addition to the cottage on Hill Common (see 225-227 above), Samuel Rundall, a tilemaker, owned three houses by the Petersham Road. One of these is at 103 below. One was at his tile kilns by the riverside, which he had acquired from Richard Goodgrome in 1654. 'Industrial hearths' were exempt from the tax, so the tile kilns themselves would not be included in the list. Rundall's other house was the larger 'Rump Hall' (see below). It seems likely that this entry refers to Rundall's cottage by the kilns (perhaps also adding in the cottage on the common). The cottage by the kiln was sold to George Carew in 1665.

102. Perkins, William                          owner        4 hearths
(Not in 1603 list; Nos. 575–579 in 1771 survey)
This cottage stood towards the southern end of the long strip of land between Moorbrook and the Petersham Road. The 1½ acres was divided into six separate quarter-acre plots by William Stone in 1638. The fifth lot (counting north to south) was bought by Henry Gray who built a cottage on it before he sold it to William Perkins in 1648. Perkins sold it to Samuel Moody in 1673. William Perkins was one of the group of Richmond watermen who were fined in 1664 for failure to repair the highways.

?103. Grimsell, Thomas (or Grimsdall)            tenant        2 hearths
(Not in 1603 list; part of No. 580 in 1771 survey)
This was probably a small cottage standing on the most southerly of the lots of strip land between the road and Moorbrook. This lot had been sold in 1638 to George Snelling who had built a cottage by the time he sold it to Samuel Rundall in 1646. On his death in 1672 Rundall bequeathed it to his grandson Rundall Pigg. There is no Grimsell or similar name in the manor records, but Thomas Grimsdall appears in the parish registers, with children baptised between 1660 and 1685. He died in 1689/90.

[Unidentified]
(Nos. 366–368 in 1771 survey)
'Rump Hall', a mansion with a long strip of land along the Petersham Road, occupying the site of the three most northerly lots of the former strip outside the Moorbrook

wall, was built by Jasper Lisney in the 1640s. Richard Adams purchased it in two parts, in 1649 and 1651, and sold it to Samuel Rundall in 1658. Rundall sold it to George Carew in 1665. It would probably have had more than the six hearths of entry No. 101 above, as it was used as Richmond's workhouse for some sixty years in the 18th century. (It is possibly No. 192 with nine hearths, which was obviously a last-minute entry to the chargeable list, but there is another rather more likely location for that in George Street. See pages 191 and 205.)

## Marshgate

Having completed their listing of the houses on the Hill and by the riverside, the tax assessors moved off to the eastern end of Richmond village, taking the 'green lane' across what was left of the Great Common, from a point near the park gate and the windmill, down to the Marsh Gate. Though grants of land outside the park wall near the gate had already been made, they had not yet been built on.

104. Moore, Ralph                 owner       3 hearths
(Not in 1603 list; Nos. 555–6 and 558 in 1771 survey)
Ralph Moore's cottage stood at the side of the common on the south side of the 'Marshgate Road'. It had eight acres of land in 1664 and was the nucleus of the later Spring Grove estate, but was still a modest house. It had been built by Thomas Bigg between 1603 and 1615. Moore bought it, and most of the land, from Martin Basill in 1636. He then held it until his death in 1664 when it was inherited by his daughter Frances Lorimer.

[Unidentified] (No. 94 in 1603 list; No. 557 in 1771 survey)
There were two cottages on the east side of the green lane at Marshgate, on the Mortlake boundary. The site of one was probably a grant to Clement Maunder at the end of Queen Elizabeth's reign, which had a cottage on it when Maunder's widow made over the reversion to her son Rowland in 1638. Rowland died in 1665 when his son Thomas inherited the cottage. The other cottage was built by Henry Maunder on land granted to him in 1649 and 1651. He died in 1663 when his son Michael was admitted as his heir, but his widow Alice (who remarried Henry Hall) appears to have remained in occupation. Neither Rowland nor Michael Maunder is included in the 1664 tax list, and Henry Hall is listed elsewhere – in George Street (No. 205). There are also listings elsewhere for two Mrs Halls (Senior in George Street No. 151 – and Junior in the Palace – No. 7). It is possible that these entries covered also the Marshgate cottages.

105. Manley, Mrs Elizabeth    Mother and guardian of owner       10 hearths
(No. 95 in 1603 list; No. 679 in 1771 survey)
'Pentecost House' passed through many hands from its building by Henry Pencost

(or Pentecost?) in 1580–81 to its acquisition by Richard Manley in 1654. He died four years later, leaving his widow Elizabeth as guardian for his son Richard aged ten. The house remained in Manley ownership until the end of the 17th century. In the latter half of the 18th century it was occupied by the steward of the manor and so got the rather misleading name of the 'Manor House'.

106. Best, William            owner      4 hearths
(No. 96 in 1603 list; No. 676 in 1771 survey)
This house was described as 'newly built' when sold by Roger Walter to John Preston in 1604. It stood on the easternmost half-acre strip of Upper Dunstable Shott. It was bought by William Best the elder in 1649 and inherited by his son William in 1661. The latter's widow sold it to Matthew Walker in 1695. It was on the site of the later Grena House.

*Marshgate Road (now Sheen Road) (north side)*

There were no further buildings along the Marshgate Road for over half a mile, until one came to:

107. Lever, William            owner      4 hearths
(Not in 1603 list; No. 499 in 1771 survey)
This house was built by William Lever, who had purchased in 1641 the half-acre strip of Upper Dunstable on which it stood. In 1657 he granted the reversion to his daughter Joan and her husband John Keele (Junior), whose family lived next door. William Lever died in 1657, John Keele in 1701. The house, largely rebuilt about 1750, is now Newnham House.

?108. Wood, Mr John          tenant      5 hearths
(Not in 1603 list; No. 498 in 1771 survey)
This, the predecessor of Marshgate House, was built by John Keele on a half-acre strip purchased in 1612. In 1658 he sold the house to Morgan Macklouthlen (*sic* – probably McLachlan) who was the legal occupier in 1662 when the hearth tax return recorded that the house was empty as its owner was in London, serving as footman to the Duke of York. Macklouthlen sold the house to Gilbert Urwin in 1664, but no occupier is then named. Mr Wood fits neatly in order. John Knapp bought the property in 1699 and built the present Marshgate House.

262. Ledgall, Mr ( = Nicholas Lydgould)      owner      8 hearths –
(Not in 1603 list; No. 497 in 1771 survey)                       empty
The Lydgoulds were a very old-established family in Kew and Richmond, but Nicholas and his wife Frances bought this house only in 1641. It had been built on a half-acre

strip by Thomas Man between 1604 and 1617. The house remained in the Lydgould family until purchased by Thomas Whitfield in 1680.

109. Turner, Dr ( = William Turner, LlD)       owner      12 hearths
(Not in 1603 list; No. 495 in 1771 survey)
On this site, a close of 1½ acres, a mansion and a cottage had been built by about 1640. In 1650 Dr William Turner (later Sir William) bought both from John Fifield. Sir William died in 1670 but the house remained in the ownership of his family until it was purchased by William Beyer in 1709.

110. Price, Mr (Richard Price?)       ?owner or tenant 7 hearths
(No. 97 in 1603 list; No. 494 in 1771 survey)
This must be the freehold property which stood between 109 and 113. It was one of the properties, the ownership of which was claimed from widow Mary Crome in the 1620s by the Richmond Vestry. Mrs Crome, though the legal judgement went against her, seems to have succeeded in retaining all the disputed properties. By 1654 the house was in the possession of Arthur Munday. As the title is not recorded in the manor court it is not clear whether Mr Price was owner or tenant in 1664. But it is almost certain that he was the Mr Richard Price whose children were baptised in Richmond between 1658 and 1664 and who was a juror at the Quarter Sessions in 1665.

## Marshgate (Sheen) Road (south side)

111. Keele, Robert       tenant      4 hearths
(Part of No. 99 in 1603 list; Nos. 529–30 in 1771 survey)
This house probably stood at or near the end of the island of land between the Marshgate Road and Paradise Row, which was freehold land belonging at this time to Dr William Turner. Robert Keele owned no copyhold property in this area except for a small cottage near the town pond which is otherwise accounted for (see No. 123).

112. Partridge, Lady       tenant      23 hearths
(Part of No. 99 in 1630 list; No. 528 in 1771 survey)
This is the large freehold mansion (later known as Carrington Lodge) which stood by the Marshgate (Sheen) Road, but with grounds running back to Paradise Row over a frontage (including 111 above) of some 500 feet on both roads. It was of 17th-century construction, but its date of building is uncertain. The owner in 1664 was Dr William Turner.

## Marshgate (Sheen) Road (north side continued)

113. Stobbard, Mr William ( = William Stobart) owner 22 hearths
(No. 98 in 1603 list; No. 493 in 1771 survey)
Clement Kinnersley bought the 'Scopeham's Farm' estate from George Peirce in 1639

and rebuilt the old house which stood on this site. When he sold it to William Stobart in 1654 the house was described as 'lately built of brick'. It remained in the Stobart family for nearly a century.

| | | | |
|---|---|---|---|
| ?193. | Goulston, Daniel | tenant | 2 hearths |

(Not on 1603 list; No. 491 in 1771 survey) (non-chargeable)

The last building on the north side of Marshgate Road, before reaching the open space where the village pond and the pound were situated, was a cottage built about 1640 by Matthew Moody and owned in 1664 by his son Samuel. Samuel Moody's name does not appear in the 1664 tax list, so the cottage must have been leased out. There is no evidence as to its occupant, but Daniel Goulston's name comes at an appropriate point in the non-chargeable list. Daniel (born 1628, died 1681, children baptised 1653-1676) was probably a son of Lawrence 'Senior'.

### Marshgate (Sheen) Road (south side continued)

| | | | |
|---|---|---|---|
| 114. | Vertue, Mrs (= Eizabeth Vertue, widow) | tenant | 7 hearths |
| 115. | Peirson, Richard (or Pierson) | tenant | 2 hearths |

(No. 100 in 1603 list; Nos. 217–18 in 1771 survey)

This property, which had belonged to Edmund Bird at the beginning of the century, was inherited in 1614 from Thomas Larkyn by his daughter Margaret wife of Richard (later Sir Richard) Manley. Their second son Richard inherited it in 1645 and built an extra small cottage. Title passed in 1658 to his son, a third Richard, then aged 10, with widow Elizabeth Manley as her son's guardian. Elizabeth Vertue was the widow of the Rev. Henry Vertue, Vicar of All Hallows, Honey Lane, London (who died in 1660); she died in 1673. By 1669 another cottage had been built on the property and when the inhabitants of the three houses were listed in 1677 one of them was Richard Pierson. (He had a daughter baptised in Richmond in March 1667/8 and died in February 1719/20.)

| | | | |
|---|---|---|---|
| 116. | Keele, John | owner | 6 hearths |

(No. 101 in 1603 list; Nos. 214–16 in 1771 survey)

This had been the *Goat Tavern* until 1634 when it came into the ownership of Mary Odling. Her son Dr Edward Odling MD sold it to John Keele in 1657. Keele held it until 1681 when it passed to John Michell on an unredeemed mortgage. The property was later developed as Union Court, etc.

### Middle Row

| | | | |
|---|---|---|---|
| ?117. | Watson, Samuel | tenant | 2 hearths |
| 118. | Mikalfe [sic], Enoch ( = Enoch Nicholls) | tenant | 2 hearths |

| | | |
|---|---|---|
| ?119. Tilsey, John ( = John Tinsley) | tenant | 2 hearths |
| ?196. Hewse, Thomas ( = Thomas Hughes) | tenant | 1 hearth (non-chargeable) |
| 197. Hubbert, John ( = John Hubbard) | tenant | 2 hearths (non-chargeable) |

(No. 103 in 1603 list; Nos. 220–225 in 1771 survey)

The cottage originally built by Henry Harvey in Queen Elizabeth's reign had been so added to and sub-divided that by 1664 there were five cottages on the site. They all belonged to Richard Keele, who inherited them from his father John in 1660 and left them to his daughter Elizabeth, wife of John Hopkins, on his death in 1666. The Hopkinses divided the property in 1666/7 when the occupants were given as Enoch Nicholls, John Gibson, John Hubbard, Robert Williams and John Wall. Only Nicholls and Hubbard appear in the 1664 tax list, in the chargeable and non-chargeable sections respectively, but the other three entries above seem indicated for this location by their position in the listing. Enoch Nicholls, a blacksmith, was a Quarter Sessions juror in 1662 and 1667-68. John Tinsley was a tapster who was prosecuted in 1661 for setting up as a painter without having served an apprenticeship. Two John Hubbards (presumably father and son, both labourers) were prosecuted in September 1661 for poaching. All but Samuel Watson appear in the parish registers as fathers of children baptised: Nicholls died in 1688/9, Tinsley in 1685/6, Hughes in 1677 and Hubbard (Senior) in 1689.

## World's End (the bottom end of the Kew Road, east side)

| | | |
|---|---|---|
| 120. Williams, John | owner | 7 hearths |
| 121. Clarke, Mr ( = Thomas Clarke) | owner | 12 hearths |
| 194. Braughton, Richard ( = Richard Broughton) | tenant | 2 hearths (non-chargeable) |
| 195. Kichin, William ( = William Kitchen) | tenant | 2 hearths (non-chargeable) |
| Unidentified house | | |
| 122. Thorpe, William | tenant | 4 hearths |
| ?123. Lewis, Daniel | tenant | 3 hearths |

(Nos. 107–104 in 1603 list; Nos. 473–484 in 1771 survey)

By 1664 the area along the first two hundred yards or so of the east side of the 'horse road' to Kew had been quite intensively developed with small cottages. The tax assessors started at the far end and worked back towards the town. John Williams acquired two houses (one of brick and one thatched) at the northern end in 1658. By 1673, when his son, also John, inherited, there were three on the site. There is no indication of tenants and John Williams' seven hearths in 1664 presumably represent two (or three) cottages.

South of Williams, Thomas Clarke, a bricklayer, bought two cottages in 1656. These were passed on to his daughter Mary and her husband William Butcher in 1669 and 1670. There is no indication that Clarke had added to the number of cottages, so his 12 hearths probably includes some other property (see at 192 below).

Next came Christopher Towne who had built two cottages by 1666 on a plot of land with a stable which he had purchased ten years earlier. When Towne, a victualler, died in 1666 and his wife Mary was admitted to the cottages, their occupants were Richard Broughton and William Kitchen.

The next cottage, belonging to Dorothy Painter and her son James Withers, was occupied in 1663 by Henry Hall, a gardener. His listing in 1664 with four non-chargeable hearths seems more appropriate to George Street (see 205 below), but might also cover this property.

The next property was on the site of the later *Bear Inn*. In 1663 it was owned by Margaret Moody (who had built it on a plot of land with barn which she had bought in 1651). It was then (1663) 'lately occupied by Thomas Barnes'. When her son Thomas Moody sold the cottage and barn to Thomas Eling in 1670 the occupant was George Smith. William Thorpe who married Margaret Smith in 1657 was almost certainly George's brother-in-law. (In 1662 he was a surety for Ralph Ditchfield's licence to keep an alehouse – the *Rose and Crown*, 124 below.)

The last house in this group was immediately north of the village pond (approximately where Richmond market is now). It had been built by Margaret, wife of John King, on land granted to her in 1646, and was sold by her to Robert Keele in 1663. The occupant then was Richard Broughton who evidently moved soon afterwards. When Keele sold it to Thomas Young in 1673 the occupant was Thomas Field. There is no documentary evidence to place Daniel Lewis in the house, but the order of listing makes this probable.

## George Street (north-west side)

124. Duchfield, Ralph ( = Ralph Ditchfield)       tenant- innkeeper  8 hearths
(No. 14 in 1603 list; Nos. 162–163 in 1771 survey)
The *Rose and Crown* inn at the corner of Duke's Lane and the main street was already well established when John Spicer purchased it from Arthur Munday in 1654. The lessee was then George Wilde, but Ralph Ditchfield had taken over by 1662 when he was granted a licence. He died in October 1664. John Spicer died in 1683 and his son John sold the inn to Abraham Matthews in 1683.

125. Spicer, John                                 owner          8 hearths
(Part of Nos. 14 & 15 in 1603 list; No. 161 in 1771 survey)
Immediately to the south-west of the *Rose and Crown* was a small cottage which had

originally formed part of the same premises and which John Spicer had bought in 1643. Then came a large parcel of land which Spicer purchased as a garden from Humphrey Heycock in 1660. John Spicer was a carpenter and master-builder (his sons achieved the status of 'gentlemen'). He had probably rebuilt the cottage as a substantial house by 1664. It too was sold to Abraham Matthews, in 1687.

?126. Drew, William                                    tenant              5 hearths
(Part of No. 15 in 1603 list; Nos. 159–160 in 1771 survey)
This was probably a house built by John Spicer on the central part of the garden mentioned above. When the Spicer family finally sold the property in 1716 the house had been divided into two and one of the occupants was Thomas Drew, great-nephew of the William listed here. Though there is no documentary evidence of occupation, it seems likely that the Drews had been tenants throughout this period. William Drew was described as 'yeoman', but his family all became (for several generations) carpenters or bricklayers. His children were baptised between 1620 and 1630; he died in January 1663/4. The listing may be for him – or perhaps his son William.

## George Street (south-east side)

The house immediately next to 116 (see at Marshgate Road above) was the old manse for the minister of Richmond Parish Church (No. 102 in 1603 list). Its eastern boundary was where Eton Street was developed in the 1850s. After the intended eviction of the minister (averted by his death) in 1647, the property was let in 1650 to Charles Kynaston for 32 years. Though probably sub-let by him, the house as church property may not have been included in the tax assessment.

?192. Burke, Mr (? = Valentine Clarke)                  tenant              9 hearths
(Nos. 108–109 in 1603 list; No. 212 in 1771 survey)
On the south-west side of the church property was a house which was rented from Robert Trotter and his wife Ann in 1646 by Simon Bardolph, gent. A cottage was added at this time. In 1652 and 1653 house and cottage were sold by widow Ann Trotter to George Mawhood and his wife Anne (who was Simon Bardolph's daughter). George Mawhood died at the end of 1653 and the cottage passed through the ownership of three of his daughters in turn before being sold in April 1664 to Giles Davies, a merchant and grocer, who was the husband of another daughter. The main house remained in the hands of widow Anne (who remarried William Short) until her death in 1659 when it was left to the five surviving daughters jointly. In 1664 Giles Davies acquired all the shares held by his four sisters-in-law. The house was at that time occupied by Valentine Clarke. His name does not appear in the 1664 tax list or in the parish registers. There seem to be two possible explanations. If Valentine Clarke was

related to Thomas Clarke (see 121 above) some eight of the 12 hearths assessed to 'Mr Clarke' might relate to this property. Alternatively the nine hearths of 'Mr Burke' – the very last entry in the chargeable list and obviously a 'postscript' – may belong here, or is Burke a misreading for Clarke? There is still a gable end of this house remaining at No. 38A George Street.

?198. Goose, John                                    tenant                    5 hearths
                                                     (non-chargeable)

(Part of Nos. 110–112 in 1603 list; Nos. 204–205 in 1771 survey)
The next house belonged to John Smith and his wife Elizabeth from 1650 to 1687. By 1687 it had been divided into two. There is no reference to its occupancy between 1629 and 1687. John Smith's name does not appear in the 1664 tax list, but John Goose's comes at an appropriate point in the list of non-chargeable properties. Goose was a husbandman, and was one of those presented in 1662 for failure to attend church.

127. Presturge, Mr ( = Thomas Prestwick)             owner                     5 hearths
(Part of Nos. 110–112 in 1603 list; No. 203 in 1771 survey)
Originally part of the same property as the previous entry, this was the site of the early 16th-century 'kilnhouse'. The two properties were divided in 1629, and this house was bought in 1633 by John Child and his wife Elizabeth. It was inherited in 1661 by their daughter Mary, wife of Thomas Prestwick. When Prestwick sold it to Giles Davies in January 1664/5 it had been in his own occupation.

128. Peachmond, Mr Christopher ( = Chistopher Peachman)   tenant     6 hearths
(No. 113 in 1603 list; No. 202 in 1771 survey)
The house at the corner of Church Lane came into the hands of the Manley family in 1614. In 1659 Margaret Manley and her husband William Powell sold it to Philip Owen as 'a messuage, yard and garden in the occupation of Christopher Peachman'. Owen, who died in 1667, left 'Peachman's house' to his daughter Jane Brent and her son Philip Brent.

## Church Yard

?191. Smith, Walter                                  owner                     4 hearths
199. Smith, widow ( = Margaret Smith)                owner                     1 hearth
                                                     (non-chargeable )
?200. Wyn, Anthony ( = Anthony Wynn)                 tenant                    2 hearths
                                                     (non-chargeable)
201. Bradshaw, James                                 tenant                    2 hearths
                                                     (non-chargeable)

(Part of Nos. 110–112 in 1603 list; Nos. 206–211 in 1771 survey)

On the north-east side of the churchyard were two buildings, divided into three or four separate dwellings, all belonging to the parish clerk, Walter Smith, who succeeded his father William in that office in 1653. At the end nearer Paradise Row was a house built by William Smith on land granted to him in 1639. After his death his widow Margaret continued to enjoy a life interest (she died in 1673) but Walter held the reversionary right. It is inherently improbable that the parish clerk's home had only one hearth, so it is almost certain that the 'postscript' entry for Walter Smith should be included here. His mother was probably living in the 17th-century equivalent of a 'granny flat' – a divided off part of the main house.

Closer to the east end of the church was another house, divided into two cottages about 1604, which was purchased by Walter Smith and his wife from Elizabeth Child in 1661. Its occupants then were James Bradshaw and widow Mary Lawson. Evidently Anthony Wynn had succeeded widow Lawson in occupation by 1664. He died, with two of his family, in the plague summer of 1665.

## Church Lane (now Church Court) (west side)

129. Jordan, Andrew ( = Andrew Gordon)      tenant      2 hearths
(No. 115 in 1603 list; Nos. 199–201 in 1771 survey)

The house nearest to the churchyard on the west side of Church Lane was inherited by Charles, son of Samuel and Margaret Blayton, in 1653. The tenant of the house at that date is not named, but when part of the garden was sold in 1649 it was in the occupation of Andrew Gordon. The property was sold to Jonah Smith in 1668 and he subsequently divided it into three houses. Andrew Gordon was still occupying the southernmost of these in 1687.

130. Mander, Margery ( = Margery Maunder)      tenant      6 hearths
?131. Reasey, John (? = John Vesey)      tenant      5 hearths
(Nos. 116–117 in 1603 list; Nos. 197–198 in 1771 survey)

The two freehold houses at the corner of Church Lane and George Street appear to have been increased to four by 1664. (These two and those at 142 and 143 below.) These two were in 1649 in the ownership of Harrington Drayton (who bought the patch of garden from 129 mentioned above) and in the occupation of Rowland Maunder. Margery was the widow of Rowland Maunder who died in August 1650. The houses were owned by William Drayton in 1668.

No John Reasey is traceable in manor or parish records, but there is a John Vesey. His cottage in Brewers Lane (see No. 203 below) is unlikely to have been recorded at this point, and as that appears to have been leased out, Vesey was presumably living in rented premises elsewhere. This listing seems very probably to relate to him. John Vaizey 'of Richmond, baker', stood surety in July 1662 for Gilbert Grimes.

*George Street (north-west side)*

| | | |
|---|---|---|
| 132. Knowles, James | tenant | 2 hearths |
| 133. Mudey, Margaret ( = Margaret Moody) | owner | 2 hearths |
| 134. Skinner, John | tenant | 5 hearths |

(No. 17 in 1603 list; Nos. 154–156 in 1771 survey)

The two cottages which existed in 1604 were in the hands of the Downing (or Downham) family from 1614 to 1650–51. One of them, apparently standing back from the street, was called the *White Lion* in 1638. In 1662 the two houses were purchased by Margaret Moody. In May 1666 they were occupied by James Knowles and Elizabeth Skinner (widow of John who died in October 1665). James Knowles issued a halfpenny trade token, at the *Drapers' Arms* in Richmond in 1664. The name of the *White Lion*, however, occurs again at this place in the 1720s. John Skinner, a candle-maker, issued a trade token in 1658.

About 1614 a 'new small messuage' had been erected on the north-eastern side of the *Three Pigeons* (see 135 below) and Robert King, then owner of the *Three Pigeons*, sold it off to his tenant Robert Trotter. In 1648, then occupied by William Downham, it came into the hands of Margaret Moody, and in the following year she acquired a piece of land at the back from the Downhams. It was occupied by Margaret Moody's daughter Sarah Goodhall and her husband John in 1660, but Margaret herself had apparently moved in by 1664. Sarah Goodhall succeeded to all three houses on Margaret's death in August 1666.

| | | |
|---|---|---|
| 135. Stanley, Thomas | owner-innkeeper | 11 hearths |

(No. 20 in 1603 list; Nos. 152–153 in 1771 survey)

At the south-east corner of Brewer's Lane the Lily Pott tavern had become the *Three Pigeons and Lilypot* by 1624. The change of name probably coincided with a rebuilding by George Charley who acquired the inn in 1614, for it was described as the 'new brick house at the sign of *Three Pigeons*' in 1629. It had almost certainly been rebuilt by 1624 when George Charley sold it to Helen Hill. It had at that time '11 spaces, viz. hall, parlour, kitchen, buttery, shop, cellar and 5 chambers' as well as three stables and a courtyard. Thomas Stanley purchased the inn from Helen Hill's son Thomas Bunn in 1651. He remained landlord until his death in 1693. It was then continued by his widow Martha and his daughter Elizabeth. In 1714 it was acquired as a site for the new parochial free school.

| | | |
|---|---|---|
| ?202. Wolfe, widow | tenant | 2 hearths |

(Part of No. 20 in 1603 list; part of No. 153 in 1771 survey)   (non-chargeable)

There were two or three small cottages built round the yard of the *Three Pigeons*. One is mentioned above (at 132–134). Another was quite likely to have been occupied by the widow of Francis Wolfe, who had been the innkeeper of the *Three Pigeons* before

Thomas Stanley and who had died in 1661. Another cottage belonged to John Child and is noted at 141 below.

## Brewer's Lane

The tax assessor turns up Brewer's Lane towards the Green, noting houses on either side as he comes to them.

| | | |
|---|---|---|
| 136. Nicholson, Mary | owner | 5 hearths |

(No. 24 in 1603 list; Nos. 125–126 in 1771 survey)
The first building on the left after the corner cottage (left to be dealt with later in George Street) was the *King's Arms* alehouse, purchased by Thomas and Mary Nicholson in 1650. It first appears under that name in 1619, but the reference in 1650 is the last use of the name, so the Nicholsons may have turned it back into a private residence. Thomas Nicholson died in 1655; his widow Mary in 1677, leaving the house to her nephew Thomas Hewson.

| | | |
|---|---|---|
| 203. Cooke, James | tenant<br>(non-chargeable) | 2 hearths |
| [248. Carter, George | tenant | ?2 hearths |

(No. 25 in 1603 list; Nos. 127–128 in 1771 survey)    (non-chargeable)]
Next door to the *King's Arms* was a pair of cottages belonging to John Vesey (see at 131 above). Vesey mortgaged them to John Turnbull in 1664 and lost ownership to Turnbull in 1665; they were recorded in July 1664 as occupied by George Carter and Hugh Carter, but in 1673 as occupied by George Carter and James Cooke. It would seem that Cooke had just moved in when the 1664 assessment was made. George Carter's assessment for 11 hearths, all non-chargeable, has already been remarked upon (see No. 248 – at page 161). It is probable that two hearths here made up part of that total.

| | | |
|---|---|---|
| 137. Smith, Jeffrey | owner | 3 hearths |

(Part of No. 20 in 1603 list; No. 152 in 1771 survey)
Almost opposite the *King's Arms* was a small cottage of three rooms, sold off from the *Three Pigeons* property by George Charley in 1619. It was purchased in 1653 by Jeffrey Smith, crossbow-maker. He lived there until his death in 1673 when it passed in turn to his sons John and (in 1678) Richard Smith.

| | | |
|---|---|---|
| ?204. Warren, Henry | tenant | 3 hearths |

(Part of No. 20 in 1603 list; part of No. 151 in 1771 survey)   (non-chargeable)
The cottage next to the one above was mortgaged by George Charley and his son James to Simon Pointer in 1648, and came into the hands of Jeffrey Smith by 1657.

There is no evidence as to its occupancy in 1664. Henry Warren was living in a small cottage in Old Palace Lane (see at No. 11 above) when it was sold in April 1664. He may have moved here to Brewer's Lane. He died in January 1671/2.

| | | |
|---|---|---|
| 138. Smith, Robert | tenant | 5 hearths |
| 139. Lewis, John | tenant | 2 hearths |

(Part of No. 19 in 1603 list; No. 151 in 1771 survey)

The next property on the right, going up Brewer's Lane, was the house that by 1690 became the *Magpye* tavern. It, together with a smaller cottage was acquired by Jeffrey Smith in 1655 and sold by him to Alexander Bower in 1657. Jeffrey Smith, however, was still listed as occupant of one of the cottages in 1673 (when Charles Bower inherited from Alexander) and it may be that Robert (?a nephew) was living in it in 1664. John Lewis, a cordwainer, seems from the order of listing to be the other tenant. He was a constable in 1668 when charged with dereliction of duty for refusing to arrest a wrongdoer for whom a warrant had been issued.

| | | |
|---|---|---|
| 140. Bower, Alexander | owner | 12 hearths |

(Part of Nos. 26–30 in 1603 list; Nos. 94, 129 and 148–150 in 1771 survey)

In addition to the two properties just mentioned, Alexander Bower owned the property adjoining them on the north side which he had bought in 1655 (this was the former cottage of William Brewer). He also acquired, in a series of deals between 1655 and 1662, the house at No. 14 The Green and the four shops at the top end of the left side of Brewer's Lane. One of these shops is accounted for in the next entry and two of the other three may be the non-chargeable entries following that. It seems likely that one shop, the house at 14 The Green and the former Brewer cottage added up to the 12 hearths assessed here. Alexander Bower died in 1678 when his son Charles inherited all his property.

| | | |
|---|---|---|
| 141. Chyld, John ( = John Child) | tenant and owner | 5 hearths |

(Part of Nos. 26–30 in 1603 list; part of No. 129 and part of No. 153 in 1771 survey)

John Child was occupying the shop nearest the Green in 1661, but this was unlikely to account for more than two or three hearths. The others probably belonged to the cottage immediately behind the *Three Pigeons* inn, which John Child sold to Thomas Stanley, the innkeeper, in 1681. Child's acquisition of this property has not been traced; it was probably a cottage which James Charley (grandson of George) sold to Joseph Day in 1638 and the latter bequeathed to Henry Day in 1653.

| | | |
|---|---|---|
| ?245: Davis, Lewis | tenant | 1 hearth* |
| ?246. Horton, John | tenant | 2 hearths* |
| ?247. Ellyott, John | tenant | 3 hearths* |
| | | *(all non-chargeable) |

(Part of Nos. 26–30 in 1603 list; parts of No. 129 in 1771 survey)

These three entries, coming as they do immediately before that for George Carter (No. 248 above) may be presumed to relate to properties in the Brewer's Lane or Green (south side) area. Lewis Davis can be placed in Brewer's Lane in 1658/9 in the Vesey house (No. 203 above) but had evidently moved out of it by 1664. 'Hobson' and 'Elliott' (no first names) occur in a list of five occupants of Brewer's Lane punished by the manor court in 1659 for throwing 'draught' (sewage) into the lane. 'Hobson' may be a misreading for Horton; the parish registers confirm the existence of a John Horton (died January 1657/8) and a John Horton Junior (children baptised 1644 and 1647, died January 1680/1). There is no information as to the occupancy of three of Alexander Bower's four shops, and these three probably account for two, or all three, of them.

## George Street (south-east side)

The tax assessor returns to the corner of Church Lane to continue along the south-east side of George Street.

| | | |
|---|---|---|
| 142. Draton, William ( = William Drayton) | owner | 5 hearths |
| ?143. Fuller, Mrs | tenant | 6 hearths |

(Part of Nos. 116–117 in 1603 list; No. 196 on 1771 survey)

William Drayton was the heir, probably the son, of Harrington Drayton. The freehold property at this corner appears to have included two more houses in addition to Nos. 130 and 131. There is no clue as to the identity of Mrs Fuller, who is fitted in here solely by virtue of the order of listing. William Drayton was one of the two constables in 1668 who were charged with dereliction of duty (see at 139 above).

| | | |
|---|---|---|
| 144. Mudey, Matthew ( = Matthew Moody) | owner | 9 hearths |
| 145. Parford, Abraham ( = Rev Abiel Borfett ) | tenant | 10 hearths |

(No. 118 in 1603 list; Nos. 194 and 195 in 1771 survey)

There were two 'cottages' in this corner of the former Clarke estate when Sir Richard Manley sold them to John King in 1633. By 1656 both had been rebuilt as substantial houses and had come into the ownership of Matthew Moody the younger. Moody himself lived, as his father had done, in the north-easterly one; the other was rented out. The Rev. Abiel Borfett, minister of Richmond Parish Church from 1660 to 1696, had become the tenant by 1661. By 1703 this house had become the *White Horse* inn, which was rebuilt and renamed the *Greyhound* by 1726. Matthew Moody was one of the two churchwardens accused of misappropriation of poor relief funds in 1665.

| | | |
|---|---|---|
| 146. Nash, Mr John | tenant | 9 hearths |
| 147. Griffin, Morgan | tenant | 4 hearths |

148. Foist, Jervise ( = Jarvis or Gervase Foster)    tenant    2 hearths
(No. 119 in 1603 list; Nos. 189–193 in 1771 survey)
Most of the Clarke estate was sold by Henry Clarke (a brother of Robert) to Sir
Richard Manley in 1630 and by him to John Gregory in 1649. This group of three
houses was sold by Gregory to Robert Wilkins, a clockmaker, and his wife Margaret
in 1659, and by them to Barbara, wife of William Short Esquire in 1661. The occupants
in 1661 were listed as John Nash, Morgan Griffin and Gervase Foster. The same tenants
were recorded in 1670 when Barbara's son and two daughters inherited the three
properties. The large house, the most north-easterly, was where Mr Nash had his
school in 1651. He died in February 1665/6. Jarvis Foster (as his name appears in the
parish resisters) was a bargeman. He married Anne Hill of Lambeth in April 1654, had
eight children baptised between 1656 and 1671, and died in 1690. Morgan Griffin is not
mentioned in the registers.

149. Lageat, William ( = William Leggatt)    tenant    3 hearths
(No. 120 in 1603 list; Nos. 184–188 in 1771 survey)
Though listed at this point, this property did not face onto George Street. It lay
behind the group 146–148 above, stretching right through to Red Lion Street, by the
side of the churchyard. It had also been sold by John Gregory to Robert Wilkins in
1651. In 1661 it was described as an orchard with a tenement occupied by William
Leggatt. Robert Wilkins died in February 1659–60; his heir was his son, also Robert.
By 1671, when Robert Wilkins the younger passed ownership to his brother Edmund,
a brewhouse had been built on the property. It was approached by a lane from the
main street, which survived first as Artichoke Alley and now as Victoria Place.

150. Wilkinse, Edward ( = Edmund Wilkins)    tenant    3 hearths
151. Hall, Mrs, Senior    tenant    5 hearths
?205. Hall, Henry    tenant    4 hearths
(Part of No. 121 in 1603 list; Nos. 178–183 in 1771 survey)   (non-chargeable)
On the south-west side of the lane and orchard mentioned. above, Robert Wilkins
owned another three cottages, one by the main street, one a little way down the lane,
and one further down, beside the orchard (with an entrance to Red Lion Street).
None of the names of the occupants in 1672, when Wilkins sold this property to
Thomas Eling Junior, occurs in the 1664 tax list. These three entries in the chargeable
and non-chargeable lists are the next in order. It clearly makes sense that Edmund
Wilkins should be living in a house belonging to his brother. There are other locations
where Henry Hall's name or that of a Mrs Hall might be appropriate (e.g. at Marshgate),
but to put these entries there would be a major aberration in the pattern of listing.
Henry Hall was a 'gardener' (i.e. market gardener). He died in 1680.

152. Wilkins, Margaret              owner        3 hearths
(Part of No. 121 in 1603 list; Nos. 175–177 in 1771 survey)
Margaret, widow of Robert Wilkins the clockmaker, released all rights in the family property to her son Robert in 1668 (the young Robert had still been a minor when his father died). At that time (1668) she was living in the cottage at the south-western end of the Wilkins property. The land stretched right through to Red Lion Street. When sold by the younger Robert Wilkins in 1671 to Richard Johnson, a carpenter, Johnson was already in occupation of the cottage.

## George Street (north-west side)

The tax assessor at this point returns to the north-west side of George Street, starting with the cottage at the corner of Brewer's Lane.

?153. Cowley, Thomas               tenant     2 hearths
?154. Baybee, William ( = William Bibby)     tenant     2 hearths
?155. Eatton, Anthony ( = Anthony Eaton)     tenant     2 hearths
(No. 21-23 in 1603 list; Nos. 123–124 in 1771 survey)
These cottages cannot be identified with certainty, but the entries are located here by order of listing. John Cogdell bought three cottages by the end of Brewer's Lane in 1604. By 1629 when his son Thomas Cogdell inherited, there seem to have been four on the site. The occupants of two of the cottages are named in 1642, and of all four in 1692 when Thomas Cogdell died. But these names have no relevance to the 1664 tax list.

    Thomas Cowley married in 1642 and died in 1689. He is probably identical with Thomas Cowling, waterman of Richmond, who was charged at the October Sessions in 1662 with an assault on some women who were 'almost drowned' (an argument over fares?). William Bibby, cordwainer, was a juror in 1665. Anthony Eaton was charged in 1667 with setting up and exercising 'the art, mystery and manual occupation of a barber' without having served an apprenticeship in that trade. He may be the Anthony Eaton, tailor, who died in 1698.

156. Shellin, George ( = George Snelling)    father of owner  1 hearth
?157. Deane, Thomas                   tenant         2 hearths
(Part of Nos. 31–37 in 1603 list; Nos. 121–122 in 1771 survey)
In 1661 George Snelling made over to his son Henry two cottages on the north-west side of the main street, adjoining the property mentioned above. One was occupied by himself and the other by Edward Ball. George did not die until 1670 so it is likely that he was the 'George Shellin' of the tax list. Thomas Deane (married in 1645) who had lived on The Green at the corner of Brewer's Lane until April 1664 (see at Nos.

32–33 above) had probably just moved into this cottage, vacated by Edward Ball (or Bell) who moved to a larger house a few doors away (161).

| | | |
|---|---|---|
| 158. Hamerton, Jacob | owner | 2 hearths |
| 159. Mander, William ( = William Maunder) | owner | 4 hearths |
| 160. Cowen, George ( = George Cowing) | tenant | 2 hearths |
| 206. Prichat, William ( = William Pritchard) | tenant (non-chargeable) | 2 hearths |
| 161. Bell, Edward | tenant | 5 hearths |

(Part of Nos. 31–37 in 1603 list; Nos. 117–120 in 1771 survey)
The two previous cottages (156 and 157) and this group all stood at the back of Mary Crome's property facing the Green (see 34 and 35 above). Mary's son Daniel Crome sold them to Edward Munday in 1649 and the latter's son Arthur divided up the property in 1651.

Jacob Hamerton, Arthur Munday's brother-in-law, and his wife Ann, had the first two cottages, counting from the north. They kept one for themselves and sold the larger one to William Maunder in 1664. The other two cottages (there were only four in 1651) went to Arthur's sister Jane Munday who later married Henry Stridwick. The Stridwicks subdivided one of these into two smaller cottages and in 1662 sold these two, occupied by George Cowing and William Pritchard, to Luke Chynnel. (The Chynnel property was on the site now occupied by Boots.) In 1666 the Stridwicks sold the other house, described as 'a brick house occupied by Edward Bell', to John Child. This last house remained in the ownership of the Child family well into the 18th century, when it became the *Black Boy* inn.

| | | |
|---|---|---|
| 207. Garrett, James | tenant | 2 hearths |

(Part of Nos. 39–42 in 1603 list; No. 116 in 1771 survey)   (non-chargeable)
The next four cottages had all belonged to Thomas Gisby; this one he had made over to Isabella Spurling in 1586. It stayed in the hands of heirs of Isabella Spurling until 1628. It was purchased in 1654 by Philip Owen. When he made it over to his daughter Joan, wife of Daniel Brent, in 1665 it was occupied by James Garrett. Garrett died in September 1667.

| | | |
|---|---|---|
| 162. Bodeycott, Moses ( = Moses Boddicott) | tenant | 4 hearths |

(Part of Nos. 39–42 in 1603 list; No. 115 in the 1771 survey)
This was just a yard with barns when sold by Thomas Gisbie Junior in 1613. George Charley built a house on it between 1615 and 1628. When John Spicer bought it in 1657 the occupant was William Leaver, but when he sold it twenty years later the occupant was Moses Boddicott (who had obviously moved in by 1664). Moses Boddicott was a victualler, but there is no evidence that this house was a tavern.

163. Spicer, James        owner      2 hearths
(Part of Nos. 39–42 in 1603 list; No. 114 in 1771 survey)
This cottage, just repaired by him, was sold by Thomas Gisbie Junior in 1638 to Thomas Charley, and the latter's niece, Mary Gotobed, sold it to James Spicer in 1646. Spicer lived there until 1675 when he sold it to Samuel Moody. James Spicer had children baptised in Richmond from 1647 to 1666. He died in 1675.

208. Greene, William        tenant      2 hearths
(Part of Nos. 39–42 in 1603 list; No. 113 in 1771 survey)    (non-chargeable)
In 1638 Thomas Gisbie Junior not only repaired the cottage above, but built this new one next to it. In 1658 (having been previously mortgaged to John Bunckle) it came into the ownership of Gisbie's aunt Ann Strickson. When in 1659 she relinquished her rights in the property to Bunckle the cottage was occupied by William Greene. He was still shown as occupant when Bunckle's widow Elizabeth and her new husband John Bond sold it to Thomas Yonge, waterman, in 1663. It remained in the ownership of Yonge's descendants for over 100 years.

## George Street (south-east side continued)

On reaching Pensioners' Alley, the tax assessor returns to the south-east side of the street.

?164. Downing, John (or Downham?)      tenant      2 hearths
?165. Browne, Robert              tenant      2 hearths
(No. 122 in 1603 list; Nos. 172–174 in 1771 survey)
This was the only part of the former Clarke estate not sold to Robert Wilkins. In 1649 Ambrose Lovell bought a cottage with orchard and barn and, separately, another barn and stable with yard. He built a new brick house, which he was occupying in 1651 when he mortgaged the cottage and orchard and one barn to Margaret Moody. In 1659 title to this latter part of the property passed to Matthew Moody, blacksmith, and in 1667 Matthew Moody bought from Lovell the other house 'lately occupied by Ambrose Lovell and now by John Udale'. Neither Lovell nor Udale appears in the 1664 tax list, so these entries, given the order of listing, would appear to be the tenants in that year. Udale does not appear in the parish registers. John Downham had children baptised in Richmond from 1653 to 1669. He is probably the John son of William baptised in 1626 and the John, waterman, who died in August 1700. It does not seem likely that the Robert Browne here was the one who was later going to develop Richmond Wells.

166. Ashley, Mr George ( = George Astley)      ex-owner      8 hearths
167. Ashley, Mr William ( = William Astley)      owner      10 hearths

(Nos. 123–124 in 1603 list; Nos. 168–171 in 1771 survey)
The large house and cottage next to the *Red Lion* had been divided by 1611 into three dwellings. (One was rented by Sir William Segar, Garter King of Arms, from 1621 to his death in 1633.) In 1651 George Astley purchased the 'messuage now three tenements'. In October 1663 he made over to his son William Astley 'two messuages newly erected in the garden near the old house of George Astley', and in February 1663/4 he also made over his own 'old house'. George Astley died in 1666; William in 1677 (succeeded by his son William who sold the property in 1681).

### George Street (north-west side continued)

| | | |
|---|---|---|
| ?168. Peirse, Thomas | tenant | 3 hearths |
| ?169. Young, Thomas | tenant | 3 hearths |
| ?181. Pennar, John ( = John Pennard) | tenant | 1 hearth |
| 182. Tomkins, Jonathan | tenant | 2 hearths |

(Part of No. 43 in 1603 list; Nos. 101–103 and 112 in 1771 survey)
The next entries on the north-west side of the street should be for the houses at the George Street end of the Pensioners' Alley property, owned at this time by Richard Burnham (see at 228–243 above, listed after No. 36 on pages 161-2). The difficulty in identifying the component dwellings on this property has been mentioned there. Apart from the order of listing, the only clue helping to tie in these entries is that in 1680 Elizabeth Burnham's cottage (one of the three-hearth ones) was bordered on the east by a tenement 'lately occupied by Jonathan Tomkins' (the two-hearth one). Next to the former Tomkins house was a very tiny cottage indeed, by the entrance to the alley, which could very well be one of the few single-hearth listings. John Pennard had children baptised in 1664–69, but then vanishes from the registers. Jonathan Tomkins's children were baptised 1660–74; he died in 1684. Thomas Young was a waterman, married in 1654, with children from 1655 to 1666, died in March 1706/7. Thomas Peirce was probably the son of William, baptised in February 1627/8; his children were baptised 1655–63, and then he too disappears from the registers. But it is also possible that the Pennard and Tomkins entries are 'postscripts' and could belong elsewhere.

| | | |
|---|---|---|
| 170. King, John | former owner | 4 hearths |
| ?171. Biggs, Henry | tenant | 2 hearths |

(Part of Nos. 44–46 in 1603 list; No. 98 in 1771 survey)
In 1658 John King inherited from his father John, the owner of the *Queen's Arms* (see at 62 etc above) three tenements, with haylofts, stables, a barn and a yard on the north-east side of the inn yard, abutting on the houses of Pensioners' Alley. The stables were bought by Thomas Eling in 1663 (see 60); the houses John made over to his brother Robert. There is no indication of the occupancy of the houses (except that John was himself living in one in 1660) until 1680 when Robert King's widow (by

then widowed again) Mary Harris sold them to Thomas Eling junior. Only one of the names occurring in 1680 is in the 1664 list – that of Bartholomew Warner, who was more probably in Water Lane in 1664.

172. Crose, Richard, senior ( = Richard Cross)  owner   2 hearths
(Part of Nos. 44–46 in 1603 list; No. 100 in 1771 survey)
The house, at the end of John King's little row, facing onto George Street, which belonged to Isabella Spurling in 1616, was sold by her grandson Robert Wilks to Richard Cross in 1633. He lived there until his death about 1680.

## George Street (south-east side)

As he had already listed the houses past the entrance to the former Queen's Arms inn yard, the assessor crosses the main street a last time to take in the *Red Lyon* inn and the houses close to it.

173. Crose, Richard, junior ( = Richard Cross)  tenant   4 hearths
174. Boulton, William          tenant   4 hearths
175. Farley, William       owner-innkeeper 12 hearths
(No. 125 in 1603 list; Nos. 164–167 in 1771 survey)
The *Red Lyon* had belonged to Alexander Slaney from 1563, but in 1603 it was in the hands of Elizabeth Boone. She died in 1605, leaving it to her son Michael Meriall. By 1615 when Michael Meriall's ownership was challenged (unsuccessfully) by Jasper Slaney, two cottages had been divided off from the main property. Bernard Hide acquired it from Meriall in 1624 but had the property confiscated from him in 1630 because he had 'allowed it to fall down and to go to ruin'. His son was readmitted, to make a surrender to Thomas Smallpiece, who presumably restored the property before selling it to Edward Farley in 1635. From Edward it passed to his son William in 1655. William Farley held the inn until 1672 when John Spiller foreclosed on a mortgage. William issued a trade token (undated) 'at ye Read Lion'. There is no record of the occupancy of the cottages, but as the listings for Richard Cross Junior and William Boulton come before that for William Farley, and as the cottages were on the north-east side of the inn, they seem to fit neatly. Boulton was variously described as 'labourer', 'waterman' and 'cheese-monger' when he made various appearances at the Sessions in 1661 to answer a charge of assault.

## ?Red Lion Street

?176. Pullmer, Robert ( = Robert Palmer)  ?tenant   1 hearth
?177. Eling, Thomas, Junior      ?tenant   6 hearths
(?part of No. 81 in 1603 list; part of No. 247 in 1771 survey)

The location of these properties is uncertain, but they may have stood behind the Red Lyon, at the north end of the close of freehold land which ran up beside Hill Street (see 78-81). Almost certainly Robert Palmer and Thomas Eling Junior were near neighbours of William Boulton (see immediately above) as they stood surety for him in 1661. Palmer had children baptised in Richmond from 1668 onwards and died in 1687, but cannot be traced in the manor records. The only copyhold property owned by Thomas Eling Junior in 1664 was the house occupied by Susan Tillman and listed under her name (209, see at 62 above).

| | | |
|---|---|---|
| 178. Drew, Thomas | owner | 4 hearths |

(Not in 1603 list; No. 260 in 1771 survey)
Thomas Drew, yeoman, acquired two acres of copyhold land at the west end of Church Shott of the upper Richmond field in 1658 and 1663. By the 1680s he had built three cottages on them. His own – presumably built by 1664 – was on the south-side of the lane behind the Red Lyon.

| | | |
|---|---|---|
| ?179. Mowbray, Mr William | ? | 5 hearths |
| ?180. Gibson, Francis | ? | 4 hearths |

(Not in 1603 list; ?No. 261 in 1771 survey)
These might be Thomas Drew's other two cottages, if he had built them by 1664. Or these entries may be 'postscripts' (especially if Nos. 181 and 182 are placed in that category instead of by Pensioners' Alley). Mr Mowbray is untraced; Francis Gibson had children baptised 1645–71, was a Quarter Sessions juror in 1662 and died in 1673.

## West Sheen

Having no doubt refreshed himself at the *Red Lyon*, the assessor goes off to the hamlet of West Sheen (see No. 126 in 1603 list).

| | | |
|---|---|---|
| 184. Lisle, the Lord Viscount | owner (crown lease) | 34 hearths |
| 185. Crofts, the Lord | owner (crown lease) | 22 hearths |
| 186. Dingley, Sir John | tenant | 13 hearths |
| 187. Blackman, Capt | tenant | 10 hearths |
| 188. Cheer, Mr Thomas ( = Thomas Cheke?) | tenant | 5 hearths |
| 189. Wormall, Mr | tenant | 8 hearths |

Philip, Viscount Lisle (later Earl of Leicester), had been resident at the former Shene Charterhouse since 1651, and was able to secure a formal grant of the whole site in 1660. He built himself a new mansion.

In 1661 he assigned part of the site to Lord Bellasys, who in turn assigned his interest to Lord Crofts in 1662. The portion assigned to Bellasys included Master

Wormall's house, and a document signed by Bellasys some three weeks after the deed of assignment notes that the assignment also included 'the messuage demised to Captain Jeremy Blackman and other messuages'.

Sir John Dingley was already established in part of the former Charterhouse buildings when they were surveyed in 1649 prior to their sale by Parliament as surplus crown property. He occupied a range of the former lay brothers' cloister, 'with six rooms below stairs and seven rooms above stairs'. As this would account exactly for 13 hearths, he was presumably in the same quarters in 1664. He died in December 1671 and has a memorial in the parish church.

'Mr Thomas Cheer' in this context must also be a resident of West Sheen. Although the parish registers confirm the existence in Richmond of a family named variously Chare, Cheare, Cheere in the 1660s and '70s, it contains no Thomas. A likelier explanation is that this is Mr Thomas Cheke (or Cheek) who married Lord Lisle's daughter Dorothy in Richmond in 1668.

## Uncertain Locations

| | |
|---|---|
| 190. Doutey, Mr | 4 hearths |
| (191. Smith, Walter | 4 hearths) |
| 192. Burke, Mr | 9 hearths |

These three entries, following those for West Sheen, are obviously postscripts. That for Walter Smith undoubtedly belongs in the churchyard, and has been included there above. Possible locations for Mr Burke's nine hearths are Rump Hall (see after No. 103) or George Street (see after No. 126). Mr Doutey's might be almost any one of the properties noted above as 'unidentified'.

# KEW

The 29 entries for Kew (21 assessed houses; six non-chargeable; two empty) were not listed in geographical sequence, but (with just two exceptions) in order of size. Most can, however, be located from the manorial records, and at least tentative identifications can be made of others.

## By the Kew-Brentford Ferry

1. The Honble Earl of Ancram ( = Charles, 2nd Earl)

owner        35 hearths

(Nos. 127–131 in 1603 list; Nos. 760–762 in 1771 survey)
This was the largest property in Richmond or Kew and represents the Earl's freehold mansion – his father and he had already sold all the copyhold. Though Ancram may

have been still in occupation in 1664, he had already lost title (through an unredeemed mortgage) to Sir John Brownlow.

### Kew Green (north side)

3.   Trevor, Sir Thomas                                       owner            26 hearths
(No. 132 in 1603 list; No. 763 in 1771 survey)
In 1664 Kew Green still extended to a point west of the 'Dutch House' (now Kew Palace), built in 1631 by the merchant Samuel Fortrey. The house was sold in 1656 by Samuel, son of the builder, to his sister Mary and her husband Sir Thomas Trevor. After Mary's death her nephew William Fortrey sold the house in 1697 to Sir Richard Levett, whose daughter Mary Thoroton leased it to Queen Caroline in 1729. It was purchased by George III in 1781.

?8.   Rutt, Mr ( = Joseph Rutt)                               tenant           2 hearths
?22.   Eger, Miles ( = Miles Eager)                           tenant           4 hearths
                                                              (non-chargeable)

?23.   Stacey, Thomas                                         tenant           2 hearths
(No. 133 in 1603 list; parts of No. 763 in 1771 survey)   (non-chargeable)
In 1658 Sir Thomas Trevor purchased three cottages which had been built on grants of land from the edge of the Green and stood in front of part of the Dutch House grounds. The inhabitants' names are not recorded but the three above are likely. Joseph and Sarah Rutt had a daughter baptised in Richmond in March 1664/5 and buried in August 1669. Miles Eager had sons baptised in 1653 and 1655. Thomas Stacey had children baptised 1638–54, and died in November 1664.

?6.   Tolleat, Mr ( = John Tallet or Tollet)                  tenant           9 hearths
(No. 134 in 1603 list; Nos. 769–770 in 1771 survey)
John Tallet or Tollet had children baptised between 1645 and 1654, but is not traceable in the manor records. As his house is one of the largest not positively identified, it is likely to be the one, owned in 1664 by Sir Henry and Dorothy Capell, which stood between Somers' Close and the Green.

9.   Wakefield, Mrs ( = Thomasine Wakefield)                  owner            4 hearths
5.   Breedon, Mr                                              tenant           7 hearths
(Nos. 135–136 in 1603 list; part of Nos. 766 and 768 in 1771 survey)
In 1650 Arthur Manley acquired three cottages built on land from the edge of The Green, and rebuilt them as two houses. On his death (about 1662) he left them to his sister Thomasine Wakefield and his brother John Manley. Thomasine lived in the more westerly house (later bought by Sir Peter Lely). Mr Breedon's occupancy of the

other house (where the Herbarium now stands) is confirmed by an entry in the manor records relating to the adjacent property, but nothing else is known of him. Thomasine Wakefield died in March 1671/2.

| | | | |
|---|---|---|---|
| 14. | Fillpott, Edward ( = Edward Philpot) | owner | 4 hearths |
| 29. | Merryday, John ( = John Meredith) | owner | 2 hearths empty |

(No. 137 in 1603 list; respectively Nos. 772–3 and 775 and Nos. 774 and 776 in 1771 survey) A house existed here by 1615. In 1644 William Philpot purchased it from John Smithies and divided it into two. William's son Edward inherited the larger, more westerly, house in 1663. The other (of four rooms, though rated for only two hearths) went to Mary, wife of John Meredith, who was probably Edward's sister. Both houses were rebuilt by Michael Pew in 1697.

| | | | |
|---|---|---|---|
| 19. | Robbison, Thomas ( = Thomas Robinson) | tenant | 1 hearth |

(No. 138 in 1603 list; Nos. 777–779 in 1771 survey) A cottage and land from the Green was purchased by Simon Poynter in 1648. In 1666 when his widow Margaret discharged a mortgage on it, the occupant was Thomas Robinson. Her son William Poynter sold the property to John Smithies in 1687.

| | | | |
|---|---|---|---|
| 11. | Jynks, William | owner | 5 hearths |

(No. 139 in 1603 list; Nos. 780–782 in 1771 survey) This house was bought from Richard Ewer by William Jynks, fisherman, in 1647. In 1665 part of the land was divided off and given to William's son Henry who had just married. William lived until January 1680/1 when his son Humphrey inherited the original house. The site is that of 63–67 Kew Green.

| | | | |
|---|---|---|---|
| 7. | Mrs Martin (? = Mrs Murden) | tenant | 7 hearths |

(Not in 1603 list; Nos. 783–784 in 1771 survey) The land on which this house was built was granted from The Green between 1611 and 1619. A cottage was built, but had collapsed by 1648 when Thomas Smith bought the property and built a new house. His widow sold it in 1669 to Jeremiah Murden and his wife, who were already in occupation. 'Mrs Martin' was probably Jeremiah's mother. The property remained in the Murden family until 1739.

| | | | |
|---|---|---|---|
| 26. | Hayes, Walter | tenant (non-chargeable) | 1 hearth |
| 15. | Butterfield, Richard | owner | 2 hearths |

(Not in 1603 list; No. 785 in 1771 survey) Richard Butterfield received a grant of land on the edge of The Green in 1641, and built two cottages. The westerly one, described as 'lately erected' when he sold it to Simon Poynter in April 1664, may have been occupied by Walter Hayes, by then quite elderly. His second wife Jennet who died in 1640 had been Richard Butterfield's sister. Hayes, whose children's baptisms range from 1620 to 1644, died in August 1666. Richard Butterfield died in 1671; his widow Elizabeth sold the cottages in 1680. The site is that of Beaconsfield House.

| | | | |
|---|---|---|---|
| 24. | Nickells, John ( = ?Thomas Nicholls) | tenant | 2 hearths* |
| 27. | Raire, Humphrey ( = Humphrey Reare) | tenant | 1 hearth* |
| 25. | Evings, James ( = James Evans) | owner | 2 hearths* |
| | | | (*non-chargeable) |

(Not in 1603 list; No. 786 in 1771 survey)

James Evans built three cottages on land granted to him in 1648. When he mortgaged them in 1663 to Stephen Poynter, the occupants were listed as Thomas Nicholls, Humphrey Reare and James Evans. James Evans died in 1666 and his son made over the property to Margaret Pointer widow (who then married Jeremiah Ewer. These three cottages, on the site of the later *Rose and Crown* inn, were in 1664 the easternmost buildings on the north side of Kew Green.

*Kew Green (south side)*

| | | | |
|---|---|---|---|
| 2. | Capell, Sir Henry | owner | 25 hearths |

(No. 140 in 1603 list; No. 729 in 1771 survey)

Kew Park with its lodge was acquired by Sir Arthur Gorges from Morgan Awberry in 1605 and was sold by Gorges' son, another Arthur, to Richard Bennett in 1634. It is not clear which of these owners developed the lodge into a substantial mansion (later to become, after further rebuilding, a royal home – the 'White House').

Richard Bennett died in 1658 and the property was inherited by his daughter Dorothy, wife of Sir Henry Capell, a brother of the Earl of Essex. It was Sir Henry who first started to plant the grounds with rare plants and trees.

| | | | |
|---|---|---|---|
| 16. | Garlin, widow ( = Joanna Garland or Garlyn.) | tenant | 2 hearths |

(Part of No. 141 in 1603 list; Nos. 731–732 in 1771 survey)

On a piece of land adjacent to the park, which he acquired from Alexander Prescott in 1606, Sir Arthur Gorges built a cottage. It was let by Richard Bennett to Christopher Garlyn or Garland in 1648 and again on a 21-year lease in 1657. Although Joanna, Christopher's widow (he died in 1660), owned the tiny cottage listed at 21 below, this slightly larger rented one was her home in 1664.

| | | | |
|---|---|---|---|
| 13. | Nickson, James (=James Nixon) | tenant | 4 hearths |

(Part of No. 141 in 1603 list; No. 733 in 1771 survey)

This house, sold in 1603 by the Earl of Derby to Alexander Prescott, belonged in 1664 to John Smither who had bought it from Prescott's nephew. The house and five acres of land were occupied by James Nixon in 1669, when it was inherited by Robert Smither.

?18. Martin, John (? = John Murden)          tenant          3 hearths
(Nos. 142–145 in 1603 list; Nos. 739–40 in 1771 survey)
Sir Arthur Gorges bought the former Ware cottage in 1606. In 1647 it was granted on a long lease to William Ingram – from whom the lease passed to his sister Elizabeth wife of Robert Ridley. William Cosbrooke occupied the cottage in 1647, but had gone by 1665. John Martin is untraceable, but a John Murden, brother of Jeremiah, is a possible tenant.

17.   Stubbs, widow ( = Catherine Stubbs)        owner          2 hearths
20.   Stubbs, William                     owner's son     1 hearth
(Part of No. 146 in 1603 list; No. 741 in 1771 survey)
Henry Cuckney sold to John Stubbs in 1627 a cottage which appears to have been built on land granted from the Green in 1602. John Stubbs died in 1660 and his widow Catherine in 1675. In 1675 she had one cottage on the site and her son William another. This listing shows that the second cottage had been built, or divided off, by 1664. The property was bought in 1684 by Richard Mountenay.

4.   Mountenay, Mr Richard            owner          16 hearths
(Part of No. 146 in 1603 list; No. 747 in 1771 survey)
In 1614 Henry Cuckney had sold the larger, eastern, part of his holding 'with a messuage newly erected' to John Garrett. It was acquired in 1656 by Richard Mountenay and remained in his family until 1739. The site of this house and the two cottages above (17 and 20) became Cambridge Cottage and King's Cottage.

10.   Benum, John ( = John Benham)          tenant          5 hearths
(No. 147 in 1603 list; Nos. 748–752 in 1771 survey)
Henry Peake sold this house to Joan, wife of John Atkins, in 1626. Joan died in 1647/8 and Atkins remarried. After his death the widow sold it to John Poole who was the owner in 1664. When John Poole died in 1669 his daughter Ann sold part of the property to John Benham. While it is not stated that he was already in occupation, it seems likely that his entry fits here.

21.   Sinior, Job ( = Job Symes)           tenant          1 hearth
(No. 148 in 1603 list; Nos. 753–754 in 1771 survey)
Christopher Garlyn bought this cottage in 1634. In 1661 his widow Joanna obtained

a licence to let the cottage, then occupied by Job Symes and Thomas Garlyn.

28. Haye, Thomas ( = Thomas Hayes)                owner                4 hearths
(Not in 1603 list; Nos. 755–757 in 1771 survey)                                empty

The last piece of land on the south side of The Green was granted in 1609 to Nathaniel Hayes. He built a cottage which, on his death in 1651, was inherited by his son Thomas, who then held it until 1675. This was in the early 18th century the site of the *Rising Sun* tavern, which became the *Coach and Horses* – and changed its location to the east side of the Green about 1774.

*Kew Green (east side)*

12. Garlin, Thomas ( = Thomas Garlyn or Garland) owner                4 hearths
(Not in 1603 list; Nos. 806–11 in 1771 survey)

There was only one house on the east side of The Green in 1664. It had been built on a grant of land made to Joanna Franklin and her son Robert in 1635. It was purchased in 1658 by Thomas Garlyn. He was the Kew ferryman. In 1667 he was prosecuted for failing to attend regularly for his duties.

# 14

## *The Building Boom of the 1680s to 1725*

THE NUMBER OF HOUSES in Richmond almost doubled in the period from 1603 to 1664. The rate of increase remained almost unchanged up to 1703, the next date at which we have a convenient summary document in the form of a 'survey of the manor' – though this is little more than a rental with notes as to the properties concerned (which only sometimes include location). An analysis of the 1703 survey, putting its entries in a geographical sequence similar to those of 1603 and 1664 –and the 1771 manor survey – will be found at Appendix 9.

The next document which enables us to check the building stock is the Richmond poor rate assessment book of 1726, the earliest surviving of what was once an unbroken series of rate books up to 1890. (During World War II a misguided but over-patriotic librarian sent for pulping the books for 1766–68, 1772–79, and thereafter nine out of every ten years, without copying in any form, without even scrutiny to record any famous names!) The 1726 book is analysed at Appendix 10. It reveals a much more rapid growth than previously, or indeed than subsequently. The number of houses rose from 262 in 1664 to 357 in 1703, to 533 in 1726, to 694 in 1771. The rate of growth from 1703 to 1726 is more than three times that for the preceding period and more than twice that for the 45 years to follow.

In fact the sudden boom in building activity began some years earlier than 1703. I date it from the 1680s partly because we suddenly become aware at that point of new circumstances and new techniques, and partly because it is from that period that a good stock of Richmond housing survives until today.

The analysis of Richmond houses in 1664 in Chapter 13 shows that, while some of the increase in the previous 60 years had been the result of development of new areas such as the Hill and the Marshgate Road, much of it was a thickening-up process where an owner would build an extra cottage or two in his garden or yard – or would subdivide his existing premises to produce an extra small cottage.

From about 1680 this pattern, though continuing to some extent, was increasingly overlaid by new trends – the rebuilding of old cottages into substantial new brick houses, the development of large new houses in the fields, speculative developments, even of whole terraces or, in one instance, of a 'housing estate' with really large mansions. Behind the change lay one vital factor – money.

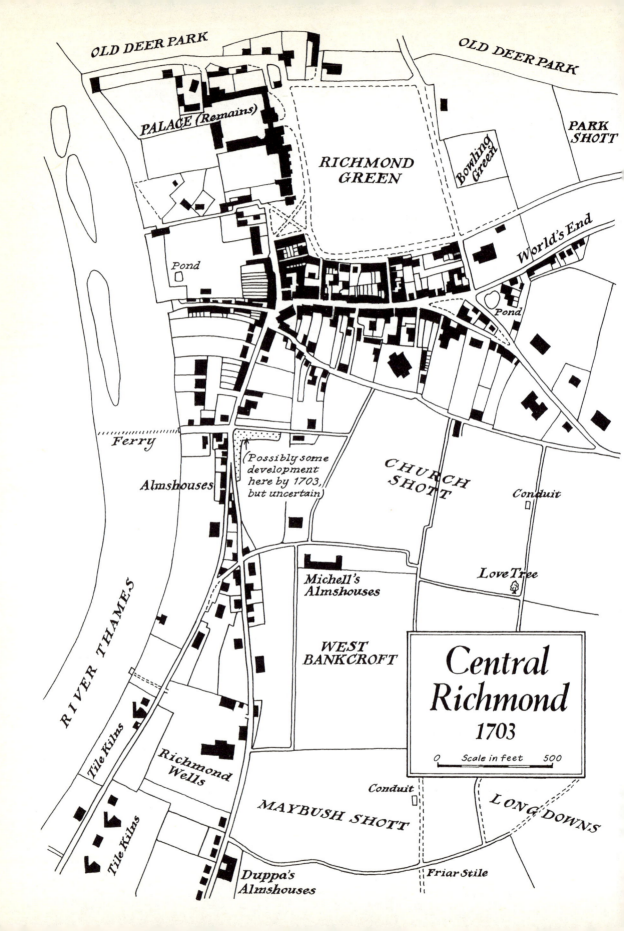

OLD DEER PARK

OLD DEER PARK

PARK
SHOTT

PALACE (Remains)

RICHMOND
GREEN

Bowling
Green

World's End

Pond

Pond

Ferry

(Possibly some
development
here by 1703,
but uncertain)

CHURCH
SHOTT

Conduit

Almshouses

Love Tree

Michell's
Almshouses

WEST
BANKCROFT

Central
Richmond
1703

0    Scale in feet    500

RIVER THAMES

Tile Kilns

Richmond
Wells

Conduit

LONG DOWNS

MAYBUSH SHOTT

Tile Kilns

Friar Stile

Duppa's
Almshouses

*Plate 17*

The houses between Water Lane (on the left) and Ferry Hill (on the right) – detail from the painting of a view of Richmond Palace by an unknown Flemish artist, c.1630. Sir Thomas Thynne's house is the one standing up in the centre; Bishop Duppa's is the gable end next to it on the left. Mr. Weld's house is the gable end to the right of the small square tower. The tall building on the right by the trees is probably a barn. The small cottage of widow Packer is well down Ferry Hill towards the river.

The houses at the top of Ferry Hill and along the first part of the Lower Road to Petersham c.1630. Detail from the view of Richmond Palace by an unknown Flemish artist. (Fitzwilliam Museum, Cambridge)

A view of Richmond from the top of the Hill *in the 1630s (aquatint c.1810 from an original drawing by Wenceslaus Hollar in the Queen's collection at Windsor). The Palace can be seen in the distance; the cottages on the right are on the site of the* Roebuck *and Nos. 1-3 The Terrace.*

*Plate 18*

*Marshgate House, 36 Sheen Road, built by John Knapp, c.1700. (Richmond Public Library, local studies collection)*

*Clarence House in the Vineyard. The four bays on the right represent Nathaniel Rawlins's original house. (The porch and the ground-floor bay are later additions, as is the wing on the left.) (Richmond Public Library, local studies collection)*

*The Rosary and the Hollies, Ormond Road, built by Nathaniel Rawlins, c.1697-99. (Photo by the author)*

*Plate 19*

*Old Palace Terrace (photograph by the author, c.1965).*

*Old Palace Place (on the left) and Old Friars (photograph by Tetley-Shelley, 1998)*

*Plate 20*

*The riverside development of the 1690s. The two large mansions in the centre are Hotham House (left) and Heron House. Their neighbour on the right was rebuilt in the 1820s. Just to the left of Hotham House can be seen the first house in the terrace facing Hill Street. (Detail from an engraving published in 1755 after an earlier [?c.1720] painting attributed to Tillemans.)*

*John Price's development at the north-east end of Richmond Green and Little Green is seen in this detail from the 'Prospect of Richmond' print published in 1726.*

London had for years been generating capital by trade. By the 1680s there was a great deal of surplus capital around. There were really only two ways to make use of it – by more trading, including merchant venturing in the new companies being set up to trade with remote parts of the world, or by investing in real estate.

For city merchants, the idea of having an extra house out of the city, but within fairly easy reach, became attractive. For the landed gentry and nobility, also, there was much to be said for possession of a mansion or villa in the country near London, in addition to their real country seat in the shires, to which they and their families could retreat for a few days' respite from duties at court or the social whirl, or when infectious disease was sweeping the capital.

The banks of the Thames, to the west of London, were particularly pleasant areas in which to establish such second or third houses. While some preferred to go out to the north or north-west of the city, or to the south or south-east, communities such as Putney, Richmond, Petersham and Twickenham were favoured by many. And the vestiges of royal interest in Richmond (James II's 'nursery' at Richmond Palace, William III's new-found interest in the Lodge in the Old Deer Park) were an added bonus – a factor which of course became much more important after the new Prince of Wales (the future George II) settled there in 1718.

For a special class of rich merchant, there was another consideration. The Jews, readmitted to England by Cromwell, were flourishing in the city, but within a virtual ghetto. Charles II's Portuguese queen, Catherine of Braganza, had encouraged the immigration to London of Sephardic Jews from Portugal and Spain. The arrival on the throne of 'Dutch William' encouraged further immigration of Ashkenazi Jews from Amsterdam and Hamburg. They had done well in trade, they had been officially permitted to become brokers, they had established their synagogues (Sephardic in Gracechurch Lane, and later at Bevis Marks, Ashkenazi in Duke's Place), 12 of them were admitted in 1697 to the Royal Exchange, they had built up large reserves of cash, but – they were not being admitted to London society.

Many of them did have a desire – even a felt need – to show themselves the social equals of the English gentry whose wealth they could now equal – and in Richmond they saw an opportunity. There was a more relaxed atmosphere about the 'summer society' which was developing in Richmond, and there the Jews could mix with and be socially accepted by their English neighbours. (Somewhat later in the 18th century they were even recorded as attending meetings of the Vestry and playing cards at an Anglican clergyman's house.) So quite a lot of Jewish money came into the development of Richmond at this time and Jewish names (especially Sephardic) are by no means rare in the earliest surviving Richmond rate books.

Whether Jew or Gentile, the new investors in Richmond property proceeded mainly in one of two ways. They might acquire an existing house perhaps by direct purchase or perhaps by renting it first, then by granting the owner a mortgage, then by taking title if the mortgage remained unredeemed, and then they would rebuild it. Or they might buy up some contiguous strips of land in the fields near the town, until they had a little estate of, say, two or three acres, and then build thereon.

Others would invest more heavily than just acquiring a new house for themselves. Having secured a suitable site, they would finance a whole speculative development.

Richmond already had a well-established building trade, available to carry out the new owners' commissions. But some of the master-builders, themselves carpenters or bricklayers by trade, began to see the opportunity to make more money by building new houses themselves for sale or lease to the gentry. They would often finance these developments by means of 'progressive mortgages': buy up some old properties, mortgage them, use the money to rebuild and sell one, use the proceeds to build another, mortgage that even before it could be sold, and move on to a third, and so on.

These master-builders/developers began to adopt a new description of their trade: 'architect'. The manor records name eight 'architects' between 1691 and 1698.

As I hope to deal in greater detail with these architects and builders and their works in another book, I shall merely note here a few examples of the various types of development referred to above.

✝

*Plate 18*

A good example of a house acquired by stages and then rebuilt is Marshgate House at 36 Sheen Road. Assessed for five hearths in 1664, it belonged to John Young, yeoman. It had been built, in the first half of the 17th century, at what was then the edge of town, on a half-acre strip of the Upper Dunstable Shott of the Upper Field. John Young, who died in April 1684, had left it by will to his eldest son John – a London citizen and carman – who was lax about seeking admission. The house was let, so why bother? Finally, he was admitted on 20 April 1693 to 'a messuage now occupied by Mr Pickering and stables, outhouses, an orchard, a garden and yards'. Within the next couple of years Mr Pickering moved out and Mr Knapp moved in.

John Knapp came from a family of city merchants – members of the Haberdashers' Company. His London house was in Bearbinders Lane (behind the site on which the Mansion House was built). He joined the newly founded 'Company of Merchant Adventurers Trading to the North-West Part of America'. On 28 March 1695 the manor court recorded that John Young had mortgaged to him (for £63) the 'messuage formerly occupied by Mr Pickering and now by John Knapp merchant, and stables ... [etc, as before]'. On 26 September 1699, John Young having failed to pay the £84 16s. od. by then due, John Knapp was duly admitted to ownership. He then rebuilt. Though the exact date of the house is not known, by the time that the manor survey of 1703 was compiled John Knapp was listed as owner of a 'capital messuage and garden in the fields to Marshgate'. He died in 1720 but the house remained in the ownership of members of his family until 1788.

✠

Nathaniel Rawlins, citizen and haberdasher, was one of those who built up an estate in the fields. Some of the consolidation had been done already. Thomas Drew, a local bricklayer, had acquired two half-acre strips close to the western end of Church Shott in the 1660s and built three small houses – two facing onto the lane behind the *Red Lion*, and the other half-way between that lane and the lane leading to the Vineyard. Then in 1682 Felix Stokes, a London scissors-merchant, bought the acre to the west of Drew's land as well as one of Drew's houses and part of his land, and the strip on the east of Drew's. This last he promptly sold to another Londoner, Francis Sandell, a haberdasher. In 1691 Drew sold one of his remaining cottages to William Stafford, a London cooper.

In 1695 Rawlins appeared on the scene, perhaps introduced by his fellow haberdasher Francis Sandell, most of whose land he bought in March. By December he had also acquired Stafford's house and all of Stokes's holding. He began to build. Moving temporarily into one of the existing houses, he started to erect a mansion at the southern end of his little estate, by the lane leading to the Vineyard. A footpath led up from the church to this lane through the land Rawlins had purchased. In April 1696 he was fined 3s. 4d. for 'turning the Church way'. He had diverted this footpath to give himself a better forecourt, which dates pretty closely his building of what is now (after enlargement) Clarence House in the Vineyard. The bend is still there in Patten Alley. *Plate 18*

With his new house completed, Rawlins demolished the house in the centre of his property (built originally by Thomas Drew) and erected, more or less on the same site, a pair of houses. He probably started work on these in 1697 or 1698, and he had certainly finished them by 1700. Built as a semi-detached, mirror-image pair, back-to-back, on four storeys they must be just about unique as a house design at that time. *Plate 18* Pairs of cottages were common, terraced construction of town houses was becoming fashionable, but this pair were built in what were still largely fields. Rawlins must have intended them for his two daughters, and in October 1700 he made over to them a quarter acre of land facing the houses across the footpath that led to Ferry Hill (now Ormond Road). This land was developed as coachhouse, stables and stable yard for the houses, which acquired in the 19th century the names of The Rosary and The Hollies.

Rawlins purchased other property in the town, including three houses in Paradise Row newly built by the bricklayer and 'architect' John Drew, Thomas's son. Rawlins may well have employed Drew to build Clarence House, The Rosary and The Hollies, but there is no documentary proof. We know that Rawlins also acquired most, if not all, of the freehold close between his Clarence House land and the road up the hill, and he may well be responsible for some of the original development of houses on the south side of Ormond Road and up Hill Rise.

✠

Another rich Londoner who participated in the redevelopment of Richmond in the 1690s was Vertue Radford, an attorney of Gray's Inn, son of the Rev. William Radford, master of Richmond's grammar school (see Chapter 21). Vertue, born in January 1657/8, had married his third wife in Westminster Abbey in May 1687. She was Susan, the daughter of Lord Chief Justice Sir Robert Wright. He had inherited two houses from his father and two more from his brothers: one he had sold already, the other three were perhaps not considered sufficiently grand for the Lord Chief Justice's son-in-law. In May 1688 he sold all three and purchased the large house by the corner of The Green which had been put together by Sir William Parkhurst in the 1630s out of three earlier houses. It had 21 hearths in 1664. He probably employed the local builder William Wollins to *Plate 19*  rebuild the entire front, one room deep, and to put a new skin wall on the back (but leaving the back rooms of the old houses). The new house (given the name of Old Palace Place about 1850) was worth at least £600 (the amount of a mortgage Radford had raised on it, which he repaid before selling the house in 1692).

But this was only a part of Vertue Radford's investment. In July 1689 he purchased for £900 the whole site, more or less facing the new house, on which the Charterhouse of Shene had once had a water conduit head and five houses, and where a single mansion had stood since the early years of the century. William Wollins was the 'architect' and builder of the terrace of seven houses facing the Green which was completed by 1692, of the row of shops built on the back part of the site separated from the houses by 'the Paved Alley', and of two other houses facing King Street at *Plate 19*  the end of the alley which were sold to Richard Hawes, a local brewer. The houses in the terrace (since 1850 called 'Old Palace Terrace') were sold in 1692 and '93 by Radford to Hawes, Thomas Smith (whose wife was a Radford) and Edward Darrell, a London bookseller who also bought the shops in Paved Alley (now Paved Court) and Radford's mansion.

Another major speculative development financed by London money was the 'Richmond Riverside' project of the 1690s. John Saunders, a London merchant, married Ann Scutt. She inherited from her step-father John Antill a house at the corner of Hill Street and Ferry Hill. In 1693 he bought up from Joyce, widow of Thomas Weld, all the property on the north side of Ferry Hill which had once been the Wright estate. *Plate 20*  On it he set out to build a terrace of five houses facing Hill Street and three substantial mansions facing the river. (The latter backed onto a new courtyard with access to Hill Street, called Herring Court.) He died early in January 1694/5 leaving the work only partially completed, and bequeathing the whole to his widow Ann. Having won a case in Chancery brought against her by a nephew of Joyce Weld, she pressed ahead with the development, mortgaging it for the enormous sum of £2846 to another London citizen and member of the Coopers' Company, Nathaniel Wood. But by the time this mortgage was recorded in the manor records Ann Saunders widow had become Mrs Nathaniel Wood. Anne died in 1696 or early 1697 but the development was duly completed and Nathaniel Wood was admitted to the ownership in May 1699. Of this project just Heron House, very much restored, still remains.

It is probable, though not absolutely certain, that one of Mr Wood's first tenants in one of the mansions overlooking the river was Sir Solomon de Medina, the first Jew to receive an English knighthood. Solomon was an army contractor. He had helped to supply the provisions for William III's expedition to Ireland. He was currently supplying the British forces in Flanders. On Saturday 18 November 1699, 'His majestie went to Hampton Court ... and dined with Mr Medina, a rich Jew, at Richmond'. In 1700 he was knighted by the King at Hampton Court. Another early occupant of the houses in Herring Court (later called Heron Court) was the Ashkenazi Moses Hart. When Hart moved to Isleworth in 1716 his house was taken over by Moses de Medina, Solomon's nephew. By 1718 Moses de Medina was joined as a neighbour by the merchant Isaac Fernandez Nunes.

'Bridge House', as it was later known, by the south side of Ferry Hill, was built for himself by the then minister of Richmond parish, Abiell Borfett, in the 1680s. In 1721 Moses de Medina moved there from his house on the north side of Ferry Hill – perhaps trying to get a bit farther away from the 'smoak, filth and stench' emitted by the chimney of the Collins family's new brewery at the foot of Water Lane, which led to a combined protest by Medina, Nunez, Dr Caleb Cotesworth and Sir Philip Jackson, a Director of the Bank of England. Cotesworth and Jackson were both neighbours.

A third generation of the de Medina family, 'Mr Modenah Junior' (Moses' son Abraham) is shown in the 1726 ratebook as living in the large house which stood in the six-acre close by the riverside (once the 'Windeyarde' or Vineyard Close), on what was later to be the site of Northumberland House. This land by now all belonged to John Darrell, but it was part of the estate which had been purchased in 1681 by Sir James Butler whose principal house was on the east side of Richmond Hill – now the Old Vicarage School. (The interior of the house displays its late 17th-century origins; its Gothic castle exterior was a remodelling of 1809.)

Butler had acquired (and probably rebuilt) the house in 1681. A year later he was instrumental in inspiring the town's first piped water supply. On 23 March 1682/3 Peter Wally (Whalley or Whaley) was granted a patent for 14 years for the use of an engine he had invented to convey water from the Thames to the house of Sir James Butler. The point at which the pump was installed was immediately to the south-west of the house which is now the *Hobart Hall Hotel*.

The success of this was soon evident to Butler's neighbours and others, and they pressed Wally to supply them also. On 19 June 1685 he submitted a petition, referring to the late King's grant of a patent, and praying leave to supply the town of Richmond with water. The petition was referred to the Surveyor-General who commented on

13 October 1685 that the inhabitants of Richmond were very keen, and he therefore recommended that Wally be granted licence to 'lay pipes through the streets and wastes and erect conduits or receptacles for water'.

Permission was duly given and Wally set about laying his pipes. Judging from one found in the late 19th century in the Terrace Gardens they were large hollowed-out tree trunks. Within a few years he had probably supplied the town. The manor court was not entirely happy about the result. In April 1694 Peter Whaley (*sic*) was presented in the court 'for not amending his water pipes and the highways where they lye'– and was fined 13s. 4d. Nevertheless the 'waterworks' flourished and by 1726 were being run by Sylvanus Lawrence, a carpenter who had a cottage nearby on the other side of the Petersham Road.

*Old wooden water pipe in the Terrace Gardens*
*(from Somers Gascoyne: Recollections of Richmond).*

✠

John Drew's name has already been mentioned as one of the architects who went in for speculative development on their own account. William Wollins was another. Between them they developed the area which is now 1–23 Sheen Road. Another developer was Michael Pew, son of a Kew brewer. We can study him at work on The Terrace, Richmond Hill. (Incidentally, it was probably he who first-laid out the Terrace Walk, planted with a double row of trees.)

*Plate 17*  Henry Goldstone who died in 1692/93 owned three little cottages on the highest part of Richmond Hill. In October 1696 his widow Margaret (who had married meanwhile John Taylor) and his two sons Henry and John sold these cottages to Michael Pew and his wife Mary. To the north of these was another cottage which seems to have been an alehouse, called originally the *Adam and Eve* (1693–96) and then either the *Half Moon and Key* or the *Cross Keys* (in January 1696/7). This had been given by Henry Goldstone (the father) to his son John and John's wife in 1677, but they made it over to John's brother Henry Junior and his wife Helena (née Avery) at the time of their marriage in 1681. Helena died, leaving her rights in this property to her brother John Avery, and in April 1694 he sold it to John Badger, 'architect'.

On 9 January 1696/7 the manor court recorded the purchase of this cottage called (by now) the *Half Moon and Key* from John Badger by Michael Pew. It also recorded a recovery process by Michael Pew and his wife Mary of 'two brick messuages ... now in course of construction in and on the land on which formerly stood three cottages ... [etc]'. On 7 April 1697 the Pews mortgaged one of the 'newly erected' houses on this site for £100 to William Beamond, and in July 1699 Beamond surrendered his interest to William Hickey. On 4 April 1700 Michael Pew formally made over this house (3 The Terrace) to William Hickey.

Then in October 1700 was recorded the mortgage, to Richard Hughes of Petersham, for £100, of the second of the new houses built in place of the three cottages. This was redeemed; and in April 1701 William Beamond lent £200 on a mortgage on this house and 'a messuage ... adjoining the aforesaid on the north'. Finally on 31 March 1703 is recorded the sale by Beamond and Pew to Richard Holland of both these houses (1 and 2 The Terrace), both already let to tenants.

Leonard Knyff's picture of *circa* 1720 shows that Nos. 1 and 2 had been constructed *Plate 36* as a unified pair, while No. 3 was a smaller, somewhat less pretentious affair. (The viewing gallery on the top of Nos. 1 and 2 is the first record of such a feature in Richmond.) It is clear from this, as from the documentation mentioned, that Pew completed and raised money on just one of the houses before he was able to finish the second. The delay enabled him to plan the second and third as a pair, though he appears to have finished No. 2 some months ahead of No. 1.

Later, William Hickey left No. 3 and the garden next to it, with other properties, to trustees for the poor. About 1730 they built No. 4 in the garden next to No. 3, and they appear to have reconstructed No. 3 so that 3 and 4 became a matching pair *Plate 36* similar to 1 and 2. (See the picture of 1749 by Augustine Heckel.) No. 3 was completely rebuilt in 1760, and Nos. 1 and 2 were almost completely rebuilt in the 1870s, so No. 4 (restored) is the only one left that has preserved anything of its original appearance.

✠

The most important of the Richmond architect-developers at this time was John Price. His major contribution to the Richmond scene was the development of the north-east side of Richmond Green and the Little Green. Between 1705 and 1710 he purchased some 12 acres of land in that area. On the land he set out to build mansions for rent or sale to the rich or noble. One of his first tenants (from 1710 to 1718) was the East India merchant Elihu Yale. The whole development proceeded by fits and starts until 1727, by which time Price had built a row of four large mansions facing the *Plate 20* main part of the Green, with a complex of smaller houses and stables in the corner by Sheen Lane, three mansions and two smaller houses facing Little Green, and several houses along the Kew Foot Lane (now Parkshot) probably including the terrace at 7–9 Parkshot. Among John Price's other known work in Richmond were the north aisle of the parish church, and Nos. 7 and 17 The Green, all of which survive *Plate 21* (while, alas, none of the grand mansions do).

It is very evident from the analysis of the 1726 houses (Appendix 10) that a lot of the growth at this time was along the Kew Foot Lane and the Kew Horse Lane (now Kew Road). Another area where many new houses were built was on the eastern side of Richmond Hill, spreading along Paradise Row and the Vineyard.

As mentioned above, there are many noteworthy buildings in Richmond and Kew surviving from this period. One of the finest, whose builder we do know, is Trumpeters' House built on the site of the former Middle Gate of Richmond Palace by John Yeomans, master bricklayer of Hampton, for the diplomat and statesman Richard Hill in 1703–04.

But in most cases, even if we know for whom the houses were built and when, we know nothing of the architects or builders. A bare list does not do them credit, but it would be worse to ignore them all together.

In approximate chronological order we may note:

| | | |
|---|---|---|
| *Plate 19* | Old Friars, Richmond Green | *c.*1700 |
| | Lissoy and 3–7 Ormond Road | *c.*1700–1715 |
| *Plate 21* | 10–12 The Green | 1705–15 |
| | Old Court House, The Green | 1707–08 (doorway and bow added later) |
| | Halford House, Halford Road | *c.*1710 (original block) |
| | 17–19 Kew Green | 1717 |
| | Stanley Cottage and Crawford Cottage (now parts of Richmond Gate Hotel) | *c.*1720 (with added Regency balconies) |
| | Vineyard House | *c.*1720 |
| | 18–22 Kew Green | *c.*1720 |
| | 1–3 Michell's Terrace, Kew Foot Road | 1720–25 |
| | The Herbarium, Kew Green | 1720s |
| | 22 Richmond Green | 1724 |
| *Plate 21* | Maids of Honour Row, Richmond Green | 1724–25 |
| | 29 Kew Green | *c.*1725 |
| | 1–5 Church Terrace | *c.*1725 |
| | 52–56 Kew Green | 1726 |

and of rather uncertain date, but before 1725:

5 Hill Street
77 and 83 Kew Green

# 15

# Richmond Trades
## in the Seventeenth and Eighteenth Centuries

IT IS ONLY RARELY that one comes across evidence of the occupation of any inhabitant of Richmond, other than important courtiers, before the 17th century. Of course the earliest records contain many vocational surnames – Clerk, Chaplain, Driver, Shepherd, Gardener, etc – which may sometimes denote the occupation of their bearers, but which may already have been inherited from an earlier ancestor. Somewhat later, the posts held by palace officials and servants were often noted when they acquired land in the manor.

However, from the 17th century onwards there is more information. Occupations are more frequently shown in manorial and other court records, in apprenticeship bonds, and at times in the parish registers. In 1603 the clerk of the manor court only rarely inserted the occupation of persons mentioned, but as the century progressed this information was recorded with increasing frequency. Not many records of the Surrey law courts have yet been published: there are assize records for the reign of Elizabeth I,[1] and quarter sessions records from 1659 to 1668.[2] There are published Surrey apprenticeship records from 563 to 1731 (but only two entries before 1664 refer to Richmond tradesmen).[3]

At times the ministers of the parish church, or the parish clerks, were conscientious about recording details in the parish registers,[4] at others not. From 1699 to 1708 nearly every entry in the baptismal register, and a high proportion of those in the burial register, included the trade, or the social standing, of the father or of the deceased, as well as his place of residence – Richmond or Kew or elsewhere. Towards 1708 a slackness developed; the proportion of entries naming occupations declined, then ceased altogether in 1709.

In 1721 the practice of giving the father's trade in the baptismal register was revived. This time it was kept up fairly well for 20 years. Then from 1741 such entries became less frequent, though there were some at least in each year up until 1759, when the registers in question were closed and new ones opened, which gave no occupations. In this second period, however, there are relatively few indications of trade in the burial registers.

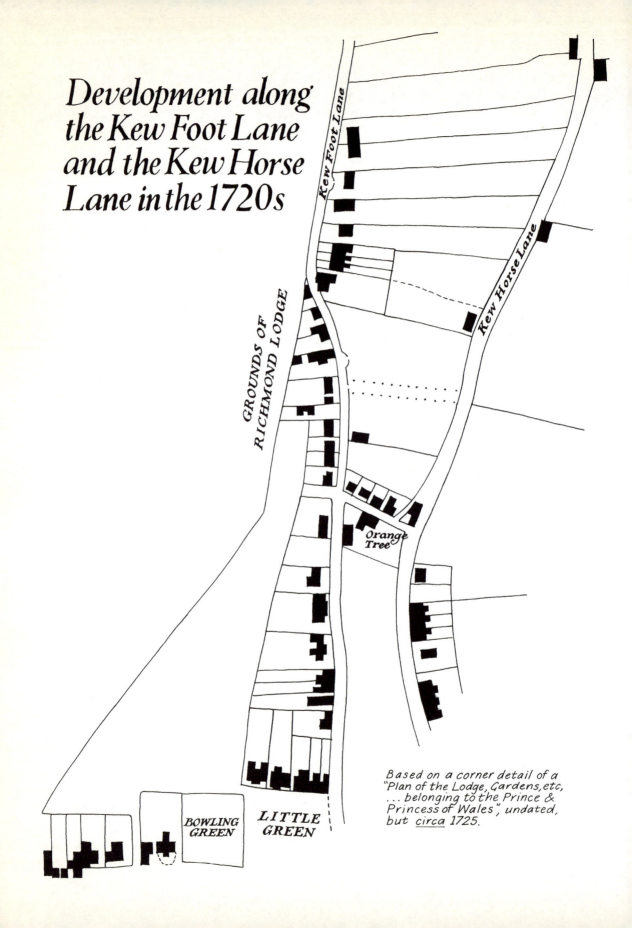

# Development along the Kew Foot Lane and the Kew Horse Lane in the 1720s

Kew Foot Lane

Kew Horse Lane

GROUNDS OF RICHMOND LODGE

Orange Tree

BOWLING GREEN

LITTLE GREEN

Based on a corner detail of a "Plan of the Lodge, Gardens, etc, ... belonging to the Prince & Princess of Wales", undated, but *circa* 1725.

From these sources it has been possible to construct three lists: one, based mainly on manorial records, from 1603 to 1700; and two based mainly on the parish registers, for 1699 to 1708 and for 1721 to 1759. The appearance of the *Universal British Directory* in 1795 enables one to produce an analysis for that year to round off the 18th century.

✝

## *The Seventeenth Century (see Table 1, p.225)*

Those whose occupations are stated in the manor records were mostly the manorial tenants holding property from the lord, but sometimes the occupations of sub-tenants are also noted. In general, therefore, the information is relevant to the wealthier and more established members of the community. Many of these were gentry and these have been excluded from this exercise unless they were professional men with professions clearly stated (e.g. some Doctors of Law or Medicine).

Nor have persons been included who were resident outside Richmond and Kew – usually named as heirs to the property of local people. (Some of course later became residents.) Those recorded as 'citizens of London' however pose a different problem. Some were local people plying their trades locally who were, however, members of one of the City companies (e.g. goldsmiths or vintners); others were rich Londoners who – especially towards the end of the 17th century – were acquiring second homes and land in Richmond. It is well-nigh impossible to separate these two categories and at least they all had a property in Richmond, so they are all included here. For convenience they are referred to below as 'Londoners', although most if not all were probably Richmond residents for at least part of the year.

The manor records from 1603 to 1700 yielded the occupations of 234 persons who were certainly following their trades in Richmond, and of 14 in Kew. There are no less than 97 'Londoners' to add to this total (with the reservation that some of them were probably not trading locally). Eliminating duplications, a further 18 names can be added from the relatively few apprenticeship records that have survived from this period, making an overall total of 363.

The results are tabulated by groups. There is an inevitable distortion, as a lot of the poorer inhabitants were not identified by both name and occupation in the manor records. For instance, in this entire period only four persons were described as 'labourers'; and for obvious reasons no servants (though there must have been many) are listed. The results do, however, give us some picture of the economic life of the community and of the relative importance of various sectors.

The largest group is that concerned with the building and woodworking trades, with a total of 56 – only seven of them 'Londoners' – or almost 16 per cent of the overall total. A third of these were carpenters, twice as numerous as the bricklayers. Bricks were not much used for domestic building in this area until the later part of the century, and it comes as no surprise to find that while almost half the carpenters' names occur before 1650 the first mention of a bricklayer is in 1656. There are eight tilemakers – all names identifiable with the tile kilns along the Petersham Road – but only two brickmakers (both mentioned in the 1670s). The eight 'architects' are all from the 1690s when this term came into use to describe master builders, especially those who were engaging on their own account in the speculative building boom that swept Richmond at that time; and three of them had previously figured in the list of carpenters.

Next in order of magnitude come three groups of about the same size: 52 in 'land-based' occupations, 49 in the catering and drinks industries and 49 in the food and chandlery trades. In considering those on the land, a word of caution should be inserted about the use of the term 'yeoman'. While many of those so listed were indeed the owners and cultivators of significant estates in the Richmond fields, there does seem also to have been a tendency to describe as 'yeomen' other prosperous inhabitants who just failed to qualify as 'gentlemen'. There is an element of double counting here: some of those described at one date as 'yeoman' figure also at another time as e.g. a miller, a victualler, a blacksmith, a carpenter. But this usage is not so frequent as to distort the pattern significantly: while the number of yeoman landowners may be a little overstated, there would certainly have been more than four labourers working on the land. It is interesting that of the six 'gardeners' (i.e. market garden proprietors) listed, two were in Kew.

The figures for the catering and drinks trades fall into two almost equal halves – those concerned with selling to the public through inns, taverns and beershops (25) and those concerned with the preparation and distribution of alcoholic drinks (24). The brewers were almost all locally-based; but the vintners were mostly – and the wine-coopers entirely – 'Londoners'.

The food trades were dominated by bakers (19) and butchers and 'fleshmongers' (9). It is probable that many of the 13 'Londoners' in this group (salters, grocers, fishmongers and a poulterer) were actually trading in Richmond. The total absence of any greengrocers or fruitsellers is to be accounted for both by direct sales from the 'gardeners' and by the general custom of growing fruit and vegetables in back gardens.

The river-based trades (34 – just over 91 of the total) do not appear quite as important as they do in the early 18th century, but this may be simply a distortion resulting from the non-identification of the sub-tenants of small cottages such as those likely to be occupied by the poorer watermen and fishermen. Kew, proportionately to its population, is well represented in this sector.

The merchants, including drapers and haberdashers, are strongly London-based. Most of those in this category, whether 'Londoners' or not, come into the records only in the second half of the century, but their incidence is fairly evenly spaced from the 1650s up to 1700. The same is true of the cloth-making group; but – rather surprisingly – six of the eight 'Londoner' merchant-tailors were in Richmond before 1640. The embroiderers are all from the earlier years of the century; but there is no shoemaker or cordwainer identified before 1659.

As one would expect, blacksmiths and farriers were numerous. However, as in the early 18th century, there is little evidence of overland traffic in goods: just one carter and one carman are identified.

Among the more specialised manufacturers two categories stand out: the goldsmiths (all 'Londoners' but most of them probably doing business locally, at least while there was still a royal court at Richmond Palace) and the Kew rope-makers. One crossbow-maker still plied his trade in Richmond in the 1650s and '60s – but in the '70s and '80s we find two clockmakers as a token of increasing sophistication.

The final category are the professional classes. The 'clerks' were probably all in holy orders: they include William Radford who was Richmond's schoolmaster in the 1660s and '70s and Abiel Borfett, Minister of St Mary Magdalene Church. One might be tempted to add the names of another couple of schoolmasters known from other sources. Equally one could add other known distinguished lawyers to the two Doctors of Laws listed, but these appeared in the manorial records as 'gentlemen' or 'esquires'. Five Doctors of Medicine (two of them 'Londoners') are so identified, but there were probably more physicians in the town and certainly some apothecaries as well as the barber-surgeons.

TABLE I
## SEVENTEENTH CENTURY

| Group | Trade | Richmond | Citizens of London | Kew | Total | Approx. %age of whole |
|---|---|---|---|---|---|---|
| I RIVER-BASED | | | | | | |
| | Waterman | 15 | | 3 | 18 | |
| | Ferryman | 3 | | | 3 | |
| | Bargeman | 2 | | | 3 | |
| | Lighterman | 1 | | | 1 | |
| | Fisherman | 8 | | 2 | 10 | |
| Group Total | | 29 | | 5 | 34 | 9 |
| 2 LAND | Gardener | 4 | | 2 | 6 | |
| | Yeoman | 33 | | 1 | 34 | |
| | Husbandman | 8 | | | 8 | |
| | Labourer | 4 | | | 4 | |
| Group Total | | 49 | | 3 | | 15 |
| 3 BUILDING & WOOD-WORKING | Carpenter | 15 | 3 | | 18 | |
| | Joiner | 3 | | | 3 | |
| | Turner | 1 | | | 1 | |

| Group | Trade | Richmond | Citizens of London | Kew | Total | Approx. %age of whole |
|---|---|---|---|---|---|---|
| | Carver | I | | | I | |
| | Bricklayer | 8 | I | | 9 | |
| | Brickmaker | I | | I | 2 | |
| | Tilemaker | 8 | | | 8 | |
| | Architect | 8 | | | 8 | |
| | Plumber | I | 2 | | 3 | |
| | Glazier | I | I | | 2 | |
| | Painter-stainer | I | | | I | |
| *Group Total* | | 48 | 7 | I | 56 | 16 |
| 4 SMITHING | Blacksmith | 9 | I | | 10 | |
| | Farrier | 5 | | | 5 | |
| *Group Total* | | 14 | I | | 15 | 4 |
| 5 CLOTH MAKING | Clothmaker | I | | | I | |
| | Clothworker | | I | | I | |
| | Weaver | | 2 | | 2 | |
| | Silkweaver | I | | | I | |
| | Tapestryweaver | | I | | I | |
| | Dyer | | I | | I | |
| *Group Total* | | 2 | 5 | | 7 | 2 |
| 6 CLOTHING | Tailor | 6 | | | 6 | |
| | Merchant tailor | | 8 | | 8 | |
| | Embroiderer | 2 | 2 | | 4 | |
| | Hatband maker | I | | | I | |
| | Girdler | | I | | I | |
| | Shoemaker | 2 | | | 2 | |
| | Cordwainer | 4 | I | | 5 | |
| *Group Total* | | 15 | 12 | | 27 | 7 |
| 7 OTHER MANUFACTURES | Wheelwright | 2 | | | 2 | |
| | Saddler | | I | | I | |
| | Founder (of bells?) | | I | | I | |
| | Crossbow-maker | I | | | I | |
| | Ropemaker | | | 4 | 4 | |
| | Goldsmith | | 6 | | 6 | |
| | Clockmaker | I | I | | 2 | |
| | Cutler | | I | | I | |
| | Scissor-merchant | | 2 | | 2 | |
| *Group Total* | | 4 | 12 | 4 | 20 | 5 |
| 8 CATERING & DRINKS | Innholder | 2 | | | 2 | |
| | Victualler | 11 | I | | 12 | |
| | Beerseller/Alehouse Kpr | 11 | | | 11 | |

| Group | Trade | Richmond | Citizens of London | Kew | Total | Approx. %age of whole |
|---|---|---|---|---|---|---|
| | Brewer | 5 | I | I | 7 | |
| | Distiller | | I | | I | |
| | Vintner | 2 | IO | | I2 | |
| | Wine-cooper | | 4 | | 4 | |
| *Group Total* | | 3I | I7 | I | 49 | I4 |
| 9 FOOD & DOMESTIC SUPPLIES | Baker | I9 | | | I9 | |
| | Butcher | 6 | | | 6 | |
| | Fleshmonger | 3 | | | 3 | |
| | Poulterer | | I | | I | |
| | Fishmonger | | 3 | | 3 | |
| | Salter | | 5 | | 5 | |
| | Grocer | | 3 | | 3 | |
| | Miller | 4 | | | 4 | |
| | Chandler | 3 | | | 3 | |
| | Cornchandler | I | | | I | |
| | Tallowchandler | | I | | I | |
| *Group Total* | | 36 | I3 | | 49 | I4 |
| IO MERCHANTS | Merchant | 2 | II | | I3 | |
| | Mercer | 4 | 2 | | 6 | |
| | Draper | 3 | I | | 4 | |
| | Haberdasher | | 7 | | 7 | |
| *Group Total* | | 9 | 2I | | 30 | 8 |
| II LAND TRANSPORT | Carrier | I | | | I | |
| | Carman | | I | | I | |
| *Group Total* | | I | I | | 2 | - |
| I2 PROFESSIONAL | Clerk | 6 | | | 6 | |
| | Doctor of Laws | 2 | | | 2 | |
| | Doctor of Medicine | 3 | 2 | | 5 | |
| | Pharmacist | I | | | I | |
| | Barber-surgeon | I | I | | 2 | |
| | Bailiff | I | | | I | |
| | Scrivener | | 2 | | 2 | |
| | Stationer | | I | | I | |
| | Bookseller | | I | | I | |
| | Herald-painter | | I | | I | |
| *Group Total* | | I4 | 8 | | 22 | 6 |
| GRAND TOTAL | | 252 | 97 | I4 | 363 | IOO |

## 1699–1708 (see Table 2)

Table 2, while constructed on the same principle as Table 1, has a slightly different make-up, reflecting its source in the parish registers. There are separate columns for the trades of the fathers of children baptised, for additional (only) names which appear as fathers of children buried, and for adult burials (in some cases the wife rather than the man himself). The 'total' column is for the entire parish which at this time included Kew – and the extra column noting those whose residence is given as Kew have already been included in the total.

As a broad generalisation one may assume that those in the first column represent the younger adult population, that those in the second column were a bit older (as they had no children baptised during the period, but only children buried) and that those in the third column were often significantly older.

Each tradesman is counted once only, however many entries concern him, provided that he remained at the same trade or within the same group of trades. Mobility between skilled trades was virtually nil, and the amount of double-counting is in fact small and is almost entirely confined to those on the labourer list, some of whom figure also among the watermen or gardeners. One or two other duplications are natural progressions: a gardener becomes a vintner; a waterman sets up as a victualler (i.e. innkeeper).

The figures, thus collated, reveal some interesting points. Something like one-eighth of the working population in 1699 to 1708 were watermen, while not a single carter or drayman is recorded in this period. There must have been a few, but the primacy of river over road as a means of transport is very evident. The importance of market-gardening in the Richmond area is equally clearly demonstrated. The 'gardeners' were mostly the owners of plots growing vegetables and fruit for the market – in London as well as locally. Some had large holdings and would themselves have been significant employers of those in the labourer category. The building and wood-working trades are also very strongly represented, as would be natural in a fast-growing little town – and it should be borne in mind that the master-builders were usually either carpenters or bricklayers by trade.

The clothing trades (especially shoemakers) and the food and drink trade again account for large sections of the total.

There were many burials recorded of persons resident in London. But this time we are dealing not with 'Londoners' acquiring property in Richmond, but more likely with people who had come to Richmond as invalids in the hope that the healthy situation and clean air (even the waters at Richmond Wells!) might help their recovery. By far the greatest proportion is children – the sons and daughters of Londoners, then wives and widows outnumber the men. All have specified London addresses, so they have been excluded from this table.

TABLE 2
## 1699-1708

| Group | Trade | Baptism Reg | Burial (children) | Burial (adults) | Total | Approx %age of whole | Kew (incl in total) |
|---|---|---|---|---|---|---|---|
| 1 RIVER-BASED | Waterman | 33 | 5 | 14 | 52 | | 3 |
| | Bargeman | 1 | | | 1 | | |
| | Fisherman | 10 | | 3 | 13 | | 2 |
| Group total | | 44 | 5 | 17 | 66 | 16 | 5 |
| | | | | | | | |
| 2 LAND | Farmer | 3 | | | 3 | | |
| | Husbandman | 2 | | 1 | 3 | | |
| | Gardener | 28 | 2 | 8 | 38 | | 7 |
| Group total | | 33 | 2 | 9 | 44 | 11 | 7 |
| | | | | | | | |
| 3 BUILDING & WOOD WORKING | Carpenter | 15 | 4 | 3 | 22 | | |
| | Sawyer | 4 | | | 4 | | |
| | Joiner | 9 | 1 | 1 | 11 | | 2 |
| | Turner | | | 1 | 1 | | |
| | Carver | 1 | | | 1 | | |
| | Bricklayer | 6 | 1 | 3 | 10 | | 1 |
| | Tilemaker | 2 | 1 | | 3 | | |
| | Mason | 1 | | | 1 | | |
| | Plumber | 1 | | | 1 | | |
| | Glazier | 2 | | 3 | 5 | | |
| | Painter | 2 | | 1 | 3 | | |
| | Plasterer | 2 | | | 2 | | |
| | Paviour | 1 | | | 1 | | |
| Group total | | 46 | 7 | 12 | 65 | 16 | 3 |
| | | | | | | | |
| 4 METAL WORKING | Blacksmith | 6 | | 1 | 7 | | 1 |
| | Farrier | 4 | | 1 | 5 | | |
| | Brazier | 1 | | | 1 | | |
| Group total | | 11 | | 2 | 13 | 3 | 1 |
| | | | | | | | |
| 5 CLOTH MAKING | Weaver | 2 | | | 2 | | |
| | Dyer | 1 | | | 1 | | |
| Group total | | 3 | | | 3 | 1 | 0 |
| | | | | | | | |
| 6 CLOTHING | Tailor | 6 | | 3 | 9 | | |
| | Glover | 1 | | | 1 | | |
| | Hatter | 2 | | | 2 | | |
| | Shoemaker | 10 | | 6 | 16 | | |
| Group total | | 19 | | 9 | 28 | 7 | 0 |
| | | | | | | | |
| 7 OTHER MANUFACTURES | Rope maker | 1 | 1 | | 2 | | |
| | Saddler | 3 | | | 3 | | |
| | Watchmaker | 1 | | | 1 | | |
| Group total | | 5 | | | 6 | 1.5 | 0 |

| Group | Trade | Baptism Reg | Burial (children) | Burial (adults) | Total | Approx %age of whole | Kew (incl in total) |
|---|---|---|---|---|---|---|---|
| 8 CATERING | Victualler | 5 | | 3 | 8 | | |
| & DRINKS | Brewer | 1 | | | 1 | | |
| | Vintner | 3 | | 1 | 4 | | |
| | Cooper | 1 | | | 1 | | |
| *Group total* | | 10 | | 4 | 14 | 3.5 | 0 |
| 9 FOOD & | Baker | 7 | | 2 | 9 | | |
| DOMESTIC | Butcher | 5 | | | 5 | | |
| SUPPLIES | Poulterer | 3 | | | 3 | | |
| | Fishmonger | 2 | | | 2 | | |
| | Grocer | 1 | 2 | | 3 | | |
| | Confectioner | | | 1 | 1 | | |
| | Pastrycook | 1 | | | 1 | | |
| | Miller | 1 | | | 1 | | |
| | Cornchandler | 2 | | | 2 | | |
| | Chandler | 4 | | 2 | 6 | | 1 |
| | Ironmonger | 1 | | | 1 | | |
| | Coalman | 1 | | | 1 | | |
| | Timber-merchant | | | 1 | 1 | | |
| *Group total* | | 28 | 2 | 6 | 36 | 9 | 1 |
| 10 MERCHANTS | Draper | 1 | 1 | | 2 | | |
| *Group total* | | 1 | 1 | | 2 | | 0 |
| 11 LAND | Coachman | 6 | 1 | | 7 | | 1 |
| TRANSPORT | Postman | 1 | | | 1 | | |
| *Group total* | | 7 | 1 | | 8 | 2 | 1 |
| 12 PROFESSIONAL | Minister | | | 1 | 1 | | |
| | Parish clerk | 1 | | 1 | 2 | | |
| | Bailiff | 1 | | 1 | 2 | | |
| | Surgeon | 1 | | 3 | 4 | | |
| | Apothecary | 2 | 1 | | 3 | | 1 |
| | Barber | 6 | | 1 | 7 | | 2 |
| | Schoolmaster | | | 1 | 1 | | |
| *Group total* | | 11 | 1 | 8 | 20 | 5 | 3 |
| 13 LABOURERS | Labourer | 65 | 5 | 21 | 91 | 23.5 | 11 |
| 14 SERVANTS | Servant | 5 | | 5 | 10 | 2.5 | |
| 15 MISC | Sailor | 1 | 1 | | 2 | | |
| GRAND TOTAL | | 289 | 26 | 93 | 408 | 100 | 32 |

## 1721-1759 (See Table 3)

There are far fewer details for this period in the burial register. Kew now had its own chapel and registers, but no details at all of occupations are noted in them, so Table 3 covers Richmond only. Otherwise, the same considerations apply as mentioned above for Table 2.

Some changes in pattern are apparent. There is a big increase in the proportion of victuallers and brewers. Road transport has finally become more important. The growing sophistication of life in Richmond can be seen in the professional and miscellaneous categories – the musicians, the prompter (at the theatre?), the broker and the lawyer, the writing master. Richmond's high-technology industry is launched with a bevy of watchmakers and a maker of mathematical instruments.

Another point which may appear significant, but which must be treated with considerable caution, is the apparent sharp drop in the proportion of 'labourers' in the second period (7%) as compared with the first (22%). Perhaps the relatively prosperous labourers of Richmond apprenticed their children to recognised trades; there are certainly instances of this in the Surrey apprenticeship records. But more likely the parish clerk in 1721–59 just omitted 'labourer' in many cases where this should have been recorded as the occupation. Even in the early years of this period there are quite a lot of entries with no trade shown – and they certainly do not all refer to 'gentlemen' and above. Moreover, some who might previously have been recorded as labourers now figure as 'gardeners' – the large number so described must include workmen as well as market-garden owners.

TABLE 3

### 1721–1759

| Group | Trade | Baptism Reg | Burial (children) | Burial (adults) | Total | Approx %age of whole |
|---|---|---|---|---|---|---|
| 1 RIVER-BASED | Waterman | 40 | 1 | 4 | 45 | |
| | Fisherman | 4 | | 1 | 5 | |
| | Boat-builder | 1 | | | 1 | |
| *Group total* | | 45 | 1 | 5 | 51 | 11 |
| 2 LAND | Husbandman | 8 | | | 8 | |
| | Gardener | 49 | | 8 | 57 | |
| *Group total* | | 57 | | 8 | 65 | 14 |
| 3 BUILDING | Carpenter | 35 | | | 35 | |
| & WOOD- | Sawyer | 2 | | | 2 | |
| WORKING | Joiner | 9 | | | 9 | |
| | Turner | 2 | | | 2 | |
| | Carver | 1 | | | 1 | |

| Group | Trade | Baptism Reg | Burial (children) | Burial (adults) | Total | Approx %age of whole |
|---|---|---|---|---|---|---|
| | Cabinetmaker | 3 | | | 3 | |
| | Bricklayer | 25 | 1 | | 26 | |
| | Mason | 3 | | | 3 | |
| | Plumber | 1 | | 1 | 2 | |
| | Glazier | 3 | | | 3 | |
| | Painter | 1 | | 1 | 2 | |
| | Plasterer | 1 | | | 1 | |
| Group total | | 86 | 1 | 2 | 89 | 20 |
| 4 METAL WORKING | Blacksmith | 6 | | | 6 | |
| | Farrier | 8 | | | 8 | |
| | Brazier | 1 | | 1 | 2 | |
| Group total | | 15 | | 1 | 16 | 3.5 |
| 5 CLOTH MAKING | Weaver | 2 | | | 2 | |
| | Dyer | 1 | | | 1 | |
| Group total | | 3 | | | 3 | 1 |
| 6 CLOTHING | Tailor | 9 | 1 | | 10 | |
| | Glover | 1 | | | 1 | |
| | Breeches maker | 3 | | | 3 | |
| | Shoemaker | 14 | | 4 | 18 | |
| Group total | | 27 | 1 | 4 | 32 | 7 |
| 7 OTHER MANUFACTURES | Wheelwright | 3 | | | 3 | |
| | Saddler | 1 | | | 1 | |
| | Basketmaker | 2 | | | 2 | |
| | Watchmaker | 4 | | 1 | 5 | |
| | Mathematical instrument maker | 1 | | | 1 | |
| Group total | | 11 | | 1 | 12 | 2.5 |
| 8 CATERING & DRINKS | Victualler | 24 | 1 | | 25 | |
| | Brewer | 5 | | 1 | 6 | |
| | Vintner | 1 | | | 1 | |
| | Cooper | 4 | | | 4 | |
| Group total | | 34 | 1 | 1 | 36 | 8 |
| 9 FOOD & DOMESTIC SUPPLIES | Baker | 7 | | 2 | 9 | |
| | Butcher | 11 | | 2 | 13 | |
| | Poulterer | 5 | | | 5 | |
| | Fishmonger | 1 | | | 1 | |
| | Grocer | 2 | | | 2 | |
| | Corn chandler | 1 | | | 1 | |
| | Chandler | 4 | | | 4 | |

| Group | Trade | Baptism Reg | Burial (children) | Burial (adults) | Total | Approx %age of whole |
|---|---|---|---|---|---|---|
| | Tallow chandler | 1 | | | 1 | |
| | Coalman | 1 | | | 1 | |
| Group total | | 33 | | 4 | 37 | 8 |
| | | | | | | |
| 10 MERCHANTS | Draper | 1 | | | 1 | |
| | Shopkeeper | 2 | | | 2 | |
| Group total | | 3 | | | 3 | 1 |
| | | | | | | |
| 11 LAND | Coachman | 11 | | 1 | 12 | |
| TRANSPORT | Drayman | 4 | | | 4 | |
| | Carter | 2 | | | 2 | |
| | Ass-man | 2 | | | 2 | |
| Group total | | 19 | | 1 | 20 | 4.5 |
| | | | | | | |
| 12 PROFESSIONAL | Minister | | | 1 | 1 | |
| | Parish clerk | | | 1 | 1 | |
| | Proctor | 1 | | | 1 | |
| | Surgeon | 5 | | | 5 | |
| | Doctor of Med. | 1 | | | 1 | |
| | Apothecary | 4 | | | 4 | |
| | Lawyer | 1 | | | 1 | |
| | Schoolteacher | 1 | | | 1 | |
| | Writing master | 1 | | | 1 | |
| | Broker | 1 | | | 1 | |
| Group total | | 15 | | 2 | 17 | 3.5 |
| | | | | | | |
| 13 LABOURERS | Labourer | 32 | | | 32 | 7 |
| | | | | | | |
| 14 SERVANTS | Groom | 2 | | | 2 | |
| | Ostler | 3 | | | 3 | |
| | Servant | 4 | | 1 | 5 | |
| | Gamekeeper | 1 | | 1 | 2 | |
| Group total | | 10 | | 2 | 12 | 3 |
| | | | | | | |
| 15 MISCELLANEOUS | Barber | 6 | | | 6 | |
| | Peruque-maker | 2 | | | 2 | |
| | Sexton | | | 1 | 1 | |
| | Beadle | 1 | | | 1 | |
| | Chimney sweep | 4 | | | 4 | |
| | Musician | 3 | | | 3 | |
| | Prompter | 1 | | | 1 | |
| | Drawer | 1 | | | 1 | |
| | Soldier | 4 | | 5 | 9 | |
| Group total | | 22 | | 6 | 28 | 6 |
| | | | | | | |
| GRAND TOTAL | | 412 | 4 | 37 | 453 | 100 |

## 1795 (See Table 4)

The *Universal British Directory*, published in 1795, lists both gentry and tradesmen, but for Richmond only. There is no list for Kew.

Under the heading of 'gentry' the directory lists 11 members of the peerage, headed by the Duke of Clarence and the Duke of Buccleuch, six baronets or knights or their widows, 17 esquires, 40 gentlemen and six serving officers. The Russian Ambassador also had a house in the town. These are not included in the table, but some gentlemen who were listed under their professions are: five members of the clergy, five surgeons and one attorney.

In the commercial section the directory lists five innkeepers and 22 victuallers, as well as two brewers, three liquor merchants and one brandy merchant. There were in fact 30 licensed premises in the town that year. Accommodation was also provided by three 'lodging-house keepers'.

Among the shopkeepers those providing clothing and food were still the most numerous. Of the clothing trades, 13 boot and shoe-makers and 11 tailors head the list, but there were seven 'mantua-makers' (a mantua was a woman's loose outer gown – and these were perhaps general dressmakers, for no one is listed as such) and four stay-makers. Included in the clothing category is the 'silk stocking cleaner to the Duke of Clarence'. Eleven hairdressers and two perfumiers attended to the coiffures and toilette of the gentry and the more prosperous tradespeople.

The greater sophistication of the town in the late 18th century – in comparison with previous lists – can be seen in the listing of three clockmakers, two china shops, one toyshop and four stationers (two of whom were also bookbinders) and a 'calendarer'. There were more drapers and haberdashers, and six 'hucksters', selling assorted small and fancy goods.

A greater variety is evident too among the food suppliers, with fruiterers and a greengrocer, milkmen, butter-men and tea merchants appearing on the list. Some fruit and vegetables were no doubt also sold by the four (market) gardeners and perhaps the one farmer listed.

The building trades were still strongly represented; and furniture-making was becoming more specialised with chair-makers and upholsterers listed as well as the traditional cabinet-makers.

An undertaker, an auctioneer and a pawnbroker provided their necessary services; as did a postmaster and a letter carrier. Medical attention was provided by a chemist and a midwife in addition to the five surgeons.

The town was beginning to acquire the reputation as a place for education which it particularly enjoyed in the 19th century. Already there were eight schoolmasters listed, three of whom ran boarding schools for boys – and three ladies had boarding schools for girls. Two music masters and a dancing master added extra accomplishments

– and one may probably assume that the three 'musicians' were likely also to take a pupil or two.

One of the big changes from the earlier part of the century was the increased use of road transport, and there were now five coachmasters in the town – and one horse dealer. Employees such as coachmen and draymen would not be mentioned in this list. Only two watermen are listed, but there must still have been many others; these two were perhaps major employers – while their employees and those plying individually for hire were not considered worthy of inclusion.

Another evident difference between this list and previous ones, resulting from the nature of the list itself, is the total absence from it of servants and labourers. There were of course many in both categories, but one would not expect to find them listed in a commercial directory.

The first official census, taken in 1801, only six years later, reported a population of 4,628 for Richmond (excluding Kew), living in 823 houses (there were an additional 65 houses currently unoccupied). The total figures from the directory are: gentry (including clergy, surgeons and the attorney) 92, tradespeople, etc, 276. Assuming that there was as yet little multiple occupancy of houses, the directory accounts for the occupations of over 40 per cent of the families in the town. Most of the remainder must be assumed to be those working for hire as servants, labourers, shop assistants, laundresses, watermen, etc.

TABLE 4

1795

| Group | Trade | Number | Approx %age of total |
|---|---|---|---|
| 1 RIVER-BASED | Waterman | 2 | 1 |
| 2 LAND | Farmer | 1 | |
| | Gardener | 4 | |
| Group total | | 5 | 2 |
| 3 BUILDING | Carpenter | 15 | |
| WOOD-WORKING & | Bricklayer | 6 | |
| FURNITURE | Stonemason | 2 | |
| | Glazier | 4 | |
| | Plumber | 2 | |
| | Painter | 4 | |
| | Plasterer | 2 | |
| | Cabinet maker | 4 | |
| | Chair maker | 2 | |
| | Upholsterer | 3 | |
| Group total | | 44 | 15 |

| Group | Trade | Number | Approx %age of total |
|---|---|---|---|
| 4 METAL WORKING | Smith | 3 | |
| | Farrier | 1 | |
| | Whitesmith/Brazier | 2 | |
| *Group total* | | 6 | 2 |
| 5 CLOTH MAKING | | 0 | - |
| 6 CLOTHING | Tailor | 11 | |
| | Hatter | 3 | |
| | Stay maker | 4 | |
| | Mantua maker | 7 | |
| | Breeches maker | 1 | |
| | Shoemaker | 13 | |
| | Glover | 1 | |
| | Umbrella maker | 1 | |
| | Silk stocking cleaner | 1 | |
| *Group total* | | 42 | 15 |
| 7 OTHER MANUFACTURES | Clock maker | 3 | |
| | Basket maker | 1 | |
| | Fishing tackle maker | 1 | |
| *Group total* | | 5 | 2 |
| 8 CATERING & DRINKS | Innkeeper | 5 | |
| | Lodging house keeper | 3 | |
| | Victualler | 22 | |
| | Brewer | 2 | |
| | Liquor/Brandy merchant | 4 | |
| | Cooper | 1 | |
| *Group total* | | 37 | 13 |
| 9 FOOD & DOMESTIC SUPPLIES | Baker | 7 | |
| | Butcher | 8 | |
| | Poulterer | 3 | |
| | Fishmonger | 2 | |
| | Grocer | 16 | |
| | Greengrocer | 1 | |
| | Fruiterer | 2 | |
| | Confectioner | 2 | |
| | Muffin maker | 1 | |
| | Milkman | 4 | |
| | Butter man | 3 | |
| | Tea merchant | 2 | |
| | Corn chandler | 2 | |

| Group | Trade | Number | Approx %age of total |
|---|---|---|---|
| | Tallow chandler | 4 | |
| | Coal merchant | 7 | |
| | Ironmonger | 2 | |
| *Group total* | | 66 | 23 |
| 10 MERCHANTS | Draper | 6 | |
| | Haberdasher | 3 | |
| | Clothes shop | 1 | |
| | China shop | 2 | |
| | Huckster | 6 | |
| | Toy shop | 1 | |
| | Pawnbroker | 1 | |
| *Group total* | | 20 | 7 |
| 11 LAND TRANSPORT | Coachmasters | 5 | |
| | Coach & harness-makers | 2 | |
| | Saddler | 1 | |
| | Horse dealer | 1 | |
| *Group total* | | 9 | 3 |
| 12 PROFESSIONAL | Clergy | 5 | |
| | Surgeon | 5 | |
| | Chemist | 1 | |
| | Midwife | 1 | |
| | Attorney | 1 | |
| | Schoolmaster | 8 | |
| | Schoolmistress | 3 | |
| | Dancing master | 1 | |
| | Music master | 2 | |
| | Musician | 3 | |
| *Group total* | | 30 | 10 |
| 13 LABOURERS | | 0 | - |
| 14 SERVANTS | | 0 | - |
| 15 MISCELLANEOUS | Postmaster | 1 | |
| | Letter carrier | 1 | |
| | Stationer | 4 | |
| | Calendarer | 1 | |
| | Hairdresser | 11 | |
| | Perfumier | 2 | |
| | Undertaker | 1 | |
| *Group total* | | 21 | 7 |
| GRAND TOTAL | | 287 | 100 |

# 16

## *Richmond Hostelries in the Eighteenth Century*

IN THE HISTORY of Richmond's drinking houses, the years 1724–26 produce a great breakthrough. From 1724 survive the earliest annual licensing records;[1] from 1726 the earliest annual rate books.[2]

Although there are gaps in the licensing records (13 years are missing between 1749 and 1769), these give the names of the licensees for each year as granted by the justices at the petty sessions in September. In 1729–30 some names of alehouses are also given, and in 1732–35 most are named. The names of houses are again recorded in the Victuallers' Recognizances between 1822 and 1826. The names of many of the inns and taverns can also be found in the manorial records, and this source reveals the names of their owners, and sometimes of the occupants (i.e. the licensees). The manorial survey of 1771 and the rental of 1774 are especially useful. From the rate books, in an almost unbroken series from 1726 to 1771, one can find nearly all the persons whose names are in the licensing records and can place their residence within the town. Sometimes this enables us to place a named tavern not otherwise locatable. Often it enables us, working from the bases of 1732–35 and 1771, to produce a full list of licensees for a particular house. Not infrequently it reveals that the licensees have moved from one house to another. A person's name may appear regularly in the licensing returns for twenty or thirty years – but in that time he may have been the licensee of, say, three different houses.

Although the information we have for the period between 1771 and 1822 is not as complete – as the ratebooks survive for only every tenth year – there is a useful list of victuallers in the *Universal British Directory* of 1795.[3] The land tax returns, from 1780 to 1832, are also a valuable source.[4] Although these tax assessments were levied on the landowners, and are listed under their names, the returns usually include the names of the occupants of each property and give the names of inns, taverns and alehouses. This is, however, a steadily diminishing asset, as increasingly more and more landowners commuted their tax for a capital sum which had the effect of freezing the record at the date of commutation.

The study of 17th-century hostelries in Chapter 10 concluded by mentioning a few establishments which were probably founded before 1700 although the first mention of them only occurs a year or two later. Including these, there were some 18 licensed premises known to be in business in 1703 (although the manor survey of that year' only names nine of them). By 1726 we can identify 47 houses by name (there were a few other licensees whose names appeared for one or two years only, and even if their addresses can be found there is no hope of identifying a name for their premises). Of these extra premises fifteen or so appear to have identifiable origins in the period 1703–24, while 13 more make their first appearance in the records in 1724 (although almost certainly most of these were flourishing before that date) and three can be placed as established in 1725–26. Only two of the 1700–03 list had closed by the early 1720s: the *Three Pigeons and Lilypot* (lately the *Castle and Trumpet*) had been bought up as a site for the parochial school in 1714; the old *White Horse* on the Green had been demolished and replaced by the two new dwelling houses at No. 22 in 1725. The original *Ship* in King Street succumbed in 1726, passing on its name and trade to the *Six Bells* next door, which then continued as the *Ship*, expanding into a part of the *Feathers* in the 1780s and becoming the *Old Ship* in the 1790s.

It is very apparent from the rating assessments in 1726 that three inns were in a class of their own: the *Dog* (which changed its name to the *Talbot* in the 1730s) was assessed at an annual rentable value (RV) of £75; the *Red Lion* and the *Feathers* were both assessed at an RV of £60. Nothing else came near – the newly rebuilt and

*The* Talbot Hotel *(from an engraved letterhead).*

renamed *Greyhound* in George Street (formerly *White Horse*) was rated at £28; the inn called the *Half Moon*, which appears to have stood between the Green and George Street (entered from a passage between 23 and 24 The Green), and which closed in 1734, was rated at £20. No other licensed premises were valued at over £16 RV. Yet among the new names of the first quarter of the 18th century were many of the pubs which are still flourishing today or which closed only in recent years.

One of the first of these is now the *Prince's Head* on the Green. In the 1703 survey mentioned above there is an entry for Michael Flayle for 'two houses at the corner of Paved Alley facing the Green' – no suggestion there that they may be alehouses. Yet on 15 January 1704/5 the manor rolls record the sale by Michael Flayle to John Collins of his messuage called the *Punch Bowl*; and on 31 December 1705 is recorded the further sale by Flayle to Collins of the adjoining messuage called the *Duke of Ormond's Head*, at the corner of Pensioners' Alley. Collins merged these two into a single establishment under the name of the *Duke of Ormond's Head* (assessed at £12 in 1726). The Duke was, of course, not only a popular national figure, but a local landowner. Despite his flight into France and impeachment in 1715, the name '*Ormond's Head*' is still found in 1732–35, but the tavern had become simply the *Duke's Head* by 1761 and was changed to the *Prince's Head* shortly before 1780.

The *Angel and Crown* in Church Court was probably founded about this time, though the evidence is not conclusive. We know that it was licensed in 1724 (and assessed at £10 RV in 1726). Its licensee then was Alexander Smith. But in 1732 the next house on the south side in Church Court was said to abut 'the house of Jonah Smith lately occupied by William Doe' on the north; William Doe had been described in the parish registers as a victualler when his son Thomas was baptised in October 1707. So there is a presumption that William Doe may have been dispensing his victuals at the *Angel and Crown* by 1707.

An alehouse called the *Cock* makes a fleeting appearance at 14 King Street in 1708 and 1709 only. It was next door to the *Thistle and Crown* at 13 King Street, which was part of the rebuilt *Angel* or *Half Moon*, and had adopted the name of *Thistle and Crown* or *Crown and Thistle* by 1724 (its RV was £9). This was damaged by fire in 1753, and was rebuilt, then changed its name to the *New Ship* about 1793. It survived under that name for just one hundred years, being closed down in 1893.

The house with a pediment at No. 17 The Green was built by John Price between 1705 and 1711. It was occupied from 1711 (at least) until his death in March 1723/4 by John Lawrence. Mary Lawrence (widow or daughter) was a licensee in 1724. A series of mortgages taken out on the house by John Price from 1711 to 1727 all mention John Lawrence as present or late occupant, but make no mention whether or not the premises were being used commercially. The next occupant after the Lawrences was John Litchfield (from 1727) and a note of empty premises in the rate book for that year includes 'Litchfield – coffee house – half year'. When John Price finally sold the premises in 1733 it was as 'the messuage lately known as the *Italian Coffee House*'. So one can say that it was possibly a coffee house from 1711, probably from 1724 and certainly from 1727.

In 1731 Mrs Joyce Baldwin took over the management, and in 1737 it was '*the London Coffee House* occupied by Joyce Baldwin'. It appears to have been enlarged about 1744–45 when its RV was increased from £18 to £25. Joyce Baldwin died in March – April 1756 and was succeeded as licensee by her son Isaac. Isaac Baldwin ceased to be the licensee in 1763 but remained listed as ratepayer until his death in 1785 (by which time it was the *Richmond Coffee House*). In 1792 his daughter Mary Baldwin sold 'the late coffee house' to John Fox. A Daniel Harris whose name appears as a licensee from 1763 to 1793, but whose name never once appears in the rate books, was probably the manager of the coffee house for Isaac Baldwin (who actually purchased the premises, hitherto leased, in 1776) and then for his daughter.

To this house the members of White's Club in London resorted at week-ends. It was Horace Walpole who commented, in a letter to Horace Mann written on Sunday 4 June 1749:[6]

> As I passed over the Green I saw Lord Bath, Lord Lonsdale and half a dozen more of the White's Club sauntering at the door of a house which they had taken there, and come to every Saturday and Sunday to play at Whisk [*sic* – whist].

One of the whist players wrote a little political poem which was published in *Richmond Notes* in 1867.[7] One verse suffices to confirm Walpole's observation:

> From White's we'll move th'expensive scene
> And steal away to Richmond Green;
> There free from noise and riot,
> Polly each morn shall fill our tea,
> Spread bread and butter – and then we
> Each night get drunk in quiet.

Another coffee house was situated at 30 The Green, a freehold house built facing north-east onto the Green behind the corner house of old Palace Terrace. This was evidently built after the Terrace was finished, but it appears to have been there by December 1711 when William Beaumond left two houses (Nos. 29 and 30) to his wife Jane and then to his niece Phoebe Hudson. In 1725 William Larcum (who had presumably bought the house from Jane Beaumond) was granted a licence to let 'his coffee house on Greenside occupied by Daniel Austin'. Austin appears in the lists of licences from 1724 to 1733; he was buried in August 1734 and his wife Mary was licensed in September 1734 at 'the coffee house'. However, she seems to have left by the time the 1735 rates were assessed, and with two brief tenancies in 1736-37 (neither of the names appears in the licensees' lists) the house remained empty until 1744, though still listed as '*Mr Austin's Coffee House*' until 1742. Its occupants after 1744 were not licensed.

In the decade between 1715 and 1725–26 we come across no fewer than 25 new names of licensed premises. For about half of these we can allocate a likely starting date (often related to the building of the house). The others are those which appear for the first time in the licensing list of 1724 but which may have opened up some years before. Some disappeared again quite quickly; some have lasted even to the present day.

Among those which can be more or less dated are several important survivors (all of them relatively small in the 1720s):

The *Three Pigeons* on its old site on the east side of the Petersham Road is first mentioned by name in the manor records in June 1715. In the whole period between 1724 and 1853 just four families appear as licensees: Skeggs (1724–52), Choun (1753-65), Raymond (1768–1816) and Hare (1817–53). It was a relatively small house (RV £8 in 1726) until enlarged in the early 19th century. The name and licence were moved across the road to the riverside site in 1870.

The *Three Tuns* at 80 George Street appears in 1724 but was probably opened in 1716 when the house was purchased by the victualler Moses Boddicott. Its occupants were unlicensed after 1737. The *Crown* at 6–7 King Street was another relatively short-lived house. It was 'formerly occupied by Jane Wickes and now by John Bacon' in 1718. Bacon appears as a victualler in the baptism registers in 1701. William Wickes (the husband of Jane) was described as a victualler when he was buried in May 1704. Jane Wickes survived at least until August 1708. So whether this was a tavern at the time of the Wickeses is uncertain, as is the date when John Bacon took over. He was the licensee in 1724 and until 1732 and was then followed by his wife Jane and his daughter Susan until 1746. In 1747 the house was unoccupied and in 1748 it was rebuilt as two (unlicensed) dwellings. The *Lion and Lamb*, at 28 George Street (the corner of Church Court), was apparently run by Ralph Bostock from 1719 to 1724 (when he died in August) and then by his widow until her death in November 1735. It was not thereafter licensed.

*Plate 22*     As far as it is possible to tell from the manor records, the first building to be erected on the site of the *Black Horse* at Marshgate was put up in 1718. This site was the tip of an acre and a half strip of land at the eastern end of the Upper Dunstable Shott. This tip was cut off from the rest by the Marshgate Road. In April 1718 the owner Andrew Mackean was licensed to let 'a new built brick house at Marshgate and garden, stables, coachhouse, outhouses, etc'. This appears to be an addition to his existing houses on the north side of the road; so it may well be that the lease was to Jeremiah Dimsdale who was the licensee of the *Black Horse* by 1724. It was a relatively small house in 1726 (RV £8), significantly enlarged for the first time in the 1790s. It was rebuilt in 1904 on the same site and still trades in the same place under the same sign.

Not far from the *Black Horse* were two other smaller taverns. The original *Red Cow* was almost certainly along Worple Way, on the south side thereof, on a piece of freehold land, where Alberta Court now stands. John Smithers (licensed from 1725) was the first known licensee, but the alehouse could have been there earlier. The name and licence were transferred to the present site some 150 yards away in Sheen Road in 1789. The *Coach and Horses* was in the same area, but its site has not been exactly identified. Its first known licensee from 1724–36 was William Phelps. His successor in the rate books does not appear in the licensing lists, and then the entry for this property disappears altogether – suddenly to crop up again from 1751 to 1757 among some miscellaneous 'afterthought' entries as 'Chaffin Martin at the *Coach and Horses*' (RV £7). And that is the last we hear of that.

Another house which is still trading in the same place under the same sign is the *Roebuck* on Richmond Hill. The cottage in question was one of a 'newly erected' pair in October 1703 when it was occupied by the owner's 28-year-old son John Jefferys. In 1701 John Jefferys was described in the parish registers as a labourer, in 1705 as a gardener; he was still 'labourer' when his mother made the cottage over into his ownership in April 1710. However in 1717/18, when his wife died and left him some other property which she had inherited, he was noted in the manor rolls as 'victualler'. It seems likely, therefore, that he opened the *Roebuck* as an alehouse between 1710 and 1717. It is clearly shown in both of Leonard Knyff's views of the scene from Richmond Hill, painted about 1720. The Roebuck was one of the smallest licensed houses in 1726 (RV only £5), but had been enlarged by 1742 (RV £12) and again by 1780 (RV £22); in the 1830s and '40s it expanded into a small hotel.

*Plate 22*

The next two taverns to be noted can be dated quite closely. Both were situated on the land which John Price had bought for development – in the section that lay between the foot lane and the horse lane to Kew. Both were on parts which Price had sold off undeveloped (though it is always possible that he built the houses after the sale). John Hope had bought in 1713 the strip of land which lies on the south side of what is now Clarence Street. He died in October 1718 and in April 1720 his son John Hope (who was a victualler) was admitted to the land with 'a brick messuage recently built'. By June 1721 the younger John Hope had built three more houses on the land. One of these (probably the one built by 1720) was the original *Orange Tree*, which was situated on Clarence Street, nearer to the foot lane (Parkshot) end than the Kew Road end. In 1808 this building was replaced by the '*New Orange Tree*', more or less on the present site (which was itself rebuilt about 1898).

The strip of land to the south of that sold to Hope had been purchased in 1716 from John Price by Edward Richardson, who sold it on almost at once to Thomas Egger. In April 1720 the manor court recorded the sale by Egger of the ground with a barn to Richard Brookes, victualler, and the mortgage by Brookes of a new messuage called the *Lamb*. This building (assessed for £10 in 1726) was renamed the *White Lion* when it was taken over by the famous 'dwarf' publican Cornelius Caton in 1747.

*Plate 23*

Caton was the only Richmond publican to be celebrated by an engraving published in the year of his death. He was Richmond born, fourth son of a sawyer, Edward Caton, who seems to have arrived in Richmond with three brothers in the mid-1680s. Cornelius was baptised in Richmond Church on 11 October 1696. By 1626 he was living in Duke Street, just behind the *Rose and Crown* and, as he is said to have raised himself from 'pot boy to head waiter', we may perhaps guess that this rise was achieved at the *Rose and Crown*. He seems to have first set up in business on his own account when he held a 'brandy licence' for the sale of spirits in 1733-35. No doubt he continued in this trade, but in 1736 new legislation imposed such a stiff tax on the retail sale of spirits and such a high licensing fee that the whole system broke down. There were riots; no more licences were taken out; spirits were just sold illegally. In 1743 the 1736 act was repealed and a moderate excise duty (on the manufacture of spirits) and a low licensing fee were introduced. From September 1745 Cornelius held a full licence as a victualler. This was the origin of the *Coffee House Tavern* (see page 249 below). Then in late 1747 or the first half of 1748 he moved to become licensee of the *Lamb*, which became the *White Lion* possibly at the time of Caton's arrival. He remained there until his death in November 1770.

The *White Lion* continued to flourish for a while after Caton's death, but there were several gaps between tenancies in the late '70s and '80s. It closed in 1790, but was reopened, very briefly, as the *Old White Lion* in 1812. The building still survives, at 31–33 Kew Road.

Another tavern which made a modest start at this time, to blossom into greater glory soon after, was the *Castle* at 37 George Street. This was an early to mid-17th-century mansion with two gables at the front (one of which still survives). It had been the home of Simon Bardolph from 1646 to 1654 and later occupants included the Countess of Longford, John Cranenburgh (an important merchant) in 1694, Lady Haversham and a Dr Cole MD (resident in 1719). At some time between 1719 and 1724 it became a tavern, then an inn. It was assessed for only £8 in 1726, but for £40 in 1733 and for £60 in 1752, figures which bring it into the same category as the *Talbot* or the *Feathers*. In 1759 the then licensee John Halford bought a larger mansion in Hill Street and transferred the business there (see page 250).

Several other new licensed houses in or off George Street appear at this time. In what is now the lower end of Sheen Road, but was then considered as part of George Street, the *George* was trading in 1724. It was part of a new terrace of houses built by William Wollins (who leased the ground from William Manley in 1687). In 1724 Manley sold the whole terrace to the victualler Moses Boddicott, but whether it was Boddicott who then installed the first known licensee at the *George*, John Lane, by September 1724, we do not know. At an unknown date, probably in the 1760s, the tavern was renamed the *Marquis of Granby's Head*. John Manners, Marquess of Granby, the oldest son of the Duke of Rutland, was a successful general in the Seven Years' War and was at the height of his popularity in 1763. The earliest reference traced to the tavern under its new name is in 1777 when a branch of the Amicable Society of Tradesmen was established there. The premises were rebuilt in 1808, but continued as a public house under the name of the *Marquis of Granby* until the early 1980s.

In the island block of buildings between George Street (or Lower George Street) and the Kew Road was the *Angel*. There is a slight puzzle about the origins of this

Plate 21

The south side of Richmond Green, a drawing by Thomas Way, 1900. Nos. 10-12 are on the left. The house in the centre, with a pediment, is No. 17, built by John Price, and Richmond's principal coffee house in the 18th century.

Maids of Honour Row – just built – is seen in this detail from the 'Prospect of Richmond' print published in 1726.

*Plate 22*

*The* Black Horse Inn, *c.1830. (Richmond Public Library, local studies collection)*

*The* Roebuck *tavern about 1720. Detail from Leonard Knyff's view from Richmond Hill. (LBRUT)*

*Plate 23*

*Cornelius Caton, a contemporary engraving.*
*(British Library, CRACH 1, TAB 1, b1, Vol. 6)*

*Plate 24*

*The* White Cross *and Collins' brewery, 1840s. (Richmond Public Library, local studies collection)*

*The* Duke's Head *tavern near the Park gate at the top of what is now Queen's Road, as drawn by Augustin Heckel, who was about to take up residence in the house just below it.*

*Plate 25*

*The* Star and Garter, c.1740 *(anonymous drawing).* *(Richmond Public Library, local studies collection)*

*The* Star and Garter *in 1803 (from James Brewer's trade card).* *(Richmond Public Library, local studies collection)*

*Plate 26*

*Thomas Way's drawing of the* Red Lion *tavern in 1900.*

*The* Marlborough, *formerly* Rose Cottage, *hotel in Friar's Stile Road. (The gables of the roof can still be seen behind later shop fronts, while the liquor business has developed in the tap room seen on the right.) (Richmond Public Library, local studies collection)*

*Plate 27*

*Mid-19th-century watercolours of the three principal taverns on Kew Green: below left, the Rose and Crown; right, the Coach and Horses; bottom, the King's Arms. (Richmond Public Library, Local Studies Collection)*

*Plate 28*

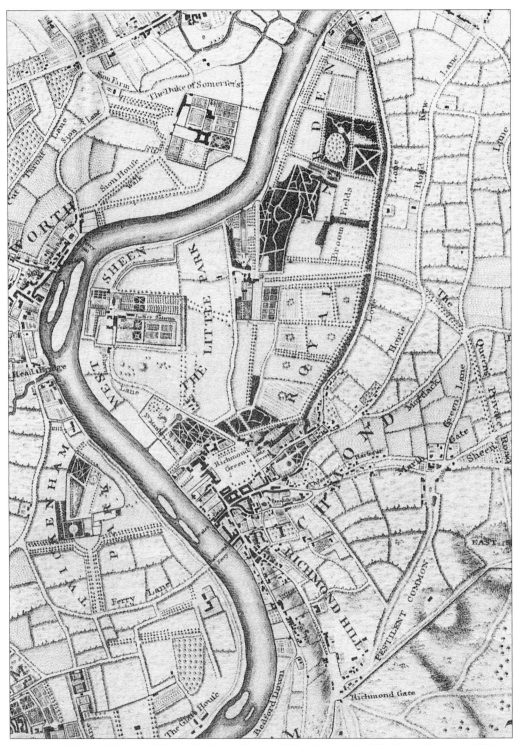

*Richmond in the 1740s. Detail from John Rocque's map of 'The Country Ten Miles Round London', 1746.*

house. It can be followed back in the manor rolls from 'the messuage called the Angel occupied by Sarah Fellows' in 1763, when Robert Lander inherited it from Jane Lander, to 1704 when Jane Drew's cottage was inherited by Mary Drew 'now wife of George Lander'. The occupants can be traced back year by year in the rate books from Sarah Fellows in 1763 to Edward Richardson in 1726. Edward Richardson appears in the licensing returns from 1724 to 1734 (and in 1729 to 1734 is stated to be at the *Angel*). But in 1719 Edward Richardson was occupying a house belonging to Richard Hawes the brewer which was next door to George Lander's. And in 1716, when he bought the land from John Price mentioned above, he was already a victualler. Perhaps he had opened an alehouse in Hawes' property by 1716 – and perhaps he then moved it to Lander's between 1719 and 1724. This tavern, enlarged in the last decade of the 18th century, was renamed the *Rose and Crown* in 1805. As such it survived until 1890 when 'Bug Island' was redeveloped. Its last landlord became the first landlord of the new *Imperial* public house built on the site.

The *Black Boy* at 65 George Street, with a still, was first noted as in the occupation of Sampson King, a distiller, in 1723-24; but by September 1724 the licensee was Robert Cross. The last known licensee, from 1748 onwards, was Edward Martin who died in 1767. According to an article by Richard Crisp in Hiscoke's *Richmond Notes* for July 1863, 'the house in which Mr Bamford resides in George Street was about a century or so since a small inn called the *Black Boy*, the niche in the brickwork in front, which still exists, contained a large carved figure of the said Black Boy as the sign.'

Almost opposite the *Black Boy* was the original *Sun* alehouse (RV £9) at 19 George Street. The house had been built by John Price about 1703, but it is not until 1726 that it can be definitely identified as an alehouse licensed to James Cowart. It changed its name to the *King's Head* by 1780 and was last licensed in 1793. Just two doors away was the *Two Brewers* at 17 George Street. It is not certain when this first became an alehouse. In January 1700/1 the house was occupied by Robert Biggs (who was described as a victualler when he was buried in 1715). In 1728 it was 'formerly occupied by Robert Biggs and now by Richard Bonsey' – and Bonsey held a licence from 1724 to 1733 (specifically at the *Two Brewers* in 1732 and '33). The house was rebuilt in 1735-36, and renamed the *Artichoke* about 1757. It seems to have been enlarged somewhat in 1770 (increase in RV from £12 to £18 in 1771). In 1860 the name was changed again, to the *Foresters' Arms* and it ceased to be an alehouse in 1914 when taken over by Henekey's wine and spirit merchants as a shop. Some elements of the 19th-century building can still be seen in the side of W.H. Smith's store (and cast iron columns which were part of its façade remain concealed within the present larger columns of the store front windows).

On the north-west side of George Street there was a building which was reached up a passage between Nos. 72 and 73 (and apparently also by a passage between 23 and 24 The Green). This had a RV of £20 and was occupied from 1726 to 1734 by Henry

Ratcliffe, who was licensed from 1724 to 1734 (specifically at the *Half Moon* in 1729–30 and 1732–34). He was described as an innkeeper in the parish registers in 1731–32 and as a victualler in 1733–34; and was buried in June 1735. For three years the property stood empty; then the later occupants do not seem to have been licensed, Margaret Lee being the occupant from 1768 to 1774. But the house then appears to have amalgamated with one immediately adjacent under the name of the *White Hart*. In July 1774 Henry Bell surrendered to Edward Collins the '*White Hart* (formerly two messuages now converted to one) lately occupied by Mr Fearne, Robert Richmond and Mrs Lee, and now occupied by Brown, Robert Richmond and Mrs Lee'. Robert Richmond figures in the licensing lists from 1771 to 1773, but as landlord of the *Cricketers*.

The famous old *Red Lion Inn* was beginning to run into difficulties by the third decade of the 18th century. A mortgage for £730 could not be redeemed, and in 1733 the mortgage was foreclosed. For two years the inn stood empty; then on 28 February 1736/7 a notice was published in the *Evening Post* that 'the old Red Lion Inn ... kept by Henry Fudge, peruke-maker, is now opened, where Gentlemen, Ladies and others will be entertained in the best manner'. Henry Fudge lasted only two years; then William Popplewell took over, but moved to the *Talbot* in 1739. For two years the rate books recorded 'late Popplewell'; in 1742 'late the *Red Lion*'. In April 1742 the premises were described as 'a messuage now divided into three, formerly known as the Red Lion'. One of the parts divided off survived for a few years as an alehouse called the *Plough*. It was licensed from 1724 to 1745 and again for one year in 1748. By 1751 it stood empty as 'the old Plough'. The original *Plough* at the top of Ferry Hill had become the *King's Head* by 1724.

In Paved Alley an alehouse called the *Haunch of Venison* existed from 1724 to 1741. Another alehouse of which little is known is the *Cross Keys* in a freehold house at 8 Hill Street which was licensed from 1724 to 1756 (one of its proprietors being the peruke-maker Henry Fudge for five years before he tried his luck at the *Red Lion*). Opposite, at the corner of Hill Street and Water Lane, the *White Hart* was a much more successful house. The building itself and the two houses immediately adjacent to it (which became the *Maids of Honour* pastrycooks' shop) were built about 1690–91 by John Smithies. At what point the corner house became a tavern is not known. Edward Goodall, known to be its proprietor from 1724 until his death in January 1739/40, was certainly in Richmond from 1716 onwards, as he had children baptised there. The *White Hart* continued to be licensed under the same name and in the same place until 1914. It was then taken over by Farrow's Bank and rebuilt.

A little way down Water Lane the *Royal Oak* alehouse was a going concern by 1724. It closed as a public house about 1790 (but was revived about 1850 until 1873). There is a puzzle concerning the next house to be mentioned – which is the well-known *White Cross*. This started life as the *Waterman's Arms* – but where? Thomas Collier, identified as landlord of the *Waterman's Arms* in 1726 and in 1732–35, was

*The* White Hart *tavern and the Maids of Honour pastrycook's shop at the corner of Hill Street and Water Lane – an engraving from the 1890s, but evidently based on a drawing of the 1830s. On the left is the Bertie/ Shewell house, built in the second or third decade of the 18th century – and renovated in 1985. (Beresford Chancellor,* History of Richmond, *p.177)*

licensed from 1726 to 1741. He appears in the rate books for 1726 and 1727 in a position which seems clearly to be a cottage in the middle of the south side of Water Lane. Then from 1728 onwards the position of his listing changes to the north side of the lane, next to the malthouse, the site where the *White Cross* stands today. As this site was Crown land, under a head lease to John Darrell of 'Old Palace Place', it is difficult to ascertain what was built on it when. Nor can we be sure when the name was changed. Perhaps Samuel Cross, who succeeded Collier as proprietor in 1742, or his sister-in-law Ann Cross who was licensee from 1743 to 1755, were responsible for the change to the *White Cross* (which had certainly happened before 1771). The house was rebuilt by 1835 and had an extra storey added by 1880. It is still going strong.

*Plate 24*

There are just four more establishments to complete the tally of those operating in 1726 – and they lie on or below the hill. Passing the *Dog* tavern, which became the *Talbot Inn* by 1746, there was an alehouse at what is now 10-16 Hill Rise. This was a freehold property, probably first built in 1705–10. The house is known to have been licensed from 1724 to 1783, in which time it had no less than four names. Originally the *King's Arms*, it became the *Bell* in 1734. By 1771 it was the *Fox and Hounds* and by 1780 the *Duke's Head*. The premises were rebuilt as two houses in the 1820s.

Somewhat further up, at what is now 20 Richmond Hill, was a house called the *Swan*. It is mentioned as such in the manor records in 1747, 1748 and 1759, and it was occupied by known victuallers in 1720 and 1734–35. But it figures very seldom in the rate books and no licensee is specifically linked to it by name, so its existence and history are a little vague. Below, in the Petersham Road, the original *Blue Anchor* alehouse, with a malthouse attached, was built in the 'parish close' by the river about 1720. It is known to have been licensed from 1724 to 1765. It was pulled down in 1769–70 and replaced by a substantial house. The malthouse was not demolished until the 1820s, when the mansion of 1770 was enlarged for Lady Ann Bingham (today the *Bingham Hall Hotel*).

At the top of the hill, the *White Lion* had become the *Bull's Head* tavern, and remained until it was replaced by The Wick in 1775. Round the corner, at the top of what is now Queen's Road, John Christopher, who probably came first to Richmond about 1717, took a lease of a house just outside the park gate which had been described in 1703 as the 'old cakehouse'. By 1724 this was the *Punchbowl* tavern. In 1738 John Christopher moved across the road to found the *Star and Garter* and Charles Slaughter (or Slater), who had for a few years had an alehouse called the *Duke's Head* in George Street, took over the *Punchbowl*, enlarged it and renamed it the *Duke's Head*. His sign,

*Plate 24*

portrayed in an engraving by Augustin Heckel, undoubtedly showed the head of William Duke of Cumberland, son of George II, as there is a reference in 1743 to 'Mr Slater's at the Prince William's Head upon the Hill'.

Although it was wholly in Petersham, the *Star and Garter* was so fully a part of the Richmond scene, and later such an important part, that it must be considered here. In 1738 John Christopher obtained from the Earl of Dysart, lord of the manor of Petersham, a grant of land on the top edge of Petersham Common, facing the gate

*Plate 25*

of Richmond Park. Here he built the first *Star and Garter*, a quite small tavern without any guest accommodation. His sons Samuel and Joseph, who took over the tavern after John Christopher's death, had the grant renewed in their joint names, mortgaged the property (in 1758) and at once built a new and larger building adjacent to the original one. They enlarged again, with a third block, in the late 1760s. The house, now an important inn, was taken over in 1801 by James Brewer, who again made

*Plate 25*

substantial enlargements – but ruined himself in the process. Under Joseph Ellis (from 1822 to 1858) it achieved fame and prosperity, and after being taken over by a limited company in 1864 it was progressively rebuilt. Closed shortly before World War I, it was taken over as a home for disabled ex-servicemen and was demolished in 1920 to be replaced by the Royal Star and Garter Home, opened in 1924.

The *Duke's Head* in George Street, mentioned above, was one of four taverns which made brief appearances in the 1730s. It adjoined the *Castle*. After Charles Slater moved up the hill, it continued to be licensed until 1746. It seems possible that an alehouse called the *King's Head* existed between 1733 and 1740 on the north side of the Marshgate Road, almost opposite the present site of the *Red Cow*. A house called the *Goat* makes a single appearance in Middle Row, next to the *Angel* in 1736. And in Petersham Road, the *Green Man* is found in 1734 and '35.

In 1737 Hannah Laycock, widow of John who had been landlord of the *Duke of Ormond's Head* until his death in 1736, purchased a nearby house; recently rebuilt, on the Green. In 1741 she installed her son-in-law William Sawyer as the first licensee. Although the name is not recorded until 1770 this tavern was probably from the outset the *Cricket Players* (as it was called in 1770) or the *Cricketers* (first used in 1771). From 1770 to 1779 a half-share in the house was owned by Samuel Whitbread, just beginning to build up his brewery and public-house company. The premises were enlarged or rebuilt in the 1820s–30s but were then destroyed by a serious fire in August 1844 and completely rebuilt. Apart from the rebuilding in 1844 the *Cricketers* has an unbroken history from 1741 to the present day.

Another house that makes its first appearance in 1745 was in Duke Street. Three houses immediately behind the yard of the *Rose and Crown* had been built by John Price between 1717 and 1725. A brewhouse at the back was part of the same property. Cornelius Caton, probably occupying what is now No. 2 Duke Street, appears in the rate books from 1726 until 1747. As mentioned above, he held a brandy licence from 1733 to 1735 and a full licence from 1745. In 1747 he moved to the *White Lion* in the Kew Road. The property was linked by ownership to the *London Coffee House* at 17 The Green, and it was perhaps this link which led to the Duke Street house being given the name of the *Coffee House Tavern*. Henry Hunt, a distiller and brewer, succeeded Caton as licensee from 1746 to 1762, but was in occupation of two adjacent houses. From 1772 these became two quite separate licensed premises – No. 2 Duke Street being the *Coffee House Tavern* and No. 3 the *Three Tuns*. The *Coffee House Tavern* became a 'wine and spirit vaults', which acquired the name of the *Cobwebs* about 1890, and then became an ordinary pub under that name until changed to the *Racing Page* in 1990. The *Three Tuns* continued until 1910.

At 51 George Street the *White Lion* (mentioned once in 1638 but not again in the 17th century) was flourishing under John Wellbeloved from 1721 to 1729 and then Joseph Balley (specifically licensed at the *White Lion* in 1734). Balley was succeeded by John Tasker who changed the name to the *Swan* (licensed there in 1735). The house continued as licensed premises until 1750 but it and adjacent buildings were rebuilt in 1751-53 and no subsequent occupants held a licence.

A new *Red Lion* tavern was opened in a newly-built house in Red Lion Street in 1753. (Its location was approximately where the bookshop and Chinese restaurant, both preserving the Red Lion name, now stand.) Never aspiring to the status enjoyed by its former namesake, this quite modest tavern stood until demolished in 1909. *Plate 26*

It was probably in the 1750s that the house at 17 Parkshot (then the Kew Foot Lane) became firmly established as a coffee house, though it does appear that one or two earlier occupants may have held licences very briefly. The *Kew Foot Lane Coffee House* is so named in 1771. Thomas Sell, who held the licence in 1785-86, appears in the land tax returns as owning 'late Kew Lane Coffee House' in 1787–89. It was probably in 1790 that the premises were renamed the *Sun*, though the first positive reference by this name is in 1794. As the *Sun* the house still flourishes today.

In 1758 Thomas Goodwin appears for the first time as occupant of the house, belonging to the Hickey Trust, at the corner of Petersham Road (east side) and Compass Hill (north side). There are no licensing records extant for that year or for 1759, but Goodwin appears from 1760 to 1765. He was succeeded as occupant by William Harvey and the 1774 manor rental identifies Harvey as tenant of the messuage, outhouses and yards called the *Rising Sun*. About ten years later the name and licence of the *Three Compasses* (see page 116) was transferred to the former *Rising Sun* (although the change of name is not shown in the land tax returns until 1790). Towards the end of the 19th century the tavern, somewhat enlarged, revised its name to the *Compasses Hotel*; and so remained until 1939 when the premises were demolished to widen the Petersham Road.

A very short lived venture in 1758 was 'the *White House* on Richmond Hill close to the Park Gate'. An advertisement of 1758 announces the opening of this establishment by Mr Wildman of Bedford Head, Southampton Street, London. It was presumably either the old *Punchbowl-Duke's Head* revived or an adjacent property. But Mr Wildman's name does not appear in the licensing lists – nor is he even in the rate books until 1762–64 when he is listed in the house between the former *Duke's Head* and the park gate. This house and the *Duke's Head* were demolished for the Duke of Ancaster's new mansion.

In 1759, as already mentioned, Mr John Halford transferred the name and licence of the *Castle* from the old premises in George Street to the mansion recently built by Dr Caleb Cotesworth in Hill Street. At the same time he opened, on its north-west side in Hill Street, a tavern, which was in effect the hotel tap, called the *King's Arms*.

The Castle Hotel
*(from Beresford Chancellor,* History of Richmond, *p.179)*

The latter, although it remained for a long time in the same ownership as the *Castle*, became a separate establishment about 1815 and adopted the new name of the *Spread Eagle* from about 1820. The hotel was closed in the late 1870s – and became the site of the new Richmond Town Hall; its assembly rooms, rebuilt by Joseph Ellis in the 1830s, were only finally demolished as part of the Richmond Riverside project of the 1980s; the *Spread Eagle* closed as a public house in 1909.

An alehouse whose name I have been unable to trace evidently existed at 7 George Street from 1757 to 1782, as all the occupants in that time noted in the rate books are also to be found in the licensing records. The last landlord was William Waterman who retired in 1779 from the *Feathers* inn, which was then closed down and converted into shops and offices. Three other well known taverns closed in the 1770s and '80s: the *Bull's Head* on the Hill in 1775, the original *Three Compasses* on Compass Hill in 1782, and the *Rose and Crown* at the corner of George Street and Duke Street in 1789. Two new houses replaced ones that had gone. The new *Blue Anchor* in Kew Road (on its present site) opened in 1779 and the new *Red Cow* in Marshgate (Sheen) Road replaced the old alehouse of that name in 1789.

With these changes Richmond's establishment of drinking houses became settled and almost unchanged for the next 40 to 50 years. There were (excluding the *Star and Garter*) 31 licensed premises in Richmond in 1790; 29 of them were still open in 1830. The original *Sun* (renamed the *King's Arms* in 1780) in George Street closed in 1793; the *White Lion* in Kew Road closed in 1790 (though revived briefly in 1812). In their place just the *Rose Cottage Hotel* (now the *Marlborough*) in Friar's Stile Road joined the list in 1828, promoted from its previous status as 'tea garden'.

*Plate 26*

Of the explosion of small alehouses which followed the passage into law of the Beer Act of 1830 I have written elsewhere.* Suffice it to say that by 1880 the total number of licensed premises in Richmond had risen to 73.

✠

## 18th-Century Hostelries in Kew

Owing to the lack of rate books it is much more difficult to trace successfully the history of the Kew taverns and alehouses – there were no substantial inns in the 18th century. But at least we start with a clear picture – I have not been able to trace a single alehouse in Kew before 1700.

The earliest references occur on 15 January 1704/5 when two presentments were made in the manor court for encroachments on Kew Green: of Elizabeth Nixon, widow, victualler, at the sign of the *Rose and Crown*; and of Charles Lawson, victualler, at the sign of the *Rising Sun*.

The original site of the *Rose and Crown* was on the south side of the Green, at No. 47. From 1680 this was part of the Capell estate. In April 1697 Lady Dorothy Capell was granted a licence to let for 21 years a 'cottage on Kew Green between the land of John Smither south and west and John Stubbs east and the way by the Green north, formerly occupied by William Ingram'. Ingram was a gardener, already in occupation by 1658/9, so it is unlikely that the house was already an alehouse. Lady Capell's tenant was Elizabeth, widow of James Nixon (who died in January 1696/7). After her death in April 1709 Lady Capell granted a new lease to Elizabeth's son

* 'Public Houses in Richmond 1790–1880' by John Cloake in *Richmond History* No. 20 (1999) pp.9–18.

Arthur Nixon in 1711. Arthur Nixon's executor was one John Hayter, who is noted as innkeeper at the *Rose and Crown* in 1721. In 1726 Joseph Williams was rated at the *Rose and Crown*. In May 1729, however, Hayter granted a sub-lease of the premises to James Smith, schoolmaster (see Chapter 21), so the *Rose and Crown* may be presumed to have moved by then to its new site – see below.

The *Rising Sun* was established in a cottage at 11–15 Kew Green. This had been inherited by Mary, wife of Michael Layton, and granddaughter of the original grantee, in 1675. When her son, another Michael Layton, inherited it in 1700 there is no indication that it was an alehouse. Nor is there any indication of when it was let to the victualler Charles Lawson. Michael Layton himself appeared in the licensing records from 1724 to 1743 (specifically at the *Rising Sun* in 1729–30 and 1732–35) and his widow then took over from 1744 to 1748. There may have been another licensee from 1749 to '53, but then from 1753 to 1765 William Gainforth was licensed. At some point before 1763 he changed the name of the establishment to the *Coach and Horses*, and he bought the house himself in June 1763 from Isaac Layton who had inherited on Michael's death a few months before. By 1769 he had closed down at this location and moved to the east side of the Green.

By the 1720s there were some other alehouses. In August 1719 William Cox was granted a licence to let the house called the *Cock and Hoop* to William Dudley. This same house was occupied in 1733 by Elizabeth Flavell. Thomas Flavell had been licensed from 1724 to 1730 and specifically at the *Ewe and Lamb* in 1729–30, and Elizabeth Flavell was licensed from 1732 to 41 (at the *Ewe and Lamb* in 1732 and '34). This house was on the east side of Kew Green, probably on the site of the later *Coach and Horses*.

From 1724 to 1732 John Hughes and from 1733 to 1743 Richard Loveday were licensed (specifically at the *Rose* in 1729–30 and 1732–35). This house was on the north side of the Green, towards the western end, and probably belonged to the brewer Richard Hawes.

One other tavern existed at Kew in 1724 – the *Swan* on Brentford Ait. This stood on the eastern part of the ait, called Mattingshawe, which belonged to charity trustees (for the poor of Fulham and Hammersmith). It was leased to Steven West, who held a licence from 1724 to 1743 (specifically at the *Swan* in 1729–30 and 1732–35). West also purchased in 1737 the adjacent central portion of the ait which he held in copyhold. He was followed by his brother Henry West from 1749 to 1784, then by Henry's son Henry to 1790 and then by the latter's widow Sarah in 1791. Under the Wests the *Swan* gained a reputation as a good eel-house. In 1780 the diarist William Hickey 'dined upon the island off the town of Brentford, where there is a house famous for dressing pitchcocked eels and also for stewing the same fish'. Though Hickey does not mention it, the house also developed a reputation for rowdiness and immorality.

In 1793 Thomas Samuel Maycock (who had been licensee of the *Red Cow* in Richmond) bought out the West heirs. Neither he nor Matthew Bowden, to whom he immediately leased the property, figure in the licensing returns after 1793, but the *Swan* certainly continued – we know that Samuel Payton was licensee from 1804 to 1808 – and there are other names of licensees which might well fill all the gaps if there were a way of sorting them out. The tavern had now become the *Three Swans*, and it continued to cause annoyance to its neighbours perhaps threefold! In 1811 Robert Hunter (then living in the mansion at Kew which is now the Herbarium of the Royal Botanic Gardens) wrote: 'Brentford Ait is a great nuisance to this parish and the neighbourhood on both sides of the river ... [because of the] house of entertainment which has long been a harbour for men and women of the worst description, where riotous and indecent scenes are often exhibited during the summer months and on Sundays'.[8] In May 1812 Hunter bought out both the part of the ait on which stood 'a tearoom with yards and gardens' and the lease of Mattingshawe with a messuage called the *Three Swans* as assigned to Maycock in 1793. Hunter at once closed down the establishment, demolished the buildings, and applied for – and was granted – permission to fill up the pond on the island that had been used for catching fish.

The little row of four cottages on the north side of the Kew Green pond was built in 1726, and one of them seems to have been turned at once into an alehouse called the *Peterboat*. The first licensee may have been a John Manger (1727–28), but from 1730 to 1735 Ralph Cheshire was licensed specifically at the *Peterboat*, and he continued to hold a licence until 1741.

In 1729 the *Rose and Crown* moved from the building on the south side of the Green which now became Kew's schoolroom nicknamed 'Hell' – to the site which it still occupies today at 79 Kew Green. Its first licensee there was Joseph Pybus (from 1729 to 1738/9), followed by Robert Frime from 1738 to 1765. There had been three *Plate 27* houses together on this site, and for the first thirty years it was just the central one which was the alehouse. Then in April 1759, on the death of the owner Thomas Howlett, the manor rolls record the inheritance by Thomas Howlett Warren of 'two messuages and stables on the north side of Kew Green, lately occupied by Robert Frime and Edward Hobbs, which together with the messuage occupied by Robert Frime first mentioned are laid into one now in his occupation known as the *Rose and Crown*'. The old building of the 1750s was replaced by a 'mock Tudor' one in the early 20th century.

It seems probable that an alehouse was in business for a while in the Richmond Road (now Kew Road) in the 1740s to '60s, as a succession of licensees at that time appear to fit with what is known of John Dillman's tenants at this house. The house, at the end of the row called Gloucester Cottages, was listed as a tavern called the *Royal Standard* in the 1841 census.

There is no clear proof that the new *Coach and Horses*, opened by Edward Soundy at No. 8 on the east side of the Green in 1769, was on the same site as the former *Cock* *Plate 27* *and Hoop* and *Ewe and Lamb*, but it seems quite probable – and there was certainly a link in the licensees. John Bone, the first husband of Mary sister of Francis Engleheart, was licensee of the *Ewe and Lamb* in 1742–43. He died in 1744, when the widow Mary married John Gater. Mary's daughter, Anne Bone, married Thomas Richmond who was licensee of the *Coach and Horses* from 1780 to 1793. The succeeding generations of the Richmond family produced almost as many – and as good miniature artists and portrait painters as their Engleheart cousins. There appears to have been a very brief gap in the house's history as licensed premises; for when John Cox Engleheart inherited the property in 1810 from John Dillman Engleheart it was described as 'the former *Coach and Horses*, now converted into a dwelling house occupied by James Haverfield'. This can only have been a brief interlude as Samuel Payton was licensee there until 1808 and Benjamin Cussell certainly from 1818 (and it is probable that the house was relicensed from 1815 when a new lease was granted). That lease was taken over in 1831 by the brewers Young and Bainbridge, who purchased the freehold in 1898. Though the house has been enlarged and altered, some of the original structure of the 1760s can still be seen.

Plate 27   The last public house to be opened in Kew in the 18th century was the *King's Arms*, built in 1773 by George Schennerstadt on a piece of land he had just purchased from the Earl of Bute. The premises have remained on the same site until the present day, although they were rebuilt in mock-Tudor style shortly after the rebuilding of Kew Bridge in 1903. They have recently been stripped of their old name, to become a pizza restaurant trading as 'Ask'.

# 17

## *'The Prospect of Richmond'*

PUBLISHED IN OCTOBER 1726 by Overton and Hoole, the well-known, but rare, engraving *Plate 30* of 'The Prospect of Richmond in Surry' gives a good overall impression of the little town as it was at that date. The Green is the nucleus, but King Street, Hill Street and George Street are fully developed. Some houses are spreading out along the riverside and up the Hill along the roads to Kew and East Sheen and there are already a few scattered mansions in the fields.

The engraving is also, though untrustworthy, the first 'map' to show the centre of the town. The unknown artist seems to have rendered fairly and faithfully many of the buildings, though he made a number of serious topographical errors. Even in the areas that are shown inaccurately it is possible to identify many of the buildings, so a detailed analysis of the engraving can not only serve to point out the errors and omissions. but makes possible another study of just how far the town had developed at a given date, and – for the first time – a broad look at its architecture.

The 'Prospect' is analysed below in some 18 sections, each separately depicted, but it will be useful to refer back from time to time to the complete picture. (It should be borne in mind that the view is from the north-west, so that broadly speaking east is to the left and west to the right.)

✠

## A. *The Palace Area*

The artist of The Prospect appears to have taken careful note of these buildings as seen from the Green, but to have failed altogether to go round to the river side, as he has omitted about half of the area.

Starting from the upper left corner, he has depicted the central five-bay building of Tudor Place (built in the 1650s in the site of the former palace tennis court) and a two-bay wing beyond it. The similar wing on the near side was hidden by Maids of Honour Row (and was indeed partly tucked in behind No. 1 of that Row, which was built around it). Maids of Honour Row is accurately drawn, with its four houses of five bays each. Built in 1725 it is probably the newest building shown in The Prospect.

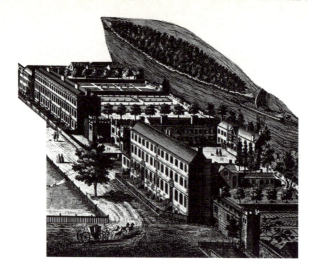

Next comes the remaining part of the old Palace. We cannot see the main gateway – the gateway visible is that which led into the former 'Winecellar Court'. That part of the building and the wing beyond it which projects forward beside No. 4 Maids of Honour Row were demolished in the early 1740s, and replaced by the 'mock-Tudor' bay which today balances the real Tudor one next to the main gate. The tower visible here is the smaller bay in the centre of the present building, of which the lower part is original.

On the near side of the gateway are the pair of houses built in 1707, which are today 'Old Court House' and 'Wentworth House'. The Prospect shows that they were originally an identical pair, but Old Court House had a bow added in front (and a splendid new doorway inserted) in the late 18th century, while Wentworth House was entirely remodelled to the designs of Henry Laxton after it suffered severe gale damage in the 1850s. Even today, the original pattern of fenestration is visible in the flat part of the façade. The original elaborately carved broken-pediment doorheads on these houses must have impressed our artist! Adjoining Old Court House the small cottage which still survives today, as part of the house, can be seen by the entrance to the Palace.

In the foreground is a small remaining part of the original palace front wall, ending in a corner turret. This stands on the site of the 19th-century Garrick House and the 20th-century Garrick Close. In front of the tower, a small fenced enclosure shows the garden of the house replaced by the Theatre Royal some thirty years later.

In Old Palace Yard, the Wardrobe building can be seen on the far side, and Trumpeters' House on the right. The Prospect reveals that the central gable of the latter was originally half-timbered, and shows the columns on each side of the gable on which the trumpeter figures (which had formerly adorned the Middle Gate on this site) were reinstated. Trumpeters' House, built in 1703–04, is seen here without its wings which (together with the great portico on the river front) were added in the mid-1740s.

On the near side of Old Palace Yard can be seen the workshops and stables which had been converted out of the low range of Tudor buildings on this side of the courtyard (now the site of Stable Cottages).

In the area by the river, which has been omitted from The Prospect, there was in fact little of interest, except the gardens, in 1726. In a line with Trumpeters' House there was a row of small houses and stables converted from the domestic offices of the Palace, and by the riverside (on the site of Asgill House) there was a brewhouse. At the other end of the site, by Friar's Lane, were a number of houses, built onto or converted from the old garden galleries, of which four (rather squeezed up) are shown. The Earl of Cholmondeley had not yet started to build his house by the river.

In the river itself The Prospect shows a single large island where today are just two tiny islets. This large island was in fact an accretion of three originally separate ayts which had evidently become joined up by 1726 (though this is not noted in the manor rolls until 1760). It was, however, somewhat eroded between the date of The Prospect and the end of the 18th century and was then – so the story goes – cut in half by the Duke of Queensberry, with the result that the two portions were more rapidly reduced by the river until they dwindled to their present size. The Ordnance Survey map of the 1860s shows the two tiny islets of today, but also shows that the full island was still at that date uncovered at low tide (before the half-tide weir was built).

## B. From Friar's Lane to Water Lane

This crowded area is one of the most difficult parts of The Prospect to interpret, though the frontage to King Street and the backs of the Water Lane cottages are clear enough.

Visible beyond Tudor Place (at the lowest point of this section), but reduced to a very insignificant scale, are 'Old Friars' and 'Old Palace Place', both refronted at the end of the 17th century. 'Oak House' and Nos. 16–17 King Street had not yet been built, so the next buildings (with two gables facing King Street and three towards Friar's Lane and the Palace) are likely to be the stables of Old Palace Place on the site of Nos. 15–17 King Street.

Nos. 12–14 King Street had been rebuilt in 1701–02, so are probably represented by the building with three mansard windows on the top floor – and with a shop awning or pentice on the ground-floor front. No. 13 was the *Thistle and Crown* tavern – later the *New Ship*. Beyond this building, the older one with a similar pentice but with two gables facing the street and large mullioned first-storey windows is probably No. 11.

The next lot of shops are largely obscured by the big tree (called the 'stocks tree', for the village stocks were at its foot) and only the last building in King Street is clearly visible. This was the *Feathers* inn, which though of Tudor origin (when it was called the *Golden Hind*) had probably been largely rebuilt in the late 17th or early 18th century.

Though they cannot be separately identified, the backs of the dozen or so cottages which lined the north-west side of Water Lane can be seen; then comes a larger (but quite low) building facing the river. This last may represent the tavern, originally called the *Waterman's Arms* but later the *White Cross*, which is known to have been in business from about 1728, but which may have been built by 1726.

The problems in this area are the several large buildings that are shown as standing between those fronting on King Street and the river. At the back of the King Street shops and the Water Lane cottages was the site of the one-time Observant Friary – and most of it was by this time gardens occupied with Old Palace Place and Old Friars. However, there was an old malthouse and brewhouse in the corner by the lower part of Water Lane, and this may be represented by the building which shows a row of four connected gables. There was also an old house (on 'The Retreat' site) dating from the mid-17th century which may be the building which appears with two (very white) gables with a single window in each just to the right of the stocks tree. The buildings immediately behind those which I have identified as Nos. 11 and 12–14 King Street may be just that – additional buildings at the rear of and forming part of these properties, so outside the 'Friars wall'.

But this explanation cannot apply to the large house with a six-bay front and three mansard windows which stands quite close to the river at the Friars Lane end of the area, or to the building (with a gable which seems to have concave sides) adjacent to it. As the Friars was a Crown leasehold, there is little detail to be found of the buildings on it from one lease to the next – and there were no leases of the Friars between 1698 and 1753. The ratebooks (from 1726) do not suggest the existence of any large house in this area except that of Mr George Smith which was on the 'Palace' side of Friars

Lane about half-way down. I think that this large house shown in The Prospect must be Mr Smith's, which has got a little misplaced. If that is so, the curious gable could perhaps belong to the old palace bargehouse which was at the extreme south-west corner of the Friars and was included in the new lease to the Earl of Cholmondeley in 1730, but which fell down a few years later.

*C. The Green and George Street (north-west side) from King Street to Brewers Lane*

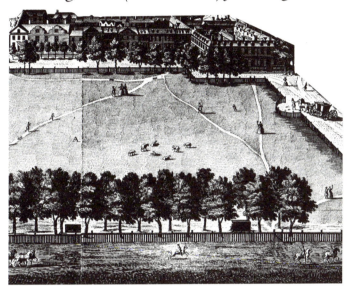

It will be noticed that the Green was at this time enclosed by a fence and that there were gates giving access to the paths that crossed it. Although it was already primarily a public place for recreation (see the bench and the sheltered seat under the avenue of elms in the foreground) it was still used for the pasturing of animals – and our artist has included a half-dozen sheep. Though the engraving shows some of the old-established footpaths on the Green, it omits the paths leading from the Palace to Brewer's Lane and to the corner of Duke Street, which still exist and which were probably the earliest of all.

Also of interest is the turning circle for coaches opposite Maids of Honour Row. Such semi-circular indents into the property facing a house were a not uncommon feature of 18th-century townscapes.

The depiction of the buildings facing the Green in this area may be adjudged as fairly accurate – but there are a few errors. Old Palace Terrace (built in 1692) and 29–32 The Green are faithfully rendered though a little condensed, but behind them we see only the rear of the King Street and George Street houses, with no sign of Paved Court and its shops – the north-east side of which was fully developed also in 1692. Similarly, there is no indication of Pensioners' Alley (now Golden Court) except a single long roof (at the same height as the Old Palace Terrace houses) and a solitary building standing behind Old Palace Terrace. The latter must represent the cottages on the south-west side of the original Golden Court which was in the centre of this side of Pensioners' Alley. The *Duke of Ormond's Head* tavern (now *Prince's Head*) seems to have been lost in this corner, as is the house which had the entrance of Pensioners' Alley through it.

Then followed (and shown in The Prospect), from right to left, the house which a bit later became the *Cricketers* (two bays) and another house 'new built' in 1712 (three bays). Then there is the pair of houses (now No. 22 The Green) (three bays each) built in 1725 on the site of the former *White Horse* tavern. To the left of these, No. 20 (three bays), 19 (with a pediment) and 18 (three bays) were still in a single ownership in 1726. Then comes the other pedimented house (No. 17), built by John Price about 1710, which was Richmond's coffee house for much of the 18th century. Next is a small house (No. 16) built about 1704 and then a pair of older houses (Nos. 14 and 15) with 'Jacobean' gables and mullioned windows. This was an early 17th-century building divided into two by 1725. No. 13 on the corner of Brewer's Lane was probably rebuilt about 1700, and has of course been again rebuilt subsequently.

A single continuous roof depicts the shops of the south-west side of Brewer's Lane. There is little point in trying to identify the backs of the houses facing onto to George Street, but one may perhaps assume that the taller buildings immediately adjacent to Brewer's Lane were the work of Henry Trippett, architect, who redeveloped 55–58 George Street in the 1690s. In the space between the Green houses and the George Street houses another building or buildings can be seen, with four white gable ends. This I suppose to represent (though not quite in the right place) the house and long room behind Nos. 70–72 George Street which appear to have been a tavern (the *Half Moon* and later the *White Hart*).

## D. The Green and George Street (north-west side) from Brewer's Lane to Duke Street

Notice again on the Green in this section the sheltered bench seat under the elm avenue called 'High Walk' and also the benches round the single large tree on the north-east side.

This is an area where the artist has again omitted a significant number of buildings, and has squashed up some of those that he does show. The three newish houses at Nos. 10–12 by the corner of Brewer's Lane (built between 1705 and 1715) are reduced to a single structure of five bays – where there should be nine. Next to them is an old 16th-/early 17th-century building with two gables and mullioned windows. This must be the house at Nos. 8–9, not rebuilt as two until the 1740s, where William Radford set up his grammar school in the 1660s and in which later lived Dr Brady, who was both minister of Richmond parish church and headmaster of the grammar school. He

has generally been believed to have been the first master of St Mary's Charity School founded in 1713, but this appears to be an error (see Chapter 21). The charity school itself, built in 1714, was on the north corner of Brewer's Lane and George Street; its rear elevation as seen in The Prospect looks to be short of windows and pretty grim!)

After Nos. 8–9 The Prospect shows only two more buildings facing the Green before the corner of Duke Street. The one on the corner is recognisably No. 1 The Green; the other is almost hidden by a tree. These were in fact four houses in 1726 between Nos. 8–9 and No. 1, at least one of which (No. 7) had been built by John Price in 1703, though the others were probably older. But none of the houses in The Prospect here bear any resemblance to No. 7. My guess is that is the building shown, behind the tree, represents Nos. 2 and 3.

In Duke Street (then Duke's Lane) a hanging sign near the George Street end betokens the *Rose and Crown* inn, which actually faced onto George Street at the corner, and the rear elevation of which is presumably shown by the three windows set fairly close together. It is not really possible to identify the backs of the other George Street houses shown, but the building which lies between the two rows may be a brewhouse which was at the rear of No. 50 George Street.

In the open area at the far end of Duke Street can be seen a small wooden cabin. This was the original watch-house and lock-up, replaced by a new building in 'The Square' in 1730. It was probably very similar to the one surviving at Petersham. It would have been used by the village constable to shut up a drunk or felon if the need should arise.

## E. From Water Lane to Ferry Hill

The topography is very distorted here, for the length of Hill Street is greatly exaggerated.

Along the south-eastern side of Water Lane in the foreground can be seen the roofs, descending towards the river, of three distinct blocks of buildings. There were in fact by this time probably 15 separate buildings along this side of the lane, but they did fall into three groups. Starting from the riverside there was first a group of four (in 1720, expanded to six, but then reduced to four again by 1728, with the establishment

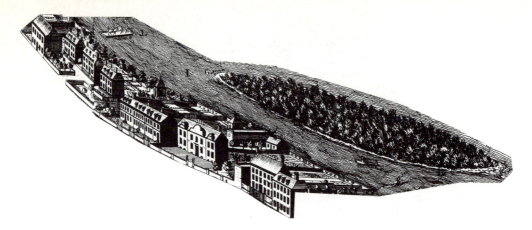

in that year of Collins' brewery at the foot of the lane). The original four had been divided about 1703 out of a single house (originally built about 1600) and were purchased by John and William Collins in 1728. Next came a group of five cottages dating from the mid-17th century which by 1725 were in four different ownerships, then another five houses, two older and three built by John Smithies in 1688–89. These were now in the ownership of Richard Toy.

At the corner of Hill Street was a group of three further houses built by Smithies in 1690–91 in replacement of two older houses and also owned in 1725 by Richard Toy. These show in The Prospect as a single five-bayed house facing Hill Street. No. 1 Hill Street was already the *White Hart* tavern; No. 3 (originally two houses) was occupied by Elizabeth Bullen, who was carrying on the business of her late husband, the pastrycook who invented the Maids of Honour tartlet.

Next, going up Hill Street, was the substantial house which had belonged to Sir Richard and Lady Chaworth (until 1690) and then to her heirs of the Bertie family (until 1718) and was now in 1725–26 owned by Thomas Shewell. It had been rebuilt not long before the date of The Prospect, but whether by the Berties or by Shewell is not clear. It is the house (5 Hill Street) which became the Ritz, then the Gaumont, Cinema and which was restored as 'Centenary House' in 1983–86. The apparently windowless building adjoining it on the south side, which projects forward to the line of the street, was probably a stable. It was still there in the early 20th century, as is shown in old photographs.

Beyond this, we see in The Prospect the long low mansion with a trifoliate centre gable belonging to, and recently built by, Dr Caleb Cotesworth. This later became the Castle Hotel, and is now the site of the Richmond Old Town Hall.

Between the Cotesworth house and Ferry Lane was the great 'riverside development project' of the 1690s – a row of five houses facing Hill Street and three mansions facing the river, with access from the newly constructed Herring (later Heron) Court. (It may have been in order to show the three mansions in their entirety that the artist of The Prospect elongated the scene, for the row of five houses, clearly depicted here, in fact extended right up to the entrance to Herring Court.) The project had been started in 1694–95 by a London merchant John Saunders whose wife had inherited the house which stood on the south side of the entrance to Herring Court, at the corner of Ferry Hill. That house had first been built in the 1640s, but judging from its appearance in The Prospect it was perhaps also rebuilt in the 1690s. Of the whole project just Heron House, the central mansion facing the river, has survived much renovated.

Both Dr Cotesworth's house and the future Hotham House (the most northerly of the three riverside mansions) appear to have gazebos by the river. Cotesworth's has also a long low building at right angles to the river bank (? a boathouse) and another small building adjacent to it.

On the river a ferry boat can be seen crossing to the Twickenham side, and what is now called 'Corporation Island' appears thickly covered with scrub.

*F. George Street and Red Lion Street up to the Church*

This area is very distorted as the artist has sited most of Red Lion Street where Hill Street should be. However, we can follow the frontage of George Street, starting with the old *Red Lyon* inn at the corner opposite the stocks tree and at the same time note what we might expect to find in Red Lion Street. The gables and mullioned windows of the inn – and still more the oriel window and gothic arched main door in the right-hand block – proclaim its age. The right-hand block at least appears to be of the mid-16th century, although the stepped gables to the left may be of the early 17th. Notice the two inn signs hanging on 'gallows' right across the street. The inn buildings along Red Lion Street probably include the block with two gabled dormer windows and the more modern house next to it.

To the left of the inn, facing George Street, is a more recent building, of five bays. This may be interpreted as the two large houses that stood on the sites of 7–8 and

9–10 George Street (built about 1660) behind which was also an older house (perhaps the one sticking out at right angles to the inn buildings along Red Lion Street). Next is a four-bay building (two houses at 11–12 George Street), then a gap with a house apparently standing some way back from the street. This feature can be clearly identified as still existing on the 1771 manor map and shows that we are at 13–14 George Street (now Marks and Spencer). The small single-storey building to the left of the gap is part of the same property.

Next to this, another five-bay building* (without dormers or mansards) is the two houses at 15-16 George Street, then we have the old *Two Brewers* tavern (later the *Artichoke* and later still the *Foresters' Arms*) – now the site of W.H. Smith. This is, I think, shown by the three-gabled building with an older fenestration pattern. At this point there should be another gap in the buildings, where later Artichoke Alley and Victoria Place came into George Street, but which in 1726 gave access to another house right behind the *Two Brewers* (we can see that in the picture). This alley led also to the large area where there was in the 1670s an orchard and a brewhouse, which lasted until William Lewis transferred his brewing operation to the riverside by the Petersham Road in the 1720s. It seems possible that the large square building with an irregular window pattern which juts out from the Red Lion Street buildings as shown in The Prospect is intended as the brewhouse.

To the left of the *Two Brewers*, a building shown with five bays must represent no fewer than five houses (at 18–22 George Street) for next comes the recognisable façade of the *Greyhound* inn (just rebuilt and renamed from *White Horse* at this time) with six bays and a large gibbet from which hangs the sign. The coach entrance is hidden by the facing houses. Finally, at the corner of Church Court, a three-bay front represents the two houses at Nos. 25–28.

On this side of Church Court there were at this time three houses, which are not individually distinguishable in the picture, but one can see the projecting sign of the *Angel and Crown*. Then the artist has inserted a quite imaginary crescent of small cottages surrounding the south western side of the churchyard. This brings us back to Red Lion Street which, in The Prospect, has now turned off at right angles from its previous alignment. The buildings shown in this area cannot be reconciled with reality. There were, in fact, a few small cottages along this part of the north side of Red Lion Street – not more than four at this date, and perhaps a few outbuildings connected with the brewhouse.

It is, of course, possible that the substantial house shown at the point where Red Lion Street appears to turn was in fact one of the buildings in Hill Street – as some of the others previously noted might also be. The lower part of Hill Street (up as far as Castle Yard) had been developed by this time.

---

* There is a slight slippage here in the joining together of the two sheets of the original engraving.

*G. Between George Street-Sheen Road and Paradise Road, from Church Court northwards*

We can begin here with the parish church, at this time with a cupola on its tower and with a porch on the north aisle (built by John Price in 1700–03). The old central nave with the Tudor chancel projecting at the east end, and the roof of the south aisle built about 1610–14 can also be seen. On the tower is what appears to be a clock face – a clock was installed in 1702, when the tower and some bells were repaired. It is not known exactly when the cupola on the tower was erected; it may have been in 1702 or when further repairs were needed after the great storm of 1703.

To the left of the church is Church Walk where the buildings shown are not, as those shown on the other side of the churchyard, imaginary – but are much exaggerated. The six (at least) substantial houses depicted by the artist were in reality just six small cottages. At the far, southern, end was a schoolroom, which may be the building jutting out behind the row of cottages. In Church Court there were no buildings on the north-east side, except the corner one facing George Street.

The frontage along George Street is more accurately portrayed. At the corner of Church Court is the large house occupied at this time by Richmond's apothecary, Thomas Eeles, and apparently of fairly recent construction. Next to this is an older house with an irregular frontage; it was actually two houses in 1726. Another, newer, house stood behind these and is so depicted. Then we have the two 'Dutch' gables of the *Castle* tavern (the left-hand one of which still survives above a shop in Lower George Street). Before being turned into a tavern in the early 1720s this house, probably built in the early 17th century, had been for a while the residence of nobility – the Countess of Longford (in the 1690s) and Lady Haversham.

Then follows another row of older, and smaller, buildings: two gables, a flat front of two bays and another three gables. These were the houses developed on what had been, until the Commonwealth, the glebe of the residence of the minister serving Richmond parish church. Since 1650 it had been rented out – but the first real details are only given in 1751 when there were five houses on this frontage – and one at the back at the Paradise Road end of the land (but that one may have been built after 1726). It seems likely that a part, at least, of the gabled buildings may be the former 'church house' itself.

In front of these buildings stands the little island group known at this time as 'Middle Row' (which had degenerated into 'Bug Island' before they were mostly demolished and rebuilt in 1889–90). The Prospect shows, correctly, that there were two buildings facing back along George Street and five (one in two parts) facing north. The one on the corner was rebuilt only a few years ago. The second one (which had been previously two) was the *Angel* tavern later renamed the *Rose and Crown*.

Next to the church properties are the products of two late 17th-/early 18th-century developments. The first of these is represented by two three-bay houses and was the work of John Drew, architect, *circa* 1714. In fact the first of these represents three houses and the second two houses – and there was an entrance between them into Union Court (presumably represented at this time by the buildings shown at the rear here). These buildings are now Nos. 1–9 Sheen Road.

The other development, shown in The Prospect by two six-bay buildings with a central pedimented three-bay section, was developed by William Wollins, the builder of Old Palace Terrace, who leased three old houses on the site in 1687 and rebuilt a row of six (Nos. 11–21 Sheen Road).

Drew had also built three houses at the Paradise Road end of his site, and Wollins had built one. The Prospect shows one quite large, but rather unprepossessing, building behind Wollins' terrace (with a smaller house or wing attached). This may well be the house that Wollins built, but another possibility is that it represents the workshop of John Drew in his timberyard on the site of Union Court. Of Drew's three houses there is no sign.

Along Sheen Road, we next come to one of Richmond's vanished 'stately homes': the large mansion with two wings built not long before. It was occupied in 1664 by Lady Partridge and later by Sir Charles Lyttleton. (It was later called Carrington Lodge and later still the wings were divided off into separate houses. It was demolished in the late 1940s.) The building behind it is its stable block.

Near the junction of Paradise Road and Sheen Road (on the site now occupied by the Christian Science Church) is Egerton House, said to have been built about 1710 and demolished in the early 1930s.

### H. *From Red Lion Street to the Vineyard, west of Church Terrace*

This is another confused area, because the artist seems to have mixed up Ormond Road and the Vineyard – and even then to have misplaced some (and mislaid other) buildings. However, the buildings he has shown are identifiable.

A relatively small but long and straight building in the bottom right-hand corner of this area represents houses on Hill Street (some of which may, of course, have got mixed up with the Red Lion Street ones in area F). Above this is the large complex

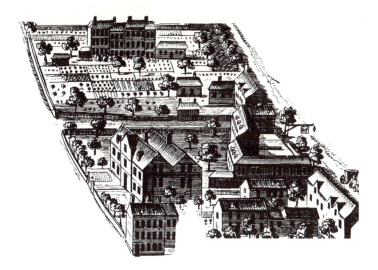

of buildings which constituted the *Dog* (later *Talbot*) inn. If the artist is to be trusted it had an open garden to the street at this time (note the inn sign).

To its left are the double gables of The Rosary and The Hollies in Ormond Road, built about 1697–99 – a back-to-back semi-detached pair. The front of The Hollies can be seen, with five bays and apparently with a central gable (which was in reality probably only a small dormer window). The road beyond these should therefore be Ormond Road but it continues to the left as the Vineyard (see area K). Even so, the houses of Ormond Row on its south side, built in the early years of the 18th century, have been shifted en bloc even further south up the hill; they appear at the very top of this area of the picture. One or two small outhouses are dotted about the gardens, and a smallish building above the Ormond Road – Hill Rise corner stands for all those houses yet developed up the hill from Ormond Road to the Vineyard (probably six by 1726). Conspicuously absent from the picture are both Clarence House (built 1696) and Michell's Almshouses (built in the late 1690s) in the Vineyard.

At the northern end of this area (the bottom in the picture) a few buildings are shown fronting on Red Lion Street. Opposite the church at the corner of Church Terrace are two houses, apparently of five and two bays respectively. Though now demolished these can be identified from old photographs as Church House and its neighbour. To their right are three cottages, one of them standing behind the others. These had been built in the late 17th century by Thomas Drew.

## I. The riverside, south of Ferry Hill

One of the most obvious topographical errors in The Prospect is the merging into one of the Lower Road (now Petersham Road) and Richmond Hill. However the buildings shown on the river side of the Lower Road do mostly belong there.

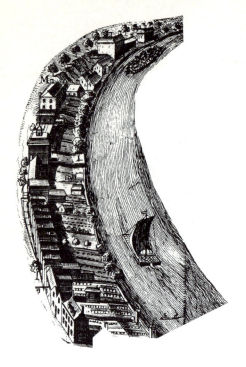

They start, at the northern (bottom) end with the largish building of the *Plough* (later *King's Head*) tavern at the corner of Ferry Hill itself. Neither Bridge House (built in the 1680s) nor the cottage lower down Ferry Hill is shown. The tavern is followed by a house with two gables facing the street, and then one with a flat front, of which no other details are shown. There were indeed two houses on the Lower Road south of the *Plough*, the second of which had been rebuilt in the 1680s.

Then follows a line of eight small roofs, all identical, which are clearly Queen Elizabeth's Almshouses founded in 1600 for eight aged women – although other evidence suggests that these were in fact built in two blocks of four rather than a continuous row of eight.

These are followed by a somewhat larger building end-on to the road, a house facing the road (with three trees in front) and a tall house surmounted by a cupola. The latter is the mansion which preceded Northumberland House and which had a close of '6 acres' between the road and the river – the ancient 'Wyndeyarde' (?Vineyard). There does not seem to be any documentary evidence of the date of erection of the house depicted here; it looks as though it might well date from the late 17th century when it was owned by Sir James Butler. It was rebuilt again about 1739/40. The two smaller buildings were probably a stable and another outbuilding.

Beyond this mansion is another small building and then another larger one. These show the initial development of the six-acre close which was undertaken when John Darrell became its owner in 1720. There were in fact three houses here by 1726, from the evidence of the rate book. They were to develop into Bellevue, Ivy Hall (now the *Hobart Hall Hotel*) and Gothic House (demolished in the 1930s). Then follows a small building closer to the river which almost certainly belonged to the waterworks established in the 1680s by Peter Wally to supply the town with river water (at that date still clear and drinkable) through a system of piped mains.

At this point our artist seems to have realised that he has forgotten about the hill, for he marks 'M – The Hill' in the road and draws a steep slope between the road and the river. On the other side of the road (see area J) we begin to have the buildings south of Friar's Stile Road! But by the riverside at the foot of this hilly slope is a group of small buildings which can only be the tile kilns. Of the development of Church

Close by the riverside (the Paragon, the *Blue Anchor* tavern and its malthouse and two other houses) which was begun in the early 1720s but not completed until 1734 there is no trace at all – unless it is represented (out of order) by the large house and two smaller buildings which then follow. There is, however, another candidate for the large house – the riverside mansion which was to be rebuilt in the 1760s by the Earl of Cardigan and became Buccleuch House. If this is a correct identification, the smaller buildings can only be outbuildings, for the site of Devonshire Lodge was not developed until after 1729.

Glover's Island appears to have floated a considerable way down river, being depicted here rather than in its correct location upstream of the river bend.

### J. Richmond Hill, south of the Vineyard

As noted above, one road in The Prospect has to serve both for the Petersham Road and Richmond Hill. For most of its length it is the slope of the hillside between which is omitted – so we are given no glimpse of Richmond Wells, the *Bull's Head* tavern (on the site of The Wick) or of the other houses in this area. On the left of the road as depicted are mainly the buildings on the eastern side of the Hill, but the very first one shown – a large mansion with a cupola – poses a problem. This could, given its relationship to the Ormond Road terrace, be Holbrook House, already

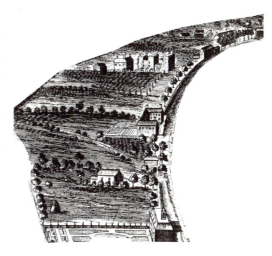

dominating its neighbours on Hill Rise by 1726. But another possibility is that it represents Rump Hall on the Petersham Road which was about to become, for nearly sixty years, Richmond's workhouse.

The next feature above this is a small building standing a little way in from the road. If the previous mansion was Holbrook House, this might be the stable that Penkethman used as a theatre. It hardly looks like the late 17th-century mansion that, 'Gothicized' in 1809, is now the Old Vicarage School. There was nothing else but a few small cottages between the Vineyard and Friar's Stile Road. (Thomas Chapman's theatre was not built until 1730.)

Next comes the unmistakeable building of Duppa's Almshouses, just past the corner of Friar's Stile Road, built in 1661–62 round three sides of an open-fronted (though railed) courtyard. Then a real puzzle: set at right angles to the road are what appear to be (from left to right) a small barn, a small house and three tall houses linked by smaller buildings. There were no buildings at all in the fields to the east of the Hill in 1726, so I conjecture that the artist has drawn here the buildings that actually stood at this time on The Terrace, to the south of the almshouses: a small cottage, the *Roebuck* tavern and Nos. 1–3 The Terrace. There should be no gaps between the three houses and No. 3 should in 1726 be still somewhat lower than Nos. 1 and 2 but this is the only explanation for this row of buildings that seems to make any sense.

Continuing along the Hill, the next house is probably Mansfield House (now part of the *Richmond Hill Hotel*), then follows a row (largely hidden by the Terrace trees) which would be the five cottages by this time standing in front of the site of the windmill (which had just been demolished about 1725). Beyond these again are a small house and a larger one adjoining, which stood at the top of Queen's Road just outside the Park Gate. The larger one was a tavern, the *Punchbowl* (later the *Duke's Head*), kept at this time by John Christopher who 12 years later was to build the first *Star and Garter* tavern at the top of Petersham Common. A little way to the left can be seen the house which was later occupied by Augustin Heckel, and a small stable which stood on the site of the *Lass of Richmond Hill*.

### K. *South of Paradise Road (or Row – as it was then called)*

Despite the confusion of the areas to the west, the few houses in this section are individually readily identifiable.

At the bottom right-hand corner, facing the churchyard, is No. 1 Church Terrace, and behind it the roofs of the other houses in the Terrace are indicated. These had just been built in 1725.

To the left (east) of No. 1 Church Terrace are what appear to be two small cottages facing Paradise Row. The first and smaller of these may be the little cottage which already existed on the site of what is now the Moss Tree cafe. The second is the house which stood on the northern edge of the grounds of Halford House. Behind them, the house standing midway between Paradise Row and the Vineyard is the original core of Halford House itself, built about 1710.

Behind this again is seen a house on the south side of the Vineyard. Newark House was not yet built, but there were some small cottages on and adjoining its site. This perhaps represents them. The lane at the right edge of this section is Patten Alley – which continued up the Hill on the line of Lancaster Park – but owing to the confusion between Ormond Road and the Vineyard it is not really possible to say which bit is which. Its importance seems greatly exaggerated – and it certainly had no coach-turning circle. (There was one in Ormond Road, opposite The Rosary and The Hollies.)

At the left (east) end of the Vineyard is a three-storey house facing north and an adjacent group of two or three houses facing west. These represent Vineyard House, built *circa* 1720, and its immediate neighbours. The line of trees running north from Vineyard House (on the line of the present Vineyard Passage) marked the eastern boundary of 'Stanley's Vineyard' in 1726.

## L. *South of Marshgate (Sheen) Road*

Three buildings are shown on the south side of Sheen Road (then called Marshgate Road). The one nearest to the Paradise Road corner was occupied in 1726 by Mr Henry Collings. It is probably the house which still stands in front of the telephone exchange. The low building between this and the next house is probably its stables.

The large five-bay house shown towards the left edge of The Prospect represents the pair of houses built about 1717 – Court Lodge and Spring House (Nos. 43 and 45 Sheen Road respectively).

Above this in The Prospect can be seen another large house with a long low building to its right and a small building to its left. The house is more or less in line with the Vineyard and could be taken for Mount Ararat – except that Mount Ararat was not built until the late 1730s. My guess is that the artist has jumped right over to the only other important building that stood a short distance north of the Marshgate

Road and has drawn here the Marquis of Lothian's mansion (later called Spring Grove) towards the bottom of what is now Queen's Road. There was already another substantial house (the future Grove Lodge) just to the north of it in 1726, for which the small shed or cottage can hardly serve. The long low building might be a stable; there was no other house south of Lord Lothian's.

## M.  Between Sheen Road and the roads to Kew

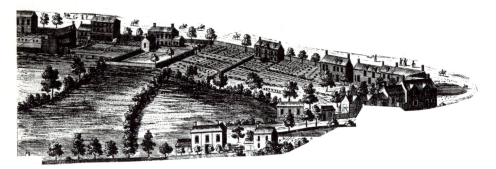

At the point where the Sheen Road and the Kew Road diverge was the village pond (now the site of Dome Buildings), seen on the right of this section of The Prospect. Beyond this the little development that had yet taken place along the Kew Road was known as 'World's End'. The largish house here, nearest to the pond, must represent the *Bear* tavern (later *Brown Bear* and now Next's store). There were in fact 12 cottages on the north side of the tavern by 1726 – only a selection are shown .

Beyond these, the Kew Road as shown in the engraving just peters out; but a bit closer to the spectator are two houses on the east side of the Kew Foot Lane (today's Parkshot). These are certainly misplaced by the artist, as the only houses yet built on this side of the road were those on the land that had been Price's, a good deal further north. By 1726 there were three of them, but whether Price built them is uncertain. In each case he had sold the land shortly before the houses were built, but this may have been on the understanding that he would erect the new house for the purchaser. One of these (built 1720-21) stood on the south side of Sun Alley; one (built 1717-20) on the site of the *Sun* inn. The original *Orange Tree* tavern was built about half way down Clarence Street between 1718 and 1720; but by 1721 three other small houses had been built in a row along Clarence Street between this house and the Kew Foot Lane. As a guess, the larger of the two houses shown in The Prospect is intended to show the one that later became the *Sun*, the smaller one to the right is the one by Sun Alley, and the house behind the *Orange Tree* is omitted altogether, as is the tavern itself.

On the south-east of the *Bear* there were a 'great barn' and a couple of cottages; then, after a space (later called The Square – where the 1870 fire station was built), another cottage with a blacksmith's shop. These must be the first group of buildings, shown as apparently all standing by the Marshgate (now Sheen) Road, leading up from the pond, though the 'Square' is reduced to just a small gap. In fact all but the blacksmith's cottage faced the pond, rather than the Marshgate Road.

There is then a substantial break before we come to the first of the large mansions along this road. It is depicted as having – seen from the back – a slightly projecting central bay with a pediment, set between a two-bay block on both sides – two storeys high but with dormer windows in the roof. This portrays the house described as 'lately built' when acquired by William Stobart in 1654. It was owned by the Stobart family for a hundred years. It was one of Richmond's largest mansions and was occupied by Richard Cullen as tenant at the time of The Prospect.

A small cottage (on the same property) and a house on the adjoining plot are ignored by the artist who merely draws gardens, then jumps straight to another large mansion owned and occupied at this time by William Beyer. The former home of Sir William Turner, it dated from the 1630s and is shown as a five-bay, two-storey house (with dormer windows), with a single-storey extension on the western (right) side and a wooden barn or stable at the rear. This house later became 'Lichfield House' (on the site of part of Lichfield Court).

Then follows a house of five bays and three storeys which stands for the pair of houses, 34 and 36 Sheen Road (the latter being 'Marshgate House'). It is probably only Marshgate House that is in fact depicted, as rebuilt by John Knapp, the London merchant, in 1699. The small wing on the east (left) side of the house and the tall barn at its rear were part of the same property. At the edge of the picture, separated by too wide a gap from Marshgate House, is a much simpler house – the predecessor cottage of Newnham House which was not rebuilt until after the date of The Prospect.

It is rather intriguing that the artist (or the engraver) of The Prospect, marking the road at this point (G), should describe it in the key as 'the road to Clapham'. Not 'Marshgate' or 'East Sheen' or 'Putney' or even 'London'. Perhaps he had a vision of the South Circular Road! Or did he perhaps live himself in Clapham?

## N. *South-east side of Little Green*

The dominant feature here is the large mansion at the corner of Duke Street. From its 'Dutch' gables and its large mullioned windows it can probably be dated to the '20s or '30s of the 17th century, when its owner was William Duke. In 1726 it was the property of John Michell, grandson of Duke's widow. In 1763–64 it became Richmond Academy, the school run by three generations of the Delafosse family who rebuilt the old house.

To its left stands a house that was built, probably in the early years of the 18th century, on a strip of land, outside the original Duke holding, which had originally been part of The Green. By 1725 it was part of the Michel estate, but was leased out.

## O. *The north-east sides of the Green and Little Green*

Here The Prospect shows, in considerable detail, the development undertaken by the Richmond architect, John Price, in the early 18th century. In 1705–08 Price bought up all the estate in this area – freehold, Crown leasehold and copyhold – that had been put together by Sir Robert Pye in the 1630s and sold by him to Sir Thomas Nott in 1640. The property stretched back on the west side of Kew Foot Lane (now Parkshot) from the Green as far as the northern side of what is now the Parkshot Centre, together with land on the east side of the lane from Parkshot House to Clarence Street. On the land facing the Green Price built mansions to sell or rent to the nobility or to rich merchants; elsewhere he built houses for the Richmond middle class.

At the north-western corner he built a complex of three houses, three cottages, coachhouses and stables. Of these all that is visible in The Prospect is the one large mansion in the foreground, its front protruding beyond those of the others in the row. Price himself lived there. Then there were three more large mansions. In 1725 the nearest was rented by John James Heidegger, the Master of the Revels to the King and manager of the Opera House in the Haymarket; the second (marked 'C' in the engraving) had been sold to Colonel Charles Floyer and the third (marked 'D'), after being rented for a while by Elihu Yale, was sold to Colonel John Duncombe. Behind Duncombe's house can be seen 'the great room' (or banqueting hall) which Duncombe had added to the original property. Beyond Duncombe's house can be seen another garden. This had very recently been made out of what had been (since 1664) a public bowling green.

In 1729 Queen Caroline bought Duncombe's house and garden and demolished the house to make a new entrance from the Green to the grounds of Richmond Lodge. In 1730 she also took over the bowling green garden, but it was not until 1765 that the Richmond Vestry allowed this to be formally incorporated into the royal gardens.

On the north-east side of Little Green (which, unlike the main Green, was unfenced) Price built three more large mansions and a pair of smaller houses. The central mansion (marked 'E') was rented in succession to the Marquess of Hertford, Lord Castleton and the Earl of Scarbrough and then to Dr Collier, vicar of Kingston and Richmond, who was there in 1726.

The nearest mansion in this Little Green row was sold outright by Price to Francis Cade in 1711; the rest of the row, including the two smaller houses, were sold to Dame Elizabeth Thorold (later Countess of Northampton) in 1724.

Immediately behind the mansions facing Little Green can be seen the backs of three houses facing the Kew Foot Lane: these stood on the south side of, and on the site of, the present railway line. The Prospect shows them as standing well back from the road; in fact they were right by it. At the left edge of the picture is the back of another house on the west side of this lane. This was No. 7 Parkshot, the end house of a short terrace built here by Price – all now part of the site of the Magistrates' Court. It was described as 'newly built' in 1721.

*P. The Upper Field, the Common and Richmond Park*

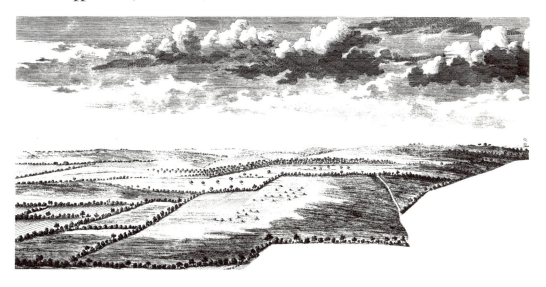

Clearly to be seen running across some two-thirds of this section of The Prospect is the wall of Richmond Park (marked 'N'). In front of it an open space lies between it and the hedges marking the limit of the Upper Field – this is what remained of the Richmond Great Common before most of it was granted in 1786 to the Vestry and enclosed. The artist shows a curious dog-leg in both the field hedge and the park wall, which had no basis in reality. He shows a house, within the Park, at the centre of this section of the wall. This may perhaps be intended to portray the 'pesthouse', built in the later part of the 17th century – though this should be outside the wall and farther to the south (right).

One other building is shown in a dip in the hills a little above and to the left of the last-noted house. Could this represent Old Lodge? Over to the far left are another house and a smaller building – perhaps a barn. These may be on the site of Bog (now Holly) Lodge – but all this is very speculative.

On the far right, the tower on the horizon has been identified by the artist as 'Kingston' church (marked 'Q'). It could have been seen from The Terrace on Richmond Hill, but hardly over the wooded slopes of Richmond Park!

## Q. *Petersham*

Barely discernible here in the shadowed slope of the hill are some of the buildings of Petersham. From left to right, they appear to be: a small cottage (?the *Plough and Harrow*, later *Dysart Arms*); the church; Petersham House; then after a gap – Douglas House; and, over to the right, Ham House. Missing is the great mansion of 'New Park', destroyed by fire five years before the making of The Prospect and not yet rebuilt as 'Petersham Lodge'.

*Plate 29*

*Chapman's Theatre on Richmond Hill.*

*William Penkethman*

*Theophilus Cibber*

*(all from Richmond Public Library, local studies collection)*

*Plate 30*

*The Prospect of Richmond.*

*Plate 31*

*The Richmond Theatre (from the* Theatric Tourist, *1805). On the right is the manager's house, where Edmund Kean died.*

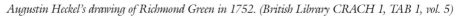

*Augustin Heckel's drawing of Richmond Green in 1752. (British Library CRACH 1, TAB 1, vol. 5)*

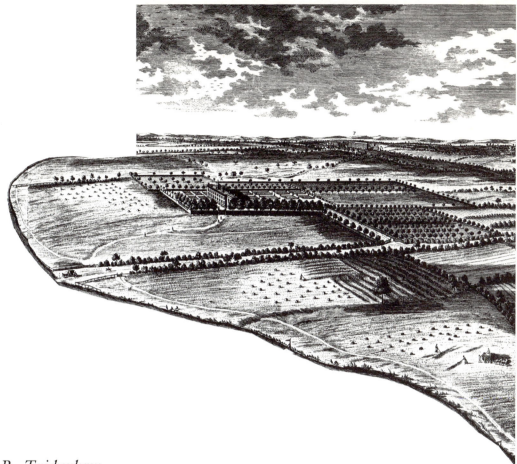

## R. Twickenham

Running across the centre of this section of The Prospect is the road from the Richmond Ferry, and dominating the scene is the mansion at this time occupied by Sir James Ash, which was later to be called 'Cambridge Park'.

Some features of the village of Twickenham can be seen in the centre background. Most prominent is the long terrace of Montpelier Row (just below the 'P' mark). A group of riverside houses to its left may include Mount Lebanon, then one can just make out the tower of Twickenham Church.

Marble Hill House had not yet been built (it was finished in 1728). Construction may have begun by 1726, but our artist does not show anything on the site. The small cottage seen at 11 o'clock from Sir James Ash's house, between it and the river, was probably on the site later occupied by the house called 'Little Marble Hill'.

The view emphasises the wide open expanse of the Twickenham meadows. From the depiction of hay-making one may surmise that the artist drew his original picture in late June or July 1726.

# 18

## *Fashionable Richmond*

ON 11 JULY 1696 the *Post Boy* newspaper carried an advertisement:

> At Richmond New Wells a Concert of Music both vocal and instrumental will be performed on Monday next, at noon, by principal bands and the best voices. Composed new for the day by Mr Frank. The songs will be printed and sold there.

A week later the *Post Boy*, reported that:

> A great concourse of persons of quality being there, it was desired the rate of coming in should be doubled, viz to make it 6d each again. At the desire of several persons of quality Mr Abel will sing on Monday 11 August, at five precisely in the Great Room, and will perform in English, Latin, Spanish, Italian and French, accompanied by instrumental music. The actual dancing will begin at eight, price 5 shillings each ticket. The tide of flood begins at one o'clock and flows till five, and ebbs till twelve, for the conveniency of returning.

It is with the opening of the New Wells in 1696 that one can perhaps mark the establishment of 'fashionable Richmond'. Already some of the fine new houses of this period were built – the development between Water Lane and Ferry Hill, the row that became 'Old Palace Terrace'. More were going up apace all around; within a few years there would be three major new houses at the top of the hill near the windmill and in front of them a walk with a double avenue of trees for all to admire the view over Hill Common and the Thames where once Bishop Duppa had had his favourite seat.

The nobility and gentry were moving into the town for the summer, as were the rich merchants. Statesmen bought houses in the town. King William III had ordered improvements and enlargements to the old hunting lodge in James I's Richmond Park (the Old Deer Park of today). In 1702 the Duke of Ormonde, a most popular figure, who had married a first cousin of Queens Mary and Anne and who would become the successor to the Duke of Marlborough as Commander-in-Chief of the British army, took over a lease of this lodge. Nobility leased John Price's new mansions on Richmond Green – as did the fabulously rich East India merchant Elihu Yale.

In his account of England in 1724 John Mackay wrote:

Here are men of all professions and all religions Jews and Gentiles, Papists and Dissenters – so that be one's inclination what it may, you will find one's own stamp to converse with. If you love books, every gentleman hath a library ready at your service; if you will make love, a stranger is everywhere welcome. At play, they will indeed be a great deal too cunning for you; even the ladies think it no crime to pawn handsomely; and for drinking, you may be matched from night to morning. Field exercise, also, as much as anywhere. In short, for a man of no business, whose time hangs on his hand, recommend me to Richmond.

*Plate 28*

The medicinal springs on the hillside, in the estate called Moorbrook, had been discovered some twenty or more years before, probably by the apothecary Thomas Warner who had taken a 31-year lease of the property from Michaelmas 1656. Warner must have started to develop the commercial potential, but he left little evidence in the way of advertisements or buildings. The earliest known notice is a letter from John Speke to his brother Hugh dated 14 June 1679 in which he wrote 'My mother is still at Richmond drinking Epsom waters'.[1] The water of the chalybeate spring evidently had something of the same quality as that of Epsom, already become famous. In his *Natural History of the Chalybeate Waters of England*, published in 1699, Benjamin Allen wrote of Richmond's spring: 'This water purgeth well, but I think scarce so much as Epsom or Acton, but more smoothly', which may be quite a recommendation in its way!

It would seem probable that it was Robert Brown, whose wife Eleanor inherited the Wells property from her parents (through trustees) in 1680 (when it was still in Warner's occupation) who himself built the new entertainment complex and launched the 'New Wells'. Most curiously, there is no known picture of them, and there is not even a formal note of any of the buildings until 1727 when widow Mary Robinson of St Clement Danes (who had become proprietor in 1721) let to Joseph and William Pearson at £60 a year:

'the Great. Room commonly called the dancing room; the room called the Coffee Room with the chambers over it and cellars under it; the room called the Booksellers Room – all in a place called Richmond Wells'[2]

Mary Robinson mortgaged the whole property for £4,000 in 1731. The heir of the assignee of this mortgage sold it to John Armitage (who owned the Coffee House at 17 The Green) in 1740. By this time the Wells was a flourishing institution. 'There are balls at Richmond every Monday and Thursday evening during the summer season' noted John Mackay in 1724. An advertisement in the *Daily Post* of 16 September 1721 mentions that the Wells were open every day.

The Great Room there is made extremely pleasant and. commodious for the Reception of Gentlemen and Ladies. As also a good Set of Musick, that play every Morning and Evening and on Thursdays and Saturdays .it will be accompany'd with the Trumpet, French Horn and German Flute.

In May 1722 the same newspaper revealed that:

Richmond Wells are now open, and will continue every day for the Summer Season, by the Proprietors of the last Year; where there is an extraordinary Set of Musick to play Morning and Evening every Day, and on every Monday will be an extraordinary Concert, composed by the Masters from the opera in which Mr Kitch will perform several Pieces on the Flute and Hautboy. N. B. There are made a commodious Pair of Stairs for the Convenience of the Company that come by Water.[3]

The Great Room and other associated rooms as let by Mary Robinson in 1727 were only a part of the Wells buildings. An inventory attached to a lease granted by John Armitage in 1752 appears to refer to the same accommodation, now listing the rooms with somewhat different names: the Assembly Room [the former Great Room?], Card Room, Parlor, Upstairs, Kitchen, Coffee Room and Lamp Room.[4] These were probably all within one 'Assembly Rooms' building. Manorial documents[5] enable us to identify other parts of the Wells complex, some of them apparently added by John Armitage. 'A building fronting the upper highway to Petersham called the Banquetting House' is mentioned in 1740 and is described as 'newly built' in 1749. It is probably the building called 'the High House' in the rate books. In 1752 we are told that it stood on the site of the house formerly occupied by Thomas Warner and Robert Brown. The 'Long Room' of 1740 and 1749 was 'situated between the two highways; another messuage 'lately finished by John Armitage facing the Long Room' is identified in 1749 as 'the Wells House lately occupied by Lady Seabright'. There was also a large Mews House and an adjacent house with coachhouse and stables at the bottom end of the property by the lower road to Petersham, which presumably provided 'parking' for coaches, stabling for visitors' horses and food and drink for the coachmen. However, at this time it is probable that the greater part of the Company would come by water.

✠

*Plate 29*     It is possible that the well-known London comic actor William Penkethman was first brought to Richmond as a master of ceremonies for the balls at the Wells. But in 1718 he launched a new form of entertainment for the summer visitors by putting on a brief theatre season. He had played at Drury Lane since 1692, played also at the Haymarket and at the Bartholomew Fair. He opened a theatre at Greenwich in 1710. His Richmond season in 1718 may have been staged in a barn on the hill (at 46–62 Hill Rise in today's terms) which belonged to Nathaniel Rawlins and which seems to have been used for a performance by the Duke of Southampton's Company in the summer of 1714.

Richmond was about to be graced by a reappearance of royal residents. On 13 April 1718 Edward Harley, son of the Earl of Oxford, wrote to his sister Abigail:

> The King has sent word to my Lord Grantham, that if 'he lends or sells the Duke of Ormonde's house at Richmond to the Prince, he will seize it as being forfeited to the Crown. He has likewise forbad the players letting them come to the play house. You can see how very near a happy reconciliation is like to be.[6]

Despite this typical bit of Hanoverian heir-baiting, neither the Earl of Grantham (Ormonde's brother-in-law) nor William Penkethman was deterred by His Majesty's bluster. Grantham made over the lease to George Prince of Wales who was ensconced in Richmond Lodge with his wife Princess Caroline by the summer of 1718. Penkethman opened his theatre in Rawlins's barn in time to receive the Prince and Princess as honoured patrons twice during that summer season.[7]

Rawlins's barn was evidently not ideal and for his 1719 season Penkethman moved next door, taking over a barn that 'had been part of John Scott's 'Royal Ass House' (64–70 Hill Rise). Scott's own business card shows what an important facility he was providing, especially as 'self-drive' transport for visitors: 'At King William's Royal Ass House a little above ye ferry on Richmond Hill asses milk is sold. Also asses are bought and sold there, or let to such as desire to keep them at their own houses by – John Scott'. Penkethman opened the season on 6 June speaking a specially written prologue with an ass standing by his side.

> ... As all the World was first made out of Chaos,
> From a dark, dirty Barn I rais'd this Play-house.
> This End, where Palaces are seen to Day,
> And Tragick Kings their Regal Power Display;
> Was fill'd with unthrash'd Corn, and mouldy Hay.
> On these two Sides that now are fill'd with Beaus,
> Were Twelve Assnego's tied in goodly rows:
> This Plaintiff Ass was Lord of all the Race,
> and was in full Possession of the Place ... [etc][8]

Penkethman continued to present a summer season of plays from June or July to August each year up to 1724. He had a house at Richmond (and indeed moved in 1725) and had by this time really become a sort of Master of Ceremonies for the town. On 28 May 1724, being the King's birthday, Penkethman staged a demonstration of loyalty, illuminating the windows of his house on the Hill (probably the house immediately below the *Dog Tavern* on Hill Street) and hoisting 'a fine silk Flag'. A song composed for the occasion was sung by Mrs Hill to the accompaniment of trumpet and hautboy, and 'the Gentlemen and Ladies were treated with wine etc. and the Commonality with a Barrel of Ale'.[9]

On 1 August Penkethman celebrated the anniversary of the Hanoverian succession 'at his new House upon Richmond Hill [probably Crawford Cottage – now the northernmost element of the *Richmond Gate Hotel*] ... with his usual Rejoycings, his Flag spread, Musick, Bonfires, and his Windows finely illuminated, and several Sorts of Liquors distributed among the Multitude without Doors'.[10]

On 20 September 1725 Penkethman died at his house at Richmond and he was buried in the parish church four days later. His theatre died with him.

Thomas Chapman, another comedian, had been a leading member of Penkethman's company at Richmond in 1724. In 1730 he decided to renew the summer theatrical season, but with a purpose-built playhouse. The *Daily Journal* of 4 June 1730 reported from Richmond:

> There is building, and almost finish'd here, a small, but very neat and regular THEATRE, a little higher on the Hill than where the late Mr Penkethman's stood. We hear it will be open'd next week by a Company of Comedians from the Theatre Royal in Lincoln's Inn Field and that their first play will be the Recruiting Officer ... and that they design to perform three or four Times a Week during the Summer Season, which we expect will be a very good one.

The *Daily Journal* reported on 14 July that 'the Company ... meet with universal Approbation and Encouragement'.

*Plate 29* Chapman's theatre stood just above the corner of Hill Rise and the Vineyard at what are now 10–14 Richmond Hill. He put on a theatrical season, originally ending in July, but later extended, every year until his death in 1747, and continued active personally both in playing and management. One of the plays which he put on in 1730 was the new 'Beggar's Opera' in which he played the Beggar. Other roles which he played at Richmond included Justice Swallow in the 'Merry Wives of Windsor', Prince Hal in 'Henry IV part 1', Richard III, and Peacham in a later production (1740) of the 'Beggar's Opera'. In the 1740s he also started to play at Twickenham and stretched his Richmond-Twickenham season into September.

Thomas Chapman died at Richmond of fever on 14 July 1747 and like Penkethman was buried in the parish church (on 17 July). His wife Hannah picked up the torch. She had herself been an actress and dancer, performing at Richmond in 1730–32. Then she seems to have taken over the office-cum-house next door and to have found her métier in management. Whether she actually ran the company after her husband's death is uncertain, but she continued to run the theatre (now known in the rate books as 'Mrs Chapman's music room') and the company continued to perform in it. They put on several performances for her benefit in each season up to 1753. There is no record of any further activity at the theatre or 'music room' until 1756 when

*Plate 29*

Theophilus Cibber made a cunning attempt to outwit the Licensing Act by advertising a 'cephalic snuff' business at his 'warehouse (late called the theatre)' where the public who purchased 'cephalic snuff' might – quite by chance – witness rehearsals at his 'histrionic academy for the instruction of young persons of genius, in the art of acting'. As a part of the students' training there would be frequent 'public rehearsals without hire, gain or reward'.

This ingenious device was brought to an abrupt end by Cibber's drowning on the way to Ireland in 1758. Mrs Chapman was buried on 5 July 1763, but the dying throes of the 'playhouse on the Hill' in 1762–64 were described by Dibdin as 'a kind of summer frolic, for, whatever celebrated actors, and sometimes actresses, happened to be in town, they were sure, either for pleasure, or from invitation, to take a trip to Richmond, and perform on a Saturday...'.[11]

Now, however, a rival Richmond theatre entered into competition. James Dance, the eldest son of the well-known London architect George Dance the elder – and elder brother of George the younger – was an actor. He had settled in Edinburgh and taken as a mistress the actress Catherine L'Amour. He assumed the stage name of James Love. The architect Robert Mylne was responsible for a reconciliation of James and his family, which led to James's return to London and his appearance at Drury Lane in 1762. However, James wanted to set up his own theatre. He obtained the financial backing of his uncle Richard Horne and of the latter's son-in-law, Colonel James Hubbald.

At the corner of Richmond Green where the lane ran down by the side of the former palace grounds to the one-time 'Crane Wharf' stood an old mansion. It was an 'island' site, with the lane on two sides, the Green in front and a footway on the other side, dividing the site from the palace grounds. The house had probably been built in the first years of the 17th century (though it may have been rebuilt when it belonged to the 'architect' Michael Pew from 1703 to 1707). Its owner in 1764 was Edward Philips Pew, a watchmaker of Brentford.

Pew sold the house to one Robert Watts (recorded in the manor rolls on 28 April 1764). His role in the operation is not clearly established; he was to sell the property on to James Hubbald in 1765 (recorded on 8 July), but it was during Watts' ownership that the old house was demolished and the new theatre built. James Love had the moral support of David Garrick, who wrote to him from Paris on 27 January 1765: 'I most heartily wish you success in yr great undertaking. I shall be glad to have you so near me [i.e. near Garrick's house at Hampton] and shall look upon yr Academy as a kind of nursery to ye Drury Lane garden – prosper the plough'.[12]

In June 1765 the *St James's Chronicle* stated that the theatre had been 'planned and built by Mr Sanderson'; but the *Dramatic Mirror* (published about 1804) says that it was built by a Richmond bricklayer named Alder 'from a model of Old Drury under the direction of Mr Butler architect and principal machinist of that theatre'. 'In it,' said a contemporary newspaper,[13] 'every imperfection in either the Royal theatres of Drury Lane or Covent Garden is carefully avoided, and every advantage retained; the boxes form a kind of crescent, which renders them commodious; the lobby is as spacious as either of the above theatres; there is but one gallery, which, however, turns out to the advantage of the audience, as it prevents the necessity of having pillars which obstruct the view. The pitt is small, but that seems no inconveniency, as the principal part of the spectators occupy the boxes; a handsome space is allowed for the orchestra; and the panels, in place of being ornamented with a gingerbread stucco, are painted of a dark colour, which gives the stage an additional degree of light when the curtain is drawn up. The scenes are elegant, and by the connoisseurs the whole is reckoned for its size to be much the best constructed theatre in the British dominions.'

*Plate 31*

The theatre was opened on Saturday, 15 June 1765, with the appropriately named comic opera 'Love in a Village'. Mr Love started the proceedings by reciting a prologue specially written for him by Garrick. The first season was only a moderate success, and moreover Love had problems over his licence. Garrick intervened on his behalf, writing on 24 February 1766 to Sir Robert Wilmot, the Lord Chamberlain's deputy: 'The bearer of this note is Mr Love who belongs to our theatre and one for whom I have the greatest regard. He apply'd for a licence last year for his Playhouse in Richmond, which he has built and decorated at great expence: He was promis'd one and the office gave him leave to perform, till the proper instrument could be made out. He now desires to renew his petition and I shall take it as a particular favour if you would please assist him with your advice. He ... has ventured a great deal of money to establish an Entertainment at Richmond that does him credit.'[14] The 1766 season, after some improvements to the theatre, including an enlargement of the stage, was much more successful and the new theatre was well and truly launched.

The Playhouse on the Hill struggled on for a while under the management of Thomas Davis and Ned Shuter. 'Mr Davis,' said an advertisement of 1765, 'has had the house entirely repaired.' In 1767 Shuter opened on 6 June with a prologue written for him by George Colman, the playwright who had just built for himself the riverside mansion in Richmond that was later known as Northumberland House. It was an ironic commentary on the competition. It opened thus:

> Welcome ye Generous, Polite, and Fair,
> Who to our lowly Roof this night repair!
> Who come, invited by our humble Bill,
> To the Old Theatre on Richmond Hill;
> Where to those guests, whose Taste not over-nice is,
> We serve up common Fare – at common Prices!
> No Cornice here, no Frieze to feast your Eyes,
> No Galleries on Dorick Pillars rise;

No gaudy Paintings on the Roof we deal in
To break your Necks with looking towards the Ceiling;
No Theatre we boast superbly built,
A Gingerbread Round O, a Cockpit gilt;
But a plain Booth, of Boards ill put together,
To raise a Stage, and Keep out Wind and Weather ...[15]

The Theatre on the Green put on the same play on the same night. On 13 June Shuter had to cancel his proposed performance of 'Love in a Village'. The Old Theatre put on a final short season in September-October 1767, after the Theatre on the Green had closed. The last performance on 10 October was of 'The Beggar's Opera'. By 1774 the old Playhouse had become 'a dissenters' meeting house'.[16] From the 1780s it was leased to Samuel Smith, who owned the bakery on the north side of the Hill Rise/ Vineyard corner, as a grain store. Smith's lease expired in 1816, but he was still assessed for 'the old theatre' in the 1820 ratebook. By 1830 it had vanished from the record.

As the Theatre vanished from the Hill, so did the Wells – at almost the same moment.

By 1730 the character of the entertainment at Richmond Wells was beginning to change. The *Craftsman* of 11 January 1730 carried the advertisement:

This is to give notice to all Gentlemen and Ladies, that Richmond Wells are now open, and continue so daily, where attendance is given for gentlemen and ladies who have a mind either to raffle for gold chains, equipages, or any other curious toys, and fine old china, and likewise play at quadrille, ombre, whist, etc; and on Saturdays and Mondays during the summer season there will be dancing as usual.

Although the Wells maintained their popularity until the mid-century, and were still advertising Assemblies in 1755, the emphasis on card playing and gambling rather than the concerts and balls began to lead to a fairly rapid deterioration. The wealthier patrons withdrew their support, admission prices were lowered and rowdies began to make the place a nuisance, particularly to the neighbours.

In the mansion that had once been Sir James Butler's, close by on the other side of the road up the hill, there now lived two spinster ladies, the Misses Susanna and Rebecca Houblon. They were daughters of Sir John Houblon, first Governor of the Bank of England, whose widow had taken over the house and installed her young family in it shortly after her husband's death in 1712. They were not short of money. John Armitage, the proprietor of the Wells, of the Coffee House on the Green, of the Coffee House Tavern and the *Three Tuns* in Duke's Lane, chronically was. He had mortgaged the entire Wells property for a mere £800 to Edward Oram in 1750. In 1763 Susanna Houblon made her move. She purchased from Armitage the Assembly Room and the Wells House and two other of the ancillary buildings, together with about a third of the land – all that part facing onto the Upper Highway. Armitage, who had already in 1749 sold a lot of the original Wells land to his neighbour on the south, was left with the Mews House and the stable complex, a house that he was already leasing to a private individual (at this time the Jewish merchant Joseph Gompertz) and a large paddock. Miss Houblon not only purchased the Wells buildings but shut them down. She had the holding enfranchised in 1773 and then demolished the buildings. After Robert Sayer had purchased Armitage's houses and grounds in 1776 Susanna Houblon sold him the now empty field where the Wells had been. It became part of the grounds of Cardigan House – and today part of the Terrace Gardens.

Another major change was wrought on the Hill at this time. In 1767 the former tile kilns and all the ground on which they stood – and from which clay had been dug out – on the south-west side of Hill Common were bought up by the Duke of Montagu, who added them to the grounds of his mansion by the river, joining the two parts of his property by the grotto-tunnel under the Petersham Road which still exists.

The closure of Richmond Wells in 1763 and the suppression of the tile kilns in 1767 greatly enhanced the amenity of houses on the upper part of the Hill. The late 1760s and early 1770s saw an eruption of building activity in the area. The way was led by Edward Collins, the town's leading brewer, who bought up a lot of the cottages that had been built south of the Wells on land granted out of the Hill Common, and

Plate 32

replaced them with a new mansion (later Lansdowne House) opposite the end of Friar's Stile Road in 1765. Mr Christopher Blanchard, playing card maker to the King, had his house at 3 The Terrace, which was leased from the Hickey Trustees, rebuilt in 1768. The architect was possibly Sir Robert Taylor, possibly James Paine. Sir William Richardson enlarged his house (the future Doughty House) about 1769 and the owners of the *Star and Garter Inn* added a second new block by 1770. In 1771–72 Sir Joshua

Plate 32

Reynolds, who had bought a small cottage on the edge of Petersham Common, got Sir William Chambers to design a new country villa for him (Wick House – see page 289). Peregrine, Duke of Ancaster, who had already acquired the two small properties outside the park gates, finally rebuilt one as Ancaster House and demolished the other in 1774. In that year Charles Pearce built Downe House on what had been an empty site next to the Duppa Alms houses. And finally in 1774 the Hickey Trustees, recognising that the ramshackle timber buildings of the *Bull's Head* tavern were no longer fitting for the area, offered the site on a building lease for one or two 'good substantial brick dwelling house or houses'. Lady St Aubyn took the lease (as owner of St Michael's Mount in Cornwall she would have been accustomed to the way the wind howls up the hillside from the Thames!) and Robert Mylne designed for her the very elegant villa known as 'The Wick'.

The opportunity of this rebuilding was taken to extend the Terrace Walk up as far as the *Star and Garter* – the footpath is in Richmond, Wick House and the Common in Petersham. It had been extended northwards to the edge of Collins' estate in 1766, though initially with only a single row of trees, and now became one of the favourite places in which the fashionable gentry could parade to show themselves off to each other.

*Plate 33*

With the closure of the Wells, Richmond had – for the moment – no Assembly Rooms, but the new Theatre on the Green was able to fill the gap. *The Theatric Tourist*, a publication of 1805, while considering Richmond – on account of its managers – to be generally 'a bad theatrical resort', is nevertheless lavish in praise of the building:

Internally considered, we may pronounce this House a model for theatrical architects. Before the curtain are commodious Boxes and a roomy Pit, with every convenience. Behind it are twenty-four feet depth of stage, terminated by an arch, beyond which the stage may occasionally be lengthened twenty feet ... There is no convenience or accommodation which may not be found ... the great facility with which the Theatre may be converted into an elegant ball-room, that has served as a pattern for many others. The Pit and Stage are completely furnished with a temporary flooring; the fronts of the Boxes taken down; by which means their seats appear but as so many benches to surround the room; the entrance is from the centre Box. The wings being removed, a complete framework, painted by a capital artist, reduces the sides of the Stage to a level with the Boxes. A tremendous piece of machinery forms a ceiling of one entire mass ... the terror of the actor. An inclosure of the front seats of the Gallery forms an excellent orchestra. The Stage doors serve as avenues to places of refection, which are well laid out, and every way appropriate. Through the arch (before mentioned) is a capacious card room, two handsome glass chandeliers are suspended. In short, the whole is so complete, and the metamorphose accomplished in so short a time, that any stranger who witnessed a performance on the Monday evening, would scarcely credit that the Tuesday's ball was conducted in the self same area.

Music for dancing was a regular feature of the Wells and of the Theatre, and as already mentioned in the early days of the Wells concerts with solo singers and instrumentalists were a regular feature. An early advertisement just for a concert was published in the *Post Boy* on 14 July 1705:

This present Saturday, being the 14th of July, at Richmond Wells, will be an extraordinary Consort of Vocal and Instrumental Musick viz, three part songs, set by Mr Eccles and perform'd before the Queen on Her Birthday. And a two-part song set by Mr Henry Purcell, never printed, nor perform'd in Publick. Also some solos on the violin by a scholar of Signior Gasparinis, who never perform'd in Publick before. To begin exactly at half an hour after six of the clock, and for those whose Business requires their return to London, the conveniency of the Tide will permit the same night. Tickets may be had at Will's and Robin's Coffee Houses near the Royal Exchange, at White's Coffee House on Richmond Green, and at the Wells, at Half a Crown each Ticket.

Although local talent was sometimes called upon, most of the concerts were performed by visiting musicians. It would be nice to know for sure in which category Mr Henry Purcell, had he been still alive, would have fallen. He is believed to have been a resident of Richmond, and he wrote a delightful song 'On the Brow of Richmond Hill', but so far no clue has been found as to a residence here. After his death in 1695, his widow certainly lived in Richmond, and died there in February 1705/6.

John James Heidegger, Manager of the Queen's (later the King's) Theatre in the Haymarket, was a Richmond resident, but contributed little to the musical life of the town. As Master of the Revels to George II, as manager of the Royal Academy of Music (where Handel was Master of the Orchestra) as well as his work in the Haymarket, where he helped to introduce and to popularise Italian opera, he was no doubt far too busy to help with Richmond concerts. He lived in succession in two of John Price's houses on the north-east side of Richmond Green from the 1720s until 1740, then for two or three years in Old Palace Terrace, and finally, from 1745 until his death in 1749, at 4 Maids of Honour Row (where he had his scene painter Antonio Joli come out to decorate the ground-floor front room).

Alleged to be Handel's equal as an organist, though not as a composer, was Dr John Worgan, organist and resident composer at Vauxhall Gardens from 1751 to 1774, and organist at several London churches, who lived at 1 Maids of Honour Row for a few years up to 1780 and then, until his death in 1790, at Nightingale Cottage, the house on Hill Common which stood where the *Petersham Hotel* is today.

Later in the 19th century some of the leading musicians of the day had houses in Richmond. John Christian Bach is known to have been one, but his home has not been traced. When it was rumoured that he was about to give up this house, the local tradesmen pressed for settlement of their accounts. It was found that his housekeeper had forged receipts for over £1,000 and had absconded with the money. He moved to Paddington in 1781 and died on 1 January 1782, owing some £4,000.

Bach was leader of the group who played regularly for King George III and Queen Charlotte. He would organise quartets or quintets, inviting his friends to stay at the *King's Arms* inn on Kew Green – from where they would meet to practise at the house of Louis Albert, one of the royal pages. Karl Friedrich Abel who played the viola da gamba, the violinist Wilhelm Cramer and the oboist John Christian Fischer were the regulars. The flautist Johann Baptist Wendling took part sometimes.

Another musician with a Richmond home at this time was Frederick Nicolay, a violinist. He lived from 1769 until about 1780 in the large mansion on Hill Rise that was later called Holbrook House. It was leased from Crofton Ross, successor in title to Nathaniel Rawlins, and had about half an acre of land. Nicolay wrote to Capability Brown to ask for the latter's help in laying out his garden: 'I am in very great distress and trouble which one coup d'oeil of yours ... would soon relieve me from. I hope it is no offence to wish for a miniature picture from a Raphael.'[17] Brown's reply is unrecorded!

Painters were also attracted to the Richmond area. Sir Peter Lely had a house on Kew Green, Kneller at Whitton, Thomas Hudson and Samuel Scott lived in Twickenham. Peter Tillemans lived for the last two years of his life in Halford House, Richmond, and painted a number of local scenes before his death in 1734. Peter Casteels was a brother-in-law of Peter Tillemans and accompanied him from Antwerp to London in 1708. He was employed from 1735 as a textile designer by a calico printing works at Merton Abbey and came to Richmond when the works were moved to West Sheen about 1745. He died in Richmond in 1749. Augustine Heckel, a gold chaser from Augsberg, migrated to London in the 1720s and soon became established as one of the leading masters of his trade. Having made a sufficient fortune he retired to Richmond in 1747, took a house at the top of Queen's Road, and amused himself by turning out sketches of the houses and scenery in the area. He was quickly taken up by the print sellers – and engravings of his views are our best visual picture of mid-18th-century Richmond.

Joshua Reynolds was one of those who invested in a house in Richmond (or to be precise, Petersham – for it stands on Petersham Common, though facing Richmond Hill). He persuaded his friend (but rival in the Royal Academy) William Chambers to build for him a relatively modest house on this site which he had acquired. Wick House, built in 1771–72, was intended originally to be just a place to entertain friends to dinner or to come for a week-end rest, but Reynolds kept changing his mind, to Chambers' great annoyance, and the house, though exceedingly plain, ended up costing twice what had been intended. From beside it Reynolds, the great portraitist, painted his only known landscape, a not very successful 'View from Richmond Hill'.

William Marlow followed his master Samuel Scott as tenant of the manor house at Twickenham, and painted a number of local views. Thomas Gainsborough and Johann Zoffany are both buried at Kew. There, a school of miniature painters developed. Jeremiah Meyer, who lived on Kew Green in a small house at the corner of Ferry Lane, was miniature painter to Queen Charlotte and enamel painter to George III. His younger contemporary George Engleheart, son of a Kew master-plasterer, was even better known as a miniaturist and founded a family dynasty of painters. The Englehearts were related by marriage to another family of artists (mostly miniaturists) descended from Thomas Richmond, landlord of the *Coach and Horses* on Kew Green, who married a cousin of George Engleheart.

The famous Joseph Mallord William Turner lived for 16 years in Sandycombe Road, Twickenham, and painted views of Richmond Bridge and many of Richmond Hill, including the great panorama of the party held in the gardens on the Hill to celebrate the Prince Regent's birthday – itself a celebration of 'fashionable Richmond'.

✢

Although the story of the royal estates has been fully told in my *Palaces and Parks of Richmond and Kew*, the contribution of royalty to making Richmond the fashionable resort it became in the 18th century must be mentioned here. George I had no residence at Richmond and even when he decided to build a lodge in Richmond Park, where he enjoyed hunting with Sir Robert Walpole, who had virtually made the Park his own, it was not finished before he died. White Lodge, as it is called today, was completed for George II and Queen Caroline.

George and Caroline, as already mentioned, had settled in the Lodge in Richmond Old Park in 1718. Caroline, with the help of Charles Bridgeman and William Kent, transformed the grounds north of the Lodge into 'Richmond Gardens' and extended the estate by leasing extra property at Kew, including the Dutch House. Their son Prince Frederick took over the house in Kew Park, which Kent enlarged and embellished as 'The White House', and with his wife Princess Augusta started to enlarge the estate and lay out 'Kew Gardens', including a section for exotic plants. After his death in 1751 Augusta carried on with these plans, and Sir William Chambers filled her grounds with classical temples and oriental follies such as the famous pagoda – about the only one of the ornamental buildings that was constructed of solid and enduring materials. (The master bricklayer was Richmond's Solomon Brown, whose name should be as revered as that of Chambers.)

When George III inherited Richmond Lodge and Gardens from his grandfather in 1760 he developed plans to rebuild the Lodge as a major palace. It was not, however, until the end of the decade that work was actually started – and that proceeded slowly, for the King was paying for it out of his own pocket. In 1772 Princess Augusta died, and George inherited her lease of the Kew property. He abandoned the plans for a new palace at Richmond, and somehow persuaded the Board of Works to pay for the renovation and enlargement of the White House by William Chambers. The old Richmond Lodge and, eventually, the foundations of the new intended palace were demolished. At Kew, the 'botanic garden' flourished with the support of both King and Queen.

At the beginning of the 19th century George III's urge to build a new palace was given the opportunity to express itself. The King was at last able to buy the Kew estate from the heirs of the Earl of Essex who had been his landlord. He commissioned James Wyatt to build him a new palace by the river in the Gothic style – and proceeded to demolish the White House. The 'castellated Palace' was completed externally but never occupied. George became almost blind by 1806 – and his attacks of porphyria lapsed into virtually permanent 'madness' by 1810. Queen Charlotte died in 1818 at the Dutch House – now elevated to the title of 'Kew Palace'. The empty and unmourned castle was demolished ten years later.

This bald account of the principal works undertaken by the royal family on their major houses in the Richmond/Kew estate provides a framework against which should be seen a very real and often close association with, and commitment to, the local community. George II and George III had farms here – and the latter in particular enjoyed being a gentleman farmer and stock-breeder. Even more he enjoyed his role of lord of the manor (of which more in Chapter 20). Though the royals were not, of course, in permanent residence, they spent several months in Richmond, or later Kew, every summer (until the 1790s when Windsor began to be preferred). They lived here with a minimum of protocol. George II and Caroline allowed suitable visitors to wander around the grounds to admire Caroline's 'Hermitage' or 'Merlin's Cave'. George III and Charlotte simply opened their grounds to the public for a day each week – Richmond Gardens on Sundays and Kew Gardens on Mondays – and would often sneak off along 'the Queen's Private Road' to the White Lodge in Richmond Park to avoid the crowds, although at other times, as Mrs Papendiek says, they 'were to be seen at the windows speaking to their friends, and the royal children amusing themselves in their own gardens'.[18] Lady Mary Coke reported the King as remarking that 'he never liked his gardens on a Monday, they seemed so dirty'.[19]

George III would sometimes walk around the town. A sad little tale is told of the time when he was recuperating at Kew from his very severe bout of madness in 1788, when he had had to be repeatedly restrained in a straitjacket. He wanted to test whether he had recovered physically as well as mentally. Accompanied by a doctor and his equerry (who recorded the incident) he set off from Kew to walk up the hill to the new workhouse on the common by Richmond Park, which had just been built at His Majesty's expense. He was taken round it and had lunch there, eating the ordinary fare. Then the Workhouse Master, with more enthusiasm than tact, took the King off 'to see their Madhouse', discoursing on the use of 'strait waistcoats every now and then'. The King was fortunately unruffled; and continued his walk to the Terrace, to point out the view of Windsor, then down into the town where he stopped at the pastrycooks to eat some Maids of Honour cheesecakes (and to make his companions have some too) and to the Green to call on General Fitzwilliam and arrange for the General's Welsh harper to be sent up to Kew so that the King might hear him play.[20]

This little story, though shedding light on the King's recovery, is of more interest in the picture it conveys of a genial, cheerful 'squire' at home with his tenants – and this is, I believe, exactly how the King saw himself. And the King and Queen were certainly extremely popular in Kew.

The renewed presence of royalty in the town, though it was a more relaxed presence than in the days of Henry VII or Queen Elizabeth, was in itself enough to attract more courtiers to the town whether, more rarely, as householders or as summer visitors. It is unsurprising that only relatively few of the better houses in Richmond were occupied by their owners. The great majority were leased out – and then often sub-let. (Which makes the destruction of those rate books – see page 211 particularly irresponsible!)

✠

This was probably one of the reasons why many of the émigrés who came to England at the time of the French Revolution made their homes in Richmond. Of course many of them had English friends at court who had houses in Richmond, or were accustomed to spend time there in the summer, but the availability of rentable accommodation must have been an additional attraction. Then once the first nucleus was well-established a further community would grow up around them. Though living in straitened circumstances the French nobility both kept up a social life of their own and participated in that of their English friends. The letters of Horace Walpole, *Plate 37* Mary Berry and George Selwyn, for example, are full of them. 'Mesdames de Biron and Cambis have taken houses on Richmond Green,' reported Walpole on 14 May 1790, 'as well as les Boufflers and Madame de Roncherolles'.

The Comtesse de Boufflers and her daughter-in-law Amélie lived first on the Hill and then in the house at the corner of the Green now called Cedar Grove, which was rebuilt in 1813. The Boufflers went to their neighbour's, Lord Fitzwilliam's, house next door on the Green to listen to the organ – and the Duke of Clarence admired Amélie's playing on the harp.

The Vicomtesse de Cambis was a niece of Mme de Boufflers. She had once been a nun and George Selwyn thought her beautiful as a Madonna. She stayed in Richmond until her death in 1809 and is one of the many émigrés buried in the Vineyard Passage burial ground.

The Duchesse de Biron was one of the four members of a little group of princesses, friends from childhood, and all free-thinkers, three of whom (and the husband of the fourth) settled in Richmond. They called themselves 'les princesses combinées' and their salons in Paris had been the meeting place for constitutionalists. She was one of the émigrés who optimistically returned to France too soon – and was guillotined.

Another of the group was the Princesse de Hénin, whose husband was the brother of Mme de Cambis. She came to England in 1792 and after an initial stay at another émigrés centre – Juniper Hall near Mickleham in Surrey – came to Richmond in 1793 and rented the house later called The Rosary in Ormond Road. She shared this house with the Comte de Lally-Tollendal, the most eloquent spokesman of the constitutionalists in the earliest phase of the revolution, but who fled to Switzerland at the time of the march on Versailles. 'Their age should have guaranteed them from scandal,' wrote Mme de Hénin's niece, 'but they were nevertheless the butt of considerable ridicule.'[21]

This niece, the young Marquise de la Tour du Pin, who wrote a famous and fascinating memoir of her exile in England and later in America, arrived in 1798 with her family to stay with her aunt in Richmond. But she 'found sharing a house with Mme de Hénin intolerable. She gave us such poor accommodation that we could not receive visitors – we had only two small bedrooms on the ground floor ... It was only

*Plate 32*

A View from Richmond looking towards Twickenham *by William Marlow. The mansion on the left is the one built by Edward Collins on the site of the future Lansdowne House. The large house with outbuildings seen at the bottom of the hill was the Mews House and stabling belonging to the former Wells – the fence of which is visible on the right. (Sotheby & Co.)*

*Wick House, Richmond Hill, as built originally for Sir Joshua Reynolds by Sir William Chambers in 1771-2. (British Library, CRACH1, TAB1, b1, vol. 5)*

*Plate 33*

Richmond Hill, *an engraving published in 1782 from a drawing by Henry William Bunbury.*

The Terrace, *watercolour drawing by Thomas Rowlandson, c.1805. (Ownership untraced)*

*Plate 34*

*...ichmond Parish Church in 1807, ...owing the Tudor chancel. Note ...so the glimpse of houses in Church ...ourt and George Street.*

*...udith Levy in an engraving of ...803. (Richmond Public Library, ...cal studies collection)*

*...hn Lewis, the Richmond brewer, ...ho won the battle for pedestrian ...cess to the Park (engraving from ...portrait in the Old Town Hall).*

MRS JUDITH LEVY.
*The Rich Jewess usually called*
*The Queen of Richmond Green.*
*Pub. by R. S. Kirby, April 1. 1803, Paternoster row.*

Plate 35

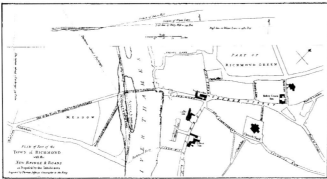

The first Kew Bridge, from a contemporary engraving.

The inhabitants' proposal for a bridge situated at the end of Water Lane. The sections at the top show the approach slopes at the Ferry Hill and Water Lane sites. (Plan by Thomas Jefferys, 1773.)

James Paine's design for Richmond Bridge. (The tollhouse at the Twickenham end, on the right, was omitted when the bridge was built.) (Royal Institute of British Architects)

in the evenings that we joined my aunt in her pretty salon on the first floor ... I had to admit that our characters were not compatible.'[22]

The Duchesse de Bouillon, a third member of the 'princesses combinées', also came to Richmond in 1798, a little after Mme de la Tour du Pin. Mme de Hénin took a small apartment for her, somewhere quite close to The Rosary. Her arrival cheered up Mme de la Tour's social life, for there were more invitations from such as the Duchess of Devonshire and Lady Bessborough. It cheered up her domestic life too, as Mme de Bouillon moved in with Mme de Hénin and allowed the de la Tour du Pin family to rent her apartment. Later Mme de la Tour du Pin moved to a small house on, or just off, Richmond Green.

One of the more flamboyant members of the French community was the Comtesse de Balbi, former mistress of the Comte de Provence (the future Louis XVIII). She rented Reynolds' former residence, Wick House, on Richmond Hill. George Selwyn wrote in 1790 that he had dined with her at the *Castle Hotel*: 'Mme la Cse Balbi chooses to give a dinner there to all her friends, the Mesdames Boufflers, the Comte de Boisqelin.'

Chateaubriand spent a part of the summer of 1799 in Richmond; and Mme de Staël stayed with her last lover (and eventual husband) at Gothick House in the Petersham Road in 1813–14. A writer who stayed longer – and founded an important English family – was the Swiss-born Jacques Mallet du Pan. The editor of the Paris *Mercure*, he fled from Napoleon's wrath. 'He died at the home of his friend Count Lally-Tolendal', records his tombstone in Vineyard Passage.

There were many others whose names appear in the Vineyard Passage Burial Ground, in the register of the recently-established Catholic chapel in Richmond, or in other documents. Some went back to France too soon, like Mme de Biron or Amélie de Boufflers, and were guillotined – a fate narrowly escaped by Mme de Hénin when she went to test the water in 1797. Some died in Richmond. Some lived to see the monarchy restored in France and then returned. A very few lived through it all and decided to stay in Richmond. One of these was the Marquis de Thuisy, who came here about 1792 and lived with his wife at Old Court House on Richmond Green. He helped Mme de la Tour du Pin with her ironing. He had three sons born in Richmond – and was still resident in 1825.

The French were generally welcomed in Richmond – and even the problems which might well have arisen a decade earlier on account of the penal legislation against Catholics had been removed by the passage of the Act of 1791 allowing Catholics freedom of worship. There seem to have been some xenophobes, however. The Vestry in 1793 records that 'some idle and disorderly persons in the town have of late made a practice of assaulting and gravely abusing several of the Foreign residents in the town without any just cause'.[23] The beadle was to be particularly attentive in discovering such persons.

✠

The 1791 Act had also permitted the opening at No. 1 The Vineyard in 1791–92 of a Roman Catholic chapel by Robert Wheble, a Richmond resident of a well-known Catholic family, and of a Roman Catholic School, in Clarence House almost opposite, by Timothy Eeles at about the same time.[24] The French exiles made use of the chapel, and a French priest was appointed to the school, and probably also to serve the chapel, though he soon quarrelled with Eeles and was replaced by an Irish priest, who was himself an exile from France. In 1824 by the beneficence of Elizabeth Doughty, of Doughty House on Richmond Hill and the Priory in Kew, the chapel was replaced by a new church dedicated to St Elizabeth of Portugal which stood next door to Clarence House.

Not far away, in Ormond Passage, an alley leading from the end of Ormond Row to the (new) *Red Lion* pub, a small 'Bethlehem' Chapel was built for a Calvinist

*The Congregational and Roman Catholic churches in The Vineyard in 1832. St Elizabeth's Church was greatly enlarged and given a new tower in 1903 (from The Picturesque Pocket Companion, c.1843).*

dissenting congregation in 1797. While the few Richmond Catholics had previously had to go to Isleworth, to a chapel maintained by the Earl of Shrewsbury, the dissenters had been better catered for. Though Mortlake had been the big local centre for dissenters in the 17th century, there were evidently some in Richmond. Peter Sterry's Academy flourished under Lord Lisle's aegis at Sheen Place. There were several prosecutions in the 1660s for failure to attend church, and William Salter and Anne Poores of Richmond were among a group of six (including others from Brentford, Isleworth and Chelsea) who were sentenced to prison at the Guildford Assizes in 1665 because 'they had assembled together with other evildoers at the house of William Salter in Richmond on 28 May under colour of the exercise of religion not allowed by the liturgy and practice of the Church of England'. The date at which a 'meeting house' was first established in Richmond is unknown but by 1726 Mrs Flood's house, on the northern corner of Hill Rise and the Vineyard, was noted in the rate books as 'late the meeting house'. Soon after the old theatre on the hill closed in 1767, it was taken over as a 'dissenters' meeting house' (so described in the 1774 rental). It was indeed the venue for a meeting in 1773 addressed by the controversial young preacher Rowland Hill which – as was often the case with his meetings – broke up in a riot.

Where the dissenters met when this building was rented out to the baker is not known. The Methodists rented rooms in Water Lane in 1810, in the Marshgate Road in 1824 and in Paradise Road from 1830. The Strict Baptists built their Rehobeth Chapel in Parkshot in 1829 and the Congregationalists their church next to St Elizabeth's in the Vineyard in 1831.

Except for those now worshipping at St Anne's on Kew Green, the parish church of St Mary Magdalene in Richmond had to cope with the increasing population – and therefore congregation – throughout the 18th century. The Vestry repeatedly worried about the need to provide extra seating. The gallery put up in the south aisle in 1683 and the new north aisle and gallery built by John Price in 1699-1703 soon proved inadequate. In 1750 the main body of the church and the whole south aisle (with a new gallery) was rebuilt to the designs of Robert Morris, a brother of the more famous Roger. That expansion had to suffice until the building of St John the Divine in 1831.

*Plate 34*

The only faith for which no provision appears to have been made locally was the Jewish. The leaders of the Richmond community were so committed to the building of their synagogues in London that they don't seem to have cared that there was none in or near Richmond. Solomon de Medina contributed largely to the building of the Sephardic synagogue in Bevis Marks, Moses Hart to the Ashkenazi one at Duke's Place. Hart's daughter, Judith Levi, resident from 1754 to 1802 in 4 Maids of Honour Row – and known locally as 'the Queen of Richmond Green' – contributed £4,000 to the rebuilding of the Duke's Place Synagoque.

*Plate 34*

The most notable of the Jews resident in Richmond in the 18th century, whose homes are revealed by the rate books, are listed in Appendix II. Moses Hart had another daughter whose name is connected with a Richmond property, Rachel the youngest – wife of Michael Adolphus. In 1756 the Earl of Cholmondeley sold to Moses Hart (who was still resident in his mansion by the Thames at Isleworth) the brewhouse and its land by Crane Piece and 'six ruinous tenements' formerly part of the Palace. The brewhouse had, since 1753, been occupied by Hart's son-in-law Michael Adolphus. It stood by the old wharf and had been converted from the foundations ('the rockhouse') of some gigantic feature – perhaps a mount to be topped by a river god – planned for the gardens of Henry Prince of Wales in 1610–12. The six tenements were part of what was left of the kitchens and domestic premises on the south side of the 'tradesmen's entrance' to the Palace. Moses Hart at once pulled down the six old tenements and applied for a new lease of the whole premises. But he died before this could be granted – and the new lease was made out in February 1757 in the name of Lazarus Simons, Michael Adolphus and Joseph Martin, Hart's executors.[25] In 1759 and 1760 the property is still listed in the rate books under the name of Michael Adolphus, but with a nil assessment (probably indicating that it was empty); then in 1761 and 1762 it is shown as 'late Michael Adolphus' with a rentable value of £24; in 1763 as 'Sir Charles Asgill' with RV of £72.

For this was the site on which Sir Robert Taylor built the splendid classical villa 'Asgill House' for Sir Charles who had been Lord Mayor of London in 1757–58 and who had a new lease in his own name for 50 years in September 1762, by which time the house had been completed.[26]

*Plate 37*

Asgill House was one of the series of new riverside mansions which were developed in Richmond about the middle of the 18th century. Next to it, Trumpeters' House was enlarged by the addition of two wings and its great portico facing the river. Then, moving towards the east, the Earl of Cholmondeley's new house, right by the riverside path, was built in the late 1740s. He was still occupying the remains of the palace (Old Palace and the Gate House and the Wardrobe) when he started building a new library by the river. In 1739 he had got a new lease which included 'a piece of waste by the Thames abutting north-east on the new Library and gardens of the Earl of Cholmondeley ... with such part of the new Library as is erected on the said ground ... reserving to the tenants of the Manor the full liberty of passage and of towing

*Plate 38*

barges'.[27] He built the new mansion onto the library a few years later. It was finished before 1749, as pictures by both Joli and Heckel testify.

We have already noted the 1690s development between Water Lane and Ferry Hill; then beyond Ferry Hill and 'Bridge House' (to give it its later name), also of the late 17th century, came the house, first called Bath House, then Camborne House and finally Northumberland House, built for George Colman the Elder, after he had inherited a fortune from his uncle by marriage and former guardian, the Earl of Bath, in 1766. Garrick wrote to Colman in that year: 'Saunderson tells me they have laid the timbers for the first floor of your house at Richmond. It rises magnificently to the ferry passengers; you will be surprised to find yourself master of a chateau at your return.'

Along the Petersham Road, Bellevue probably dates from about 1752 when the rentable value of the house on the site doubled. The assessment for Ivy Hall rose from £20 to £58 when taken over by the Countess of Buckinghamshire in 1758. After her death in 1762 her younger son, the Hon Henry Hobart, lived there until 1800 (though renting it briefly to the Duke of Clarence in 1789). The former 'Gothic House' (demolished in 1938) was a cottage built in 1743, much enlarged in 1761–62 and gothicised about 1800. Midhurst (another casualty of the 1930s) was built in 1751. Next to this came the four houses of the 'Paragon' built in the 1720s, and then two large mansions, of which only one survives. Bingham Villa, as it was then called, was constructed for Lady Ann Bingham in the 1820s, but out of a house which replaced the *Blue Anchor* tavern in 1770 and the former adjacent malthouse. Next was Riverdale House (demolished 1930s), put together out of two former houses about 1780 and also much enlarged in the 1820s.

Finally, by the riverside towards the boundary between Richmond and Petersham stood a house which belonged to the Perkins family of fishermen, and which had been rented to the Earl Ferrers in the 1720s. As an unusually chatty entry in the manor rolls tells us:

> John Perkins repaired the buildings and built stables and leased the premises to the Earl of Cardigan [from 1742] for 21 years to expire at Michaelmas 1763 for £52 10s. 0d. per annum. In 1761 the Earl of Cardigan proposed to pull down the old house and rebuild it and by a document dated 29 April 1761 John Perkins granted to the Earl of Cardigan a lease for 60 years. And the Earl had demolished the old house and started to rebuild when he discovered that John Perkins was only tenant for life and had no power to grant such a lease. So an Act of Parliament was passed in 1762 to vest the site from 1 June in trustees ...[28]

Then in 1765, by direction of John Perkins, the trustees sold the whole property, including 'the new mansion house of the Earl of Cardigan', to Dr Cutts Barton, who was Cardigan's attorney. In 1766 the Earl was advanced to the rank of Duke of Montagu, and on his death in 1790 the property was inherited by his daughter Elizabeth, wife of the Duke of Buccleuch and Queensberry. So the house became in turn Montagu House and Buccleuch House, by which name it was still known when purchased by the Council and demolished (to widen the Petersham Road) in the 1930s, when its grounds became a public garden known as 'Buccleuch Gardens'.

✠

The whole environment of the riverside had of course been drastically changed by the building of Richmond Bridge in the 1770s. The ferry at Kew had already been replaced by a bridge in 1758–59. It had been built by Robert Tunstall, owner of the ferry, and was designed by John Barnard. It had 11 arches, of which two at each end were of stone and the seven in the centre of timber. (The central span was 50 feet.) It was, of course, to be financed by tolls – just one penny for a pedestrian. 2,000 people paid their penny on the day it was opened, 7 June 1759.

This, of course, excited the people of Richmond who began to consider the replacement of their ancient ferry by a bridge. When the ferry proprietor, William Windham, came up with a plan for a wooden bridge on the site of the ferry and proposed a parliamentary bill to enable the King to grant him the freehold of the ferry as a preliminary step, it was found by the Parish Trustees (i.e. the Council, see Chapter 20) on 7 March 1772 to be 'very prejudicial to the inhabitants' because it was

*Plate 35*

in the wrong place. The Trustees formally opposed the bill.[29] What they, and most of the residents of Richmond, wanted was a bridge sited at the end of Water Lane. The lane, to be widened, would provide a much gentler slope and easier approach *Plate 35* from the main street, George Street, than the steep Ferry Hill. The residents, led by Henry Hobart, produced an engraved plan to illustrate their proposal for a stone bridge to be built on this site. However, this excellent scheme would have required a few hundred yards of new access road on the Twickenham bank – and the owner of the land there flatly refused permission.

In the end a compromise was reached in 1773, and incorporated in an Act of Parliament. The bridge would have to be on the Ferry Hill site, but the access would be improved and the new construction would be wholly of stone. The interests of William Windham and Henry Holland (to whom Windham had sub-let the ferry) were to be bought out by a body of Bridge Commissioners, headed by Henry Hobart. *Plate 35* A design by James Paine and Kenton Cruse was approved. In August 1774 Henry Hobart laid the first stone. The bridge was opened to pedestrians by September 1776, and to vehicles in January 1777, and was finally completed in December of that year. Construction was financed by the issue of tontine shares, the dividends on which were found from tolls. (The tolls were abolished and the toll houses at the Richmond end of the bridge were pulled down in March 1859, after the death of the last surviving holder of the tontine shares.)

The wooden bridge at Kew was not very satisfactory. In 1774 it was damaged by a collision and remained closed for two years. By 1782 more repairs were needed. Robert Tunstall, proprietor, son of the original builder, decided to get James Paine, whose Richmond Bridge had been much admired, to design a stone bridge for Kew. This, of nine arches, was begun in 1783 and completed in September 1789 when George III led 'a great concourse of carriages' across it.

The completion of the bridges led to a determination on the part of the London Corporation, in whom was vested the right to control river traffic on the Thames as far up as Staines, to improve the arrangements in the area of Richmond and Kew. The King himself had already made improvements to the riverside foot paths and tow path, but by an Act of 1777 the Corporation proposed to make a proper towing path, to allow horses to be used, on the Surrey bank from the King's bargehouse at Kew to Water Lane in Richmond. In November 1778, without the backing of any further legislation, the Corporation determined, at the request of barge masters, to continue this towing path under and beyond the new bridge. They proposed to do this without taking any land from those whose properties came down to the water's edge, but by making a new embankment along the side of the river – which would, of course, cut off the riverside proprietors from the water. They ran into a lot of opposition. George Colman in particular in July 1779 hired thugs to attack the Corporation's workmen and to cut down the piles being sunk for the new embankment. City marshals and a file of soldiers were required to restore order. Colman tried to prosecute the Corporation's employees, but the Court at Kingston would not proceed against them and, when he later tried to sue for injury done to his premises by the construction of the towing path, he lost.

One person, however, had the necessary clout to prevent the construction of the towing path on or in front of his land – the Duke of Montagu. And so it is that the riverside walk today does not continue through Buccleuch Gardens into Petersham Meadows. It is still necessary to come up from the river to the Petersham Road and then turn down again on the Petersham side of the old boundary.

There was one other way in which the bridging of the river affected, if somewhat indirectly, the geography of Richmond. Once the river was bridged at Kew, the old public road from the former Kew-Brentford Ferry to Richmond Green, which ran right through the King's estate, was of less use. He was able, as explained in Chapter 20, to secure its closure in 1766. This encouraged him to contemplate other deals to enlarge and consolidate the royal estate. The very complete and accurate survey of Richmond manor prepared in 1771 was undoubtedly a by-product of this concern. *Plate 40* With his proposed new palace in mind, in the late 1760s he bought out all the crown leases of property at the hamlet of West Sheen – the one-time site of the Charterhouse of Shene – and by 1772 he had demolished all the remaining buildings there.

For the past 25 years, the part of the West Sheen site that was in lease to Sir John Buckworth and his heirs had been rented to Richard Andrews, a calico printer, who moved his works here from Merton. Richard Crisp, writing in the 1860s, said:

> There were numerous persons employed at this calico-printing establishment, both male and female, and as they all worked piecework, as it is termed, earned a very considerable rate of wages. An aged inhabitant of Richmond once informed us that his father had frequently told him about these large works, and that the numbers of work people there, as they earnt high wages, were a saucy and independent lot; in fact that at one time Richmond was overrun by the calico-printers.[30]

This project, which appears to have continued for a while after the West Sheen site was lost – though its whereabouts has not been traced – was one of Richmond's very few industries.* Of course, since Tudor times Richmond's principal industry, if one may call it that, has been catering for the visitors – foreigners, courtiers, rich London merchants, poor London daytrippers, and all. But of manufacture Richmond had seen very little. The tile kilns set up between the Petersham Road and the river in the time of Elizabeth I, re-establishing themselves on the east side of the Petersham

---

* In evidence given to the Parliamentary Committee on Manufactures, Commerce and Shipping in 1833 a Mr James Thomson, calico printer of Primrose, near Clithero, Lancs, stated that the establishment of calico printing in Britain 'dates from about the year 1690 when a small print ground was established on the banks of the Thames at Richmond, by a Frenchman who in all probability was a refugee after the revocation of the edict of Nantes'. However, no coroborative evidence for this assertion has been traced; nor does there appear to be any reason why Mr Thomson should have inside information about events in Richmond a century and a half before.

Road in the 17th century and despoiling the Hill Common from then until 1766, was one. The brewing of beer was another. A number of relatively small breweries can be identified in the 17th century. In the 18th two sites were predominant. The brewery of the Collins family was established at the river end of Water Lane in the 1720s – and supplied at least a dozen 'tied houses' as the Collinses bought up many of the taverns in the town. And by the riverside, where tilekilns had been, just to the south of 'Riverdale House', William Lewis removed his brewery from mid-town about 1725. *Plate 34* His son John is more renowned for his spirited defence of the right of Richmond residents to walk and drive in Richmond Park (on roads that were there long before the park walls or the deer) than for his brewing. His brewery was in fact destroyed by severe floods – but he was by then a local hero and the minister of the parish church organised a collection for his benefit.[31]

✠

Calico printing, the making of tiles and the brewing of beer certainly did not constitute a manufacturing base in the eyes of the citizens of Richmond. The 'Case of the Inhabitants with respect to a Bridge intended to be built by William Windham Esq ... ,' as presented to Parliament, apart from all the arguments about location and materials, sums up Richmond as they saw it in 1773:

> That the Town of Richmond is a Place of no Manufacture, but depends chiefly upon the Residence of Persons of Prosperity and Fortune; who are invited to live there from the Agreeableness of its Situation, and more particularly from the Beauty of the River Thames, which extends itself along the Borders of the said Town, from one End to the other. That on the Banks of the River Thames are the Houses and Estates of many Persons of Rank and Fortune, as well as others, commanding a fine View of the River up and down, and also of Richmond-Hill and the adjacent Country.

with reference also to: '... the Company who resort there at various Times, particularly during the Summer Season, for Pleasure and Entertainment.'

# 19

## *The Consolidation of the Big Estates*

RICHMOND NEVER HAD an enclosure act. (One in 1832 affected just the Kew meadows and the land which George IV wanted to enclose from the end of Kew Green.) But the land in the strips in the common fields was never redistributed by act of Parliament, for the process of consolidation and enclosure had taken place gradually, voluntarily and effectively throughout the 17th and 18th centuries.

Not many of the estates noted in 1620 survived intact. The Jones estate appears to have escaped break-up until 1705; much of the Payne estate can be traced in the hands of a single owner (Sir William Turner) and then his heirs and successors in title. The Gorges estate was sold in 1634 to Richard Bennett – and passed intact to his Capell descendants. Most of the rest were dispersed.

The Portman freehold estate descended with the baronetcy in turn through the sons of Sir John (Henry died 1623, John died 1624, Hugh died 1630) until it came into the hands of the youngest, William, who had inherited the copyhold lands directly from his father. Once he had his hands on the whole estate, he sold it in 1630: a single house with seven acres of ground to the merchant Samuel Fortrey who promptly built the so-called 'Dutch House' (now Kew Palace), the rest to the Scottish courtier Sir Robert Carr of Ancrum. Carr, who was in a sense William Portman's brother-in-law, having married as his second wife the widow of Sir Henry Portman, 2nd Bart, was ennobled as Earl of Ancram in 1633. A close friend of Charles I (he had been in his service since the young Charles was first granted his own household in 1617), Ancram sold to Richard Bennett his copyhold lands in Kew in 1648, but ended his days as a penniless exile, dying in Amsterdam in 1654. His successor as Earl of Ancram was Charles, his elder son by his second wife, to whom the estates in Richmond and Kew were quickly passed by the younger son Stanley, who initially inherited the copyhold under the 'Borough English' custom of the manor. Charles was beset by creditors. He sold off all the Richmond lands and Kew Heath in a series of separate (many of them small) transactions between 1656 and 1662. He was finally able to mortgage what remained of the freehold estate at Kew and the great mansion there (under a deal with a 1,000-year term) in 1659 to Sir John Brownlow. The mortgage was foreclosed in 1663/4. The estate, which included not only the house but 63 acres of freehold land in closes between Kew Park and Field and the river and also the 18 acres of 'Ware Ground' on the east side of the Green, passed from the Brownlow family to the Levetts in 1700, was rented by Queen Caroline in 1728–29 and was eventually purchased (except for the Ware Ground) by George III and Queen Charlotte from Levett Blackborne in 1781.

☩

Richard Bennett, who put together the other big estate at Kew by purchase of both the Gorges estate and another part of the Portman/Ancram estate, so that he ended up owning almost the whole of the original Kew Field (including Kew Park), was the son of Thomas Bennett, a London alderman and mercer, who served as Sheriff in 1613–14, and died in 1620, and his wife Dorothy May (daughter of Richard May of Rawmere in Sussex and sister of Sir Humphrey May, Chancellor of the Duchy of Lancaster). A great-uncle, Sir Thomas Bennett had been Lord Mayor of London in 1603–04, and an uncle, Sir John, was Chancellor to James I's wife, Anne of Denmark. Through the Mays, he was related to Sir William Herrick – and this may perhaps have been the connection which first brought him to the area. He purchased the entire estate of Sir Arthur Gorges in 1634–36 (and sold 64 acres of the land in Kew Field to Robert Earl of Ancram).

In October 1644 Ancram mortgaged all his copyhold lands in Kew (together with nine acres of Aldey in Richmond) to Bennett, and in December 1648 Bennett took full title to the estate. In the meantime Bennett, a royalist, had been declared a 'delinquent', but had leased the house and grounds at Kew and decamped to Cornwall. In 1647 the lease at Kew was taken over by Edmond Prideaux, a leading lawyer and a strong Parliamentarian (who was appointed Solicitor General in October 1648), but he moved to the Dutch House when Bennett returned in 1648 to confess his delinquency and 'compound' for a fine of £400 to regain his estates.

Richard Bennett had no son. When he died in April 1658 his heir in Kew was his youngest daughter Dorothy (still only 16 years old but already married to the Hon Henry Capell, a son of Arthur Lord Capell). Henry in due course was ennobled as Lord Capell of Tewkesbury, but died without heirs in 1696. His brother Arthur had been made Earl of Essex, and when Dorothy died in 1721, it was her great-niece Elizabeth Capell (daughter of the 2nd Earl) who was the heir. Elizabeth married first in 1717 Samuel Molyneux M P (who died in 1727) and then in 1730 Dr Nathaniel St André. The St Andrés leased the Kew estate to Frederick Prince of Wales and the principal house – the one-time Lodge of Kew Park – was improved and enlarged by William Kent to become 'the White House'. Elizabeth St André's heir was William Anne Capell, 4th Earl of Essex, and it was not until after his death in 1799 that King George III and Queen Charlotte were eventually able to purchase the estate from his heirs.

☩

Turning to the estates in the Richmond fields, Dorothy Wright's lands had an entailed reversion to Lionel Wright, which he passed to his nephew Charles in 1632. A year later, still some five years before Lady Dorothy's death, Charles sold the reversion to Richard Burnham. The holding was split up in the 1660s by Burnham's widow Elizabeth. The copyhold Payne lands followed a similar pattern, while it appears that almost all the freehold Payne lands were purchased by Dr (later Sir) William Turner in the 1650s.

The Peirce estate was mostly inherited from Stephen Peirce by his son George in 1630 (a small part went to Stephen Peirce Junior in 1628, and from him to George in 1635). George Peirce sold the entire holding to Clement Kynnersley in 1639; and Kynnersley at once started to split up the estate.

Similarly Richard Clarke's estate, inherited by his brother Henry Clarke in 1617, was sold by the latter to Sir Richard Manley in 1630. Manley sold off some parcels separately, but the greater parts were purchased by John Gregory and Clement Kynnersley in 1649 and they then split up the holdings.

Mary Crome's estate was inherited by Daniel Crome her son in 1636, but he then split it up, however selling quite a lot of it to Edward Munday in 1649. Munday divided his portion still further.

George Charley's holding was inherited more or less intact in turn by Thomas Charley, his son, in 1628 and then by the latter's brother James in 1638. James Charley sold it immediately to Joseph Day, from whom it descended to his son Henry Day in 1653. Each of the Charleys and Days made several transactions involving the purchase and sale of houses and cottages in the town, but they made almost no sales of land in the fields. Thomas Charley sold 1¼ acres, Joseph Day ½ acre and Henry Day 1½ acres. So Henry Day still had 23 acres to sell to John Spicer in 1657. John Spicer broke up the estate.

The Smith and Burd holdings were fragmented almost immediately after 1620. Thomas Smythe sold most of his land to John Gregory in 1621. Bartholomew Smith died and his widow Winifred married a John Coles. They sold her land to John Tompson in 1626 and he subsequently dispersed it.

✝

A number of persons were actively engaged in the land market in Richmond in the mid-17th century – buying, selling and exchanging plots of land, either as brokers or as principals building up more consolidated holdings. Foremost among these were:

*John Gregory*, a 'yeoman', in whose name are recorded 19 acts of purchase between 1618 and 1657, including most of the Clarke estate, a considerable part of the Peirce estate (purchased from Kynnersley in 1656) and part of the Ancram estate. He disposed of it all by 1658, in 20 different sales, the principal purchasers being Robert Wilkins, Clement Kynnersley and Thomas Eling.

*John Keele the elder*, blacksmith, made his first purchase of property in Richmond in 1605. Over the next forty years he purchased a total of 9 acres of land in the fields, but it was not until the 1650s that he began to buy up land more intensively. His son John, who inherited 16 acres from his father in January 1661/2, threw himself into the game, buying, selling or exchanging several properties each year. Another son Robert also dabbled in the land market.

*William Leaver*, yeoman, who was Keele's next door neighbour and whose daughter Jane married John Keele Junior, was another dealer in this market from 1641 onwards. At one point he owned some 13 acres, but by his death in 1675 his remaining estate was just a single cottage.

*Clement Kynnersley*, Esquire, was the biggest operator in the Richmond land market. He started by buying the entire Peirce estate in 1639, then after some sporadic purchases in the 1640s he purchased in July 1649 17 acres and one acre of mead directly from Richard Manley, and from John Gregory a further 15 acres and an acre of mead which had been part of the Clarke/Manley estate. With a pool of some 90 acres to draw on, Kynnersley began to redistribute the land in 1654. In that year he sold 9 acres in Aldey to Richard Manley and a mansion and 15 acres to William Stobart. In 1656 he sold 17½ acres to Thomas Eling and 16½ to John Gregory. In 1657 he sold 41½ acres to William Turner. In the next two years came a series of further adjustments: he bought some land from Eling and the Earl of Ancram and bought some back from Gregory. He exchanged some land with Turner, and sold him a few acres more. When he died in 1662 he left to his wife Dorothy and his son Philip just one solid block of 8 acres of land by the road to Mortlake and a 2-acre close between the horse and foot roads to Kew, on the north-east side of Mr Michell's mansion. Dorothy and Philip Kynnersley sold these at once to William Turner.

*Thomas Eling*, a butcher, was a somewhat later starter in the land market game, but a major player once he got going. His first venture was to buy Walnut Tree Ait in 1652, followed by 3¾ acres of the former Crome lands purchased from Arthur Munday in 1654. Then in 1656 he bought from John Gregory the *Black Bull* tavern, which he turned into his shop and slaughterhouse, together with ¾ acre of land; and three months later he bought 17 acres of land from Clement Kynnersley. He made his first sales in 1657, of ½ acre each to John Antill and to Kynnersley. Then came more purchases in 1658: an acre from Ancram, 7¾ acres from John Gregory, ½ acre each from Christopher Towne and from John Michell. These were followed by more disposals: ½-acre and 1 acre in two separate deals to John Michell, 5 acres to William Turner, 5½ acres to John Keele the elder. After those sales he made no more deals for five years.

From 1663 onwards Thomas Eling engaged in 36 more recorded land deals before his death in 1697; while his son, Thomas Eling Junior, started to become involved in 1667. Few of these were large purchases or sales: an acre or two here or there, sometimes a single ¼-acre, often a mixed bag of, say, three parcels of land, one of an acre, one of ½ acre, one of ¼ acre. Several were exchanges of land. The largest transactions were a deal with William Turner in 1663 whereby Eling gave up 4¼ acres in Parkshot in exchange for 2½ acres in the same shott, and the purchase of 6 acres, in two closes of 4 acres and 2 acres, by Thomas Eling Junior from John Keele in 1667 and then the sale of the 4-acre close to John Young in 1669.

*William Turner*, Doctor of Laws, knighted in 1663, began to acquire property in Richmond in 1650. Although he did resell some of the land he purchased, his major interest was not in dealing but in building up an estate for himself. His first purchases were of a house and adjacent cottage on the north side of the road to Marshgate. Here he made his home, probably rebuilding the house. Two years later he acquired the reversion (after the death of Rebecca) of the Payne copyhold lands. It seems likely that it was in 1654 that he purchased the freehold Payne estate. (Looking at entries concerning the transfer of pieces of land adjacent to Payne freeholds, it seems that the transaction may have taken place between the end of March and the end of October 1654.)

In 1657 Dr Turner bought 41½ acres from Clement Kynnersley, some of it former Peirce and some former Clarke land. He bought another house adjoining his existing property from the Earl of Ancram, together with ¾ acre; and he bought ¼ acre from John Gregory. In 1658 he bought 5 acres from Thomas Eling and, in April 1659, 3¼ acres from Richard Burnham (former Wright land). He also exchanged three pieces of land totalling one acre for similar parcels belonging to Kynnersley. Then in October 1659 he exchanged some land with William Leaver, bought 3¾ acres more from Clement Kynnersley and 6 acres from the Earl of Ancram.

There was a brief pause before Turner bought 3 acres from Robert Keele in 1662 and the 8 acres and the 2-acre close already mentioned from Dorothy and Philip Kynnersley in 1663. Later in 1663 Turner exchanged 2½ acres in Parkshot for 4¼ acres in the same shott belonging to Thomas Eling. In 1664 he purchased some small pieces of land from Richard Hussey, William Stobart and John Antill and engaged in two unequal exchanges: 2 acres to John Keele in return for 3½; and 4 acres from Sir William Bolton in return for just one half-acre. He bought another acre from James Spicer in 1665 and got 6 acres in exchange for 4 acres in a deal with William Leaver.

In 1666 Sir William Turner made his will, and surrendered all his lands 'to its use'. He bought a last 2 acres in 1669 and in October 1670 he died. He left one of his houses (between the junction of the Marshgate Road and Paradise Road) to a daughter by his first marriage who was the wife of Anthony Horsmanden; the whole of the rest of his estate went to his widow Frances. She died in January 1684/5, leaving a son Brian, who died unmarried in August 1687, and a daughter Frances who then, with her husband Captain David Lloyd, inherited the estate, which then included more than 100 acres of copyhold land, in addition to all the freehold. Virtually unchanged, the estate was inherited by the Lloyds' children David and Briana in 1712–15 and was sold by them to Charles Selwyn in 1720.

Charles Selwyn had come to Richmond in 1718 as a member of the household of the Prince of Wales and Princess Caroline, who settled in Richmond Lodge in the Old Deer Park as their country residence. Selwyn took a lease of a house in the hamlet of West Sheen, which had developed on the site of the former Charterhouse. Two years later he purchased the Turner/ Lloyd estate. He continued to live in West Sheen until his death in 1749, and the houses which had belonged to Turner were leased or sold off. Charles Selwyn left his estate to his nephew William who built a house at Larkfield Lodge (just off the road to Mortlake) and later moved to a house built for him in 1810 by the Kew Road. This was called Pagoda House, and later Selwyn Court, and stood on the site of the later (but now redeveloped) Christ Church. The estate, somewhat enlarged in the later 18th and early 19th centuries, then developed with housing in the mid-19th century, can be traced through some 50 street names which have some Selwyn family connection or association.

⊹

William Turner was not the only dealer in land to build up a sizeable estate for himself. Among the others were Matthew Moody, blacksmith (died 1649) and his sons Matthew, a farrier (died 1702) and Samuel, goldsmith (died 1708/9). Samuel left land including a brewhouse which was mortgaged by his grandson Thomas Newman to Sara Thayer, from whom the mortgage was bought by John Collins, up to then a baker but thereafter brewer. Matthew Moody the younger left an estate which descended to his granddaughter Alice, who married John Collins' son William. Although much of the estate which was built up over several generations by Collins brewers was town property – inns and taverns – there was also a considerable holding in the fields, especially Marsh Furze Shott, Long Downs and Pennards Butts, by the late 18th century.

John Michell the Younger (died 1739) was another who acquired a lot of land, though he disposed of much of it during his lifetime (some of which found its way to the Selwyn estate).

William Stobart acquired 2 acres in 1653, then purchased from Clement Kynnersley a newly built mansion on the north side of the Marshgate (now Sheen) Road, together with 15 acres of scattered lands in the fields. By the end of the decade he had two more houses in the town. He sold about half the land to various persons and his widow and heirs counted their property more in houses, gardens and adjacent closes than in holdings in the fields. Nevertheless it was Stobart land that provided the nucleus for the estate of Dr John Baker in Upper Dunstable in the 1770s.

Sir James Butler was another whose estate, though significant, was mostly outside the fields, having been built up largely between the river and the freehold closes on the north-east side of Richmond Hill. Much of the work of putting this estate together was done by George Carew in the 1660s and '70s. The property which Carew mortgaged to Butler for £2,500 in 1681 did, however, include also the 35 acres of Kew Heath south of the Mortlake Road and 10 acres in the shot adjoining Bayley's Bank, as well as some 6 acres in two closes in Parkshott. Butler left the estate by will to John Chappell, 'formerly my clerk, for his faithful services'. John Chappell (who raised a mortgage on the estate of £3675 and settled in Norwich) sold the whole in 1719 to Edward Darrell, the London bookseller who had purchased the house now called 'Old Palace Place', part of the newly built Old Palace Terrace and all the shops in Paved Court from Vertue Radford in 1692. Darrell died very shortly after making this major purchase and left it – indeed all his freehold and copyhold property in Richmond – to his younger son John Darrell in lieu of a £6,000 legacy. John was still a minor when he was admitted to the property in 1720, his uncle Robert being appointed as guardian. In 1749 John surrendered to John Dillman of Kew Green, the German-born gardener of Prince Frederick, the 35 acres of Kew Heath, the 10 acres in Bank Shott and the 6 acres in Park Shott. This land was inherited by Dillman's son-in-law John Dillman Engleheart in 1760, and (with the addition in 1778 of the other 10 acres of Kew Heath north of the Mortlake Road) remained the Engleheart estate until developed in the 19th century. The Darrell estate itself was broken up in the first two decades of the 19th century.

Some other smaller estates were built up in particular areas: for example, that of Matthew Walker at Marshgate or those of Samuel Rundall and his son-in-law Isaac Pigg, both tilemakers, in the areas of the riverside, the Hill Common and the land behind the Windmill on the Great Common.

In all the many deals that gradually put these estates, large or small, together we can see an underlying pattern. It is like one of those puzzles where a block of wood has to be manoeuvred from one corner of a pattern to the corner diagonally opposite, by moving every other piece in the pattern two or three times just to liberate the one we are really interested in. Sometimes in a single move, sometimes in two or three, contiguous strips are brought and then held under the same ownership. Turner and some others mentioned were interested in retaining the land. Gregory, the Keeles, Leaver, Kynnersley, the Elings were not essentially building up estates for themselves. If they had a little land left over at the end of their lives it was usually promptly sold by their heirs. They were simply dealing. Unfortunately we do not have any record of the monetary values of their transactions, but we must assume that they made a reasonable profit from their dealing – and that the usual way in which that profit was generated was by providing the buyer at a premium with land adjacent to that which he already owned, so that he might eventually have, instead of scattered strips, a field of several acres.

By way of illustration, let us consider a couple of examples. The first is a relatively simple series of deals in the East or Heath Field, covering 3 acres of land all copyhold.

In 1620 these three acres were in five strips: from north to south, ½ acre of Clarke, ½ acre of Peirce, 1 acre of Bartholomew Smythe, ½ acre of Peirce and ½ acre of Mary Crome. The Clarke ½-acre was part of the estate sold to Richard Manley in 1630. It was sold to John Gregory in 1649 and by him to Thomas Eling in 1658. Eling disposed of it almost at once to John Keele who sold it to John Spicer in 1664. Spicer already owned the next parcel to the south. That and the other Peirce half-acre had been sold by George Peirce to Clement Kynnersley in 1639. Kynnersley sold them to John Spicer in 1657. He already owned the land in between and the land on the south.

The acre strip in the centre of the 3 acres we are considering had belonged to Bartholomew Smythe in right of his wife Winifred (née Haynes). When he died she married John Coles, and in 1626 John and Winifred Coles sold a holding of 5¾ acres (which included this one acre) to John Tompson. Tompson sold the acre in 1631 to Gregory – and in 1656 Gregory sold it to John Spicer.

The Crome half-acre, inherited by Daniel Crome, was sold by him to Edward Munday in 1644 and by Munday to John Spicer in 1649. It was 'by the Friar's Stile'. So by 1664 John Spicer had 3 acres all contiguous, in a single field. It was the site on which the house called 'Home Castle' was later to be built. That same 3-acre field lasted well into the 19th century (though built on at the north-west end).

Another illustration of the process, this time more complicated because it involves freehold land as well as copyhold, may be the ground in Church Shott lying to the north-east of Conduit Field. This by the early 18th century was a single field of 6¼ acres. (In present-day terms this is the land stretching from just north-east of Halford Road up to and including Mount Ararat Road.) We will consider its composition and its consolidation, strip by strip from south-west to north-east.

There was first a half-acre owned in 1620 by Bartholomew Smythe and his wife. This was sold to John Gregory in 1622, and by Gregory to John Tompson in 1626. Tompson sold it to John Michell in 1657 and the younger John Michell inherited it in 1662. It was in the occupation of William Turner (as a tenant) in 1676. John Michell sold it to Frances Lloyd in 1712 as 'a half acre enclosed by William Turner and now occupied by Ann Vandeput'.

Next to this was ¾ acre, allegedly free land belonging to Sir Henry Portman, but surrendered as copyhold by the Earl of Ancram in 1657 to Thomas Stanley, landlord of the *Three Pigeons and Lily Pot*. The latter's second wife Martha inherited it on his death and, dying herself in 1699, left it (with another 12 acres) to her daughter Elizabeth Stanley.

Next was a holding of 1½ acres, purchased by Sir Robert Wright and his wife Dorothy from John Bird in 1606, and held by Dorothy in 1620. As mentioned above, the reversion in Dame Dorothy's lands was sold by Charles Wright to Richard Burnham in 1633. In April 1659 Richard Burnham sold the 12 acres to William Turner who already had the adjacent land on the east – a freehold acre of the Wright/Payne estate.

*Plate 36*

*The Terrace and the view from Richmond Hill, about 1720, oil painting attributed to Leonard Knyff. In the right foreground are the houses of 1-3 The Terrace and the Roebuck Tavern. Above them can be seen Bishop Duppa's Almshouses. Towards the left Trumpeters' House stands out by the riverside, but does not yet have its portico. (London Borough of Richmond upon Thames)*

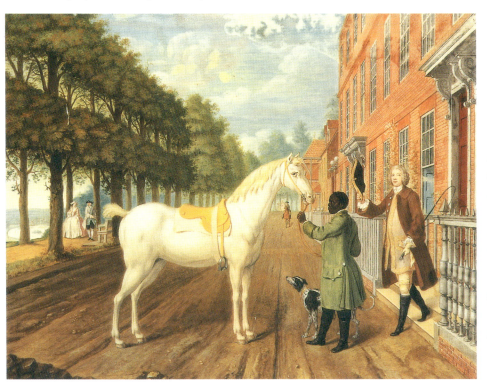

*The Terrace, Richmond Hill, 1749. Painting in gouache signed and dated by Augustin Heckel. The Roebuck and Nos. 1 and 2 The Terrace are unchanged but No.3 has been rebuilt to make a pair with No.4, built about 1730. The gentleman about to mount his horse is probably Sir William Richardson, who was occupying No.4 in 1749, following a fire in his new-built house next door (on the site of Doughty House). (Sotheby & Co.)*

*Plate 37*

Society on Richmond
Green, *a drawing by
Thomas Rowlandson,
showing on the left the
house of Earl
Fitzwilliam. (Victoria
and Albert Museum,
no. 1817-1900)*

Asgill House – *a
drawing by Thomas
Rowlandson. (LBRUT)*

*Plate 38*

*This painting by Antonio Joli, c.1749, shows the newly-completed Cholmondeley House, the library of which (built first) is the wing of the building closest to the viewer, with an apsidal end and an elaborate doorway to the riverside walk. Beyond the house is the White Cross tavern, then Collins' brewery and the three mansions of Herring Court. At the top of the Hill can be seen the neat row of trees on The Terrace, the Star and Garter tavern and the summer house in the park built by Walpole. (Private Collection)*

Plate 39

# Street Lighting
## in 1772

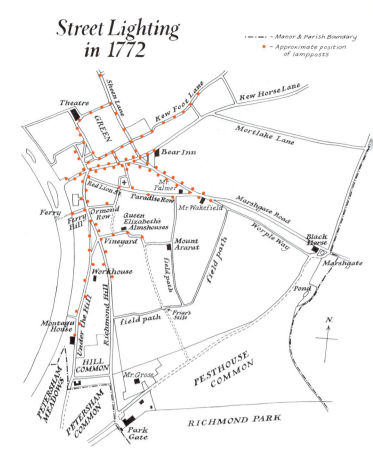

# Nightwatch Patrols
## in 1772

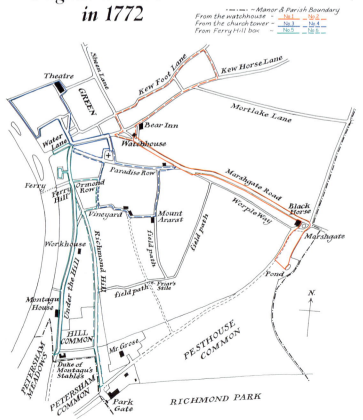

A rood of Portman copyhold land came next. This was sold directly by the Earl of Ancram to William Turner in July 1659. Then came another ¼ acre of Dorothy Wright and another ½ acre of Payne land (Vincent in 1559) which came to Turner in the same transaction as those mentioned above.

A freehold half-acre belonging to the Jones estate came next, and this was presumably sold in or about 1705 to the Lloyds. Then was a half-acre of the Peirce estate (Scopeham's lands or Parkins' Farm) which belonged to Parkins in 1559 and to Stephen Peirce in 1620. George Peirce inherited it in 1630 and sold it along with the whole estate to Clement Kynnersley in 1639. Kynnersley sold this half-acre to William Stobart in 1654 and Stobart sold it to Turner in 1664.

The last item in this particular sequence is the half-acre strip at the old Charterhouse conduit head – in Crown ownership since the suppression of the Charterhouse in 1538. This was acquired, together with the former Charterhouse land on the Green (site of Old Palace Terrace and Paved Court) by John Thorpe, and sold by him to Humphrey Michell in 1669. Humphrey sold it to his nephew John Michell in 1689. But in 1656 the Manor Court had noted that the conduit and the ground on which it stood had been 'in the year 1655 inclosed within the farm yard of Dr William Turner, by what right we do not know'.

So in the 1670s there was a block of land of 6¼ acres. At the west and east ends were the two half-acres belonging to John Michell, one of which Turner had enclosed within his own property in 1655 and the other had been in Turner's occupation by 1676. Next at the west end was the ¾ acre belonging to Thomas Stanley. In the middle was a half-acre of Jones land. The other 4 acres belonged to William Turner. We may assume that he rented the 2¼ acres not in his ownership. Almost certainly Turner enclosed this 6¼ acres as a single field. Elizabeth Stanley eventually sold her land to the same person who bought the Turner mansion close by, suggesting that there was a link there also.

From Turner, knighted in 1663, the land was inherited by his widow Frances, then his son Bryan, then his daughter Frances Lloyd. David and Briana, the children of Frances Lloyd, sold the land, together with their entire estate, to Charles Selwyn in 1720. This was one of the only portions of the former Turner estate which did not remain in the Selwyn family for the next century. Charles Selwyn sold this field (both the freehold and copyhold elements) in 1729 to Robert Darrell and it was still in the latter's ownership and occupation in 1774. His heir Edward Darrell sold it to one John Jeffreys in 1814 and Jeffreys to George Robinson in 1825.

These two examples may serve to illustrate the process. It continued through the 18th century. By 1771 most of the main estates that were to underlie, and to an extent dictate the shape of, the housing developments of the latter part of the 19th century had already been formed. It is quite interesting to compare the plan of some of the larger estates in 1771 as revealed in the manor survey with those of 1851 as shown in the tithe map:

| 1771 | 1851 |
| --- | --- |
| Royal estates (including that of Princess Dowager of Wales): parts in Kew at north end of Richmond Gardens and parts of Kew Gardens still leased, from Blackborne and Essex. | Royal estates now including those leased elements. Enlargement at south end of Kew Gardens and north of Richmond Green, and at west end of Kew Green. |
| Ware Ground belonging to Blackborne. | Ware Ground now 'Priory Estate' (Doughty). |
| Kew Heath north of Mortlake Road – Middleton. Kew Heath south of Mortlake Road – Engleheart. | Kew Heath – all Engleheart. |
| Selwyn estate – much of Lower Field, plus half of Lower Dunstable and substantial blocks in Upper Dunstable, Church Shott. Long and Short Downs. | Selwyn estate – land in Parkshot sold to Crown, but holding east of Kew Road consolidated. Some land in Upper Field apparently given up – but perhaps not shown because built on. |
| Collins estate – very large blocks in Marsh Furze Shott, east end of Church Shott, Long Downs, Pennard's Butts and West Bancroft. Darrell – large block in Church Shott. | George Robinson estate – about half of Collins' holdings in Marsh Furze and Long Downs, plus land formerly Darrell's in Church Shott and some land in Upper Dunstable. |
| Houblon estate – large blocks in Maybush Shot and West Bancroft. | Doughty estate – smaller holdings in Maybush Shot and West Bancroft (but plus Ware Ground at Kew). |
| Floyer estate – east end of Marsh Furze Shott and Cox's Close | Price estate – eastern half of Marsh Furze Shott, all of Pennard's Butts and half of Aldey. |

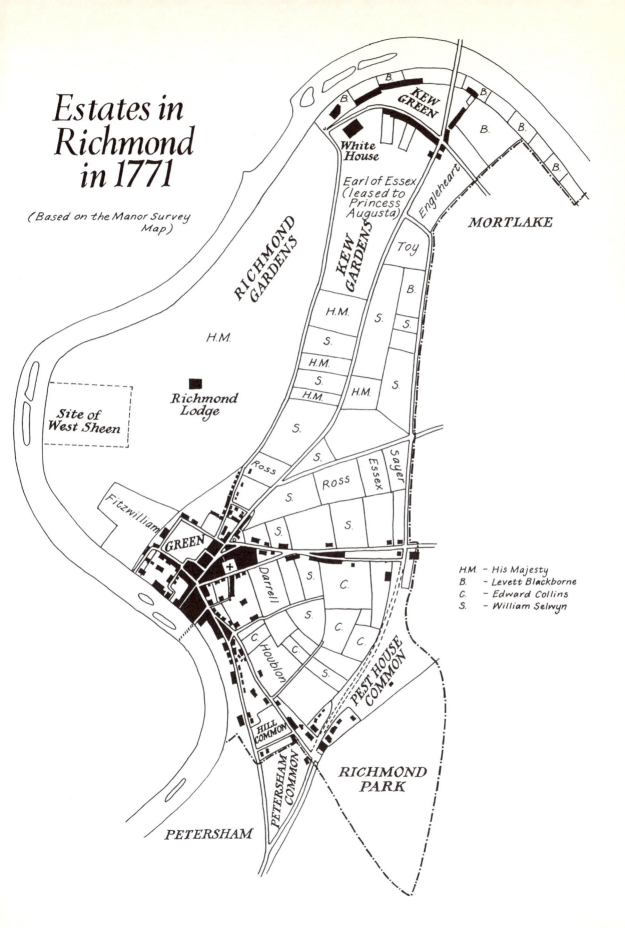

Estates in
Richmond
in 1771

(Based on the Manor Survey
Map)

KEW
GREEN

White
House

Earl of Essex
(leased to
Princess
Augusta)

Engleheart

MORTLAKE

RICHMOND
GARDENS

KEW
GARDENS

Toy

B.

H.M.

S.

S.

H.M.

S.

S.

H.M.

H.M.

H.M.

Richmond
Lodge

Site of
West Sheen

S.

S.

S.

Ross

Fitzwilliam

Ross

Essex

Sayer

GREEN

S.

S.

S.

Darrell

C.

H.M. – His Majesty
B. – Levett Blackborne
C. – Edward Collins
S. – William Selwyn

C.

C.

Houblon

C.

C.

S.

PEST HOUSE COMMON

HILL
COMMON

PETERSHAM COMMON

RICHMOND
PARK

PETERSHAM

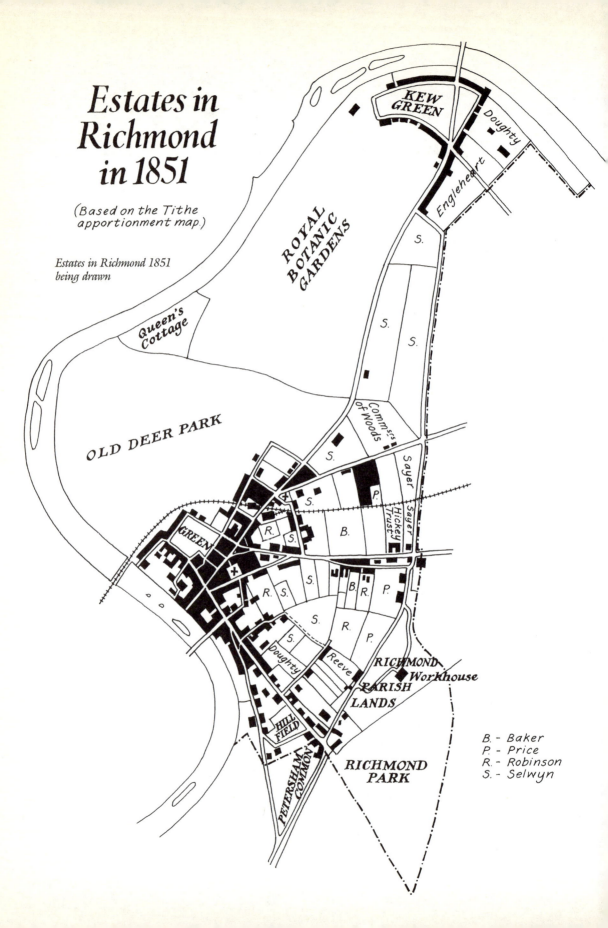

# Estates in
# Richmond
# in 1851

(Based on the Tithe
apportionment map.)

Estates in Richmond 1851
being drawn

ROYAL
BOTANIC
GARDENS

KEW
GREEN

Doughty

Englehedrt

S.

S.

S.

Queen's
Cottage

Comm.ʳˢ
of Woods

S.

OLD DEER PARK

S.

Sayer

P.

Hickey
Trust

GREEN

R.

S.

B.

Sayer

R.

S.

B. R.

P.

R. S.

B. R.

P.

S.

S.

R.

P.

Doughty

Reeve

RICHMOND
Workhouse

S.

Hill
Field

Doughty

RICHMOND
PARISH
LANDS

PETERSHAM
COMMON

RICHMOND
PARK

B. – Baker
P. – Price
R. – Robinson
S. – Selwyn

# 20

## *Local Government from the Seventeenth to the Nineteenth Centuries*

THE LORD OF THE MANOR and his steward and the manorial courts, as described in Chapter 4, with their officers, the headborough, the constable and the aleconner, continued to provide the principal local government for Richmond until well into the 17th century. In 1628 Richmond finally won its full independence from Kingston. For some time the inhabitants had been chafing under the arrangement – a hang-over from centuries before – that the Court Leet of the borough of Kingston had jurisdiction over Richmond and the appointment of the manorial officers. Various petitions had been presented by the inhabitants, and in 1622 and 1624 the Prince of Wales' own council had supported them, but to no avail. By 1626, however, Prince Charles was King, and the inhabitants tried again – with another petition. 'Kingston skimmeth away the cream from your Majesty', it pointed out.

Coincidentally, but from Richmond's point of view most providentially, Kingston was at this time contesting a claim from Hampton for a right to hold a market, and was seeking a confirmation of its borough charter. The King ordered two committees to look into these two cases. Conveniently the one considering the Court Leet supported Richmond, but Kingston was appeased because their right to a market was upheld against Hampton. Kingston was to have a new charter in which its jurisdiction over Richmond, Petersham and Ham would be surrendered, but its right to hold three annual fairs and to hold the only market for seven miles would be confirmed. Sir Robert Douglas, already Steward of the manor of Richmond, was formally appointed as steward for life of the new Richmond Court Leet on 13 October 1628.[1] It held its first meeting at Richmond Palace on 15 April 1629.[2] Its jurisdiction extended to Kew, as part of the manor of Richmond, but also to Petersham and Ham – and for each locality a full team of officers – headborough (or tithingman), constable and aleconner – was appointed.

*Plate 41*

The Court Leet had wider powers than the Court Baron, but as a matter of convenience it was normally convened on the same day at the same place, with the same panel of jurors. It is hardly surprising, therefore, that it very quickly became little more than a curtain-raiser to the Court Baron, appointing the manorial officials, but leaving all 'presentments' to be handled by the latter. While the main part of the Court's business was always the registration of changes of property ownership, it is in these presentments that we often learn rather more about what was exercising the minds of the inhabitants. The Court was an embryonic planning authority: it would order repairs to be carried out to buildings in need of maintenance; it would require the removal of any building encroaching on highways or public open space – or would recommend that the Lord grant land to legitimise such encroachment. It was an embryonic highways authority, requiring any impediment to be cleared away, bridges to be repaired, road surfaces to be patched, dangerous places to be properly fenced. It was an embryonic health authority: it was always quick to punish those who threw waste or night soil into the public streets: it was constantly requiring the manorial tenants to scour their ditches; it was on the alert for nuisances caused by the running of residents' 'sinks' (i.e. drains) into the roads or open spaces or – worst of all – into water supplies such as the town pond or conduit heads. It was an embryonic amenity, heritage, and community defence group – and often surprisingly outspoken in its complaints about the actions of the lord of the manor himself. This was a well-established tradition.

In the early 15th century there were repeated presentments of Thomas Holgill, who was temporary lord of the manor by lease, about his misdeeds at his weir (see pages 32-3). In 1494 there were complaints against hawking or hunting within the manor by any persons except 'of the kynges blode', and against those who, when the King was in residence, 'cast loose their horses into the meadows, corn and fields without leave or permission' – both thinly disguised attacks on the members of the royal court.[3] In the early 1650s, following the sale by Parliament of Richmond Palace and the Old Deer Park, there was a constant stream of complaints against the new owners for closing ancient rights of way or encroaching on the Green.

In 1652 the jurors of the Manor Court actually rebelled (politely) when the new lord of the manor intimated his intention to replace a 'chequer rail' in front of the Palace by a brick wall:

... which desire of the Lord this Homage doth not think proper to assent unto without the good liking of the free and copyhold tenants of the said Manor and having had some conference with many of them concerning the same this Homage doth find much unwillingness in them to concur therein by reason (as they affirm) there hath been many inclosures and encroachments made by some new farmer or farmers of the Park whereby the usual cartways both to Kew and to Sheene are much straitened and have endeavoured to take away the Common footway leading to Sheene and thence to Brainford and likewise their cart horse and foot way to the Thames by the ancient footway called the Crane Wharf ... and therefore this Homage doth desire that the Lord ... will be pleased to declare his intention as to the restoring of these former rights and enjoyments of those particulars so taken from them, which this Homage doth conceive will be a fit and necessary expedient to the obtaining of his own desires ...'[4]

Brave men – they probably would not have dared to be quite so outspoken to Queen Elizabeth or Charles I; but they would not have had the need. Charles may have enclosed his new Richmond Park against the wishes of the inhabitants, but he would never have tampered with Richmond Green and the roads there.

Among other matters which came within the Court's competence were the sorting out of minor boundary disputes between neighbours (and orders to make or repair fences and hedges), the regulation of the pasturing of livestock, the removal of earth or brushwood from the commons, and maintaining the quality of bread and ale, and always the maintenance and preservation of the 'Customs of the Manor' whenever and in whatever way they might be threatened.

✠

In the meantime, alongside the manorial jurisdiction, a new local government body was beginning to develop. It would perhaps be more correct to say that an organisation every bit as old as the manor was beginning to extend its responsibilities into this new field. This was the ecclesiastical parish, and what gave it the impulse to grow in importance and scope was the poor law legislation of the 16th century.

Most earlier legislation in this field had simply been directed to the problem of vagabonds and 'sturdy beggars'. Care of the sick and aged poor was a matter for the church, in particular the monasteries, with their endowments, their almoners, their hospitals and hospices, their herbalists and dispensers. Suddenly in the 1530s this whole structure was brought crashing down. With the dissolution of the monasteries the safety net which underlay the social order in England was removed. It was fortunate, if perhaps not wholly coincidental, that ideas about the relief of the poor were already beginning to change. In 1531 a new distinction was clearly drawn between the 'aged, poor and impotent persons' whom it was right and proper – and a Christian duty – to sustain with alms, and the able-bodied who were to be hounded to work. Any beggar not licensed by the Justices of the Peace as a deserving case was to be punished by flogging or the stocks, and vagrants were to be sent back to their place of birth – or at least to the place where they had last lived for a period of at least three years.

It was perhaps this insistence that the beggar be sent back to a place of origin that underlay a new concept introduced in 1536 – that the parish should be made legally responsible for the relief of its own poor, to be funded by a systematic collection of alms to be made by the churchwardens or persons specially appointed. As the monasteries closed all over the country in the next three years, this responsibility – and the institution of the alms collection – became of vital importance.

These principles survived the many changes in the detail of poor law legislation during the remainder of the 16th century. In 1552 the annual appointment of collectors of alms, and the keeping of registers of donors and of the impotent poor was made mandatory for every parish. In 1563 the obligation to contribute alms was made compulsory. In 1572 the office of 'Overseer of the Poor' was created and the Justices were to appoint four annually for every parish. In 1576 Courts of Quarter Sessions were authorised to build 'Houses of Correction' where both the needy poor and the able-bodied beggars could be set to work.

The system was codified in the Poor Relief Acts of 1598 and 1601. These introduced the element of a defined and assessed rate for the relief of the poor to be levied on the inhabitants of each parish instead of the collection of compulsory but undefined 'alms'.

So by 1601 the parish, and officials who derived no standing from the manor, were legally exercising powers, including the levying of a money rate, for a purpose that was not essentially the maintenance of the church buildings, its ministers, its rites and services. The government of the parish, which apart from the ecclesiastical hierarchy, had been a matter for church wardens and parish meetings, began itself to become an issue. If rates were to be assessed on the value of real estate then the principal householders of the parish were going to ensure that they had a major say – the development of vestries, as self-appointed and self-perpetuating executive councils, was an inevitable step. Sometimes these just grew; in Richmond a 'Select Vestry' was established by licence of the Bishop of Winchester in 1614.

The manor courts continued to exercise their jurisdiction, and on some issues we see the manor courts and the vestry working closely together: in particular in attempts to keep out 'strangers' who might become a burden on the parish. Encouraged by the Acts of Settlement of the second half of the 17th century, authorising the expulsion within forty days of any newcomer who was not occupying property of the annual value of £10, the manor court records contain frequent orders to inhabitants to get rid of lodgers unless they, the inhabitants, were prepared to indemnify the parish against any possible eventual claim for relief by the lodgers.

We have a case where the constable – a manor officer – presents to the Vestry 'certain strangers and inmates, which had crept into the Parish and were likely to be a charge to this Parish (if not timely removed)'. The vestry, therefore, ordered that the constable should see them all removed out of the said parish, unless they could find sufficient security to discharge the parish of them before the next meeting of the vestry, and the constable is hereby required to give an account to the Vestry then meeting.[5] In July 1654 Thomas Raymond was even required 'to remove his wife's mother out of the Parish within a fortnight'. In 1658 the fines levied in the Manor Court for feeding swine in Brewer's Lane and Church Lane were 6s. 8d.; those for 'entertaining strangers as inmates in his house' 20 shillings a month.[6]

The vestry, of course, also continued to manage the ecclesiastical business of the parish – necessary repairs to the church structure, the renting out of the lands which endowed the maintenance of the church, the allocation of pews, etc. The period of the Commonwealth gave the vestrymen a new taste of power. No longer was the appointment of the minister to look after the spiritual needs of Richmond parish and its church to be left as a matter for nomination by the vicar of Kingston. When the minister was turned out by the Commonwealth authorities (but successfully defied their attempts to sequestrate his house, by dying before the order could be enforced), it was the vestry who twice appointed new ministers – and who made the necessary arrangements for services when the benefice was vacant. Even after the restoration, when Richmond parish was again firmly under the control of the vicar of Kingston, the gentlemen of the Richmond vestry made clear to the vicar whom he should appoint as minister of Richmond. Then in 1651 the vestry levied a rate for paving – admittedly it was to pave Brewer's Lane and Church Court to improve access to the church, but here we have what may be a first taste of the exercise of a wider civil power.

For a hundred years after the establishment of Richmond's Select Vestry, it was run by the local gentry – there were very few members who did not at least rate a 'Mr' before or 'gent' after their name. There were 12 members, apart from the minister. And in this time, while becoming more powerful and influential, it still seems to have concerned itself mainly with matters either of church management or of poor law administration. Then, in the early 18th century, judging from the surviving records, the Select Vestry began to abdicate power to a general parish meeting. There is no obvious reason for this, but there are virtually no minutes of the vestry of any interest from 1715 onwards. Instead, from that time, the book of 'parish general meetings' begins to record matters other than the appointment of parish officers.

The first major achievement of the Parish Meeting was the establishment of a workhouse for Richmond in 1729. This was first set up in some cottages by the *Orange Tree* tavern, which belonged to Joseph Maston, one of the overseers of the poor in that year. This was a purely temporary arrangement while a search was made for larger premises. In May 1730 it was agreed to take a lease of the oldish mansion in the Petersham Road called 'Rump Hall'. Together with a smaller house adjacent, it was 'much out of repair yet of a size sufficient to contain all the poor requiring relief of the parish'.[7]

The objective was to move the poor into a place where they could be fed and sheltered and looked after by a nurse, and tended if necessary by a doctor, more conveniently and economically than by the provision of pensions and special allowances for medical care as had hitherto been the case. Rump Hall was duly taken and thoroughly repaired. The poor who were reliant on parish relief were moved into the new workhouse, a master and a matron were appointed; and it was agreed in May 1734 that the churchwardens and the overseers of the poor should take weekly turns as visitors, to check 'whether the Master, the Matron and the poor there are in order and in their proper stations, their meat and drink wholesome, their chambers kept clean'.[8]

The workhouse was considered to be a great success; it was agreed that 'No new Pensioner ought to be admitted to the Pension list nor rents paid ... to or for any person whatsoever within the said Parish ... whilst a Workhouse is subsisting within the same where every Person intitled to Relief and [who] shall apply for it ought to be admitted to be there maintained and employed if able'.[9]

A new body of trustees was set up to consider the government of the Workhouse and on 28 March 1737 a comprehensive set of orders for its administration was agreed. Contracts were to be placed for the supply of meat, beer, groceries, candles, etc, after bidding by competitive tender; there were to be three meals a day; the poor were to attend the parish church twice every Sunday and to have daily prayers 'read in the family'. Boys and girls were 'to be placed as convenient with sober families' for wages of 4d. a day plus small beer (or an extra penny wage) – the wages to be paid to the trustees. There were to be no out-pensioners except 'infectious and lunatick persons': and no rents were to be paid without the express approval of the trustees.[10] (As Rump Hall filled up it gradually became necessary, however, to resume the system of out-pensioners.)

Alongside the official provision of relief, private charity also continued to play its part in providing for the poor. Most reasonably wealthy persons made some bequests for the poor in their wills. Sometimes these were of short-term benefit only, but some more generously provided perpetual endowments for clothing, coal, food or annual cash gifts. Most generous of all were the grants to endow almshouses.

Richmond's first almshouses, for eight poor women, were founded in 1600 by Sir George Wright. They were built on the west side of the 'lower road to Petersham, a little to the south of Ferry Hill and were known – later at least – as Queen Elizabeth's. It is said that the Queen's arms were transferred to the new buildings in the Vineyard in 1767.[11]

*Plate 42*  These were followed in 1661 by the almshouses founded by Brian Duppa, Bishop of Winchester, a long-time Richmond resident. It is said that while living in Richmond in retirement during the Commonwealth, having been ejected from his former see of Salisbury, he had vowed to found almshouses if his former pupil, Charles Prince of Wales, was restored to the throne. With the restoration, Duppa was made Bishop of Winchester, but he retained his house in Richmond (on the site where the Old Town Hall now stands) as all his official residences had been damaged during the civil wars. Duppa was as good as his word and built his almshouses, for 10 poor women, at the top of the hill, just south of the lane leading to the Friar's Stile.

*Plate 42*  The first almshouses for men were those founded in the Vineyard by Humphrey Michel and his nephew John in 1695–97. These were for 10 old men. Michel's Almshouses, though rebuilt, are still on their original site. Queen Elizabeth's were moved to a new site in the Vineyard in 1767 and were followed there by Bishop Duppa's in 1852.

By the early 18th century therefore there were three almshouse foundations providing accommodation for 28 of Richmond's aged poor. In 1769 a fourth, again for women, was established by the sisters Rebecca and Susanna Houblon on land which they owned on the south side of the Marshgate Road. These almshouses, in three blocks round an enclosed garden, have never been completely rebuilt and are therefore the oldest ones now standing in Richmond.

These foundations were all run by bodies of trustees, independent of manor court, vestry or parish meeting – and indeed of each other. But inevitably the same names of 'the good and the great' (or in the case of the General Parish Meeting, not so great, even if equally good) occur in the records of any and all of these various bodies. Such coordination as might be required was supplied by individuals, who were also responsible from time to time for some useful pieces of cross-fertilisation.

It is apparent from the records that by 1730 the parish meeting was beginning to take an active interest in wider community matters. They resolved to build a new 'watch house', and then to build 'a convenient house adjoining to the new intended watch house to contain the two fire engines'.[12] Policing and fire control had been added to poor relief as a parish, not a manor, responsibility. In October 1739 the parish meeting took another important step along this path in establishing for the first time a regular paid watch. They noted that: 'For several years past the Watch of this Parish was only irregularly summoned. Its maintenance and support were unequally levied.' (Some people paid a shilling, some sixpence, some nothing.) 'Many inconveniences may happen by Fire and Irregularities committed by loose and disorderly Persons in the Night during the Winter Season without any possibility of being discovered till the like fatal Calamities are past recovery.' It noted, too, that 'some of the inhabitants think they are neither obliged to watch nor to pay their quotas'.

*Plate 43*

The meeting therefore adopted a proposal that a watch, consisting of a beadle, the constable or headborough, and three 'fit and able' watchmen, should keep watch from 11 p.m. to 5 a.m. each night from 1 November to the end of February. The watchmen might be chosen from among the casual poor on the parish list – men with families 'and in need of relief during the said four months when work is commonly scarce'. The beadle was to have an allowance of 10d. a night, the watchmen 6d. each 'and extra for fire and candles'. The total cost would be £1 6s. 10d. per week – to be paid at the workhouse.[13]

It is not quite clear from this whether the constable and/or headborough, one of whom was to be present each night, were to receive an allowance for watching. These were manorial officers, and traditionally unpaid. What is particularly interesting is that a duty was being laid upon them here, not by the manor court but by a General

Parish Meeting, and that in the performance of that duty they were apparently to be under the control of the Beadle, a paid parish officer.

*Plate 43*

The beadle was by origin a person appointed by the parish to keep order in church during services – to prevent gaming, keep out animals, stop the children from playing or fighting, perhaps even to awake the heavy snorers. From this beginning, other tasks of a generally supervisory order were put upon him – the responsibility for the watch, the task of looking after the fire engines. He was given regular wages and was later to have an official uniform and wand of office. And in Richmond in 1755 he was even provided with official accommodation: 'The enginehouse and watchhouse to be raised with one storey over, the same consisting of two rooms for the conveniency of the Beadle of the Parish and also for the better conveniency of his looking after the fire engines'.[14] (In 1745 the General Meeting had considered a report on the fire engines: the small one was fairly good; the large one very bad – a new engine was purchased at a cost of £30.)[15]

Evidently the General Parish Meeting, run by the minister and the churchwardens, was rapidly becoming more and more important, while the select vestry had virtually ceased to function. The last recorded entry in the vestry minute book is a bare note that a meeting was held on 3 December 1749. But on 3 April 1749 what had hitherto been 'the parish general meeting' met for the first time under a new title of 'General Vestry'.

✠

This development, if democratically desirable, had considerable drawbacks. The 'General Vestry' had no defined powers. It was soon discovered to be a cumbersome and inefficient instrument for local government. In 1766, when King George III negotiated the first of his series of deals with the inhabitants of Richmond, the opportunity was taken to improve the local government structure. This was a matter in which the King, as lord of the manor, took a strong personal interest.

The primary purpose of this deal was to close the old public road from the Brentford-Kew Ferry which ran right across the royal estates, within two hundred yards of the King's house at Richmond Lodge. The road had become of less importance since the opening of the first Kew Bridge in 1759. The King proposed, in return, to improve at his own expense both the towpath and the 'horse road to Kew' all the way from Kew Bridge to the *Bear* inn at the outskirts of Richmond and to maintain this road in perpetuity. This was agreed and incorporated in an Act of Parliament in 1766.[16] By the same Act a new body of a 'Board of Trustees' was established to take over all local government functions from the general vestry – which would confine itself to church affairs. The trustees, 31 in number, were originally nominated, but were then to be elected on a rotational system of five each year. They were to have powers to levy not just a poor rate but also a highways rate (to pay for paving, cleaning and lighting of the streets and for the establishment of a proper night watch).

✟

The new trustees set about their tasks with a will. Their first concern was to confirm the orders for the conduct of the workhouse and the relief of the poor. By 1766 there were 72 inmates in the workhouse and 35 poor people being aided by pensions outside. Their next priority was to ask the King for a grant of land on the Common to build a new workhouse, and at the same time to protest about the way in which the Hill Common was being despoiled by the tilemakers' unrestrained digging of clay and to suggest that it might be granted for use as pasture only. All this was put into a petition to the King. His reply, delivered through James Sayer, deputy steward of the manor (but also one of the trustees), was very forthcoming. The King agreed to put an immediate stop to the illegal digging of clay. As for grants of common land, the steward would be instructed to make grants on the usual basis, provided that there should be no building on the Hill Common and provided that the business was pursued through the manor courts and shown to be agreeable to the inhabitants generally. The trustees failed to follow up on this. The main reason appears to be that they just couldn't figure out how they were going to finance the building of a workhouse if they were given the land on which to build it. In the meantime they soldiered on with Rump Hall – and turned their attention to other business.

They commissioned a report on what needed to be done to tidy up the streets, and followed this up quite promptly by letting a contract (at £17 a year) for street cleaning. They set about repairing the road up the Hill from Ormond Row right up to the park gate (and authorised the occupants of the houses from what are now Downe House to Doughty House to lay at their own expense a pavement of Purbeck stone slabs). In 1769 they settled the names of some streets: the High Street to be henceforth George Street, Duke's Lane to be Duke Street, Church Lane to be Church Court, Magpye Alley to be Brewer's Lane, Furbelow Street to be King Street.

The security of the town was another early major preoccupation. In August 1768 the Trustees chose John Gibson and John Stedwell as 'Two Able Men to Patrole and Clear the Streets and other Places of this Parish from all idle and disorderly Persons, Beggars, Vagrants, etc, and to watch from Michaelmas untill Lady Day from Ten o'Clock in the Evening till seven in the Morning – And from Lady Day to Michaelmas from Eleven of the Clock in the Evening till five in the Morning to Proclaim both the Hour of the Night and also the Weather'. They were also to act as messengers for the trustees. They would be paid £20 a year and were to have an official uniform: 'a Brown Surtout Coat the Cape and Cuffs to be faced with Scarlet trimmed with Gold Lace' (to be made by Mr Barnsley, tailor) and 'a Gold Laced Hat' (to be furnished by Mr Guildharr, hatter). Mr Joseph Pybus, who was the Manor Bailiff, and who had been temporarily employed as 'messenger' by the trustees, was to be discharged and given one guinea for his trouble.[17]

A couple of weeks later, detailed instructions were issued to the 'messengers'. These stressed that any 'Idle and disorderly Persons, Rogues, Vagabonds and Beggars' were to be driven out of the parish 'or if you shall perceive any suspicious or incorrigible you are then to carry them before some Justice of the Peace to be dealt with according to law'. It was pointed out that the legal basis for these actions was the Vagrants Act of 17 George II – and recited the definitions of 'idle and disorderly', 'rogues and vagabonds' and 'incorrigible' contained therein. It was made clear that the two 'messengers' were to take turns at night duty – and that other tasks were to examine and report on all 'Annoyances Obstructions or Incroachments' in the streets – and to keep them clear of swine.[18]

This enlarged role for the beadles – for that was what the 'messengers' were and were very soon openly called – was a clear encroachment into what had been the sphere of the manorial constable, but it seems to have passed without comment by the manor court.

In June 1771 the trustees resolved that the streets should be lit at night from 1 September to 1 April and by the following January they had installed 100 lamps at a total cost including posts, brackets, etc, of £71 18s. 9d. For lighting the lamps and full servicing, including the cost of oil, they agreed to pay 100 guineas for the full seven-month period: Details of the location of the 100 lamps[19] were recorded and are shown on Plate 39. They ordered 100 more lamps for the next winter – and determined to supply their own oil from a store to be set up in the workhouse.

The trustees also decided in 1771 that 'because of frequent burglaries and robberies' their one-man patrol at night was insufficient and that they should set up a proper night watch of six men with regular beats. The beadle was to ring a bell for five minutes before 10 o'clock each evening, by which time the watch should muster by the church belfry. The initial beats were specified (see Plate 39), but the clerk to the trustees was authorised to change them from time to time. There would be two setting out from the belfry, two setting out from the watchhouse, and two to set out from a new small watchhouse to be set up at Ferry Hill. Each watchman would be paid 10 shillings a week.[20]

A bit later in the same year the trustees opposed the building of a new bridge at Ferry Hill – which would be 'very prejudicial to the inhabitants because it was in the wrong place' – but to no avail. In 1773 they bought a new fire engine for £40 to replace the small one, by then over 50 years old. In 1774 they did much work on paving the streets. By 1777 obelisks had been built at each end of George Street with public water pumps installed. They then fitted screw nozzles to be compatible with the hoses on the fire engines, so that these pumps could be used in case of fire. In 1774 the King made another deal with the inhabitants, closing Sheen Lane, the old road to the Charterhouse site which was now entirely back in the King's hands, in return for improvements to the road and towing path by the river. But this deal had no local government spin-off.

In the late 1770s there was a lot of fuss about collection of the rates, and one inhabitant brought a case against the overseers at the Quarter Sessions. It was agreed that some assessments were wrong. An examination in 1780 of the rate books for 1778 showed that over 10 per cent of the rates due had remained uncollected. In the same year the trustees were again concerned about the condition of the old workhouse. James Sayer, now steward of the manor, suggested to them that they might consider using the old pesthouse on the Common, which for some years had had no use other than housing the manor bailiff. He was sure that the Queen (to whom the manor had been formally granted by George III in 1770) would agree a grant.[21] The trustees set up a committee to consider this proposition. The result was a determination by the trustees in February 1781 that the Act of 1766 'is defective and that several additional powers are necessary to carry into effectual execution the several powers with which the Trustees are invested by the provisions of the Act'.[22]

Another committee submitted a detailed report in June 1781: it agreed that a new workhouse was indeed needed – the present one was incapable of holding the numbers necessary. It was leasehold and determinable in 10 years. But extra powers were needed if the trustees were to be able to build a new workhouse. New clauses would have to be clearly and carefully drafted.[23]

Although the trustees did this time obtain the approval of the manor court (on 12 August 1780) for a proposed grant of 16 acres, 2 roods and 30 perches of land on Pesthouse Common, and Mr Sayer on the same occasion confirmed the Queen's willingness to grant the land, it took them until February 1785 to come up with the draft of a new bill which would give them the powers they deemed necessary. They forwarded it to the House of Commons with an explanatory petition emphasising the need both for a new workhouse and for a new cemetery, as the churchyard was rapidly becoming full. There was nothing in the petition or the bill about the grant of land that the Trustees hoped to receive – this was a matter, as they thought, for the King and Queen and not for Parliament.

At this point Mr Sayer appears to have intervened again. There is no record of what he said or to whom, but it seems fairly clear that he – or the King – felt that such a substantial grant of land from the royal demesne should perhaps have parliamentary sanction. Though the grant of lands in a royal manor was hardly the 'alienation of Crown lands' forbidden by the Civil List Act of 1702, this was a rather larger affair than the odd acre here or there. Moreover, there was another point. Nothing had been said up to now about any *quid pro quo* for the grant of common, but the King, who had in 1772 inherited his mother's lease of the grounds at Kew which lay alongside the northern part of his Richmond estate, would dearly like to close the narrow lane –

called 'Love Lane' – the top end of the 'foot lane' from Richmond Green to Kew – which divided the two estates. The King would be happy to provide a new public path to the Kew Road from the point of closure. The closure of a public right of way required parliamentary sanction. Why not put all this into the bill?

The trustees seem to have adopted the idea with alacrity, pausing only to obtain the consent of the Kew vestry, as part of Love Lane lay within Kew. By April a new petition in the name of 'the landowners in the Manor of Richmond and the inhabitants of the Parishes of Richmond and Kew' was submitted to the House of Commons. This referred to the bill seeking the powers already before the House, and then to the understanding that their Majesties would grant land from the Commons for a workhouse and to everyone's desire to close the 'extremely dangerous ... real nuisance' of Love Lane, and asked that these points be added to the bill.[24]

The bill was duly passed into law and received the Royal Assent on 13 June 1785. It replaced the board of trustees by a new, enlarged and elected vestry with extended powers. The vestry, like the board of trustees, was to have 31 members. New members would be elected whenever a place became vacant through death or resignation. The bill empowered the King and Queen to grant to the vestry land on the commons and it empowered the Vestry to enclose the land required for a new workhouse and a new burial ground. It forbade any building on Hill Common. It provided that the poor of Kew should be admitted to the Richmond workhouse. And it authorised the closure of Love Lane.[25]

On 18 October 1786 the King and Queen Charlotte formally granted to the new Richmond vestry the whole of what remained of Hill Common and a large part of Pesthouse Common (more than twice the area that had been mentioned in the Manor Court). The grant specified that the land on Pesthouse Common not actually used for workhouse or burial ground should be held in trust for the 'employment and support' of the poor of the parish of Richmond. And so the vestry became the original trustees of what is now called 'the Richmond Parish Lands Charity'.*

Though progress with the workhouse, etc, had to await the royal grant, the Act of 1785 was all that was needed to establish the new Vestry. Present at its first meeting on 4 July 1785 were the minister and the two churchwardens, *ex officio*, one 'Honourable', 11 'Esquires', one other 'Reverend' and three 'Gentlemen'.[26] An elected body it might be – but the people of Richmond were still to be represented by their gentry. This body as then established was to remain the local government of Richmond until 1890.

☩

Reference has been made above to the Kew Vestry and the Parish of Kew. The chapel of St Anne on Kew Green since its consecration in 1714 had the status of a

---

* For a detailed history of this charity, and its lands, see J. Cloake, *Royal Bounty: The Richmond Parish Lands Charity 1786–1991*, published by the Trustees of the Richmond Parish Lands Charity, 1992.

*Plate 40*

*The Manor Survey of 1771. The register of property was accompanied by a set of large-scale plans – detailed and accurately surveyed. From these a number of single-sheet maps were drawn, to several different scales. This is one of them. (PRO MR699)*

Plate 41

(136)

Manor of
Richmond
als
Westsheene &
Petersham & Ham
in the County of
x x Surry x x

**A ffirst Court Leetor View** of ffranc pleg held
for the said Manors at the Palace of our Lord the King called
Richmond Place Scituate within the Manor of Richmond afores: the
Fifteenth Day of the Month of Aprill in the fifth Year of the Reign of
Charles by the grace of God of Great Britain France and Ireland
King Defender of the ffaith and so forth 1629 by Robert Lewis Esq
Deputy Steward of s: Manors by vertue of severall Letters Patents under
the great Seal bearing date at Westm:           Days of the Month       in the
fourth Year of our s: Kings Reign By which s: Letters Patents our s: King
hath created Ordained and Constituted A Court or View of ffranc pleg for s:
Manors to be held for ever w:thin his Manor of Richmond &c. twice in a
Year Annually According to the Law in that case provided

Essoins

Robert Dye & Richard Manley Kn:ts because they are in the Kings Service
Martin Bassill Essoined by           his Servant

| Sworn for our Lord the King | | | Sworn for our Lord the King |
|---|---|---|---|
| Dixey Hickman Esq | W:m Clifton | | |
| Nich: Bird gen | Henry Collins | | |
| Rob: Trotter | Rich: Cavard | | |
| Tho: Acton | Edw: Chapman | | |
| Rob: Deane | Henry Perkins | | |
| Rich: Lovell | James Scott | | |
| Jn: Gregory | Henry Lane | | |
| Tho: Jenkins | Roger Rawling | | |
| Rob: Heather | | | |

WHO being Sworn & Charged in & upon certain Articles of this Court ON their
Oath say That William Slingsby Kn: W:m Seager Kn: and 84 Others are Inhabitants
& Residents within the Jurisdiction of this View of ffranc Pleg & this Day have made
Default of their Custom Therefore Amerce each of them . . 2:

**Richmond**
Constable — And in the Office of Constable of Richmond have chose Tho: Brooker who is
Sworn into that Office

Tythingman — And in the Office of Tythingmen there have chose Nich: Ansell & Richard
Davyes who are Sworn &c

Aleconner — And in the Office of Aleconner ~ ~ ~ have chosen Tho: Nelam & Will:m
Rutter Junior who are Sworn &c

**Kew**
Constable — And in the Office of Constable of Kew have chose Rich: Jorden who is Sworn &c

Tythingman — And in the Office of Tythingman there have chosen William Hill who is Sworn &c

Aleconner — And in the Office of Aleconner ~ ~ ~ have chose John Adkins who is Sworn &c

**Petersham**
Constable — And in the Office of Constable of Petersham have chose James Scott who is
Sworn &c

Tythingman — And in the Office of Tythingman there have chose Jn: Tanner who is Sworn &c

Aleconner — And in the Office of Aleconner ~ ~ ~ have chose Robert Heather who is Sworn &c

*Record of the first Court Leet held at Richmond Palace on 15 April 1629 (PRO: LR3/71 p.136).*

*Plate 42*

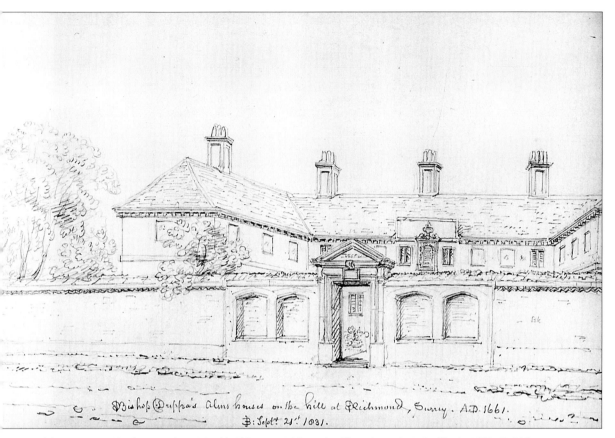

*Bishop Duppa's Almshouses – the original buildings on Richmond Hill, as drawn by J. Buckler in 1831. (British Library, Add MS 36388, f. 271)*

*Michel's Almshouses as originally built (from a drawing by John Pullen made in 1716). (Richmond Public Library, local studies collection)*

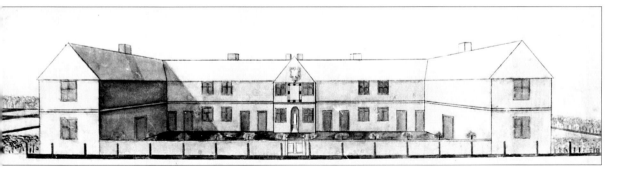

*Plate 43*

*The Richmond Watchhouse in 1754, with the pound and stocks at the left. The building behind it, with a hanging sign, may be the* Bear *inn.*

*This photograph shows the three Beadles of the constituent parishes of the Borough of Richmond: Petersham (on the left), Richmond (centre) and Kew (right), all in their traditional uniforms with their staves of office. (From the* Richmond Herald *Christmas supplement 1913.)*

*(Both from Richmond Public Library, local studies collection)*

The late Mr. W. Bennett.    The late Mr. H. Head.    Mr. George Viner (Kew).

chapel of ease within the parish and vicarage of Kingston. But it had its own vestry, collected its own poor rate, and kept its own registers. Then in 1769 a rather remarkable decision was taken – to create a new separate vicarage by merging Kew with Petersham, while leaving Richmond as part of the vicarage of Kingston. The only conceivable justification for this move might be that Mr David Bellamy was at the time curate of both churches at Petersham and at Kew; but as the formal appointment of a new vicar was not to be made until he died (in 1788), this does not seem very logical. However, Kew became a separate parish church. (The parishes of Kew and Petersham remained united in a single vicarage until separated by an Act of 1850, which did not become fully effective until 1891. The vicarage of Richmond was finally separated from that of Kingston in 1849.)

The Richmond vestry were annoyed by the stipulation in the 1785 Act that the poor of Kew were to be admitted into their new workhouse. But when they then found that – after all that worry about how to finance the building – King George III proposed to pay for the erection of the workhouse out of his own pocket there was not much they could do about it. It was agreed with the Kew vestrymen in March 1788 that the parish of Kew should pay Richmond 3s. 6d. a week per head for the upkeep of any Kew parishioners in the workhouse and that Kew should be directly responsible for their 'clothes, physic and burials'. Another problem was settled two years later when Kew agreed to indemnify Richmond for all charges 'on account of the birth of an illegitimate child in the workhouse of this [Richmond] parish on the body of any woman sent from the said parish of Kew'.[27]

The new workhouse, designed by Kenton Couse, was formally handed over to the Richmond vestry in April 1787; and in May they agreed that the adjacent old 'pesthouse' should be demolished. In its place was to go a new infirmary and accommodation for lunatics – this addition to the original, plan being paid for by the Vestry, not the King. The first removals of poor from Rump Hall to the new workhouse took place in October 1787; and by April 1788 the former was sub-let for the remainder of the lease term, an interesting point being that the tenant, one Richard Howat, was 'to indemnify the parish against any charges on account of settlements to employees in the manufacture of calico printing'[28] – an indication that this business was still being conducted in Richmond despite the reintegration of its original site into the royal estates.

I have written elsewhere in some detail about the Vestry's management of the workhouse prior to 1834* when the new Poor Law Amendment Act removed the responsibility for workhouses from individual parishes and gave it to new Boards of Guardians set up for 'Unions' of parishes. The Richmond Union, which took over in 1836, was to cover Richmond, Kew, Petersham, Mortlake and Barnes. In some areas the new dispensation was no doubt an improvement; in Richmond it was a severe set-

* John Cloake, *Royal Bounty, op cit.*

*The Richmond workhouse, an engraving of 1899 (from
Smoers Gascoyne's* Recollections of Richmond).

back. The commissioners who had drawn up a report on all Poor Law authorities in England before the new arrangements were decided upon had singled out Richmond as a fine example to others and had actually suggested that the new legislation should be based on the appropriate portions of the 1785 Richmond Act. The Richmond vestry protested most strongly about the new arrangements, but to no avail.

The vestry had other tasks and concerns beyond the administration of the workhouse and the 'parish lands' (some of which were used as a farm for the workhouse and the rest leased out as pasture). One of the very first was the building of a new watchhouse, for which a contract was placed in October 1785.[29] Another was the state of the fire engines; and here it is of interest that in September 1789 the trustees agreed that the bill for their maintenance and repair was a proper charge on the poor rate.[30]

The urgent requirement for a new burial ground was met without the need to use any of the new lands on the former Pesthouse Common. In March and April 1790 it was agreed that a 'half acre' of land belonging to the church estate, which lay between Paradise Row and the Vineyard and was therefore conveniently close to the parish church and the existing churchyard, should be extended by purchasing another, adjacent 'half acre', which had some small buildings on it, and that these together might form the new burial ground. £350 was to be paid to Mr Edward Collins, the brewer, the owner of this extra parcel of land – of which the trustees of the church estate would contribute £240.[31] This plan also suggested the solution to another problem. The vestry had been meeting in a room in Church Walk which they had rented from Clement Smith, their clerk (and former clerk to the parish trustees) who had recently died (early in 1787). They wanted to have some proper permanent accommodation, so they decided in June 1790 that 'the spot on which houses now

*The Vestry Hall in the 1880s (from Somers Gascoyne:*
Recollections of Richmond).

stand on the ground purchased for the new burial ground would be suitable'. Mr
Faulkener, surveyor, produced the design.[32] By Lady Day 1790 the Vestry were
established in their new premises;[33] and on 22 December 1791 the Bishop of London
(on behalf of the Bishop of Winchester) consecrated the new 'Vineyard burial ground'.[34]      *Plate 44*
It was more than 50 years before the need arose, in the late 1840s, to reconsider the
establishment of a cemetery on the parish lands.

Other main concerns of the vestry at this time were the watch, street lighting and
the state of the roads. In December 1793 major changes were made in the beats to be
patrolled by the night watch, which were now to be 10 in number, each beginning
at a separate point, but grouped in five pairs (out and back by different routes).[35] In
September 1803 it was decided that the watch should consist of two sergeants, 14
watchmen (seven per night, on alternate duty) and four supernumeraries.[36] Then on
13 January 1840 responsibility for policing the town was assumed by the newly-formed
Metropolitan Police.[37]

☩

The vestry was not primarily concerned with public morals, but it was occasionally
faced with matters that at least touched on this aspect of life in the town. In July 1799
Mr Frederick Barnard (whose house faced the bridge at the corner of Ormond Row)
asked the Vestry to ban men and boys from bathing (naked, of course, in those days)
near the bridge. He was told that the vestry had no powers to issue such a ban. But
when he returned to the charge a year later, with the backing of Sir George Baker and
Sir John Day, the vestry agreed at least to put up a notice reading 'For the better
Preservation of Decency and Good Manners in the Public Walk ... recommend to all
persons desirous of bathing not to bathe after 9 a.m.'.[38] It was not until July 1818 that
this was superseded by another notice forbidding bathing between 7 a.m. and 10 p.m.

328 / COTTAGES AND COMMON FIELDS OF RICHMOND AND KEW

in the river anywhere from the Petersham boundary to 'beyond the towpath gate adjoining His Majesty's farm'.[39]

Nor could the vestrymen ban undesirable social events. But they did unanimously in September 1799 declare their 'disapprobation of having any public masquerade in Richmond' and agreed that this should be conveyed to Mr Nevill, manager of the Richmond Theatre, whose advertisement for such a masquerade had precipitated the matter.[40] Undesirable sports could, however, be prosecuted with the full weight of the law. In February 1814 the beadle was instructed to 'give notice by bell' that all persons kicking football in the streets on Shrove Tuesday will be prosecuted;[41] and a month later two special constables were appointed to prevent improper sports on the Green or in the streets during the Sabbath.[42] The Shrove Tuesday town football tradition died hard. It was noted in 1840, after the Metropolitan Police had taken over responsibility, that extra police had to be sent to Richmond on Shrove Tuesday to stop the football in the streets.[43]

Street lighting, after the major installation made by the trustees in the 1770s, remained at much the same level – of some 200 lamps. In September 1803, for example, a contract was agreed with John Deane for lighting 202 lamps (each to have two burners) for six months from 29 September to 25 March, from sunset to first light, at a cost of 18s. 1½d. per lamp.[44] Then in September 1825 the momentous decision was taken to light the town with gas.[45] In July 1827 a seven-year contract was agreed with the Brentford Gas Company to supply pipes and 65 lanterns with posts to be lit from sunset to daybreak for nine months a year at a cost of £4 a lamp. The streets to be lit were described as 'from Kew Lodge to the Star and Garter' and 'from the Black Horse to the Duchess of Buccleuch's and Mrs Palmer's'.[46] Oil lights were still to be provided elsewhere, and until the gas lamps were installed. Extra gas lamps were put up in Ormond Road and Red Lion Street in 1828 and along the Kew Road in 1829.[47] Although there were initial complaints about the quality of the light, the Brentford Company continued to supply the gas lighting until 1849, by which time the new Richmond Gas Company had been established (in 1846), had set up its works in the Lower Mortlake Road by Manor Road, and was ready to take over supplying the town.

Keeping the roads in repair was no great problem as long as the vestry had control over the workhouse. The able-bodied poor were a good source of labour for necessary jobs. They were used in 1789 to repair the drain in Magpie Alley.[48] Their use as watchmen has been mentioned above. In 1796–97 some of them were first invited to volunteer, then enrolled by ballot, in the County Supplementary Militia (with a bounty of 4 (later 5) guineas for the volunteers and of 2½ guineas for the conscripts).[49] They were certainly used on occasion to pave and repair the roads. By 1805 King Street and Duke Street had been paved, and the paving of George Street was just being started, but these jobs seem to have been done by contract.[50] However, in May 1824 the road over Pesthouse Common from the *Star and Garter* down to Marshgate which 'from its badness is impassible in winter months' was ordered to be repaired throughout its length under the supervision of the Workhouse Master.[51] (A report in 1821 had pointed out that in such work 'many hands are employed which would otherwise be idling their time and a continued burthen to the Parish'.)[52]

A frequent preoccupation was the state of Hill Common and The Terrace, and as early as 1792 the fencing of the sides, filling of holes, etc, was considered to be a suitable job for the 'workhouse people'.[53] The decision taken in 1797 to let out the Common in two closes for pasture, followed by the agreement with Mr Brent of Nightingale Cottage in 1810, allowing him to divert the road round the land he was leasing (thus creating the present alignment of Nightingale Lane) took care of the ground itself and its hedges and fences throughout nearly all the rest of the century, but the condition of The Terrace Walk itself and the trees there continued to cause anxiety. The alignment of the trees on The Terrace has changed over the years. In the 1840s and '50s the largest and oldest were 'between the Terrace Walk and the road', rooted where the narrow pavement by the roadway is today. The vestry in January 1844 asserted to the Commissioners of Woods their belief that their grant of Hill Common included everything up to the highway itself, including the land on which these trees stood. Two of the trees opposite the *Roebuck* stables were decayed and in a dangerous state, and the vestry intended to take them down.[54] They were allowed to get away with this, and in 1849 they determined to lop and top all the trees on the Hill Terrace.[55] In 1850 the hedge between the Field and the Terrace was repaired.[56] In 1860 general improvements to the Terrace Walk were agreed.[57] A resolution adopted in April 1859 seems only too applicable today: 'The attention of the Duke of Buccleuch and the Marquess of Lansdowne is to be called to the obstruction to the landscape scenery from the Terrace, Richmond Hill, caused by the height and overgrowth of the trees on their properties – and that they be requested to take steps for the abatement of the same'.[58] Today it is the vestry's successors themselves who are responsible for such overgrowth destroying the views, especially that of the river from the top of Petersham Common, but to some extent those from The Terrace also.

A part of the initial problem with the Hill Common was identified by the vestry's committee in 1792: 'drains from houses on the hill onto the common are a great nuisance,' and it was recommended that a new main drain be made 'to be carried to the common sewer which discharges into the river'.[59] 'Common sewer' at that time still tended to have its old meaning of an open stream, used as water supply (though not usually for drinking), irrigation, drainage and sewerage at the whim of the adjacent landowners. But the fouling of such streams by overflowing 'sinks', or by the erection over them of 'houses of office' (i.e. privies), was a practice which the vestry and the manor court united in banning or attempting to ban.

Drinking water still came partly from the springs on the slopes of the Hill, partly from wells and partly from the wooden pipes conveying the river water pumped out by the 'waterworks' in the Petersham Road. The river, though not yet filthy, was hardly clean. The waterworks had been privately owned since they were set up by Peter Walley in the 1680s. In 1835, in an attempt to improve the quality of the supply, *Plate 44* a new company was formed. It installed a new pumping engine and water tower, but the water supplied was still untreated and unfiltered river water.

The vestry faced a problem. They were becoming acutely aware of the need for a much improved system of drainage and sewerage throughout the town, but they were firmly instructed by their legal adviser that they had no powers under the 1785 Act which would allow them to use the highway rate (let alone the poor rate) to construct sewers.[60] Once again, in 1826, they resolved to seek new powers by amendment of the parliamentary act under which they functioned. There was much discussion and debate about this but nothing had been settled when the problem appeared to be resolved by the establishment of the Metropolitan Commissioners of Sewers and the inclusion of Richmond within their district. The Board's Surveyor recommended in 1849 the construction of several main sewers and subsidiary house drainage. (The map provided with his report [see page 354] is a valuable link between the manor survey map of 1771 and the first Ordnance Survey large-scale plans of the 1860s.) The cost was ultimately to be borne by the parish, but the Commissioners started work as soon as the vestry had approved the plan – only to run out of funds before the scheme was completed.[61]

At this time the condition of the water being taken from the river began to deteriorate badly. An artesian well sunk by the water company in 1859 was not a success and in 1860, under pressure from a committee of residents, approaches were made by the Richmond company to the bigger companies who supplied London. This led to the take-over of the Richmond company by the Southwark and Vauxhall Company, followed by constant friction between the inhabitants and the company and eventually leading to the establishment by the vestry of a new Richmond water company drawing its supplies from artesian wells. But this story, like that of the completion of the sewers, runs well beyond the temporal limits of this book.

So there we will leave the history of Richmond's local government. There is one aspect of the vestry's stewardship still to be considered – the development of the parish lands – but that will more appropriately be included in the next chapter. And by the 1850s the manor courts and officials had ceased to play any meaningful part, beyond being a court of record for the conveyance of copyhold property – until the system of copyhold tenure was abolished in 1922. But it would be interesting to know exactly what functions were performed in the 1920s by the two headboroughs and one constable appointed for Richmond, the constable/headborough for Kew, the aleconner for the manor as a whole, and the herdsmen for Richmond and for Kew, appointed by the Court Leet. The Court Leet was presided by the Deputy Steward and its homage was by then one foreman and one other; the Court Baron consisted of the Deputy Steward and one single juror!

# 21

# *Schools in Richmond up to 1825*

## *Sixteenth Century*

It is probable that the first schools established in Richmond were associated with the Charterhouse and the Palace.

By the early 16th century a number of Charterhouses had set up schools in which the instruction was not that given by a monk or lay brother to a monastic novice but rather teaching by learned laymen (or at least non-monastic clerics) to lay pupils. Although it is not stated anywhere that there was such a school at the Shene Charterhouse, we know that Reginald Pole, the future cardinal, was sent to Shene to study at the age of seven and that he remained there for five years before going on to university.[1] If there was indeed a school at Shene, as this might suggest, it would have been closed down when the monastery was dissolved in 1538.

There is clear evidence for the existence of a school for the choristers of the Chapel Royal at Richmond. In 1581 Henry Harvey was 'presented' (i.e. indicted) at the manor court on many counts. Among his alleged misdeeds was that he had built a barn and a shed 'on royal ground, formerly part of the garden belonging to the school for the choristers of the Chapel'.[2] As most of the charges concerned the grounds of the former Friary, adjacent to which was Harvey's house, it is probable that the school had used the Friary buildings next to the Palace.

## *The Grammar School and Richmond Academy*

The Rev William Radford (*c.*1620-1673) had officiated at some marriages in Richmond parish church in the last years of the Commonwealth, but does not appear to have been officially appointed as minister. In 1660 a new minister was appointed. Radford was then granted, by the Surrey Commissary Court on 26 September 1662, a licence for the teaching of boys.[3] By 1664[4] he was living in an old house on the site of Nos. 8-9 The Green (which he purchased in February 1664/5),[5] and which was presumably the location of his school. It was assessed for 10 hearths. He died in October 1673 and was buried in Richmond as 'William Radford, schoolmaster' on 20 October. The records of Winchester College, to which he had been admitted in 1634 aged 14, state that he was 'Master of Richmond Grammar School'. This appellation seems to have lasted for at least fifty years – and perhaps until 1764.

Radford's widow was still living in the house in 1679[6] (she died in 1681), and it was owned by his son Vertue Radford, an attorney, until 1692, but there is no other record of occupancy during that period. It seems probable, however, in the light of what follows, that the school continued in being.

In 1692, when Vertue Radford sold the house, its occupant was Christopher Johnson, clerk.[7] In 1694 and again in 1699 Christopher Johnson is mentioned as a former curate of Richmond and now 'schoolmaster of Richmond' in documents concerning a case which he had brought in the ecclesiastical courts against the minister, Abiel Borfett.[8] He had acquired a doctorate of Divinity by 1701. Two whole pews in the parish church were allotted to Dr Johnson 'for young gentlemen of his school' in January 1701/2.[9] Johnson was still occupying 8-9 The Green in 1705,[10] and was buried in Richmond on 6 January 1710/1. He thus appears to have been a successor (possibly the direct successor) of Radford as Master of the Grammar School.

Dr Nicholas Brady, who had become minister of the parish church in succession to Borfett in 1696,[11] then took over both the house and the school. (There was no appointed residence for the minister at that time.) His benign rule at the school is praised in a letter from a pupil to *The Spectator*, dated 5 September 1711:[12]

> Mr Spectator,
>
> I am a boy of fourteen years of age, and have for this last year been under the tuition of a doctor of divinity, who has taken the school of this place under his care. From the gentleman's great tenderness to me and friendship to my father, I am very happy learning my book with pleasure. We never leave off our diversions any further than to salute him at hours of play when he pleases to look on. It is impossible for any of us to love our own parents better than we do him. He never gives any of us a harsh word, and we think it is the greatest punishment in the world when he will not speak to any of us. My brother and I are both together inditing this letter. He is a year older than I am, but is now ready to break his heart that the doctor has not taken any notice of him these three days. If you please print this he will see it, and, we hope, taking it for my brother's earnest desire to be restored to his favour, he will again smile upon him.
>
> Your most obedient servant,
> T. S.

Dr Brady was a well-known character. He had become famed as a preacher at St Michael's Wood Street and at St Katharine Cree in London, where he had been before coming to Richmond. He was chaplain to William III and Mary and then to Queen Anne, as well as to the Duke of Ormonde's Regiment of Horse. His doctorate was bestowed by Dublin University in 1699. He collaborated with Nahum Tate in producing the metrical version of the Psalms, and many of his sermons and other writings were published.[13]

In 1718 Dr Brady, while remaining minister of the parish church, was succeeded as master of the school by Daniel Mackenzie.[14] In his reply to the questionnaire of a Bishop's Visitation in 1725, Dr Brady mentioned 'a grammar school under Mr Mckensie, licensed by the then bishop of the diocese'.[15] Daniel Mackenzie appears as ratepayer at 8-9 The Green from 1726 (the earliest surviving rate book) until 1732 and as 'schoolmaster' is named in the manor rolls in 1742[16] as a former occupant of the premises.

In 1733 Richard Comber replaced Mackenzie in the ratebooks. He is named as 'schoolmaster' as occupant of the premises in the 1740s in the manor records,[17] and as 'writing master' in the parish registers when his son James was baptised in January 1735/6. About 1744 the house was divided into two (it was probably rebuilt at that point as two houses) and Comber remained in possession of No. 9.[18] He continued to pay the rates until 1754; but was buried on 29 January 1755. Mrs Comber is shown as ratepayer in 1755, then James Comber in 1756 and '57. James died in December 1757 and the ratepayer for 1758 was a Mr D'Ind. Stephen D'Ind, schoolmaster of Richmond, aged 23, married Ann Comber aged 21 (presumably Richard's daughter and James's sister) by licence in April 1758[19] and had a son baptised in Richmond in June 1759. But he then disappears from the Richmond records – and the ratepayer for 9 The Green in 1759 was 'Mr Delafosse'. Presumably he had taken over the school.

The Rev. Charles Delafosse continued as ratepayer at 9 The Green until 1764, but in that year his name also appears in the ratebooks for the first time at the large house that stood between the Kew Road and Little Green on the north-east side of Duke Street. Here Mr Delafosse established in 1764 his 'Richmond Academy' – presumably taking with him his pupils from 9 The Green, whose occupants thereafter were not schoolmasters.

It thus appears that the Richmond Academy was the direct successor of the Grammar School founded a century earlier by William Radford.

In an advertisement in the London newspapers in 1764 Mr Delafosse stated that he 'is removed into the house late Colonel Soulegre's on Richmond Green, which he doubts not will give full satisfaction to all such parents and guardians as shall please to view the premises'. He described the house as 'roomy and elegant, the gardens extensive, the play-place study walled round and in full view of the master's parlour; there is also a commodious place for exercise in rainy or cold weather'. The advertisement claimed that, 'notwithstanding Mr Delafosse has such accommodation for his boarders as few, if any, private schools in the Kingdom can equal, yet his terms are extremely moderate, and every article relative to health, morals, and education will assuredly be duly attended to'.

*Richmond Academy (from Beresford Chancellor's* History and Antiquities of Richmond, *etc., 1894, based on a drawing of 1820).*

It is not at all clear when the mansion shown in the 'Prospect of Richmond' was replaced by the building illustrated here. The likeliest date is perhaps indicated in the ratebooks by a sharp rise in rentable value (of £570) between 1745 and 1748, with the building shown as empty in 1746 and unlisted in 1747. There was a further increase of 20 per cent between 1759 and 1760, but then the assessment appears to have been halved when Delafosse took over, not reaching the 1760 figure again until 1838. The reason for this may be that three other houses and a coachhouse, built on the Duke Street and Kew Horse Road edges of the property, and hitherto rated with the main house, were now rented out separately.

The Academy was to flourish under three generations of Delafosses for over seventy years. After the death of the Rev. Charles Delafosse in 1778, the next head was the Rev. Robert Mark Delafosse (who was curate of Petersham under the Rev. Daniel Bellamy from 1780 until the latter's death in 1788 and then remained as curate-in-charge until his own death, aged 62, in 1819).[20] He retired, however, as head of the school in 1811, handing over to his son, the Rev. Daniel Charles Delafosse (who also assisted at St Peter's in Petersham both before and after his father's death). D.C. Delafosse ran the school until 1838.

The most famous alumnus of the Academy was the explorer and writer Sir Richard Burton, who was one of D.C. Delafosse's pupils for about a year in the early 1830s. His father (who had made his home at Tours in France) was visiting England with the family and had rented 1 Maids of Honour Row on the Green. Most of the Academy pupils were boarders, but Richard (aged 10) and his younger brother Edward (aged six) attended as day boys. The fees were £33 10s. od. a term – a very large sum for a day boy at that time. Richard wrote a brief account of his time at the school,[21] his memory of it largely dominated by the awfulness of school food!

[The school] consisted of a large block of buildings (detached) ... In those days it had a kind of paling round a paddock, forming a parallelogram, which enclosed some fine old elm trees. One side was occupied by the house and the other by the schoolroom. In the upper storeys of the former were the dormitories with their small white beds, giving the idea of the Lilliput Hospital; a kind of outhouse attached to the dwelling was the place where the boys fed at two long tables stretching the length of the room ... The schoolroom was the usual scene of hacked and well-used benches and ink-stained desks, everything looking as mean and uncomfortable as possible.

Theo Rev. Charles was a bluff and portly man, with dark hair and short whiskers, whose grand aquiline nose took a prodigious deal of snuff, and was not over-active with the rod. He was rather a favourite with the boys ...

Breakfast at 8 a.m. consisting of very blue milk and water, in chipped and broken-handled mugs of the same colour. The boys were allowed tea from home, but it was a perpetual battle to get a single drink of it. The substantials were a wedge of bread with a glazing of butter. The epicures used to collect the glazing to the end of the slice in order to convert it into a final *bonne bouche*.

The dinner at one o'clock began with stickjaw (pudding) and ended with meat – the latter was as badly cooked as possible, black out and blue inside, gristly and sinewy. The vegetables were potatoes which could serve for grapeshot, and the hateful carrot.

At least the Burton brothers could escape home at 5 p.m. and have a decent evening meal. And they would take extra supplies from home to school with them: 'packets of ham, polony and saveloy ... and half-finished bottles of Bordeaux'.

The school was closed for a while when several boys died in a measles epidemic; and then Burton's father took the family back to Tours. Some two years later three more pupils at the school, including the 15-year-old son of Lord Elibank (who was buried at Petersham), died of an attack of scarlet fever. The dangers of contagion in the schools of that time were high, and Delafosse's Academy was certainly not below the general standards of the day. Indeed its reputation, as well as its fees, were high. In Evans' *Guide to Richmond*, first published in 1824, it was described as 'a large establishment for young gentlemen, of classical celebrity'.

After the retirement of D.C. Delafosse in 1838, the school was transformed into a girls' school for daughters of naval officers, under the name of 'Hope House'. This continued until 1856, when it became a 'Cavalry College', but was almost immediately destroyed by fire. The rebuilt college remained as a school of one kind or another for a further sixty years; and the building still stands today as an office of Barclay's Bank.

## Various seventeenth-century schools

A pew list for Richmond parish church in 1649[22] shows that there were two schools established in Richmond at that time. The larger one was that of Mr John Nash, for whom and his family and scholars two whole pews were allotted. Many of the pews seated ten to twelve adults, so Mr Nash may have had well over twenty pupils. The other school was that of Mr Roberts whose family and scholars were allotted just one pew.

The name of Mr Nash, but not that of Mr Roberts, figures in the church rate assessment of 1651 (for paving the 'church lane', i.e. Brewer's Lane and Church Court).[23] Beyond the baptisms of three children of George Roberts from 1647 to 1650, no other trace of him has been found. Mr Nash, however, appears in the hearth tax assessment of 1664, assessed for nine hearths at a house on the south-east of George Street (on the site which is now No. 23).[24] He was buried in Richmond on 14 February 1665/6. His widow Ann occupied the house for some years after his death, but there is no further indication of a school there.

In January 1655/6 one Robert Mossom submitted to the Council of State a petition saying that since his sequestration from Teddington church in 1650 (for no greater offence than reading from the Book of Common Prayer) he had been earning his living as a schoolmaster in Richmond.[25] (Mildred, a daughter of Robert Mossom, was baptised in Richmond on 3 August 1653.) A declaration of the Council had now banned sequestered priests from teaching, which would deprive him, his wife and six small children, of their livelihood. He submitted two certificates (one from a JP) of his good conduct as a teacher and begged to be licensed to continue teaching. His petition was granted. The location of his school has not been traced, but it seems possible that he may have taken over from Mr Roberts. No Mossom or similar name appears in the 1664 hearth tax list.

A school house, which may possibly have been that used by Mr Roberts and/or Mr Mossom, was situated at the end of the garden of No. 1 The Green. This is mentioned when it and No. 1 The Green were surrendered at the Manor Court of 11 April 1665[26] by Dorothy Painter and her son James Withers (a surgeon) to John Williams and his wife Unica. There is, however, no further mention of the schoolhouse when the Williamses surrendered the property to their son in 1673.[27]

In June 1658 John Bentley Esq, who lived in the large house on the western corner of the Green (on the site now Cedar Grove), put forward a proposal for the foundation of a free school.[28] He asked for a grant of one acre of land on the north-east side of the Green on which to build the school, and for three acres of the Common by Marshgate (to be used as an endowment for the school) – for which grants he would pay £40 'for the public use of the Parish'. The Manor Court approved the proposal and asked the lord of the manor to grant the land, which they had staked out.

However, this came to nothing. Possibly the imminence of the restoration (which would probably have invalidated the grant in any case) made the lord reluctant to approve it. As it was, John Bentley's death in March 1660/1 put an end to the idea.

At some date between 1664 and 1693 Walter Smith, the parish clerk, who at that time owned all the strip of land on the north-east side of the churchyard (now Church

Walk), built a schoolroom at its southern end, by Paradise Row. In 1693 he made the schoolroom over to his son William.[29] It seems likely that Walter and William Smith were themselves the masters for this school. There is no clear evidence that it continued without interruption after their deaths (both died in 1699); but Benjamin Lyon who was in occupation of the property in 1780 and 1790 was described in 1795 as a schoolmaster;[30] and a schoolroom on almost the same site existed into the mid-19th century.

The 'wife of John Spilman of Richmond, schoolmaster' was buried on 29 April 1700. Spilman himself was buried on 17 June 1711 (but no description of his trade or profession was then recorded). His name has not been found in the manor rolls, so where he taught or lived is unknown.

What, if only we had a little more information about it, might well be the most interesting of all Richmond's mid-17th-century educational establishments was the Puritan academy founded by Peter Sterry.[31]

Sterry, who was one of Oliver Cromwell's chaplains, retired from the political scene after his master's death in 1658 to become the private chaplain to Lord Lisle at his house at West Sheen (on the site of the former Charterhouse). Sterry had, however, had connections with Richmond – and perhaps a house there – for some years before 1658, as he was one of the two influential local gentlemen who had supported Robert Mossom's petition in January 1655/6, saying that he had 'had several children with Mr Mossom'. (A 'Fraunc. Sterry' – possibly a son Francis or possibly a more distant relation – was buried in Richmond in September 1651.)

At West Sheen Sterry, imbued like his patron Lord Lisle with neoplatonist ideas, founded a small utopian society, primarily to provide academic instruction for nonconformists who were excluded from the universities by the Test Acts. The community consisted of himself, his wife, two sons and two daughters, and his pupils. Of the latter a few names are known: Robert Liddell, Matthew Hutton and a Mr Laiton. Sterry was the only tutor. He approached West Sheen, in the words of N.I. Matar, 'as a place of discipline and teaching, based on a study of the Bible, the classics and the Neoplatonists'. How long the academy survived is unknown; Matar says it lasted well after Sterry's death in 1672. There is no mention of Sterry in the hearth tax returns of 1664, but he may have been occupying part of Lord Lisle's own mansion.

## The Charity School (St Mary's)

The eventual establishment of a free charity school, attached to the parish church, came in 1713. It was funded by subscription and the list of subscribers was headed by Queen Anne and included such names as the Duke and Duchess of Ormonde, Lord Cholmondeley and the rich East India merchant Elihu Yale, then living on the Green).[32] Margaret, the widow of Sir Peter Vanderputt, purchased as a site for the school the old inn, known for most of the 17th century as the *Three Pigeons and Lily Pot* but which had lately changed its name to the *Castle* or *Castle and Trumpet*, together with two adjacent cottages. This property, on the north side of the corner of Brewer's Lane and George Street, was vested in trustees in April 1714 'for the support, maintenance and keeping up of a Charity School which is now erecting in Richmond ... for the learning and instruction and teaching of poor children who shall from time to time be put and placed there for that purpose'.[33] Lady Vanderputt appears to have paid herself for the building of the school. That a considerable number of pupils were expected is shown by the decision of the Vestry in November 1713 to take down three pews 'at the lower end of the South Gallary in Order to make seats for the Accommodation of the Children of the Charity School'.[34]

The minister, Dr Nicholas Brady, is said to have been the first schoolmaster, but this may result from a confusion with his mastership of the Grammar School. Certainly, by 1725, when he was replying to the Bishop's questionnaire, he stated that 'Mr Jones and Mrs Dix are the master and mistress; and very well qualified for their employments'.[35] Some 50 boys and a like number of girls were attending the school. 'Evan Jones, schoolmaster of Richmond' was mentioned in the will of William Hickey in 1727. He died in November 1756. (Mary Dix, widow, died in January 1733/4.) The children were issued with blue gowns and wore numbered circular metal badges.

*Plate 45*

By 1788, when another Bishop's Visitation questionnaire was answered by the Rev. Thomas Wakefield, attendance seems to have dropped to 34 boys and 34 girls. The teachers were then Samuel Goff* and Elizabeth Richardson.[36]

The school continued at the Brewer's Lane-George Street corner until 1854 when it moved to Eton Street. In his *Guide to Richmond*, published in 1824, John Evans wrote of it:[37] 'It is conducted upon Mr Bell's system, combining all the children of the poor residing in the parish; thirty-six boys and thirty-six girls are annually clothed, and as they go out others of the parishioners' children are clothed to that number ... At this time are educated one hundred and forty boys and about eighty girls in this excellent charity.'

## Other eighteenth-century schools

Dr Brady's report in 1725[38] mentioned the charity school and the Grammar School 'and several petty schools that make no figure'. Where these latter were (apart possibly from the one started by the Smiths) we do not know. The only unattached 18th-century schoolmaster traced before the 1790s is a Peter Seyer whose son was baptised on 6 July 1753. There is only one entry for such a name in the rate books of the period: that for a 'Mr Seere' (later spelled Sayer) at No. 4 Ormond Row (Road) from 1751 to

---

* Samuel Goff was described as 'of Mortlake' when he married in Richmond in 1770; but was probably the Samuel baptised at Richmond in January 1744/5, son of William, landlord of the *Duke's Head* tavern on Richmond Green (now the *Prince's Head*).

1760. He may, of course, have been a teacher at the charity school, or at the Smiths' school, or he may have had his own school in this house.

Mr Wakefield in 1788[39] mentioned that there were 'several common pay schools in the parish and some boarding schools for both sexes' as well as 'a boys and girls Sunday school supported by subscription'.

The *Universal British Directory* of 1795 enables us to identify some of these private schools. Apart from Mr Delafosse's Academy on Richmond Green, there were:

(i) Mr William Cundall's Academy. This appears from the rate books to have been in 1790 at No. 1 The Vineyard (the house which a little later was to serve as a Roman Catholic chapel prior to the building of St Elizabeth's), but to have moved in 1791 to Paradise Row (a house on the site of the present multi-storey car park).

(ii) Mr Timothy Eeles' boarding school for Roman Catholic boys at Clarence House in the Vineyard. This has been written about by Noel Hughes in his book on *The Richmond Catholic Mission 1791-1826*. It appears to have been established after 1790 and to have closed down in 1797-98. Its most famous pupil was Bernardo O'Higgins, the liberator of Chile.

(iii) Mr William Brewster's boarding school for boys – location not yet identified.

(iv) Mrs Bayssalance's boarding school for girls – location not yet identified.

(v) Mrs Budd's Ladies' boarding school. At No. 11 The Green in 1790. It moved to Old Friars on Richmond Green between 1800 and 1810 and remained there until the 1840s.

(vi) Mrs Jones's Ladies' boarding school in the Marshgate Road. This was a large house next door to Upper Dunstable House (about where No. 90 Sheen Road is today).

(vii) Mrs Williamson's Ladies' boarding school. (In 1780, '90 and 1800 Mrs Sophia Williamson occupied the southernmost of the terrace houses to the south of the *Castle Hotel* in Hill Street, by the entrance to Heron Court.)

(viii) Benjamin Lyon schoolmaster – as noted above this was probably the school at the corner of Church Walk and Paradise Road.

(ix) John Smith schoolmaster, who was at 30 The Green in 1790 (succeeded there from 1800-20 by Dr Clement Smith).

(x) Robert Smith schoolmaster – who occupied in 1790 a large house on the northern corner of Hill Street (now Hill Rise) and Compass Hill.

(xi) George Wright schoolmaster – location not yet identified.

(xii) Not listed in the Directories but known to exist from correspondence in 1793 (see Noel Hughes *op. cit.* pp.33-34) was a school for Roman Catholic girls run by Miss Havers and Miss Nicols in the Kew Foot Road. (The names do not appear in the 1790 rate book.)

There was also a school set up in the new Workhouse built in 1785-86. Instruction seems to have been given by the Master and Matron of the Workhouse – both to the children housed there and to illiterate adult inmates.

## Richmond Private Schools in 1825

The guide to *Richmond and its Vicinity* published by John Evans in 1824 (with a second edition in 1825) lists 20 private schools, both day and boarding.[40]

Apart from Mr Delafosse's Academy on Richmond Green, the others listed (with some notes added as to locations) were:

Miss Pettingale 'who receives a limited number of young ladies to educate' – on Richmond Green (probably between No. 2 and No. 8, but not exactly identified).

Mrs Budd's 'establishment for young ladies' on Richmond Green (at 'Old Friars').

Miss Wright on Richmond Green (Nos. 23-24).

Rev. J. White, 'Centre House', Richmond Green (probably No. 3 Old Palace Terrace).

Miss Kershaw, Kew Foot Lane (No. 37).

Rev. J.E. Denham 'who receives a few private pupils' at Lumley Lodge (said to be in Kew Road, but actually in the Lower Mortlake Road, approximately where Salisbury Road is now).

Miss Pritchard's 'establishment for young ladies', said to be at Upper Dunstable House, Marshgate Road (but actually at *Lower* Dunstable House, now 93 Sheen Road).

The Misses James 'who have a select seminary for young ladies, in the house occupied by the late Lady Suffield' in the Vineyard (probably now 'Vineyard House').

Mrs Howlings in the Vineyard.

Plate 45   Rev. Mr Allan at Mount Ararat Lodge, Vineyard. The school was a small detached building at the south end of Mount Ararat House. It was described by an ex-pupil, F.S. Ellis, as 'a wretched sham-Gothic schoolroom built, I believe, with a special view to keeping the boys in a freezing condition during the winter.'[41]

Mr W.H. Butt's Catholic School in the Vineyard (in Clarence House – opened in 1822 under the name of 'Richmond College', but closed by 1830).

Miss Fisher on the Rise of the Hill (at what is now 6-8 Richmond Hill).

The Misses Gosling at 'Ivy House', Church Row (now Church Terrace.)

Miss Turner 'a preparatory establishment for young gentlemen' in Church Row.

Mr W Gibbons in George Street – location not identified.

Mrs Gibbons – boys' preparatory in George Street – location not identified.

Miss Budd, 'an establishment for young ladies of great respectability' at Gothic House in the Lower (now Petersham) Road.

Rev. Robert Gream, 'who educates young gentlemen, sons of noblemen, and others, for the

*Plate 44*

*The Vestry Hall in Richmond in 1831, a watercolour by T. Hassell. (British Library CRACH 1, TAB 1, b1, Vol. 6)*

*The new equipment for the waterworks in the Petersham Road, 1835 (lithograph by R. Cartwright). (Richmond Public Library, local studies collection)*

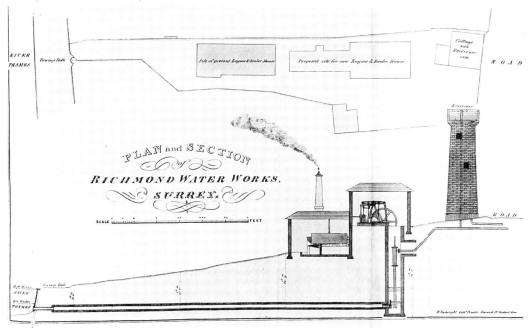

*Plate 45*

*A badge worn by a pupil at the free parochial school, founded in 1713. (Museum of Richmond)*

*The Schoolhouse (on the right) at Mount Ararat. (Richmond Public Library, local studies collection)*

*The first King's School at Kew in 1827, drawing by J. Buckler. (British Library, Add MS 36388, f.249)*

*Mount Ararat Lodge.*

*Richmond, Surrey.*

*King's Free School on Kew Green.*

*Jun. 9th 1827*

*Plate 46*

*Upper Dunstable House, 1825.
(British Library CRACH 1,
TAB 1, b1, Vol. 6)*

*Prince's Street and, beyond it,
Waterloo Place, c.1890.
(Richmond Public Library, local
studies collection)*

*Plate 47*

*The chapel in the centre of the main block of the Hickey Almshouses, built in 1834. (Photo by author)*

*Church Estate Almshouses. (Richmond Public Library, local studies collection)*

Universities' in a 'handsome residence, with an extensive lawn, well adapted for their reception' in the Lower Road (at Ivy Hall).

Rev. W. Bewsher, 'who has a large establishment for young gentlemen' in the Lower Road (at Bellevue Lodge).

The guide also lists 15 'private tutors', six for music, two for 'classics and writing' and one for classics alone, two for French and one for French and Italian, two for 'writing and mathematics (or arithmetic)' and one for drawing.

## Early Schools at Kew

In his reply to the Bishop's Visitation questionnaire in 1725, the Rev. Hugh Lewis, curate, stated that there was 'no school in the hamlet'.[42] He did, however, mention the bequest of Lady Dorothy Capell of £100 per annum to be distributed to 12 charity schools. Kew's share was to be used to put out poor children of Kew as apprentices until a charity school was established there.

The school set up in the building known as 'Hell' on the south side of Kew Green, which was part of the Kew House (later White House) estate and which is mentioned in 1731 in the documents of the lease of that estate to Frederick Prince of Wales,[43] was therefore of quite recent creation and it would seem that this building had been the original site of the *Rose and Crown* tavern. James Smith, the schoolmaster, was at first an under-tenant of John Hayter, who was described as innholder of the *Rose and Crown* in 1721, and Joseph Williams (licensed from 1725 to 1728) was assessed for rates for the *Rose and Crown*, apparently at this location, in 1726[44] Hayter's sub-lease to Smith was dated 8 May 1729,[45] so the establishment of the school can reasonably be dated from mid-1729. Smith was given a new lease by the St Andrés in January 1730.[46]

The school presumably remained in this location until, at least, 1761, for Prince Frederick paid for 'repairs to the schoolhouse' in the years 1759-60 and 1760-61.[47] A minute of the Kew Vestry dated 30 December 1742 refers to a subscription for a 'charity school now erecting in this place', but nothing seems to have come of this initiative. By 1767, however, Hell House was said to be occupied by Princess Augusta's servants.[48] Where the school had gone is unknown.

After the enlargement of St Anne's in 1770, the school was transferred to the pew-keeper's room in the south aisle. Then in April 1778 a committee of the Kew Vestry was set up to consider the establishment both of a charity school and of a workhouse.[49] In December 1778 William Hudson was appointed, with a salary of £21 a year, as master of the charity school, which it was proposed to build next to the cottage used as a poor-house at the corner of the Richmond Road and Sandy Lane.*[50] Two years

---

* At this period Sandy Lane (now Sandycombe Road) continued into the Kew Road by way of what is now Broomfield Road.

later this project was abandoned; it was decided to house the poor children in a lean-to of the poor house and to continue to use the schoolroom in the church.[51] So it was that, when James Corve, curate, replied to another Bishop's Visitation questionnaire on 18 February 1788,[52] he listed one school with five scholars, of which Hudson was the master, appointed by the vestry. Lady Capell's charity was then producing £11 per annum for the school (being a twelfth share of £132).

The idea of a separate workhouse for Kew had been abandoned in 1780 when arrangements were made to send the Kew poor to the Barnes workhouse. When a new workhouse was built in Richmond in 1785-86, the Kew vestry negotiated with the Richmond authorities and by April 1788 it had been agreed to accept the Kew poor, including the poor children, there.[53] The Kew schoolmaster and the 'housekeeper of the schoolhouse' were both given notice.

Kew was without a school again until 1810, when a new school project was agreed by the vestry in February. Thomas Henry Ellisby was appointed both as schoolmaster and as vestry clerk, and a room to be used as a schoolhouse was rented at 27 The Green from Mr George Pepper.[54] The school remained there until 1824 when the enclosure of the Kew meadows provided an opportunity to acquire a site for a new school building. The Vestry gave up some rights to Lammas land and rights of way to Miss Elizabeth Doughty, who in return ceded to them a piece of land north of the pond as a site for a new free school.[55] The school was built in the Gothic style, *Plate 45* matching Miss Doughty's 'Priory' and its lodge gate on the Green. It was opened in 1826 – and, by command of George IV, was given the name of the King's Free School.

It became the Queen's School on Queen Victoria's accession and has since changed its name according to the sex of the sovereign. It was rebuilt as a three-storey building on the same site in 1887 and remained there until moved to new premises in Cumberland Road in 1970.

# 22

# *The End of the Fields*

THE DECISIVE DATE in the 19th-century development of Richmond is of course 1846 when the 'Richmond Railway' opened, conveying passengers from a new Richmond station to the terminus of the London and South Western Railway at Nine Elms. From that moment onwards, Richmond's character was doomed to change, from fashionable resort to dormitory suburb.

However, that change had begun even before the railway arrived. The bridging of the river at Kew in the late 1750s and then at Richmond in the 1770s had made a significant difference to the traffic pattern. Access to Richmond – and through Richmond to Twickenham – was becoming much easier. New coach proprietors set up services into London. By 1830 there was even an omnibus, 'The Pilot', and by the end of that decade there were five omnibuses a day to the Bank and five to St Paul's. Travel by river was made faster, if not always safer, by the introduction of river steamers. By 1843 there were six in each direction daily.

More members of the middle classes began to move out from London to Richmond. Inevitably there was an increase also in the artisan and labouring classes – the servants, gardeners, laundresses, coachmen needed to support the better off, and the shopkeepers, shop assistants, skilled tradesmen to supply their needs.

The population growth is reflected in the housing stock. In the 50 years between the manor survey of 1771 and the census of 1821 the number of houses in the Parish of Richmond had increased by some 40 per cent, from 694 to 1,003. By 1841 another 45 per cent growth had brought the total to 1,454. In Kew 68 houses in 1771 had become 120 in 1821 and 183 in 1841.

A great part of this increase had been, especially before the 1820s, a 'thickening-up' of areas already partly developed. Along George Street, in Brewer's Lane and Red Lion Street, in the 'World's End' area on the eastern side of the Kew Road, by the riverside and along the Petersham Road new terraces of houses and cottages were being built, often in place of a single previous house, sometimes filling in what had previously been an empty space. Some of these were substantial villas like those in St Helena Terrace or Spring Terrace in the Marshgate Road; some were smaller villas like those in the Petersham Road; some were shophouses, such as those in Hill Street and Hill Rise; some were small cottages such as Bath Buildings in Asgill (now Old Palace) Lane.

But some of this new building had begun to encroach on the area of the common fields and the traditional open pastures. Such development was often in two stages: first, a number of (usually detached) houses built facing an existing road, or a field path made up into a road, each retaining a long garden representing the original field strip on one end of which the house was built: second, rows of houses built at right angles to the existing roads, in one (or two or three adjacent) strips.

One area which had experienced this first phase of development between 1771 and 1810 was that of the former Kew Heath, south of the lane to Mortlake. This had been purchased by John Dillman, Prince Frederick's German-born gardener, in 1749 from John Darrell, and had been bequeathed by Dillman in 1760 to his great nephew and principal heir, John Dillman Engleheart. There was just one cottage on the land in 1771. Engleheart started to build at once. By 1774 there were two new houses building by the corner of the Mortlake Road, six already in a group a little further south and three at the southern end of the land near the point where the 'Sandy Lane' from Richmond, having turned sharply west from its course up the manor boundary, ran into the Kew Road. By the time of his death in 1810, there was a total of 22 houses spread along the frontage between the Mortlake Road and Sandy Lane, including the row of large houses at the northern end and the mansion later called Gloucester House.

The northern part of Kew Heath above the Mortlake Road had already been developed with houses facing the Green and the inn called the *Coach and Horses* when Engleheart acquired it in 1778, but the former Ware Ground, to the north of this, was only turned from pasture into a private estate when purchased by Elizabeth Doughty in 1809. She had the architect J.B. Papworth design her a 'Priory' – a sort of extended summer pavilion with a chapel and library, all in Gothic style – and a lodge cottage, also Gothic, at the Kew Green end of a new driveway.

The whole of Kew Field and most of Parkshot in the Lower Richmond Field was now of course part of the royal estate. George III had continued to expand the estate southwards in Parkshot below the end of Kew Gardens until he made his deal with the people of Richmond and Kew in 1785 to close 'Love Lane', the public right of way between Richmond Gardens and Kew Gardens. This involved his making a new path from the point of closure on the Kew Foot Lane through to the Kew Horse Road (or Kew Road as it would henceforth be called) on the line of what is now Old Deer Park Gardens. After making this path he sold off the piece of land which lay to its south (which had been his most recent acquisition).

To the south of the new path, between the Kew Foot Lane on the west and the Kew Road on the east, was what was left of the former Park Shott, with a group of cottages at its southern end (by the lane which is now Clarence Street) and some

*Rosedale in Kew Foot Road, in about 1820.*

twenty houses dotted along the east side of Kew Foot Lane, up as far as Rosedale, the house that had belonged to James Thomson the poet and which was purchased early in the 19th century by the Hon. Ashley Cooper, who succeeded as 6th Earl of Shaftesbury in 1811. There was a little extra development along the Kew Road side before 1800, and some new houses including 'Kew Lodge' were built at the eastern end of the ground sold back by the King. Apart from the fairly dense group of freehold cottages by Clarence Street, this was all 'phase 1 development'.

Then, around the turn of the century, came the first signs of phase 2 – the construction of some cottages in the rear of the three houses of Michell's Terrace, on freehold land belonging to the Michell Trustees, and of some more 'at the back' (as the rate book describes them) of the houses in the Kew Road north of Clarence Street. By the 1840s these had become dense rows of cottages – 48 in 'Sweeps' Alley' behind the Michell property, some 25 rather larger and more salubrious cottages in St John's Grove. In the 1850s another row of larger houses was built just to the south of 'Rosedale'. These were Shaftesbury Villas – originally a cul-de-sac entered from the Kew Foot Road end only.

There is some confusion about the nomenclature of the Michell cottages. The first group were named as Sweeps' Alley in the 1830 rate book; by 1840 there were 40 cottages in Sweeps' Alley plus another eight called Wilson's buildings. In 1850 all 48 are included as Sweeps' Alley. The Sewer Commission map of 1849 shows these as being mostly aligned along the northern edge of this piece of Michell property, with another eight on the southern edge. The 60-inch Ordnance Survey plan of 1867 names 'Night and Morning Row' as running by the southern edge of the Michell property (with 16 more buildings on its south side, not on Michell land). The layout of the Sweeps' Alley buildings appears the same as in 1849, but there is now another row on the adjoining ground to their north – Benn's Cottages. Later maps show a blank space where Sweeps' Alley had been.

In 1866 the Michell Trustees leased to the builder James Long for a 60-year term the land 'on which several cottages had been erected, called "Night and Morning Row" and also a piece of ground adjoining on which several houses called "Nelson's Buildings" were standing', Long undertaking to pull down the existing buildings and to erect 28 cottages on the site of Night and Morning Row and three houses or shops on the other piece of land. By September 1867 eleven of the new houses called 'Michel's Row' had been leased; by September 1868 a further eleven. Then, as Long had not carried out his undertaking, the trustees took back the buildings he had not yet demolished and themselves built the last six cottages of Michel's Row and the three shops – facing onto the Kew Road. Now a vestry minute of June 1868 about a report on the housing of the poor refers to Sweeps' Alley and 'Michel's Buildings' as being in bad condition, but comments that 'the pulling down of Night and Morning Row has removed the worst'. From this it would seem that Sweeps' Alley *was* Night and Morning Row, but Alderman Somers Gascoyne in his *Recollections of Richmond* published in 1898 refers to the Shrove Tuesday football games between teams coming from Water Lane and 'Night and Morning Row (now Michell's Row)'.

In 1808 the Michel trustees also developed another row on their land a little further north – 'Old Deer Park Cottages' built by a Mr Steell, are now the southern side of Rosedale Road. To complete the story of this area, the Shaftesbury estate was sold for development in 1866 and 'Rosedale' became the Richmond Hospital in 1868. Evelyn and Jocelyn Roads were then fairly rapidly built up.

On the eastern side of the Kew Road, the old cottages of 'World's End' seem to have been mostly replaced by more substantial buildings in the 1770s and '80s, but there were still only one or two houses between them and the junction with the lane to Mortlake. Between these two roads, however, Charles Selwyn had leased out a triangle of land extending some 350 feet along each road from the corner. Here another intense little development, with some 35 cottages and houses facing the Kew Road and 25 along the Mortlake Road, was started in the 1770s and completed by 1790. At its northern limit on the Kew Road was the new *Blue Anchor* tavern. Then in 1810 William Selwyn built a new mansion for himself in the fields a little further up towards Kew: Pagoda House, facing the southernmost edge of the royal property.

Selwyn's previous house had been Larkfield, one of only two mansions on the south side of the Mortlake Road. (The other, built for John Boddington in 1762, was later called Lumley Lodge.) These two represented the entire development along the road (east of Blue Anchor Alley) until the 1820s. Then came an immediate 'Phase 2' development, a few houses facing the main road being little more than end features for a series of rows of very small cottages built at right angles to the road. This was the beginning of 'New Richmond', a mini-suburb to house the working class. Development in the '20s included in the western row (eventually all called Twenty Row) a score of cottages named Day's, Martin's and Long's, and a southern extension on the same line called New Richmond Place. A little row of one larger house (originally called Gothic House and later the *Castle* tavern) and four cottages led to the next north-south line, Cross Row (later called West Sheen Vale) and Botten's Place. New Richmond Place with some 20 small cottages and Botten's Place with 25 even smaller were not completed until the 1830s. They ran right down to the boundary between Lower Dunstable, on which they stood, and Upper Dunstable. When the railway was built in the early 1840s along this boundary, but mostly in Lower Dunstable, both roads had to be cropped a little at the southern end, losing four or five houses. The third row of New Richmond, called Crofton Terrace, originally of 48 houses, built in the late 1830s, suffered the same fate. It was linked to the others only by the Mortlake Road at the top and a little cross lane at the bottom. Ironically, one of the houses lost to the railway was a little alehouse, called the *Railway Tavern*.

The larger houses in Sheendale Road, originally called Sheen Dale Villas on the west side and Ross Villas on the east, and those in Crown Terrace, further east again, were somewhat later additions. *Plate 53*

Another area where growth of housing in the fields was evident by the 1820s was towards the middle part of Marshgate Road and its junction with the old Worple Way. There were already Upper Dunstable House, on the north side of the road, and a few cottages on the strip of land between the two roads – and a little group around the farm which stood at the east end of the present Worple Way (in the 18th century the lane continued right along to the back of the *Black Horse* tavern). In the 1770s Dr Baker, the owner of Upper Dunstable House, built Lower Dunstable House, almost opposite. His son, Sir Robert Baker, purchased from the developer's heirs another little group of cottages that were built in the 1780s just to the east of Upper Dunstable House. The latter was itself rebuilt in the first years of the 19th century. *Plate 46*

On the south side of Worple Way, the hundred yards or so of land to the east of the field path which came down past Houblon's Almshouses was built up with cottages between 1770 and 1810, and some more were built on the north side of Worple Way. The *Red Cow* tavern moved in 1789 from its original site at the east end of this development to an almost new building facing the Marshgate Road. The land on which most of these new cottages were built, and then stretching up the hillside to their south, had been purchased from Edward Collins by Thomas Hillier in 1803. On its eastern side George Robinson acquired most of the rest of the Collins holdings in the fields, including what was by then one large field by Marshgate and another stretching up the hill on the east side of the field path which is now Albany Passage. In 1821, perhaps anticipating further development to come, he turned the lower field, at the Marshgate end, into a brickfield.

There were other developments along the Marshgate Road in the 1820s. On Robinson's own land, between the road and Worple Way, three cottages were built called Mount Pleasant, and immediately adjoining on their east, a row of seven called

Belvedere Place. Further west, a row of six substantial houses called Spring Crescent stood on the south side of the Marshgate Road and its extension into Paradise Road. Down towards the centre of town, the complex of Union Court now occupied the land to the east of the former church glebe; and opposite it 24 new cottages were built by Black Ditch, the stream which drained out of the village pond, along Kew Road and Mortlake Road, into the Mortlake marsh. These became Prince's Street and Waterloo Place.

*Plate 46*

Then, at the eastern end of the road came an important new development. The Hickey Trust had a lot of property with valuable housing. They enfranchised it in 1817 and were then able to charge enhanced rents. They rapidly built up a capital surplus which the Trustees decided to use in buying a field on which to build a new block of almshouses. The Hickey Almshouses were on a grander scale than any of the earlier foundations. They were built in 1834 to the designs of Lewis Vulliamy, and provided 10 houses each for men and women, with a chapel and gate lodge cottages for a porter and a nurse. (The Almshouses have been expanding periodically ever since over parts of the field which the Trustees bought at Marshgate: 29 units have been added to the original foundation over the years.)

*Plate 47*

The trustees of the Church Estates, who had been authorised in 1820 to let out their land on building leases, also found themselves building up capital. They followed the Hickey Trustees' example – and indeed their geographical lead also, and built 10 almshouses designed by W.C. Stow, on the plot immediately westward of Hickey's in 1844. A little further west, on the south side of Marshgate Road, eight quite large villas were built in the area called Peldon, between the road and the footpath part of Worple Way, in the 1840s.

*Plate 47*

✠

In the town itself, the '20s and '30s were a period both of expansion at the edges and of consolidation at the centre. Red Lion Street was an area of growth, with new houses being built on the land on either side of the *Red Lion* tavern, filling up the space between Ormond Road and Red Lion Street and Church Terrace. By the churchyard the 10 cottages called Wellington Place were built by 1830 and eight Caroline Cottages by 1838. Artichoke Alley had 15 cottages by the end of the 1830s. By the riverside a big boost to development was given by the sale in 1833 of the Crown freehold land between the palace site and Water Lane. This was quickly followed by the building of St Helena Terrace in 1834-35, of Queensberry Place and of the Villa Retreat – with Retreat Road opened up to provide access. The old Cholmondeley (later Queensberry) House by the riverside was demolished in 1831 to be replaced by a new Queensberry Villa set further back. At the other end of the palace site Asgill (now Old Palace) Lane was developed with two rows of cottages and small houses – Bath Buildings in 1810 and Bath Terrace in the 1830s.

*Artichoke Alley*

*(Both illustrations from Somers Gascoyne,* Recollections of Richmond, c.*1899)*

*Ormond Passage, from Red Lion Street*

Turning up the hill, the 1830s saw the creation of two new terraces of shop-houses in Hill Street. The 1690s mansion in Herring Square which stood nearest to the bridge was pulled down and rebuilt about 1820 for Joshua Jonathan Smith, a Lord Mayor of London. In 1835 this was turned into a hotel, the *Royal*. Then in 1839 a new terrace was built up in what had been its garden, facing onto Hill Street and turning the corner into Bridge Street. This 'Royal Terrace' was the work of one Leonard W. Lloyd who had taken over the hotel in 1838, but he went bankrupt as a result of overspending on the project.

Almost opposite, the gardens which during the 18th century had been rented by the proprietors of the *Talbot Inn*, were also built up with a new terrace of shop-houses, so that the line of buildings at last became continuous from Red Lion Street to Ormond Road, apart from the entrance into Castle Yard (where the *Castle Hotel*'s stables were) between the two rows.

A little further up the hill, York Place (now 10-18 Richmond Hill) was built in the 1820s. To the south of the Michel Almshouses, Lancaster House rose in the early 1830s, to be joined by Lancaster Place (28-40 Richmond Hill) and Mews in the '40s.

✠

This town of 7,760 persons in 1841 (with another 923 in Kew) was still in the main a riverside resort, to which the richer Londoners came out to stay in the summer, or even, now that the roads were better and safer, came out to dine on summer evenings or to lunch on Sundays. Joseph Ellis had enlarged the *Star and Garter Hotel* again; he had taken over the *Castle Hotel* and built new assembly rooms there just in time for the celebrations of Queen Victoria's coronation. The Austrian Ambassador gave a *Plate 48* grand party for the occasion at the *Castle*; the special French envoy, Marshal Soult, stayed at the *Star and Garter*.

There was still a sprinkling of aristocratic inhabitants: the Duke of Buccleuch down by the river, the Marquess of Lansdowne and the Earl of Cardigan in the two large mansions standing on the slopes of the hill, the Countess of Mansfield in a mansion now part of the *Richmond Hill Hotel*, the Earl of Shaftesbury in the Kew Foot Road, and the Duke of Cambridge at Kew (where his brother, formerly Duke of Cumberland but now King of Hanover, also maintained a residence). A list of the resident gentry, headed by a score of baronets and knights, would be long indeed.

The intellectual and artistic life of the town continued to flourish. Subscription concerts had been started in the 1790s by Clement Smith, the organist who lived at 3 Ormond Road – and his neighbour William Tibbs. The latter's death in 1809 had been marked by a special benefit concert for his wife and family, for which the famous soprano Madame Catalani travelled specially from Italy to sing. Paganini played in Richmond at the theatre in 1834; and Messrs Etherington, the musical instrument dealers in Hill Street, who took over the management of the subscription concerts, prevailed on the great Jullien to conduct for them in 1849. Etherington's advertisement for 1853 promised a 30-man orchestra, two pianists and two vocalists.

At the theatre the long and successful management of Charles Klanert had been succeeded by two years under the famous actor-manager Edmund Kean, who died in the house attached to the theatre in 1833. Though the management since had changed almost every year, the seasons were successful (until 1844 when it closed down for five years). In 1837 for the first time the theatre was lit by gas, introduced in the street lighting 10 years earlier.

Painting was currently represented by Thomas Christopher Hofland, who painted a number of extremely pleasant and competent views from Richmond Hill and one, at least, of Richmond Bridge. He lived from 1840 to 1842 in The Hollies in Ormond

Road with his wife Barbara, a writer primarily of books for children but also author of the first book devoted to illustrating *Richmond and its surrounding Scenery*, with 24 full-plate engravings by W.B. Cooke, who was also the publisher, and 10 vignettes in the text. This had been issued in 1832, soon after Richmond's very first guide book, Evans' guide to *Richmond and its Vicinity* published locally in 1824, and not long after an enormous epic poem 'Richmond Hill' by Thomas Maurice in 1807. Each of these, Barbara Hofland in particular, wrote up some of the history,* but the first real history of Richmond, Richard Crisp's *Richmond and its Inhabitants from the Olden Times*, was not published until 1866.

Another well known woman writer who, with her sister, spent her summers in Richmond was Mary Berry. Charles Dickens summered in Petersham, and regularly celebrated his wedding anniversary with a dinner at the *Star and Garter*. Thackeray, an occasional visitor, much preferred to stay at Rose Cottage, the first building to have been erected (in the 1820s) on 'the lane to the Friar's Stile', and turned by its proprietor Maria Gibbins from a teahouse into a small hotel about 1840.

The increase in population had finally put too great a strain on the resources of the parish church. It could be enlarged no more. As an alternative to pulling it down and erecting an altogether larger building, it was decided to build a new church, on the northern edge of the town where housing development had begun to produce a new, if for the moment mostly poorer, congregation. To the designs of Lewis Vulliamy the church of St John the Divine was erected on the south-east side of the Kew Road, a little south of its junction with the Mortlake Road, in 1831-36. In 1838 St *Plate 48* John's was made into a separate ecclesiastical parish (though remaining within the parish of Richmond as an administrative unit of civil government). A new house was built for its incumbent near Kew Lodge on the other side of the Kew Road.

At Kew itself a major change had taken place, though it was not yet, in the early 1840s, very visible. The new Queen had agreed to hand over responsibility for the maintenance of most of Richmond and Kew Gardens to the state. In March 1840 control was formally transferred to the Commissioners of Woods and Forests. A year later William Jackson Hooker, Professor of Botany at Glasgow University, was appointed Director of the Royal Botanic Gardens at Kew. For a start he had control only of the original small botanic garden, but he opened this at once to visitors; there were 9,000 in 1841. By 1843 he had another 50 acres and could start planning new gates, the great Palm House and a new landscape layout.

☩

These changes were important, but of much greater significance was the railway. As early as 1836 a group of entrepreneurs had put forward a proposal for a 'City of London and Richmond Railway'. It was to run from the south side of London Bridge

---

* Based largely on the pioneer works on Surrey by Daniel Lysons (1792) and by Manning and Bray (1804-14).

to a new terminal close to the new St John's Church in Kew Road. As most of its length in the built-up areas of Southwark and Lambeth was to be carried on brick viaducts, it proved too costly and the scheme was abandoned – but has left us with an engraving of the viaduct and another one of the rather splendid terminal station proposed for Richmond.

*Plate 49*

In 1838, however, the London and South Western Railway opened its line from the London terminus at Nine Elms to Southampton. This came fairly close to Richmond, passing through Wimbledon and Kingston (the station now called Surbiton). In 1844 the Richmond promoters, among them the MP, the Hon. C.P. Villiers; Sir Thomas Reeve, a developing landowner; Joseph Ellis of the *Star and Garter Hotel*; Thomas Long and James Davy, both developer-builders; and one or two of the other local gentry came up with a new project: the 'Richmond and West End Junction Railway' would build a line from Richmond to join the LSWR at Falcon Bridge (now Clapham Junction) and the 'West End Junction' bit – a line by-passing the Nine Elms terminus, through Vauxhall to a new station at the south end of Waterloo Bridge. Eventually, the prospectus suggested, the line might be extended across the Thames to a terminus on the north bank. It was also suggested that a branch line might be built to Kew Bridge and Brentford. This proposal had, of course, been discussed with the LSWR and it was understood that they would operate the trains. Further negotiations resulted in an agreement that the LSWR would themselves build the proposed extension from Nine Elms to Waterloo.

The project was supported by the LSWR in the parliamentary hearings, and by the Richmond vestry, but opposed by the parishes of Putney and Mortlake – and the vested interests in the coaching and steamer businesses. Public opinion in Richmond was very divided. Some were vehemently opposed, believing that the whole character of Richmond would be destroyed; others saw it as an opportunity for growth and in general most people were reassured that, with the line coming in along the southern edge of Lower Dunstable, very little built-up property would be affected. The parliamentary bill passed both houses and received the royal assent on 21 July 1845. The new line was opened on 22 July 1846. A 16-coach train for the directors and their guests, drawn by the locomotive 'Crescent', chugged its way from Nine Elms to the new station at Richmond (on the site now occupied by the multi-storey car park).

The LSWR ran 17 trains a day with fares originally set at 1s. 4d. (first class), 1s. 0d. (second class) and 8d. (third class), but reduced after much criticism to 1s., 10d., and 6d. respectively. Negotiations proceeded for a merger between the LSWR and the Richmond company, and in January 1847 the LSWR took over full ownership.

It was never seriously intended that the railway should stop at Richmond once it had arrived there. In 1845 the Board of Trade had commented favourably on the possibility of an extension to Staines. By 1846 there were two projects for a line to Staines and two for a connection between London and Windsor. From these a single proposal backed by the Richmond company and the LSWR emerged – the Windsor, Staines and South Western Railway, which would construct a line from Richmond to Staines, and then on to Windsor. The idea of a railway bridge over the Thames was bitterly opposed by the Richmond vestry, who suggested a tunnel instead: 'irreparable damage and injury to the beauty and scenery of one of the most favourite and beautiful walks in the Parish by a railway bridge over the Thames here and the embankment on both sides'. However the project received parliamentary sanction and the line from Richmond to Datchet was opened on 22 August 1848. Richmond was no longer a terminus and, rather than pull down Station No. 1, the LSWR converted it into a goods depot and built a new Station No. 2 for the through line between the Kew Road and Parkshot, both roads now with bridges crossing the railway.

*Plate 49*

Although the 'Hounslow loop' from Barnes, crossing the river to Kew Bridge Station and on to join the Staines Line at Feltham was opened in 1850, it was not until the 1860s that the LSWR, partly if not wholly motivated by the desire to keep other railway operators out of 'their' south-west London territory, proposed to build a line from Richmond through Kew to Turnham Green, Hammersmith, Shepherd's Bush and Kensington. The line was opened on 1 January 1869. This was soon to permit a link with the North London line at Gunnersbury and, a bit later, with the District Railway at Hammersmith. It required the construction of yet another station (No. 3) at Richmond, again a terminus on the east side of the Kew Road, and on the north side of the through tracks; and a new Kew Gardens station, with the unusual feature (for a small station) of a pavilion and bar attached as there was no refreshment facility yet in the Royal Botanic Gardens, was also opened. This line, from the point where it was crossed by the Mortlake Road at the manor boundary, in fact ran up to the railway bridge at Kew through land that was in the parish and manor of Mortlake, and Kew Gardens Station lay well over a hundred yards outside the boundary of Richmond. A new road was made, linking it to the corner of Sandy Lane and then curving up through the east side of the Engleheart estate, about to be developed.

✠

Once the railway had established itself – which it did very quickly – the surge out of London of the middle classes (from upper middle to lower middle) accelerated. New villas (from large detached to small terraced) mushroomed in the fields.

Along the Mortlake Road, St Mary's Grove, Adelaide Villas and Townshend Villas were developed beside and behind the Hickey Almshouses. The almshouses built by the Hickey and Church trustees served as a spur to the Richmond vestry, as trustees of the Parish Lands Charity on Pesthouse Common. The vestrymen saw how rich these other bodies were getting from the rents from built-up land as compared with the meagre return they were getting from leasing land as pasture. They obtained a Chancery order in 1845 allowing them to grant building leases of not more than 90

*Plate 50*

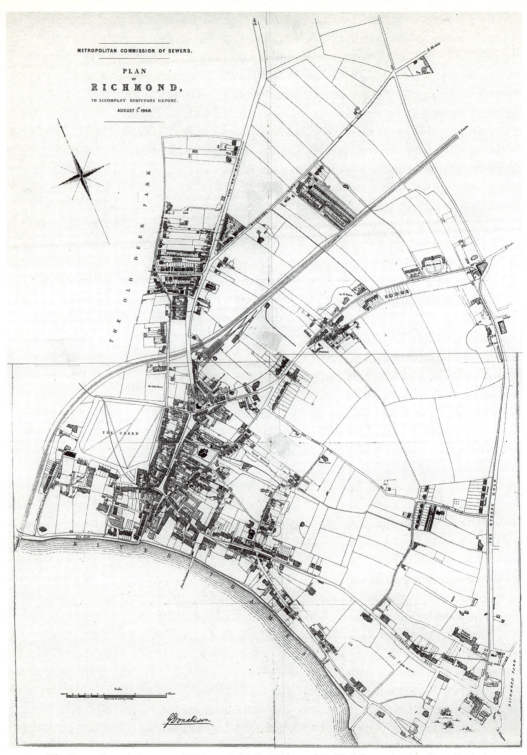

*The Sewers Commission map of Richmond, 1849. (Richmond Public Library; local studies collection)*

years' term for the best rents that could be had. By 1863 the whole Queen's Road frontage of the parish lands had been covered by rows of substantial villas, and Cambrian, Parkhill and Pyrland Roads behind them had been fully developed.

On the other side of Queen's Road the Wesleyans had taken over 'Squire Williams's' estate, originally put together by the Swiss jeweller Francis Grose in the 1740s, and had built their new Institute, a theological and missionary college, in 1842/3. Below *Plate 50* this was some land which had been part of the parish lands grant but which the vestry had been given permission to sell in 1849. On this, sold off in separate lots, new homes began to appear. To the north again were two new rows of villas – Park Villas West, built in the '50s, and Park Villas East (originally called Marlborough Terrace) dating from the late '40s. These were at one end of Park Road, the first road to be developed on the slope between Friar's Stile Road and Queen's Road. The developer was Sir Thomas Newby Reeve, and at the other end of his property here he built Rothesay Villas in Friar's Stile Road, extending from what is now Marlborough Road to the still extant 'Burlington House'. In the next decade Park Road was completed, and was parallelled by Marlborough Villas (on the north side only of Marlborough Road) and Alma Villas (on the south side only of Rosemont Road). Between Rose Cottage and Marlborough Road five new shophouses, Foxton Terrace, went up in the early '60s. On the north side of Friar's Stile Road a single development in the '50s of large semi-detached villas was named Montague Terrace.

The new growth of population in the Queen's Road – Friar's Stile Road area, and its likely spread as Mr Robinson began to consider developing his fields, led the Vestry to consider putting a new church in the parish lands area. But their lawyers were dubious about the proposal – as trustees they had to secure maximum benefit for the beneficiaries (who should have been the poor of Richmond but were in fact those inhabitants who had to pay the poor rate), and the order in Chancery had told them explicitly to get the best rents they could.

Mr Charles Jasper Selwyn came to the rescue. In 1857 he offered a plot of land at the corner of his estate, by the end of Friar's Stile Road. St Matthias Church was built, to the designs of Sir George Gilbert Scott, on the site and was consecrated in August 1858 – though its landmark spire was not completed until 1862. To its north-west the road down the hill past Mount Ararat was still a mere lane; to its north-east George Robinson had laid out the new King's Road in time for it to be shown with dotted lines on the Ordnance map surveyed in 1863 (but not published until 1868). The road *Plate 52* started to be lined with large villas in the 1870s.

Down in the town, the extension of the railway through the southern edge of the Old Deer Park and sweeping round to the new railway bridge had made Fitzwilliam (or Pembroke) House on the north-west side of the Green untenable. It was demolished and the row of Pembroke Villas was built in its place in the very early 1850s. The railway cutting had sliced off a small portion of the park at the corner on the north-east side of the Green, where a small bridge was built to retain access between the Green and the Park. This proved rather a blessing to the vestry. In 1849 it had finally been agreed that Richmond should become an independent vicarage – separated from Kingston. King's College, Cambridge, who were the patrons of the living, agreed provided that the parish built a suitable new residence for the new vicar. The vestry *Plate 51* were still trying to raise the money for this when the Commissioners of Woods offered the site at the corner of the Green.

Beside St John's Church a new road was opened up between Kew Road and the Marshgate Road, with groups of villas along it, including Medina, St John's, Friston and Sidney. By 1852 the vestry had determined that the entire road should be called Church Road. To its east was another row, built in the late 1830s, called Dunstable Villas. In 1868 Sir Charles Selwyn, as he had then become, donated the land to enable Church Road to be extended up the hill from the Marshgate Road to St Matthias. It was all on Selwyn land, as were the roads developed off it between Church Road and Mount Ararat Road – Dynevor, Royston, Chislehurst.

With the development of the Robinson estate and that part of the Selwyn estate south of the Marshgate Road, already about half of the field on the hillside had begun to disappear. The late 1860s and 1870s saw a big advance in this process. Mr John Maxwell, publisher, vestryman, and husband of Mary Braddon the novelist, bought up at auction in 1865 some parts of the Robinson estate and built houses in Marchmont Road, crossing King's Road – and a bit later in Audley Road, named for two of his wife's best-known works: *John Marchmont's Legacy* and *Lady Audley's Secret*. To the south of Worple Way the Hillier land was developed with Albert Road and Prince's

*St Matthias Church*
*(vignette by Rook & Co.,*
*published 21 January 1862).*

*Plate 48*

The Austrian Ambassador's fête at the Castle Hotel *in honour of Queen Victoria's coronation. The assembly rooms are the range on the left; in the background is the rear of the main hotel building. (Engraving by H. Adlard from a drawing by T. Allom c.1838).*

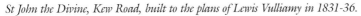

*St John the Divine, Kew Road, built to the plans of Lewis Vulliamy in 1831-36.*

*Plate 49*

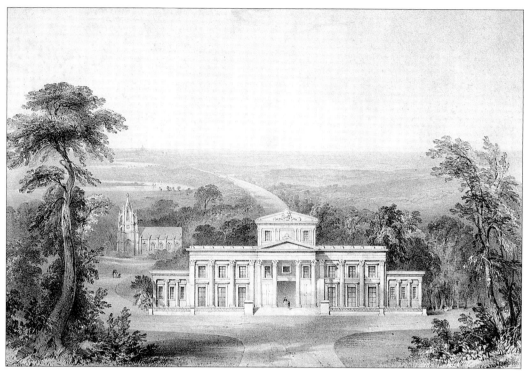

*The proposed terminal station at Richmond for the City of London and Richmond Railway, designed by Charles John Blunt, 1836. (Richmond Public Library, local studies collection)*

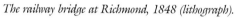

*The railway bridge at Richmond, 1848 (lithograph).*

*Plate 50*

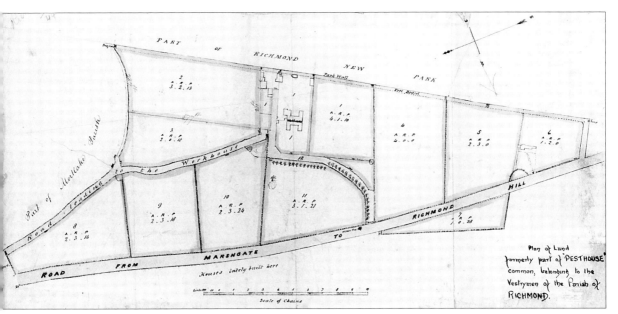

*The Richmond parish lands on Pesthouse Common in the late 1840s, a plan accompanying some lease documents (Trustees of Richmond Parish Lands Charity).*

*The Wesleyan Institute, c.1840 (engraving by H. Adlard from a drawing by T. Allom).*

*Plate 51*

*Victorian Mansions*

*Glebe House on Richmond Green, built as the new Richmond Vicarage in 1852; demolished 1967. (Author's photograph, 1965)*

*78 Richmond Hill, built on the former Cardigan/Lansdown land at the south-west end of Maybush Shott. It was 'Metcalfe's Hydro' in 1905 when this postcard was used. Now part of the site of the 'Hillbrow' flats.*

*Belle Vue House, Petersham Road, with its terraced garden down to the river in the 1890s when it was the home of Sir Edward Hertslet. Built (together with 1 and 2 Bellevue Place – on the left) about 1790, it was enlarged about 1840, and the new wing on the right was added in the 1860s. (Photograph courtesy of Sheila Hertslet-Hodges)*

Plate 52

*Ordnance Survey,*
*6 inches to 1 mile map of*
*Richmond surveyed in*
*1863, and first published*
*in 1868, but revised to*
*show the new railway line*
*through Kew. (Richmond*
*Public Library, local*
*studies collection)*

*Plate 53*

*Castlegate, the militia headquarters in the Lower Mortlake Road. (Richmond Public Library, local studies collection)*

*Cottages in the Lower Mortlake Road. (Photo by the author)*

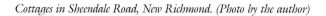

*Cottages in Sheendale Road, New Richmond. (Photo by the author)*

Plate 54

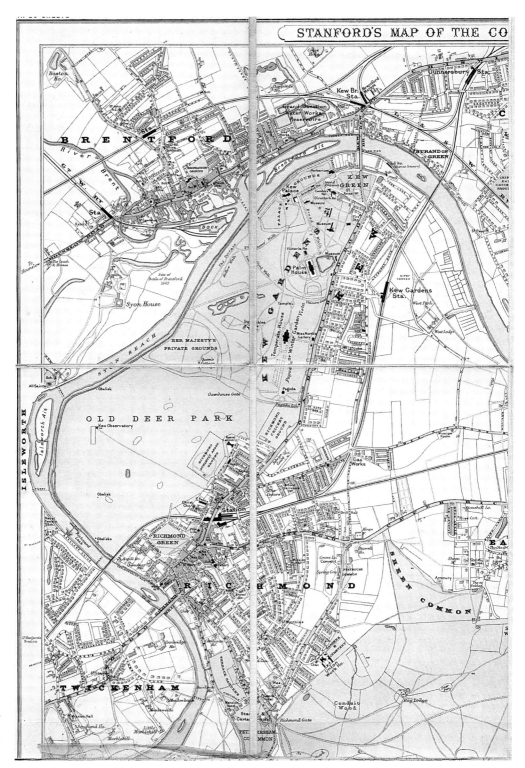

*Edward Stanford
4 inches to 1 mile
map published 1894.
(Richmond Public
Library, local studies
collection)*

*Plate 55*

*Spring Grove – the front to Queen's Road in 1899. (Richmond Public Library, local studies collection)*

*Grove Lodge (called at this time Marsh Gate House), c.1825 (British Library CRACH 1, TAB 1, b1, Vol. 6).*

Road in the '70s. Mount Ararat Road was widened and began to have villas built at its top end about 1865, and this growth was extended through Selwyn land in the late '70s. The first houses were built in Onslow Road, and a new terrace on the north side of Friar's Stile Road in the '60s; and a new row of cottages was built facing Alma Villas and the whole road – never quite opened through to Queen's Road at the southern end – was renamed Rosemont Road about 1866. These developments were more or less completed in the 1880s when Onslow Road, Montague Road, Marlborough Road and Cardigan Road were filled up with houses and new terraces were built in Friar's Stile Road. In Queen's Road new villas filled the gap between the Wesleyan Institute and Park Villas West.

On the north side of Marshgate Road the grounds of Upper Dunstable House were developed as Sheen Park, and just to their east the new Holy Trinity Church was built in 1870 and beside it and behind the almshouses Townshend Road, Townshend Terrace and Adelaide Road.

In the Mortlake Road the Larkfield House grounds were developed with Larkfield Road and an extension to St John's Villas in the 1870s, and Lumley Lodge was replaced by Jessie Terrace (later Cedar Terrace) about 1880. The 'New Richmond' development crept steadily eastwards, filling the land between the Mortlake Road and the new railway line up through Kew, with the building of Victoria Villas about 1870, then the Holy Trinity Schools, and finally Trinity Cottages and St George's Place in 1866.

Much of the northern side of the Mortlake Road, east of Blue Anchor Alley, was Selwyn land, but to the east of this was a large field belonging to the Crown. In its western corner, by the road, the barracks for the Surrey Militia had been built in 1856, with a drill ground behind. The buildings looked like the front wall of a castle and acquired the name Castlegate. After the building was given up in 1875 (in favour of a new castle in Kingston) it was bought by Thomas Cave MP and converted by him into 37 separate dwellings for lease at affordable rents to the poor – a private philanthropic anticipation of council housing. The land to the east of Castlegate was developed with Raleigh Road in the 1880s.

*Plate 53*

The north side of the road, up to Blue Anchor Alley, had the name of St John's Place, but *Kelly's Directory* for 1891/2 gives the buildings there the additional name of 'Selwyn's Model Cottages'. In that year a new house appears to the east of the alley and then, after a gap, Nos. 1-52 Compton Terrace between there and Castlegate (the first four houses of Compton Terrace – at the east end – were recorded in 1887). By 1894/5 the line of building on the north side of the road up to Castlegate was complete, with two houses, then Nos. 1-8 Crumpsell Villas, 1-67 Compton Terrace and five new shops called Pagoda Parade before the new south end of Pagoda Avenue came in to the west of what were now called 'Castlegate Dwellings'.

*Plate 53*

☩

To the north lay land which had become all Selwyn property, up to the part of Sandy Lane which turned round into the Kew Road. In 1868 there stood on this land just Sir Charles Selwyn's Pagoda House, and three cottages, Pagoda Cottage, Rose Cottage and Ivy Lodge. To its north there was still only a ribbon development from Sandy Lane up to the Mortlake Lane on the Kew Road frontage of the Engleheart estate. This estate was enfranchised in 1868 to John Gardner Engleheart, and a part to him and a brother as trustees for their aunt Lucy (Gardner). As a result of the opening of Kew Gardens Station in 1869 the new wide approach avenue from the station to the Sandy Lane corner was continued in a double sweep across the Engleheart lands. One branch curled back to the Kew Road (and was named Kew Gardens Road); a branch road off it (Prince's Road), led back to Sandy Lane. The other branch swept up to the Mortlake Road in a gentle curve (Cumberland Road). These roads, as also the part of the Engleheart estate north of the Mortlake Road, where Gloucester Road was developed by 1872, were soon lined with houses.

To the north of the Engleheart estate, the 'Priory' was sold in 1875 (and again in 1877) and its grounds were divided into two roughly equal parts, one to go with the 'Priory' itself (which had been enlarged into a substantial mansion since Miss Doughty's time), and the other to go with Priory Lodge, a 'Tudor-style house' (as it was described in the sale catalogue) with which went the 'Gothic' lodge gate on Kew Green and another small house on the Kew Green frontage. Priory Road and Priory Terrace (facing Kew Green) were developed by 1884, Forest Road in the late '80s, the houses north of Priory Road facing the Pond and Bradfield Gardens only by 1900.

*Plate 54*

The opening of the railway through Kew also spurred development on the rest of the Selwyn estate – or at least its northern part. The map of 1894 shows an interesting pattern. Starting from the northern end there is now a continuous line of villas along the Kew Road down to just south of Eversfield Road. On the south side of that part of Sandy Lane turning into Kew Road (which was separately renamed Broomfield Road in 1895) is a line of villas; then there are east-west turnings off Kew Road in order (from north to south): Lichfield, Holmesdale, Branston and Hatherley Roads, The Avenue, and Eversfield Road. Only Lichfield Road and The Avenue continue right through to Sandycombe Road (as Sandy Lane was renamed by the vestry in 1884). The others are terminated by a new Ennerdale Road, so sited that the ends of the back gardens of the houses on its east side reproduce exactly the old boundary between Middle Shott by the Kew Road and the Bank Shott by the Mortlake border. That Lichfield Road runs right through is a reminder that at the north end of both shotts was a single 20-acre field. There is another curious feature of this development. The roads in Middle Shott are lined with sizable houses. But, apart from Lawn Crescent, a late development, the houses in Bank Shott, in culs-de-sac off Sandycombe Road, are much smaller, and in the cases of Battenburg (now Windsor) Road, Alexandra Road, Victoria Cottages and Elizabeth Cottages, as small as the early developments of New Richmond or Sweeps' Alley.

Apart from The Avenue, originally intended as a route to Kew Gardens from the new station (the location of which was, however, changed), these show a steady development from north to south. Then there was a gap until another string of eight houses along the Kew Road and a little square of development at Lion Gate Gardens and the northern side of Stanmore Road. Pagoda Avenue, Selwyn Avenue and Beaumont Avenue had been laid out by 1894, but there were only 10 houses in Pagoda Avenue and nine in Selwyn Avenue.

Sandy Lane (or Sandycombe Road) was in Richmond, but the manor boundary lay along its eastern verge. Some terraced cottages were built on the west side in the course of the Selwyn estate development, but on the east side a long and almost unbroken string of small cottages was put up, terrace by terrace, starting in the early 1880s (many still bear the date of 1882). These, and Kew Gardens Station, only became part of Richmond when the Borough, newly chartered in 1890, took over not only Petersham and Kew, but the part of Mortlake since called North Sheen, in 1892. But that is another story.

✝

This survey has now covered almost all the area of the fields except those lying close to the east side of Richmond Hill. Up to the Vineyard they were already to a considerable extent built up by 1840. Hermitage Villas (later Road, and later just 'The Hermitage') were developed in the grounds of the Hermitage, the southernmost house of Church Terrace, in the 1850s; Halford Road was built in the grounds of Halford House in the first half of the 1880s. Lancaster Park and Ellerker Gardens, developed respectively in the late 1880s and the early 1890s, in the gardens of Lancaster House and Ellerker House (now the Old Vicarage School) similarly commemorate the names of the estates in which they were built, which together occupied almost the whole of West Bancroft. The southern end of Maybush Shot had been acquired by the owners of Cardigan House. Cardigan Road was laid out there in the late 1870s; originally the two sections had different names – Lansdowne Road, running into Richmond Hill, commemorated Lansdowne House which had stood on the west side of the Hill opposite the end of Friar's Stile Road, and which had been demolished in the early 1870s. It was then renamed as part of Cardigan Road in 1900. By then large mansions filled the frontage to Richmond Hill up to Friar's Stile Road.

*Plate 51*

So, by the end of the 19th century there were only two patches remaining of the original Richmond and Kew Fields. One was the part of the Selwyn estate close to Pagoda House (which was renamed Selwyn Court in 1878). The estate was sold in 1890; Selwyn Court itself was demolished in 1895 to be replaced by Christ Church. But it was not until just before the First World War that the gap between Eversfield Road and Lion Gate Gardens was filled by Walpole and Fitzwilliam Roads and that the section below Battenburg Road was laid out with Temple, Dudley, Gordon, Burdett and Gainsborough Roads, and not until after the war that those roads were built up. The last corner of the Selwyn estate to be developed was a part acquired by the Council for council housing – Windham and Braddon Roads, built up in the early 1930s.

The other last remnant of the fields was the Rugge-Price estate, occupying the western side of Queen's Road from Marshgate up almost to Park Road. This estate had been put together by Matthew Walker in the 1680s, then divided into halves by his will. The northern half nearer to Marshgate came eventually into the hands of the Phelp family. It had the original house, later called 'Grove Lodge'. The southern half with 'a messuage lately erected' was mortgaged to George Martin in 1694. Martin and Walker's heir Robert Ferrer sold this to William Triggs Esq in 1699, and Triggs sold the 'brick messuage recently built' to the Marquess of Lothian in 1716. This house, probably totally rebuilt, but certainly greatly altered, called 'Spring Grove', was purchased in 1797 by Charles Price. A banker and a member of the Ironmongers' Company (of which he was Master in 1798), Price served as Lord Mayor of London in 1802-03 and was duly rewarded with a baronetcy in January 1804. In 1813 he also purchased Grove Lodge, which had been for the last forty years the house of Lord Willoughby de Broke. Grove Lodge was then rented out, but Spring Grove remained the Price family home until the time of the 6th Baronet, Sir Charles Rugge-Price, who succeeded his father in 1892. (The father had added the name Rugge in 1874.)

*Plate 55*

*Plate 55*

Sir Charles intended to sell the estate for development in 1899, but the sale was not completed. He continued to live at Spring Grove until his death in 1927. However, a large part of the land was sold, and between 1904 and 1909 Marchmont Road was extended through to Queen's Road, and Spring Grove Road and Denbigh Gardens (west side only) were built. Behind the eight houses in Peldon a new Peldon Avenue of 50 houses was opened up (destroyed by bombing in September 1940 and replaced twenty years later by the highrise Pelden Court flats). When Spring Grove House was finally demolished in 1934 the east side of Denbigh Gardens could be built up in what had been gardens of the house. Much later, Queen's Crescent was built on the site of the house itself. Grove Lodge had been rented out as a Marist Convent. When the Marists moved to Sunningdale the site was redeveloped in 1945 as the St Edward the Confessor School, later merged into Christ's School.

That was really the end of the common fields of Richmond and Kew. We may also consider that the rebuilding of Middle Row, degenerated into 'Bug Island', in 1889-90, the slum clearance schemes along Red Lion Street in 1909, the demolition of many of the smallest cottages in the Kew Foot Road area and of almost all those in New Richmond after World War II virtually put an end also to the cottages. For any cottages that still remain, such as those in the Alberts, or Waterloo Place or Vine Row, are now the highly desirable small residences of the almost rich. It is not the end of the story of Richmond's development; but the replacement of houses by flats and office blocks, and the many fascinating new features of social and community life in the second half of the 19th and the 20th centuries is a whole new book.

# APPENDIX I

## *Variations of the Place-Names Shene and Kew*

| A. | SHENE | First noted | Source |
|---|---|---|---|
| | Sceon | 951 | Will of Bishop Theodred |
| | Sceanes | 1130 | Pipe Roll |
| | Schene | 1194 | Pipe Roll |
| | Sienes | 1204 | Curia Regis Roll |
| | Cernes* | c.1207 | Book of Fees (Testa de Nevill) |
| | Shenes | 1210-12 | Red Book of Exchequer |
| | Syenes | 1212 | Book of Fees |
| | Scrernis* | 1212-17 | Red Book |
| | Scien | 1214 | Curia Regis Roll |
| | Scenes | 1216 | Harleian Charter |
| | Seenes | 1218-19 | Curia Regis Roll |
| | Senes | 1219 | Book of Fees |
| | Shenys | 1220 | Curia Regis Roll |
| | Shene | 1230 | Surrey Feet of Fines |
| | Schenes | 1238 | Book of Fees |
| | Chenes | 1241 | Close Roll |
| | Westshenes | 1250 | Curia Regis Roll |
| | Sethnes* | 1250 | Book of Fees |
| | Senis | 1250 | Book of Fees |
| | Schene | 1255 | Close Roll |
| | West Shene | 1258 | Surrey Feet of Fines |
| | Shen | 1292 | Inquisitions Post Mortem |
| | Scene | 1302 | Patent Roll |
| | Sheen | 1445 | Privy Council |
| | Kyngston Shene | 1480 | William of Worcester |
| | Kyngshene | 1487 | Surrey Wills |

It is interesting also to note the phonetic (in Spanish) spelling of Xin, used by the Spanish Ambassador in 1498! In the same year the Milanese Ambassador got nearer the mark with Shyn.

---

* Probably clerical errors rather than genuinely variant spellings.

**B.** **KEW**

| | First noted | Source |
|---|---|---|
| Cahiho* | 1201 | Pipe Roll |
| Caiho* | 1202 | Pipe Roll |
| Cayho | c1314 | Extent of Manor |
| Cayesho | c1314 | Extent of Manor |
| Cayhow | c1314 | Extent of Manor |
| Cyho | c1314 | Extent of Manor |
| Kayo (juxta Braynford)† | 1330 | St Swithins Accounts |
| Kayho (juxta Braynford)† | 1330 | St Swithins Accounts |
| Keyho | 1375 | Merton Abbey records |
| Cayu | c1413 | Petition |
| Keyhowe | 1415 | Manor Roll |
| Cayhoo | 1417 | Manor Roll |
| Kayhowe | 1440 | Surrey Feet of Fines |
| Kayhough | 1491 | Manor Roll |
| Kayhoo | 1493 | Manor Roll |
| Kayheo | 1500 | Manor Roll |
| Keyo | 1500 | Manor Roll |
| Keyowe | 1513/4 | Manor Roll |
| Kayhow | 1522 | Surrey Feet of Fines |
| Keyhoe | 1524 | Surrey Feet of Fines |
| Kayooo | 1533 | Surrey Feet of Fines |
| Kew | 1533 | Surrey Feet of Fines |
| Keyhow | 1534 | Manor Roll |
| Cewe foreanempst Braynford | 1537 | CLPFD |
| Keew | 1538 | CLPFD |
| Kewe | 1538 | CLPFD |
| Kayehowe | 1539 | Manor Roll |
| Cayo | 1539 | Manor Roll |
| Kaio | 1540 | CLPFD |
| Kyeo | 1545 | CLPFD |

* These first two occurrences are as a surname 'de Cahiho' etc, and are not in the context of this area, so may not be relevant.
† The spelling occurs with and without the 'juxta Braynford' suffix.

# APPENDIX 2

# *The Extent of the Manor of Shene c.1314*

This document, in the Public Record Office (reference SCII/638), appears to be part of a regular manorial roll. It is on both sides of a single piece of parchment, written in a clear but very small hand, with many abbreviations. It is undated; but the date can be quite closely ascertained (see Chapter 3). The full translation below is entirely the work of the present author. The marginal rubrics are as in the original.

TRANSLATION – EXTENT OF THE MANOR OF SHENE – *circa* 1314

WALTER WALDESCHAFT holds two carucates of land in Turbevile of the Manor of Schene and pays annually 18 shillings at the quarter days: at the feast of St Michael 7s, at the feast of the Nativity of our Lord 4s, at Easter 3s, and at the feast of St John the Baptist 4s. And he owes suit at the lord's court every three weeks. And if he should die holding this tenement he is liable for a heriot, and if he were to die elsewhere in his own demesne he would pay nothing for having such demesne, but if he should die elsewhere and have no demesne elsewhere then he would be liable, etc.                   Sum –– 18s

holding in fee +RALPH POSTEL holds one messuage and three acres of land and pays nothing annually except suit at the lord's court as above; and he is liable for a heriot.

holding in fee WILLIAM ATTE CHURCHE holds one messuage and a curtilage and pays annually 2 shillings at the quarter days named above by equal instalments. And he owes suit as above; and he reaps for two days at harvest time and has an allowance of two meals a day, and the work is worth 2d a day; and he lifts hay for one day with food provided by the lord, and the work is worth ld. And he is liable for a heriot:                   Sum –– 2s

holding in fee JOHN LE CLERKE holds one messuage and half a curtilage and half an acre of land, and he pays annually 13 pence at the four quarter days above named, viz: at the feast of St Michael 4d and at each other quarter day 3d. And he does service and receives allowances in all respects as the aforesaid William atte Churche.                   Sum –– 13d

holding as above +MARY widow PAROLE holds one messuage and half a curtilage and pays annually 6 pence on two quarter days, viz: at the feast of St Michael and at Easter in equal instalments. And she makes one appearance at the lord's court each year, viz: at the feast of St Michael. And she is liable for a heriot.
                   Sum –– [*blank*]

holding as above +ISABELL DE BINGATES holds one messuage and 10 acres of land and one acre of meadow and pays annually 6s 8d at the four quarter days by equal instalments. And she owes suit every three weeks. And she is liable for a heriot.

[*Entry deleted*: CHRISTEN DE (?Nautarum Sinus)[1]]

holding as above   JOHN LE WALSCHE holds one messuage and 9 acres of land and one acre of meadow and pays annually 12 pence on two quarter days as above. And he owes suit as above. And he is liable for a heriot.

holding as above   JOHN LE SCHEPHURDE holds one messuage and four and a half acres and one rood of land, and he pays annually 15½ pence, viz: at the feast of St Michael. And he owes suit as above. And he is liable for a heriot.

holding as above   +HENRY LE MELEWARD holds one messuage and an acre and a half and one rood of land, and he pays 3d at the feast of St Michael. [*deleted* – And he owes suit as above.] And he is liable for a heriot.

holding as above   JOHN VALENTYN holds one messuage and 10 acres of land and pays annually 2 shillings at the four quarter days above named by equal instalments. And he owes suit as above. And he is liable for a heriot. And at harvest time he reaps on every other day when the lord shall assign the corn which is to be reaped by him, and for two days he receives for each day one loaf priced at ½d and fish priced at ¼d, and on a third day for dinner sufficient bread and cheese and two hot dishes of meat or fish and two [cakes?] priced at ¼d.

holding as above   +STEPHEN LOMBARD holds one messuage and 8 and a half acres and one rood of land and one acre of meadow, and pays 2d at the feast of St Michael. And he makes one appearance at the court at the feast of St Michael. And [*left blank-might have been intended to read 'he is liable for a heriot'*]

holding as above   DENIS LE LAD holds one messuage and [*deleted*:4 and a half acres of land] five acres of land and one acre and a half of meadow, and pays at the feast of St Michael one penny, and one more at the feast of the birth of St John the Baptist. And he is liable for a heriot. And he is free from all service. [*Added in margin*] And he also has a pasture for two horses, 4 oxen, 4 cows, 6 steers and heifers and for [200?] sheep. And he also has, a pasture for 12 pigs, formerly belonging to John de Valletorte, where the lord's pigs also use the same land, as is shown by a certain charter of the said John de Valletorte.

holding as above   RICHARD DE VALTORT holds one acre and one rood of land and pays annually one penny at the feast of St Michael in full discharge.

holding as above   THOMAS ATTE BOSCO [WOOD] holds 36 acres of land and four acres of meadow and pays annually 14 pence at the feast of St Michael. And he does service if he is present in the lands. And he is liable for a heriot if he should die in the said tenement.

holding as above   +ALICE widow of HENRY WARRE holds 4 virgates of land above and pays annually 8 shillings at the feast of St Michael. And she owes suit at the lord's court every three weeks. And she is liable for a heriot if she should die in the said tenement, as above.

+ at the court.

☩

RICHARD DE CAYHO holds in villenage one messuage, 20 and a half acres of land and two acres of meadow, and pays annually 3 shillings and 10 pence at the four quarter days by equal instalments. And he owes suit at the lord's court every three weeks. And he hoes for a half day without food, but if he works for a whole day he receives food, viz: one loaf priced at ½d and fish priced at ¼d, and the half day's work is worth 1d. And he mows for 2 days and receives nothing except a gift of

[1] Nautarum Sinus is Rotherhithe; but the reading is very dubious.

as much grass as he can lift with his scythe[2], and the day's work is worth 4d. And he lifts hay for 2 days without food, and the day's work is worth 1d. If he does not mow or lift the hay he is to receive nothing.[3] And at harvest time he reaps with two men every other day, with food provided by the lord, and for any third day he receives allowances as John Valentyn, as appears above. And on the first day of May he gives 6d for the right of pannage. And he pays merchet. And he gives 10 eggs at Easter.

ALICE DE CAYESHO holds as above one messuage, 18 acres of land and two acres of meadow, and pays annually 2 shillings and 10 pence on the aforesaid quarterdays by equal instalments. And she does service in all respects as the aforesaid Richard. And the aforesaid Richard and Alice jointly provide cartage for one cartload of fuel before Christmas, and they may return home on the same day. And the aforesaid Richard and Alice jointly cart the lord's corn for two days at harvest time, with food provided by the lord, viz: three meals. And they jointly cart hay for the lord for one day, with food provided by the lord as above.

JOHN HO holds in villenage one messuage, 14 and a half acres of land and 2 acres of meadow, and pays annually 3 shillings at the aforesaid quarterdays by equal instalments. And he owes suit of court as above. And he threshes and winnows half a quarter of wheat without food; and gives 10 eggs at Easter. And he hoes as the aforesaid Richard, etc. And at harvest time he provides two men for reaping the lord's corn as does the aforesaid Richard, with food provided by the lord as for the aforesaid Richard. And he ploughs at Lent each year in whatever place at the will of the lord for seven full days[4] with food provided by the lord. And he harrows for half a day. If he does not do the ploughing he is to receive nothing. And with one man he mows the lord's meadow on whatever day the lord's meadow is to be mown; and with one man he lifts the lord's hay for as long as is needed to lift all the lord's hay; and for the lifting of the hay the lord provides food which will be carried to the fields – and by custom they have a sheep worth 2 shillings at the time of the haymaking. And at harvest time he carts the lord's corn for 2 days, with food provided by the lord. And he pays merchet. And he makes 2 quarters of malt.

JOHN LE CLERKE DE CAYESHO holds as above one messuage, 18 acres of land and 2 acres of meadow, and pays annually 3 shillings and 5 pence, viz: at Easter 11d and on each of the other days 10d. And he does service in all respects as the aforesaid John Ho, except that he does not thresh and winnow, nor plough. But he carts fuel as the aforesaid Richard de Cayesho.

RICHARD LOVE holds in villenage, etc, one messuage, 9 acres of arable land and 1 acre of meadow, and pays annually 2 shillings at the four quarterdays by equal instalments. And he owes suit; and threshes and winnows 2 bushels of wheat, and hoes and mows as the aforesaid John;[5] and lifts hay as above. And with one man he reaps at harvest time on every other day, the lord providing food as above. And at harvest time he carts the lord's corn for one day. And he ploughs the demesne land each year for 7 full days, the lord providing food. And he gives 5 eggs at Easter. And he pays merchet. And he makes one quarter of malt.

JOHN CAYHOW holds as above one messuage, 9 acres of land and 1 acre of meadow, and pays annually 18 pence at the four quarterdays by equal instalments. And he does service in all respects as the aforesaid Richard Love. And he carts animal dung in the fields for the lord as above to half a virgate of land. And he guards the lord's sheep in the field at the time of shearing, the lord providing food (or he receives ¾d). And during Lent he provides one man with a horse (if he has a horse) for harrowing for half a day. And he digs for half a day without food provided. And he pays merchet. And he makes one quarter of malt.

---

[2] A not uncommon form of payment — quite a lot of hay could be balanced and lifted on the handle of a scythe.
[3] Presumably the meaning is that if he does not finish the work he is to get no payment.
[4] The word used here is 'lux' — daylight, i.e. the whole period from sunrise to sunset.
[5] John Ho is presumably intended.

ALICE widow CARPENTER holds one messuage, 9 acres of land and 1 acre of meadow, and pays annually 18 pence at the four quarterdays by equal instalments. And she does service in all respects as the aforesaid John le Cayhow. And she makes one quarter of malt. And she provides one hurdle every other year.

ISABELL BINNEGATES holds one messuage, 9 acres of land and 1 acre of meadow, and pays nothing. And she does service in all respects as the aforesaid Alice. And she washes the lord's sheep for half a day and shears for half a day, the lord providing food (or she receives ¾d). And she makes malt and provides a hurdle as above.

WILLIAM LE DRIVERE holds 9 acres of land and 1 acre of meadow, and pays annually 2 shillings at the four quarter days by equal instalments. And he does service in all respects as the aforesaid Alice. And he washes and shears as above; and provides a hurdle as above.

CRISTEN widow SIMON holds one messuage, 9 acres of land and 1 acre of meadow, and pays and does service in all respects as the aforesaid Alice. And she washes and shears as above. And she makes one quarter of malt and provides a hurdle as above.

JOHN GOIONN holds one messuage, 9 acres of land and 1 acre of meadow, and pays and does service each year as the aforesaid Alice. And he washes and shears as above.

GILBERT BINNEGATE holds one messuage, 9 acres of land and 1 acre of meadow, and does service and pays as [*deleted*: the aforesaid Alice and guards ...] the aforesaid John le Cayhow.

THOMAS LE THRISHERE holds one messuage, 9 acres of land and one acre of meadow, and pays annually 18 pence at the four quarterdays by equal instalments. And he does service in all respects as Isabell de Binnegates. And he buys one hurdle every other year for the lord's enclosure. And he makes two quarters of malt.

JOHN ERMITE holds one messuage, 9 acres of land and one acre of meadow, and he pays and does service in all respects as Thomas le Thrishere.

[*Space is left here for one entry, indicated by a marginal mark, but not inserted.*]

GILBERT HO holds one messuage, 13 and a half acres of land and one and a half acres of meadow, and pays annually 2 shillings and 8 pence at the four quarterdays by equal instalments.[6]

ADAM LADDE holds one messuage, 13 and a half acres of land and one and a half acres of meadow, and pays annually 2 shillings and 3 pence at the four quarterdays by equal etc. And he threshes and winnows 3 bushels of wheat [at any place within the demesne?]. And he carts dung as above. And he hoes, and mows and lifts hay as above, and ploughs as above. And he does service in all respects as aforesaid for one virgate and a half of land. And he makes five and a half quarters of malt. And he provides hurdles, viz: one year two hurdles and the next year following one hurdle, and so on year by year.

ANNE widow WARY holds one messuage, 18 acres of land and 2 acres of meadow, and pays annually 3 shillings at the four quarterdays by equal instalments. And she threshes and winnows half a quarter of wheat. And she carts dung as above. And she makes 2 quarters of malt. And she gives one hurdle a year. And she hoes for half a day; and mows with one man for each day when the lord's meadow is to be mown; and she lifts and carts hay for as long as is needed for all the hay to be lifted. And at harvest time she provides 2 men every other day for reaping the lord's corn, with food provided by the lord as above. And she carts the lord's corn for 2 days at harvest time, with food provided by the lord as above. And she ploughs as above. And she owes suit and merchet. And [*deleted*: she gives for four meadows) she pays at the feast of St Michael 1 penny for the right of pannage; and for any meadow she pays for half a year ½d; and if she has no pigs nor piglets she gives nothing. And she gives one hurdle each year[7]. And she gives 10 eggs. And she

---

[6] There is no mention in this entry of any services owed, but Adam Ladde (next entry) appears to do service for twice his own holding. It appears that for some reason Adam Ladde performs Gilbert Ho's services as well as his own.

[7] This sentence appears to be repetitive.

[repairs?] four hurdles twice a year for the lord's pale. And she harrows for half a day. And she fixes one hurdle with the lord's fastenings.

GILBERT VAGGE holds one messuage, 18 acres of land and 2 acres of meadow and pays annually 4 shillings at the four quarterdays as above by equal instalments as above. And he does service in all respects as the aforesaid Anne, except that he gives a hurdle only every other year and he does not make malt. But he brings the sheep to the shearing and takes them back to the fields.

MAUD LE PALMER holds one messuage, 18 acres of land [and all as above?], and pays annually 3 shillings at the four quarterdays by equal instalments, etc. And she does service in all respects as the aforesaid Anne, except that she folds the fleeces.

MAUD DE BINNEGATES holds as above and pays annually 4 shillings at the four quarterdays by equal etc. And she does service in all respects as the said Gilbert Vagge, except that she does not give a hurdle, and she washes and shears the lord's sheep for two half-days.

ADAM BIGGE holds as above and pays annually 3 shillings and 6 pence at the four quarterdays by equal etc. And he does service in all respects as the aforesaid Anne, except that he provides 5 men every other day at harvest time, with food provided by the lord, and each one of them has a dinner priced at ¾d. And he provides two men on each day for mowing the lord's meadow when the meadow is to be mown.

GILBERT DE CYHO holds as above and pays annually 3 shillings at the quarterdays as above. And he does service in all respects as the aforesaid Maud le Palmer.

WILLIAM THOMAS holds as above and pays annually 4 shillings at the quarterdays as above. And he does service in all respects as the aforesaid Maud de Binnegates.

JOHN PARGENT holds as above and pays annually 3 shillings at the quarterdays as above. And he does service in all respects as the aforesaid Anne.

MAUD BALIS holds as above and pays annually 3 shillings at the quarterdays as above. And she does service in all respects as the aforesaid Anne.

GILBERT BONDE holds as above and pays annually 4 shillings at the quarterdays as above. And he does service as the aforesaid Maud de Binnegates, except that he carries a rod at the sheep shearing.

fine 3s  JOHN RANDULPH holds as above and pays annually 3 shillings at the days as above. And he does service in all respects as the aforesaid Maud le Palmer.

William Drivere
John le Ermite
John Goionn
Total of aforesaid rents 113s 9 ½d
fine 3s
fine 5s  JOHN LE WALSCH came to the court and made a fine that he might hold for three years a virgate of land which is of the hereditament of John [d'Amer?] which he holds by demise from the said John to the said [devisee?], paying therefor an annual rent of 3 shillings at the quarterdays above named by equal etc, and doing service in all respects as the aforesaid Anne, except that he makes nothing, but he prepares the sheepfold.

Thomas le Thrishere
John Goionn
William Drivere
John Ermite
fine 20s  ROBERT LADDE came to the court and made a fine for relief of his lands out of the hands of the lord, which were seized because the aforesaid Robert said that he was a free man, and afterwards it was found by the inquest and by his own admission that he was born a bondsman. And he is to give 20 shillings to the lord

(sureties: John le Walsche, John Ermite, William le Drivere, John Goionn, Richard de Valtort and Gilbert le Cyho). And the tenement was restored to him and he did homage for one messuage, 18 acres of land and two acres of meadow. And he pays annually 3 shillings at the quarterdays above named by equal etc. And he does service in all respects as the aforesaid Maud le Palmer.

recognizance 20s All tenants, both freemen and villeins, recognized the lord and gave 20s.

DENIS LADDE came and made a fine for relief out of the hands of the lord of his lands which were seized and that he might hold the same without other service because he is a carter, and that they might be free in perpetuity. And he gave as a fine 40 shillings, viz: at the feast of All Saints next following 20 shillings and at the feast of the Nativity of our Lord 10 shillings and at the feast of the Purification of the Blessed Mary 10 shillings (sureties: Sir Hugh de Hausche. and Ralph Wakemer). And he did homage for (as shown elsewhere).

# APPENDIX 3

## *The Shene Manorial Accounts 1313-22: Prices*

(Note: the famine years were 1315-16, 1316-17 and 1321-22)

### 1. Grain and allied products

|   |   |   |   |
|---|---|---|---|
| a. | Wheat per quarter | 1313-4 | 6s |
|   |   | 1314-5 | 10s 8d |
|   |   | 1315-6 | 20s |
|   |   | 1316-7 | 16s |
|   |   | 1317-8 | 9s |
|   |   | 1320-1 | 6s 8d |
|   |   | 1321-2 | 17s |
| b. | Oats per quarter | 1313-4 | 2s-2s 8d |
|   |   | 1314-5 | 2s-3s |
|   |   | 1315-6 | 3s-4s |
|   |   | 1316-7 | 5s |
|   |   | 1317-8 | 3s-5s |
|   |   | 1319-20 | 1s 6d-1s 8d |
|   |   | 1320 | 1s 8d |
|   |   | 1321-2 | 2s 2d |
| c. | Barley per quarter | 1314-5 | 5s 4d |
|   |   | 1315-6 | 15s |
|   |   | 1317-8 | 7s |
|   |   | 1320-1 | 4s 4d |
|   |   | 1321-2 | 8s |
| d. | Rye per quarter | 1313-4 | 5s-6s 8d |
|   |   | 1314-5 | 6s 4d-10s 8d |
|   |   | 1315-6 | 17s-18s 8d |
|   |   | 1316-7 | 13s 4d |
|   |   | 1317-8 | 6s 4d-6s 8d |
|   |   | 1320-1 | 3s 4d |
| e. | Malt per quarter | 1313-4 | 6s 8d |
| f. | Bran per quarter | 1317 | 1s 4d |

### 2. Other crops

|   |   |   |   |   |
|---|---|---|---|---|
| a. | Peas per quarter | 1313-4 | 3s 4d |   |
| b. | Haras (a kind of pulse) | 1313-4 | 4s 8d |   |
|   | per quarter | 1316-7 | 5s 4d |   |
|   |   | 1319-20 | 3s |   |
| c. | Vetches (lentils) per quarter | 1321-22 | | 6s 8d |
| d. | Beans per quarter | 1319-20 | | 3s 4d |
| e. | Apples per quarter | 1315 | | 2s |
|   |   | 1316 | | 1s 4d |

### 3. Livestock and related products

| | | | |
|---|---|---|---|
| a. | Horses | 1316 | 10s |
| | | 1317 | 17s-24s |
| | | 1321 | 19s 6d-40s |
| b. | Oxen | 1314 | 14s-16s |
| | | 1316 | 10s- 13s 4d |
| | | 1317 | 13s 4d-20s |
| | | 1321 | 13s 4d-17s |
| c. | Bulls | 1317 | 18s |
| d. | Cows | 1314 | 10s |
| | | 1315 | 16s |
| | | 1316 | 10s-15s |
| | | 1317 | 22s |
| e. | Rams | 1321 | 2s 2½d |
| f. | Sheep | 1314 | 1s-1s 6d |
| | | 1315 | 1s 2d-1s 4d |
| | | 1321 | 1s 8d-2s |
| g. | Lambs | 1321 | 4d |
| h. | Pigs (incl. Boars) | 1315 | 4s 4d |
| i. | Wool per pet (7 lb) | 1313-4 | 2s 8d |
| | | 1314-5 | 2s 5d |
| | per unshorn sheepskin | 1321-2 | 5d |
| j. | Hides (oxen or cows) | 1319 | 1s 8d |
| k. | Cheese per ¼-pisa | | 12s |
| l. | Eggs per 120 | 1316 | 5d |
| | | 1317 | 4d |
| | | 1321 | 4d |

### 4. Fish

| | | | |
|---|---|---|---|
| a. | Herring per 1000 | 1317 | 11s 8d |
| b. | Salmon each | 1314 | 3s approx |
| | | 1315 | 2s 4d |
| | | 1316 | 3s 5d |
| | | 1317 | 4s 4d |
| c. | Sturgeon each | 1316 | 24s |

### 5. Agricultural implements, etc.

| | | | |
|---|---|---|---|
| a. | Plough shares each | 1316 & 1321 | 8d |
| b. | Plough shoes each | 1317 | 3½d |
| | | 1320 | 3d |
| c. | Cart wheels per pair | 1316 | 2s |
| d. | Clouts (for cart axles) | 1316, 17 & 21 | 1d |
| e. | Clout nails per 100 | 1316, 17 & 21 | 1½d |
| f. | Hurdles each | 1317 | 1¼d-1½d |
| | | 1320 | 1½d |
| | | 1321 | 1¼d |

### 6. Building materials, metals, etc.

| | | | |
|---|---|---|---|
| a. | Tiles per 1000 | 1314 | 3s 0½d |
| b. | Tile pins per 1000 | 1314 | 1¼d |
| c. | Oak laths | 1317 | 6d |
| | | 1321 | 4¼d |
| d. | Sap laths per 100 | 1321 | 22d |
| e. | Lath nails per 1000 | 1317 | 3d-10d |
| | | 1321 | 5d |

| f. | Spike nails per 1000 | 1317 | 10d |
| | | 1321 | 9d |
| g. | Lime per quarter | 1321 | 8d |
| h. | Tar per gallon | 1313 | 8d |
| | | 1314 | 5½d |
| i. | Iron per 8 lbs | 1324 | 5d |
| j. | Lead per lb | 1321 | ½d |
| k. | Brass per quarter | 1317 | 1s 4d |
| l. | Locks & keys per piece | 1320 | 5d |

## 7. Miscellaneous

| a. | Salt per 3 bushels | 1315 | 3s |
| | | 1316 | 3s |
| | | 1317 | 1s 8d-2s 2d |
| | | 1319 | 1s 5¼d-2s |
| | | 1320 | 1s 3d |
| b. | Candles per lb | 1314 & 15 | 2d |
| c. | Wax per lb | 1317, 20 & 21 | 6d |
| d. | Grease per gallon | 1314 | 1s 2d |
| e. | Canvas per ell | 1321 | 3d |
| f. | Rope per tey | 1321 | 1s 6d |
| g. | Salmon nets | 1314 | 45s 8d |
| | | 1316 | 17s 6d |
| | | 1317 | 22s |
| | | 1319 | 26s 6d |
| h. | Herring nets per piece | 1320 | 2s 6d-5s |
| i. | Bast cords per 220 | 1320 | 4s |
| j. | Hempen thread per lb | 1321 | 2s |
| k. | Tan per quarter | 1321 | 1s 4d |
| l. | 9-gallon brass pot | 1314 | 12s |
| m. | Glass lamp & chain | 1321 | 3d |
| n. | Strigil | 1321 | 2d |

## 8. Labour costs

| a. | Mowing per acre | 1321 | 3d |
| b. | Threshing: wheat, rye per qr | 1314, 15, 17, 20 & 21 | 3d |
| | barley, haras, beans per qr | 1314, 16, 17, 20 & 21 | 2d |
| | oats per qr | 1314, 20 & 21 | 1d |
| c. | Winnowing per qr | 1316 & 17 | ¼d |
| d. | Thatcher per day | 1314, 15, 17 & 21 | 4d |
| | Thatcher's assistant per day | 1314, 16, 17 | 2d |
| | | 1321 | 1½d |
| e. | Tiler per day | 1314 | 4d |
| | Tiler's assistant per day | 1314 | 3d |
| f. | Carpenter per day | 1314 | 4d |
| | | 1316, 17, 21 | 4d-5d |
| | | 1320 | 5d |
| g. | Sawyer (2 men for 1 day) | 1321 | 42d |
| h. | Plasterer per day | 1316 | 3d |
| i. | Fisherman per year | 1315 | 16s |
| j. | Cartage: 50 qrs of oats from Shene to London | 1316 | 2s 1d (i.e. ½d per qr) |

# APPENDIX 4

# *The Shotts of the Common Fields of Richmond and Kew*

The term 'furlong' for a division of the open fields appears to predate the usage of 'shott', but it survived only in the Kew Field. There are many variant names for some of the divisions, and the dates of first usage encountered are given below: but often the usages overlapped. It was rare for the entries in the manor rolls to give particulars of the strips in the fields when they changed hands before the 17th century, as most transfers were in 'whole' or 'half tenements, so the Rayneford terrier of 1559 is a very useful source of early names. Some of the field divisions are not identifiable by any name until the Richmond manor terrier of *circa* 1620.

The sub-divisions of the furlong or shott into strips were said to 'shoot' in a given direction: thus, for example, Upper Dunstable Shott which ran from east to west had its strips 'shooting north to south'.

**A. Kew Field** (all shotts shooting north to south), between the Kew 'horse road' on the east and the 'foot lane' to the ferry on the west.

1. *Tinderland*, the northernmost shott. abutting the Green. Kew Park (first mentioned in 1560) appears to have been formed out of its western portion. The name 'Tinderland' is first mentioned in 1577. There were two headland strips at the north.

2. *Park Furlong* abutted Kew Park and Tinderland on its north side. Its name before the formation of Kew Park is unknown. Although there are references to land here as 'by the Park corner' from 1578, the name of Park Furlong is not found before 1620.

3. *Brickkiln Furlong* abutted Park Furlong on its north side. It is named as Brickkiln Furlong in the 1620 terrier. The date of establishment and the exact site of the kiln are unknown, but a note on the church lands in 1596 refers to three half acres 'in Kew fields near ye Brickhouse', and there is a later reference to the digging of clay for bricks in these half acres.

4. *Foxholes* (first mentioned in 1552) abutted Brickkiln Furlong on its north side. and the Lower Richmond Field on the south. It was only about half the width of the other shotts and was perhaps a later addition to the field. It was divided into a few short, broad strips.

5. *West Deane* is mentioned as a part of Kew Field in 1504, East Deane in 1517, and 'Dean Head' in 1578. After the division of Kew Field (except Tinderland) between the Earl of Ancram and Richard Bennett in 1648 by a north-south line, the names of East Dene and West Dene seem to have been revived briefly. The 'Dean Head hedge' formed the south limit of this division, but the name of Dean Head seems to have been used for Foxholes plus a northern part of Park Shott in the Richmond field. The location of the original 'West Deane' of 1504 is uncertain, but it may have been the part of the field which I believe to have lain to the west of the footway to the ferry and to have been absorbed into the freehold estate there.

## B. LOWER FIELD OF RICHMOND

In the early 17th century the Lower Field had a very different character from the Upper Field. Whereas the latter was almost entirely divided into strips of one acre or a half-acre, this was the case in the Lower Field only in the southern two-thirds of Park Shott. The northern part of Park Shott, Middle Shott, Bank Shott and (to some extent) Lower Shott had much larger holdings of land – in some cases up to 20 acres or 18 acres in a single parcel. As these lands adjoined what remained of the manor warren to the west and Kew Heath to the north it seems likely that they were the result of assarting at a period later than the original division into strips.

A part, some 35 acres, of the Lower Field, on the west of the 'foot lane' to Kew Ferry, was purchased by King James I in 1605-07 to add to his new park. It is possible that the area to the west of this (also included in this park) known as the 'Lord's Pieces' had also been part of the original lower field, though reserved by the Lord as demesne land.

1.  *Path Furlong*, the name used in the Rayneford terrier in 1559, covered all the land which was known as *Park Shott* after the formation of King James's park, as well as the land purchased by the King for the park. Before this purchase, the 'path', or Kew foot lane, ran through more than half of this field. There were however alternative names in use:

>   1(a)  *Fagge Furlong*, first mentioned in 1550, appears to have been the northern end of Path Furlong or Park Shott. Fagge had the meaning of a left-over piece (as in fag-end), from which it may be conjectured that this was indeed the last part of the common fields to be recovered from the waste and distributed to manorial tenants. The present Kew Road was known as 'Fagge Lane' as early as 1492, and this name survived in use for a while after the formation of the park.

>   1(b)  *Crab Tree Shott*, a name found only in a single entry in 1621, appears to refer to the southern part of Park Shott and may have been a usage contemporaneous with that of Fagge Furlong which had survived in a partial recitation in 1621 of an earlier (but now lost) entry.

*Park Shott* was used for the whole field, from Richmond Green up to the Kew Field, on the west side of Fagge Lane or the Kew horse road, once the Park was formed. The strips shot from east to west.

2.  *Middle Shott* is found as a name in 1607, but the 1620 terrier calls it the *Shott butting the highway to Kew*. Its divisions shot east to west, but were, in 1620, only some eight large holdings. (Rayneford had no land here, so the name in use in 1559 is unknown.)

3.  *The Shott butting on Baylie's Bank* is the 1620 name for the land along the Mortlake border south of Kew Heath. 'Baylie's Bank' or 'Mortlake Bank' was within the manor of Mortlake. This shott was later known simply as Bank Shott. Its divisions shot east to west, but were also mostly large holdings. The 20-acre holding at the north end of both Middle Shott and Bank Shott was allotted to Bank Shott by the 1620 terrier. It had belonged in 1559 to Rayneford but was then described as at 'P..den way by Shepperd's Cross', which appears to refer to the end of Sandy Lane (now Broom field Road) rather than to a field division.

4.  *Lower Shott* (shooting north-south) was the triangular area between the highways to Kew and Mortlake, and it is sometimes so described. The 1620 terrier calls it the *Lower Shott butting the highway to Mortlake*.

## C. THE UPPER FIELD OF RICHMOND

1.  *Nether Downstede* (1559)
    *Nether Dunstead* (1606)
    *Lower Dunstel* (1567)
    *Lower Dunstable* (from 1578)
    *Lower Shott of the Upper Field* (1615)

are all variants of what eventually became settled as Lower Dunstable Shott (shooting north-south), the northernmost shott of the Upper Field, on the south side of the highway to Mortlake.

2.  *Aldey* (1491)
    *The Alders*

were closes between the east end of Lower Dunstable and the manor boundary. It is probable that they had been reclaimed from the marsh at a relatively early date.

3.  *Upper Downstede* (1559)
    *Upper Dunstead* (1606)
    *Upper Dunstel* (1567)
    *Upper Dunstable* (from 1578)

Upper Dunstable (shooting north-south) abutted Lower Dunstable on its north side. On the south its boundary was the old road to East Sheen which followed the line of Worple Way and Peldon Passage up to Marshgate, rather than that of the later Marshgate(now Sheen) Road. 'Marshgate' was where the road had a gate across it at the manor boundary. There was an extensive marsh on the Mortlake side: a somewhat smaller one on the Richmond side.

4a. *Church Furlong* (1550)
    *Church Shott*
    *Conduit Shott* (rare)

The western end of this shott (shooting north-west to south east) began a little to the east of what is now Hill Street and Hill Rise, being separated from the road by a private freehold close. The variable factor was its eastern limit. In 1559 'Church Furlong' was used only for the land up to the conduit (on the line of Mount Ararat Road). More frequently it was used to cover all the land up to the field path which is now Albany Passage. In the 1620 terrier Church Shott extended all the way to the Great Common south of Marshgate.

4b. *East Furlong* (1559)

The name is found only in the Rayneford terrier, and was used for all the land from the conduit (Mount Ararat Road) to the Common.

4c. *The Marsh* (1567)
    *Marsh Furlong* (1578)
    *Marsh Furze Shott* (1606)

The eastern end (or extension) of Church Shott, from Albany Passage to the Common. The strips (shooting north to south) were longer here than those further west. The eastern end of the shott was reclaimed from the marsh only in the late 16th century.

5.  *West Baynecroft* (1559)
    *West Bancroft* (from 1550)

A small shott, shooting east to west, on the slope of the hill, stretching southwards from the Vineyard Lane about two-thirds of the way up towards Friar's Stile Lane. It was separated from the road up the hill by a private freehold close, and its eastern boundary was a field path on the line of Onslow Road which led to the Friar's Stile.

6.  *East Baynecroft* (1559)
    *East Bancroft*

Another small shott, also shooting east to west, on the east side of West Bancroft and stretching from the Vineyard Lane to as far south as West Bancroft. Its eastern boundary in the northern part was on the line of Mount Ararat Road, but the strips in the southern third of the shott extended beyond this line to abut the westernmost strip of Long Downs.

7.  *Short Downe Furlong* (1559)
    *Redde Condyt Furlong* (1569)
    *Maybush Shott*

Alternative names for the shott, shooting north-west to south-east, which lay between the southern end of the two Bancrofts and the Friar's Stile Lane. At the west end it extended right up to the highway on Richmond Hill, and its eastern end was on the line of Mount Ararat Road. The old Red Conduit stood in this shott.

8.  *East Field Shott* (1578)
    *Common Shott* (1679)
    *Long Common Shott*
    *Shott abutting the Heath*
    *Heath Shott* (1668)

A variety of names applied to the whole shott comprising the two distinct parts noted at 8a and 8b below. The name East Field Shott was used in the 1620 terrier. Heath Shott was the most common usage.

8a.  *Upper South Field* (1550)
     *East Downe* (1559)
     [North (*sic*) Down abutting the Great Common (1615)]

The southernmost part of the Upper Field, shooting north west to south-east. It was bounded on the north-west by the Friar's Stile Lane and on the south-east by the Great Common. It was divided from the road on the hill by a parcel of waste ground which was granted into private hands in the 16th century. (The southern corner of the field was just behind the present Doughty House on The Terrace.) The north-eastern boundary was a path (through a strip and not a field path) which connected the end of the Friar's Stile Lane (at a point between 8 and 10 King's Road) with the 'Brunningham Stile' giving access to the Common (at the north side of Queen's Court). The Friar's Stile (a name first found in 1631) was at the head of the present Marlborough Road. The 'North Down' name, found in a single entry in 1615, was probably a clerical error for 'South Down'.

8b.  *South Downe* (1559)
     *Pennard's Butts* (1691)

A small shott, shooting east to west, between East Down and Marsh Furze Shott, abutting Long Downs on the west and the Great Common on the east. It was trapezoid in shape, with its northern end almost twice as long as its (very short) southern end. Though it appears quite distinctive on the map it was seldom differentiated from East Down, and the two together were known by the names given at 8 above. The name 'Pennard's Butts' suggests the possibility that there were archery butts here. Richard Pennard, a tilemaker, died in 1655, and John Pennard had children baptised in the 1660s, but there is no evidence to link either of them to this location. The boundary with Marsh Furze Shott was known as the Withy Hedge (1497) or Withy Cross Hedge (1567).

9.    *Long Downe* (1559)
      *Long Downs*

With 10 below, this formed an almost triangular area surrounded by other shotts: clockwise from the north – Church Shott, Marsh Furze Shott, Heath Shott, Maybush Shott and West Bancroft. The strips shot north to south, but there were two groups of headlands shooting east-west at the north side: one against the Marsh Furze Shott boundary at Withy Hedge, and the other against the Church Shott boundary. The latter group of headlands were known collectively as *Love Tree Field* (the 'Love Tree' stood at the corner of the Vineyard and Mount Ararat Road).

10.    *Short Downs* (1564)

This was the very small western corner of the triangle, between Love Tree Field on the north and the extended strips of East Bancroft on the south. It seems likely that it was originally part of Long Downs, but was given this name (its strips, shooting north-south, were very short) when it fell into disuse for Maybush Shott (7 above).

# APPENDIX 5

# *The Population of the Manor*

Until 1801, when the first census was held, it is only possible to estimate the population of Richmond from such indications as the number of manorial tenants or the number of houses. The latter figure can only be calculated with any degree of accuracy from 1603 onwards, as the manorial records are complete and continuous from that date. But the former can be assessed from various lists of tenants which appear in the records from the earliest times. An overlap in the period from 1603 to 1703 is helpful in correlating the two sets of figures.

## *Number of Manorial Tenants*

The manorial extent of *circa* 1314 gives us an exact figure of land-holding tenants at this early date. The next exact figure comes only in 1649, when all tenants were listed in the parliamentary survey of the manor prior to its sale. But the Manor Court always listed those attending, together with (often incomplete) lists of defaulters and, sometimes, also those whose homage was still due to be made. In 1553 and 1628 there are lists which appear to be virtually complete. Rough estimates for other periods can be made by taking a series of court records and noting all the names of jurors and defaulters listed and any others whose surrenders of property show them to have been tenants, even though they do not appear in the lists. (These estimates are likely to be a little on the low wide.) A manor survey made in 1703 provides an accurate figure for that year – which can be closely reconciled with surviving rentals for 1702 and 1704. Thereafter, figures for number of tenants bear no meaningful relationship to population.

## *Number of Houses*

A detailed study of the manor records permits a fairly close estimate to be worked out of the number of houses standing in Richmond and Kew in the early 17th century. This exercise has been attempted for 1603 and 1620. For 1664 the Hearth Tax returns provide accurate figures, even differentiating between occupied and empty houses. Another estimate, based on the 'survey' of the manor made in that year, has been calculated for 1703. The manor survey of 1771 allows another accurate figure to be computed. From 1801 onwards the numbers of occupied and unoccupied houses (including in the latter figure those still in the course of construction) are given in the census returns.

## *Estimating the Total Population*

For some time it was assumed that the average size of a medieval family unit was some five persons. However, a very detailed study of *British Medieval Population* was published by Josiah Cox Russell in 1948. Russell reckoned that for the medieval period a multiplying factor of 3.5 per house gives a fair figure of the total population, and went on to argue that the same factor could be applied to lists of manorial tenants. While this might be true for country manors, I doubt if it is applicable without considerable modification to a case like Shene or Richmond, where the presence of a royal palace would have affected the population pattern, attracting tradesmen and merchants as well as courtiers, who may have leased their houses from manorial tenants who owned several each. There is clear evidence that, by the 17th century at least, the number of houses in Richmond far exceeded the number of manorial tenants. As it has in any case been argued by other authorities that Professor Russell's 3.5 factor was on the low side, I have adopted in table 1 a factor of 3.75 for the earlier periods and a sliding scale thereafter.

When we first have reasonably accurate figures for both population and number of houses, in 1801, the multiplying factor is 5.4 (for the entire house stock) or 5.9 (if only the occupied houses are counted). Ten years later these factors had risen to a peak of 6.1 and 6.5 respectively. Thereafter they drop off through the 19th century to 5.1 and 5.4. There was clearly an element of multiple occupancy in these early 19th-century figures (in 1801 there were 1,184 families in Richmond and Kew living in the 895 occupied houses, or approximately four families for every three houses). There was also from the mid-17th century onwards a gradual increase in average family size due to a longer life expectancy and a falling infant mortality rate. While it may be reasonable to retain the factor of 3.75 for 'houses to total population' up to the mid-17th century, I have increased this in Table 2 to 4 for 1664, 4.5 for 1703 and 5 for 1771.

As for the estimates derived from the number of manorial tenants, a comparison of these figures with the house figures shows that in 1603 the number of houses was already more than 1½ times the number of tenants and that both in the mid-17th century and in 1703 the number of houses was about double that of the number of tenants. We should therefore increase the factors accordingly, giving us 'tenants to total population' factors of 6 in 1603, 7.5 in 1649 and 9 in 1703. As this may be assumed to be a continuing trend at least from early Tudor times onwards a process of intercalation suggests the use of factors 4.5 for 1504-6, 5.25 for 1553, 6 for 1603-7 and 6.5 for 1628.

These factors I have applied in the Tables 1 and 2 below; but it must be emphasized that the resultant population estimates can only be *very* approximate, and that the earlier figures in particular (based on tenants only) may be a bit on the low side.

After 1703 Richmond began to be more of a town than a village. The number of manorial tenants becomes an irrelevance. The number of houses doubled by 1771, and showed another rapid increase to 1801. There was actually a small drop in the following decade, but the rise continued again in the period 1811-21. The census figures for the 19th century in Table 3 may not be completely accurate, but are much more so than my earlier estimates. From 1821 the rate of increase was accelerating all the time until the 1880s. By 1891 most of the land in Richmond that was not parks, commons or royal gardens had been built on, and the population was approaching its present level.

That the increases in population were due to migration into the town rather than an indigenous growth may seem fairly obvious, but it is amply borne out by a comparison of the baptism and burial entries in the parish registers in the 17th and 18th centuries (Table 4). There were few decades in which the number of baptisms exceeded the number of burials. Even discounting the high number of burials in plague years, the population was hardly self-sustaining.

**TABLE I**

*Number of manorial tenants and estimated population in Shene/Richmond and Kew 1314-1703*

| Date | Source | Reference | No. of tenants | Factor | Est. Population |
|------|--------|-----------|----------------|--------|-----------------|
| 1314 | Extent of manor | PRO SC11/638 | 42 | 3.75 | 158 |
| 1413-22 | Court lists (estimate) | PRO LR3/101/1 | 50 | 3.75 | 187 |
| 1504-06 | Court lists (estimate) | PRO LR3/101/2 | 50 | 4.5 | 225 |
| 1553 | Court list | SyRO 578/1 | 53 | 5.25 | 278 |
| 1603-07 | Court lists (estimate) | PRO LR3/71 pp1-49 | 100 | 6 | 600 |
| 1628 | Court list | PRO LR3/71 p107 | 109 | 6.5 | 709 |
| 1649 | Parliamentary survey | PRO E320/R25 | 145 | 7.5 | 1088 |
| 1703 | Manor survey | PRO LR2/226 pp166ff | 197 | 9 | 1773 |

**TABLE 2**

*Number of houses and estimated population 1603-1771*

| Date | Richmond | | | Kew | | | Whole manor | | | Factor | Estimated population | | |
|------|----------|-------|-------|-----|-------|-------|-------------|-------|-------|--------|----------|-----|-------|
| | Occ. | Empty | Total | Occ. | Empty | Total | Occ. | Empty | Total | | Richmond | Kew | Total |
| 1603 | | | 137 | | | 20 | | | 157 | 3.75 | 513 | 75 | 588 |
| 1620 | | | 161 | | | 18 | | | 179 | 3.75 | 604 | 67 | 671 |
| 1664* | 257 | 5 | 262 | 27 | 2 | 29 | 284 | 7 | 291 | 4 | 1048 | 116 | 1164 |
| 1703 | | | 357 | | | 34 | | | 391 | 4.5 | 1606 | 153 | 1759 |
| 1771† | | | 694 | | | 68 | | | 762 | 5 | 3470 | 340 | 3810 |

\* Hearth tax returns (PRO E179/188/481)]

† Manor survey (PRO CRES 5/346)

**TABLE 3**

*Number of houses and reported population from census returns 1801-1891*

| Date | Richmond | | | Kew | | | Whole manor | | | Factor* | Population | | |
|------|----------|--------|-------|-----|--------|-------|-------------|--------|-------|---------|----------|-----|-------|
| | Occ. | Empty† | Total | Occ. | Empty† | Total | Occ. | Empty† | Total | | Richmond | Kew | Total |
| 1801 | 823 | 65 | 888 | 72 | 13 | 85 | 895 | 78 | 973 | 5.4 | 4628 | 424 | 5252 |
| 1811 | 816 | 59 | 875 | 73 | 3 | 76 | 889 | 62 | 951 | 6.1 | 5219 | 560 | 5779 |
| 1821 | 976 | 28 | 1003 | 111 | 9 | 120 | 1087 | 36 | 1123 | 5.9 | 5994 | 683 | 6677 |
| 1831 | 1166 | 52 | 1218 | 130 | 8 | 138 | 1296 | 60 | 1356 | 6.0 | 7273 | 837 | 8080 |
| 1841 | 1321 | 132 | 1454 | 176 | 7 | 183 | 1497 | 139 | 1636 | 5.3 | 7760 | 923 | 8683 |
| 1851 | 1542 | 82 | 1624 | 176 | 5 | 181 | 1718 | 87 | 1805 | 5.7 | 9255 | 1009 | 10264 |
| 1861 | 1841 | 112 | 1953 | 192 | 3 | 195 | 2033 | 115 | 2148 | 5.6 | 10926 | 1102 | 12028 |
| 1871 | 2566 | 332 | 2898 | 180 | 28 | 208 | 2746 | 360 | 3106 | 5.2 | 15113 | 1033 | 16146 |
| 1881 | 3457 | 304 | 3761 | 287 | 31 | 318 | 3744 | 335 | 4079 | 5.1 | 19068 | 1670 | 20738 |
| 1891 | 4185 | 243 | 4428 | 376 | 40 | 416 | 4561 | 283 | 4844 | 5.1 | 22684 | 2076 | 24760 |

\* The factor shown here is the average ocupancy per house standing (occupied, empty or under construction), in order to enable a more direct comparison with the figures in Table 2. The average occupancy per occupied house was up to 0.5 higher.

† 'Empty' here includes houses under construction (noted separately in the original returns).

**TABLE 4**

*Baptisms and burials recorded in the Richmond Parish Registers 1596-1780*

Notes:

(1)   Before 1596 and in the years 1609-1613 inclusive the records are evidently very incomplete. The period 1609-13 has been excluded from the figures below.

(2)   Years are counted from 1 January to 31 December throughout.

(3)   To highlight the incidence of plague, the burials for some decades have been broken down. (Richmond was relatively little affected by the plague of 1665, the burials in that year being only ten more than the average for the decade.)

| Period | Baptisms Total | Yearly average | Period | Burials Total | Yearly average |
|---|---|---|---|---|---|
| 1596-1600 | 89 | 18 | 1596-1600 | 136 | 27 |
| 1601-1608 | 233 | 29 | 1601-1608 | 269 | 27 |
| | | | 1601-1602 | 42 | 21 |
| | | | 1603 | 90 | 90 |
| | | | 1604 | 64 | 64 |
| | | | 1605-1608 | 73 | 18 |
| 1614-1620 | 318 | 45 | 1614-1620 | 184 | 26 |
| 1621-1630 | 367 | 37 | 1621-1630 | 515 | 52 |
| | | | 1621-1624 | 180 | 45 |
| | | | 1625 | 174 | 174 |
| | | | 1626-1630 | 161 | 32 |
| 1631-1640 | 447 | 45 | 1631-1640 | 413 | 41 |
| | | | 1631-1639 | 309 | 34 |
| | | | 1640 | 104 | 104 |
| 1641-1650 | 427 | 43 | 1641-1650 | 417 | 42 |
| | | | 1641-1642 | 99 | 50 |
| | | | 1643 | 74 | 74 |
| | | | 1644-1650 | 244 | 35 |
| 1651-1660 | 318 | 32 | 1651-1660 | 421 | 42 |
| 1661-1670 | 471 | 47 | 1661-1670 | 409 | 41 |
| 1671-1680 | 563 | 56 | 1671-1680 | 579 | 58 |
| 1681-1690 | 625 | 62 | 1681-1690 | 651 | 65 |
| 1691-1700 | 662 | 66 | 1691-1700 | 637 | 64 |
| 1701-1710 | 814 | 81 | 1701-1710 | 682 | 68 |
| 1711-1720 | 854 | 85 | 1711-1720 | 902 | 90 |
| 1721-1730 | 855 | 86 | 1721-1730 | 1055 | 106 |
| 1731-1740 | 895 | 90 | 1731-1740 | 1005 | 101 |
| 1741-1750 | 744 | 74 | 1741-1750 | 980 | 98 |
| 1751-1760 | 872 | 87 | 1751-1760 | 1110 | 111 |
| 1761-1770 | 1071 | 107 | 1761-1770 | 1133 | 113 |
| 1771-1780 | 1211 | 121 | 1771-1780 | 1168 | 117 |

In a return dated 1788 the minister of Richmond parish stated that the average number of baptisms per year was 128 and of burials 110.

# APPENDIX 6

## *The Manor Court Rolls and Books of Shene and Richmond*

After the odd survivals noted in the first two entries below, the Public Record Office holds a fairly complete series of rolls from 1485 to 1588 (with gaps as shown). From 1603 to 1937 the rolls are complete. Except for the Commonwealth period, all are in Latin up to 1732.

The roll entries from 1603 to 1688 were collated (partly summarised) and translated into English in the 18th century and are contained in a single large volume (LR3/71). A separate book contains an index to these entries (LR3/72).

From 1638 to 1935 there is also a series of books, mostly individually indexed (and with some overlapping), which contain the same entries as the rolls. The books are, of course, much easier to handle than the rolls. Most of the books have indexes – not always correct or complete.

Except for the 14th-century survival, all these records up to 1792 are in the Land Revenue Office series (LR); after 1792 they are in the Crown Estate series (CRES).

The list below shows only what I have found to be the most convenient sources for the dates shown.

| | |
|---|---|
| SC2/205/5 (odd pages) | Oct 1348 – 1350 |
| LR3/101/1 (rolls) | Feb 1404/5 – Jun 1405 |
| " | Jul 1413 – Apr 1422 |
| " | 1441 & Nov 1445 – Nov 1452 |
| LR3/101/2 " | Nov 1485 – Nov   1508 (?gaps 1486,88,93,95) |
| 101/3 " | 1509 – Jun 1533 (gap 1520-27) |
| 101/4 " | Jun 1534 – Feb 1544/5 (gap 1545-47) |
| 101/5 " | Dec 1547 – Apr 1553 (gap 1553-58) |
| 101/6 " | Apr 1559 – Apr 1588 (gap 1589-1602) |
| LR3/71&72 (books) | Jun 1603 – Jul 1688 and index thereto |
| 78 " | 1679 – May 1689 |
| 79 " | Jun 1690 – Jan 1700/1 |
| { 80 " | Oct 1700 – Apr 1705 (legible, but no index) |
| { 94 " | Oct 1700 – May 1706 (bad copy, but with index) |
| 95 " | Jun 1706 – Oct 1710 |
| 81 " | Apr 1711 – Nov 1716 |
| 82 " | Apr 1717 – Oct 1720 |
| 83 " | Apr 1721 – Jan 1725/6 |
| 84 " | Apr 1726 – 9 Sep 1731 |

| | | |
|---|---|---|
| LR3/85 | " | 14 Sep 1731 – Aug 1737 |
| 86 | " | Apr 1738 – Nov 1744 |
| 87 | " | Apr 1745 – Nov 1751 |
| 88 | " | Apr 1752 – Dec 1758 |
| 89 | " | Jan 1759 – 28 Apr 1764 |
| 90 | " | 28 Apr 1764 – 12 May 1768 |
| 91 | " | 23 May 1768 – Apr 1775 |
| 92 | " | Aug 1775 – Apr 1784 |
| 93 | " | Jul 1784 – May 1792 |
| | | |
| CRES5/325 (books) | | 1792 – 1802 |
| 326 | " | 1802 – 1810 |
| 327 | " | 1810 – 1815 |
| 328 | " | 1816 – 1822 |
| 329 | " | Aug 1822 – May 1832 |
| 330 | " | Aug 1832 – Oct 1837 |
| 331 | " | Jan 1838 – 25 Aug 1845 |
| 332 | " | 25 Aug 1845 – Feb 1855 |
| 333 | " | Apr 1855 – 8 May 1861 |
| 334 | " | 16 May 1861 – 13 Apr 1866 |
| 335 | " | 18 Apr 1866 – Sep 1870 |
| 336 | " | 1870 – 1875 |
| 337 | " | Jun 1875 – May 1880 |
| 338 | " | 1880 – 1884 |
| 339 | " | Jan 1885 – Jun 1890 |
| 340 | " | 1890 – 1895 |
| 341 | " | Apr 1895 – 24 Oct 1901 |
| 342 | " | 24 Oct 1901 – 13 Nov 1906 |
| 343 | " | 13 Nov 1906 – Feb 1911 |
| 344 | " | Jan 1912 – Feb 1922 |
| 345 | " | Mar 1922 – Oct 1935 |

Other key manorial documents are:

| | | |
|---|---|---|
| SC11/638 | Extent of the manor | c.1314 |
| LR2/203, pp.134-144 | Terrier of the manor | c.1620 |
| LR2/226, ff 166-182 | Survey of the manor | 1703 |
| CRES5/346 | Survey of the manor | 1771 |
| MP1/1/545 | Detailed plans of the manor | 1771 |
| CRES5/88 & 89 | Manor title book (starting dates vary, but none before 18th century; apparently maintained up to c.1815. Contains some errors.) | |

# APPENDIX 7

# *The Tenements of the Manor up to 1620*

The histories of some tenements can be traced back as far as the 1314 extent of the manor – assuming a descent of property in a single family. But such early links are essentially speculative, given the paucity of surviving manor rolls before the reign of Henry VII. Even after 1485, the gaps in the records still necessitate a certain amount of speculation to provide probable links between earlier and later documented evidences of title. The conjectural material is sidelined below: often it is itself documented – the conjecture is as to whether it belongs to the context.

The order in which the tenements are listed here is arbitrary; they are grouped together when they have come into the same ownership.

A number of freehold estates of different sizes are noted. While the Wylde-Raynford-Duke estate contained land in the common fields of Richmond approximately equal to four normal tenements, the Devonshire estate and part of the Merton Priory estate were entirely outside the common fields: and those parts of the Merton estate in the fields were never really considered as a tenement, nor were the lands belonging to the parish church (which almost certainly derived from Merton holdings). However, they are listed here for the sake of completeness.

The evidence for the postulated links is indicated briefly.

To avoid overburdening the text references have not been quoted where, as in most cases, the sources are the manor rolls (see list of these by dates at Appendix 6).

## *1. Freehold tenement of 19 acres and a one-acre close of mead*

This tenement, originally copyhold, may have belonged to Richard Blackett.

1 November 1517. Grant to Charles Somerset, Earl of Worcester, Chamberlain, messuage and a virgate of land at Kew and an acre of mead behind the aforesaid messuage, held by copy of court roll – which virgate contains 19 acres – and by special licence ... to be held in socage. [together with some other land].

1526.       By his will the Earl of Worcester left his estates to his wife, with remainder to his son George Somerset.

7 June 1538. [Thomas Cromwell's accounts] To Sir George Somerset for purchase of his house at Kew £200.

15 July 1538. [Thomas Cromwell's accounts] From my Lord of Suffolk for the house at Kew £200.

24 August 1545. Death of Charles Brandon, Duke of Suffolk. By his will he left to his wife Katherine 'my house of Kew ... and all my houses, lands, tenements ... in Kew aforesaid for the term of her life'.

The widow Katherine (in her own right Baroness Willoughby d'Eresby) married Richard Bertie in 1552. What happened to the house is uncertain. (Katherine and her husband were in exile on the continent from January 1554/5 until the death of Queen Mary, but Katherine did not die until 1580.)

The house may be 'the house at Kew' mentioned in a warrant for a grant in freehold to 'Mr Kempe of the Privy Chamber' in 1558. But it then came into the ownership of Lord Mordaunt. John, first Lord Mordaunt, died in 1562, succeeded by his son John.

19 April 1564. 'The former messuage called Suffolk Place in Kew in the hands of Lord Mordaunt is devastated and destroyed by the said Mordaunt and is seized into the hands of the Lord'.

The property was regranted to one of the successors in title to the Dudley estate at Kew (see tenement No. 2), probably to Thomas Gardiner. It was part of the Portman freehold estate by the 1590s.

The *capital messuage* of this tenement was by the riverside at Kew, and was rebuilt as a mansion by the Earl of Worcester, who leased it to Charles Duke of Suffolk in the 1520s, and sold it to him in 1538. It was destroyed by 1564.

## 2. Devonshire lands at Kew – freehold

The origin of this freehold may lie in the marriage dowries of the Belet family in the 12th and 13th centuries.

The lands appear to have come into the ownership of Sir Hugh Courtenay by the time of Edward IV and to have been inherited by his son Edward, created Earl of Devonshire in 1485. The lands were somewhere between 30 and 40 acres in extent – all contiguous – and contained a mansion house.

William Courtenay, son of Earl Edward and husband of Princess Elizabeth Plantagenet, attainted 1504. Estate escheated to Crown.

Edward Earl of Devonshire died 1509.

William Courtenay released and restored to estates 1511. Died 1511.

His son Henry Courtenay allowed to succeed to the earldom and granted full restoration of rights 1512. Created Marquess of Exeter 1525.

Henry Marquess of Exeter attainted and executed 1538. Estate forfeit.

His son Edward imprisoned until 1553, when he was released and the house and lands at Kew were regranted to him 28 September 1553.

Edward Earl of Devonshire arrested and exiled 1554. Died 1556.

Marchioness of Exeter probably in possession of Kew estate until her death in 1558.

29 December 1558. Lands of Earl of Devonshire granted to Robert Dudley, Lord Dudley (together with other property at Kew).

13 May 1562. Robert Dudley sale to Francis Pope, merchant tailor, for £728.

c.1562. Francis Pope sale to Thomas Gardiner, goldsmith and teller of the Exchequer.

1575. Thomas Gardiner in debt to Crown – surrenders estate.

28 September 1575. Grant to Thomas Handford and Kenard Delaber.

18 May 1576. Handford and Delaber sale to Thomas Peerson.

February 1576/7. Thomas Peerson sale to Thomas Sackville, Lord Buckhurst.

10 July 1591. Lord Buckhurst sale to Anthony Mason als Wickes.

May 1592. Anthony Mason sale to Hugh Portman.

7 March 1603/4. Death of Sir Hugh Portman – brother John Portman. (Knighted 1605, created baronet 1611.)

4 December 1612. Death of Sir John Portman Bt – son Sir Henry Portman Bt (who held the freehold Portman estates in 1620).

The *capital messuage* of this holding was by the riverside at Kew, to the south of the Brentford-Kew ferry. It was probably demolished by Dudley.

## 3. Merton Priory lands – freehold

17 February 1219. Alice Belet – Prior of Merton – 6 acres and 3 acres mead.

*circa* 1242. Lands belonging to Merton Priory include the church with lands in Shene 20s, and land of the same 5s.

1250.   The Prior of Merton held 41s in rents and 8½ acres of pasture and 1 acre of mead worth 10s.

1375.   Merton Priory assigns to the Vicar of Kingston lands at Shene for a manse and curtilege (see 3A below).

1539. Lands of former Merton Priory include 'land and tenement called Prystes' 20s. and 'meadow called Keyomead and 16 acres of pasture 46s 8d.

1 June 1539. Grant for life to Ralph Annesley includes Prystes in Shene and Kewmead in Kew.

28 May 1544. Reversionary grant to Richard Taverner of lands granted to Ralph Annesley includes 'Pristes *als* Merton Landes in Shene' and 'Meadow called Kewmead and 16 acres of pasture in Kew'.

12 July 1546. Licence to Richard Taverner to alienate to Augustine Hynde, alderman of London, lands called Pristes *als* Merton Lands in Shene and meadow called Keyomead and 16 acres of land in Kew.

16 August 1554 (date of probate). By his will dated 23 June 1554 Augustine Hynde left to his eldest son Rowland Hynde: 'the lands called Pristes or Merton Lands in Shene alias West Shene alias Richmond and the Meadow called Keyo Mede and pasture containing 16 acres, occupied by myself and James Parkyns'.

2 September 1594. Licence to Rowland Hynde to alienate his tenements and lands in Richmond to Hugh Portman.

Then as for (2) above.

Note: six different half-acre strips in the Richmond fields can be identified from the Raynford terrier and/or the manor rolls as having been held by Merton Priory – all these were in Portman ownership in 1620.

## 3A. Richmond Parish Church Lands – freehold

This 'church estate' probably derived from the 1375 grant from Merton Priory.

Apart from the manse and its glebe (No. 102 in the 1603 list) and the Church Close by the riverside, 5¾ acres of land in the fields (4¼ acres in Richmond Upper Field, 1½ acres in Kew Field), plus ½ acre of mead were listed in vestry minutes of 1596, the 1620 terrier and vestry minutes of 1621 and 1634.

## 4. Whole tenement of 20 acres – Walton's

Richard Walton is listed as a manorial tenant 1413-18.

Alice widow of John Walton held a messuage and 20 acres in 1418.

18 November 1445. William Walton admitted to land formerly of Richard Walton, and noted as a tenant 1449.

1452. John Walton listed as a manorial tenant.

24 November 1485. John Maiken – wife Isabella for life with remainder to Thomas Aleyn – tenement and virgate of land formerly Walton's.

24 October 1499. Isabella Maykyn (widow of John) deceased – heir Thomas Aleyn. Whole tenement called Walton's containing a virgate of land.

20 May 1501. Thomas Aleyn admitted to whole tenement called Walton's.

17 April 1505. Thomas Alen – conditional surrender to Henry Wyatt – messuage and virgate anciently called Walton's.

6 November 1509. Thomas Alen – Adam Halydaye. Tenement of 20 acres and 1 acre mead.

27 May 1532. Adam Halydaye deceased – heir is relative William Halydaye. Whole tenement of 20 acres and 1 acre mead.

11 December 1539. William Halydaye – Augustine Hynde (after the expiry of a ten-year lease to John Becke) 20 acres and 1 acre mead.

The *capital messuage* of this tenement is unknown but may have been in the large Portman property on Richmond Green (No. 15 in the 1603 list).

Now see tenements 4-10 below.

## 5. Half tenement of 10 acres – South's

1348-50. John South listed as a manorial tenant.

17 February 1404/5. Grant to Thomas atte Mill of messuage and 10 acres, formerly of John South and his wife Mavill, and afterwards of Henry Br... and then of William Colchester.

1415-1422. Mentions of Thomas and William atte Mille (as manorial tenants) and of John atte Mille and Alice atte Mille.

1446-52. Mentions of Ralph, William and Thomas atte Mille.

24 November 1485. William Mille deceased – Robert Mille – Thomas Hart cottage and half a virgate called Southe's containing 10 acres.

1496-1505. Edward Hart listed as a manorial tenant. He presumably inherited the half tenement from Thomas *circa* 1495-6.

22 June 1506. Edward Hart – John Oxenbridge – 10 acres parcel of a tenement called Southe's.

29 April 1538. John Oxenbrigge, chaplain, deceased – relative William Horethorne half tenement of 10 acres and ½ acre mead (and 3 cottages).

4 December 1542. William Horethorne *als* Sparrowe – Augustine Hynde 10 acres parcel of a tenement called Southe's.

The *capital messuage* of this tenement was probably 51-54 George Street and 1-3 Brewer's Lane (No. 20 in 1603 list). It was sold by Thomas or Edward Hart. Thomas Knolles sold the 'cottage and garden called Southe's' to John Smith and his wife Alice in 1502.

Now see tenements 4-10 below.

## 6. Whole tenement of 20 acres

This tenement appears to have resulted from the amalgamation in 1485 of two half-tenements which had belonged to Robert atte Mille and William Hunt.* There are mentions of John Hunt in 1419 and of Richard Hunt and his wife Alice in 1441.

1485. Robert atte Mille decd – Thomas Hart – 10 acres [this was extra to No. 5].

1485. William Hunt – Thomas Hart – cottage and half virgate. Edward Hart (listed as manorial tenant from 1496) presumably inherited from Thomas.

22 June 1506. Edward Hart – John Oxenbridgge – barn and garden and whole tenement of 20 acres and 1 acre mead.

29 April 1538. John Oxenbrigge, chaplain, deceased – relative William Horethorne whole tenement of 20 acres and 1 acre mead.

4 December. 1542. William Horethorne *als* Sparrowe – Augustine Hynde tenement and curtilege, 20 acres and 1 acre mead, being a whole tenement.

---

* For the atte Mille family see tenement No.5.

The *capital messuage* of this tenement is unknown. It may have been in the large Portman property on Richmond Green (No. 15 in 1603 list).

Now see tenements 4-10 below.

## 7. Half tenement of 10 acres

John Pykwell was a manorial tenant 1414-22, and 1445-49. He died in 1452.

22 November 1452. Nicholas Pykewell owed suit for a cottage and 10 acres.

Nicholas Pykewell is listed as a manorial tenant 1487-92.

14 July 1494 Nicholas Pykewell – son John Pykewell half tenement of a cottage and garden and 10 acres.

29 April 1499. The cottage was sold off – see below.

5 April 1500 [entry torn and only part legible]. John Pykewell – Robert Fawkon ... 10 acres.

4 December 1542. Robert Fawkon – Augustine Hynde 10 acres and ½ acre mead formerly of John Pykewell.

The *capital messuage* of this tenement was on the site of Heron Square, Hill Street (No. 80 in 1603 list). It was sold off by John Pykewell in 1499:

29 April 1499. John Pykewell – John Pyke and wife Joan cottage and croft, parcel of the tenement of John Pykewell, abutting the tenement and croft of John Pyke and wife Joan (formerly of Thomas Vernon) south, the land of John Hough north, the highway from West Shene to Petersham east and the Thames west.

Now see tenements 4-10 below.

## 8. Whole tenement of 20 acres

The Thorne (or at Thorne) family appear in the 15th-century rolls – Adam at Thorne was a manorial tenant 1413-14 and John at Thorne 1415-19.

Emma Thorne owed suit of court in 1415-16.

1419. Richard at Thorne deceased – Roger Thorne – messuage and 20 acres. Roger Thorne was a manorial tenant 1449-52 and Robert Thorne in 1452.

The tenement had come into the ownership of Robert Bradshaw by the time of Henry VII's accession (the 1502 transaction noted below indicates that the later entries relate to Thorne's tenement).

1486. Robert Bradshaw – William Lawles and wife Margaret 20 acres.

[19 April 1502. William Lawles – Thomas Denys – a garden formerly Thorne's.]

1504. Grant to Alice, wife of John Man and late wife of Thomas Denys, whole tenement of messuage and 20 acres late of William Lawles.

16 July 1539. John Aman – Thomas Denys (and release to Denys from John Parrett and wife Agnes, who was Thomas Denys's daughter).

16 July 1539. Thomas Denys – John Aman for life with reversion to himself – tenement of 20 acres and 1 acre mead, late of William Lawles. [These transactions were in implementation of a decree by the King's Council.]

8 July 1541. John Aman admitted and surrendered reversion to Thomas Denys – tenement of 20 acres and 1 acre mead.

The tenement was then split up:

8 December 1541. Thomas Denys – Augustine Hynde – reversion to 13½ acres and 1 acre mead (John Aman had surrendered 3½ acres of this to Robert Fawkon who surrendered them to Augustine Hynde on 4 December 1542, when Denys repeated his surrender.)

23 February 1544/5. John Aman and wife – conditional surrender to Augustine Hynde cottage and

garden.

20 November 1547. John Aman and wife – John Sherborne and wife Katherine cottage, garden, barn and 10 acres.

1 December 1550. John Sherborne and wife Katherine – Augustine Hynde cottage, garden, barn and 10 acres.

1 December 1550 (after obtaining a grant of an extra ¼ acre). Thomas Denys – Robert Rutter and wife Katherine 1 acre and 3 roods.

1 December 1550. Thomas Denys – self and wife Joan – messuage and 5 acres.

30 May 1556. Thomas Denys and wife Joan – Richard Clyffe – 2 houses and 5 acres.

The *capital messuage* of this tenement was probably in the large Portman property on Richmond Green (No. 15 in 1603 list). By 1620 the 1½ acres of the tenement surrendered to Robert Rutter in 1550 were in the ownership of John Keele, and the 5 acres surrendered to Richard Clyffe in 1556 in that of Henry Cuckney.

Now see tenements 4-10 below.

## 9. Whole tenement of 20 acres – Makyn's

The earliest mention of the Makyn family was in 1385 when John Maykyn of King's Shene was prosecuted for using unlawful fishing nets.

On 26 June 1405 William Rockingham and wife Agnes surrendered to John Makyn and wife Joan a half tenement of a messuage and 10 acres.

John Makyn is noted as a manorial tenant 1413-22, Clement Makyn 1413-22, and Thomas Makyn 1413-21.

18 November 1445. Clement Makyn died holding a messuage and 20 acres and an island.

1446. Clement Makyn and wife Alice – Alice for life (but she is now dead) with remainder to son Stephen Makyn tenement of messuage, 20 acres and an island.

This tenement descended in the family to Robert Makyn who was noted as a manorial tenant in 1485.

17 October 1491. Robert Makyn deceased – former wife Joan (now Joan Lacy) and daughters Joan Statham and Margaret Smythe – tenement of a messuage and virgate of land in Kew.

The tenement was then divided between the daughters:

(a)  14 February 1513/4. Thomas Statham and wife Joan – daughter Alice – reversion of half of 20 acres in Kew.

30 June 1534. Alice wife of Thomas Dover (daughter of Thomas Statham) – John Becke and wife Dorothy – reversion after the death of Joan Statham former wife of Thomas Statham to half a tenement called Makyn's in Kew.

(b)  13 June 1530 John Smythe of Kew and wife Margaret – son Robert Smythe – half tenement formerly of Robert Makyn.

5 June 1531. Robert Smythe – John Smythe – Thomas Flower all lands and tenements formerly of Robert Makyn.

14 June 1535. Thomas Flower – John Becke and wife Dorothy – all lands and tenements formerly of Robert Makyn.

18 July 1536. John Becke – conditional surrender to Cuthbert ... preant, apothecary, of tenement of 20 acres and 1 acre mead in Kew.

16 July 1539. John Becke – Augustine Hynde and wife Margaret – Charles Duke of Suffolk (subiect to mortaage of 1536) tenement of 20 acres and 1 acre mead in Kew.

These lands were mortgaged by Charles Duke of Suffolk to Augustine Hynde, to whom the title reverted on the Duke's death in 1545.

The *capital messuage* of this tenement was by the riverside in Kew (No. 132 in 1603 list).

Now see tenements 4-10 below.

## 10. Whole tenement at Kew of 20 acres with an island – Lydgold's

Robert Lydgold was a manorial tenant 1404-22, and John Lydgold in 1413 (mentioned again in 1419).

John Lytgold (or Litegold) was a tenant 1449-52. On 12 November 1449 he leased to William Bower his island called Litegold's.

Presumably this tenement descended in the family to Robert Lydgold, listed as a manorial tenant 1489-1503.

27 July 1504. Robert Litgold sold 1 acre to Thomas Byrche and gave ½ acre to his daughter Alice wife of Richard Brown. The remainder 'a tenement in Kew and 18½ acres' went to his wife Edith with reversion to his son Thomas.

6 November 1509. Edith Lytgold, widow of Robert made a conditional surrender to Robert Staynford and his wife Alice (daughter of Robert Lytgold) of a tenement of 20 acres in Kew.

8 May 1520. Robert Staynford and wife Alice – son Thomas Staynford (property unspecified).

1521-27. Thomas Staynford – Sir George Somerset.

12 November 1538. Sir George Somerset – John Becke – self and wife Margaret and John Becke and wife Margaret conditional surrender to Augustine Hynde – whole tenement of 20 acres and 1 acre of mead in Kew formerly of Robert Lydgold and an eyot in the Thames.

16 July 1539. John Becke – Augustine Hynde and wife Margaret – Charles Duke of Suffolk – whole tenement of 20 acres and 1 acre mead and an eyot in Kew, formerly of Sir George Somerset.

Charles Duke of Suffolk mortgaged 12½ acres of this tenement to Augustine Hynde, to whom the title reverted on the Duke's death in 1545.

23 February 1544/5. Release by Sir George Somerset to Augustine Hynde whole tenement of 20 acres and 1 acre mead in Kew and an eyot in the Thames. The property was then divided, the messuage, 12½ acres and the island going to Augustine Hynde, and the remaining 7½ acres apparently descending as follows:

7½ acres    Charles Duke of Suffolk's daughter Eleanor (d 1547) married Henry Lord Clifford, later Earl of Cumberland. Their daughter Margaret (d 1596) married Henry Stanley, Lord Strange (who succeeded as 4th Earl of Derby 1572 and died in 1593).

In 1565-67 Edward Bulman and his wife Joan prosecuted a suit against Henry Lord Strange and his wife Margaret in respect of a barn and 5½ acres [sic] in Kew, Bulman claiming that Robert Lydgold had had only a term of 50 years (now expired) in this property. Bulman had previously brought a suit in 1560-61 against John Hynde in respect of the messuage, the other 12½ acres and the acre of mead [actually the island] saying that the tenement had once belonged to John Lydgold. Robert, a relative of John, had left the property to Thomas Lydgold who died without an heir. It should then have been granted to Richard Lydgold, whose son was William Lydgold the younger, whose son was William Lydgold the barber, whose daughter was Joan, wife of Edward Bulman. Judgment was given in favour of the Bulmans, but John Hynd never surrendered the land. Bulman's suit against Lord Strange failed.

The 4th Earl's son Ferdinand succeeded as 5th Earl of Derby in 1593, but died in 1594 when his brother William became 6th Earl.

9 June 1603. William Earl of Derby – Alexander Prescott – cottage and 7½ acres in Kew.

28 May 1606. Alexander Prescott – self and wife Elizabeth – cottage and 7½ acres in Kew field.

Alexander Prescott was buried 4 July 1608. His widow Elizabeth married John Burd who held the land in 1620 (with reversion granted in 1616 to Richard Prescott, brother of Alexander).

The *capital messuage* of this tenement was by the riverside in Kew (No. 132 in 1603 list). Now see tenements 4-10 below.

*Tenements 4-10*

Augustine Hynde held from these tenements a total of 106 acres, 4½ acres of mead and two islands.

23 June 1554. By his will (proved 16 August 1554) Augustine Hynde citizen and alderman of London bequeathed his youngest son John Hynde all his copyhold property in Kew and Shene *als* Richmond.

Augustine Hynde had also acquired an extra 2 acres from Thomas Denys in 1541, and John Hynde purchased 1½ acres from James Ware in 1578 and 1588, as well as acquiring some extra islands (by Richmond Palace).

John Hynde's total known holdings amounted to 109½ acres, 5 acres of mead and 6 islands (plus Kew Heath in whole or in part).

1589-1602. Transfer of title from John Hynde to Sir Hugh Portman, either by direct sale or possibly by sale from Hynde to Lord Buckhurst or to Anthony Mason and thence to Sir Hugh Portman.

9 June 1603. Sir Hugh Portman granted licences to let the house at Kew called the Farm House to George Hudson for 21 years and to let the house by Richmond Green to William Dunn for 21 years.

2 May 1604. John Portman granted licence to let all customary tenements, etc, 'descended to him on the death of his brother Hugh Portman Kt'. [The admission of John Portman to the property, which presumably took place at this court, was not recorded.]

30 September 1607. Sir John Portman (knighted in 1605) sold to the King for his new park 3¾ acres and 61 perches of land.

5 October 1619. Death of Sir John Portman presented. Proclamation for heir – youngest son William Portman (who was not in fact admitted until 1627).

## 11. The freehold estate of Wylde, Raynford, Duke, Jones

This estate probably had its origin in a 12th-century dowry. It may have been the freehold land (quantity unspecified) held by Roger de Burun and his wife Matilda (née Belet) in 1214 and by William Colville and Matilda (one carucate) in 1220.

1250. Geoffrey de Wherry held 4 virgates of land.

1314. Alice, widow of Henry Warre (a corruption of Wherry?) held 4 virgates as freehold.

To these 4 virgates were probably added another 20 acres by 1478.

9 April 1478. Recovery by William Gray to John de Orkan of 'one messuage, 100 acres of land, 8 acres of meadow and 3 acres of wood in Kayo'. [Hildyard papers]

This estate was then sold to Sir Thomas Urswick. In all the following documents its size is stated to be exactly twice what it was in reality.

11 March 1478/9. Sir Thomas Urswick, chief justice of the King's Bench – John Aleyn citizen and goldsmith of London. '2 messuages, 200 acres of land, 16 acres of meadow, 6 acres of wood in Shene and Kew, formerly of John Goyern'. [Hildyard papers].

18 September 1489. John Aleyn – John Breteyne, clerk, professor of sacred theology, Richard Segrum, clerk, Master of Arts, Thomas Salle gent, William Amyas gent, Richard Swanne, skinner, and William Tenacres, merchant, '2 messuages [as above] formerly of John Goyern, which Aleyn had by grant of Sir Thomas Urswyk and John Browne gent'. [Richmond Public Library].

This estate then came into the hands of the Wylde family whose names appear in the Richmond records from 1498 onwards. In 1498 'Margaret Wylde, tenant dwelling at Kew' was due to render homage. William Wylde is mentioned in 1499, and the heirs of John Wylde in 1500. In 1522 Henry Wylde, son of John, sold 3 acres of freehold meadow. Winifred, widow of Thomas Wylde, married Sir John Raynford.

1535-36. John Raynford a manorial tenant.

11 December 1539. Sir John Raynford and Lady Winifred conditionally surrendered to John Hale of Kew all their land and tenements in Richmond and Kew.

1552. Sir John Raynford, tenant in right of his wife Winifred (former wife of Thomas Wylde) presented for demising to John Hayle for a term of 40 years without a licence.

September 1559. Death of Sir John Raynford. A terrier lists his lands in Richmond, but appears to lack the last page – so nothing about holdings in Kew.

14 July 1561. Sir George Howard granted custody of Winifred, late wife of Sir John Raynford and daughter of John Pimpe late of Nettlested, Kent, 'a lunatic enjoying lucid intervals ... with custody of her lands in Kent, Suffolk and Surrey'.

13 April 1576. Lady Winifred Raynford, late wife of John Raynford Kt and formerly wife of Thomas Wylde held for her life by free charter 2 messuages, 200 acres of land, 16 acres of meadows and 6 acres of woodland in Richmond, Shene and Kew ... and on her death Thomas Duke paid a relief ... and Thomas Duke came to the court because someone had said the tenements were customary and not free, and he showed the charter and proved his title and that they were free property. [Thomas Duke was the son of George Duke of Cossington and his wife Ann, daughter of William Wylde of Camberwell.]

8 February 1575/6. Thomas Duke – Wyatt Wylde. A moiety of 5 messuages, 200 acres, 30 acres of meadow, 10 acres of pasture and 12 acres of wood in Shene als Richmond, Kew and Kingston on Thames. [Hildyard papers.]

It appears likely (though no documentary confirmation has been found) that the part of the estate handed over to Wyatt Wylde was the 'George Farm' as the lands in the Richmond fields were now called, together with the house in the five-acre close on the north-east side of Hill Street (No. 81 in 1603 list). This property was sold, probably just before the end of Queen Elizabeth's reign, to Duncan Jones, who appears to have leased it to William Dawborne.

*(George Farm in Richmond)*

17 December 1604. Reference to Dawborne's Close against Richmond Ferry (i.e. the five-acre close with the house). That the property had but recently changed hands is indicated by an entry at the same court:

17 December 1604. Heirs of the George Farm 'to show their evidence concerning the said farm and lands therewith occupied'.

There are six further references in the manor rolls to land held by Dawborne up to 1616 – all identifiable with land previously held by Raynford and held in 1620 by Jones – and in 1617 a reference to land formerly occupied by Dawborne. That Jones and not Dawborne was the owner of the freehold seems to be confirmed by:

24 February 1606/7. £28 6s 10d paid to Thomas Smythe and William Dawborne for the use of Mr Jones in consideration that he surrender 5½ acres and 27 perches ... now enclosed in the King's park (this land is identifiable with holdings totalling 6½ acres as shown in the Raynford terrier).

Following this sale, Duncan Jones held 83½ acres in the Richmond fields in 1620.

*(Residual estate in Kew)* [Hildyard papers]

2 July 1576. Thomas Duke leased to William Wright for 43 years the capital messuage or farm in Kew and 100 acres of arable, meadow, pasture and woodland in Shene and Kew which were parcel of the dower of Dame Winifred Raynford deceased.

30 March 1577. William Wright assigned the lease to Lord Buckhurst.

30 March 1590. Lord Buckhurst assigned the lease to Anthony Mason *alias* Weeks.

1592. Sub-lease by Anthony Mason to William Hickman.

Easter term 1604. Thomas Duke and son Edward Duke – William Duke. 4 messuages, 60 acres of land, 10 acres of meadow, 40 acres of pasture and 10 acres of wood in East Shene, West Shene and Richmond (*sic*) and a free fishery in Kew.

10 November 1609. William Duke – Walter Hickman 'capital messuage near Kew Ferry and houses and stables and arable and pasture ... containing 100 acres, in East Shene, West Shene and Kewe'.

14 February 1609/10. Walter Hickman – Sir John Portman [as last above].

William Duke retained the house by Little Green, and just two acres of land in Richmond fields, which he held in 1620.

The *capital messuage*s associated with this estate were:

(i) in Richmond on the south-east side of Little Green (No. 10 in 1603 list), held by 'Mr Duke' in 1581, which gave its name to Duke's Lane (now Duke Street) and was inherited by the Michell family.

(ii) the house in the close on the north-east side of Hill Street (No. 81 in 1603 list) identified in the Raynford terrier.

(iii) the house near the ferry at Kew (No. 127 in 1603 list) sold by William Duke to Walter Hickman in 1609 – and by Hickman to Portman.

## 12. Free tenement of 30 acres

Ascension tide 1451. Fine for sale for 100 marks by William Skerne to Richard Marshall and wife Alice – 1 messuage, 3 tofts, 30 acres of land and 3 acres of meadow and 3s 6d of rents in West Shene.

A sale by the Marshalls to William Blackett, followed by the sale (?*circa* 1490) by Blackett to Peter de Narbone.

28 June 1490. Peter de Narbone holds from the Lord (at 14s 6d quit rent) one free tenement. 3 cottages, 30 acres of land and 3 acres of meadow, formerly of William Blackett.

Descent from Peter de Narbone to John de Narbone his son, as below (at tenement No. 13 or 14).

The *capital messuage* of this tenement possibly stood in the freehold close between what are now Sheen Road and Paradise Road, stretching up to the junction of these roads (No. 99 in the 1603 list). This was owned by Wright in 1620.

Now see tenements 12-15 below.

## 13. Whole tenement of 20 acres – 'Gryffyn's'

It is possible that this tenement had belonged to John Pykewell (died 1452) or his successor Nicholas Pykewell (see tenement No. 7) as the spring on the adjacent site, granted to the Charterhouse of Shene in 1466, was called 'Pyckwell's well'.

A Nicholas Gryffyn is listed as a manorial tenant in 1446-52. In 1489 the heirs of John Gryffyn were in default for failing to attend the Manor Court.

John Hoo or Hough was listed as a manorial tenant from 1487.

4 September 1492. Matilda Tailler [*sic*] formerly Howe [*sic*] – Robert Hough – a virgate of land parcel of the tenement formerly of John Gryffyn.

There is no further mention of Robert Hough. Sir William Tyler (?husband of Matilda) who inherited 4 acres of land directly from John Howe in January 1500/1, appears to have acquired ownership by 1501.

5 April 1501. Sir William Tyler – Peter Narbon and wife Katherine. Lands called Gryffyns formerly of John Gryffyn.

29 November 1518. Peter Narbon deceased – son Anthony Narbon – brother John Narbon. Lands formerly of John Gryffyn and Sir William Tyler.

The *capital messuage* of this tenement was on the sites of 77-81 George Street and 22-26 King Street (all now part of Dickins and Jones store) (Nos. 44-48 in 1603 list). A part was sold off by John Gryffyn in 1494; the rest was owned by Matthew Clyderowe by 1504.

Now see tenements 12-15 below.

## 14. *Whole tenement of 20 acres – Heron's*

A William Heron is mentioned in the manor rolls in 1418. This is the only occurrence of the name in the surviving rolls before 1490.

28 June 1490. William Blackett – Peter de Narbon. Tenement and 20 acres of land called Heron's Tenement.

By his will in 1517 Peter de Norbone [*sic*] left some of his property to his son Anthony (see tenement 13 above) and the rest to his executors to hold for six years to provide for the education of Anthony's son John, but then to revert to his own son John. By 1523 John would have been in possession.

The location of this *capital messuage* is unknown.

Now see tenements 12-15 below.

## 15. *Half tenement of 10 acres*

It is possible that the half tenement surrendered by William Blackett to William Gardner on 13 September 1487 eventually came into the possession of John Narbon.

The location of its *capital messuage* is unknown.

Now see tenements 12-15 below.

*Tenements 12-15*

25 June 1545. John Narbone, son and heir of Peter Narbone, died holding a messuage and 30 acres of land and 12 acres of mead in socage at a rent of 10s 4d, and 50 acres of land and 2 acres of mead by copyhold at a rent of 10s.*

4 December 1547. John Narbone died without heirs and his land is seized to the lord.

8 July 1549. Grant to David Vincent by letters patent. Lands held by John Narbone, son of Peter Narbone late of Richmond (John Narbone having died at the Tower of London and his lands having been escheated) to hold in free socage – messuage, barn, stable and orchard, 30 acres of land and 1½ acres of mead, held in socage, and 50 acres of land and 2 acres of mead, being formerly copyhold.

22 June 1556. Sale by David Vincent to Nicholas Culverwell – ' messuage, etc, and 80 acres of land and 3½ acres of mead.

1569.   Nicholas Culverwell deceased – by will to Ezekiel Culverwell – the same.

23 March 1608. Sale by Ezekiel Culverwell for £800 to Richard Wright, with reversion to son Robert Wright and his wife Rebecca – the same.

1617. Richard Wright died. Robert Wright had predeceased his father. Robert's widow Rebecca married as her second husband Robert Payne, who held these lands in 1620.

---

* Peter de Narbone was a servant of Henry VII and was given an appointment as a Poor Knight of Windsor. He married a baseborn daughter of King Louis of France. His son John was a royal herald, being appointed Bluemantle Pursuivant in November 1528 and Richmond Herald in September 1536. John died without heirs at the Tower of London in 1540. In 1534 he had mortgaged part of his Richmond property to William Ingham and others, and Ingham appears to have been admitted as a manorial tenant in 1541. The escheat of John's lands and the regrant to David Vincent seem to have taken no account of Ingham's interest. The latter made an evidently unsuccessful attempt to claim the lands from Vincent by a suit in the Court of Requests.

## 16. Half tenement of 10 acres

In 1314 Gilbert Binnegate held in villenage a half tenement of a messuage and 9 acres of land and 1 acre of mead. This subsequently became 10 acres of land and ½ acre of mead.

29 September 1348. Gilbert Byngate – William Walshe – a messuage, 10 acres of land and ½ acre of mead. [For 15th century references to Walshe family see tenement No. 26.]

17 October 1491. Robert Walshe deceased – John Walshe Junior – carthouse and 10 acres.

4 September 1492. John Walshe – Thomas Denys Junior – barn and cartway and carthouse and 10 acres.

26 July 1503. Thomas Denys – Alice Denys in trust for son Thomas Denys – barn or carthouse and 10 acres, formerly of John Walshe.

Thomas Denys (the son) surrendered this holding to Nicholas Culverwell between 1553 and 1558.

Thomas Denys (deceased) and his wife Joan surrendered to Nicholas Culverwell (recorded 4 April 1559) a barn and 3 half-acres adjacent.

11 May 1570. Nicholas Culverwell deceased – son Nicholas Culverwell – 10 acres and 1 acre mead formerly of Thomas Denys.

10 April 1584. Nicholas Culverwell deceased – brother Ezekiel Culverwell – 10 acres and 1 acre mead which their father Nicholas Culverwell deceased held from the surrender of Thomas Denys.

The barn and 3 half-acres must have passed with the above (and No. 32) to Nicholas the Younger in 1570 and to Ezekiel in 1584. In 1591 Ezekiel lost possession as noted below.

19 April 1609. Ezekiel Culverwell, clerk – Richard Wright, with remainder to Robert Wright his eldest son and the latter's wife Rebecca – the reversion (on the death of Nicholas Culverwell his father) to 10 acres and 1 acre mead.

19 April 1609. Grant to Ezekiel Culverwell, and surrender by him to Richard Wright with remainder to Robert Wright and his wife Rebecca: barn or carthouse and 1½ acres of land which had been forfeited to the Lord because leased by Ezekiel to Thomas Pain on 2 October 1591 for a term of 29 years without licence from the Lord.

1 September 1617. Richard Wright deceased – Rebecca Payne (late wife of Robert Wright deceased) with reversion to son Lionel Wright – 10 acres and 1 acre mead.

The *capital messuage* of this tenement was possibly at 7-9 The Green (part of No. 15 and Nos. 16-17 in 1603 list).

## 17. Half tenement of 10 acres

In 1314 Isabell Bynnegates held in villenage a half tenement of a messuage, 9 acres of land and 1 acre of mead. For later 14th-century and 15th-century references to the Byngate family see at tenement No. 6.

John Byngate was listed as a manorial tenant from 1487 onwards.

14 October 1510. John Byngate – wife Joan for life with reversion to son John Byngate – messuage and 10 acres.

23 May 1529. John Byngate and wife Helen admitted to 10 acres of land of his late father John Byngate.

?after 1533. John Byngate died. His widow Helen married Edward Howe.

29 April 1538. Edward Howe and wife Elena (former wife of John Byngate) – Henry Parkyns – half tenement of 10 acres and ½-acre mead.

16 July 1539. Henry Parkyns – self and wife Alice – to their wills – half tenement formerly of John Byngate and his wife Ellen.

After death of Henry Parkyns, his widow Alice married Robert Saunders.

1 December 1550. Suit Thomas Lawrence and wife Alice (daughter of John Byngate deceased) *versus*

Robert Saunders and wife Alice over. 10 acres of land and ½ acre mead. [The Saunders won.]

19 April 1564. Robert Saunders deceased – wife Anne for life, with remainder to Roger Richbell – messuage, barn, hempstall ground and 10½ acres.

30 October 1574. Anne Saunders deceased – Roger Richbell – messuage, barn, hempstall ground and 10½ acres.

1589-1602. Roger Richbell – daughter Katherine wife of Thomas Gisby.

1589-1602. Thomas and Katherine Gisby – Humphrey Stafferton and wife Elizabeth (who may have been the Gisby's daughter).

1589-1602. Stafferton exchanged 1½ acres of land for another 1½ acres. He then dispersed the holding. Known disposals:

7 April 1602 to Sir Robert Wright and wife Dorothy – 5 acres.

9 June 1603 to William Haynes – 2 acres.

9 June 1603 to Thomas Larkyn *als* Flint – 1 acre

9 June 1603 to Thomas Bigg – 1 acre

9 June 1603 to Henry Cuckney – ½ acre mead

2 May 1604. Humphrey Stafferton deceased – wife Elizabeth for life with remainder to son Charles – messuage and 1 acre.

8 April 1605. John Holloway and wife Elizabeth (former wife of Humphrey Stafferton) admitted to messuage and 1 acre.

1625. Charles Stafferton admitted.

 *Capital messuage.* The messuage owned by Humphrey and Charles Stafferton was on the site of manor grange land (110-12) and not an original capital messuage. A possible site for the messuage of this tenement is at the corner of George Street and Brewer's Lane (Nos. 21-25 in the 1603 list). The barn and hempstall ground were on Ferry Hill.

## 18. Whole tenement of 20 acres (with an island instead of meadow)

Robert Gylle was listed as a manorial tenant 1445-52. His wife Mary was mentioned in 1445. They were probably the parents of Robert Gille below.

17 October 1491. Robert Gille deceased – wife Margery Gille – tenement of 20 acres of land and an island in the Thames.

14 July 1494. Margery Gylle – Henry Parkyns – tenement with a virgate of land and an island in the Thames at Kayhoo, formerly of Robert Gylle.

[18 April 1542 Henry Parkyns – John Foxe and wife Elizabeth – land called an eyte.]

The *capital messuage* of this tenement has not been located, but was possibly on the south-east of George Street (No. 122 in 1603 list.)

Now see tenements 18-21 below.

## 19. Whole tenement of 20 acres

The family of Ho, Hoo, Howe or Hough maintained a presence in Shene throughout the 14th and 15th centuries. The references below may apply to this tenement or to No. 20.

 In 1314 John Ho held in villeage 14½ acres of land and 2 acres of mead and Gilbert Ho held in villeage ¾ of a tenement (13½ acres of land and 1½ acres of mead). Adam Ladde who held the same amount as Gilbert Ho did service for both holdings – so there was probably a connection between them.

 Thomas Howe was listed as a manorial tenant from 1404 to 1422. On 26 March 1414 he was admitted to a whole tenement of 20 acres formerly belonging to Robert How (who was listed as a tenant from 1405 to 1421).

John Howe was listed as a tenant from 1405 to 1418.

24 November 1485. John Maiken – wife Isabella Maiken – whole tenement of a messuage and virgate of land, formerly of Robert Hoo.

16 July 1489. Isabella Makyn, widow of John Makyn – Richard Scopeham – tenement of 20 acres and 1 acre mead formerly of John Makyn.

25 December 1501. Will of Richard Scopeham leaves all lands in King's Shene *als* Richmond to son Edmund.

18 January 1501/2. Alice, widow of Richard Scopeham – son Edmund Scopeham and wife Elizabeth – all lands and tenements formerly of Richard Scopeham.

20 August 1503. Will of Edmund Scopeham (proved 2 September 1503) leaves all lands in Richmond to wife Elizabeth.

Elizabeth Scopeham sold the land to Henry Parkyns (or she married Henry Parkyns).

The *capital messuage* of this tenement was probably at the site of Old Friars, Old Palace Place and 17 King Street (Nos. 58-69 in 1603 list).

Now see tenements 18-21 below.

## 20. Whole tenement of 20 acres

For early records of Hough family see at tenement No. 19.

12 November 1449 Constance Hoo deceased – heir William William Hoo – messuage and virgate of land.

John Hough (listed as a tenant from 1487) seems to have split up the tenement at or just before his death:

*4 acres.*

18 January 1501/2 John Hough (deceased) – Sir William Tyler – 4 acres of land.

5 April 1501. Sir William Tyler – Peter Narbone and wife Katherine – 4 acres formerly of John Howe.

*Cottage and 5 acres.*

18 January 1501/2. John Hough (deceased) – widow Isabella Hough with remainder to Humphrey Hough – cottage and 5 acres.

2 March 1511/2. Isabella Hough (widow of John Hough) – Humphrey Hough (son of John Hough) – cottage and 5 acres.

*Messuage and 11 acres.*

6 November 1509 suit: Humphrey Hough *versus* Henry Prym *re* messuage and 11 acres.

14 February 1513/4. Humphrey Hough – Henry Parkyns – all lands (not specified).

The *capital messuage* of this tenement was between Hill Street and the river (No. 79 in 1603 list).

Now see tenements 18-21 below.

## 21. Whole tenement of 20 acres (or half tenement of 10 acres?)

13 September 1487. John Turner deceased – wife Joan Turner deceased – son William Turner with reversion to Thomas Fysshe – 20 acres.

13 September 1487. Joan Turner (daughter of John Turner deceased) – William Turner son of William Turner reversion to 10 acres belonging to Joan Turner former wife of her father.

13 September 1487. Joan Turner (daughter of John Turner deceased) – John Turner son of William Turner reversion to 10 acres belonging to Joan Turner former wife of her father.

Thomas Fysshe admitted to property on death or surrender of members of Turner family.

17 April 1505. Thomas Fysshe deceased. Proclamation for his brother and heir John Kyte of Hampton.

22 June 1506. John Cave and wife Elizabeth (daughter of Thomas Fysshe deceased) – surrender all property to John Knolles [inoperative as not admitted].

3 September 1508. John Cave and wife Elizabeth admitted to property.

21 November 1508. John Cave and wife Elizabeth – John Knolles – land formerly of Thomas Fysshe which he surrendered to John Cave and wife Elizabeth (his daughter and heir).

8 May 1515 [entry torn and partly illegible]. John Knollys – William Hartopp.

1 December 1528. William Hartopp – Henry Parkyns – tenement formerly of John Knollys and before of Thomas Fysshe.

The *capital messuage* of this tenement was probably on the site of 10-12 The Green and 5-13 Brewer's Lane (Nos. 16-19 in 1603 list). This site was owned by Thomas Fysshe in 1505 and had come into the ownership of Thomas Denys by 1558. It appears to be of a size only appropriate to a half-tenement, and it is not clear whether Fysshe inherited the whole tenement or only part of it.

Now see tenements 18-21 below.

*Tenements 18-21*

9 June 1533. Henry Parkyns deceased – wife Elizabeth Parkyns for her life with reversion to son John Parkyns – 3 tenements and cottages.

1533-1538. Long drawn-out suit Thomas Denys *versus* Elizabeth Parkyns widow *re* cottage, 10 acres and ½ acre mead claimed to have belonged to Thomas Denys Senior.

18 July 1536. Elizabeth Parkyns – son John Parkyns – cottage called Copthall.

1536-38. Suit: Reginald Kyte (son of John Kyte, Thomas Fysshe's brother) versus Elizabeth Parkyns *re* 12 cottages and gardens; and suit: Reginald Kyte *versus* John Parkyns *re* cottage called Copthall.

4 December 1547. Elizabeth Parkyns deceased. Son John Parkyns is heir.

4 December 1550. John Parkyns admitted to all property of his father Henry.

1560-61. Suit: John Parkyns *versus* Nicholas Beneson and wife Joan (former wife of Thomas Denys) *re* 8 cottages which Henry Parkyns surrendered to his wife Elizabeth with reversion to John Parkyns; and suit: John Parkyns *versus* Richard Gaywood and wife Williames *re* 2 cottages [as above]. Judgment for John Parkyns.

18 February 1562/3. John Parkyns – John Hopkins and Bowes Thelwell – messuage and tenement called Scopeham's Lands and close and barn and 60 acres of arable and land in Aldey containing 9 acres and 3 acres of mead in a close before the house and 4 acres in lott meadows.

23 April 1563. John Hopkins and Bowes Thelwell – Thomas (son of Gregory) Lovell – [all as above] as surrendered by John Parkyns.

13 April 1565. Thomas Lovell deceased – sister Francesca Lovell – all lands.

12 April 1577. Francesca Lovell deceased – brother Henry Lovell with remainder to brother Robert Lovell – messuage and 80 acres called Sconeham's Lands.

Henry Lovell may have sold some land before 1603, then he sold to the King for the park: on 20 February 1605/6, 4½ acres and 20 perches *and*
on 24 February 1606/7, 4 acres and 21½ perches.

7 October 1606. Henry Lovell – Rev James Fitche (Vicar of Kingston) and his wife Martha – capital messuage, and 4 closes containing 12½ acres and 4 acres of meadow and 46 acres of arable in the fields, all formerly called Scopeham's Farm and Scroope's Tenement, and lately called Parkyns' Farm or Tenement.

22 April 1612. James Fitche – Stephen Peirce – [all as above].

## 22. *Whole tenement of 20 acres*

27 July 1413. John Waler – John Frauncys – messuage, orchard and 1 virgate of land [the messuage being] near the close formerly of Robert Howe and the Church hawe.

A Hugh Fraunceys was mentioned as a manorial tenant in 1445-52.

Henry Stokes seems to have disposed of the tenement in two halves:

28 June 1490. Henry Stokes deceased – ... Goodyere - half tenement and 10 acres, formerly of Frauncys.

17 October 1491. Henry Stokes - Richard Goodyer – tenement and garden and half virgate of 10 acres, formerly of Henry Stokes and before of John Frauncys, and ½ acre of mead

| ? Richard Goodyer – John Blythe.

14 July 1494. Richard Goodyere - William Cooke. Half tenement of cottage and garden and 10 acres, formerly of Henry Stokes.

14 May 1496. John Blythe – William Cooke – half tenement of messuage and cottage and garden and 10 acres and ½ acre mead.

17 April 1505. William Cooke – wife Katherine – all lands and tenements.

22 June 1506. Edward Skerne and wife Katherine (formerly wife of William Cooke) surrendered one cottage to Thomas Parker.

27 May 1532. Lady Tyle widow (former wife of William Cooke deceased) died. Her son Thomas Cooke is heir (Clement Twyford is guardian) – tenement and 20 acres.

The *capital messuage* of this tenement was probably at 18-23 George Street (No. 119 on 1603 list). Now see tenements 22-24 below.

## 23. Half tenement of 10 acres

John Drewe is noted as a manorial tenant from 1485 to 1492, so must have acquired this holding before the accession of Henry VII. The John de Bury mentioned below cannot have been the Keeper of the New Park of Shene from 1440 to 1452, but might be his son.

14 July 1494. John Drewe deceased – heir is Elizabeth daughter of John de Bury – half tenement of a messuage and 10 acres.

16 May 1496. Grant to Elizabeth Cornwalys, daughter and heir of John de Bury – half tenement of cottage and 10 acres and ½ acre mead.

22 May 1497. Robert Cornwalys and wife Elizabeth (daughter of John de Bury late of Twickenham) – John Kempe – half tenement of 10 acres and ½ acre mead.

15 May 1498. John Kempe – Thomas Thorpe – half tenement of cottage and 10 acres and ½ acre mead, formerly of Elizabeth Cornwalys.

1499-1500. Thomas Thorpe sale to Edward Jones. (Thorpe was a manor tenant in but not after 1499: Jones in but not before 1500.)

22 May 1501. [roll torn ?Edward Jones] – Hugh Denys – cottage and 10 acres, formerly of John Kempe.

9 October 1511. Will of Hugh Denys, esquire of the King's body – house in Richmond to be sold. Mentions wife Mary and nephews John Denys and William Denys.

3 March 1511/2. Hugh Denys died seized of a half tenement of 10 acres formerly of Edward Jones and before of John Kempe. Proclamation for heirs.

   The original *capital messuage* of this tenement was between Hill Street and the river (No. 79 in 1603 list). It was probably sold off after Hugh Denys' death.

   Now see tenements 23-24 and 22-24 below.

## 24. Half tenement of 10 acres

There is no certainly identified history for this tenement before 1533, but it seems possible that it may have been Lockyer's, the existence of which is only known from the history of the property (No. 101 on 1603 list) adjacent on the east side of the church glebe, which was probably its original capital messuage.

| John Lockyer was a juror 1404-05 and 1415-22.

18 November 1445. Messuage and garden late of John Lockyer and formerly of Robert Gardyner now in hands of the Lord.

26 July 1503. Edmund Scopeham sale to Richard Recolver – close of land, parcel of the tenement called Lockyer's, between land of John Byngate to the east and the 'vicarage' of Richmond to the west.

29 May 1504. Richard Recolver to William Prentes – close of land between tenement of John Byngate east and tenement of Recolver west.

22 June 1506. William Prentes to Thomas Pole [largely illegible, but referring to property 'formerly called Lockyer's'].

6 November 1509.⎱ Thomas Pole (late Groom of the Wardrobe) deceased – brother William
3 March 1515/6. ⎰ Pole of London – cottage and garden [roll torn at this point].

27 May 1532. Thomas Poole former Groom of the Wardrobe to John Chaundler – cottage, stable, garden and croft.

9 June 1533. John Chaundler to self and wife Mary with reversion to son John Chaundler – cottage, barn, stable, garden and croft formerly of Thomas Pole who was a Groom of the Wardrobe temp. Henry VII.

15 September 1539. John Chaundler and wife Mary to John Narbone – cottage, stable, garden and croft.

27 May 1548. Hugh Narbone – Thomas Gybson – cottage, stable, garden and close.

16 July 1549. Richard Narbone – Thomas Gybson of London, clothworker – cottage, stable, garden and close adjoining said cottage, formerly of John Chaundler.

25 April 1552. Thomas Gybson to William Whyte, Groom of the Wardrobe – cottage, stable, garden and close formerly of John Chaundler.

15 April 1575. Richard Manning and wife Rachel (youngest daughter and heir of William Whyte deceased) to Thomas Garrett – cottage, stable, garden and close formerly of John Chaundler.

30 March 1579. Thomas Garrett to Thomas Gisbie – as above.

4 April 1583. Thomas Gisbie to William Boon – cottage in Richmond called the Sign of the Goat and stable and garden adjacent.

Now see tenements 23 and 24 and 22-24 below.

*Tenements 23 and 24*

9 June 1533. Sir Giles Capell and wife Mary (formerly wife of Hugh Denys) surrendered (on 8 September 1532) to Clement Twyford – half tenement in the possession of ... Cooke; and tenement and cottage and 10 acres and ½ acre of mead.

'Master' Twyford was listed as a manorial tenant in 1535-36. He was the guardian of Thomas Cooke (see tenement No. 22), so it is almost certain that these two half-tenements went to Thomas Cooke.

*Tenements 22-24*

Apart from tenement at No. 25, which he still held at his death, Thomas Cooke held another two whole tenements in 1535. These appear to be the whole tenement at No. 22 and the two half tenements at 23 and 24.

14 June 1535. Thomas Cooke, son of William Cooke – Ralph Annesley – cottage and garden and 2 virgates of land.

Ralph Annesley's widow probably married as her second husband Jeffrey Perryns, who is listed as a manorial tenant in 1550 and 1554. There are five references in the Raynford terrier of 1559 to land of 'Perryns late Ansley' – all but one relating to land later held by the Clarkes. Perryns must have died about 1559, when the widow married as a third husband ... Cartledge, very shortly before her own death.

11 July 1559. Elizabeth Cartelage (formerly wife of Ralph Annesley) deceased – George Annesley (son of Robert Annesley deceased who was son of Ralph Annesley) one whole tenement of 20 acres and 1 acre mead and 3 cottages and another tenement of 20 acres and 1 acre mead called the *Katheryn Whele*.

28 March 1571. George Annesley – Henry Deacon, serjeant plumber to the Queen – whole tenement of 20 acres and 1 acre mead and 3 cottages and another whole tenement of 20 acres and 1 acre mead called the *Catheren Whele*.

Henry Deacon appears as a manorial tenant from 1571 to 1584. He died in September 1592. His heir to the tenements was his daughter Joan, who had married Robert Clarke of the Inner Temple. Deacon had built up a considerable estate out of several cottages to the south-west of the church, and either he or Clarke built a large mansion there.

28 April 1606. Robert Clarke deceased – son Richard Clarke – great capital messuage and gardens, orchards, etc, and 40 acres land and 2 acres mead and 2 cottages.

15 May 1615. Richard Clarke – himself for life, then to brother Henry, sister Elizabeth and sister Joan, brother John and brother Lawrence in tail – all property (except 2 cottages) formerly of his father Robert.

31 March 1617. Richard Clarke deceased – brother Henry Clarke – all customary messuages and land in entail as by surrender of 15 May 1615.

## 25. *Whole tenement of 20 acres*

John Prymme and his wife Alice are mentioned in the manor rolls for 1421 and 1422. He may have held this tenement. The name does not occur again in the surviving mid-15th-century rolls, but reappears at the beginning of Henry VII's reign.

16 July 1489. John Prym deceased – wife Joan for life with reversion to John Walshe – tenement of 20 acres and 1 acre mead (see also will of John Prein (*sic*) probate Kingston 21 October 1488).

18 January 1501/2. John Walshe – Robert Elyott, yeoman of the Crown, and wife Joan – tenement of 20 acres and 1 acre mead.

14 October 1510. Robert Elyott deceased – wife Joan – all his estate.

Either Joan Elyott married John Mellyneck (Bailiff of the Manor Court) or she sold the tenement to him. Then John Mellyneck sold the tenement to Owen Holland.

23 May 1529. Owen Holland – self and wife Ethelreda – cottage and tenement of 20 acres, formerly of John Mellyneck.

Owen Holland sold the tenement to Thomas Cooke.

12 November 1538. Thomas Cooke died seised of a tenement and 8 cottages – proclamation for heir.

15 September 1539. Thomas Cooke's daughter Katherine (a minor) is recognized as heir to 20 acres, 1 acre mead and 8 cottages.

1 December 1550. Katherine (daughter of Thomas Cooke) wife of John Hall admitted to 20 acres, 1 acre mead and 8 cottages.

24 March 1550/1. John Hall and wife Katherine sold to John Gwyldmyn ½ acre.

24 March 1550/1. John Hall and wife Katherine – Henry Naylor tenement containing 19½ acres, 1 acre mead and 8 cottages.

Henry Naylor appears frequently as a manorial tenant up to 1580. The date of his death is unknown, but his heir was Mary Crome, who held this land in the 1620s (so stated in minutes of Richmond vestry).

The *capital messuage* of this tenement was the *Crown* at 16-20 The Green and 59-65 George Street (Nos. 31-37 in 1603 list). It remained attached to the tenement until the death of Mary Crome.

## 26. Free half tenement of 10 acres

In 1314 Isabell de Binnegates held a messuage and 10 acres of land and 1 acre of mead in free socage. Gilbert de Byngate was taxed in Shene in 1332.

29 September 1348. Gilbert Byngate – William Walshe – 10 acres of land and 1 acre of mead.

There are several early 15th-century references to the Walshe family as manorial tenants (Robert 1404-05; John 1404-19; Edmund and wife Joan 1415; Mavill 1418; Henry 1419: heirs of Elena 1421; Thomas 1445.)

17 October 1491. Robert Walshe deceased – John Walshe Senior – free tenement and 10 acres.

4 September 1492. Thomas Denys held a free tenement at the east end of the village of Shene with 10 acres, formerly of John Walshe. (The Thomas Denys of 1492 was the father (or grandfather?) of Thomas Denys mentioned next below.)

31 August 1558. Thomas Denys – Allen Matthews and Robert Saunders [churchwardens] – half a free tenement viz: a messuage between the lands of Nicholas Culverwell east, the highway south, land of the heirs of Auaustine Hynde north and land of John Parkyns west, together with 10 acres of land and ½ acre of mead (free) – inscribed in manor rolls by request of the parish council on 4 April 1559.

Despite the above this half tenement was sold by Thomas Denys's widow Joan and her new husband Nicholas Beneson to Henry Naylor, from whom it was inherited by Mary Crome before 1603.

Mary Crome held the land in 1620 and was sued for its return by the vestry in 1626 – but without success.

The *capital messuage* of this tenement was the house 'at the east end of the village' on the site of Lichfield Court, Sheen Road (No. 97 in the 1603 list). It remained attached to the tenement until the death of Mary Crome.

## 27. Whole tenement of 19 acres and a 1-acre close of mead

Thomas Byrche (or Brykke) was listed as a manorial tenant from 1497.

17 April 1505. Thomas Brykke – Charles Somerset Kt – messuage and virgate of land containing 19 acres and 1 acre of mead behind the messuage in Kew.

1526. By his will Charles Somerset, Earl of Worcester, left his estates to his widow Eleanor, with remainder to his son George Somerset.

George Somerset rearranged his lands to create a park of 19 acres (copyhold) at the west end of Tenderland Furlong and a belt of freehold land, to the west of the path to the ferry.

1553-58. Sir George Somerset died leaving the estate at Kew to his widow Thomasine with remainder to his youngest son William Somerset.

1 April 1560. Sir George Somerset deceased – son William Somerset – 19 acres at Kew in the Park on which is built a messuage called the Lodge, formerly in the tenure of Thomasine Thomas, widow of Sir George.

3 May 1566. William Somerset – Dr William Awberry – 19 acres [as above].

4 May 1587. Dr William Awberry and wife Winifred – son Morgan Awberry and wife Joan – 19 acres at Kew in the Park.

30 September 1605. Morgan Awberry and wife Joan – Sir Arthur Gorges and wife Elizabeth – 19 acres at Kew in the Park.

20 February 1606/7. Sir Arthur Gorges and wife Elizabeth – selves for lives with remainder to son Arthur – all properties surrendered to them by Morgan Awberry and wife Joan.

The *capital messuage* of this tenement was by the riverside at Kew (No. 134 in 1603 list).

## 28. Half tenement of 10 acres

The family of 'atte Ware' (originally probably 'at the Weir') is the oldest one traceable in Kew, the first mention being of a Roger at Were in 1234.

William atte Ware is mentioned in 1349.

Robert atte Ware was a manorial tenant 1404-22. In 1417 he and his wife Honora made over a piece of land in Kew to John atte Ware and wife Joan. John atte Ware is noted as a manorial tenant 1418-22.

Clement at Wer is noted as a tenant in 1445, John Were in 1449, and Robert atte Were in 1452.

This tenement presumably descended in the family to Stephen att Were, as a tenant from 1487.

18 January 1501/2. Stephen at Were of Kew deceased – son William at Were – half tenement of 10 acres at Kew.

1502-31. William at Were is listed as a manorial tenant.

5 June 1531. William Atwere – self and wife Joan – half tenement of 10 acres in Kew occupied by William Atwere.

This tenement passed into the ownership of Ralph at Ware, recorded as a manorial tenant 1532-54.

1554-58. Ralph at Ware – Thomas Adams and wife Joan.

Thomas Adams is recorded as a tenant up to 1576.

12 April 1577. Joan Adams deceased – James at Weere – half tenement of 10 acres in Kew which she held for her life.

James Were split up the half tenement (but most of it went to the Awberrys):

| | |
|---|---|
| 4 April 1578 to John Hynde | ½ acre |
| 4 April 1578 to William Awberry | 4 acres |
| 28 March 1580 to William Awberry | ½ acre |
| 3 April 1581 to William Awberry | 2 acres (1 of meadow) |
| 19 April 1582 to William Awberry | 4 lots of meadow |
| 4 April 1583 to William Awberry | 4 acres |
| 17 July 1587 to Morgan Awberry | messuage, curtilege and garden in Kew. |

(1 acre was returned to James Ware by Morgan Awberry and resold to John Hynde.)

The Awberry holdings were sold to Sir Arthur Gorges in 1605, the Hynde holdings became part of the Portman estate.

The *capital messuage* of this tenement was between the riverside and Kew Green (No. 135 in 1603 list).

## 29. Whole tenement of 20 acres

No history has been traced before 1492.

4 September 1492. Thomas Vernon – John Pyke, goldsmith, of London, and wife Joan – tenement of 20 acres.

The *capital messuage* of this tenement was on the site of Heron Square, Hill Street (No. 80 in 1603 list). It remained attached to the tenement until sold by John Bird to Robert Wright in 1604.

Now see at tenements 29-30 below.

## 30. Half tenement of 10 acres

William Constable appears in the manor records from 1419 to 1449. His widow Cecily who died in 1454 left her goods and chattels to her son Robert Constable. The latter was a manorial tenant in 1452 and was presented for an offence involving 'land formerly Freeman's' (see tenement No. 18).

From Robert the half tenement may have descended to John Constable.

24 November 1485. Walter Osborne, kinsman and heir of John Constable deceased, died without heirs before his admission. New grant by Lord of Manor to John Pyke, goldsmith of London, and his wife Joan of 10 acres of land formerly held by John Constable.

The *capital messuage* was on the site of Pensioners' Alley (now Golden Court) (No. 43 in 1603 list). It probably remained attached to the tenement until the time of Henry Harvey (who was in occupation in 1582).

Now see at tenements 29-30 below.

*Tenements 29 and 30*

9 September 1505. John Pyke – self and wife Isabella – all lands and tenements.

29 November 1518. John Pyke and wife Isabella – Owen Holland and wife Elizabeth – whole tenement of 20 acres now occupied by Thomas Proctor, and a half tenement of 10 acres, and a messuage and croft. Owen Holland was succeeded in title by a son of the same name.

13 April 1576. Owen Holland – Henry Harvey – all lands and tenements.

Now see below for further history of tenements 29-31.

## 31. Whole tenement of 20 acres

Elys Hawes was listed as a manorial tenant from 1489 onwards and may have acquired this tenement before 1485.

18 April 1502. Elys Hawes – wife Margaret and daughter Margaret – tenement of 20 acres.

1530. Suit between Robert Moger and wife Margaret (daughter of Elys Hawes deceased) and Robert Lyngo and wife Fredeswide (another daughter of Elys Hawes) concerning a whole tenement of 20 acres. [The Mogers appear to have won.]

30 June 1534. Robert Moger and wife Margaret – Henry Herford and wife Alice – whole tenement of 20 acres and 1 acre mead.

23 April 1563. Henry Herford (deceased) and wife Alice (later wife of John Pawles) also deceased – son Thomas Herford – all lands.

21 December 1565. Thomas Herford sold:

    3½ acres to Robert Stockden

    3½ acres to Edward Lovell

4 April 1567. Thomas Herford – William Herford – cottage adjoining the Bell inn and another cottage and 13 acres and 1 acre mead.

4 April 1567. William Herford sold 2 acres to William Smithe

1 April 1568. William Herford – Henry Herford – 12 acres (= 11 acres and 1 acre mead).

Henry Herford's name varies to Henry Harvey.

The *capital messuage* of this tenement is uncertain. Nos. 118 and 120 in the 1603 list belonged to the Herford/Harvey family.

Now see tenements 29-31 below.

*Tenements 29-31*

Henry Harvey held 41 acres and 2½ acres of mead. He appears to have sold at least 31¾ acres and 2½ acres of mead (and possibly the entire holding) to Nicholas or John Bird between 1589 and 1602.

See below at tenements 29-32 for the dispersal of the Bird estate.

## 32. Whole tenement of 20 acres

Maud de Binnegates in 1314 held in villenage a whole tenement consisting of a messuage, 18 acres and 2 acres mead. This would have become 20 acres and 1 acre mead.

The Byngate family figure in the manor records throughout the rest of the 14th and 15th centuries (Gilbert 1332; Gilbert, Thomas and John 1348; John died 1349; Thomas died 1347 – heir Julia; Alan 1404-21; William 1404; John 1414; Thomas 1417; Peter 1449; William 1449-52.

John Byngate was a manorial tenant by 1487.

14 October 1510. John Byngate – wife Joan for life, reversion to son Thomas – messuage and a virgate.

23 May 1529. John Byngate deceased – Thomas Byngate – daughter Sibyll Byngate – whole tenement of 20 acres.

16 July 1539. Sibyll Byngate died without heirs. Alice, sister of Thomas Byngate and wife of Thomas Lawrence is her heir.

27 May 1549. Thomas Lawrence and wife Alice granted licence to let to Walter Blackwell a whole tenement of 20 acres and 1 acre mead.

Thomas Lawrence is noted as a tenant up to 1552. He was succeeded in title by Robert Lawrence at a date between 1553 and 1558.

4 April 1559. Robert Lawrence deceased – wife Ann – tenement of 21 acres.

19 April 1564. William Lawrence admitted as heir to brother Robert – messuage and 20 acres.
> *either* William Lawrence leased the tenement to George Vernon and then sold it to Thomas Foster;
> *or* he sold it to Vernon who at once sold it on to Foster.

21 December 1565. Thomas Foster, Groom of the Chamber – Nicholas Culverwell – messuage of 20 acres now or lately in occupation of George Vernon.

11 May 1570. Nicholas Culverwell deceased – son Nicholas Culverwell – messuage and 20 acres formerly of William Lawrence.

10 April 1584. Nicholas Culverwell deceased – brother Ezekiel Culverwell – messuage and 20 acres held by their father Nicholas Culverwell from the surrender of William Lawrence (*sic*).

This tenement was surrendered (between 1589 and 1602) by Ezekiel Culverwell to Nicholas or John Bird. (The seven pieces of land shown in the Raynford terrier as held by 'Lawrence late Byngate' all fit into the pattern of the disposal of the Bird estate – see below.)

The *capital messuage* of this tenement may possibly have been at 11-21 Sheen Road (No. 100 in 1603 list) which was owned by John Byngate in 1503 and by Edmund Bird in 1608.

*Tenements 29-32: the Bird estate*

| | |
|---|---|
| In 1587 Nicholas Bird acquired from William Pate (tenements 33-34) | 8 acres |
| Between 1589 and 1602 Nicholas or John Bird acquired from Henry Harvey (tenements 29-31) up to | 41 acres & 2½ acres mead |
| from Ezekiel Culverwell (tenement 32) | 20 acres & 1 acre mead |
| Total (maximum) | 69 acres & 3½ acres mead |
| (minimum) – held in 1603 | 59¼ acres & 3½ acres mead |

(The doubt here is whether the 9¾ acres was sold by Harvey or the Birds – it went to Richard Wright (8 acres), Thomas Smythe (1½ acres) and Henry Naylor (¼ acre).

The estate was broken up after 1603. Known disposals:

| | |
|---|---|
| 8 April 1605 to Henry Holloway and wife Dorothy | 2 acres |
| 8 April 1605 to Thomas Smythe | 8 acres |
| 28 May 1606 to Sir Robert Wright and wife Dorothy | 11½ acres & 1½ acre mead |
| 28 May 1606 to trustees William Haynes and Thomas Smith | 38 acres & 2 acres mead |

Subsequent disposals by Haynes and Smith:

| | |
|---|---|
| 11 July 1606 to Alexander Prescott | 8 acres |
| 11 July 1606 to Henry Cuckney | 8 acres |

| | |
|---|---|
| 7 October 1606 to John Preston | ½ acre |
| 24 February 1606/7 to King James for his park | 3¼ acres |
| 22 April 1612 to Sir Arthur Gorges | 2 acres mead |
| 22 April 1612 to John Leaver | 1 acre |
| 8 April 1613 to Thomas Smith | 8½ acres |
| 8 April 1613 to William Haynes (who died before admission, so to his daughter Winifred, wife of Bartholomew Smythe) | 8½ acres |

Alexander Prescott died in 1608. His widow Elizabeth married John Burd who held the 8 acres listed above, together with 7½ acres from tenement No. 10, in 1620.

## 33. *Whole tenement of 20 acres*

The Osey family was established in Shene by the early 15th century. The transfer of a messuage and 30 acres from Hugh Osey is noted in 1421. Other Oseys, including Philip and John, are recorded in the 1440s. Nothing is known of the Leghtons.

1486. Thomas Hart and wife – John Warren and wife Joan – William Bracebrygge. Virgate of 20 acres and 1 acre of mead, formerly held by John Leghton and his wife Elizabeth and before that by John Osey.

15 May 1498. William Bracebrigge, citizen and draper – Sir Richard Gilford – whole tenement of messuage, 20 acres and 1 acre of mead, previously occupied by John Waren and wife Joan, before that by John Leghton and wife Elizabeth, and once by Philip Osey. (Sir Richard Gilford, a close associate of Henry VII and Controller of the Household from 1496, died on pilgrimage in Jerusalem in 1506.)

21 November 1508. Henry Gilford, son and heir of Sir Richard, admitted to whole tenement formerly of Sir Richard Gilford and before that of Bracebrigge.

6 November 1509. Henry Gilford – Matthew Clyderowe – whole tenement, formerly belonging to Bracebrigge.

15 June 1517. Matthew Clyderowe – Richard Broke and wife Alice – reversion of whole tenement, formerly of Bracebrigge.

13 June 1530. Richard Broke of London – John Pate and wife Anne – whole tenement of 20 acres.

18 July 1536. William Pate declared heir to 20 acres and 1 acre mead formerly held by his father John Pate.

John Pate's widow Anne may have married (?Thomas) Aleyn or Allen, as lands held by 'Allen, late Clithero [Clyderowe]' are mentioned in the Raynford terrier. As Anne had been admitted as a joint tenant in 1530, she and a new husband would have held the lands for her lifetime.

28 March 1571. William Pate – self and wife Alice – whole tenement of 20 acres formerly of Matthew Clyderowe and once of Sir Henry Gilford.

The *capital messuage* of this tenement was on the site of 7-11 Hill Street (No. 77 in 1603 list). It remained attached to the tenement until sold by William Pate and his wife Alice to Ralph Fletcher shortly before 1603 (title made good in 1606).

Now see at tenements 33-34 below.

## 34. *Half tenement of 10 acres*

John Yonge is noted in the manor rolls in 1449-52. Members of the Hunt family occur in 1419 and 1441.

13 September 1487. William Hunt deceased – wife Joan with reversion to son Edmund – a half-virgate. Joan subsequently married – Hosey (?or Osey).

22 May 1497. Joan Hosey (formerly wife of William Hunt) – son Edmund Hunt – half tenement of 10 acres and ½ acre mead, formerly of John Yonge.

18 April 1502. Edmund Hunt – Hugh a Deane and wife Agnes. Half tenement of 10 acres.

6 November 1509. Agnes a Deane widow – John Sharpe – half tenement of 10 acres.

1521-27. John Sharpe – John Crewe. (John Sharpe was still a manor tenant in 1520; John Crewe is first mentioned in 1531. Land of 'William Pate late Sharpe' is mentioned in the Raynford terrier.)

5 June 1531. John Crewe – wife Elizabeth Crewe, with reversion to John Pate – half tenement of 10 acres.

18 July 1536. William Pate pronounced heir to cottage and 10 acres held by his late father John Pate: and surrendered to Elizabeth Stede (?formerly Crewe) for her life with reversion to himself – and Elizabeth Stede leased the premises to him.

23 February 1544/5. William Pate admitted to half tenement of 10 acres, in accordance with 1531 surrender by John Crewe to his wife Elizabeth (now dead) with reversion to John Pate (now dead).

The *capital messuage* of this tenement was probably at 13-15 The Green and 12-18 Brewer's Lane (Nos. 26-30 in 1603 list). This property was owned in 1596 by John Feare *als* Deere, who acquired quite a lot of Pate's estate.

Now see tenements 33 and 34 below.

### Tenements 33 and 34

This holding, totalling 30 acres of arable and 121 acres of mead, was broken up by William Pate and his son and heir John Pate. Known disposals are:

| | |
|---|---|
| 13 March 1557/8 to Henry Naylor | 3 acres |
| 4 April 1578 to Thomas Lord Buckhurst | 10 acres |
| 4 May 1587 to Nicholas Bird | 8 acres |

4 July 1606 John Pate to Ralph Fletcher (renewing former surrender) – 8¼ acres and a close of 1½ acres and 1 acre of mead.

## 35. Whole tenement of 20 acres (Thomas's)

In 1314 William Thomas held a whole tenement of a messuage, 18 acres and 2 acres of mead.

There are references to William Thomas (taxed in 1332) and to William Thomas and John Thomas in 1348.

John Thomas was a manorial tenant 1404-22.

Now see tenements 35 and 36 below.

## 36. Whole tenement of 20 acres (Freeman's)

1418. Alice, former wife of Geoffrey Colet, is now wife of William Freeman.

1421-22. William Freeman a manor tenant.

Now see tenements 35 and 36 below.

### Tenements 35 and 36

1422. Robert Kentford was a manorial tenant.

18 November 1445. John Kentford died, holding lands formerly of Robert Kentford. His sister Cecily is his heir.

1446. Cecily Kentford admitted as heir to Robert and John Kentford – 2 messuages and 2 virgates.

*Note* – There is no evident link between the Kentfords and the Blacketts except that they both held two tenements.

William Blackett was listed as a manorial tenant from 1485.

17 October 1491. William Blackett – Richard Brampton – tenement and 20 acres and 1 acre mead

formerly of Richard Thomas and 20 acres parcel of the tenement called Freeman's.

1 December 1528. Richard Brampton deceased – son John Brampton – 2 tenements.

27 May 1532. John Brampton deceased – son John Brampton – 2 tenements, 40 acres of land and 2 acres mead.

11 April 1572. John Brampton deceased – Thomas Brampton 2 tenements containing 40 acres and all cottages, houses, etc.

20 December 1581. Thomas Brampton – Thomas Gisby – 40 acres of arable and 2 acres of mead.

The *capital messuage* of one of these tenements was probably at 21-25 The Green and 66-73 George Street (Nos. 38-42 in 1603 list). Parts of this property were sold off by Thomas Gisby Senior in the 1580s; the rest, in several parcels, by his son Thomas Gisby in 1613 and 1638. The location of the other capital messuage is unknown.

*Tenements 35 and 36 (continued)*
Thomas Gisby gradually broke up the estate.

| | |
|---|---|
| Known disposal: | |
| 27 April 1590 to William Boone Senior | 2 acres |
| Conjectural disposals: | |
| 1589-1602 to Ralph Tye | 4¾ acres |
| 1559-1602 to Nicholas Saunders | 7 acres |
| 1589-1602 to John Jewett | ½ acre |
| 1589-1602 to Thomas Bun and wife Helen | 1½ acres |
| Known disposals: | |
| 8 April 1605 to Thomas Tye | 2 acres |
| 30 September 1605 to Seth Goldstone | ½ acres |
| 20 February 1605/6 to King James I for park | ½ acre & 20p |
| 28 May 1606 to George Hudson | ½ acre |
| 24 February 1606/7 to King James I for park | ½ acre & 31p |
| 9 April 1607 to Joan Harrold | <u>2 acres</u> |
| Total disposals before death of Thomas Gisby Sr | 21¾ acres. |

21 April 1608. Thomas Gisby deceased – son Thomas Gisby – remaining estate (= 18¼ acres and 2 acres mead)

| | |
|---|---|
| Known disposals by Thomas Gisby Junior: | |
| 11 May 1608 to Ralph Fletcher | 8½ acres |
| 20 May 1610 to Richard Lovell | 1¾ acres |
| 6 May 1611 to William Fletcher | <u>8 acres & 2 acres mead</u> |
| | 18¼ acres & 2 acres mead |

# APPENDIX 8

# *Ownership of the Richmond Aits*

## 1. [Actually in Petersham, on boundary with Richmond]

|  | Henry Perkins |
| --- | --- |
| 1615 & 36 | William Perkins |
|  | James Perkins |
| 1695 | son James Perkins |
| 1733 | John Perkins |
|  | Rev Cutts Barton (for Duke of Montagu) |
| 1781 | son John Barton (for Duke of Montagu) |
|  | merged into Buccleuch House grounds |

## 2. By Church Close, Petersham Road

| 1506 | Grant to Richard Richardson |
| --- | --- |
| 1542 | Robert Fawkon – Augustine Hynde |
| 1554 | son John Hynde |
| 1590s | Sir Hugh Portman |
| 1604 | Sir John Portman |
| 1619 | Sir William Portman |
| 1630 | Sir Robert Carr, Earl of Ancram |
| 1656 | Stanley Carr |
| 1656 | Charles Carr, 2nd Earl of Ancram (by then incorporated into riverbank) |
| 1659 | Trustees for the poor of Richmond (then merged into Church Close) |
|  | Trustees for the Church Estate |

## 3. 'Bullrush Bed by the Ferry' – now Corporation Island (No. 866 in 1771 manor survey)

| 1602 | Grant to John Standen |
| --- | --- |
| 1630 | son Gilbert Standen |
| 1663 | son Ellis Standen |
| 1676 | James Perkins |
| 1691 | widow Alice Perkins |
| 1717 | son John Perkins |
| 1720 | Richard Price |
|  | William Cross |
| 1745 | William Price |
| 1775 | son William Price |
| 1789 | widow Ruth Price |
| 1790 | William Bullen |
| 1792 | Walwyn Shepherd |
| 1797 | Henry B Scudamore *et al* |
| 1802 | William Duke of Queensberry |
| 1812 | Lord Yarmouth (Later Marquess of Hertford) and wife Maria |
| 1831 | Maria Marchioness of Hertford *et al* |

| 1831 | Crown |
|------|-------|
| c.1840 | HM Commissioners of Woods |
| 1873 | Richmond Vestry |
| 1890 | Borough of Richmond |
| 1965 | London Borough of Richmond upon Thames |

## 4. Former aits at the end of Water Lane

| A) | ? | | Grant to William Pate and Alice Pate |
|----|---|---|------|
| | 1602 | | John Pate |
| | 1606 | | Robert Bayley |
| | | | [incorporated into riverside land as Bayley's wharf and house] |
| B) | 1638 | | Grant to Samuel Chambers |

## 5. Three former aits by 'The Friars'

| 1316 | Grant to Carmelites |
|------|-------|
| 1542 | Grant to John Lovell |
| | George Lovell |
| 1572 | John Hopkins and wife Julia |
| 1578 | John Hynde |
| 1590s | Sir Hugh Portman |
| 1604 | Resumed by Lord of Manor |
| 1610-11 | Incorporated into riverside land |

## 6. Ait opposite Palace (formerly three, now two) (No. 865 in 1771 manor survey)

| A | | | | B | | | | C | |
|---|---|---|---|---|---|---|---|---|---|
| 1560 | Grant to Massie Standen | | | | | | | | |
| 1574 | Edward Limcocke | | | | | | | | |
| 1575 | John Hynde | | | | | | | | |
| 1589 -1602 | Edward Standen | | | 1580 | Grant to Edward Standen | | | | |
| 1607 | Richard Standen | | | 1607 | John Standen | | | | |
| 1608 | Robert Bayley | | | | | | | | |
| 1614 | brother Wm Bayley | | | 1630 | son Gilbert Standen & wife Eliz. | | | 1619 | Grant to Augustine Redding |
| 1656 | Gilbert Standen | | | | | | | 1656 | son Wm Redding |
| 1663 | Elias Standen | | | 1663 | Elias Standen (reversion) | | | 1664 | sister Eliz. Maunder |
| | | 1669 | John Antill | | | | | 1672 | nephew Wm Perkins Jr |
| | | 1682 | son John Antill | | | | | | |
| | | 1696 | sister Eliz Antill (m James Cole) | | | | | 1695 | sons Wm & Geo Perkins [George died 1710?] |
| | | 1722 | son Thomas Cole | | | | | | |
| | | 1740 | Thomas Sayer (for Earl of Cholmondeley) | | | | | 1738 | Thos Perkins (son of Wm) |
| | | 1756 | James Sayer – Wm Walmsley & John Honour | | | | | | |
| | | 1756 | Francis, Earl Brooke | | | | | 1760 | dau Eliz. Perkins |
| | | | | | | | | 1760 | Francis, Earl Brooke |
| | | | | 1765 | John, Viscount Spencer (later Earl Spencer) | | | | |
| | | | | 1804 | son George, Earl Spencer | | | | |
| | | | | 1804 | William Duke of Queensberry | | | | |
| | | | | 1812 | Lord Yarmouth (later Marquis of Hertford) and wife Maria | | | | |
| | | | | 1831 | Maria Marchioness of Hertford *et al* | | | | |
| | | | | 1831 | Crown | | | | |
| | | | | c.1840 | HM Commissioners of Woods (as part of Crown estate) | | | | |
| | | | | 1873 | Richmond Vestry | | | | |
| | | | | 1890 | Borough of Richmond | | | | |
| | | | | 1965 | London Borough of Richmond upon Thames | | | | |

## 7. Parts of Isleworth Ait

| A (near Railshead) | | Walnut Tree Ait (No. 864 in 1771 manor survey) | | B (2 aits at northern end) | |
|---|---|---|---|---|---|
| 1617 | Grant to John Standen | 1617 | Grant to Wm Bayley | 1617 | Grants to Thos Redriffe of 2 separate aits |
| 1630 | son Gilbert Standen | | | | |
| 1663 | widow Eliz (m. Cogdell ) | 1653 | Thomas Eling | 1654 | son Thos Redriffe |
| 1666 | son Elias Standen | | | | (2 aits now one) |
| 1668 | John Antill | | | | |
| 1682 | son John Antill | 1681 | William Perkins | 1690 | widow Avis Redriffe |
| 1696 | sister Eliz Antill (m. James Cole) | 1695 | son William Perkins | 1691 | sister Martha Lewis |
| | | | | 1704 | daus Eliz. Stephens & Martha Bonwit |
| | | | | 1704 | John Stevens (half) |
| 1722 | son Thomas Cole | | | | |
| 1742 | James Wood | 1741 | Ambrose Baker | 1729 | Mary Gutteridge (half |
| | | 1754 | son James Baker | | |
| | | | Thomas Russell | 1757⎫ | James Wood |
| | | | | 1765⎭ | |
| | | 1759 | son David Russell | | [then as A – see left] |
| | | 1772 | Mary Toy | | |
| | | 1774 | Richard Toy *et al* | | |
| | | 1774 | Henry Bell | | |
| 1786 | nephew Thos. Lee | 1779 | dau Elizabeth Collett | | |
| 1794 | son William Lee | 1804 | son James Collett | | |
| 1807 | Thomas Forrow | 1811 | Elizabeth Eleanor Collett (m. –– Toby) | | |
| 1818 | Matthew Bowden | 1829 | son Wm James Toby | | |
| 1818 | Hugh 3rd Duke of Northumberland | | | | |
| 1851 | Algernon 4th Duke of Northumberland | | | | |
| 1855 | [enfranchised] | | | | |
| 1865 | George 5th Duke of Northumberland. | 1892 | nephew H G O Collett | | |
| 1867 | Algernon 6th Duke of Northumberland | 1905 | son H A A Collett | | |
| 1899 | Henry 7th Duke of Northumberland | 1922 | Norton Courlander | | |
| 1918 | Alan 8th Duke of Northumberland | | Duke of Northumberland | | |
| 1930 | Henry 9th Duke of Northumberland | | | | |
| 1933 | Middlesex County Council | | | | |
| 1965 | Greater London Council | | | | |
| 1986 | Thames Water Authority | | | | |

## 8. Brentford Ait (west part – 'The Hill' or 'Hoghole')
(No. 863 in 1771 manor survey)

| | |
|---|---|
| 1491 | Robert Gille |
| 1491 | widow Margery Gille |
| 1494 | Henry Parkyns |
| 1502 | John Foxe |
| 1533 | widow Rose Foxe |
| 1569 | Grant to Thomas Burgess |
| 1571 | Michael Staple |
| 1573 | niece Cecilia Kenyon (married John Hudson) |
| 1631 | son Richard Hudson |
| 1637 | Henry Perkins |
| 1641 | son William Perkins |
| 1695 | son George Perkins |
| 1710 | widow Anne Perkins |
| 1715 | Thomas Sawyer |

| | |
|---|---|
| 1725 | widow Anne Sawyer |
| 1726 | William Larcum |
| 1752 | son William Larkham |
| 1768 | William Strudwick |
| 1768 | son Walwyn Strudwick |
| 1776 | brother William Strudwick |
| 1781 | Samuel Ward |
| 1821 | grandson George (son of John) Ward |
| 1825 | father John Ward |
| 1825 | Crown |
| c.1840 | HM Commissioners of Woods |
| 1893 | Borough of Richmond |
| 1965 | London Borough of Richmond upon Thames |

## 9. Brentford Ait (central part – Twigg Ait)
## (No. 862 in 1771 manor survey)

| | |
|---|---|
| 1449 | John Litgold – lease to William Bower |
| 1538 | John Becke mortgage to Augustine Hynde |
| 1539 | Duke of Suffolk |
| 1545 | Augustine Hynde |
| 1603 | John Barber – Thomas Child |
| 1608 | Ezekiel Primmer |
| 1640 | brother Thomas Primmer |
| 1653 | Robert Randell |
| 1666 | son Edward Randell |
| 1687 | Edward Robinson |
| 1714 | Henry Robinson |
| 1737 | Stephen West |
| 1748 | brother Henry West |
| 1784 | widow Elizabeth West |
| 1793 | Thomas Samuel Maycock |
| 1802 | Elizabeth Legh |
| 1806 | granddau Elizabeth Hester, wife of T D Broughton |
| 1812 | Robert Hunter |
| 1813 | son John Hunter |
| 1813 | brother Robert Hunter |
| 1820 | Crown |
| 1823 | HM Commissioners of Woods |
| 1893 | Borough of Richmond |
| 1965 | London Borough of Richmond upon Thames |

## 10. Brentford Ait (east part – Mattingshawe or Makenshawe)
## (No. 862a in 1771 manor survey)

| | |
|---|---|
| 1445 | Clement Makyn |
| 1446 | Stephen Makyn |
| | John Payne |
| | William Payne |
| 1613 | seized to lord of manor (because alienated out of manor without licence) |
| 1637 | Grant to trustees of Payne's Charity, Fulham (then successive bodies of trustees) |
| 1874 | HM Commissioners of Woods |
| 1893 | Borough of Richmond |
| 1965 | London Borough of Richmond upon Thames |

# APPENDIX 9

# *The Manor Survey of 1703*

This document (LR2/226, pp.166ff) is basically a rental with some notes helping to identify – or at least locate approximately – many of the properties listed. It lists first the freeholds (but omits several), then copyholds in rough alphabetical order of tenants with the quit rents due, then the properties forming part of the 'old Palace and the demesne lands' (showing leasehold rents, rather than quit rents).

A few extra details can be gleaned from lists of quit rents in 1702 and 1704 (LR13/1/11 and 12) and from what appears to be a preparatory exercise listing some of the properties (at LR3/80, pp.123ff).

In many cases the quit rents due for a number of copyhold properties held by a single manor tenant have been lumped together to make a single total, though in others rents for the separate items are shown. The lump sums can often be broken down according to the following tariff (and when this has been done the component rents are shown in brackets):

> land 2d an acre (but 1d for a half-acre or a quarter-acre)
> cottage 4d　house 6d　larger mansion 1s or 2s
> island 2s　[grant of waste – great variation from 1d to 2s]

In two cases, those of Edward Darrell and Nathaniel Rawlins, a break-down has proved impossible.

As listed below the holdings have been rearranged into a geographical sequence similar to that used for the lists of houses in 1603 (Chapter 8), 1664 (Chapter 13), 1726 (Appendix 10) and 1771 (Appendix 12). The numbers allotted are those of the properties in the 1771 survey. The rents for lands appear very incomplete, but the larger estates include land with the houses.

## *The Manor Survey of 1703 (LR2/226, pp.166ff)*

(entries rearranged on a geographical basis)

| 1771 Survey no. | | Rents for leases |
|---|---|---|
| | **Crown land in and around the Palace** | |
| 6 | 'Ruinous building called the Gallery, late in the possession of Sir James Butler and Dr. Griffith – can hardly be made habitable without rebuilding' | --- |
| (5) | 2 tenements built by John Ayres Esq, in lease to Countess Dowager of Winchelsea | £20 |
| 5 | Messuage with garden and stable leased to Ann Hopper | £10 |
| 4 | Garden Gate House or Trumpeting House in lease to Hon Richard Hill | £15 |
| (4) | Part of a drying yard adjoining the Garden Gate house ⎱ | |
| 12 | Ruined building called the Pumphouse, stable and coachhouse and a parcel of waste adjoining, and part of the land called Fryers ⎰ in lease to Richard Hill | £2.6.8 |

| | | | |
|---|---|---|---|
| 7 | 2 ruined tenements and messuage adjoining with a garden, late in the tenure of -- Godscal | | |
| | Messuage late in the tenure of -- Lloyd | in lease to Maj Gen Cholmondeley | £40 |
| | House over gateway | | |
| | Remaining part of drying yard | | |
| 3 | Messuage with garden and brewhouse in lease to Richard Hawes | | £20 |
| 10 | Messuage in lease to Jane Armitage | | £40 |
| 11 | Messuage and garden in tenure of Thomas Smith | | |
| | 3 tenements adjacent late in the possession of -- Edridge, Joseph Rogers and Thomas Rayer | in lease to Thomas Smith | £21 |
| (11) | House with small yard adjacent to tenement of Mr Smith, in lease to Ann Darley | | £ 4 |
| (12) | House and garden called the Fryers in lease to John Lauze Esq | | £ 10 |
| 17 | Piece of ground, parcel of the Fryers ... with a wharf and a tenement in lease to Edward Darrell | | £ 4 |
| 13 | Piece of ground near the garden of Edward Darrell, in the occupation of – Wood gt. | | £ 2 |
| (12) | Small building called the Old Barge House at the corner of Mr Darrell's garden, in lease to Sylvanus Lawrence | | £1.10.0 |
| ? | Stable at end of old buildings fronting the Green, late in the tenure of Lady Waller | | £ 2 |
| 7-8 | The remaining parts in His Majesty's hands, possessed by Mr White under pretence of being housekeeper there | | --- |

**Crown land on north-west side of Green**

| | | | |
|---|---|---|---|
| 1 | 3 closes of pasture called Bentley Park | | |
| 1 | Tenement with orchard and garden, late Beamond's and a | in lease to Sir Charles Hedges | £26 |
| 1 | Tenement called the Bakehouse, with 2 little gardens | | |
| 1 | 2 tenements adjoining the premises last mentioned, late in the tenure of Rowland Corbet and William Watts | in lease to Sir Charles Hedges | £5.15.0 |
| 1 | An old stable and some other small things | | |

*Quit rents*

**North-west side of Green**

| | | | |
|---|---|---|---|
| 24 | House at NW corner of Green, late Mrs Munday's | Michael Pew | (2s 8d) |
| 22 | Capital messuage by the Green | Thomas Ewers | 3s 10d |
| 21 | Capital messuage on N side of Green | Mr Finch | 13s 0d |
| 21 | Piece of waste adjoining his garden | Sir Charles Hedges | 1d |

**North-east side of Green**

| | | | |
|---|---|---|---|
| a.b.c. N.O. | Piece of ground near the Bowling Green | Capt Knot (sic-Nott) | 2s 8d |

### Along the foot lane to Kew

| | | | |
|---|---|---|---|
| 414 | House, garden and 2 barns and half an acre | John White | 1s 0d |
| ?708 | House and barn | Isaac Pigg | (6d) |

### South-east side of Green (north of Brewer's Lane)

| | | | |
|---|---|---|---|
| 423-8 | Freehold house, garden and orchard | } John Michell | 7s 6d |
| 141 | House occupied by -- Gideon | | |
| 139-40 | 2 houses abutting Richmond Green: one in her own possession and one in possession of Mrs Campion | Mrs Eliz. Stobart | (1s 0d) |
| 135-8 | Capital messuage on south side of Richmond Green | Dr [John ] Price | 2s 0d |
| 133-4 | [Part of Radford estate] | Edward Darrell | * |
| 130-2 } 146-9 } | 3 houses adjoining Brewer's Lane and fronting the Green | Robert Browne | (1s 6d) |

### Brewer's Lane

| | | | |
|---|---|---|---|
| 150-1 | 2 messuages in Brewer's Lane | Richard Hawes Sr | (1s 0d) |
| 152 | Cottage in Brewer's Lane | William Grant | 4d |
| 126 | House in Brewer's Lane | heirs of John Child | 6d |
| 127-8 | 2 little houses in Brewer's Lane: one in her own possession, one in possession of John Payne | widow [Mary] Eling | 1s 0d |
| ? | Tenement in Brewer's Lane | widow [Ann] Eling | (4d) |
| 129 | 2 houses in Brewer's Lane | Samuel Spiers | 1s 0d |

### South-east side of Green (south of Brewer's Lane)

| | | | |
|---|---|---|---|
| 95 | Messuage at corner of Brewer's Lane, next the Green, late Mr Jones's | Mr Marriott | 1s 0d |
| 94 | House on S side of the Green | Walter Howel | (6d) |
| 93 | Cottage | John Saunders' wife | (4d) |
| 91-2 | House facing the Green, on the S side | Charles Wicks | 6d |
| 88-90 | House on S side of Richmond Green | Mr Masters | 6d |
| 86-7 | Tenement called the White Horse on | William Cross | 6d |

### Greenside

| | | | |
|---|---|---|---|
| 85 | House on the Green | William Drew | 6d |
| 84 | House on the S side of the Green | Michael Pew | (6d) |
| 83 | House on Richmond Green adjoining Pensioners' Alley NE | Philip Brent | 6d |

### Pensioners' Alley

| | | | |
|---|---|---|---|
| 82-3 | 4 cottages in Pensioners' Alley bought of one Chapman | John Brent | (1s 1d) |

| 81 & 103-4 | 3 cottages in Pensioners' Alley | } Michael Flayle | 2s od |
| 80 | 2 houses at corner of Paved Alley, facing the Green | | |
| 108 | Cottage in Pensioners' Alley | Wm Sherman | 4d |
| 109 | Cottage in Pensioners' Alley | Wm Greenbury | 4d |
| 110 | 3 cottages in Pensioners' Alley | Rowland Corbett | 1s od |
| 111 | Cottage | Alice Constable | 4d |

### South-east side of Green [Old Palace Terrace]

| 61-2 | [Parts of Radford estate] | Edward Darrell | * |
| 57-60 | 'Several tenements' | heirs of Jonah Smith | (2s od) |
| [54-5 | 2 freehold houses] | [Richard Hawes] | |

### South-west side of Green

| 29 | [Part of Radford estate] | Edward Darrell | * |
| 28 | Capital messuage and parcel of waste on W side of Green | John Wood | 2s od |
| 27-8 | 2 houses fronting the Green | Wm Boddicott | (1s 2d) |
| 26 | House at corner going down to the Friars | Joseph Fletcher | (6d) |

### King Street (SW side)

| 30-2 | 3 houses in street from stockstree to the Green | Francis Sandell | 1s 6d |
| 33 | House in street from stockstree to the Green | Wm Southwell | 6d |
| 34 | Tenement in possession of John Wilkinson in Green Street | William Street | (6d) |
| 35 | House left her by Thomas Redriffe | Martha Lewis | (4d) |
| 39 | House in street from Green to Red Lyon | John Rudel | 6d |
| 40 | House in street from Green to Red Lyon | Joseph Fletcher | (6d) |
| 41 | Tenement with sign of the Bells in street from Green to Red Lyon | William Lowndes | 6d |
| 42 | Feathers Inn Tenement in possession of John Chabener Tenement in possession of widow Leigh | } William Street | (2s od) |
| 43 | Tenement in possession of Caleb Hastings in Water Lane | | |

### Water Lane (north side)

| 44-5 | 2 cottages in Water Lane | John Martin & wife | 8d |
| 46-7 | 2 houses in Thames Street | John Vernon | 1s od |
| 48-51 | 3 cottages built by him, with garden, in Water Lane | Richard Price | 9d |
| 52 | 2 cottages and part of a barn in Water Lane | Richard and John Cross | 9d |
| 53 | House in Water Lane | William Perkins | (6d) |
| 53 | 2 tenements | Elizabeth, Ann and Martha Darling | 1s od |

## Water Lane (south side)

| | | | |
|---|---|---|---|
| 227 | Messuage in Water Lane, divided by him into four | Mr Bricknal | 6d |
| 228 | Cottage in Water Lane | Mrs John Scott | 4d |
| 229-30 | Messuage divided in two in Water Lane, in possession of Robert Kinders | John Cross | 6d |
| 231 | Tenement in Thames Lane | widow Newstrope | 6d |
| 232 | Stable or barn in Thames Lane | George Tisbury | (2d) |
| 233-4 | Divers tenements in Water Lane | John Smithies | 2s 2d |
| 236(pt) | Stable in Water Lane | Robert Bertie Esq | (2d) |

## Hill Street (west side)

| | | | |
|---|---|---|---|
| 235 | 2 houses near the Red Lyon | Walter Howel | (1s 0d) |
| 235 | Messuage against the stocks | Richard Hawes Sr | (1s 10d; |
| 236 | House and piece of ground in street from stockstree to Richmond Hill | Robert Bertie Esq | (1s 4d) |
| 237 | 2 houses in street from Stockstree to Richmond Hill | Edward Brabazon | 1s 0d |
| 237 | Capital messuage and garden in street leading up the hill | Mr Hallet | 2s 0d |
| 238-40 242-6 | Several new buildings late of John Sanders deceased, going up the Hill, and Antill's house and lands | Nathaniel Wood | 5s 0d |
| 241 | Part of house on hill turning down to the Ferry | Mrs Eliz. Antill | (3d) |

## Ferry Hill (south side)

| | | | |
|---|---|---|---|
| 275 | 2 tenements in Ferry Lane | Abell Burford (*sic* – Borfett) | 1s 0d |
| 276-7 | Cottage at upper end of Ferry Lane ('the Plough') | Wm Butcher Sr | (4d) |
| 276 | 2 tenements at corner of Ferry Lane | Thomas Farrin | 1s 0d |

## Lower Road to Petersham (west side, north to south)

| | | | |
|---|---|---|---|
| 279-80 | Almshouses | Almshouse Trustees | 8d |
| 281-4 | Major Prestwick's house [and close] | } Sir James Butler | 5s 4d |
| 285-7 | [close] | | |
| 296 | Tilekilns | | |

## Lower Road (east side, south to north)

| | | | |
|---|---|---|---|
| 585 | Parcel of waste on common near lower way to Petersham | John Vernon Jr | 1s 0d |
| 583 | House and ground on common | widow of James Perkins | (1s 0d) |
| 577-81 | 2 tenements, tilekilns and 2 pieces of ground | Randall Pigg | 2s 0d |
| 573 & 575-6 | 3 cottages | Samuel Moody | (1s 0d) |
| 574 | House and piece of waste near the tile kilns | widow Perkins | 1s 0d |

| 572 | Cottage by the tile kilns | Richard Almond | (4d) |
| 366-8 | Rump Hall | } Sir James Butler | 6d |
|  | Rutter's Piece |  | 6d |
| 364-5 (pt) | Cockdale's house | } Sir James Butler | 1s 4d |
|  | Fernes piece |  |  |
| 363-4 | House late Dewy's | Sir James Butler | 6d |
| 364-5 | Brown's orchard | Sir James Butler | 4s 0d |
| 364-5 | House late Mr George Carew's | } Sir James Butler | 8s 6d |
|  | Mr Lee's lands |  |  |

### The Hill (west side below Compass Hill)

| 297 | Houses going up Richmond Hill and cottage adjoining | William Butcher Sr | (3s 0d) |
| 298 | Cottage next Sarah Hartop's | widow Hill | 4d |
| 299 | Cottage up Richmond Hill | Sarah Hartop | 4d |
| 300-3 | 'Little old house on the brow of Richmond Hill where 'tis said Mr Hilliard apperconed at' | Thomas Rice | (4d) |
| 304-8 | Dr Thompson's estate | William Hickey | 1s 0d |

### The Hill (east side below Friar's Stile Lane)

| (?-331) | Several houses and gardens on backside of Red Lyon | Nathaniel Rawlins | * |
| 319-20 | House formerly called Poynter's | Geo Gardener | 1s 6d |
| 372 | Cottage lying above Poynter's gate | John Collins | 4d |
| 379-81 | Several houses in the way leading up the hill, over against Sir James Butler's estate. | heirs of Mrs Cogdale | 2s 8d |
| 373-6 382 | Part of John Chappell's estate | Edward Darrell | * |

### The Hill (west side above Compass Hill)

| 364-5 pt 369-71 | Old Wells | Robert Browne | (15s 11d) |
| 577-80 | Cottages on Richmond Hill near Old Wells | Richard Almond | (9d |
| 580 | Several tenements against the almshouses | Isaac Pigg | (4s 6d) |

### Hill Common (by Petersham border)

| 587 | House between Petersham and Richmond Commons | Thos Walpole & Jane Wright | 6d |
| 588 | Cottage on common near Hickey's slip | Richard Almond | (4d) |
| 589 | 3 little cottages bought of widow Eling | Mr Hickey | 1s 0d |
| 589 | 'White Lyon on Richmond Hill – sold to William Hickey' | widow [Ann] Eling [sic] | (1s 0d) |

## Top of the Hill (east side south of Friar's Stile Lane)

(Almshouses)

| | | | |
|---|---|---|---|
| 604-6 | 3 cottages, part built by her, and small garden | wife of John Saunders | (10d) |
| 605 | House near windmill | Eliz Jeffreys | 6d |
| 606 | Tenement near windmill | Isaac Pigg | (6d) |
| 607-8 | 2 houses on the hill late Pue's [sic – Pew's] | Richard Holland | 1s 0d |
| 609-11 | House late Pue's by the windmill and piece of waste before his door | Mr Hickey<br>Mr Hickey | 6d<br>2d |
| 612-13 | Cottage and 2 acres of land lately occupied by the widow of Arthur Best | Mr Hickey | 8d |
| 614 | Cottage and windmill | Thomas Matthews | 1s 0d |
| 615-16 | 2 cottages near windmill | Mary Kempson | 8d |
| 615-16 | Cottage near windmill | William Pearce | 4d |
| 618-20 | Piece of waste and 2 cottages by the windmilll | Peter Wallis | 1s 4d |
| 621 | Piece of waste | John Drew | (2s 6d) |
| 621 | Waste ground by the windmill | John Hopkins | 1s 0d |

## By the park wall, north of the gate

| | | | |
|---|---|---|---|
| 647 | House on Richmond Hill near the park gate | Edward Aldridge | 6d |
| 648 | Old cake house on the hill | heirs of Thomas Parsons | 5d |

## Marshgate (south side of road)

| | | | |
|---|---|---|---|
| 675 | Own house and late Maunder's house at Marsh Gate | Peter Wallis | 1s 4d |
| 675 | House at Marsh Gate | widow Harris | 6d |
| 554-6 | House and 2 acres near Marsh Gate | Mr Trigg | 10d |
| 558 | House late Matthew Walker's | William Trigg | 6d |

## Marshgate (north side of road)

| | | | |
|---|---|---|---|
| 679 | Messuage at Marsh Gate | } Mr Provost | 2s 0d |
| 680-82 | 3 closes of land late William Manley's | | |
| 676 | Tenement in possession of Samuel Sale (and 14 acres) | heirs of Matthew Walker | 4s 2d |

## Marshgate Road

| | | | |
|---|---|---|---|
| 533 | Barn and one acre in fields to Marsh Gate | Thomas Wall | (6d) |
| 504-5 | House by the way leading to Marsh Gate | Mrs Carter | 6d |
| 498-9 | Houses and gardens without the gate leading to Marsh Gate | Mr Young, | 1s 7d |
| 498 | Capital messuage and garden in fields to Marsh Gate | Mr Knapp | 1s 0d |
| 360 (g) | 1 acre against Knapp's house on the way to Marsh Gate | John Thorne | 2d |

| 497 | House near the field gate to Marsh Gate | Mr Whitfield | 6d |
| (350?) | Waste near the field gate in the way to Marsh Gate | Rd Hawes Jr | 1s 4d |
| 495 | [Part of Sir William Turner's estate] | Capt Lloyd | 18s 0d |
| 492-3 | Large house and garden near Richmond Gate | } Mrs Elizabeth Stobart | (3s 6d) |
| | Close next widow Young's without Richmond Gate | | |
| 491 | [Cottage] | Samuel Moody | (4d) |

## World's End (east side of Kew Lane)

| 483-4 | Part of cottage at Town's end | Michael Maunder | 2d |
| 483-4 | Part of Michael Maunder's house | Thomas Young | 2d |
| 482 | Cottage in street to Mortlake | George Smith | 4d |
| 482 | House at Town's end in the way to Mortlake | Michael Wicks | 6d |
| 480-1 | 3 cottages at World's End | Wm Butcher Sr | (1s 0d) |
| 479 | [Cottage] | Samuel Moody | (4d) |
| 477-8 | 2 little houses in the possession of William Wallins and Thomas Matthews | Mrs Eliz. Stobart | (8d) |
| 475-6 | 7 tenements at World's End | John Gardner | (3s 6d) |
| 474-5 | House with sign of the Bear against the pond | Mary Lever | 6d |
| 473 | Tenement by the town pond | Thomas Young | 6d |

## Middle Row

| 220 | 2 cottages in Middle Row | widow Drew | 8d |
| 221-2 | 2 tenements in Middle Row | Rowland Corbet | 1s 0d |
| 225 | House in Middle Row against the town pond | Mary Lever | 6d |

## London Street [George Street], north-west side up to Brewer's Lane

| 162-3 | Cottage in street leading to Middle Row | Mrs Spicer | (6d) |
| 161 | House and garden in main street by Rose and Crown | Abraham Matthews | 10d |
| 159-60 | 3 cottages and a house built by her husband against the stocks house | Mrs Spicer | (1s 6d) |
| 157-58 | 2 tenements in main street between widow Spicer's and widow Goodall's | John Price (joiner) | 1s 0d |
| 154-6 | Messuage in main street | Mrs Sarah Goodall | 1s 0d |
| 152-3 | Divers tenements | Mrs Stanley & dau Elizabeth | 4s 3d |

## London Street, north-west side, Brewer's Lane to King Street

| 123-4 | Piece of ground intermixed with tenements lately built by Henry Tippett | Mr Merriam & Mr Weatherhead | 6d |
| 123a | House in main street | John Stephens | (6d) |
| 123-4 | 2 tenements at corner of Brewer's Lane next main street | Wm Adams Jr (of Brentford) | 1s 0d |

| 121-2 | 2 tenements, one in his own possession and one occupied by John Bell | John Gardener (baker) | (1s 0d) |
| 120 | 3 small houses in London Street | Thomas Rice | (1s 0d) |
| 119 | 2 tenements in main street | John Drew | (1s 0d) |
| 118 | House in main street | Dorothy Bawke | 6d |
| 118 | House in main street | Heirs of Thomas Chilton | 6d |
| 117 | House in main street | Mrs Francis Child | 6d |
| 116 | Tenement lately occupied by Daniel Brent | John Brent | (6d) |
| 116 | 2 messuages adjoining the tenement in possession of Moses Boddicott | Charles Brent | 1s 0d |
| 115 | Barns, sheds and cowhouses in several people's possession | Mrs Eliz Stobart | (1s 0d) |
| 114 | 2 tenements facing main street | Jonathan Tomkins | 1s 0d |
| 113 | Tenement in high street | George Tisbury | (6d) |
| 111-2 | 2 tenements in London Street in possession of John Elham and John Roll | William Street | (1s 0d) |
| 100-2 | 2 houses in Thames [sic] Street in occupation of William Jaggard and William Harrold | John Vernon | 1s 0d |
| 100 | House of John Cross | Mr Barnes | 6d |
| 98-99 | Tenement in London Street in possession, of widow Jaggard and a little house adjacent | } widow [Ann] Eling | (10d) |
| 98-99 | Tenement in ownership of William Eling | | (6d) |
| 72 | Queen's Head over against the Red Lyon | Felix Fletcher | 6d |

### King Street (north-east side)

| 70 | House in possession of George Gardener, poulterer | widow of Francis Russell | 6d |
| 67-9 | [3 houses] | Thomas Eling | (1s 6d) |

### London Street (south-east side, north of Church)

| 528-30 | [Part of Sir William Turner's estate] | Mr Horsemanden | 2s 10d |
| 217-8 | Several tenements lately built by him, in possession of William Golton, William Reasin, John Edmonds, John Hedges, Matthew Drew, William Mason, —— Wadbrook, widow Purcell deceased | Major Manley | 4s 0d |
| 214-6 | 4 houses against the town pond | Henry Joyce | 2s 0d |
| 214-6 | 2 tenements on south side of the town pound | John Drew | (1s 0d) |
| 213 & 219 | [Parish lands – said to be freehold] | Robert Freeman | —— |
| 212 & 203 | 4 tenements and gardens | Robert Freeman | 4s 0d |
| 204-5 | 2 cottages in main street built by him | John Collins | 4d |
| 206-9 | Tenement in churchyard | heirs of Walter Smith | 10d |
| 210-11 | 2 tenements in churchyard | Clement Smith | 1s 0d |
| 202 | Peachman's house | John Brent | (6d) |

## London Street (south-east side, Church Court to Red Lyon)

| | | | |
|---|---|---|---|
| 199 -201 | Several tenements | heirs of Jonah Smith | (1s od) |
| 196a | Part of a garden | Job Gardener | 2d |
| 194-5 | 2 tenements: one in his own possession and the other the White Horse (and 22 acres of land) | William (son of Matthew) Moody | 4s 8d |
| 193 | Tenement in main street next the White Horse | Thomas Wall | (6d) |
| 189-192 | 5 cottages in main street | John Price, joiner | 1s 8d |
| 184-8 | Dwelling house, brewhouse and orchard, late Samuel Moody's (and 15 acres of land) | Thomas Newman | 3s od |
| 178 -83 | 3 tenements in main street | William Eling | 1s 6d |
| 175-7 | House in main street | Richard Fitzwater | 6d |
| 172-4 | 2 tenements | Matthew Moody | (1s od) |
| 168-171 | 8 houses in main street | Mr Patrick Lamb | (4s od) |
| 164-7 | The Red Lyon and tenement adjoining | Mrs Goulton | (2s od) |
| 167 | Messuage next the Red Lyon | William Boddicott | (6d) |

## 'Backside of the Red Lyon' [Red Lion Street]

| | | | |
|---|---|---|---|
| 259, 261 267-268 | Several houses and gardens on the backside of the Red Lyon | Nathaniel Rawlins | * |
| 260 | Cottage on the backside of the Red Lyon | Thomas [son of John] Drew | 4d |
| 262-263 | 2 tenements on the backside of the Red Lyon, facing the field | Francis Sendall | 1s od |
| ? | 3 tenements on the backside of the Red Lyon, facing the field | George Tisbury | (1s 4d) |

## Paradise Row

| | | | |
|---|---|---|---|
| 351 | House above the conduit | John Stephens | (6d) |

## Other Properties

| | | |
|---|---|---|
| Wayland's Farm [the George Farm] – freehold | Edward Allen | 11s 1d |
| Richmond Ferry | Lady Ashe | £3 13s 4d |
| Richmond Little Park and Lodge 'formerly leased to John Latten and others, but all now in the possession of Duke of Ormond' | Duke of Ormond | -- |
| 'In Kingston, 140 acres held of this manor, occupied by Thomas Barnes' | heirs of Sir Edward Evelyn | 18s 2d |

**West Sheen** appears to have been inadvertently omitted from the survey. The owners of property there in 1703 were:

| | |
|---|---|
| 'House formerly of the Earl of Leicester and other premises formerly in the possession of Henry Lord Brouncker' | Sir John Buckworth |
| 'The remainder including Sir William Temple's estate' | John Jeffreys |

*Note The total quit rent paid by Edward Darrell for 'Chappel's and Radford's estates' was 5 shillings. The total quit rent paid by Nathaniel Rawlins for 'several properties' was 4s 6d.

## Kew Green, south side

| 728-32 & | Capital messuage and land at Kew; and | Lady Capell | 7s 6d |
|---|---|---|---|
| 739-40 | 4 houses on south side of Kew Green | | 2s 0d |
| 733-8 | Cottage on Kew Green (and 4 acres) | Mrs Garland | 1s 0d |
| 741-7 | Capital messuage and land on south side of Kew Green | William Mounteny | 1s 9d |
| 748-53 | 2 houses on south side of Kew Green | Mrs Jackman | 1s 0d |
| 755-7 | Cottage on Kew Green near way to Mortlake | Miles Layton | 4d |

## Kew Green, north side

| 759-62 | Dwelling place in occupation of widow Gosland; and about 10 acres of orchard and garden; and 2 new-built houses, outhouses, orchards, etc in Sir Charles Eyre's possession; and Lord Plymouth's acre and 52 acres of land | Sir William Brownlowe's estate (freehold) | £1 6s 0d |
|---|---|---|---|
| 763-4 | Capital messuage formerly Lady Compton's at Kew | Sir Richard Levett | 10s 9d |
| 765 | Capital messuage on north side of Kew Green | John Lilley (Lely) | 1s 0d |
| 766 | House at Kew | Mrs Mary Eliz Brathwayt | 6d |
| 772-5 | 2 cottages at Kew on N side of Green | William Adams (of Brentford) | 8d |
| 775 | 2 cottages on north side of Kew Green | Matthew Hews | 8d |
| 777-9 | 3 tenements on north side of Kew Green | Wm Murden Sr | 1s 6d |
| 780 | Cottage at Kew | Mr Barnes | 4d |
| 781-4 | 3 cottages at Kew and a piece of ground | Jeremy Murden Sr | 1s 2d |
| 785 | Tenement at Kew | Mr Boggest | 6d |
| 786 | Tenement on north side of Kew Green | Jeremiah Murden Jr | 6d |
| 786 | Tenement adjacent to the east | William Murden Jr | 6d |
| 787-8 | House on north side of Kew Green | Humphrey Jenkes | 6d |
| 789 | Waste on north side of Kew Green | Thomas Croskal | 1s 0d |
| 798-9 | Waste plot on north side of Kew Green next to Croskal's | Edward Holden | 6d |
| 801 | Piece of ground at north-east end of Kew Green | John (son of Jeremiah) Murden | 6d |

## Kew Green, east side

| 805-7 | House called Benham's | William Cox | 6d |
|---|---|---|---|
| 808 | Cottage on Kew Green | Mrs Garland | (4d) |
| 809-11 | 3 cottages built by him on Kew Green and 10 acres and 4 lots of Kew Mead | William Cox | 4d |
| | | | 1s  10d |
| | 18 acres by Kew Green in Wm Cox's tenure | | |
| | 18 standing lots in Kew Meads | Sir William Brownlowe's estate (freehold) | |
| | 18 more in possession of one Marden | | |

## Islands

| 2 aytes | Mrs Eliz Antill | (4s) |
|---|---|---|
| ayte in Thames | widow of Jas Perkins | 2s |
| ayte at Sheen | William Perkins | 2s |
| ayte between Brentford and Kew | John Benfield | 2s |
| ayte against Kew | Edward Robinson | 2s |
| ayte at Kew | George Perkins | 2s |

## Miscellaneous land not included in holdings above

| 3 acres Bankside | Wm Adams of Mortlake | 6d |
|---|---|---|
| 12 acres | Mrs Eliz Antill | 2s |
| ½ acre Upper Dunstable | Brudenel Brown | 1d |
| rood of land near almshouses | Wm Butcher Jr | 1d |
| 3 acres | Wm Boddicott | 6d |
| rood in Church Shot | John Badger | 1d |
| rood in Church Shot bought of Wm Shearman | Henry Badger | 1d |
| 1½ acres Upper Dunstable | Mr Barnes | 3d |
| 1 acre Park Shot | heirs of Thomas | 2d |
| ½ acre Upper Dunstable | Chilton | 1d |
| 2 acres | E, A, & M Darling | 4d |
| 1 acre near Marshgate occupied Mr Barnes | Rd. Dalton | 2d |
| parcel of waste | Edw. Darrell | 2d |
| parcel of waste to enlarge his house | Thos Eling | (6d) |
| 9 acres Park Shot | Dinah Eling | 1s 6d |
| parcel of waste adjoining Green | James Ewers | 2s |
| 7 acre close occupied by Peter Thorne | James Goulton | (1s 2d) |
| ½ acre Marsh Furze bought of Mr Michell | Sir Chas Hedges | 1d |
| 1 acre Park Shot | John Hope | 2d |
| parcel of waste at Kew Bank (ex Geo Carew) | heirs of Thos Keele | 1d |
| 4 rods of waste in Upper Dunstable now used by John Keele of Mortlake for laying dung on | heirs of farmer Keele | 1d |

| | | |
|---|---|---|
| 2 acres | John Michell | 4d |
| 15 acres | Samuel Moody | 5s |
| 2 acres Park Shot | Matthew Moody | 4d |
| 1 acre Park Shot | Duke of Ormond | 2d |
| 4 rods at Sandpit in Kew | Andrew Oakly | 1d |
| 1 acre | Joseph Phelps | 2d |
| ½ acre Upper Dunstable | Thomas Rice | 1d |
| 10 acres | Francis Sandall | 1s 8d |
| ½ acre | Tobias Sedgwick | 1d |
| 10 acres | Wm Street | 1s 8d |
| parcel of ground behind Mrs Eling's house | Wm Salter | 2d |
| 3 roods at upper end of Church Shot | Wm Shearman | 12d |
| lot in Kew Mead | Robert Tunstall | 1d |
| 2 acres | Robert Wilson | 4d |

# APPENDIX 10

## *The Rate Lists of 1726*

The earliest surviving complete Richmond poor rate book dates from 1726, when the rate levied was 1s. 4d. in the £. Though the list shows only the amounts to be collected, it is a matter of simple arithmetic to calculate back to the underlying assessment figure of each property. This was the estimated annual rentable value (the concept of a 'rateable value' somewhat lower than the rentable value was not introduced until the 1840s). Comparison of the RV year by year, in relation to the neighbours, is a very important clue to the dating of works of enlargement, rebuilding, etc. (In 1751 the entire parish was reassessed at approximately one third higher than the previous figures; this was a matter of administrative convenience and as the increase applied to every building it does not indicate any alteration of structure.)

The list in the rate books is almost continuous, with no indications of separate streets, and very few even of sector. But the assessors followed a fixed geographical pattern which was hardly changed for the next 100 years. The listing starts round the Green (with a diversion up Kew Foot Lane), then goes up the west side of King Street and Hill Street to Ferry Hill. It continues along the Petersham Road ('Under the Hill'), first on the river side, then back, turns up the hill (south-west side) to the Park gates; then down again on the north-east side. Then it turns along the north-west side of George Street, includes a few properties at the south end of the Kew Road, and out along the north side of the Marshgate (now Sheen) Road; back along the south side of Marshgate Road and the south-east of George Street; finally taking in Red Lion Street, the Vineyard, Paradise Row – and out to the hamlet of West Sheen.

The names listed are of course those of the ratepayers – usually the occupants rather than the freeholders or copyholders – and often short-term tenants. A close comparison of the ratebooks of successive years up to 1771, and of the names of the ratepayers in 1771 with the 'occupiers' listed for most properties as well as the owners in the 1774 manor rental, and of both of these with the survey of 1771 which lists every owner, makes it possible to identify owner and occupier for almost every property in 1771 (see Appendix 12) and to work backwards to identify at least a great many of the properties listed in 1726. That is what is attempted in the listing below, which remains essentially in the same order as the original rate book, but shows also the 1771 survey number and an indication whether the property was new (or had been rebuilt) since the 1703 survey.

Only three complete rate assessment lists for 18th-century Kew have survived. As one of them is for the church rate in 1726 (at 1s. 6d. in the £) it is possible to extend this exercise to cover Kew also, and thus to show a more complete picture of the development by 1726.

Entries which relate to holdings of land only have been omitted here. In a few cases where it is obvious that the valuation is for both house and lands, but that the land element is vastly predominant (and possibly not even permanently attached to the house in question) I have inserted, instead of the RV as calculated, a figure (in brackets) from a future year which appears to apply to the house or 'house and garden' only. Similarly when the 1726 assessment is blank I have inserted a figure for the earliest subsequent year available. Some blanks remain – usually because the entry in question disappears completely from future rate books before any assessment has been recorded.

NOTE. Properties existing in 1703 are marked with a + in column 4. Properties known to have been rebuilt since 1703 are marked 'R'.

| Location & ratepayer | RV(£) | Details of property (if any) | Existing in 1703? | 1771 survey no. |
|---|---|---|---|---|
| **Palace site** | | | | |
| Lord Cholmondeley | 69 | Old Palace and Wardrobe | + | 7 |
| Rev John Hill | 22 | Trumpeters' House | R | 4 |
| Dame Harris | 13 | | + | Parts of |
| Baptist Hall | 8 | former kitchens area | + | 7,4 |
| widow Sawyer | 5 | | + | and 3 |
| Ralph Coleman | 4 | | + | |
| Richard Hawes | 20 | Brewhouse & house by Crane Piece | + | 3 |
| Sarah Williamson | 5 | | | ? |
| Dr Robert Wood | 24 | Old Court House | R | 6 |
| Ctss of Winchelsea | 27½ | corner of front wing | + | 5 |
| Thomas Sayer | 24 | NE side of Old Court | + | 6 |
| The Maids of Honour | 80 | 4 new houses in MOH Row | R | 8 |
| | | | | |
| **North-west side of Green** | | | | |
| Michael Pew | 20 | | + | 23-4 |
| Mrs Eliz Fetherston | 30 | | + | 22 |
| Sir Matthew Decker | 60 | site of later Fitzwilliam House | + | 21 & 1 |
| | | | | |
| **North-east side of Green** | | | | |
| late Mr Heidegger | [40 in 1727] | | | N |
| Col Charles Floyer | 35 | | | a |
| Col Dun.combe | 50 | | x | |
| Thomas Ryley | - | Houses at corner of Green | | d(?) |
| Thomas Price | 10 | | | b(?) |
| Henry Urban | 3 | | | c |
| John Greenbury | 3 | 'Duke's Yard' behind the above | | c |
| Richard Caton | - | | | c |
| Joseph Hart | 3 | | | c |
| | | | | |
| **North-east side of Little Green** | | | | |
| late Mr Cade | [30 in 1728] | | | 397 |
| Rev Collier (late Lord Hertford) | 30 | | | 398 |
| Mr Moseley | 30 | | | 400 |
| Thomas Dunn | 8 | | | 401 |
| Rev Dr Brady | [8 in 1727] | | | 401 |
| | | | | |
| **Kew Foot Lane (west side)** | | | | |
| Robert Belew | 6 | | | 402 |
| Capt More (late Salman) | 11 | | | 403 |
| Mr Beadle [Biddle] | 16 | | | 404 |
| Mr Smithies (late Dr Collier) | 28 | | | 407 |
| Mrs Davenport | 12 | | | 407 |
| Mr Henry Myler | 16 | | | 408 |
| Mr Bagnell (late Morgan) | 20 | | | 408 |
| Mr Cross | 30 | | | 409 |
| Thomas H Woodhouse | 7 | | | 411 |
| William Mason | 6 | | | 411 |
| Richard Caton | 6 | | | 411 |
| William Small | 6 | | | 411 |

| | | | | |
|---|---|---|---|---|
| Mrs Moody | 7 | | | 412 |
| Mrs Runnals [Reynolds] | 10 | | | 412 |
| William Dudley | 7 | | | 412 |
| Robert Lawson | 15 | | | 413 |
| Mrs Bell | 10 | | | 414 |
| Thomas Croskell | 4 | | + | 414 |
| William Cross | 8 | | | 414 |
| Edward Worsley (late Mrs Russell) | 8 | | | 415 |
| Thomas Early | 8 | | | 417 |
| Captain Agnew | 18 | | | 418 |

**Kew Foot Lane (east side)**

| | | | |
|---|---|---|---|
| David Bullen | 5 | | 465 |
| John Ball | 6 | | 464 |
| Mr Willis | 10 | | 463 |
| William Millichamp | 12 | | 461 |
| James Long | 3 | | 460 |
| James Vicars | - | | 459 |
| Mr Piggott | 14 | ⎤ | 457 |
| Robert Cain (late Creeth) | 15 | ⎬ Michell's Terrace | 457 |
| Mr Wood | - | ⎦ | 457 |
| Thomas Hunt (late Edward Worsley) | 5 | | 456 |
| William Benson | 5 | | 455 |
| John Chappell | 6 | | 446 |
| Edward Hide | - | | 444 |
| James Plumbr.idge | 12 | | 443 |
| Anne Baxter | 3 | | 443 |
| John Keele | 4 | | 442 |
| Edward Whitney | 4 | | ? |
| Charles South | 3 | | ? |
| John Pricklove | 5 | | ? |

**Kew Horse Road**

| | | | |
|---|---|---|---|
| widow Chester | - | | 458 |
| Samuel Edwards | - | | 452 |
| Samuel Coleman | - | | 452 |
| Daniel Harvey | 4 | | 452 |
| Richard Brooks | 10 | 'Lamb' tavern | 435 |
| Humphrey Mills | 3 | | 437 |
| John Peto | 3 | | 437 |
| -- Edmunds (late William Benson) | 5 | | 441 / 439 |
| William Grant | 2 | | 441 |
| John Hope | 15 | 'Orange Tree' | 440 |
| Robert Holway | - | ⎤ probably cottages behind Orange Tree, | 439 |
| John Woolinton | - | ⎬ close to Kew Foot | 439 |
| Henry Warlands | _ | ⎦ [in Kew Foot Lane – west side] | 439 |
| Capt Cholmondeley | 15 | | 419? |

**Kew Foot Lane (east side)**

| | | | |
|---|---|---|---|
| widow Vernon | - | (2 houses) | 433? |
| Thomas Egger | 15 | Kew Foot Lane Coffee House | 434 |
| William Meeking | 7 | | 430 |
| Mr Kennedy | 7 | | 430 |
| late Mrs Mary Bell | 12 | House facing Little Green  + | 428 |

| John Michell | 55 | The former Duke mansion | + | 423-7 |
|---|---|---|---|---|

**Duke Street**

| Nele [Cornelius] Caton | 6 | | ⎤ | 143-4 |
|---|---|---|---|---|
| William Punnell | 9 | | ⎦ | |

**Greenside**

| Nathaniel Turner | 24 | No. 1 The Green | + | 141 |
|---|---|---|---|---|
| Mrs Stobart | 33½ | (2 houses) Nos. 2 and 3 | + | 139-40 |
| Mrs Katherine Price | 20 | No. 5 | + | 136-7 |
| Dr Edward Coles | 30 | No. 7 | | 134-5 |
| Daniel Mackenzie | 30 | No. 9 – The Grammar School | + | 133 |
| Mr Spires | 14 | No. 10 | R | 132 |
| John Messenger | 5 | No. 11 | R | 131 |
| Thomas Campion | 14 | No. 12 | R | 130 |
| Samuel Harris | 4 | House in Brewer's Lane behind No. 12 | | 146-9 |
| Mrs Sara Buckeridge | 7 | No. 13 | + | 95 |
| late Holwell | - | No. 14 | + | 94 |
| Mrs Margaret Lilly | 20 | No. 15 | + | 93 |
| Mr William | 16 | No. 16 | + | 92 |
| late Lawrence | [16 in 1727] | No. 17 – Italian Coffee House | R | 91 |
| Evan Griffiths | 4 | | ⎤ | 88-90 |
| Matthew Drew | 6 | | ⎦ | |
| John Waltho | 26 | | R | 86 |
| late Lester | - | | | 87 |
| Henry Ratcliffe | 20 | | R | 85 |
| John Pew | 16 | | + | 84 |
| William Frimley | 8 | | + | 83 |
| Mr Larcum | 10 | | + | 82 |
| Joas Skinner | 8 | | | ? |
| John Booth | 5 | | + | 80 |
| John Laycock | 12 | Duke of Ormond's Head | + | 80 |
| Samuel Woodham | 8 | No. 29 | | 64 |
| Daniel Austin | 14 | No. 30 – Coffee House | | 63 |
| Thomas Fowler | 24 | No. 31 | | 61 |

**[Old Palace Terrace]**

| Thomas Fowler | 15 | No. 6 Old Palace Terrace | + | 60 |
|---|---|---|---|---|
| Major Ninian Boyd | 15 | No. 5 | + | 59 |
| Francis Clark | 15 | No. 4 | + | 58 |
| Walter Baynes | 15 | No. 3 | + | 57 |
| Mr Creton | 15 | No. 2 | + | 55 |
| Mrs Smirk | 15 | No. 1 | + | 54 |
| Dorothy Milbourn | 5 | 18 King Street | + | 54 |

**The Green (south-west side)**

| Mrs Abigail Goodhall | 30 | Old Palace Place | + | 29 |
|---|---|---|---|---|
| William Gardiner Esq | 40 | Old Friars | + | 28 |
| Mrs Susan Leighton | 12 | | + | 28 |
| Henry Collins gent | 12 | | + | 27 |
| Mrs Rebecca Fletcher | 9 | | + | 26 |

**Friars' Lane**

| John Carter | 14 | | | 15-19 |
|---|---|---|---|---|
| John Cross | 7 | | | 14 |

| | | | | |
|---|---|---|---|---|
| John Collins | 7 | | | 14 |
| Mr Shears | 10 | | | 14? |
| George Smith Esq | 30 | Houses on site of Garden Gallery | + | 11 |
| Percival Hart | 10 | Brewhouse | | 10 |

**The Green (south-west side)**

| | | | | |
|---|---|---|---|---|
| Stephen Child gent | 30 | [Tudor Place etc] | + | 10 |

**[King Street (south-west side)]**

| | | | | |
|---|---|---|---|---|
| Peter Wickham | 9 | 14 King Street | + | 30 |
| Taylor | 15 | | + | 31 |
| Susan Pitman | 9 | 13 King Street | + | 32 |
| Wm Southwell Jr | 13 | 12 King Street | + | 33 |
| Wm Southwell Sr | 8 | | | |
| John Wilkins | 13 | 11 King Street | + | 34 |
| Thomas Webb | 8 | | | 35 |
| Mrs Scovey | 12 | | | 36 |
| John Bacon | 10 | Crown tavern | | 37 |
| George Gardner | 11 | | + | 39 |
| John Maddox | | | + | 40 |
| Robert Bedford | 11 | | | |
| widow Ann Harris | 7 | Six Bells tavern | + | 41 |
| Thomas Child | 60 | (2 houses) The Feathers inn | + | 42 |

**Thames [Water] Lane (north-west side)**

| | | | | |
|---|---|---|---|---|
| John Plumbridge | 3 | | + | 42 |
| George Dennis | 3 | | + | 43 |
| Joseph Piper | 6 | | + | 44-5 |
| Thomas Terreh | 4 | | + | |
| Richard Gardener (late Richard Laws) | 3 | | + | 47 |
| Abraham Shoreman | 9 | Royal Oak alehouse | + | 48 |
| James Wright | 3 | | + | 51 |
| John Cross | 3 | | + | 51 |
| James Cross | 3 | | + | 52 |
| Thomas Charley | 3 | | + | 53 |
| William Downs | 3 | | + | 53 |
| John Juster | 3 | | + | 53 |
| Edward Greenbury (late Jas Gates) | 3 | | | 53 |
| widow Lee | - | | | 53 |
| Warwick Rhodes | 12 | malthouse | | 19/20? |
| George Dennis | - | | | 20? |

**Thames [Water] Lane (south-east side)**

| | | | | |
|---|---|---|---|---|
| William Collins | 40 | brewhouse | | 226 |
| John Clarke | - | | + | 227 |
| John Hopkins | - | | + | 229 |
| William Bell | - | | | 229 |
| Thomas Collyer | 7 | Waterman's Arms alehouse | - | 229 |
| Thomas Mason | 3 | | + | 230 |
| Edward Greenbury | 3 | | + | 231 |
| John Meads | - | | + | 232 |
| widow Ball | - | | + | 233 |
| Edward Monck | - | | + | 233 |
| John Webb | [2 in 1728] | | + | 233 |

## Hill Street (south-west side)

| | | | | |
|---|---|---|---|---|
| Edward Goodhall | 11 | *White Hart* tavern | + | 235 |
| widow Bullen | 9 | Maids of Honour pastry shop | + | 235 |
| Mr Huggs | 8 | | + | 235 |
| Thomas Shewell [Sewell] | 20 | | R? | 236 |
| Dr Caleb Cotesworth | 80 | Mansion later *Castle Hotel* | R | 237 |
| William Cross | 15 | | + | 238 |
| Randolph Greenaway | 15 | The terrace of houses | + | 238 |
| Mr Blake | 15 | later known as Clarence Terrace | 11 | 238 |
| late Smith | 15 | | + | 238 |
| William Triggs Esq | 15 | | + | 238 |
| Isaac Nunez | 70 | later Hotham House | + | 242 |
| Lady Jackson | 30 | later Heron House | + | 243 |
| John Becker | 35 | | + | 244 |
| Mr Steven | [24 in 1728] | | + | 240 |
| Richard Grosvenor | 24 | | + | 241 |
| widow King | 7 | Cottage at foot of Ferry Hill | + | 246 |

## 'Under The Hill' [Petersham Road – south-west side]

| | | | | |
|---|---|---|---|---|
| Moses Madonnah [Medina] | 38 | Bridge House | + | 275 |
| Joseph Reeves | 4 | Cottage by Ferry | + | 275 |
| William Towell | 10 | *King's Head* tavern | + | 276 |
| Evan Nelhams | 4 | | + | 277 |
| Edward Taylor | 7 | | | 277 |
| John King | 12 | | + | 278 |
| Simon Robinson | 12 | | + | 278 |
| Mr Modenah Jr [Medina] | 30 | | | 281 |
| Mrs Killner (late Mr Blackman) | 18 | | + | 281 |
| Jane Wicks | 20 | Bellevue | | 283 |
| Wm Chambers gent | 26 | Ivy Hall (now *Hobart Hall Hotel*) | | 284 |
| John King (boat-builder) | 10 | | | 287 |
| late Mrs Allen | 20 | | | 289 |
| Mrs Barnfield | 16 | | | 294 |
| Dr Wm Nelson | 16 | | | 295 |
| Ralph Platt | 3 | malthouse | | 292 |
| William Pook | 5 | *Blue Anchor* tavern | | 292 |
| William Lewis | 35 | Brewery – newly installed in place of tilekilns | R | 296 |
| Lord Ferrers | 10 | House on later Buccleuch House site | + | 574 |

## [Petersham Road – north-east side]

| | | | | |
|---|---|---|---|---|
| Lord Ferrers | 40 | | | 584 |
| John Butcher | - | | + | 583 |
| Samuel Cross | 10 | | | 582 |
| William Langley | 5 | | + | 581 |
| " (adjacent house) | 7 | | + | 581 |
| Occupants of the tilekilns | 20 | | + | 580-1 |
| Samuel Cross | 7 | | | 581 |
| John Skiggs | 8 | *Three Pigeons* alehouse | + | 578 |
| John Oxted | 3 | | + | 578 |
| John Robinson | 3 | | + | 576 |
| widow of John Oxted | 3 | | + | 576 |
| widow Joan Watson | 3 | | + | 575 |
| William Tucker | 5 | | + | 369 |
| Sylvanus Lawrence | 11 | | + | 365 |

| | | | | |
|---|---|---|---|---|
| Sylvanus Lawrence (for the waterworks) | 30 | (These were between the road and the river) | + | 285 |
| Mrs Seignoret | 18 | | + | 365 |
| Mr Salvadore | 44 | Rump Hall | + | 365-8 |
| John Perkins | 3 | | + | 362 |

**Richmond Hill (west side)**

| | | | | |
|---|---|---|---|---|
| William Butcher | 12 | | + | 297 |
| Samuel Smith | 9 | | | 298 |
| Charles Head | 6 | | + | 299 |
| Richard Anger | - | | | |
| -- King (late Head) | 8 | | | |
| William Marshall | 5 | *Three Compasses* alehouse | + | 361 |
| Christopher Needham | 20 | | + | 363 |
| widow Eling | 8 | | + | 364 |
| wi.dow Baker | 8 | | + | 364 |
| Mme Seignoret | 45 | The Wells | + | 364-5 |
| -- Taylor | - | | ? | ? |
| Mr Robinson | 36 | | + | 580 |
| Edward Beckley | 4 | | + | 580 |
| William Baker | 8 | *Bull's Head* tavern | R | 589 |

**Pesthouse Common [Queen's Road] – south side**

| | | | | |
|---|---|---|---|---|
| widow Price | 8 | | + | 647 |
| John Christopher | 8 | *Punchbowl* tavern | + | 648 |
| George Dodge | [10 in 1728] | | + | 649 |

**Pesthouse Common [Queen's Road] (north side)**

| | | | | |
|---|---|---|---|---|
| -- Morris | 5 | | + | 621 |
| James Pitman | 3 | | + | 621-2 |
| James Singleton | 5 | | + | 622 |
| William Budd | 5 | | + | 622 |
| Thomas Phelps | 5 | | + | 618-20 |

**Richmond Hill (east side)**

| | | | | |
|---|---|---|---|---|
| George Bentley | 20 | | + | 616 |
| Mrs Jackson | 20 | | + | 615 |
| Mrs Crutcher | 12 | | + | 614 |
| late Wm Penkethman | [12 in 1727] | | | 614 |
| Mrs Denney | 35 | (later Mansfield House) | | 613 |
| Mrs Flood | 15 | | | 612 |
| Mr Hill | 30 | | | 610-1 |
| Wm Hickey gent | 20 | 3 The Terrace | + | 609 |
| Ward Smith gent | 20 | 2 The Terrace | + | 608 |
| Mary Cook | 24 | 1 The Terrace | + | 607 |
| John Jeffrey | 5 | *Roebuck* alehouse | + | 605 |
| John cooper | 9½ | | + | 603 |
| [Duppa's almshouses] | | | + | |
| Lady Houblon | 53 | (later Elleker House and Old Vicarage School) | + | 382 |
| Mrs Alkin | 20 | (Penkethman theatre) | | 376 |
| William Jordan | 11 | | + | 374 |
| Mrs Frances Fisher | 11 | | + | 372 |
| Mrs Flood | 8 | ('late meeting house') | + | 322 |
| Robert Watts | 7 | | + | 319-22 |
| John Scott | 12 | ('ass house') | | 318 |

| | | | | |
|---|---|---|---|---|
| Mrs Bridger (late Westbrook) | 40 | (later Holbrook House) | | 315 |
| Philip Mendez gent | 55 | | | 313-4 |
| William Winter | 7 | *King's Arms* alehouse | | 312 |

**Ormond Row (south side)**

| | | | | |
|---|---|---|---|---|
| Charles Burt | 7 | 'Lissoy' | | 309 |
| Mrs Slaid | 6 | | Developed | 325 |
| Mr Martin | 30 | | at end 17th | |
| Robert Berry | 10 | No. 3 | or beginning | 326 |
| William Bridges | 10 | No. 4 | of 18th C but | |
| Isaac White | 8 | No. 5 | not known if | 327 |
| widow King | 12 | No. 6 | before 1703 | 328 |
| Mr Peerman | 18 | No. 7 | | 329 |
| Joseph Tallis | 30 | Ormond House | | 330 |

**Hill Street (north-east side)**

| | | | | |
|---|---|---|---|---|
| Peter Hudson | 75 | *Dog Inn* | + | 255-6 |
| William Penkethman | [12 in 1728) | | | 254 |
| William Griffin | 10 | | Uncertain if | 253 |
| Mrs Martha Bugbee | 12 | | developed | 252 |
| Edward Paine | 15 | | by 1703 | 251 |
| Mr Quartermain | 25 | 2 houses, incl *Cross Keys* alehouse | | 250 |
| William Sheerman | 10 | | | 249 |
| Richard Price | 15 | | | 247-8 |

**Paved Court**

| | | | | |
|---|---|---|---|---|
| William Cross | 5 | | + | 79 |
| Edward Hewett | 10 | (2 houses) incl *Haunch of Venison* | + | 77-8 |
| Thomas Willetts | 5 | | + | 76 |
| Thomas Wallings | 5 | | + | 75 |
| Charles Chabenor | 5 | | + | 74 |
| Ann Whitall | 5 | | + | 73 |

**[King Street] (north-east side)**

| | | | | |
|---|---|---|---|---|
| Thomas Sandell | 8 | | + | 65 |
| William Bauck | 6 | | + | 67 |
| Thomas Goring | 3 | | + | 68 |
| Thomas Russell | 10 | | + | 69 |
| John Rowles | 8 | | + | 70 |
| Thomas Eling | 6 | | + | 71 |

**[George Street] (north-west side)**

| | | | | |
|---|---|---|---|---|
| Ambrose Parish | 15 | *Queen's Head* tavern | + | 72 |
| Robert Cross Jr | 15 | *Three Tuns* tavern | + | 99 |
| Dinah Gardner | 29 | | + | 100 |

**Pensioners' Alley**

| | | | | |
|---|---|---|---|---|
| John Matthews | 5 | (Whitesmith) | + | 101 |
| Edward Haile | 4 | | | |
| Thomas Wright | 6 | | + | 102 |
| William Hildyard | 6 | | + | 103 |
| John Nelhams | 3 | | + | 112 |
| Richard Griff;n | 3 | | + | 111 |
| William Perkins Sr | 5 | | + | 113 |

**[George Street (north-west side)]**

| | | | | |
|---|---|---|---|---|
| John Rowles Sr | 6 | | | |

| | | | | |
|---|---|---|---|---|
| Moses Boddicott | 22 | | + | 115 |
| Mr Miller | [3 in 1727] | | | |
| William Cole | 4 | | | |
| Ann Brown | 4 | | | |
| Robert Cross Sr | 8 | *Black Boy* tavern | + | 117 |
| George Knight | 7 | | + | 118 |
| John Bauck | 6 | | | 118 |
| Mrs Steel | 10 | | + | 119 |
| Charles Scott | 10 | | + | 119 |
| Geoffrey Higginbotham | 5 | | | 121? |
| Ambrose Baker | 15 | | | 122 |
| Hester Trippett | 5 | | + | 123 |
| John Stevens | 6 | | + | 123 |
| Mr Goodwin | 5 | | + | 124 |
| Joseph Barnsley | 5 | | + | 124 |

**Brewer's Lane (south-west side)**

| | | | | |
|---|---|---|---|---|
| Thomas Grimsdale | 5 | | + | 125-6 |
| William Doe | 5 | | + | 127 |
| widow Halfpenny | 5 | | + | 128 |
| Samuel Spires and Mr Leggatt | 10 | (2 houses) | R | 129 |

**Brewer's Lane (north-east side)**

| | | | | |
|---|---|---|---|---|
| Joseph Halfpenny | 8 | (2 houses) | + | 150 |
| Thomas Lowder | 4 | | + | 150? |
| Thomas Pearce | 5 | *Magpie* tavern | + | 151 |
| Robert Long | 4 | | + | 152 part |
| Evan Lewis | 3 | | + | 152 part |
| William Bell | 4 | | + | 152 part |

**[George Street] (north-west side continued)**

| | | | | |
|---|---|---|---|---|
| [Parish charity school] | | | R | [152-3] |
| Sarah Goodhall | 10 | | + | 154 |
| John Wellbeloved | 10 | *White Lion* tavern | + | 155 |
| William Price | 7 | | | 156 |
| Rowland Ingrams | 18 | | | 157 |
| David Salter | 12 | | + | 158 |
| Pennel Hubbard | 18 | | | 159 |
| Thomas Drew | 7 | | + | 160 |
| Eleanor Matthews | 10 | | + | 161 |
| William Fitches | 12 | *Rose and Crown* inn | + | 162 |

**Duke's Lane**

| | | | | |
|---|---|---|---|---|
| Elizabeth Geoffrey | 6 | Cottages at back of *Rose and Crown* yard | + | 162-3 |
| William Adams* | [6 in 1738] | | + | |

*The Adams assessment included a lot of land elsewhere. The earliest assessment for the house alone is £6.

**Kew Horse Lane (east side)**
**'World's End'**

| | | | | |
|---|---|---|---|---|
| Thomas Young | - | | + | 484 |
| Michael Wickes | 3 | | + | 482 |
| Anne Smith | 3 | | + | 483 |
| Henry Wallis | 5 | | + | 480 |
| -- Hodges | 4 | | + | 481 |
| John Caton | 3 | | + | |
| Anne Moody | 3 | | | 479 |

| | | | | |
|---|---|---|---|---|
| Thomas Eggers | 5 | | + | 478 |
| widow Pearce | - | | | 477 |
| Peter Thorn | 11 | | | 476 |
| Richard Laycock | 3 | | + | 476 |
| John Tatley | 3 | | + | 476 |
| William Fry | 3 | | + | 476 |
| John Leggatt | 12 | *Bear* inn | + | 475 |
| Thomas Palmer | [12 in 1727] | | + | 475 |
| Edward Penner (late Henry Bowles) | [62 in 1729] | | + | 474 |
| Richard Gibson | [3 in 1727] | | + | 473 |
| Alex Nicholls | [4 in 1727] | | + | 473 |

**Marshgate Road (north side)**

| | | | | |
|---|---|---|---|---|
| Thomas Matthews | 8 | blacksmith's shop | + | 491 |
| Richard Cullen gent | 35 | | + | 493 |
| widow Page | 3 | | | 492 |
| James Fearn | 9 | | + | 492 |
| William Beyer Esq | 38 | [former Turner house] | + | 495 |
| widow Whitfield | 10 | | + | 497 |
| John Knapp gent | 16 | [Marshgate House] | + | 498 |
| widow Ann Young | [6 in 1727] | | + | 499 |
| Mr Moore | 12 | | ] | 500-1? |
| William Phelps | 9 | | | |
| Mrs Adams | 10 | | + | 505 |
| Mr Bromley | 16 | | | 508 |
| widow Williams | 4 | | | 509 |
| Thomas White | 25 | | | 511 |
| widow Perkins | 2½ | | | |
| Francis Collins | 7 | | | 503 |
| Charles Bagnell | 9 | | | 652 |
| Mrs Mackean | 18 | [site of Grena House] | + | 676 |
| Benjamin Lethelier | 40 | [site of Manor House] | + | 679 |

**Marshgate Road (south side)**

| | | | | |
|---|---|---|---|---|
| Lord Lothian | 50 | [Spring Grove] | + | 558 |
| Edward Owen gent | 38 | [Grove Lodge] | + | 555 |
| Ralph Ratcliffe gent | 40 | [later Kenyon House] | + | 557 |
| William Bamfield | 4 | | | 557 |
| Jeremiah Dimsdaıe | 8 | *Black Horse* tavern | | 675 |
| John Smithers | 6 | *Red Cow* alehouse | | 549 |
| William Phelps | - | *Coach and Horses* alehouse | | 549 |
| Henry Smith | 28 | | | 537 |
| Ann Moor | 5 | | | 515 |
| Henry Sheppard gent | 42 | | | 535 |
| Henry Collins | 25 | | | 533 |
| George Gough gent | 21 | | | 529 |
| Lady Vanderputt | 60 | | + | 528 |
| Mrs Hester Goulton | 8 | | | 218 |
| Samuel Savill | 8 | | | 218 |
| Steven Andrews | 8 | | | 217 |
| widow Mary Jennings | 8 | | | 217 |
| John Lane | 8 | *George* tavern | | 217 |
| Robert Carr | 12 | | + | 216 |
| George Mortimer | 20 | | + | 215 |
| John Smith | 5 | | | 214 |

| Jacob Reynolds | 4 | | + | 214 |
|---|---|---|---|---|
| Matthew Drew | 10 | | | 213 |
| Nicholas Hance | 4 | Church land | | 213 |
| William Pearce | [10 in 1732] | | | 213 |
| Henry Filjam | 8 | *Castle* tavern | + | 212 |

**Middle Row**

| William Armstrong | - | | + | 223/4 |
|---|---|---|---|---|
| Edward Richardson | 11 | (2 houses) incl *Angel* alehouse | + | 222 |
| John Wingrove | 5 | | | 221? |
| Arthur Nixon | 3 | | | |
| George Lander | 6 | | + | 221 |
| Joseph Marston | 6 | | + | 220 |

**[George Street] (south-east side)**

| Mrs Sarah Freeman | 6 | | | 212 |
|---|---|---|---|---|
| Mrs Mary Colston | 50 | | | 212 |
| John Myhill | 20 | (baker) | + | 204-5 |
| William Thornton | 9 | | + | 203 |
| Thomas Eeles | 20 | (apothecary) | + | 202 |

**Church Court**

| John Bell | 5 | | + | 202 |
|---|---|---|---|---|
| John Allum | 8 | | + | 202 |
| Charles Mordaunt | 10 | | + | 200 |
| Alexander Smith | 10 | *Angel and Crown* tavern | + | 199 |
| Henry Allum | 4 | | + | 200-1 |
| George Weekley | 15 | | | 198 |
| Robert Smith | 14 | | | 198 |

**[George Street] (south-east side)**

| Mrs Anne Bostock | 15 | *Lion and Lamb* tavern | + | 197 |
|---|---|---|---|---|
| William Hawkins | 6 | | + | 196 |
| Job Gardner | 6 | | + | 196 |
| Thomas Gregory | 12 | | + | 195 |
| Edward Oram | 28 | *Greyhound* inn | R | 194 |
| Thomas Wall | 22 | | + | 193 |
| John Cawley | 9 | | | 192 |
| Robert Wilson | 9 | | + | 192 |
| Philip Leggatt | 9 | | + | 192 |
| James Cowart | 9 | *Sun* tavern | + | 190 |
| William Kirk | 11 | | + | 189 |
| Richard Bonsey | 9 | *Two Brewers* tavern | + | 179 |
| John Stevens | 3 | | | 180 |
| Edward Barnes | 3 | | | |
| William Eling | 10 | | + | 178 |
| John Fitzwater | 8 | | | 175-6 |
| Mrs Fitzwater | 12 | | + | |
| Mr Collins | - | | + | 174 |
| Robert Mylam | 2 | | | |
| Hannah Maskell | 16 | | + | 173 |
| William Rice | 11 | | | 172 |
| Joseph Paine | 10 | | + | 171 |
| Richard Toy | 14 | | + | 171 |
| William Gardner | 12 | | + | 170 |
| Thomas Cross | 11 | | + | 169 |

| | | | | |
|---|---|---|---|---|
| George Gardner | 12 | | + | 168 |
| widow Greenborough | 5 | | + | 164-7 |
| Redmond Burke | 60 | *Red Lion* inn | + | |

**[Red Lion Street]**

| | | | | |
|---|---|---|---|---|
| Catherine Ilsley | 10 | | | 164 |
| John Sawbridge | 7 | (2 houses) | | 165 |
| Mr Stroud | 20 | | | 247 |
| Thomas James | 14 | | + | |
| widow Michell | 5 | | + | 259-261 |
| John Leatherland | 4 | | + | |
| Rev John Brown | 12 | | + | |
| Thomas Williamson | 6 | | + | 262 |
| William Frost | 3 | | + | 263 |
| Mrs Hutchenson (late Mrs Cooper) | 3 | | | 263 |
| | - | | | 269? |
| John Williamson | 7 | | | 269? |
| Henry Perkins | 4 | | | 269? |
| Robert Lyons | [3 in 1727] | | | 269? |
| John Tisbury | 3 | | | 270? |
| Thomas Crow | 4 | | | 270? |
| Edward Excell | 10 | | | 271? |
| Thomas Blizzard | - | | | 272? |
| Mr Goulton | 15 | | | 272? |

**Church Row [Terrace]**

| | | | |
|---|---|---|---|
| Mrs Fell | 12 | No. 2 | 340 |
| Mrs Lake | 12 | No. 4 | 342 |
| Mr Michell | 12 | [The Hermitage] | 343 |

**Ormond Row (north side)**

| | | | | |
|---|---|---|---|---|
| Mr da Paiba | 22 | [The Hollies] | + | 267 |
| Mr Johnson | 20 | [The Rosary] | + | 268 |

**The Vineyard**

| | | | | |
|---|---|---|---|---|
| Mr Hall | 24 | [Clarence House] | + | 331 |
| John Edwards | 3 | | | |
| Jonathan Graves | 3 | | | |
| Mr Wheeler | 6 | ?tenants of Michell's Almshouse Trustees | | 384-9? |
| Mr Bacon | 3 | | | |
| William Watts | 6 | | | |
| John Oxton [Oxenden] | 4 | | | |
| widow Harris | - | | | |

**Paradise Row (south side)**

| | | | |
|---|---|---|---|
| Andrew Arnold | 20 | Halford House | 348 |
| Daniel Skidwell | 8 | | 352 |
| William Gill | 3 | | 352 |
| Mrs Levers | - | | 349 |
| Mrs Buckworth | 16 | 'Vineyard Lodge' | 353 |
| Mrs Crouch | 20 | | 353 |

**Paradise Row (north side)**

| | | | |
|---|---|---|---|
| Mrs Cropp | 12 | | 218 |
| George Smith | 11 | | 218 |
| James Ellis | 5 | | 218 |

| | | | | |
|---|---|---|---|---|
| Sir Pierce Freak (late | | | | |
| Lady Norton) | 20 | | | 218 |
| Mrs Beverley | 16 | | | 218 |
| widow Pressey | 8 | | | 219 |

**The Vineyard**

| | | | | |
|---|---|---|---|---|
| Richard Wheeler | – | | | ? |
| Christopher Bacon | 4 | | | ? |
| William Harris | 17 | Vineyard House | | 357 |
| William Woodman | 7 | | | 358 |
| Richard Sheppard | 7 | | | 359 |
| Charles Head | 7 | | | 359 |
| Thomas Piper | 5 | | | 359? |
| Thomas Ryley | 7 | | | 359? |

**Church Walk**

| | | | | |
|---|---|---|---|---|
| Robert Smith | 5 | | + | 210 |
| Mrs Beamond | 4 | | | 209 |
| John Benstead | 3 | | | 208 |
| Hester Mordaunt | 4 | | | 207 |
| William Bell | 5 | | | 206 |

**Sheen**

| | | |
|---|---|---|
| Lady Buckworth | 60 | + |
| Walter Cary Esq | 25 | + |
| Earl of Scarborough | 80 | + |
| Charles Selwyn Esq | 27 | + |
| Edward Smith | 5 | |
| William Gurnett* | [7 in 1731] | |
| John Hayter* | [8 in 1727] | |

*The entries for William Gurnett and John Hayter contain a lot of extra lands. The earliest entries which seem to be for the houses alone are as shown above.

**Miscellaneous**

| | | |
|---|---|---|
| HRH Prince of Wales | 250 | for lands attached to Kew House |
| Duke of Argyll | 10s p.a. | for something at Sudbrook |
| John Drew | £4 p.a. | for the Bowling Green |
| — Rogers | - | for an ayt (unspecified) |
| — Lewis | - | for an ayt (unspecified) |

### KEW RATES 1726 (omitting entries for land only)

| | | |
|---|---|---|
| HRH Prince of Wales | 95 | Lands in Park |

**Riverside near Ferry**

| | | | | |
|---|---|---|---|---|
| Robert Parker | 40 | ferry | | |
| Henry Parker | 10 | house by ferry | + | |
| Sir John Brown | 20 | | + | 759-62 |
| Sir Charles Eyre | 35 | (later 'the Queen's House') | + | |

**Kew Green (south side)**

| | | | | |
|---|---|---|---|---|
| Sam Molineux Esq | 46 | (later the 'White House') | + | 729 |
| –– Cairnes Esq | 32 | house late Earl of Thomond's | | 731 |
| John Lowe | 3 | | + | |
| Rev Mr Lewis | 12 | | + | 732 |
| Mr Bradbury | 1 | for shop | + | |

| | | | | |
|---|---|---|---|---|
| Countess of Buckenburgh | 29 | | + | 733 |
| Joseph Williams | 13 | *Rose and Crown* tavern | + | 739 |
| George Harrison Esq | 26 | | + | 741-7 |
| late John Martyn (empty) | - | | + | 748-50 |
| — | — | a newly erected house | | |
| Charles Rawson | 10 | | | 751-2 |
| widow Wrencher | - | [poor] | | |
| Stephen Hall | 3 | | + | 753 |
| Thomas Dawney | 5 | | | |
| John Kingston | 8 | | | 754 |
| Michael Layton | 4 | *Rising Sun* tavern | + | 755 |
| William Machinn | 4 | | | 756 |
| late Humphrey Jenks (empty) | - | | | 757 |

**Kew Green (east side)**

| | | | | |
|---|---|---|---|---|
| Thomas Abbott | - | [poor] | + | 811 |
| Thomas Flavell | 7 | *Ewe and Lamb* tavern | + | 810 |
| widow Cox | 19 | | + | 809 |
| Mr Robert Murden | 6 | | + | 808 |
| Mrs Maine. | 15 | | R | 807 |
| Edward Reddish Esq | 15 | | | 806 |
| George Warren | 9 | one of new houses erected by pond | | |
| Joseph Bridges | - | another (excused – at sea in HM services) | | 801 |
| Thomas Pullen | 6 | another | | |
| –– Scott | 9 | the fourth | | |
| Robert Grant | 3 | [an inhabitant of Edenborough Bucks – for coachhouse, stable and garden walled in and tenement adjoining] | | 799? |

**Kew Green (north side)**

| | | | | |
|---|---|---|---|---|
| HRH | 4 | for bargehouse | | |
| Thomas Howlett | 12 | | + | 787-8 |
| Thomas Layton | 5 | | | |
| William Gardner | 3 | | + | |
| late Thomas Pullen (empty) | - | later the *Rose and Crown* | | 786 |
| John Davis | 2 | | + | |
| Mrs Saint | 11 | | + | 785 |
| John Murden | 6 | | + | |
| Col de la Bastide | 15 | | + | 781-4 |
| Mrs Ann Montigny | 10 | | + | |
| Mr Mulcaster | 13 | | | |
| John Hughes | 3 | | + | 780 |
| Richard Baxter | 6 | | + | |
| Mrs Porter | 8 | | + | 777-9 |
| Col Wynward | 15 | | + | |
| William Plaistow | 4 | | + | 775 |
| Edward Taylor | 3 | | + | 773 |
| Humphry Jenks (late widow Gunn) | 3 | | + | 772 |
| Mr Christopher Appleby | 8 | Site of Hunter House (Herbarium) | + | 766a |
| John Lely | 20 | | + | 765 |
| late Sir John Hobart | 70 | 'Dutch House' – now Kew Palace | + | 763 |

**'Eyott'**

| | | | | |
|---|---|---|---|---|
| Stephen West | 6 | for house (*Swan* tavern) | | |

# APPENDIX II

# *Some Notable 18th-Century Jewish Residents*

Solomon de Medina. Merchant and banker. Army contractor. Knighted 1700.
In Richmond (?somewhere in Herring Court) 1699.

Moses Hart
Herring Court before 1716 (when he moved to Isleworth).
Purchased site of Asgill House 1756.

Moses de Medina. Nephew of Solomon. And wife Deborah.
Herring Court 1716-21.
'Bridge House' 1721-32.

Isaac Fernandez Nunez. Merchant.
Hotham House, Herring Court 1718-29.
House on site of later Buccleuch House 1733.

Moses de Paiba. Merchant and broker.
'The Rosary', Ormond Road 1718-22.

Abraham de Medina. Son of Moses and Deborah.
House on site of later Northumberland House, Petersham Road ?1726-28.

Philip (or Moses) Mendez da Costa. Merchant.
Hill Rise 1726-34.

Joseph Tallis da Costa. Merchant
'Ormond House', Ormond Road 1726-32.

Abraham Joseph de Cappidocia. Merchant.
'Holbrook House', Hill Rise 1734-41
Hill Street 1749-51.

Abraham Levy
'Bridge House' 1737-53.

(?Moses) Mendez. Merchant. Dramatist.
7 The Green 1750-55.

Solomon Mendez. Merchant. Man of Letters. Friend of James Thomson the poet.
Kew Foot Road 1750-54.

Mr Levy
Hill Street 1752-64.

Henry Isaac
Hotham House, Herring Court 1752-58.

John Marks
3 Maids of Honour Row 1752-62 and 'Mrs Marks' 1762-79.

Michael Adolphus (nephew of Judith Levy's husband) and wife Rachel (daughter of Moses
Hart).
House on site of Asgill House 1753-60.

Judith (widow of Elias) Levy. Daughter of Moses Hart.
4 Maids of Honour Row 1754-1802.

Moses Isaac Levy (later President of Board of Deputies in 1789).
'Spring Grove House', Queen's Road 1762-67.

Abraham de Paiba. Diamond broker. Grandson of Moses de Paiba (above).
4 The Terrace, Richmond Hill 1767-75.

Jacob Abrahams
Kew Foot Road 1768-71 (?)
Kew Foot Road 1780 (a different house)

Solomon Gompertz. Diamond merchant.
House on site of Cardigan House 1768-74.

Joseph Gompertz
4 The Terrace, Richmond Hill 1780.

Alexander Abrahams
Kew Foot Road 1780.

Joshua (d 1802) and wife Judith (d 1815) Mendez da Costa
Ormond House 1780
7 Ormond Road 1785-95 (owned by them 1770-1815)

Moses Mendez da Costa, nephew of Joshua and Judith
7 Ormond Road 1815-21 (owner)

Moses Lara and wife Sara, niece of Joshua and Judith Mendez da Costa)
7 Ormond Road 1821-59 (owners)

# APPENDIX 12

# *The 1771 Survey of the Manor of Richmond*

Although the 1771 survey (CRES5/346), supplemented by its detailed plans (MP1/1/545 A-H), is much easier for the uninitiated to use than the previous lists (of 1603, 1664, 1703 and 1726), it may be helpful to reprint here a full list of the houses and other significant buildings recorded, in the same order as the previous lists (and the order of listing in the rate books), together with information not only on the owners but also on the occupants in 1771. The 'occupants' are mainly those listed in the 1771 rate book. Some, whose names do not appear in that, have been added from other sources; they are shown in square brackets. For Kew, where there is no 1771 rate list, all occupants are taken from the 1774 rental. All entries relating to land without any buildings have been omitted from this exercise.) See plans at Plates 56-58a.

| Survey No. | Description of Property | Area of lot | Owner | Occupier (rate payer) |
|---|---|---|---|---|
| | **Richmond Palace** | | | |
| 7 | Old Palace | 0-1-2.4 | Sir Charles Sheffield | Sir Charles Sheffield |
| 7a | Wardrobe | 0-3-23 | Matthew Skinner | Matthew Skinner |
| 8 | No. 1 Maids of Honour Row | ⎤ | | ⎡ John Moseley |
| 8 | No. 2 | 0-1-16 | exors. of | Lucy Burdett |
| 8 | No. 3 | | William Wallesley | Elizabeth Marks |
| 8 | No. 4 | ⎦ | | ⎣ Judith Levy |
| 10 | messuage | ⎤ 0-1-16 | Mrs Jane Child | ⎡ Mrs Jane Child |
| 10 | messuage | ⎦ | | ⎣ (late Rev Dr Sandford) |
| 11 | messuage | 0-3-24 | George Wood | George Wood |
| 12 | Cholmondeley House Spencer | 1-2-19 | Earl Spencer | Countess Cowper |
| 6 | messuage | ⎤ 0-1-08 | Cpt Lanoe | ⎡ William Robertson |
| 6 | messuage | ⎦ | " | ⎣ John Honour |
| 5 | Stables | 0-3-18 | John Honour | John Honour |
| 4 | Trumpeters' House | 3-2-08 | Mrs Way | Mrs Way |
| 3 | Asgill House | 1-3-23 | Sir Charles Asgill | ⎡ Sir Charles Asgill |
| | | | | Mrs Barnes |
| | | | | ⎣ John Whiffing |
| 9 | messuage [Asgill Lodge] | 0-0-12 | exors of Wm Walmesley | Elizabeth Le Cocq |
| | **Old Palace Lane and Green, NW side** | | | |
| 24 | Theatre | 0-0-27 | James Hubbald | James Love |
| 23 | messuage | 0-0-02 | Hannah Diamond | Mrs Diamond |
| 22 | messuage | 0-2-31 | Wm Ewer | William Ewer |
| 21 | Fitzwilliam House | 1-0-24 | Earl Fitzwilliam | Earl Fitzwilliam |
| 1 | Stables, outhouses and park | 15-1-36 | Fitzwilliam Trustees | " |
| | **Green, NE side** | | | |
| d | messuage | 0-0-15 | Henry Edmead | Lewis Shepherd |
| O | messuage | 0-0-35 | His Majesty | [late Rev Comer] |
| b | messuage | 0-0-11 | Sir John Rushout | Charles Morris |

441

| | | | | |
|---|---|---|---|---|
| c | 3 cottages | 0-0-14 | Anne Barstone | ? |
| N | capital messuage | 0-3-06 | His Majesty | [late William Mills] |
| a | capital messuage | 0-2-17 | Nicholls Esq | Augustine Floyer Esq |

**Little Green, NE side**

| | | | | |
|---|---|---|---|---|
| 397 | messuage freehold | 1-0-0 | Frances Floyer | John Glover |
| 398 | messuage freehold | 0-1-10 | Anne Barstone | James Barstone |
| 400 | messuage freehold | 0-0-25 | " | John Shaw |
| 401 | 3 messuages freehold | 0-0-15 | Bridget Foot | ⎡ Bridget Foot<br>⎢ Bridget Foot<br>⎣ Mrs Campbell |

**Kew Foot Lane. NW side**

| | | | | |
|---|---|---|---|---|
| 402 | messuage | 0-0-6 | Mary Toy | Mary Toy |
| 403 | messuage | 0-0-10 | Margaret Kitchen | Margaret Kitchen |
| 404 | messuage | 0-0-20 | Thomas Biddle | Samuel Enys Esq |
| 405 | messuage | 0-0-16 | Anne Barstone | Mrs Delia Hudson |
| 406 | messuage | 0-0-14 | " | Mr Telphard |
| 407 | 2 messuages | 0-0-32 | Thomas Tunstall<br>" | ⎡ Mr Telphard<br>⎣ James Whitley |
| 408 | 2 messuages | 0-0-38 | Isabella Baker | Isabella Baker |
| 409 | messuage | 0-0-39 | Charles Rogers | Charles Rogers |
| 411 | 4 messuages | 0-0-32 | Thomas Lynall | ⎡ John Collins<br>⎢ Gregory Barnes<br>⎢ Sarah Caton<br>⎣ Mr Deverell |
| 412 | 4 messuages | 0-1-16 | John Stone | ⎡ Sarah Caton<br>⎢ James Lavalade<br>⎢ Francis Booles<br>⎣ John Stone |
| 413 | capital messuage | 0-1-25 | John Stone | John Stone |
| 414 | 4 messuages | 0-1-16 | Daniel Bullen Sr | ⎡ Ellen Rice<br>⎢ William Fuller<br>⎢ Joseph Hurst<br>⎣ John Greenaway |
| 415 | messuage freehold | 0-1-11 | Thomas Heath | Widow Scott |
| 416 | messuage freehold | 0-0-10 | Joseph King | William Goff Sr |
| 417 | 2 messuages freehold | 0-0-13 | Joseph Joulls<br>" | ⎡ Joseph Joulls<br>⎣ Mrs Bickham |
| 418 | capital messuage | 0-1-00 | Morris Mersault | Gray Cooper Esq |
| 419 | coachhouse & stables | 0-0-08 | " | " |

**Kew Foot Lane, SE side**

| | | | | |
|---|---|---|---|---|
| 706 | capital messuage & garden (Rosedale) | 3-3-16 | George Ross | George Ross |
| 466 | 2 messuages | 0-0-10 | ⎡ Robert Smith<br>⎣ " | Robert Smith |
| 465 | 2 messuages | 1-1-34 | ⎡ Daniel Bullen<br>⎣ " | Mark Gunn<br>Daniel Bullen |
| 464 | messuage | 0-0-38 | Eliz. Ball | William Harrison |
| 463 | messuage | 0-1-00 | Jas Patterson | Sarah Patterson |
| 462 | messuage | 0-1-08 | Daniel Bullen | William Bullen |
| 461 | messuage | 0-3-02 | Richard Billingham | Hon Robert Monkton |
| 460 | coachhouse | 0-2-28 | Michell's Trust | Robert Smith |
| 459 | messuage freehold | 0-2-30 | Richard Young | Richard Whitman |
| 457 | 5 messuages | 0-2-28 | Michell's Trust | [-- Attaway]<br>James Smith<br>Richard Billingham<br>William Deverell |
| 456 | messuage freehold | 0-0-10 | Henry Bell | (John Chitty] |
| 455 | messuage freehold | 0-0-19 | Samuel Spiers | [John Hughes] |
| 444 | messuage freehold | 0-0-27 | Joseph Dell | Mrs Moore |
| 442 | 3 messuages | 0-0-17 | ⎡ Chaffin Martin<br>⎢ "<br>⎣ " | Jacob Ahraham<br>Chaffin Martin<br>? |

| | | | | |
|---|---|---|---|---|
| 439 | 3 tenements | 0-0-7 | William Larkham | [Henry Dalel |
| | | | " | [Henry Scott] |
| | | | " | [William Stevens] |
| 440 | *Orange Tree* alehouse | 0-0-27 | " | Elizabeth Larkin |
| 434 | *Kew Lane Coffee House* | 0-0-9 | Jemima Eaton | John Green |
| 433 | messuage | 0-0-19 | Francis Vernon | [Sarah Caton] |
| 432 | messuage | 0-0-10 | William Deverell | William Deverell |
| 430 | 2 messages | 0-0-8 | John Stone | John Goodall |
| | | | | Ellen Rice |
| 428 | messuage | Total area 423-428 | James Clutterbuck | William Stallard |
| 423 | capital messuage – Richmond Academy | 2-0-22 | " | Rev Charles Delafosse |

### Duke's Lane (N side) and Kew Horse Road

| | | | | |
|---|---|---|---|---|
| 425 | messuage freehold | [see above] | Jas Clutterbuck | John Scuffham |
| 426 | messuage and shop | " | " | William Warren |
| 427 | messuage and shop | | " | Joseph Hillier |
| 431 | messuage | 0-0-6 | Anne Leycock | Thomas Ledger |
| 435 | *White Lyon* alehouse | 0-0-9 | Jos. Sims | William Goff |
| 436 | messuage | 0-0-4 | " | " |
| 437 | messuage | 0-0-10 | " | Henry Clarke |
| 438 | messuage | 0-0-21 | John Stone | James Mead |
| 443 | 2 messuages freehold | 0-0-18 | Richard Guise | Benjamin Lyon |
| 445 | 3 tenements freehold | 0-0-4 | Jas. Mead | ? |
| 446 | tenement freehold | 0-0-1 | Philip Gibson | Philip Gibson |
| 447 | 3 messuages freehold | 0-0-5 | Richard Laycock | Richard Laycock |
| | | | | ? |
| | | | | ? |
| 448 | messuage freehold | 0-0-4 | Guy Parks | ? |
| 449 | messuage freehold | 0-0-4 | John Wall | ? |
| 450 | messuage freehold | 0-0-5 | John Bray | ? |
| 451 | 4 tenements freehold | 0-0-6 | Jas Gillett | ? |
| 452 | 5 tenements | 0-0-6 | John Stone | Thomas Faulkener |
| | | | " | Richard Steele |
| | | | " | James Robertson |
| | | | " | James Adams |
| | | | " | James Uoht |
| 453 | 5 tenements freehold | 0-0-8 | Solomon Brown | Robert Adam Mark |
| | | | Henry Bell (4) | ? |
| 458 | messuage freehold | 0-0-28 | Eliz. Atterbur | William Davis |
| 468 | messuage | 0-0-03 | John Alcock | John Drew |
| 469 | coachhouse | 0-0-04 | Henry Bell | Richard Billingham |
| 470 | tenement | 0-0-02 | Richard Turner | John Wood |
| 471 | 4 tenements | 0-0-09 | Daniel Bullen | Richard Long |
| | | | | [David Bullenl |
| | | | " | [ Weedon] |
| | | | " | [Richard Howard] |
| 709 | 3 tenements in 4 acre field | 4-1-23 | William Selwyn | James Singleton |
| | | | | John Bernard |

### Kew Horse Road (E side)

| | | | | |
|---|---|---|---|---|
| 694 | 2 cottages | 0-1-09 | Mary Gulliver | -- East |
| | | | | -- Perryman |
| 695 | 12 tenements freehold | 1-0-07 | Wm. Selwyn (leased to Richard Laycock) | ? |

### Mortlake Lane (S side)

| | | | | |
|---|---|---|---|---|
| 692 | capital messuage | 1-3-17 | John Boddington | John Boddington |
| 488 | messuage | 1-3-02 | Wm. Selwyn | Mrs Adams |
| 485 | messuage | 3-2-27 | Wm. Selwyn | [late Mr. Ed Collins] |

**Greenside**

| | | | | |
|---|---|---|---|---|
| 141 | messuage 1 The Green | 0-0-09 | Jas Clutterbuck | Solomon Brown |
| 140 | messuage 2 The Green | 0-0-10 | Rbt Sayer | Mrs Rebecca Walker |
| 139 | messuage 3 The Green | 0-0-09 | Rbt Sayer | Mrs Catherine Jones |
| 138 | messuage 4 The Green | 0-0-13 | John Rice | Christopher Jackson |
| 137 | messuage 6 The Green | 0-0-15 | " | Wm Gumbrell |
| 136 | messuage 6 The Green | 0-0-30 | " | " |
| 135 | messuage 7 The Green | 0-0-08 | John Perkins | Mrs Jane Ranken |
| 134 | 2 messuages | | Richard Cross | |
| | 8 The Green | 0-0-30 | | Mrs Sarah Mann |
| | 9 The Green | " | | George Brown |
| 132 | messuage 10 The Green | 0-0-06 | Jas. Brookes | Edward Fletcher |
| 131 | messuage 11 The Green | 0-0-03 | Jas. Thornton | Laurantia Haywood |
| 130 | messuage 12 The Green | 0-0-04 | Samuel Ward | Rev Spark Canham |

**Brewer's Lane (E side)**

| | | | | |
|---|---|---|---|---|
| 146 | 2 messuages | 0-0-02 | Samuel Ward | Edward Long |
| 147. | | | " | John Parish |
| 148 | 2 messuages | 0-0-03 | Joseph Toe | [Bale Thorn] |
| 149 | | | " | [Thomas Carr] |
| 150 | 2 messuages (*Magpie* Tavern) | 0-0-07 | Eliz. Jackson *et al* | Mr Bradford |
| 151 | " | | " | William Hilbough |
| 152 | messuage | 0-0-03 | Charity School Trustees | –– |
| 153 | Charity School | 0-0-08 | " | –– |

**Brewer's Lane (W side)**

| | | | | |
|---|---|---|---|---|
| 125 | 2 messuages | 0-0-02 | Henry Bell | [John Jones ] |
| 126 | | | " | [Mrs Jenkins] |
| 127 | messuage | 0-0-02 | Esther Trepett | [Joseph Stevens Sr] |
| 128 | messuage | 0-0-03 | Sarah (Cox) Poole | John Bly |
| 129 | messuage | 0-0-03 | Edward Proctor Sr | Edward Prockter Jr |

**Greenside**

| | | | | |
|---|---|---|---|---|
| 95 | messuage 13 The Green | 0-0-04 | Isaac Baldwin | Isaac David |
| 94 | messuage 14 The Green | 0-0-07 | Eliz. Long | Guy Park |
| 93 | messuage 15 The Green | 0-0-07 | Mary Collins | Mary & Sarah Guyse |
| 92 | messuage 16 The Green | 0-0-14 | " | Walwyn Strudwick |
| 91 | *Coffee House* 17 The Green | 0-0-12 | John Armitage | Isaac Baldwin |
| 90 | messuage 18 The Green | 0-0-07 | Ann Armitage | George Hannah |
| 89 | messuage 19 The Green | 0-0-04 | " | Henry Careless |
| 88 | messuage 20 The Green | 0-0-06 | " | John Clifford |
| 87 | messuage | 0-0-06 | Philip Leggett | John Martindale |
| 86 | messuage | 0-0-11 | Wm Wright | Ralph Knox |
| 85 | messuage | 0-0-05 | Mary Harrison | Margaret Lee |
| 84 | *The Cricketers* | 0-0-05 | Sam. Whitbread & Edward Collins | –– Richmond |
| 83 | messuage | 0-0-03 | Richard Cross | George Smart |
| 82 | messuage | 0-0-02 | Henry Edmead | Thomas Marsh |

**Pensioners' Alley**

| | | | | |
|---|---|---|---|---|
| 107 | stable | 0-0-01 | Wm Wright | ? |
| 108 | 2 cottages | 0-0-02 | Henry Bell | ? |
| 109 | | | " | ? |
| 110 | 5 cottages | 0-0-05 | Jonathan Smith | ? |
| 81 | 3 cottages | 0-0-03 | Edward Collins | [Thomas Harris] |
| | | | " | [George Clarke] |
| | | | " | [John Moses] |
| | | | | [Richard Harding] |
| 104 | cottage | 0-0-01 | | |
| 105 | cottage | 0-0-01 | Henry Bell | ? |
| 106 | 3 cottages | 0-0-03 | Wm Waterman | ? |

### The Green

| | | | | |
|---|---|---|---|---|
| 80 | *The Duke's Head* | 0-0-13 | Edward Colline | Benjamin Cook |
| | 2 messuages freehold | 0-0-08 | | |
| 64 | 29 The Green | | Mary Costeker | Mary Costeker |
| 63 | 30 The Green | | " | Eliz Powell [late Lovell] |
| | 2 messuages freehold | 0-0-08 | | |
| 62 | 31 The Green | | Harriet Darrell | " [Gen Brown] |
| 61 | 32 The Green | | " | " [Mrs Cranes] |

### Old Palace Terrace and King Street

| | | | | |
|---|---|---|---|---|
| 60 | messuage 6 O P T freehold | 0-0-04 | George Wood | Eliz Powell [Mr Burdett] |
| 59 | messuage 5 O P T " | 0-0-08 | " | Mrs Ann Southwell |
| 58 | messuage 4 O P T " | 0-0-08 | Mrs Jane Wood | |
| 57 | messuage 3 O P T " | 0-0-08 | Mrs Mary Bullard | |
| 55 | messuage 2 O P T " | 0-0-05 | Crutchley & Turquant | [late Barbara Walker] |
| 54 | 2 messuages 1 O P T " | 0-0-05 | " | George Patmore |
| | 18 King Street | | " | Edward Booles |
| 56 | messuage and slaughterhouse | 0-0-08 | " | Edward Rummell |
| | 19 King Street freehold | | | |

### Paved Alley

| | | | | |
|---|---|---|---|---|
| 73 | messuage freehold | 0-0-01 | Adkins | Mr Snow |
| 74 | messuage | 0-0-02 | Wm Wickham | John Simpson |
| 75 | messuage | 0-0-02 | Henry Careless | Martha Rowbotham |
| 76 | messuage | 0-0-02 | Wm Francis | John Palmer |
| 77 | messuage | 0-0-02 | John Rummell | John Rummell |
| 78 | messuage | 0-0-02 | Henry Edmead | John Smith |
| 79 | messuage | 0-0-02 | Richard Laycock | John Morse |

### King Street (N E side)

| | | | | |
|---|---|---|---|---|
| 65 | 2 messuages | 0-0-05 | Eliz. Jackson *et al* | George Walter |
| 66 | | | " | Thomas Gulliver |
| 67 | 3 messuages | | Eliz Edmead | Ann Gilbert |
| 68 | | 0-0-11 | " | Thomas Tibbs |
| 69 | | | " | Thomas Mason |
| 70 | messuage | 0-0-05 | Mary Muskall | Michael Wicks |
| 71 | messuage | 0-0-02 | Martha Fox (ex Gardner) | John Fear |

### Friars' Lane and riverside

| | | | | |
|---|---|---|---|---|
| 13 | messuage | 0-1-17 | Wm Gardiner | ? |
| 15 | 2 coachhouses | 0-1-17 | J & H Andrews | Countess Cowper |
| 16 | Sheds & boathouses | 0-0-24 | " | H-Andrews |
| 17 | messuage (Retreat House) | 1-2-20 | " | " |
| 14 | 2 messuages (Cholmondeley Walk) | 0-0-31 | " | Gen Fitzwilliam |
| | | | | Henry Edmead |
| 19 | messuage & malthouse | 0-1-18 | " | H Andrews |
| 20 | *White Cross* | 0-0-09 | " | Benjamin Holland |

### Corner of Green

| | | | | |
|---|---|---|---|---|
| 27 | messuage | 0-0-10 | Wm Chambers | Thomas Collins |
| 28 | capital messuage Old Friars | 0-0-36 | Wm Gardiner | Wm Gardiner |
| 29 | 2 messuages Old Palace Place | 0-1-15 | Edward Collins | Frederick Standert |

### King Street (W side)

| | | | | |
|---|---|---|---|---|
| 30 | messuage & shop | 0-0-08 | Mary Wickham | Mary Wickham |
| 31 | messuage & shop | 0-0-07 | Crofton Ross | James Longman |
| 32 | messuage | 0-0-07 | " | ? |
| 33 | messuage | 0-0-07 | George Walter | ? |
| 34 | messuage | 0-0-04 | John Perkins | Evan Prosser |
| 35 | messuage | 0-0-04 | Edward Proctor | Thomas Fuller |
| 36 | messuage | 0-0-08 | Thos Norton | James Burgess |
| 37 | messuage | 0-0-04 | Eliz Chilton | Allan Collyer |

| | | | | |
|---|---|---|---|---|
| 38 | messuage | 0-0-04 | " | Philip Phillips |
| 39 | messuage | 0-0-06 | Thomas Cope | Thomas Cope |
| 40 | messuage | 0-0-04 | Henry Edmead | William Guillet |
| 41 | messuage (the *Ship*) | 0-0-05 | Edward Collins | Ralph Lambert |
| 42 | *Feathers* inn | 0-0-31 | " | William Waterman |
| | **Water Lane (N side)** | | | |
| 43 | messuage | 0-0-01 | Edward Collins | [John Laver] |
| 44 | messuage | 0-0-01 | John Norton | (widow Penner] |
| 45 | messuage | 0-0-01 | Mary Rowland | ? |
| 46 | messuage | 0-0-02 | James Wood | Martha Dearlove |
| 47 | messuage | 0-0-02 | Edward Collins | [Richard Collins] |
| 48 | *Royal Oak* | 0-0-04 | Wm Price Sr | Mrs Walker |
| 49 | messuage | 0-0-02 | Wm Price Jr | ? |
| 50 | stores | 0-0-04 | Wm Price Sr | ? |
| 51 | messuage | 0-0-02 | " | ? |
| 52 | 3 messuages | 0-0-03 | Edward Collins | [Christopher Brown] |
| | | | " | [William Slewter] |
| | | | " | [Thomas Stone] |
| 53 | stable | 0-0-16 | " | Edward Collins |
| | **Water Lane (S side)** | | | |
| 226 | brewhouse | 0-0-25 | Edward Collins | Edward Collins |
| 227 | 2 messuages | 0-0-07 | " | [David Rice & Thomas Bladen] |
| 228 | messuage | 0-0-04 | Wm Armitage | [William Toy] |
| 229 | messuage | 0-0-07 | Edward Collins | [Thomas Webb] |
| 230 | messuage | 0-0-06 | Joanna Oades | [George Bolton] |
| 231 | messuage | 8-0-03 | Henry Smith | [Ann Cuff] |
| 232 | messuage | 0-0-01 | Philip Leggatt Sr | [John Northl |
| 233 | 4 messuages | 0-0-08 | Mary Toy | [Ang Rummell] |
| | | | " | [widow Adams] |
| | | | " | [Thomas Knight] |
| | | | " | [James Paine] |
| 234 | 2 messuages | 0-0-03 | Philip Leggatt | [Richard Stokes] |
| | | | " | [Thomas Edmonds] |
| | **Hill Street (W side)** | | | |
| 235 | 4 messuages | 0-0-08 | Edward Collins | [Georoe Wheelerl |
| | | | " | [widow West] |
| | | | " | [Michael Deverell] |
| | | | " | James Holbourn |
| | *(White Hart)* | | | |
| 235a | 2 messuages | 0-0-09 | Mary Toy | Thomas Burdekin |
| | | | " | Samuel Webb |
| 236 | messuage | 0-0-25 | Henry Leigh | Henry Leigh |
| 237 | *Castle Inn* | 1-1-34 | Albany Wallis | John Halford |
| 238 | 5 messuages | 0-0-11 | Nathaniel Sheppard | Mrs Gandy |
| | | | " | " |
| | | | " | Mrs Catherine Owen |
| | | | " | [Mr Ashby] |
| | | | " | Edward Smith |
| 240 | messuage | 0-0-07 | " | Mrs Mary Collins |
| 241 | messuage | 0-0-07 | " | Mrs Ann Handley |
| | **Heron Court** | | | |
| 242 | capital messuage | 0-0-39 | Eliz Phillips | Daniel. Lesuer Esq |
| 243 | capital messuage | 0-1-05 | Nathaniel Sheppard | John Chase |
| 244 | capital messuage | 0-1-21 | " | George Arbuthnott |
| 245 | 2 stables | 0-0-16 | " | -- |
| | **Ferry Hill (NW side)** | | | |
| 246 | Ferry House | 0-0-09 | Nathaniel Sheppard | Joseph King |

| | | | | |
|---|---|---|---|---|
| 275 | messuage (Bridge House) | 0-1-29 | George Tilson | George Tilson |
| 276 | *King's Head* | 0-0-14 | Eliz Jackson *et al* | William Procktor |
| | **Lower Road to Petersham** | | | |
| 277 | 3 messuages & shops | 0-0-06 | John Farnham | Mary Wickey |
| | | | " | John Farnham |
| | | | " | Miles Singleton |
| 278 | 4 messuages | 0-0-13 | John King | Hendon Alleyn |
| | | | " | Margaret Hickes |
| | | | " | Thomas Welton |
| | | | " | Eleanor Dobbinson |
| 279-280 | [late almshouses] | 0-0-22 | Almshouse Trustees | -- |
| 281 | capital messuage | 1-1-08 | Harriet Darrell | George Colman Esq |
| 283 | messuage | 0-2-16 | " | Benjamin Lyon Sr |
| 284 | capital messuage (Ivy Hall) | 0-2-09 | " | Hon Henry Hobart |
| 285 | messuage & water engine | 0-1-03 | " | John Pococke |
| 286 | messuage | 0-0-29 | " | Lady Harriet Vernon |
| 287 | messuage | 0-0-27 | " | James Crockett |
| 288 | messuage freehold | 0-0-08 | Parish Church | Mrs Martha Roberts |
| 289 | messuage freehold | 0-0-10- | " | Lady Henrietta Seabright |
| 290 | messuage freehold | 0-0-10 | " | Mrs Otley |
| 291 | messuage & stables freehold | 0-0-14 | " | Henry Leevers |
| 292 | *Blue Anchor*. malthouse freehold | 0-0-14 | " | Percival Hart |
| 293 | messuage freehold | 0-0-14 | " | Robert Brownell |
| 294 | messuage & stables freehold | 0-0-32 | " | Samuel Thorp |
| 295 | messuage freehold | 0-0-16 | " | Robert Burgess |
| 296 | messuage with brewhouse and stables | 1-0-26 | Harrick Darrell | John Lewis |
| 574 | capital mansion house | 1-1-12 | Rev Cutts Barton (for Duke of Montagu) | Duke of Montagu |
| 585 | capital messuage | 0-1-00 | Isaac Platt | Duke of Buccleuch |
| | **Lower Road to Petersham (E side)** | | | |
| 587 | coachhouse & stables | 0-2-00 | Rev Cutts Barton | Duke of Montagu |
| 588 | 3 tenements | 0-1-20 | Henry Hunt | Thomas Sheriff |
| | | | " | ? |
| | | | " | ? |
| 584 | messuage | 0-1-19 | Wm Richardson | Lady Howe |
| 583 | offices | 0-1-07 | Rev Cutts Barton | Duke of Montagu |
| 582 | 6 messuages | 0-0-34 | Chas Grantham | [widow Sellars] |
| | | | " | Susan Stagg |
| | | | " | Joseph Ricketts |
| | | | " | John Langley |
| | | | " | J T Taylor |
| | | | " | Mr Cooke |
| 579 | *Three Pigeons* | 0-0-31 | James Wood | William Raymond |
| 578 | messuage | 0-0-01 | Chas Grantham | [Joseph Marks] |
| 577 | messuage | 0-0-06 | Eliz Land | [James Wiggans] |
| 576 | messuage | 0-0-07 | Chas Farmer | [James Skeets] |
| 575 | messuage | 10-0-07 | John Grosvenor | Thomas Clark |
| 369 | capital messuage | 3-0-32 | John Armitage | Ann Armitage |
| 368 | messuage | 0-0-27 | Harriet Darrell | late John Langley |
| 367 | coachhouse | 0-0-13 | " | -- |
| 366 | workhouse | 0-0-36 | " | [Richmond Parish] |
| 365 | capital messuage | 1-0-31 | " | William Mills |
| 362 | 2 tenements | 0-0-04 | E Watts | John Baird |
| | | | " | Thomas Luckman |
| 308 | *Rising Sun* alehouse | 0-0-08 | Hickey's Trust | William Harvey |
| 307 | messuage | 0-0-11 | " | H St G Trelawney |
| 304 | 4 tenements | 0-0-07 | " | Joseph Money |
| | | | " | Edward Proctor Sr |
| | | | " | Richard Prince |

| No. | Description | | | |
|---|---|---|---|---|
| 303 | 4 messuages | 0-0-03 | Grove Wheeler<br>"<br>" | Mary Tudor<br>Henry Deal<br>Christopher Prockter |

**Upper Causeway (Richmond Hill) (W side)**

| No. | Description | | | |
|---|---|---|---|---|
| 297 | messuage | 0-0-09 | .James Brooks | Robert Smith |
| 298 | messuage | 0-0-02 | Wm Larkham | John Beazley |
| 299 | messuage | 0-0-03 | " | George Singleton |
| 300 | 3 messuages | 0-0-03 | Grove Wheeler<br>"<br>" | –– Hughes<br>George Wall<br>? |
| 301 | 3 messuages | 0-0-04 | "<br>"<br>" | [Christopher Procktor]<br>[— White]<br>[— Durant] |
| 302 | messuage | 0-0-02 | Grove Wheeler | ? |
| 305 | 2 messuages | 0-0-02 | Hickey's Trust<br>" | [Charles Prockter]<br>? |
| 306 | 2 messuages | 0-0-06 | "<br>" | Thomas Goldsmith<br>Samuel Cook |
| 361 | Three Compasses alehouse | 0-0-17 | Mary Toms | Joshua Slater |
| 363 | 2 messuages | 0-0-09 | Harriet Darrell<br>" | John New<br>[James Bacon] |
| 364 | capital messuage (Harford House) | 1-0-25 | " | Samuel Pechell |
| 370 | messuage (site of Cardigan House) | 0-1-15 | John Armitage | Solomon Gomperts |
| 371 | messuage (The Wells House) | 1-2-07 | Susanna Houblon | –– |
| 580 | capital messuage (Landdowne House | 3-2-28 | Edward Collins | Lord Molyneux |
| 589 | *Bull's Head* tavern | 0-2-27 | Hickey's Trust | Francis Baker |

**Outside Park Gate**

| No. | Description | | | |
|---|---|---|---|---|
| 647 | capital messuage (Ancaster House) | 0-0-28 | Mary Burshett | Duke of Ancaster |
| 648 | old messuage | 0-2-12 | Rowbotham Trustees | Duke of Ancaster |
| 649 | messuage | 0-2-17 | Francis Watkins | Duke of Ancaster |
| 650 | messuage | 0-0-21 | Thos H Warren | J Cookman |
| 651 | coachhouse | 0-1-11 | Marshalsea Prison Trustees | –– |

**Pesthouse Common (N side)**

| No. | Description | | | |
|---|---|---|---|---|
| 642 | messuage (Home Castle) | 4-2-00 | Sam. Spiers | Francis Watkins |
| 633 | messuage freehold | 0-2-21 | Wm Sowle | Robert Sowle |
| 625 | 2 tenements | 0-0-23 | John Hopkins<br>" | James Cutler<br>Henry Tilling |
| 624 | 2 tenements | 0-0-18 | Mrs Ann Grose<br>" | Thomas Gale<br>Hewitt Cobb |
| 622 | 5 tenements | 0-1-38 | "<br>"<br>"<br>"<br>" | James Cutler<br>James Gale<br>Benjamin Hancock<br>?<br>? |
| 621 | capital messuage | 0-3-05 | " | Ann Grose |
| 620 | messuage | 0-0-09 | Hickey's Trust | John Coleman |
| 619 | coachhouses | 0-0-35 | " | |

**Top of Hill**

| No. | Description | | | |
|---|---|---|---|---|
| 617 | messuage | 0-0-12 | Marshalsea Prison Trustees | Sarah Hosey |
| 616 | messuage | | | Gov Thomas Pownall |
| 615 | messuage | 0-0-08 | Daniel Grose | Daniel Grose |
| 614 | 2 messuages | 0-0-06 | John Stains Michell<br>" | Richard Turner |
| 613 | capital messuage (Mansfield House) | 1-0-27 | Hickey's Trust | Richard Cropp |
| 612 | messuage | 0-1-24 | " | Mary Toy |
| 611 | capital messuage (Doughty House) | 0-1-35 | " | Wm Richardson |
| 610 | messuage (4 The Terrace) | 0-0-07 | " | Abraham de Paiba |

| | | | | |
|---|---|---|---|---|
| 609 | messuage (3 The Terrace) | 0-0-13 | Hickey's Trust | Miss Blanchard |
| 608 | messuage (2 The Terrace) | 0-0-13 | Christopher Blanchard | Mrs Isabella Ford |
| 607 | messuage (1 The Terrace) | 0-0-26 | " | Mr Charles Pearce |
| 606 | messuage | 0-0-05 | Ann Toy | Mary Walpole |
| 605 | *Roebuck* tavern | 0-0-12 | Sarah Burgess | Teverson Eley |
| 604 | coachhouse | 0-1-05 | Christopher Blanchard | -- |
| 603 | messuage | 0-0-2.3 | Chas. Pearce | Mr Rolls |
| 601 | almshouses | 0-1-27 | Bishop Duppa's Trustees | -- |

### Upper Causeway, Richmond Hill (E side)

| | | | | |
|---|---|---|---|---|
| 382 | capital messuage (Elleker House) | 1-1-15 | Harriet Darrell | Mrs Rebecca Houblon |
| 381 | coachhouse | 0-0-13 | Samuel Pechell | -- |
| 380 | messuage | 0-0-03 | " | John Guize |
| 379 | messuage | 0-0-02 | " | [        ? Bayton] |
| 378 | messuage | 0-0-01 | Margaret Toms | [Mrs Kelly] |
| 377 | messuage | 0-0-04 | Eliz. Wright | John Wright |
| 376 | former playhouse | 0-0-08 | Harriet Darrell | Mr Williams |
| 374 | messuage | 0-0-16 | " | Mr Wickstone |
| 373 | messuage | 0-0-19 | " | Mrs Mary Kramer |
| 372 | messuage | 0-0-19 | " | Capt Gavin Hambleton |

### Vineyard

| | | | | |
|---|---|---|---|---|
| 375 | 3 tenements Vine Row | 0-0-07 | Harriet Darrell | Richard Malcolm |
| | | | " | John Edwards |
| | | | " | Benjamin Lyon Jr |
| 384 | 6 tenements | 0-0-24 | Michell's Almshouses Trustees | William Colebrook |
| | | | " | — Nicholson |
| | | | " | -- Huggett |
| | | | " | George Kitchen |
| | | | " | Samuel Marriage |
| 388 | Michell's almshouses | 0-0-24 | " | -- |
| 385 | messuage | 0-0-25 | Michell's Trustees | R Watts |
| 381 | capital messuage | 0-3-11 | " | Alexander Crawford |
| 387 | messuage | 0-0-10 | " | [Edward Wheatley] |
| 389-90 | messuage | 0-0-05 | " | ? |
| 357 | messuage freehold | 0-0-09 | Catherine Lesley | Hon Thomas Lesley |
| 358 | messuage freehold | 0-0-04 | Mary Toy | George Briggs |
| 359 | 2 messuages | 0-0-09 | Jas Clutterbuk | Sarah Roades |
| | | | | Isabella Badger |
| 360 | 3 messuages | 0-1-13 | " | John Whitehead |
| | | | " | John Kitchen |
| | | | " | Thomas Ansell |
| 297 | coachhouse | 0-0-30 | " | William Patoun |
| 398 | capital messuage (Mount Ararat) | 0-2-24 | Thos H Warren | Daniel Wray |
| 346 | Queen Elizabeth's almshouses | 0-0-24 | Almshouse Trustees | -- |
| 331 | Capital messuage (Clarence House) | 1-0-16 | Crofton Ross | Crofton Ross |
| 324 | coachhouse & stable freehold | 0-0-37 | " | Crofton Ross |
| 323 | coachhouse & stable freehold | 0-1-05 | " | Thomas Tunstall |

### Hill Street (E side)

| | | | | |
|---|---|---|---|---|
| 322 | messuage & shop | 0-0-04 | Eliz Stanley | Joseph Ridley |
| 321 | messuage & shop | 0-0-04 | Mary Guildharr | John Ernest Guildharr |
| 320 | messuage & shop | 0-0-03 | Crofton Ross | Charles Burt |
| 319 | messuage & shop | 0-0-04 | " | William Barker |
| 318 | messuage freehold | 0-0-31 | John Scott | John Scott |
| 317 | messuage freehold | 0-0-06 | Ann Grose | Dr Kreuter |
| 316 | messuage freehold | 0-0-07 | " | Thomas Tunstall |
| 315 | messuage freehold | 0-1-36 | Crofton Ross | Frederick Nicolay |
| 314 | messuage freehold | 0-1-14 | Jas Clithero | -- Reignier |
| 313 | messuage & coachhouses freehold | | " | Whichcote Turner |
| 312 | *Fox & Hounds* tavern freehold | 0-0-12 | Charles Triggs | John Stevens |
| 311 | messuage & shop freehold | 0-0-04 | Jas Clithero | Charles Phillips |

| 310 | messuage freehold | 0-0-01 | Ann Reeves | -- Tutton |
| 309 | messuage & shop freehold | 0-0-09 | Charles Burt | Thomas Turner |

### Ormond Row

| 325 | messuage freehold | 0-0-12 | Jas Clithero | Elizabeth Yeames |
| 326 | 2 messuages    " | 0-0-12 | John Platt | Ann Siddall |
|     |                 |        | " | Susan Popplewell |
| 327 | messuage    " | 0-0-05 | John New | Richard Turner |
| 328 | messuage    " | 0-0-10 | Jas Clithero | Charles Triggs |
| 329 | messuage    " | 0-0-17 | Mendez da Costa | John F Lynch |
| 330 | messuage (Ormond House) freehold | 0-0-36 | Mary Brown | -- Baxter |
| 338 | messuage | 0-0-05 | Edward Collins | Mary Russell |
| 266 | messuage | 0-0-14 | " | William Reynolds |
| 267 | messuage (The Hollies) | 0-0-39 | Crofton Ross | Henry Hunt |
| 268 | messuage (The Rosary) | 0-0-39 | " | John Pulley |

### Hill Street (E side)

| 256 | *Talbot Inn* freehold | 0-3-18 | Albany Wallis | Catherine Hutchins |
| 254 | messuage    " | 0-0-07 | Jos. Clifton *et al* | Joseph Clifton |
| 253 | messuage    " | 0-0-05 | Wm Griffin | William Griffin |
| 252 | messuage    " | 0-0-06 | Richard Guize | Elizabeth Tyrell |
| 251 | messuage    " | 0-0-12 | Rogers Chilton | Rogers Chilton |
| 250 | messuage    " | 0-0-04 | Sarah Lett | John Cheek |
| 249 | messuage    " | 0-0-05 | John Clark | [late Richard Harding] |
| 248 | messuage    " | 0-0-04 | Wm Price Sr | John Ballard |
| 247 | messuage    " | 0-1-07 | | William Price |

### George Street (NW side)

| 72 | *Queen's Head* tavern | 0-0-03 | Ann Lake | John Williamson |
| 99 | messuage | 0-0-03 | Wm Gumbrell | -- Piggott |
| 96 | slaughterhouse in yard | 0-0-04 | Edward Proctor | ? |
| 97 | stables in yard | 0-0-01 | Elizabeth Edmead | ? |
| 98 | messuage & shop in yard | 0-0-02 | Wm Gumbrell | [William Gumbrell] |
| 100 | messuage | 0-0-04 | Alex. L. Oades | -- Smith |
| 101 | messuage & shop | 0-0-05 | Eliz. Chilton | Mr Wheble |
| 102 | messuage | 0-0-02 | Henry Bell | James Higgins |
| 103 | messuage | 0-0-03 | Edward Collins | Richard Harding |
| 112 | cottage | 0-0-01 | Eliz. Grantham | [widow Stedwell] |
| 111 | cottage | 0-0-01 | Chas. Grantham | [Charles Avery] |
| 113 | 2 messuages | 0-0-08 | Mary Toy | John Wall |
|     |           |        | " | Robert Parham |
| 114 | messuage | 0-0-10 | Henry Bell | [-- Brown] |
| 115 | messuage & large room | 0-0-21 | Eliz. Green | Elizabeth Green |
|     |                       |        |            | Benjamin Baccum |
| 116 | 2 cottages | 0-0-03 | Mary Maskall | Mary Maskall |
|     |            |        | " | John Gibson |
| 117 | *Black Boy* | 0-0-06 | Mary Toy | Frances Martin |
| 118 | messuage | 0-0-03 | Henry Perkins | John Withall |
| 119 | messuage | 0-0-05 | Edward Paine | James Paine |
| 120 | 2 messuages | 0-0-06 | Eliz Grantham | George Booth |
|     |             |        | " | Rowland Smith |
| 121 | messuage | 0-0-04 | Elizabeth Rudd | Richard Dyke |
| 122 | messuage | 0-0-08 | Thos H Warren | Boxall Eling |
| 123 | messuage | 0-0-01 | Esther Trippett | Ann Trippett |
| 123a | messuage | 0-0-03 | Joseph Toe | Joseph Toe |
| 124 | messuage | 0-0-02 | John Barnsley | Mrs Barnsley |
| 154 | messuage | | Wm Price Sr | Benjamin Bradbury |
| 155 | messuage | 0-0-19 | " | Thomas Pownall |
| 156 | messuage | | " | Alice Collins |
| 157 | messuage | 0-0-11 | Wm Stradwick | Wm Stradwick |
| 158 | messuage & shop | 0-0-8. | Philip Leggatt Sr | Philip Leggatt Sr |
| 159 | messuage | 0-0-8 | Richard Toy | Edward Robinson |

| | | | | |
|---|---|---|---|---|
| 160 | messuage | 0-0-13 | Wm Alder | William Alder |
| 161 | messuage and slaughterhouse | 0-0-17 | Martha Paine | Thomes Paine |
| 162 | *Rose and Crown* tavern | 0-0-26 | Edward Collins | Thomas Sell |
| 163 | messuage | 0-0-03 | " | Jane Smith |

**Duke Street (S side)**

| | | | | |
|---|---|---|---|---|
| 145 | messuage | 0-0-02 | Edward Collins | John Ford |
| 144 | messuage | 0-0-11 | John Armitage | John Bray |
| 143 | messuage | | " | John Bond |
| 142 | stables | 0-0-05 | John Rice | ? |

**World's End (S end of Kew Road)**

| | | | | |
|---|---|---|---|---|
| 472 | warehouse | 0-0-12 | William Warren | ? |
| 473 | 2 messuages | 0-0-07 | William Alder | [William Alder] |
| 474 | messuage | 0-0-01 | John Gardner | Samuel Loveday |
| 475 | *Bear* alehouse | 0-0-08 | " | Samuel Loveday |
| 476 | 6 tenements | 0-0-13 | Eliz.Norden | [widow Seymour] |
| | | | " | [-- Darbourn] |
| | | | " | [John Trippettl |
| | | | " | [widow Penny] |
| | | | " | [John Counshill] |
| | | | " | ? |
| 477 | messuage | 0-0-02 | Thomas Paine | [widow Davies] |
| 478 | 2 messuages | 0-0-06 | Henry Edmead | [-- Fairbank] |
| | | | " | [John Parker] |
| 479 | 2 messuages | 0-0-05 | Sam. Loveday | William Absell |
| | | | " | Joseph White |
| 480 | 4 messuages | 0-0-09 | Henry Edmead | [James Wilson] |
| | | | " | Stephen Smith |
| | | | " | Thomas Budd |
| | | | " | [Herod Drew] |
| 481 | 2 messuages | 0-0-09 | Mary Murray | John May] |
| | | | " | Robert Richens |
| 482 | messuage | 0-0-03 | Thomas Wicks | [William Platt] |
| 483 | messuage | 0-0-02 | Joseph Reeve | [Thomas Batty] |
| 484 | messuage | 0-0-02 | Henry Bell | [John Avis] |

**Marshgate Road (N side)**

| | | | | |
|---|---|---|---|---|
| 490 | engine house | 0-0-01 | Richmond Parish | -- |
| 491 | messuage & smith's shop | 0-0-13 | Samuel Spiers | Thomas Matthews |
| 492 | 3 tenements | 0-0-14 | W Strudwick | ? |
| 493 | capital messuage | 2-2-12 | " | Mary Curtis |
| 493 | coachhouse | 0-1-13 | Earl of Hardwick | Earl of Hardwick |
| 495 | capital messuage (Lichfield House) | 1-2-30 | -- Beyer | " |
| 497 | messuage | 0-0-36 | Rebecca Knapp | Rev George Wakefield |
| 498 | messuage | 1-1-22 | Rebecca Knapp | Mrs Rebecca Knapp |
| 499 | messuage | 0-0-20 | Richard Young | Richard Belson |
| 500 | '7 new messuages & 4 still building' | 3-1-25 | Charles Pearce | -- |
| 501 | messuage | 2.1.19 | " | William Duffus |
| 503 | 3 messuages | 1-0-36 | Robert Overton | Robert Overton |
| | | | " | [Mary Drew] |
| | | | " | [-- Randall] |
| 505 | stables | 0-0-08 | George Alcock | -- |
| 506 | messuage | 0-1-24 | Richmond Parish | James Wilkes |
| 508 | messuage | 0-0-13 | George Alcock | [John Drew] |
| 509 | messuage | 0-1-24 | Charles Pearce | Elizabeth Sheppard |
| 511c | mansion house | 0-3-03 | Dr John Baker | John Baker MD |
| 652 | messuage | 3-1-29 | Alex. Laroche Oades | Richard Gurney |
| 676 | messuage | 0-1-27 | Eleanor Brown | Mrs Eleanor Brown |
| 679 | capital messuage ('Manor House') | 1-0-10 | James Sayer | James Sayer Esq |

### Marshgate Road (S side)

| | | | | |
|---|---|---|---|---|
| 557 | part of capital messuage (part in Mortlake) | 1-2-22 | Sarah & Mary Metcalf | Edmund Starkie Esq |
| 558 | capital messuage (Spring Grove) | 2-3-28 | John Townson | Sir Humphrey Morris |
| 555 | capital messuage (Grove Lodge) | 6-2-21 | Dorothy Floyer. | Peter Floyer Esq |
| 675 | *Black Horse* tavern | 0-0-26 | Thomas Prosser | Thomas Prosser |
| 549a | 6 tenements | 0-3-28 | Thomas Roberts | ? |
| 549b | 3 tenements freehold | 0-3-29 | Thomas Roberts | William Rolls *et al* |
| 546 | messuage | 1-1-10 | Edward Collins | Thomas Miles? |
| 543 | almshouses | 1-2-31 | Susanna Houblon | -- |
| 537 | messuage | 0-1-34 | Thomas Morson | Thomas Morson |
| 536 | messuage freehold | 0-1-00 | " | William Selwyn |
| 535 | coachhouse | 0-3-28 | " | -- |
| 533 | messuage | 1-0-05 | Richard Curson | Richard Curson |

### Between Marshgate Road and Worple Way

| | | | | |
|---|---|---|---|---|
| 525 | messuage | 0-1-18 | Dr Baker | [Dr Baker] |
| 520 | messuage | 0-0-07 | George Alcock | Edward Mann |
| 519 | messuage freehold | 0-0-04 | Henry Bell | " |
| 518 | messuage freehold | 0-0-04 | Francis Martin | [-- Bolton] |
| 517a | tenement freehold | 0-0-02 | Wm Sherman | ? |
| 517 | tenement freehold | 0-0-01 | Thomas Webb | ? |
| 516 | 2 messuages freehold | 0-0-06 | Henry Dennis | widow Smith |
| | | | " | Simon Redben |
| 515 | messuage | 0-0-03 | William King | Susanna Ash |
| 514 | 2 messuages | 0-0-08 | Thomas Roberts | Thomas Roberts |
| 513 | 5 tenements | 0-0-06 | Wm Waterman | all ? |

### Marshgate Road (S side)

| | | | | |
|---|---|---|---|---|
| 529 | capital messuage | 0-1-39 | Philip Palmer | Philip Palmer |
| 528 | capital messuage | 1-1-32 | Rbt Darrell | Robert Darrell |
| [218 | messuage (part of capital messuage in Paradise Rd) | | S Long | ?] |
| 217 | 3 messuages | 0-0-33 | Mary Leyburn | Ann Andrews |
| | | | " | John Hollyfield |
| | (*Granby's Head*) | | " | John Thresh |
| 216 | messuage | 6-0-08 | Jemima Eaton | Herman Baker |
| 215 | messuage | 0-0-22 | Mary Harrison | Edward Shrubsole |
| 214 | 3 messuages | 0-0-04 | Eliz Grantham | [William Fellows] |
| | | | " | William Wall |
| | | | " | [-- Burtle] |
| 213 | 4 messuages freehold | 0-0-31 | Richmond Parish | Peter Butchards |
| | | | " | Mrs Fisher |
| | | | " | John Ballance |
| | | | " | James Tasker |

### Middle Row

| | | | | |
|---|---|---|---|---|
| 225 | messuage & 2 tenements | 0-0-05 | Chaffin Martin | Chaffin Martin |
| | | | " | William Martin |
| | | | " | Francis Goff |
| 224 | messuage | 0-0-02 | Jane Sherlock | [Jane Sherlock] |
| 223 | messuage | 0-0-03 | Geo Armstrong | [Edward Mann] |
| 222 | *Angel* alehouse | 0-0-04 | Thomas Norton | Richard Whitbey |
| 221 | 2 messuages | 0-0-12 | Robert Lander | Chaffin Martin |
| | | | " | William Taylor |
| 220 | messuage | 0-0-04 | Eliz Jackson *et al* | Thomas Grimsdale |

### George Street (SE side)

| | | | | |
|---|---|---|---|---|
| 212 | 3 messuages | 1-0-22 | Wm Robinson | Joseph Mills |
| | | | " | William Barnard |
| | | | " | Elizabeth Gulliver |
| 205 | messuage | 0-0-13 | Mary Collins | Elizabeth Mihill |

*Plate 56*

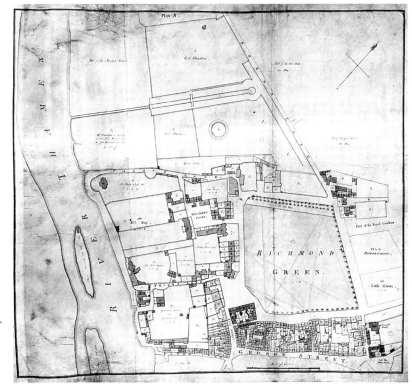

*The Manor Survey of 1771. Plans of the area round the Green, and of the development along the Kew and Marshgate Roads (PRO MP1/1/ 545 Plans A & C)*

Plate 57

*The Manor Survey of
1771. Plans of the areas
from George Street to the
Wells and from the Wells
to Richmond Park.
(PRO MP1/1/545
Plans B & E)*

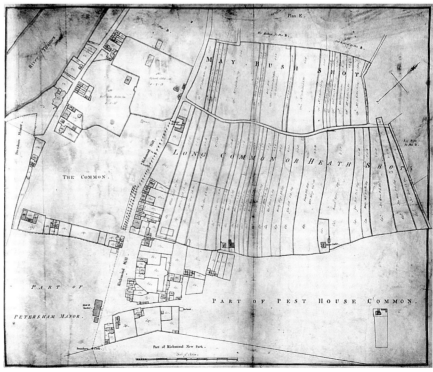

*Plate 58*

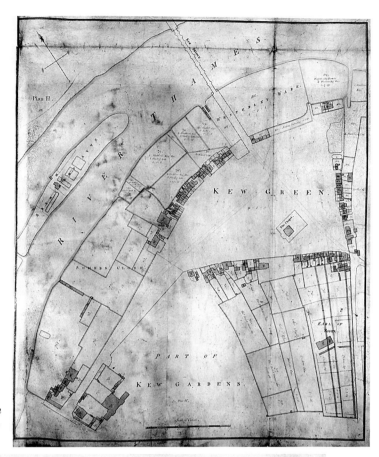

*The Manor Survey of 1771. Plan of Kew. (PRO MP1/1/545 Plan H)*

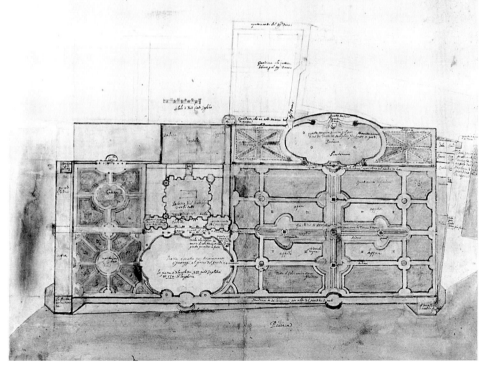

*Costantino de' Servi's project for Richmond Palace and gardens, 1611. (Archivio di Stato, Florence)*

*Plate 59*

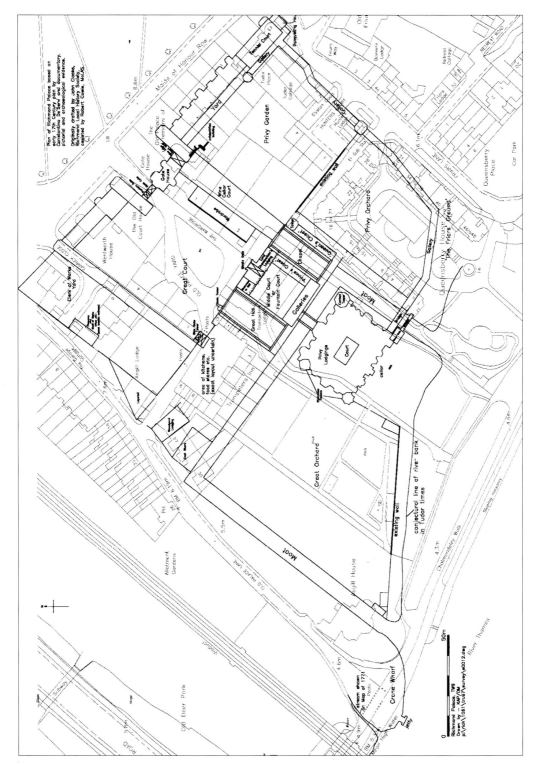

*Plan of the Tudor palace of Richmond, amended in the light of the de' Servi plan, superimposed on modern Ordnance Survey plan.*

| | | | | |
|---|---|---|---|---|
| 203 | messuage | 0-0-12 | Samuel Ward | -- Lowe |
| 202 | messuage | 0-0-22 | " | Rev George Laughton |

### Churchyard

| | | | | |
|---|---|---|---|---|
| 204 | warehouse | 0-0-05 | Samuel Ward | [Samuel Ward] |
| 206 | 2 messuages | 0-0-07 | Mary Toy | Edward Monk |
| 207 | " | | " | Mary Vaughan |
| 208 | 2 messuages | 0-0-07 | Thomas Matthew | Thomas Lawrence |
| 209 | " | | " | Sarah Butcher |
| 210 | 2 messuages | 0-0-32 | Clement Smith | Clement Smith |
| 211 | " | | | Richard Walklin |

### Church Court

| | | | | |
|---|---|---|---|---|
| 201a | messuage | 0-0-03 | Samuel Ward | William Maybank Sr |
| 201 | messuage | 0-0-03 | " | John Parkhurst |
| 200 | messuage | 0-0-05 | " | Anthony Laycock |
| 199 | *Angel and Crown* tavern | 0-0-07 | " | Samuel Chambers |

### George Street SE side (continued)

| | | | | |
|---|---|---|---|---|
| 198 | 2 messuages freehold | 0-0-07 | William Coles | Samuel Ward |
| 197 | | | " | Edward Pain |
| 196 | messuage freehold | 0-0-07 | John Gardner | John Gardner |
| 195 | messuage | 0-0-08 | Edward Collins | Philip Phillips |
| 194 | *Greyhound* inn | 0-0-32 | " | Richard Carpenter |
| 193 | messuage | 0-0-14 | Ann Shepherd | Grace Grubb |
| 192 | messuage | 0-0-10 | Mary Collins | John Rowbotham |
| 191 | messuage | 0-0-06 | " | John Sumner |
| 190 | messuage (*Sun* alehouse) | 0-0-06 | " | Thomas Phelps |
| 159 | messuage | 0-0-06 | Martha Rowbotham | John Francis |
| 188 | mews, barn, stables, etc | 0-0-37 | Mary Collins | [Edward Collins] |
| 179 | *Artichoke* alehouse | 0-0-07 | Edward Collin | Mrs Mary Skinner |
| 178 | messuage | 0-0-01 | Boxall Eling | Lewis Gunn |
| 176 | 2 messuages | 0-0-33 | John Perkins | William Prockter |
| 175 | " | | " | Mrs Scott |
| 174 | messuage, smith's shop, barn, etc. | 0-1-10 | Mary Bateman *et al* | [William Waterman] |
| 173 | messuage | 0-0-15 | Anne Allan | Thomas Pritchard |
| 172 | messuage | 0-0-15 | " | Thomas Creighton |
| 171 | messuage | 0-0-30 | Henry Bell | William Matthews |
| 170 | messuage & shop | 0-0-13 | Henry Bell | William Goter |
| 169 | messuage | 0-0-09 | " | Joseph Webster |
| 168 | messuage | 0-0-11 | " | George Rowles |
| 167 | messuage | 0-0-03 | Eliz. Ritson | William Telford |
| 166 | messuage | 0-0-17 | Mary Toy | Thomas Parke |
| 165 | messuage & slaughterhouse | 0-0-11 | Eliz. Chilton | Robert Stevens |
| 164 | messuage | 0-0-02 | Chas. Grantham | Charles Pearson |

### Red Lion Street (N side)

| | | | | |
|---|---|---|---|---|
| ?part of 165 (the old *Plough*) | | | ? | Abraham Robinson |
| ?part of 166 or 170, 171 or 173 (see above) | | | ? | Richard Gabriel |
| 177 | 2 messuages | 0-0-06 | Henry Parker | Roger Dipple |
| | | | ? | Mrs Mary Burchett |
| 180 | 5 tenements | 0-0-16 | Richard Toy | Isaac Frost |
| | | | " | [widow Dartington] |
| | | | " | [William Matthews] |
| | | | " | -- Fish? |
| | | | " | ? |
| 181 | messuage | 0-0-01 | Edward Collins | |
| 182 | messuage | 0-0-02 | Eliz. Chilton | [Jane Burt] |
| 183 | messuage | 0-0-02 | Richard Toy | ? |
| 184 | messuage | 0-0-06 | Henry Bell | Samuel Finney |
| 185 | messuage | 0-0-03 | " | [-- Pickett] |
| 186 | carpenter's shop | 0-0-12 | " | Henry Bell |
| 187 | messuage | 0-0-05 | " | George Beadle |

**Red Lyon Street (S side)**

| | | | | |
|---|---|---|---|---|
| 255 | messuage | 0-9-31 | Henry Bell | Richard Gabriel |
| 260 | messuage | 0-0-30 | " | Mary Murray |
| 261 | 4 tenements | 0-0-37 | " | Henry Bell |
| | | | " | ? |
| | | | " | ? |
| | | | " | ? |
| 262 | messuage | 0-0-05 | " | [Thomas Dounes] |
| 263 | 2 messuages | 0-0-12 | J Rouse | [J Rouse] |
| 265 | *Red Lion* alehouse | 0-0-39 | Henry Bell | Richard Bolton |
| 269 | messuage | 0-0-02 | " | William Wickham |
| 170 | messuage & smith's shop | 0-0-10 | Edward Collins | Ann Crow |
| 271 | messuage | 0-0-12 | Henry Bell | [Henry Bell] |
| 272 | 2 messuages | 0-0-22 | Saint Allum | Edward Oram |
| | | | " | Saint Allum |

**Church Row**

| | | | | |
|---|---|---|---|---|
| 339 | messuage | 0-0-15 | E Clare | Daniel Wise |
| 340 | messuage | 0-0-11 | " | Elizabeth Eeles |
| 341 | messuage | 0-0-06 | M Maskall | John Groombridge |
| 342 | messuage | 0-0-07 | " | John Wood |
| 343 | messuage | 0-0-06 | Edward Collins | Catherine Cross |
| 344 | messuage | 0-1-29 | Wm Turner | William Turner |
| 345 | coachhouse & stables | 2-0-29 | " | " |

**Paradise Row**

| | | | | |
|---|---|---|---|---|
| 347 | messuage | 0-0-16 | Henry Bell | Christopher Bacon |
| 348 | messuage | 0-1-18 | John Halford | Isaac Henckell |
| 349 | messuage | 0-0-21 | " | F E Benezer |
| 351 | 5 tenements | 0-1-20 | Richmond Parish | John Ranken |
| | | | " | ? |
| | | | " | ? |
| | | | " | ? |
| | | | " | ? |
| 353 | 2 messuages | 0-1-30 | F Beyet *et al* | Elizabeth Knapton |
| | | | " | John Price |
| 218 | capital messuage | 0-2-16 | Sarah Long | Lady Mary Compton |

**KEW – South of Green**

| | | | | |
|---|---|---|---|---|
| 729 | Palace (White House) | 5-0-16 | Earl of Essex | His Majesty |
| 731 | gatehouse | 0-14 | " | " |
| 732 | capital messuage | 0-1-08 | " | " |
| 733 | 2 messuages | 0-1-26 | Thos H Warren | T H Warren |
| | | | " | -- Bethune |
| 739 | messuage called 'Hell' | 0-1-14 | Earl of Essex | His Majesty |
| 741 | capital messuage | 0-3-38 | Ann Appleby | " |
| 747 | messuage | 0-0-21 | " | (Parnell Hawkins) |
| 748 | messuage | 0-0-12 | Wm Warren | Rev Bellamy |
| 749 | messuage | 0-0-05 | Thos H Warren | Joseph Hilliard |
| 750 | messuage | 0-0-10 | " | -- Minneys |
| 751 | messuage | 0-0-05 | " | Robert Rich |
| 752 | messuage | 0-0-05 | " | William Frime |
| 753 | messuage | 0-0-06 | J D Engleheart | Mrs Robinson |
| 754 | messuage | 0-0-09 | Ann Engleheart | Dr Majendy |
| 755 | *Coach and Horses* | 0-0-16 | Tyson Chapman | Samuel Witchenham |
| 756 | messuage | 0-0-04 | Thomas Layton | Thomas Layton |
| 757 | 2 messuages | 0-0-09 | Henry Taylor | Henry Taylor |
| | | | " | Edward Davidson |

**KEW – North of Green**

| | | | | |
|---|---|---|---|---|
| 760 | 2 messuages | 0-2-01 | Levett Blackborne | Mr Smelt |
| | | | " | George Kirby |

| 761 | capital message | 1-1-30 | " | Lady Charlotte Finch |
|---|---|---|---|---|
| 762 | capital messuage | 4-0-24 | " | Their Majesties |
| 763 | capital messuage (Dutch House) | 2-1-00 | " | |
| 765 | capital message | 0-0-36 | Chas. Douglas | [late Mordecai Green] |
| 766 | capital messuage | 1-0-04 | Peter Theobald | Peter Theobald |
| 768 | messuage | 0-1-29 | " | " |
| 772 | messuage | 0-0-03 | " | Edward Butler |
| 773 | messuage | 0-0-03 | Mary Toy | John Stringer |
| 774 | cottage | 0-0-01 | Mary Orton | Sarah Orton |
| 775 | 2 messuages | 0-0-07 | Eliz. Jackson *et al* | James Croome |
| 776 | messuage | 0-0-05 | Mary Orton | Mr Myers |
| 777 | 3 messuages | 0-0-13 | Eliz Jackson *et al* | Geo Schennerstadt |
| 778 | | | " | Mary Porter |
| 779 | | | " | –– Atkins |
| 780 | messuage | 0-0-08 | Nicholas I Hill | Mr Beaufarr |
| 781 | messuage | 0-0-05 | Thos H Warren | Frederick Albert |
| 782 | messuage | 0-0-05 | " | Lewis Albert |
| 783 | capital messuage | 0-0-28 | " | William Blair |
| 784 | messuage & coachhouse | 0-0-06 | " | –– Finlay |
| 784a | messuage | | " | Stephen Hall |
| 785 | messuage | 0-0-16 | Frances Engleheart | Mr Albert |
| 786 | *Rose and Crown* | 0-0-16 | Thos H Warren | Thomas Dell |
| 787 | messuage | 0-0-09 | " | John Andrews |
| 788 | messuage | 0-0-08 | Mrs | Newton |
| 796 | boathouse | 0-0-20 | R Tunstall | –– |
| 797 | boathouse | 0-0-22 | B Smith | –– |
| 799 | coachhouse | 0-0-23 | Thos H Warren | –– |
| 801 | 3 messuages | 0-1-08 | Nicholas Paxton | Mr Spilsbury |
| | | | " | Mary Cheshire |
| | | | " | Mr Thomas |

**KEW – east of Green**

| 804 | messuage | 0-0-16 | Thomas Fuller | James Clewley |
|---|---|---|---|---|
| 805 | shop & coachhouse | 0-0-12 | Thos H Warren | George Warren |
| 806 | messuage | 0-0-03 | " | John Haverfield |
| 807 | messuage | 0-0-03 | " | Thos Haverfield |
| 808 | messuage | 0-0-20 | " | George Warren |
| 809 | messuage | 0-0-05 | Wm Middleton | Thomas Robinson |
| 810 | messuage | 0-0-11 | " | John Pepper |
| 811 | messuage | 0-0-16 | " | Ann Engleheart |
| 812 | barn | 0-1-26 | Levett Blackbourne | –– |
| 824 | messuage | 0-1-38 | Wm Middleton | Edward Soundy |
| 825 | messuage | 0-0-21 | " | John Haverfield |

**KEW – along Richmond Road**

| 828 | messuage | 0-0-39 | J D Engleheart | J D Engleheart |
|---|---|---|---|---|
| 829 | messuage | 0-0-06 | " | late George Bone |
| 830 | messuage | 0-1-07 | " | Capt Thompson |
| 831 | messuage | 0-1-00 | " | Mrs Radford |
| 832 | 2 messuages | 0-0-08 | " | William Walker |
| | | | " | William Withers |
| 833 | messuage, stable, coachhouse | 0-0-10 | " | Sarah Simmons |
| 843 | messuage and barn | 7-2-37 | " | Mr Methold |
| 844 | 2 messuages | 0-1-00 | " | Kew Parish |
| | | | " | Mrs Edwards |
| 862 | messuage on **Brentford Ayt** | 2-3-24 | Henry West | Henry West |

# A Postscript to Palaces and Parks

When I drew the plan of Richmond Palace that figures on page 60 of *Palaces and Parks* (part 1), many of the dimensions of the outer buildings could be ascertained from Crown leases of buildings that survived the destruction of the 1650s. Other dimensions, for the Hall, Chapel, Fountain Court, etc, came from the Parliamentary Survey of 1649. But for the Privy Lodgings building, all there was to go on was the verbal description in the survey and the drawings by Wyngaerde, Hollar and the unknown artist of the Fitzwilliam painting. So the precise size, shape and location of the Privy Lodgings building remained somewhat conjectural. In the summer of 1997 a 'Time Team' excavation for Channel 4 Television attempted to find the outside walls of the building. (The programme was broadcast in January 1998.) They made some interesting discoveries, but it is now clear that none of their trenches was on the site of an outer wall of the building.[1]

Plate 58b
What has changed the picture is the chance discovery and the serendipitous identification of a drawing in the Medici archives in Florence.[2] This was published by the Canadian art historian, Dr Sabine Eiche, in *Apollo* magazine in November 1998.[3] It was at once clear when she consulted with me and showed me a photograph of the plan that this was a drawing made by Costantino de' Servi, probably soon after his arrival in Richmond in May 1611, to show Prince Henry a proposal for a completely new garden layout and for some alterations to the south face of the Privy Lodgings building. It included a detailed plan of the Privy Lodgings (as they would be after the alterations), a clear and marked indication of the former bridge over the moat dividing the Privy Lodgings from the buildings in Fountain Court, and a blocked-in (so only approximate) rectangle showing these Fountain Court buildings. There was some indication of a remaining section of garden galleries and of the outer court – and a scale in English feet.

A close comparison of the de' Servi plan with the existing drawings confirms that it was only on the south face of the building that he was planning any modification – and that was mainly in the form of the addition of two new wings and a loggia. There was some, but not much, alteration to the towers of the south face. Most of the details of towers, etc, fit closely with the drawings. It is therefore possible to accept some 9/10 of the building shown by de' Servi as depicting what stood on the ground in 1611.

The building was somewhat smaller and it was sited rather further to the west than previously believed. Its longer axis was parallel with rather than at right angles to the river.

Plate 59
When I first heard from Dr Eiche of her discovery I was working with Robert Cowie of the Museum of London Archaeological Service on the preparation of a detailed report on 'An Archaeological Survey of Richmond Palace, Surrey' – to be published in *Post Mediaeval Archaeology* in 2001. Dr Eiche was happy that we should include all her contribution – and that we should draw up a new plan of the Palace taking the de' Servi drawing into account as well as all the other evidence. That new plan, superimposed on the current Ordnance Survey plan, is reproduced here, with acknowledgements to Robert Cowie and his associates at the Museum of London Archaeological Service who worked with me in producing it[4] and of course to Sabine Eiche for her generosity in sharing her discovery ahead of its publication and for her continued interest in the Richmond site.

# *Glossary*

## 1 Measurements of length and land

| | |
|---|---|
| Acre | by statute the area contained by the length of a furlong and the breadth of a chain (640 acres = 1 square mile ). 'Acres' in the fields often varied from a half to one and a half times this size. |
| Carucate | the quantity of land considered ploughable by one ox team – normally four virgates. |
| Chain | one tenth of a furlong – 22 yards (from a surveyor's chain.) |
| Furlong | originally the length of a plough furrow – one-eighth of a mile (220 yards). Also used for a major division of a common field, notionally one furlong in width (compare shott). |
| Hide | originally a tax assessment on land; later virtually synonymous with a carucate. |
| Perch or Rod | one quarter of a chain's length – 5½ yards (but some times a rod of 6 yards length was used as a unit of measurement); also used as a measure of area – one perch or rod square. |
| Rood | an area of 40 perches or rods – one quarter of an acre. (N.B. occasionally 'yard' was also used in this sense.) |
| Shot(t) | a major division of a common field (from the length of a bowshot). |
| Virgate | the quantity of arable land considered tillable by one man – an amount which varied in different areas, but in Richmond was 20 acres. |

## 2 Land tenure

| | |
|---|---|
| Capital messuage | the main house of a tenement; later just a large messuage house. |
| Copyhold | land held from the lord of the manor, any transfer of which had to be effected by its 'surrender' to the lord for regrant. It was therefore recorded in the manor court rolls, and a 'copy' of the entry of the 'admission' of a new tenant served as the title deed. |
| Customary tenant | a tenant holding land in accordance with the customs tenant of the manor; in origin a villein, but later a copyholder. |
| Farm | the leasing of a property (or an office of profit) for a 'firm' (i.e. fixed) annual sum to a tenant or 'farmer' who was then entitled to whatever income he could make from the property or office. |
| Freehold | land held by a freeman, who could dispose of it freely within certain limits (e.g. the lord's licence might be needed for a long lease or for sale to an inhabitant of another manor). |
| Freeman | a tenant not tied to the manor, who owed homage to the lord but paid only a quit rent for his land. |
| Messuage | a house, with its immediately adjacent garden, yards, etc. |

Quit rent       an annual sum paid in quittance of any labour services.

Socage          Freehold

Tenement        the holding of a tenant; the normal 'whole tenement' was a virgate of arable land, an entitlement to the use of meadow (in Richmond notionally one acre) and a capital messuage.

Villein         a bond tenant, tied to his manor of birth, who owed the lord of the manor labour services for his landholding.

## 3 Money and taxation

Aid             a tax for some civil purpose.

Angel           ten shillings.

Crown           five shillings.

Fine            a sum of money paid to 'finish' some transaction, such as the purchase of property or of an office; later, a sum paid to 'finish' a prosecution, hence a financial penalty.

Knight's fee    the holding of land for which, originally, one knight should be provided to serve in the King's army when required. Later used as a unit of taxation (e.g. 2 marks per knight's fee).

£.s.d.          pounds, shillings, pence. 12 pence (d) = 1 shilling; 20 shillings (s) = 1 pound (£).

Mark            two-thirds of a pound (13s. 4d.).

Scutage         a tax for a military purpose.

## 4. Miscellaneous

Assart          a piece of woodland or waste cleared and converted into arable land.

Custumal        a statement of the manorial customs and the services owed by tenants.

Extent          a survey of the value of a manor and its individual tenancies.

Hawe            an enclosed piece of land, usually near to a house.

Headland        a strip of land at the end of a field in which the plough was turned, and which was later ploughed at right angles to the rest of the field.

Lease or leaze  meadow land.

Rout            a trap for fish in the form of a wheel.

Skout (scow)    a flat-bottomed boat.

Toft            a plot of land on which a building had previously stood.

Warren          an unfenced hunting ground (as distinct from an enclosed park); later a ground in which game, especially rabbits, were bred.

Weir            a trap for fish erected across a river.

# Bibliography

## I Original Documents

### i. **Public Record Office, Kew (PRO)**
The classes of documents to which reference has been made are:

| | | | |
|---|---|---|---|
| C | Chancery | 54 | Close rolls |
| | | 66 | Patent rolls |
| CP | Common Pleas | 25/2 | Feet of fines |
| CRES | Crown Estate | 2 | Leases |
| | | 5 | Manor Court rolls and books |
| | | 38 | Title deeds |
| E | Exchequer | 101 | King's Remembrancer – accounts various |
| | | 317 | Augmentation Office – parliamentary surveys |
| | | 318 | Augmentation Office – particulars for grants |
| | | 320 | Augmentation Office – particulars for sales |
| | | 364 | Pipe Office – foreign account rolls |
| | | 367 | Pipe Office – particulars for leases |
| LR | Land Revenue | 2 | Miscellaneous books and surveys |
| | | 3 | Manor Court rolls and books |
| | | 13 | Quit rolls |
| MPE, MPZ, MR | | – | Maps and plans |
| PROB | Probate Registry | 11 | Enrolments of wills |
| SC | Special Collections | 2 | Manor rolls |
| | | 6 | Ministers' accounts |
| | | 8 | Ancient petitions |
| | | 11 | Rentals and surveys |
| | | 12 | Rentals and surveys |
| SP | State Papers | – | (Volumes in chronological sequence) |

### ii. **British Library (BL)**

| | |
|---|---|
| Harleian charter 45H45 | Grant by Michael Belet |
| Add MSS 59899 | Works Accounts |

### iii. **Bodleian Library, Oxford**

| | |
|---|---|
| Dodsworth MSS 35 f10 | Exchange of Petersham with Chertsey Abbey |
| Laud MSS 723 | |

### iv. **Ashmolean Museum, Oxford**

| | |
|---|---|
| Large Vol. 4 ff 10a, 11a, 11c, 12a, 12b, 54 | Drawings of Richmond Palace by Antonis van Wyngaerde |

### v. **Surrey History Centre, Woking** (formerly Surrey County Record Office)

| | |
|---|---|
| 3/3/44 | Note about Ancram mortgage |
| 5/16 | Documents concerning Darrell estate, Richmond |
| 58/2 | Ham Manor Court rolls |
| 58/4 | Petersham Manor Court rolls |
| 2353/51/16/1 | Windeyarde Close |
| KS2/1/1 and PS3/1/1 | Petty Sessions Minute Books for the Hundreds of Kingston and Elmbridge |

QS5/10/2-5           Victuallers' recognizances 1785-1827
Kew Vestry documents
Land tax returns (microfilm copies)
vi. **Nottingham University Library**
Acc. 1325           Hildyard family papers
vii. **Richmond Public Library**, Local Studies Collection
Categories of material used (including printed material listed here for convenience) include:
     Richmond poor rate books 1726-1890
     Richmond Parish general meeting book 1597-1735
     Richmond select Vestry minute book 1614-1749
     Richmond general Vestry meeting minute book 1736-1767 (including Parish general meetings up to
         1749)
     Richmond Parish Trustees' general meeting minute books 1766-85
     Richmond Vestry meetings minute books 1785-1928
     Richmond Manor rental 1774
     Raynford terrier 1559 (typescript copy)
     F S Ellis, Recollections of Richmond (typescript)
     Topographical and subject files
     Collections of house and land sale catalogues
     Newspaper cuttings
     Street directories
     Maps
     Photographs
viii. **Hounslow Public Library**
Notes on Isleworth Ait
Enclosure award map of Isleworth 1818
Map of Parish of Isleworth by Thomas Warren 1848
ix. **Armytage family papers** (as communicated by Mr George Redmonds)
x. **Archivio di Stato, Florence**

## II Published Documents

i. **Records Commission**
Close rolls      *Rotuli litterarum clausarum in Turri Londinensis* (2v), ed. T.D. Hardy, 1833.
Patent rolls      *Calendarium rotulorum pat. in Turri Londinensis*, ed. T. Astle, 1802.
                  *Patent rolls*, ed. T.D. Hardy, 1835.
Pipe rolls      *Magnum rotulum scaccarii* (great roll of the Pipe) 31 Henry I, ed. Joseph Hunter,
                  1833.
                  *The great roll of the Pipe for 2, 3, 4, Henry II*, ed. Joseph Hunter, 1844.
                  *The great roll of the Pipe for 1 Richard I*, ed. Joseph Hunter, 1844.
                  *Rotulus cancellarii 3 John*, 1833.
*State Papers of the Reign of King Henry VIII*, 1831-52.
ii. **Public Record Office Calendars** etc (showing abbreviations used in footnotes)
*CCR*             *Calendar of Close Rolls*
*CChR*            *Calendar of Charter Rolls*
*CFR*              *Calendar of Fine Rolls*
*CIPM*            *Calendar of Inquisitions, Post-Mortem*
*CLPFD*          *Calendar of Letters and Papers, Foreign and Domestic, Henry VIII*
*CPR*              *Calendar of Patent Rolls*
*CSP Dom*       *Calendar of State Papers, Domestic*
*CSP (Venetian)*   *Calendar of State Papers (Venetian)*
*Cal Pap R*       *Calendar of Papal Registers*
*Curia Regis Rolls*
*Privy Council Acts, Proceedings*
iii. **Domesday Book**
*Surrey*, trans Sara Wood, ed. John Morris, Phillimore, Chichester, 1975.

*Middlesex*, trans Sara Wood, ed. John Morris, Phillimore, Chichester, 1975.

iv. **Historical Manuscripts Commission**

*Calendar of Portland MSS* (10v), HMSO, 1891-1931.

v. **Pipe roll Society** (one volume for each year, issued from 1884 onwards)

Pipe Rolls for 5-34 Henry II

Pipe Rolls for 2-10 Richard I

Pipe Rolls for 1-17 John

*Calendar of Exchequer Memorandum Rolls 1326-27*

vi. **Rolls Series**

No. 99 *The Red book of the Exchequer* (3v), ed. H Hall, 1896.

vii. **Surrey Archaeological Collections**

Vol. 5 (1871) includes Parliamentary Survey of Richmond Palace and Manor (1649).

Vol. 11 includes marriage (and other) licences issued by the Surrey Commissary Court.

Extra Vol. 1 (1894) – *Surrey Feet of Fines in the Public Record Office*

[Vols. 11, 12, 23, 24 and 35 include wills of Richmond people.]

viii. **Surrey Record Society**

Vol. 4: Nos. 3 (1915), 7 (1916) ⎫ *Surrey wills 1595-1608*
15 (1920), Vol. 5: No. 17 (1922) ⎭

Vol. 11: Nos. 18 (1922) and 33 (1932)    *Surrey taxation returns*

Vol. 16: Nos. 35, 36 and 39 (1934-38)    *Surrey quarter session records 1658-1666*

Vol. 17: Nos. 40 and 41 (1940)    *Surrey Hearth Tax returns 1664*

Vol. 21: Nos. 38 (1937) and 48 (1954)    *Manor Court rolls of Chertsey Abbey 1328-1347*

Vol. 34: (1994)    *Parish and Parson in 18th-century Surrey; Replies to Bishop's Visitations*

ix. **Miscellaneous published documents**

*Book of Fees (Testa de Nevill)*, PRO, HMSO London 1920-23

*Early Charters of St Paul's*, Camden Society, 3rd series, Vol. 58, 1939

*Codex Diplomaticus*, ed. J.M. Kemble , London, 1839-48

*English Historical Documents*, Vol. 1, *c.*500-1042, ed. Dorothy Whitelock, Eyre and Spottiswood, London, 1955

*The Records of Merton Priory*, ed. Alfred Heales, H. Frowde, London, 1898

*Compotus Rolls of the Obedientaries of St Swithin's Priory, Winchester*, Hampshire Record Society, 1892

*Winchester Cathedral Cartulary*, ed. A.W. Goodman,Winchester, 1927

*Diocese of Winchester, Woodlock Register*, Canterbury and York Society, 1940-1

*Parish Registers of Richmond* (2v), ed. J. Challenor Smith, Surrey Parish Register Society, 1903-5

*Documents relating to the Office of Revels in the Time of Queen Elizabeth*, ed. A. Feuillerat, Louvain, 1908

## III  *Published books – Contemporary diaries, letters, etc.*

Coke, Lady Mary, *Letters and Journals of Lady Mary Coke* (4v), ed. J.A. Home, 1889-96 (reprint 1970)

Dee, Dr John, *Privat Diary*, Camden Society (No. 19), London, 1842

Duppa, Rt Rev Brian, *The Correspondence of Bishop Brian Duppa with Sir Justinian Isham*, Northamptonshire Record Society, Vol. 17, 1955

Garrick, David, *Letters of David Garrick*, ed. D.M. Little and C.M. Kahrl, Oxford University Press (3 vols), 1963

Greville, R.F., *The Diaries of Robert Fulke Greville*, ed. E.M. Bladen, John Lane, London, 1930

Macky, John, *A Journey through England* (1714), 4th edition, John Hooke, London, 1724

Moritz, Carl Philip, *Journeys of a German in England in 1782*, trans. and ed. Reginald Nettel, Jonathan Cape, London, 1965

Papendiek, Mrs, *Court and Private Life in the Time of Queen Charlotte* (2v), ed. V.D. Broughton, R. Bentley and Son, London, 1887

Selwyn, George, *George Selwyn, his letters and his Life*, ed. E.S. Roscoe and H. Clergue, T. Fisher Unwin, London, 1899

Wakefield, Rev. Gilbert, *Memoirs of the Life of Gilbert Wakefield, written by Himself*, J. Johnson, London, 1804

Walpole, Horace, *Horace Walpole's Correspondence* (48v), ed. W.S. Lewis, Yale University Press, 1937-80
Whitlocke, Sir James, *Liber Familicus*, Camden Society (No. 70), London, 1858

## IV  *Published Books – on the history of Richmond and Kew – a selection relevant to this book (for a fuller list, see Palaces and Parks of Richmond and Kew)*

Bell, Mrs Arthur G., *The Royal Manor of Richmond with Petersham, Ham and Kew*, George Bell, London, 1907
Bingham, Frederick, *A Celebrated Old Playhouse: the History of Richmond Theatre*, Henry Vickers, London, 1886
Blomfield, David, *The Story of Kew*, Leybourne Publications, Kew, 1992
Blomfield, David, *Kew Past*, Phillimore, Chichester, 1994
Burt, Charles, *The Richmond Vestry: Notes of its History and Operations from 1614 to 1890*, Darnill, Richmond, 1890
Cassidy, George E., *Kew As It Was*, Hendon Publishing Co, Nelson, Lancs, 1978
Cave, Estella, Lady, *Memories of Old Richmond*, John Murray, London, 1922
Chancellor, E. Beresford, *The History and Antiquities of Richmond, Kew, Petersham, Ham, etc.*, Hiscoke, Richmond, 1894
Cloake, John, *The Growth of Richmond*, Richmond Society History Section 1982; new edition, Richmond Local History Society, 1990
Cloake, John, *Richmond's Great Monastery, the Charterhouse of Jesus of Bethlehem of Shene*, Richmond Local History Society, 1990
Cloake, John, *Richmond Past*, Historical Publications Ltd, London, 1991
Cloake, John, *Royal Bounty, the Richmond Parish Lands Charity 1786-1991*, Trustees of the Richmond Parish Lands Charity, Richmond, 1992
Cloake, John, '*Prospects about Richmond': mid-18th Century Drawings and Prints by Augustin Heckel*, exhibition catalogue for Museum of Richmond, 1994
Cloake, John, *Palaces and Parks of Richmond and Kew* (2v), Phillimore, Chichester, 1995 and 1996
Cloake, John (with Graham Fletcher and Shelley Churchman), *Richmond Past and Present*, Sutton Publishing, Stroud, 1999
Courlander, Kathleen, *Richmond*, Batsford, London, 1953
Crisp, Richard, *Richard and its Inhabitants from the Olden Times*, Sampson Low, London, 1866
Cundall, H.N., *Bygone Richmond*, John Lane, London, 1925
Desmond, Ray, *Kew, the History of the Royal Botanic Gardens*, Harvill Press and R.B.G., Kew, 1995
Dunbar, Janet, *A Prospect of Richmond*, Harrap, London, 1966 (revised edition White Lion Publishers, London 1973)
Essen, Richard, *Richmond and Kew*, Archive Photographic Series, Chalford Publishing Co, 1995
Evans, John, *Richmond and its Vicinity*, Darnill, Richmond, 1824
Garnett, Richard, *Richmond on the Thames*, Sealey. London, 1896
Gascoigne, Bamber, *Images of Richmond*, St Helena Press, Richmond, 1978
Gascoyne, Somers T., *Recollections of Richmond, its Institutions, and their Development*, F.W. Dimbleby, Richmond, 1898
Goldney, S., *Kew, Our Village and its Associations*, privately published, 1892
Hiscoke & Son, *Richmond Notes* (a monthly magazine), March 1863-September 1868, Hiscoke & Son, Richmond
Hofland, Barbara, *Richmond and its Surrounding Scenery*, W.B. Cooke, London, 1832
Hughes, Noel, *The Richmond Catholic Mission 1791-1826*, privately published, Richmond, 1991.
Lysons, Rev. Daniel, *The Environs of London, Vol. 1, the County of Surrey*, T. Cadell, London, 1792
Manning, Rev. Owen, and Bray, William, *The History and Antiquities of the County of Surrey* (3v), White, Cochrane, London, 1804-14
Nelson, Sir Thomas J, *Richmond Park, Extracts from the Records of Parliament and of the Corporation of London*, Blades, London, 1883.
Piper, A.C., *History of Richmond Parish Church*, privately published, 1947
Richmond Local History Society (ed. John Cloake), *Richmond in Old Photographs*, Alan Sutton, Stroud, 1990

Richmond Society History Section, *Richmond, Surrey, As It Was*, Hendon Publishing Co., Nelson, Lancs, 1976

Sherwood, Tim, *The Railways of Richmond upon Thames*, Forge Books, Wokingham, 1991

Simpson, Edwin, *The History of Kew*, privately published, 1849

Warren, Charles D., *History of St Peter's Church, Petersham*, Sidgwick & Jackson, London, 1938

Way, Thomas R., and Chapman, Frederick, *Architectural Remains of Richmond, Twickenham, Kew, Petersham and Mortlake*, John Lane, London, 1900

Wright, Mariateresa, *Vintage Richmond*, Hendon Publishing Company, Nelson, Lancs, 1978

## V Published Books – General Secondary Sources

Bennett, H.S., *Life on the English Manor 1150-1400*, Cambridge University Press, 1937

Burton, Isabel, *The Life of Captain Sir Richard F. Burton* (2v), Chapman & Hall, London, 1893

Clark, Peter, *The English Alehouse, a Social History 1200-1830*, Longmans, London, 1982

Colvin, Howard M. (gen. ed.), *The History of the King's Works* (6v), HMSO, London, 1963-82

Colvin, Howard M., *Biographical Dictionary of British Architects 1600-1840*, John Murray, London, 1978

Dugdale, Sir William, *Monasticon Anglicanum* (orig pub 1655-73) (6v in 8), ed. Henry Ellis *et al.*, London, 1817-30

Harris, John, *The Artist and the Country House*, Sotheby Parke Bernet, London, 1979

Harvey, P.D.A., *The Peasant Land Market in Mediaeval England*, Clarendon Press, Oxford, 1984

Hastings, Michael, *Sir Richard Burton*, Hodder & Stoughton, London, 1978

Holdsworth, W.S., *History of English Law* (1903), 7th ed., 1956

Holinshed, Raphael, *Chronicles of Englande, Scotlande and Irelande* (2v), London, 1577

Pinto, V. de S., *Peter Sterry, Platonist and Puritan*, Cambridge University Press, 1934

Rosenfeld, Sybil, *Strolling Players and Drama in the Provinces 1660-1765*, Cambridge University Press, 1939

Roth, Cecil, *History of the Great Synagogue*, Edward Goldston, London, 1950

Schenk, W., *Reginald Pole, Cardinal of England*, Longmans Green, London, 1950

Stow, John, *The Annales or General Chronicle of England* (1592), originally published as *Chronicles* 1580, as *Annales* 1592, revised edition R. Meighen, London, 1631

Stroud, Dorothy, *Capability Brown*, 1950 (revised edition Faber, London, 1975)

Thacker, F.S., *The Thames Highway* (2v), 1914 (new edition David & Charles, 1968)

Urwin, Alan, *Twicknam Park*, privately published, 1965

Webb, Sidney and Beatrice, *The History of Liquor Licensing in England, principally from 1700 to 1830*, Longmans Green, London, 1903

West, John, *Village Records*, Phillimore, Chichester, 1977

## VI Articles – to which reference is made in the text or which are of particular relevance to the subject of this book.

Barkas, Dr. A.A., 'Our Ancient Springs', *Richmond & Twickenham Times*, 3 April 1920

Berryman, Ron, 'The Prospect of Richmond Revisited', *Richmond History*, No. 19, 1998

Cloake, John, 'The Development of the Area between Richmond Hill and the River', *Richmond History*, No. 9, 1988, and No. 10, 1989

Cloake, John, 'The Curious Story of the Church Estate', *Richmond History*, No. 13, 1992

Cloake, John, 'Shene in 1314', *Richmond History*, No. 16, 1995

Cloake, John, 'Public Houses in Richmond. 1790-1880', *Richmond History*, No. 20, 1999

Cloake, John, 'The Plan of Richmond Palace', *Richmond History*, No. 20, 1999

Cloake, John, and Cowie, Robert, 'An Archaeological Survey of Richmond Palace, Surrey', *Post-Medieval Archaeology*, 2001

Daiches-Dubens, Rachel, 'Eighteenth Century Anglo-Jewry in and about Richmond, Surrey, *Jewish Historical Society of England, Transactions 1953-55*, Vol. 18, 1958

Eiche, Sabine, 'Prince Henry's Richmond: the Project by Costantino de' Servi', *Apollo*, November 1998

Filson, Judith, 'French Refugees in Richmond, 1789-1815', *Richmond History*, No. 7, 1986

Green, James, 'Charles Selwyn of Richmond, 1689-1749', *Richmond History*, No. 13, 1992

Greenstreet, Anthony, 'Sir Solomon de Medina of Richmond', *Richmond History*, No. 19, 1998

Hertslet, Sir Edward, 'Recollections of Richmond', 1897
Hussey, Christopher, 'Richmond Palace, Surrey', *Country Life*, 14 and 21 April 1944
Hussey, Christopher, 'Richmond Green, Surrey', *Country Life*, 5 and 12 May 1944
Hussey, Christopher, 'Asgill House, Richmond, Surrey', *Country Life*, 9 June 1944
Matar, N.I., 'Alone in our Eden: a Puritan Utopia in Restoration England', *The Seventeenth Century*, Vol. 2, No. 2, 1987
Price, Roy, 'Queensberry House', *Richmond History*, No. 13, 1992

## VII  *Periodicals – to which reference is made in the text of the book*

*The Post Boy*, 1696
*The Spectator*, 1711
*St James's Post* and *St James's Evening Post*, 1718
*Weekly Journal* and *Reed's Weekly Journal*, 1719
*The Daily Post*, 1721-2
*The Craftsman*, 1730
*The Daily Journal*, 1730
*St James's Chronicle*, 1765-7
*Richmond and Twickenham Times* (pub. 1873-date)
*Richmond Herald* (pub. 1885-1976)

# Notes

## 1 Shene: Setting the Scene, pp.1-5

[1] *English Historical Documents I c.500-1042*, ed. Dorothy Whitelock, Eyre & Spottiswood, 1955, no. 106, pp.509-11. The will is recorded in a 14th-century cartulary of Bury St Edmunds in the Cambridge University Library MS Ff 2.33.

[2] *Domesday Book: Surrey*, ed. John Morris and Sara Wood, Phillimore, 1975, Section 22.4.

[3] LR3/101/2, m8 and LR3/101/4, m3verso.

## 2 Shene in the Thirteenth Century, pp.6-12

[1] *Curia Regis Rolls* I, p.153 (Hilary term 1 John, m 12).

[2] *Ibid.* III, p.99 (Hilary term 5 John, m 2).

[3] BL Harl Charter 45H45.

[4] *Curia Regis Rolls* VII, p.168 (Trinity term, 16 John, m 8d).

[5] *Book of Fees*, p.1153.

[6] Dugdale, *Monasticon*, II, p.543.

[7] A Heales, *Records of Merton Priory*, Appx XLIX, p.xxxi.

[8] *Curia Regis Rolls* VIII, p.352 (Easter term 4 Henry III, m 24).

[9] CP2/25/2(150) (Ped Fin Surrey, Easter term 14 Henry III).

[10] *Book of Fees*, p.1237 (LTR Rolls 1/11, II, 88-92).

[11] CP2/25, no. 297(90) (Ped Fin Cos Divers, Mich 37/38 Henry III).

[12] CP2/25/283/17 (Trinity term 54 Henry III, no. 471).

[13] *Palaces and Parks* I, p.13; *see also* CPR 1272-81, p.357.

[14] *C Ch R*, p.221 (Cart 8 Edw I, n 72).

[15] *CIPM* III, p.47 (no. 65); (C133/63).

[16] *CPR* 1292-1301, pp.188, 418.

[17] *CIPM* IV, p.11, no. 26.

[18] *CPR* 1272-81, p.357 (Pat 8 Edward I, m 26).

[19] *CPR* 1301-1307, p.32.

[20] *Chancery Miscellany* (C260/15, no. 51).

[21] *CPR* 1301-1307, p.329.

[22] *Woodlock Register* I, pp.495-6, 504, 548, 554.

[23] Ped. Fin. Surrey, 2 Edward II, nos 21a and 37 (CP2/25/227/30).

## 3 Sheen in 1314, pp.13-22

[1] *CFR* 1307-19, p.184.

[2] SC11/638.

[3] The story of the Turbeville manor is given in Manning and Bray, *History of Surrey* III, pp.16-18.

[4] *Curia Regis Rolls* VIII, 1219-20, Roll 72 m 24 (p 352).

## 4 The Manorial Courts and Customs, pp.23-8

[1] SC2/205/5.

[2] LR3/101/1.

[3] There are the original rolls up to 1792, also books into which the rolls were copied covering 1603-1792, all in the LR3 series. Court rolls from 1793 to 1937 and court books from 1793 to 1935 are in the CRES5 series. Except for the Commonwealth period rolls are all in Latin until the 1720s, but those for 1603-89 were copied into an indexed book, in summarised English translation, in the 18th century (LR3/71). See Appendix 6.

[4] Surrey RO 2353/51/16/1.

[5] LR3/71, p.122.

[6] These are quoted from an undated reprint probably published in the 1860s.

[7] Surrey RO 58/2/1/6.

[8] E320 R25 (published in *Surrey Archaeological Collections* V, 1871, pp.98-99).

## 5 The Medieval Fisheries, pp.29-34

[1] F S Thacker, *The Thames Highway*, 1914 (reprint 1968), I, p.12.

[2] *Domesday Book, Middlesex*, Phillimore, 1975, Sections 3, 12 and 12.1 and *Domesday Book, Surrey*, Phillimore, 1975, Sections 1.8, 2.3, 8.14 and 22.4.

[3] Thacker, *op. cit.*, pp.14-15.

[4] *Ibid.*, p.24.

[5] *Ibid.*, p.25 (quoting City of London Letter Book F).

[6] *CChR* IV, 1327-41, 472.

[7] *Pipe Roll*, 11 Henry II (1164-65), p.111, and subsequent years (to 29 Henry II).

[8] *Curia Regis Rolls* XV, pp.13 and 190; *Early Charters of St Paul's*, Camden Society 3rd Series, LVIII, 1939, pp.259-62, quoting Fines Mx Henry III, Lib A, f 35a (No. 322).

[9] *Record Commission Calendar of Close Rolls* IV, pp.293, 392-93 (Rot Claus 25 Henry III, m 11 and 26 Henry III, m 9).

[10] SC8/128, No. 6379.

[11] *CChR* IV 1327-41, 472.

[12] Corporation of London Letter Book H.

[13] Bodleian Lib MS Laud 723, f 87v, quoted in Heales, *Merton Records*, p.285.

[14] *Ibid.*, quoted in Heales *op. cit.*, p.286.

[15] City of London archives: book Dunthorn, f 331, quoted in Heales, *op cit*, p.295.

[16] *Compotus Rolls of the Obedientiaries of St Swithin's Priory, Winchester*, Hampshire Record Society, p.253 (Rolls of the Hordarians).

[17] *Winchester Cathedral Cartulary*, pp.11 and 19, nos 25 and 45; *Calendar of Papal Registers* I, 1198-1304, pp.21, 201.

[18] J M Kemble, *Codex Diplomaticus* VI, pp.134-36.

[19] *Winchester Cathedral Cartulary*, p.155, and *Compotus Rolls*, pp.253-4.

[20] *Compotus Rolls*, p.254.

[21] Cart 3 & 4 Henry V, m 8 (text in Dugdale's *Monasticon* VI, pp.31-32).

[22] SC6/Hen VIII/3464, m 43.

23 Pat 4 Henry V, m 22.
24 LR3/101/1, mm 12, 13, 14.
25 CPR 1408-13, p.351.
26 CCR V, 1341-1417, pp.334, 348, 350.
27 CPR 1408-13, p.239.
28 SC8/185, No. 9235 (the original is in French).
29 Thacker, op. cit., pp.32-33..
30 Ibid., pp.47-49
31 Ibid., p.57.
32 Holinshed, Chronicle (1587 edition), II, p.46.
33 Prospects about Richmond, catalogue (by J. Cloake) of an exhibition of Heckel's drawings and prints at the Museum of Richmond, October 1993-February 1994, nos. 34 and 35.

## 6 The Black Death, pp.35-42

1 Holinshed, Chronicles of England, Scotland and Ireland, 1577, p.855.
2 SC6/1014/2-9.
3 Calendar of Memorandum Rolls (Exchequer) 1326-27 (in Pipe Roll series), p.331.
4 Surrey Taxation Returns, Surrey Record Society XVIII (1922) and XXXIII (1932), quoting Exchequer, KR Subsidies 184/4, m 3, m 22 (Shene).
5 Ibid.
6 SC2/205/5.
7 LR3/101/1, m 2.
8 CPR 1350-54, p.519.
9 CPR 1354-58, p.118.
10 Ibid., p.375.
11 Palaces and Parks, chapter 2.
12 Stow's Annales for a Chronicle of England, 1615 edition, p.305.
13 E364/58, rot G.
14 CPR 1436-41, p.145; E101/503/9.
15 E101/494/28, m-4. See Alan Urwin, Twicknam Park, 1965, pp.15-17.
16 Bodleian Library, Dodsworth MSS, vol. 35, f 10. The whole story is given in Manning and Bray, History of Surrey III, pp.213-14.
17 CCR, Henry V, I, p.217. See J. Cloake, 'The Early History of Ham' in Richmond History, no. 12 (1991), p.7.

## 7 The Village in the Fifteenth and Sixteenth Centuries, pp.43-50

1 Privy Council Proceedings VI, p.32.
2 CPR1461-67, p.513 (Pat 6 Edward IV, i, m17).
3 CChR V, pp.469 and 479, and CPR1441-46, p.56.
4 CPR 1476-85, p.156.
5 LR3/101/2, m 8.
6 Surrey Wills, 1484-90 (Surrey Record Soc., v5, No. 17 - 1922), p.55.
7 Ibid., p.82.
8 Br Lib, Add MS59899, pp.68v and 77.
9 A. Heales, The Records of Merton Priory (1898), App LVIII, p.xxxiv.
10 Curia Regis Rolls Calendar, VIII, p.352.
11 Heales, op. cit., App LXVI*, p.xl.
12 Ped. Fin. Surrey, Hilary term 42 Henry III, No. 17 (105).
13 Heales, op. cit., pp.260-263, quoting Dioc. Register, Wykeham, ii, pt 3, f 137a.
14 J Cloake, 'The Curious Story of the Church Estate', in Richmond History, No. 13 (1992), pp.2-16.
15 CSP/Venetian VI, i, p.107, no. 132.
16 Privy purse expenses of King Henry VIII, 25 May 1530

(CLPFD. V, p.750)
17 F S Thacker, The Thames Highway, II, p.491.
18 CLPFD Henry VIII, III, p.49, no. 152.
19 John Dee, Privat Diary (Camden Society no. 19 — 1842).
20 CPR 1441-46, p.159.
21 Augmentation office roll, 32 Henry VIII.
22 CPR 1441-46, p.145.
23 CPR 1476-85, p.171.
24 Recorded in grant to Vincent, see note 25.
25 CLPFD Henry VIII, X, p.80.
26 E310/25/139/2, f 27.
27 E310/25/141, f 9.
28 CSPDom 1591-94, p.495.
29 A. Feuillerat, The Office of Revels Documents (1908), p.298.
30 LR3/101/6, m 10.
31 LR3/101/6, m 14.
32 The Richmond Public Library local studies collection has a typescript transliteration of the Raynford terrier, with no indication of origin. It was probably made by someone with the initials W.J.M. in 1907 and bears a note, 'Read by J. Challenor Smith June 1908'. It contains many evident misreadings of names (some corrected by Smith). It is clear that the last section was missing from the document from which it was copied. I have so far been unable to identify or locate that original document, but I have no doubt whatever as to its existence in 1907 and as to the essential accuracy of the copy.
33 Respectively at: LR3/101/2, m 20; C82/454, m 1; LR3/101/6, m 25 verso; LR3/101/5, m 8; LR3/101/6, m 24.

## 8 Richmond and Kew in 1603, pp.51-84

1 CPR 1436-41, p.128.
2 E317 Surrey 46 (SAC v, pp.76-85).
3 LR2/190, pp.100-2.
4 E318/2026.
5 Privy Council Acts, III, p.56.
6 CPR 1550-53, p.305.
7 E310/25/140, p.10.
8 CRES38/1765.
9 CPR 1461-67, p.513.
10 E310/140.
11 LR2/197, p.96.
12 PCC-94 Capell.
13 E317 Surrey 46.
14 Surrey Record Office (now History Centre) 2353/51/16/1.

## 9 The Fields in 1620, pp.87-110

1 LR2/203, pp.146 and ff. The terrier is undated, but its date can be deduced from a comparison of the owners listed with the transfers of land recorded in the manor rolls.
2 LR3/71, p.115.
3 LR3/101/1, m 2.
4 LR3/101/5, m 4v.
5 LR3/101/5, m 8 and LR3/101/6, m 14, 35v.
6 LR3/101/6, m 14.
7 LR3/101/2, m 5.
8 LR3/101/6, m 5.
9 Richmond Parish Meeting Book (in Local Studies Collection, Richmond Public Library), note at beginning.
10 LR3/101/4, m 6v and CPR 1555-57, p.186. (See Palaces and Parks I, pp.171-172.)

11 The extracts from the Chertsey Abbey Court Rolls, published by the Surrey Record Soviety (Vol. 21), Nos. 38 (1937) and 48 (1954), covering the years 1328-1347, show how fragmented the Petersham holdings were.

12 Sir James Whitelocke, *Liber Familicus*, Camden Society 1858, pp.20-21.

13 PCC Wingfield 29, published in *Surrey Archaeological Collections*, vol. 24.

14 Will of Sir George Wright, PCC 7 Byrde (PROB:11/143).

15 Whitelocke, *op. cit.*, p.12.

## 10 Inns and Taverns in Richmond in the Sixteenth and Seventeenth Centuries, pp.111-18

1 *CSP Dom, Charles I*, Vol. 7, 1634-35, p.36.

2 Cundall, *Bygone Richmond*, pp.62-63, quoting Lansdowne MSS.

3 *CLPFD Henry VIII*, Vol. 3, 1519-23, pt. i, p.344, no. 932.

4 LR3/101/4 m.2 and LR3/101/6m.36v.

5 E351/3216.

6 LR3/101/6m.6.

7 LR3/101/4m.6v.

8 LR3/71 pp.174 and 186.

9 Beresford Chancellor, *History and Antiquities of Richmond ...*, pp.175-6.

10 This, and all further references to hearths in this chapter, are taken from *Surrey Hearth Tax 1664* (ed. C.A.F. Meekings), Surrey Record Society, Vol. 17 (1940).

11 Rate books.

12 Rate books and licensing records.

13 LR3/101/5m.8.

14 LR3/101/6m.12.

15 LR3/71, p.131.

16 LR3/79, p.297.

17 LR3/80, p.252.

18 LR3/81, p.77 and LR3/84, p.48.

19 LR3/101/6m.17.

20 Richmond Vestry minute book, 27 Aug. 1626.

21 LR3/71, pp.273 and 307.

22 LR3/101/6m.32.

23 LR3/71, p.195.

24 LR3/71, p.202.

25 LR3/71, p.2.

26 LR3/71, p.429.

27 LR3/71, p.41.

28 LR3/71, p.195.

29 LR3/71, p.59.

30 LR3/71, p.288.

31 LR3/71, p.349.

32 LR3/71, p.80.

33 *ibid*.

34 LR3/71, p.216.

35 LR3/71, p.240.

36 LR3/71, p.322.

37 LR3/71, p.102.

38 LR3/79, p.241.

39 LR3/95, p.40.

40 Licensing records and LR3/84, p.138 (22 Apr 1731).

41 Land tax returns.

42 LR3/71, p.107.

43 LR3/71, p.303.

44 LR3/71, p.129, etc to LR3/71, p.195.

45 LR3/71, p.187.

46 LR3/71, p.139.

47 LR3/71, p.220.

48 Parish Registers.

49 LR3/71, p.344.

50 LR3/71, p.230.

51 Licensing records.

52 LR3/71, pp.257-8.

53 LR3/71, pp.203 and 287.

54 LR3/71, p.273.

55 LR3/79, p.306.

56 LR3/95, p.109.

57 LR3/71, p.322.

58 Land tax returns.

59 LR3/71, p.359.

60 LR3/84, p.2.

61 LR3/71, pp.278 and 362.

62 LR3/71, p.302.

63 LR3/71, p.346.

64 LR3/71, p.612 (1683) — and LR3/79, p.38.

65 LR3/71, p.374.

66 LR3/80, p.117.

67 Licensing records.

68 Ratebooks.

69 LR3/71, p.327.

70 LR3/71, p.404.

71 Licensing records.

72 CRES5/326.

73 LR3/71, p.576.

74 LR3/82, p.131.

75 LR3/79, p.11.

76 Street Directories.

77 CRES5/343, p.62.

78 LR3/79, pp.102 and 188.

79 LR3/79, pp.195 and 198-9.

80 LR3/80, pp.18-19.

81 Parish registers.

82 Licensing records; LR3/84, p.50; and LR3/87, p.65.

83 LR3/85, p.92.

84 LR3/88, p.145.

85 CSP Dom, Anne 1702-3, p.82.

86 Licensing records.

87 LR3/94, pp.49-51; LR2/226, p.166 ff (Surrey)

88 Evans, *Richmond and its Vicinity* (1824), p.93.

89 Ratebooks — increase in value.

90 Sale catalogue (Richmond Public Library — house sales Vol. 5).

91 LR3/79, p.309.

92 LR3/80, p.123.

93 LR2/226, pp.166 ff.

94 According to Edward Casaubon's pioneer work in 1986 on the Richmond licensing records, to which I am greatly indebted, there was some reference in 1717 to Edward Berkley's being William Hickey's tenant at the *Bull Head* alehouse. I have not been able to identify this reference.

95 LR2/226, pp.166 ff.

96 LR3/71, p.540; John Gardiner bur 19 Apr. 1722 (parish registers)

97 Land tax returns.

## 11 Where did all the Islands Go?, pp.119-30

1 LR3/101/1, m2v.

2 LR3/101/5, m4v.

3 LR3/71, p.215.

4 E317 Surrey 45.

5 Petersham Manor Court Book, 7 August 1781.

6 LR3/101/2, m25v.

7 LR3/101/4, m13.
8 LR3/71, p.379.
9 LR3/71, p.42.
10 CRES5/325, pp.400-1.
11 LR3/71, p.37.
12 LR3/71, p.230.
13 LR3/101/6, m36v.
14 LR3/71, p.60.
15 *CPR* 1313-1317, p.514.
16 LR3/101/4, m13.
17 LR3/71, p.12.
18 LR3/101/6 m2.
19 LR3/101/6, m27.
20 LR3/71, p.422.
21 LR3/86, p.77.
22 LR3/88, pp.64-67.
23 LR3/71, p.105.
24 LR3/89, p.145.
25 Thacker, *The Thames Highway*, II, p.485.
26 CRES5/329.
27 Richmond Vestry Minute Book I, pp.202, 218 and 274.
28 LR3/71, p.100.
29 e.g. LR3/71, p.417; LR3/86, p.108.
30 LR3/71, p.100.
31 e.g. LR3/88, p.50.
32 LR3/71, p.95.
33 LR3/71, p.100.
34 LR3/71, p.326.
35 LR3/71, p.329.
36 LR3/88, p.115; LR3/93, pp.98-99.
37 LR3/93, pp.98-99.
38 LR3/86, p.108; LR3/88, p.115; LR3/93, pp.98-99.
39 CRES5/328, p.245.
40 CRES5/332, p.286.
41 CRES5/333, p.24.
42 Rental of manor of Richmond 1774 in Richmond Public Library, local studies collection.
43 CRES5/326, p.160.
44 Richmond manor records in LR3 and CRES5 series. 1922 sale is at CRES5/345, p.49.
45 Report by Adams, Thompson and Fry, consultants [in Hounslow Public Library].
46 Notes on the History of Isleworth Ait published by Hounslow Public Library.
47 CRES5/88 and 89.
48 Hounslow Public Library.
49 Hounslow Public Library.
50 CRES5/333, p.24.
51 LR3/101/1, m 11.
52 LR3/101/4, m7v.
53 LR3/101/4, m8.
54 LR3/101/4, m15.
55 LR3/101/2, m 5.
56 LR3/101/2, m 7.
57 LR3/101/2, m 18.
58 LR3/101/3, m 30.
59 LR3/101/1, m 12.
60 LR3/101/1, m 13.
61 LR3/101/6, m 14.
62 LR3/71, p.224.
63 LR3/71, p.254.
64 LR3/81, pp.124-5.
65 LR3/92, p.79.
66 CRES5/329, p.291.
67 LR3/71, p.3.
68 LR3/85, p.142.

69 LR3/71, p.76.
70 LR3/71, p.225.
71 Richmond licensing records at SyRO; and cf LR3/85, p.142.
72 LR3/87, p.30; CRES38/1793; licensing records.
73 CRES5/325, p.62; CRES38/1793; licensing records.
74 CRES5/327, pp.261, 263.
75 Title deeds at CRES38/1774.
76 Title deeds at CRES38/1793.
77 *ibid*.
78 CRES5/335, p.459.
79 CRES38/1793.

## 12 Nibbling Away at the Common Wastes, pp.131-45

1 *CPR* 1461-67, p.513 (Pat6 Ed IV pt 1, m.17).

## 13 Richmond in 1664: The Hearth Tax Returns as a Street Directory, pp.146-210

1 E179/188/481.

## 15 Richmond Trades in the Seventeenth and Eighteenth Centuries, pp.221-37

1 Calendar of Assize Records, Surrey — Elizabeth I.
2 Surrey Record Society, Vol 16, Nos. 35 (1934) for 1659-61, 36 (1935) for 1661-63, and 39 (1938) for 1663-66, and Surrey Record Publications, Vol. 9 (1951) for 1666-68.
3 *Kingston on Thames Apprenticeships 1563-1713*, Surrey Record Society, Vol. 28 (1974), and *Surrey Apprenticeships 1711-1731*, Surrey Record Society, Vol. 10, no.30 (1929).
4 The registers up to 1780 were published (in two volumes) by the Surrey Parish Register Society (1903 and 1905).

## 16 Richmond Hostelries in the Eighteenth Century, pp.238-54

1 Petty Sessions Minute Books for the Hundred of Kingston and Elmbridge (at the Surrey County Record office (now History Centre): 1723-1751 (KS2/1/1) — 1750 and 51 are missing; 1752-1794 (PS3/1/1) — 1752, 54-5, 57-9, 61-2 and 66-8 are missing; Victuallers' Recognizances 1785-1827 (QS5/10/2 to 5). There are no further licensing records surviving until 1873.
2 Richmond Poor Rate Books are in the Richmond Public Library, Local Studies Collection. Surviving are 1726-65, 1768-71, 1780, and then every 10th year to 1890. (There is also an assessment book dated 1838.)
3 Copy in Richmond Public Library Local Studies Collection.
4 Copies on microfilm at Surrey History Centre.
5 LR2/226 pp.166 ff (see Appendix 9).
6 Correspondence of Horace Walpole (Yale edition), Vol. 20, p.63.
7 Hiscoke and Son's *Richmond Notes*, No. 56, October 1867, pp.400-401.
8 Thacker, *The Thames Highway*, II, pp.492-3.

## 18 Fashionable Richmond, pp.278-300

1 *CSP Dom* 1679-80, p.176.
2 Armytage papers for which I am indebted to Mr. George Redmonds.
3 Quoted in Beresford Chancellor's *History of Richmond*, Appendix E, p.xxvii.

4 Armytage papers.
5 LR3/86, p.55 (10 April 1740); LR3/87, p.101 (30 March 1749); LR3/88, p.2 (2 April 1752).
6 Hist MSS Comm, Portland V, p.559.
7 *St James's Post*, 3 May 1718; *St James's Evening Post*, 5 May and 23 August 1718; *Weekly Journal*, 2 August 1718.
8 *Read's Weekly Journal*, 13 June 1719.
9 Sybil Rosenfeld, *Strolling Players*, p.283, quoting Latreille vol II f 112.
10 *Ibid.*, p.285, quoting Burney.
11 Rosenfeld, *op. cit.*, p.299, quoting *The Professional Life of Dibdin*, written by himself, 1803, vol. I, p.38.
12 D.M. Little and G.M. Kahrl, *Letters of David Garrick*, 1963.
13 Quoted by Frederick Bingham, *A Celebrated Old Playhouse*, 1886, pp.11-12.
14 Little and Kahrl, *op. cit.*
15 Rosenfeld, *op. cit.*, quoting *St James's Chronicle*, 6-9 June 1767.
16 Manor rental: Harriet Darrell copyhold property No. 376.
17 Dorothy Stroud, *Capability Brown*, p.221, quoting a letter in the collection of G.R.M. Pekenham.
18 Mrs Papendiek, *Court and Private Life in the Time of Queen Charlotte* (2 vols.), ed. V.D. Broughton, 1887.
19 *Letters and Journals of Lady Mary Coke*, ed. J.A. Home, 1889-96, II, p.319.
20 *Diaries of Robert Fulke Greville*, ed. E.M. Bladen.
21 *Memoirs of Madame de La Tour du Pin*, ed. and trans. Felice Harcourt, Harvill, London, 1969, p.318.
22 *Ibid.* p.321.
23 Richmond Vestry Minute Book, 11 March 1793.
24 See Noel Hughes, *The Richmond Catholic Mission, 1791-1826.*
25 E367/7187.
26 E367/7245 and 5206.
27 E367/4522.
28 LR3/89, p.325.
29 Trustees General Meeting Book 1766-77, p.253.
30 Richard Crisp, *Richmond and its Inhabitants from the Olden Time*, 1866, p.115.
31 The story of John Lewis and the battle for Richmond Park is told in *Palaces and Parks of Richmond and Kew*, vol. 2, pp.111-114.

## 20 Local Government from the Seventeenth to the Nineteenth Centuries, pp.313-30

1 *CSP Dom* 1628-29, p.350.
2 LR3/71, p.156.
3 LR3/101/2, m 7 verso.
4 LR3/71, p.316-17.
5 Vestry Meeting Book, 1 March 1651.
6 LR3/71, p.358.
7 General Parish Meeting Book, 15 September 1729.
8 GPMB, 6 May 1734.
9 *Ibid.*, 6 May 1734.
10 *Ibid.*, 28 March 1737.
11 Hiscocke's *Richmond Notes* No. 5, July 1863, p.1.
12 GPMB, 25 May 1730.
13 GPMB, 22 October. 1739.
14 GPMB, 12 May 1755.
15 GPMB, 10 June 1745.
16 Act 6 George III c. 72.
17 Trustees' General Meeting Book (TGMB) 1766-77, pp.122-23.
18 TGMB, pp.129-132.
19 *Ibid.*, p.240.
20 *Ibid.*, p.245.
21 TGMB 1778-1785, p.102.
22 *Ibid.*, p.120.
23 *Ibid.*, p.134.
24 *Ibid.*, p.278.
25 Act 25 George III, c. 41.
26 Vestry Book A, 1785-92, p.1.
27 Vestry Book A, pp.277 and 406.
28 *Ibid.*, p.282.
29 *Ibid.*, p.28.
30 *Ibid.*, p.378.
31 *Ibid.*, pp.399, 410, 412.
32 *Ibid.*, p.425.
33 *Ibid.*, p.453.
34 *Ibid.*, p.517.
35 Vestry Book B (1792-1804), pp.50-51.
36 *Ibid.*, p.488.
37 Vestry Book E (1829-1842), pp.461, 463, 465.
38 Vestry Book B, pp.273 and 306.
39 Vestry book D (1816-29), p.101.
40 Vestry Book B, p.287.
41 Vestry Book C (1804-1816), p.447.
42 *Ibid.*, p.454.
43 Vestry Book E, p.468.
44 Vestry Book B, p.488.
45 Vestry Book D, p.415.
46 *Ibid.*, p.486.
47 *Ibid.*, pp.494, 534, 538.
48 Vestry Book A, p.338.
49 Vestry Book B, pp.178, 192.
50 Vestry Book C, p.75.
51 Vestry Book D, p.354.
52 *Ibid.*, p.218.
53 Vestry Book B, p.9.
54 Vestry Book F (1842-1852), p.63.
55 *Ibid.*, p.290.
56 *Ibid.*, p.362.
57 Vestry Book G (1853-1863), pp.339, 346.
58 *Ibid.*, p.292.
59 Vestry Book B, p.9.
60 Vestry Book D, p.410.
61 Charles Burt, *The Richmond Vestry*, Richmond 1890, pp.18-19.

## 21 Schools in Richmond up to 1825, pp.331-42

1 W Schenk, *Reginald Pole, Cardinal of England*, 1950, p.1.
2 LR3/101/6, m 30.
3 Licences granted by the Commissary Court of Surrey, *Surrey Archaeological Collections XI*, pp.205 ff.
4 *The Surrey hearth tax 1664: Surrey Record Society Vol. 17*, 1940, based on PRO E179/188/481.
5 LR3/71, p.397.
6 LR3/71, p.516.
7 LR3/79, p.86.
8 Richmond Select Vestry minutes (Richmond Local Studies Collection).
9 *Ibid.*, 25 January 1701/2.
10 LR3/80, pp.279-280.
11 A C Piper, *History of Richmond Parish Church*, 1946, p.87.
12 *The Spectator* No. 168, 1711, quoted in A C Piper, *op. cit.*, p.88.
13 A C Piper, *op. cit.*, pp.87-89.
14 *Ibid.*, p.80 (though in incorrect context of charity school).

[15] *Parson and Parish in Eighteenth Century Surrey: Replies to Bishops' Visitations*, Surrey Record Society, Vol. 34, 1994, p.52.

[16] LR3/86.

[17] LR3/86, p.85 and LR3/87, p.2.

[18] LR3/87, p.2 and evidence of ratebooks.

[19] A.R. Bax, *Allegations for Marriage Licences issued by the Commissary Court of Surrey between 1673 and 1770*, 1907, p.374.

[20] Charles D. Warren, *History of St Peter's Church, Petersham*, 1938, pp.42 and 99.

[21] Quoted by Michael Hastings, *Sir Richard Burton*, 1978, pp.26-28.

[22] Richmond Select Vestry minutes.

[23] *Ibid.*

[24] Hearth Tax 1664 (see note 4 above).

[25] *Calendar of State Papers (Commonwealth)* IX, p.134.

[26] LR3/71, p.405.

[27] LR3/71, p.445.

[28] LR3/71, p.363.

[29] LR3/79, p.107.

[30] *Universal British Directory*, 1795.

[31] For Peter Sterry and his academy see: V. de S. Pinto, *Peter Sterry, Platonist and Puritan*, 1934, and articles by N.I. Matar in *Notes and Queries 29*, 1982, pp.45-46 and in *The Seventeenth Century*, Vol. 2, No. 2, 1987, pp.189-198.

[32] A C Piper, *op. cit.*, pp.79-80.

[33] LR3/81, p.77. For confirmation that the actual purchase was made by Lady Vanderputt see LR3/84, p.48.

[34] Richmond Select Vestry minutes, 21 September 1713.

[35] *Parson and Parish ...*, Surrey Record Society, Vol. 34, p.52.

[36] *Ibid.*, p.131.

[37] John Evans, *Richmond and its Vicinity* (1824, revised edition 1825), pp.65-66.

[38] *Parson and Parish*, p.52.

[39] *Ibid*, p.131.

[40] Evans, *Richmond and its Vicinity*, pp.194-195.

[41] A loose page from a booklet entitled *Recollections of Richmond* by F.S. Ellis — in the local studies collection of the Richmond Public Library.

[42] *Parson and Parish ...* Surrey Record Society, Vol. 34, p.36.

[43] CRES38/1765 and 1766.

[44] Kew rate list for 1726 among Vestry documents, Surrey RO.

[45] CRES2/1245.

[46] *Ibid.*

[47] Duchy of Cornwall: Household accounts of Frederick Prince of Wales, XLIII (Jan 1759-Jan1760) and XLIV (Jan 1760-Jan 1761).

[48] See the cartoon about 'Lord Bute's erections' on Kew Green in the *Political Register*, May 1767 (illustrated at p.130 of *Palaces and Parks*, Vol II.)

[49] Surrey RO (now Surrey History Centre, Woking) — Kew Vestry order book 1758-1791, 20 April 1778.

[50] *Ibid.*, 4 December 1778.

[51] *Ibid.*, 8 November 1780.

[52] *Parson and Parish ...*, Surrey Record Society, Vol 34, p.116.

[53] Richmond Vestry minute book A, p.277, and Kew Vestry order book, 7 April 1788.

[54] Surrey RO (now Surrey History Centre) — Kew Vestry book, 21 February 1810.

[55] *Ibid.*, 16 and 29 July 1824. For instrument of enclosure see PRO WORK24/7/1.

## Postscript to *Palaces and Parks*, p.456

[1] See *Time Team 1998: the Site Reports*. Channel 4 Television, 1998, pp.4-10.

[2] Archivio di Stato, Florence, Miscellanea Medicea 93, ins.3. n 106.

[3] Sabine Eiche, 'Prince Henry's Richmond: The project by Costantino de' Servi' in *Apollo*, November 1998, pp.10-14.

[4] It was also published in *Richmond History* No. 20 (the Journal of the Richmond Local History Society) in May 1999, pp.50-54 and (in a slightly modified form) in my *Richmond Palace – its History and its Plan* published by the Richmond Local History Society in March 2001.

# Index